Lecture Notes in Artificial Intelligence   11697

Subseries of Lecture Notes in Computer Science

More information about this series at http://www.springer.com/series/1244

Kamil Ekštein (Ed.)

Text, Speech, and Dialogue

22nd International Conference, TSD 2019
Ljubljana, Slovenia, September 11–13, 2019
Proceedings

 Springer

Editor
Kamil Ekštein
University of West Bohemia
Pilsen, Czech Republic

ISSN 0302-9743   ISSN 1611-3349 (electronic)
Lecture Notes in Artificial Intelligence
ISBN 978-3-030-27946-2   ISBN 978-3-030-27947-9 (eBook)
https://doi.org/10.1007/978-3-030-27947-9

LNCS Sublibrary: SL7 – Artificial Intelligence

This Springer imprint is published by the registered company Springer Nature Switzerland AG
The registered company address is: Gewerbestrasse 11, 6330 Cham, Switzerland

Preface

The annual International Conference on Text, Speech, and Dialogue (TSD), which emerged in 1998, constitutes a recognized platform for the presentation and discussion of state-of-the-art technology and recent achievements in computer processing of natural language. It has become a broad interdisciplinary forum, interweaving the topics of speech technology and language processing. The conference attracts researchers not only from Central and Eastern Europe but also from other parts of the world. Indeed, one of its goals has always been bringing together NLP researchers with various interests from different parts of the world and to promote their mutual co-operation. One of the ambitions of the conference is, as its name suggests, not only to deal with dialogue systems but also to improve dialogue among researchers in areas of NLP, i.e., among the "text" and the "speech" and the "dialogue" people.

The TSD 2019 was again a very special year: The TSD conference got truly international as it left the Czech Republic for the first time in its 22-year-long history. The Program Committee decided that the existing good repute of the conference might be further boosted by embedding it into the group of international conferences not only by international participants but also by changing venues around the world and involving local Organizing Committees from different countries. In order to make this beginning of the new era as smooth as possible, we picked a destination in Central Europe not far from the country of TSD origin, the Czech Republic. Thanks to long-lasting co-operation and friendship with the ASR & NLP researchers from the University of Ljubljana, Slovenia, the choice was thus easier. The first non-Czech venue of the TSD conference was therefore the beautiful Slovenian capital Ljubljana.

The TSD 2019 conference was held on the campus of the co-organizing institution, the Faculty of Electrical Engineering of the University of Ljubljana, during September 11–13, 2019. The conference schedule and the keynote topic was again co-ordinated with the Interspeech Conference and TSD 2019 was listed as an Interspeech 2019 satellite event. Like its predecessors, TSD 2019 highlighted the importance of language and speech processing to both the academic and scientific worlds and their most recent breakthroughs in current applications. Experienced researchers and professionals as well as newcomers in the field found in the TSD conference a forum to communicate with people sharing similar interests.

This volume contains a collection of submitted papers presented at the conference. Each of them was thoroughly reviewed by three members of the conference reviewing team consisting of more than 60 top specialists in the conference topic areas. A total of 33 accepted papers out of 73 submitted, altogether contributed by 174 authors and co-authors, were selected by the Program Committee for presentation at the conference and for publication in this book. Theoretical and more general contributions were presented in common (plenary) sessions. Problem-oriented sessions as well as panel discussions then brought together specialists in narrower problem areas with the aim of exchanging knowledge and skills resulting from research projects of all kinds.

Last but not least, we would like to express our gratitude to the authors for providing their papers on time, to the members of the conference reviewing team and the Program Committee for their careful reviews and paper selection, and to the editors for their hard work preparing this volume. Special thanks go to the members of both local Organizing Committees for their tireless effort and enthusiasm during the conference organization.

September 2019

Kamil Ekštein
Miloslav Konopík

Organization

The 22nd International Conference on Text, Speech, and Dialogue – TSD 2019 – was organized by the NTIS (New Technologies for the Information Society) P2 Research Centre of the Faculty of Applied Sciences, University of West Bohemia in Plzeň (Pilsen), Czech Republic, in co-operation with the Faculty of Electrical Engineering, University of Ljubljana, Ljubljana, Slovenia, and co-organized by the Faculty of Informatics, Masaryk University in Brno, Czech Republic.

The conference website is located at http://www.kiv.zcu.cz/tsd2019/ or http://www.tsdconference.org/.

Program Committee

Elmar Nöth (General Chair), Germany
Rodrigo Agerri, Spain
Eneko Agirre, Spain
Vladimír Benko, Slovakia
Archna Bhatia, USA
Jan Černocký, Czech Republic
Simon Dobrišek, Slovenia
Kamil Ekštein, Czech Republic
Karina Evgrafova, Russia
Yevhen Fedorov, Ukraine
Volker Fischer, Germany
Darja Fišer, Slovenia
Eleni Galiotou, Greece
Björn Gambäck, Norway
Radovan Garabík, Slovakia
Alexander Gelbukh, Mexico
Louise Guthrie, USA
Tino Haderlein, Germany
Jan Hajič, Czech Republic
Eva Hajičová, Czech Republic
Yannis Haralambous, France
Hynek Hermansky, USA
Jaroslava Hlaváčová, Czech Republic
Aleš Horák, Czech Republic
Eduard Hovy, USA
Denis Jouvet, France
Maria Khokhlova, Russia
Aidar Khusainov, Russia
Daniil Kocharov, Russia

Miloslav Konopík, Czech Republic
Ivan Kopeček, Czech Republic
Valia Kordoni, Germany
Evgeny Kotelnikov, Russia
Pavel Král, Czech Republic
Siegfried Kunzmann, USA
Nikola Ljubešić, Croatia
Natalija Loukachevitch, Russia
Bernardo Magnini, Italy
Oleksandr Marchenko, Ukraine
Václav Matoušek, Czech Republic
France Mihelič, Slovenia
Roman Mouček, Czech Republic
Agnieszka Mykowiecka, Poland
Hermann Ney, Germany
Juan Rafael Orozco-Arroyave, Colombia
Karel Pala, Czech Republic
Nikola Pavešić, Slovenia
Maciej Piasecki, Poland
Josef Psutka, Czech Republic
James Pustejovsky, USA
German Rigau, Spain
Leon Rothkrantz, The Netherlands
Anna Rumshisky, USA
Milan Rusko, Slovakia
Pavel Rychlý, Czech Republic
Mykola Sazhok, Ukraine
Pavel Skrelin, Russia
Pavel Smrž, Czech Republic

Petr Sojka, Czech Republic
Georg Stemmer, Germany
Marko Robnik Šikonja, Slovenia
Vitomir Štruc, Slovenia
Marko Tadić, Croatia
Jan Trmal, Czech Republic
Tamas Varadi, Hungary
Zygmunt Vetulani, Poland

Aleksander Wawer, Poland
Pascal Wiggers, The Netherlands
Yorick Wilks, UK
Marcin Wolinski, Poland
Alina Wróblewska, Poland
Victor Zakharov, Russia
Jerneja Žganec Gros, Slovenia

Local Organizing Committee (Plzeň Team)

Miloslav Konopík (Chair)
Václav Matoušek (Chair Emeritus)
Lucie Tauchenová (Secretary)
Kamil Ekštein

Pavel Král
Roman Mouček
Ondřej Pražók
Jakub Sido

Local Organizing Committee (Ljubljana Team)

Simon Dobrišek (Chair)
Vitomir Štruc (Co-chair)
Kaja Dobrovoljc

Martin Pernuš
Olga Zakrajšek

Keynote Speakers

The organizers would like to thank the following respected scientists and researchers for delivering their keynote talks:

Ryan Cotterell
Denis Jouvet

Bhiksha Raj
Aline Villavicencio

Acknowledgments

The organizers would like to give special thanks to the following reviewers who substantially contributed to the successful completion of the TSD 2019 review process by voluntarily agreeing to deliver reviews beyond their duties:

Anuj Goyal
Ondřej Pražák

Carlos Ariel Ferrer Riesgo
Jakub Sido

Sponsoring Institutions

The organizers would like to express their immense gratitude to the following establishments for providing extra funding that helped to keep the conference fees reasonable:

Springer-Verlag GmbH, Heidelberg, Germany
CLARIN.SI, Ljubljana, Slovenia

Abstracts of Invited Talks

Mitigating Gender Bias in Morphologically Rich Languages

Ryan Cotterell

Department of Computer Science and Technology, Natural Language and Information Processing Research Group, University of Cambridge, William Gates Building, 15 JJ Thomson Avenue, Cambridge CB3 0FD, UK
https://www.cl.cam.ac.uk/research/nl/
ryan.cotterell@jhu.edu

Abstract. Gender bias exists in corpora of all of the world's languages: the bias is a function what people talk about, not of the grammar of a language. For this reason, data-driven systems in NLP that are trained on this data will inherit such bias. Evidence of bias can be found in all sorts of NLP technologies: word vectors, language models, coreference systems and even machine translation. Most of the research done to mitigate gender bias in natural language corpora, however, has focused solely on English. For instance, in an attempt to remove gender bias in English corpora, NLP practitioners often augment corpora by swapping gendered words: i.e., if "he is a smart doctor" appears, add the sentence "she is a smart doctor" to the corpus as well before training a model. The broader research question asked in this talk is the following: How can we mitigate gender bias in corpora from any of the world's languages, not just in English? As an example, the simple swapping heuristic for English will not generalize to most of the world's languages. Indeed, such a solution would not even apply to German, since it marks gender on both nouns and adjectives and requires gender agreement throughout a sentence. In the context of German, this task is far more complicated: mapping "er ist ein kluger Arzt" to "sie ist eine kluge Ärztin" requires more than simply swapping "er" with "sie" and "Arzt" with "Ärztin"–one also has to modify the article ("ein") and the adjective ("klug"). In this talk, we present a machine-learning solution to this problem: we develop a novel neural random field that generates such sentence-to-sentence transformations, enforcing agreement with respect to gender. We explain how to perform inference and morphological reinflection to generate such transformations without any labeled training examples. Empirically, we illustrate that the model manages to reduce gender bias in corpora without sacrificing grammaticality with a novel metric of gender bias. Additionally, we discuss concrete applications to coreference resolution and machine translation.

Adversarial Attacks on ML Systems

Bhiksha Raj

Language Technologies Institute, School of Computer Science,
Carnegie Mellon University, 5000 Forbes Avenue, Pittsburgh, PA 15213, USA
http://mlsp.cs.cmu.edu/people/bhiksha/
bhiksha@cs.cmu.edu

Abstract. As neural network classifiers become increasingly successful at various tasks ranging from speech recognition and image classification to various natural language processing tasks and even recognizing malware, a second, somewhat disturbing discovery has also been made. It is possible to fool these systems with carefully crafted inputs that appear to the lay observer to be natural data, but cause the neural network to misclassify in random or even targeted ways.

In this talk we will discuss why such attacks are possible, and the problem of designing, identifying, and avoiding attacks by such crafted "adversarial" inputs.

Multiword Expressions and Idiomaticity: How Much of the Sailing Has Been Plain?

Aline Villavicencio[1,2]

[1] Department of Computer Science, University of Sheffield, UK
www.sheffield.ac.uk/dcs
[2] Institute of Informatics, Federal University of Rio Grande do Sul, Brazil
www.inf.ufrgs.br
a.villavicencio@sheffield.ac.uk

Extended Abstract

Much progress has been made in designing accurate word representations [2–4], with improvements for language technology applications like machine translation and text simplification. Precise natural language understanding requires adequate treatments both of single words and of larger units. In particular, one commonly held assumption for constructing the representation for larger units like expressions, phrases and sentences, is that the meaning of the unit can be constructed from the meanings of its parts, in what is known as the Compositionality Principle. While it allows an interpretation to be generated even for unseen combinations of known words, it may not be adequate for expressions like idioms, verb-particle constructions and compound nouns as they often display idiomaticity. For instance, this is the case of *loan shark* with the meaning of a person who lends money at extremely high interest rates (rather than a fish that can be borrowed). Therefore it is important to identify which words in a sentence form an expression [5], and whether an expression is idiomatic [1, 6] and should be treated as a unit, as this determines if it can be interpreted from a combination of the meanings of their component words or not. In this talk I discuss advances on the identification and treatment of multiword expressions in texts, focusing in particular on techniques for modelling idiomaticity.

Acknowledgements. This talk includes joint work with Carlos Ramisch, Marco Idiart, Silvio Cordeiro, Rodrigo Wilkens, Felipe Paula and Leonardo Zilio.

References

1. Cordeiro, S., Villavicencio, A., Idiart, M., Ramisch, C.: Unsupervised compositionality prediction of nominal compounds. Comput. Linguist. **45**(1), 1–57 (2019). https://doi.org/10.1162/coli_a_00341

2. Lin, D.: Automatic retrieval and clustering of similar words. In: Boitet, C., Whitelock, P. (eds.) 36th Annual Meeting of the Association for Computational Linguistics and 17th International Conference on Computational Linguistics, COLING-ACL 1998, 10–14 August 1998, Université de Montréal, Montréal, Quebec, Canada. Proceedings of the Conference, pp. 768–774. Morgan Kaufmann Publishers/ACL (1998)
3. Mikolov, T., Sutskever, I., Chen, K., Corrado, G., Dean, J.: Distributed representations of words and phrases and their compositionality. CoRR abs/1310.4546 (2013). http://arxiv.org/abs/1310.4546
4. Peters, M.E., et al.: Deep contextualized word representations. In: Walker, M.A., Ji, H., Stent, A. (eds.) Proceedings of the 2018 Conference of the North American Chapter of the Association for Computational Linguistics: Human Language Technologies, NAACL-HLT 2018, New Orleans, Louisiana, USA, 1–6 June 2018, vol. 1 (Long Papers), pp. 2227–2237. Association for Computational Linguistics (2018)
5. Ramisch, C.: Multiword Expressions Acquisition - A Generic and Open Framework. Theory and Applications of Natural Language Processing, Springer, Switzerland (2015). https://doi.org/10.1007/978-3-319-09207-2
6. Reddy, S., McCarthy, D., Manandhar, S.: An empirical study on compositionality in compound nouns. In: Fifth International Joint Conference on Natural Language Processing, IJCNLP 2011, Chiang Mai, Thailand, 8–13 November 2011, pp. 210–218. The Association for Computer Linguistics (2011)

Contents

Keynote Talks

Speech Processing and Prosody 3
   Denis Jouvet

Text

Using a Database of Multiword Expressions in Dependency Parsing 19
   Tomáš Jelínek

Explicit Discourse Argument Extraction for German 32
   Peter Bourgonje and Manfred Stede

Consonance as a Stylistic Feature for Authorship Attribution
of Historical Texts. 45
   Lubomir Ivanov and Brandon Neilsen

Bidirectional LSTM Tagger for Latvian Grammatical Error Detection 58
   Daiga Deksne

Methods for Assessing Theme Adherence in Student Thesis 69
   Mikhail Tikhomirov, Natalia Loukachevitch, and Boris Dobrov

Natural Language Analysis to Detect Parkinson's Disease 82
   P. A. Pérez-Toro, J. C. Vásquez-Correa, M. Strauss,
   J. R. Orozco-Arroyave, and E. Nöth

Using Auto-Encoder BiLSTM Neural Network for Czech
Grapheme-to-Phoneme Conversion 91
   Markéta Jůzová and Jakub Vít

The FRENK Datasets of Socially Unacceptable Discourse in Slovene
and English 103
   Nikola Ljubešić, Darja Fišer, and Tomaž Erjavec

KAS-term: Extracting Slovene Terms from Doctoral Theses via Supervised
Machine Learning 115
   Nikola Ljubešić, Darja Fišer, and Tomaž Erjavec

A Self-organizing Feature Map for Arabic Word Extraction 127
   Hassina Bouressace and János Csirik

Czech Text Processing with Contextual Embeddings: POS Tagging,
Lemmatization, Parsing and NER   137
   Milan Straka, Jana Straková, and Jan Hajič

On GDPR Compliance of Companies' Privacy Policies   151
   Nicolas M. Müller, Daniel Kowatsch, Pascal Debus, Donika Mirdita,
   and Konstantin Böttinger

A Semi-automatic Structure Learning Method for Language Modeling.   160
   Vitor Pera

Coreference in English OntoNotes: Properties and Genre Differences   171
   Berfin Aktaş, Tatjana Scheffler, and Manfred Stede

The TransBank Aligner: Cross-Sentence Alignment with Deep
Neural Networks.   185
   Ahmad Aghaebrahimian, Michael Ustaszewski, and Andy Stauder

Exploiting Large Unlabeled Data in Automatic Evaluation of Coherence
in Czech   197
   Michal Novák, Jiří Mírovský, Kateřina Rysová, and Magdaléna Rysová

Examining Structure of Word Embeddings with PCA   211
   Tomáš Musil

Semantic Structure of Russian Prepositional Constructions   224
   Victor Zakharov and Irina Azarova

Explicit and Implicit Discourse Relations in the Prague
Discourse Treebank.   236
   Šárka Zikánová, Jiří Mírovský, and Pavlína Synková

Speech

On Practical Aspects of Multi-condition Training Based on Augmentation
for Reverberation-/Noise-Robust Speech Recognition.   251
   Jiri Malek and Jindrich Zdansky

Evaluation of Synthetic Speech by GMM-Based Continuous Detection
of Emotional States.   264
   Jiří Přibil, Anna Přibilová, and Jindřich Matoušek

Deep Representation Learning for Orca Call Type Classification.   274
   Christian Bergler, Manuel Schmitt, Rachael Xi Cheng,
   Hendrik Schröter, Andreas Maier, Volker Barth, Michael Weber,
   and Elmar Nöth

On Using Stateful LSTM Networks for Key-Phrase Detection 287
  Martin Bulín, Luboš Šmídl, and Jan Švec

Consonant-to-Vowel/Vowel-to-Consonant Transitions to Analyze
the Speech of Cochlear Implant Users 299
  T. Arias-Vergara, J. R. Orozco-Arroyave, S. Gollwitzer, M. Schuster,
  and E. Nöth

Czech Speech Synthesis with Generative Neural Vocoder 307
  Jakub Vít, Zdeněk Hanzlíček, and Jindřich Matoušek

Linguistic Resources Construction: Towards Disfluency Processing
in Spontaneous Tunisian Dialect Speech 316
  Emna Boughariou, Younès Bahou, and Lamia Hadrich Bleguith

Comparing Front-End Enhancement Techniques and Multiconditioned
Training for Robust Automatic Speech Recognition. 329
  Meet H. Soni, Sonal Joshi, and Ashish Panda

Label-Driven Time-Frequency Masking for Robust Speech
Command Recognition 341
  Meet Soni, Imran Sheikh, and Sunil Kumar Kopparapu

A Comparison of Hybrid and End-to-End Models
for Syllable Recognition. 352
  Sebastian P. Bayerl and Korbinian Riedhammer

LSTM-Based Speech Segmentation for TTS Synthesis. 361
  Zdeněk Hanzlíček, Jakub Vít, and Daniel Tihelka

Spoken Language Identification Using Language Bottleneck Features 373
  Malo Grisard, Petr Motlicek, Wissem Allouchi, Michael Baeriswyl,
  Alexandros Lazaridis, and Qingran Zhan

Dialogue

Question-Answering Dialog System for Large Audiovisual Archives 385
  Adam Chýlek, Luboš Šmídl, and Jan Švec

Crowd-Sourced Collection of Task-Oriented Human-Human Dialogues
in a Multi-domain Scenario 398
  Norbert Braunschweiler, Panagiotis Papadakos, Margarita Kotti,
  Yannis Marketakis, and Yannis Tzitzikas

Author Index 413

Keynote Talks

Speech Processing and Prosody

Denis Jouvet[(✉)]

Université de Lorraine, CNRS, Inria, LORIA, 54000 Nancy, France
`denis.jouvet@loria.fr`

Abstract. The prosody of the speech signal conveys information over
the linguistic content of the message: prosody structures the utterance,
and also brings information on speaker's attitude and speaker's emotion. Duration of sounds, energy and fundamental frequency are the
prosodic features. However their automatic computation and usage are
not obvious. Sound duration features are usually extracted from speech
recognition results or from a force speech-text alignment. Although the
resulting segmentation is usually acceptable on clean native speech data,
performance degrades on noisy or not non-native speech. Many algorithms have been developed for computing the fundamental frequency,
they lead to rather good performance on clean speech, but again, performance degrades in noisy conditions. However, in some applications,
as for example in computer assisted language learning, the relevance of
the prosodic features is critical; indeed, the quality of the diagnostic
on the learner's pronunciation will heavily depend on the precision and
reliability of the estimated prosodic parameters. The paper considers
the computation of prosodic features, shows the limitations of automatic
approaches, and discusses the problem of computing confidence measures
on such features. Then the paper discusses the role of prosodic features
and how they can be handled for automatic processing in some tasks such
as the detection of discourse particles, the characterization of emotions,
the classification of sentence modalities, as well as in computer assisted
language learning and in expressive speech synthesis.

Keywords: Prosody · Speech processing · Prosodic features ·
Fundamental frequency

1 Introduction

In speech communication, prosody conveys various types of information over the
linguistic content of the messages. For example, prosody structures the utterances, thus playing a role similar to punctuation in written texts; and provides
ways to emphasize words or parts of the messages that the speaker think are
important. Prosody also conveys information on the speaker's attitude and emotional state.

The prosody of the speech is often neglected in automatic speech recognition
as well as in manual transcription of speech corpora. On the other side expressive

© Springer Nature Switzerland AG 2019
K. Ekštein (Ed.): TSD 2019, LNAI 11697, pp. 3–15, 2019.
https://doi.org/10.1007/978-3-030-27947-9_1

speech is now attracting more and more interest in some speech sciences, such as for speech synthesis [44] and for automatic recognition of emotions [32]. For a long time text-to-speech (TTS) synthesis research was focused on delivering good quality and intelligible speech. Such systems are currently used in information delivery services, as for example in call center automation, in navigation systems, and in voice assistants. The speech style was then typically a "reading style", which resulted from the style of the speech data used to develop TTS systems (reading of a large set of sentences). Although a reading style is acceptable for occasional interactions, TTS systems should benefit from more variability and expressivity in the generated synthetic speech, for example, for lengthy interactions between machines and humans, or for entertainment applications. This is the goal of recent or emerging research on expressive speech synthesis.

Prosody is a suprasegmental information, i.e., is defined on segments larger than the phones. Several variables are used to characterize the prosody. This includes the fundamental frequency, the duration of the sounds, and the energy of the sounds. Most of the time it is the evolution of these variables over time, or their relative values that bring prosody information.

Forced speech-text alignment is used to obtain word and phone segmentations of speech signals. Assuming that a precise transcription is available, forced speech-text alignment provides good segmentation results on clean speech signals. However there exists conditions where performance degrades, as for example, on noisy signals, or when dealing with dysfluencies of spontaneous speech, or when processing non-native speech. Similarly, many algorithms have been developed for computing the fundamental frequency. They work well on good quality speech signals, but their performance degrades on noisy speech signals.

The paper is organized as follows. Section 2 details the features and their automatic computation. Section 3 deals with the reliability of the prosodic features. Section 4 discusses the use of prosodic features in various speech applications. Finally a conclusion ends the paper.

2   Computing Prosodic Features

The computation of the prosodic parameters involves the computation of the phone duration, of the fundamental frequency, and of the phone energy.

2.1   Phone Duration

The phone duration is determined from a phonetic segmentation of the speech signal. Such segmentation can be done manually using some speech visualization tool such as Praat [9], or automatically using forced speech-text alignment procedures. Although automatic speech-text alignment provides good results on clean speech data, some manual checking and corrections may be necessary, especially when dealing with spontaneous speech if all speech dysfluencies are not marked in the transcription and properly processed, when processing non-native speech, or in noisy conditions.

2.2 Fundamental Frequency

The fundamental frequency (F0) is an important prosody feature. It corresponds to the frequency of vibration of the vocal folds. Many algorithms have been developed in the past to compute the fundamental frequency of speech signals, they are generally referred to as pitch detection algorithms. Several algorithms operate in the time domain. This is the case of those based on the auto-correlation function (ACF) [8], of the robust algorithm for pitch tracking (RAPT) [52], of the YIN approach [12] and the time domain excitation extraction based on a minimum perturbation operator (TEMPO) [27,28]. Some algorithms operate in the frequency domain as the sawtooth waveform inspired pitch estimator (SWIPE) [11]. Other algorithms combine processing in the time and in the frequency domains. This is the case of the pitch detection of the Aurora algorithm [49] initially developed for distributed speech recognition, and the nearly defect-free F0 (NDF) estimation algorithm [26]. More recently, new algorithms have also been released, as for example the robust epoch and pitch estimator (REAPER). A pitch tracker has also been developed for automatic speech recognition of tonal languages within the Kaldi toolkit [18]. Their accuracy and reliability is discussed later in Sect. 3.3

2.3 Phone Energy

The raw local energy of speech signals is quite easy to compute, and is part of many sets of acoustic features. However getting the phone energy implies some choices: should it be an average value over the whole phone segment, or and estimation in the middle of the phone segment. What is the impact when applied to non stationary sounds such as plosives and diphthongs. Errors on the phone boundaries will also affect the estimation.

Other phenomena must also be taken into account. The energy of the speech signal not only depends on the speaker, but is also dependent on the distance and position between the speaker's mouths and the microphone, on the type of microphone and on the transmission channel. All these variability sources complicates the actual usage of the energy feature. Comparing phone energy between sounds that belong to the same utterance is reasonable, as we can assume that the above acquisition factors do not vary too much within an utterance. However comparing phone energy between speech utterances collected in different conditions may not be reliable, and can lead to unexpected results.

3 Reliabity of Prosodic Features

This section discusses the reliability of the prosodic features, especially when computed automatically on spontaneous speech, on non-native speech, or on noisy data.

3.1 Speech-Text Alignments

Speech-text alignment relies on matching the speech signal with a sequence of acoustic models that corresponds to the possible pronunciation variants of the corresponding text. Hence a correct prediction of the pronunciation variants of the words is critical. Usually pronunciation variants are extracted from available pronunciation dictionaries for words present in those dictionaries, and using some grapheme-to-phoneme converters for other words. Well known approaches of grapheme-to-phoneme converters are based on joint multigram models [7], on weighted finite-states transducers [38], on conditional random fields [19], and more recently on neural networks, either long-short term memory recurrent neural networks [43] or sequence-to-sequence neural net models [56]. In practice it is important to predict all possible pronunciation variants. As any individual grapheme-to-phoneme converter may make mistakes, it is interesting to combine several converters. Predicting the pronunciation variants of names of persons, locations, etc., is more complicated, in particular when dealing with foreign names, which can be pronounced as in the original language, or pronounced using pronunciation rules of the current language, or a mix of both. Some papers have investigated using the origin of the proper names in the prediction process [20].

The speech signal is affected by many variability sources [6], which include speaker, environment noise, channel transmission, etc. Frequently strong accent or non-native accent implies non-standard pronunciation variants, consequently this will introduce mismatches in the alignment process; unless specific pronunciation variants are taken into account. Nevertheless, it should be noted that it is almost impossible to predict all possible non-native pronunciation variants of each word, as non-native variants depends on both the mother tongue and the target language. This would lead to too numerous variants which will be harmful for the alignment process. Spontaneous speech dysfluencies, such as false starts implies matching portions of the signal with partial pronunciation of words that are not always properly predicted. Automatic alignment performance also degrades on noisy signals, which are typical of spontaneous speech signals. Other problems come the manual transcription of the speech signals, which may contain some spelling errors, and some unforeseen notations due to variability in annotation protocols [17].

Most of the speech-text alignment systems relies on acoustic Markov models (with Gaussian mixture models or hybrid approaches with neural network models). In both cases, the structure of the model is a three-state model, which means that are least three acoustic frames must be aligned with each phone model. Consequently this implies a minimum duration of three frames for each phone segment. Conventional acoustic analysis compute frames every 10 ms, leading to a minimum duration of 30 ms, which appears to be too long in some cases in rapid speaking styles. This lead to investigating the usage of a smaller frame shift (5 ms instead of 10 ms) for speech-text alignment [21]. It should also be noted that parametric speech synthesis systems such as HTS [57] and MERLIN [55] relies also on 5 ms frame shifts.

3.2   Phone Duration

The duration of the phones are obtained from the phone segmentation. Hence the quality of the estimated duration of the phones depends on the accuracy and precision of the phone boundaries. For automatic speech-text alignments, the precision of the boundaries depends on the frame shift used: either 10 ms or 5 ms shift. The accuracy depends on the quality of the acoustic models used. Also, some boundaries are clearly marked in the spectrum space, as for example between vowels and fricatives or plosives. On the opposite, boundaries between vowels and sem-vowels or liquids are much less obvious, and often their position is error prone in automatic alignments.

In many cases the automatic speech-text alignment relies on a two step process. A first alignment is carried out using context dependent phone models. Such models provide a refine modeling of the contextual influence of adjacent phones, and thus are relevant to find the best pronunciation variant for each word occurrence. Once the best pronunciation variant has bee determined for each word occurrence a new alignment is carried out using context-independent phone models, as such models lead to a better determination of time position of the phone boundaries.

3.3   Fundamental Frequency

In order to better understand the performance of the various pitch detection algorithms, a set of experiments has been conducted to evaluate and compare their performance on clean speech and on noisy speech [23]. Two speech corpora have been used for the evaluations: the pitch-tracking database from Graz University of Technology (PTDB-TUG) [41] which contains clean English speech signals from 20 speakers, and the SPEECON [16] corpus which contains Spanish speech signals recorded in various real environments from 60 speakers with close-talk and distant microphones placed at different distances from the speakers. This corpora have been developed for pitch tracking evaluation, and are thus provided with reference pitch values.

On clean speech data, large performance variations are observed across speakers, and the average F0 frame error on the PTDB-TUG data varies between 5% and 8% for the 15 approaches that were considered in [23]. According to a recent bibliometric survey [51] the most frequently used pitch detection algorithms are Praat [8], RAPT [52], STRAIGHT [27,28], YIN [12], and SWIPE [11]. On clean speech signals the ACF algorithm from Praat, and the RAPT algorithms are the two approaches that provides the best performance (average performance of 5% F0 frame error on the 20 speakers of the PTDB-TUG corpus). However, at around 10 dB SNR, the best approaches are RAPT, REAPER, and NDF. An analysis of the results shows that when the level of noise increases, the performance degrades, and the voicing decision is always the main cause of errors. In many cases, the dominant error is the mis-classification of voiced frames as unvoiced. Babble noise is also more harmful than the other types of noise. However all algorithms do not behave the same way with respect to the type of noise and the SNR level.

Currently there is no indication of the reliability of the estimated F0 values provided by the various pitch detection algorithms. Some preliminary work has been carried out in this direction [14], but further studies are still necessary.

4   Prosodic Features in Automatic Speech Processing

Following the presentation of the prosodic features in Sect. 2 and a discussion about the reliability of those features in Sect. 3, this section presents and comments some usage of prosodic features in automatic speech processing.

4.1   Computer Assisted Language Learning

In the last decades there has been enormous progress in the domain of computer assisted foreign language learning (e.g. [15, 48, 53]). When focusing on the pronunciation, the main problem is the automatic detection of mispronunciations. This is achieved using approaches derived from automatic speech recognition technology. Common approaches computes goodness of pronunciation scores [54] which amounts to computing log likelihood ratio between a forced alignment corresponding to the expected pronunciation and another alignment over an unconstrained phonetic loop. Other approaches introduce frequent mispronunciation variants in the pronunciation lexicon for directly detecting some mispronunciations, and also getting better phonetic segmentation of non-native pronunciations [24].

Besides the correct pronunciation of the expected phones, another aspect to consider is the lexical stress, especially when such phenomenon is not present in the mother tongue. Reliable estimation of the fundamental frequency and of the phone segments is mandatory if one wants to provide relevant feedback to the learner. For example, segmentation reliability of vowels depends on the nature of the adjacent phones [37]. And to avoid providing wrong and useless feedbacks, one should also consider the case where the learner did not pronounce the expected word or expression [10, 40].

4.2   Structuring Speech Utterances

As mentioned before, prosody helps structuring the speech utterances, thus playing a role similar to punctuation in written texts. Although it is associated with the syntactic structure, the prosodic structure is a priori independent of it.

For the French language, an automatic detection of the prosodic structure has been proposed, based on a theoretical description of prosodic trees; the framework was first developed for prepared speech [36], was later adapted for the semi-spontaneous speech in [46], and further revisited and applied on various types of speech material [2] including spontaneous speech. The approach is based on the assumption that there is a prosodic structure that organizes hierarchically the prosodic groups. Such structure results from contrasts of melodic slopes observed on stressed syllables. Thus, for French, the vowel duration and F0 movements are measured on word final syllables, and the prosodic structure is build by considering the inversion and amplitude of the melodic slopes.

Later an analysis of links between punctuation marks and automatically detected prosodic structures has been conducted on large speech corpora [3] that were manually transcribed and punctuated. Inserting punctuation symbols is somewhat subjective and may vary with annotators. Nevertheless it was interesting to note that more than 85% of the punctuation symbols match with the end of automatically detected prosodic groups.

4.3   Sentence Modality

Several studies have been conducted in the past with respect to the detection of the modality of the sentences, as for example for modeling and detecting the discourse structures [25], for distinguishing statements from questions [30, 35], for enriching automatic transcription outputs [29], and for helping creating summaries of meetings [42].

Experiments have been conducted to evaluate various classifications approaches for identifying questions and statements on French data [39]. It was observed that using linguistic features alone provides better results than when using prosodic features only. With linguistic features there is a small drop in performance when using sequences of words resulting from automatic speech recognition than when using reference transcriptions. However, when dealing with automatic speech transcription data, combining prosodic and linguistic features slightly improved the classification performance.

4.4   Prosodic Correlates of Discourse Particles

Discourse particles are small words or expressions (such as "well", "so", "let's see") that are frequently used in spoken language; they play an important role to steer the flow of the dialogue or to convey various attitudes of the speaker [50]. When such words or expressions are used as discourse particles, their semantic load differ from its usual lexical meaning. Hence the proper detection of discourse particles is important in some applications, as for example for relevant speech understanding, or for speech translation.

A large set of French speech corpora have been used for investigating some discourse particles and for studying their prosodic correlates. The speech corpora used were forced aligned in the ORFEO project[1]. These corpora exhibit various speaking styles ranging from prepared speech (story telling, and broadcast news) to spontaneous speech (interviews and interactions). A set of words that are frequently used as discourse particles in French have been chosen. This include *"alors"* ("then", "what's up"), *"bon"* ("well", "all right"), *"donc"* ("thus", "therefore"), *"quoi"* ("what"), etc. About 1000 occurrences per word have been randomly selected and annotated as discourse particle or not. It was interesting to observe that the frequency of usage of these words as discourse particles increases significantly with the spontaneity of speech data [1, 22].

---

[1] ORFEO project: http://www.projet-orfeo.fr/.

The prosodic correlates of these words have been investigated. This include also the position of the word in its prosodic group, determined automatically as described above in Sect. 4.2. Experiments have also been carried out on automatic classification of the occurrences as discourse particle or not using their prosodic characteristics [13, 22].

When a word occurrence was used as a discourse particle, its pragmatic function was also annotated. The pragmatic function typically indicates the role of the discourse particle in structuring the speech flow, as for example: introduction, conclusion, interruption, etc. Prosodic correlates have been analyzed with respect to the pragmatic functions of the discourse particles [33] As different discourse particles sharing a same pragmatic function often exhibits a set of similar prosodic patterns, experiments have been conducted to investigate their interchangeability [34] when using only textual information, or when using audio plus textual information.

4.5   Expressive Speech

Since a few years research on expressive speech synthesis is attracting more and more attention. A few emotions are considered, typically, anger, joy, surprise, sadness, fear and disgust. The speech material necessary to build emotional speech synthesis systems is obtained by having the speaker uttering predefined set of sentences while acting the various emotions. Such approaches lead to good quality emotional speech synthesis systems.

Such data, in French, has also been used to investigate the differences in the speech signal among the various emotions. Many features vary with the emotion styles: vowel duration, vowel energy, and fundamental frequency. For example the fundamental frequency is on average much higher than in neutral speech for the anger and joy styles, and lower than in neutral speech for the sadness and disgust styles [5]. The range of variation of the fundamental frequency is also much larger for anger speech, and much smaller for sadness speech. With respect to pronunciaton variants, phoneme changes between neutral and emotional speech have been investigated, and a high percentage of schwa omissions has been observed for disgust, fear and joy [4].

Besides investigating the phonetic and prosodic realization of emotional speech, some research is carried out to ease the development of expressive speech synthesis systems using deep learning approaches, and to avoid a specific recording of emotional data from the speech synthesis speaker. Preliminary experiments have investigated the use of transfert learning [31].

For many years, the general approach for the recognition of emotion in speech signals was based on computing a very large set of features on the speech segment, and then providing this huge vector to a classifier [47]. Now deep learning approaches are also used for speech emotion recognition [45].

5   Conclusion

This paper has summarized some research activities relating to prosody in automatic speech processing. After a presentation of the prosodic features, that is the fundamental frequency, the phone duration and the phone energy, we have detailed their computation and discussed their reliability.

In the second part of the paper, we have presented and discussed some research activities dealing with the use of prosodic features. This includes computer assisted language learning, structuring speech utterances, sentence modality, prosodic correlates of discourse particles, and expressive speech.

Forced speech-text alignment and detection of fundamental frequency works rather well on clean speech transcriptions and clean speech signals. However, their performance degrades when dealing with spontaneous speech or noisy signals, which is typical of every day speech. One critical point that received so far very little attention, and needs to be investigated further is the estimation of confidence measures on the computed features. That is, similarly to automatic speech recognition systems that provides confidence measures associated to the recognized words, it would be very useful to have confidence measures associated to the phone segment boundaries, and to the estimated fundamental frequency values. Such confidence measures would be useful for the usage of the prosodic features. For example, in computer assisted language learning, this would allows to obtain a confidence score on the diagnosis, and thus this would lead to much more relevant feedback to the learners.

References

1. Bartkova, K., Dargnat, M., Jouvet, D., Lee, L.: Annotation of discourse particles in French over a large variety of speech corpora. In: ACor4French - Les corpus annotés du français, TALN 2017 - Traitement Automatique des Langues Naturelles. Orléans, France, June 2017. https://hal.inria.fr/hal-01585540
2. Bartkova, K., Jouvet, D.: Automatic detection of the prosodic structures of speech utterances. In: Železný, M., Habernal, I., Ronzhin, A. (eds.) SPECOM 2013. LNCS (LNAI), vol. 8113, pp. 1–8. Springer, Cham (2013). https://doi.org/10.1007/978-3-319-01931-4_1
3. Bartkova, K., Jouvet, D.: Links between manual punctuation marks and automatically detected prosodic structures. In: Speech Prosody 2014, Dublin, Ireland, May 2014. https://hal.archives-ouvertes.fr/hal-00998031
4. Bartkova, K., Jouvet, D.: Analysis of prosodic correlates of emotional speech data. In: 9th Tutorial and Research Workshop on Experimental Linguistics, ExLing 2018, Paris, France, August 2018. https://hal.inria.fr/hal-01889932
5. Bartkova, K., Jouvet, D., Delais-Roussarie, E.: Prosodic parameters and prosodic structures of French emotional data. In: Speech Prosody 2016, Boston, USA, May 2016. https://hal.inria.fr/hal-01293516
6. Benzeghiba, M., et al.: Automatic speech recognition and speech variability: a review. Speech Commun. **49**, 763–786 (2007). https://hal.inria.fr/inria-00616506
7. Bisani, M., Ney, H.: Joint-sequence models for grapheme-to-phoneme conversion. Speech Commun. **50**(5), 434–451 (2008)

8. Boersma, P.: Accurate short-term analysis of the fundamental frequency and the harmonics-to-noise ratio of a sampled sound. In: Proceedings of the Institute of Phonetic Sciences, Amsterdam, vol. 17, pp. 97–110 (1993)

9. Boersma, P., Weenink, D.: Praat: doing phonetics by computer [computer program]. Version 6.0.20 (2011)

10. Bonneau, A., et al.: Gestion d'erreurs pour la fiabilisation des retours automatiques en apprentissage de la prosodie d'une langue seconde. Traitement Automatique des Langues **53**(3) (2013). https://hal.inria.fr/hal-00834278

11. Camacho, A., Harris, J.G.: A sawtooth waveform inspired pitch estimator for speech and music. J. Acoust. Soc. Am. **124**(3), 1638–1652 (2008)

12. de Cheveigné, A., Kawahara, H.: YIN, a fundamental frequency estimator for speech and music. J. Acoust. Soc. Am. **111**(4), 1917–1930 (2002)

13. Dargnat, M., Bartkova, K., Jouvet, D.: Discourse particles in French: prosodic parameters extraction and analysis. In: Dediu, A.-H., Martín-Vide, C., Vicsi, K. (eds.) SLSP 2015. LNCS (LNAI), vol. 9449, pp. 39–49. Springer, Cham (2015). https://doi.org/10.1007/978-3-319-25789-1_5. https://hal.inria.fr/hal-01184197

14. Deng, B., Jouvet, D., Laprie, Y., Steiner, I., Sini, A.: Towards confidence measures on fundamental frequency estimations. In: IEEE International Conference on Acoustics, Speech and Signal Processing, New Orleans, USA, March 2017. https://hal.inria.fr/hal-01493168

15. Eskenazi, M.: An overview of spoken language technology for education. Speech Commun. **51**(10), 832–844 (2009)

16. European Language Resources Association (ELRA): Speecon manually pitch-marked reference database for Spanish, ISLRN : 866–498-919-979-7, ELRA ID: ELRA-S0218, Catalogue ELRA. (http://catalog.elra.info/)

17. Fohr, D., Mella, O., Jouvet, D.: De l'importance de l'homogénéisation des conventions de transcription pour l'alignement automatique de corpus oraux de parole spontanée. In: 8es Journées Internationales de Linguistique de Corpus (JLC2015). Orléans, France, September 2015. https://hal.inria.fr/hal-01183352

18. Ghahremani, P., BabaAli, B., Povey, D., Riedhammer, K., Trmal, J., Khudanpur, S.: A pitch extraction algorithm tuned for automatic speech recognition. In: IEEE International Conference on Acoustics, Speech, and Signal Processing, pp. 2494–2498 (2014)

19. Illina, I., Fohr, D., Jouvet, D.: Multiple pronunciation generation using grapheme-to-phoneme conversion based on conditional random fields. In: XIV International Conference "Speech and Computer" (SPECOM 2011), Kazan, Russia, September 2011. https://hal.inria.fr/inria-00616325

20. Illina, I., Fohr, D., Jouvet, D.: Génération des prononciations de noms propres à l'aide des champs aéatoires conditionnels. In: JEP-TALN-RECITAL 2012, Grenoble, France, June 2012. https://hal.inria.fr/hal-00753381

21. Jouvet, D., Bartkova, K.: Acoustical frame rate and pronunciation variant statistics. In: Dediu, A.-H., Martín-Vide, C., Vicsi, K. (eds.) SLSP 2015. LNCS (LNAI), vol. 9449, pp. 123–134. Springer, Cham (2015). https://doi.org/10.1007/978-3-319-25789-1_12. https://hal.inria.fr/hal-01184195

22. Jouvet, D., Bartkova, K., Dargnat, M., Lee, L.: Analysis and automatic classification of some discourse particles on a large set of french spoken corpora. In: 5th International Conference on Statistical Language and Speech Processing, SLSP 2017, Le Mans, France, October 2017. https://hal.inria.fr/hal-01585567

23. Jouvet, D., Laprie, Y.: Performance analysis of several pitch detection algorithms on simulated and real noisy speech data. In: 25th European Signal Processing Conference, EUSIPCO 2017, Kos, Greece, August 2017. https://hal.inria.fr/hal-01585554

24. Jouvet, D., Mesbahi, L., Bonneau, A., Fohr, D., Illina, I., Laprie, Y.: Impact of pronunciation variant frequency on automatic non-native speech segmentation. In: 5th Language and Technology Conference - LTC 2011, Poznan, Poland, pp. 145–148, November 2011. https://hal.archives-ouvertes.fr/hal-00639118

25. Jurafsky, D., et al.: Automatic detection of discourse structure for speech recognition and understanding. In: 1997 IEEE Workshop on Automatic Speech Recognition and Understanding Proceedings, pp. 88–95. IEEE (1997)

26. Kawahara, H., de Cheveigné, A., Banno, H., Takahashi, T., Irino, T.: Nearly defect-free F0 trajectory extraction for expressive speech modifications based on STRAIGHT. In: Interspeech, pp. 537–540 (2005)

27. Kawahara, H., Estill, J., Fujimura, O.: Aperiodicity extraction and control using mixed mode excitation and group delay manipulation for a high quality speech analysis, modification and synthesis system straight. In: MAVEBA, pp. 59–64 (2001)

28. Kawahara, H., Katayose, H., De Cheveigné, A., Patterson, R.D.: Fixed point analysis of frequency to instantaneous frequency mapping for accurate estimation of F0 and periodicity. In: Eurospeech, pp. 2781–2784 (1999)

29. Kolář, J., Lamel, L.: Development and evaluation of automatic punctuation for French and English speech-to-text. In: Thirteenth Annual Conference of the International Speech Communication Association (2012)

30. Král, P., Kleckova, J., Cerisara, C.: Sentence modality recognition in French based on prosody. In: International Conference on Enformatika, Systems Sciences and Engineering-ESSE, vol. 8, pp. 185–188. Citeseer (2005)

31. Kulkarni, A., Vincent, C., Denis, J.: Layer adaptation for transfer of expressivity in speech synthesis. In: 9th Language and Technology Conference Proceedings of LTC 2019 (2019)

32. Lanjewar, R.B., Chaudhari, D.: Speech emotion recognition: a review. Int. J. Innov. Technol. Explor. Eng. (IJITEE) **2**, 68–71 (2013)

33. Lee, L., Bartkova, K., Dargnat, M., Jouvet, D.: Prosodic and pragmatic values of discourse particles in French. In: 9th Tutorial and Research Workshop on Experimental Linguistics, ExLing 2018, Paris, France, August 2018. https://hal.inria.fr/hal-01889925

34. Lee, L., Bartkova, K., Jouvet, D., Dargnat, M., Yvon, K.: Can prosody meet pragmatics? Case of discourse particles in French. In: To Appear in Proceedings of ICPhS 2019. International Congress of Phonetic Sciences (2019)

35. Margolis, A., Ostendorf, M.: Question detection in spoken conversations using textual conversations. In: Proceedings of the 49th Annual Meeting of the Association for Computational Linguistics: Human Language Technologies: Short Papers-Volume 2, pp. 118–124. Association for Computational Linguistics (2011)

36. Martin, P.: Prosodic and rhythmic structures in French. Linguistics **25**(5), 925–950 (1987)

37. Mesbahi, L., Jouvet, D., Bonneau, A., Fohr, D., Illina, I., Laprie, Y.: Reliability of non-native speech automatic segmentation for prosodic feedback. In: Workshop on Speech and Language Technology in Education - SLaTE 2011. ISCA, Venise, August 2011. https://hal.inria.fr/inria-00614930

38. Novak, J.R., Minematsu, N., Hirose, K.: Phonetisaurus: exploring grapheme-to-phoneme conversion with joint n-gram models in the WFST framework. Nat. Lang. Eng. **22**(6), 907–938 (2016)
39. Orosanu, L., Jouvet, D.: Combining lexical and prosodic features for automatic detection of sentence modality in French. In: Dediu, A.-H., Martín-Vide, C., Vicsi, K. (eds.) SLSP 2015. LNCS (LNAI), vol. 9449, pp. 207–218. Springer, Cham (2015). https://doi.org/10.1007/978-3-319-25789-1_20. https://hal.inria.fr/hal-01184196
40. Orosanu, L., Jouvet, D., Fohr, D., Illina, I., Bonneau, A.: Combining criteria for the detection of incorrect entries of non-native speech in the context of foreign language learning. In: SLT 2012–4th IEEE Workshop on Spoken Language Technology, Miami, United States, December 2012. https://hal.inria.fr/hal-00753458
41. Pirker, G., Wohlmayr, M., Petrik, S., Pernkopf, F.: A pitch tracking corpus with evaluation on multipitch tracking scenario. In: Interspeech, pp. 1509–1512 (2011)
42. Quang, V.M., Castelli, E., Yên, P.N.: A decision tree-based method for speech processing: question sentence detection. In: Wang, L., Jiao, L., Shi, G., Li, X., Liu, J. (eds.) FSKD 2006. LNCS (LNAI), vol. 4223, pp. 1205–1212. Springer, Heidelberg (2006). https://doi.org/10.1007/11881599_150
43. Rao, K., Peng, F., Sak, H., Beaufays, F.: Grapheme-to-phoneme conversion using long short-term memory recurrent neural networks. In: 2015 IEEE International Conference on Acoustics, Speech and Signal Processing (ICASSP), pp. 4225–4229. IEEE (2015)
44. Schröder, M.: Expressive speech synthesis: past, present, and possible futures. In: Tao, J., Tan, T. (eds.) Affective Information Processing, pp. 111–126. Springer, London (2009). https://doi.org/10.1007/978-1-84800-306-4_7
45. Schuller, B.W.: Speech emotion recognition: two decades in a nutshell, benchmarks, and ongoing trends. Commun. ACM **61**(5), 90–99 (2018)
46. Segal, N., Bartkova, K.: Prosodic structure representation for boundary detection in spontaneous French. In: Proceedings of ICPhS, pp. 1197–1200 (2007)
47. Sethu, V., Epps, J., Ambikairajah, E.: Speech based emotion recognition. In: Ogunfunmi, T., Togneri, R., Narasimha, M.S. (eds.) Speech and Audio Processing for Coding, Enhancement and Recognition, pp. 197–228. Springer, New York (2015). https://doi.org/10.1007/978-1-4939-1456-2_7
48. Shadiev, R., Hwang, W.Y., Huang, Y.M.: Review of research on mobile language learning in authentic environments. Comput. Assist. Lang. Learn. **30**(3–4), 284–303 (2017)
49. Sorin, A., et al.: The ETSI extended distributed speech recognition (DSR) standards: client side processing and tonal language recognition evaluation. In: IEEE International Conference on Acoustics, Speech, and Signal Processing, vol. 1, pp. 129–132 (2004)
50. Stede, M., Schmitz, B.: Discourse particles and discourse functions. Mach. Transl. **15**(1–2), 125–147 (2000)
51. Strömbergsson, S.: Today's most frequently used f 0 estimation methods, and their accuracy in estimating male and female pitch in clean speech. In: Interspeech 2016, pp. 525–529 (2016)
52. Talkin, D.: A robust algorithm for pitch tracking (RAPT). In: Kleijn, W.B., Paliwal, K.K. (eds.) Speech Coding and Synthesis, pp. 495–518. Elsevier, Amsterdam (1995)
53. Viberg, O., Grönlund, Å.: Mobile assisted language learning: a literature review. In: 11th World Conference on Mobile and Contextual Learning (2012)
54. Witt, S.M., Young, S.J.: Phone-level pronunciation scoring and assessment for interactive language learning. Speech Commun. **30**(2–3), 95–108 (2000)

55. Wu, Z., Watts, O., King, S.: Merlin: an open source neural network speech synthesis system. In: SSW, pp. 202–207 (2016)
56. Yao, K., Zweig, G.: Sequence-to-sequence neural net models for grapheme-to-phoneme conversion. arXiv preprint arXiv:1506.00196 (2015)
57. Zen, H., et al.: The HMM-based speech synthesis system (HTS) version 2.0. In: SSW, pp. 294–299. Citeseer (2007)

Text

Using a Database of Multiword Expressions in Dependency Parsing

Tomáš Jelínek[(✉)]

Faculty of Arts, Institute of Theoretical and Computational Linguistics,
Charles University, Prague, Czech Republic
tomas.jelinek@ff.cuni.cz

Abstract. Identifying and correctly handling multiword expressions is critical for understanding a language system and for properly functioning NLP tools. This paper presents a database of multiword expressions (MWE) we build for the Czech language which currently contains more than 7,000 entries. It contains detailed information about the properties of MWEs, e.g. about their idiomaticity and variability. The database also contains manually verified dependency structures of MWEs. We show one of the possible uses of the database: identification and correction of parsing errors in sentences containing MWEs.

Keywords: Multiword expressions · Dependency parsing ·
MWE database

1 Introduction

Handling multiword expressions in NLP tasks can be tricky. If such an expression is not correctly recognized as such, it can confuse software tools and render the results of processing a given sentence useless. This is why a lot of effort is dedicated to this NLP domain, with workshops (e.g. [14]) and shared tasks (e.g. [20]) aimed at solving specific problems of this task.

We adopt the definition of multiword expressions of Baldwin and Kim [1]: "Multiword expressions (MWEs) are lexical items that: (a) can be decomposed into multiple lexemes; and (b) display lexical, syntactic, semantic, pragmatic and/or statistical idiomaticity", adding morphological idiomaticity (i.e. multiword expressions in which at least one word form is used exclusively in this MWE) to the list.

In order to categorize MWEs and facilitate work with them, several electronic databases of multiword expressions of various languages have been created in recent years, for example [5,7] or [8].

In this paper, we present a database of Czech multiword expressions, consisting of more than 7000 entries. Each MWE is assigned a type (such as verbal idiom, stereotyped comparison, proverb etc.); morphological, syntactic, semantic, lexical and pragmatic idiomaticity and variability is recorded, as well as other

© Springer Nature Switzerland AG 2019
K. Ekštein (Ed.): TSD 2019, LNAI 11697, pp. 19–31, 2019.
https://doi.org/10.1007/978-3-030-27947-9_2

useful data, among which dependency syntactic structure of the expression. The entries in this database can be linked to MWEs identified automatically in texts (in corpora). We use syntactic annotation of MWEs contained in the database to correct their parses: 92% of identified errors are corrected.

2 "A Pain in the Neck for NLP"

"Syntactically idiomatic MWEs can lead to parsing problems, due to nonconformance with patterns of word combination as predicted by the grammar," Sag states in his famous article [19]. There is, for example, a multiword expression *být s to (něco udělat)* 'to be able to (do something)' in Czech, consisting of the verb *být* 'to be', the preposition *s* 'from'/'with' and the demonstrative pronoun *to* 'it'. The preposition *s* governs the accusative case in this multiword expression, which is unusual, since it generally governs the genitive or instrumental case. The accusative case with this preposition appears only in two MWEs: *být s to* and *kdo s koho* lit. 'who from whom': 'a showdown, who wins against the other'. The MWE *být s to* governs an obligatory infinitive. In dependency syntax, it is unclear which token should be the governing node for the infinitive. In Prague Dependency Treebank 3.0 (PDT) [9], the pronoun *to* has been chosen, with the preposition *s* marked as a particle or part of a MWE **AuxY** and not as a preposition **AuxP**. As the syntactic function **AuxY** is ambiguous, the automatic conversion from the PDT format to the Universal Dependencies annotation system is at a loss what to do: for the 22 occurrences of *být s to* in PDT, it generates 10 combinations of UD dependency relations for the preposition *s* and the pronoun *to* with nmod – cc, cc – acl and nmod – advmod the most prominent (see Fig. 1 for an example of incorrect conversion in the UD PDT corpus and the structure we think the sentence should have according to UD annotation rules), in 13 cases the pronoun governs the preposition and in 9 cases the preposition governs the pronoun. Few of these constructions come even close to

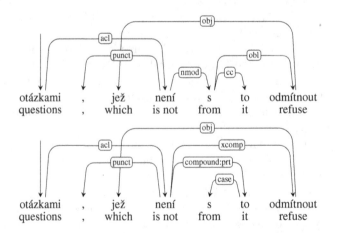

Fig. 1. Automatically generated and correct UD representation of MWE *být s to*

correctly represent the MWE according to UD annotation rules. This shows how a relatively simple and frequent MWE can complicate automatic processing of sentences when not handled properly.

3 Syntactic Representation of Multiword Expressions

The question of how to represent multiword expressions in dependency syntactic structure has been much discussed in recent years. The opinion prevails that it is necessary to differentiate between different types of multiword expressions and reflect these differences in the dependency structure. In the Universal Dependencies annotation system [18], there are, for example, three special labels of syntactic relations (deprel) for words which are part of a MWE: **fixed** for grammaticized expressions (*in spite of*), **flathead** for headless MWEs like names and dates and **compound** for noun compounds such as *phone book* or phrasal verbs, e.g. *find out*. Other multiword expressions (including more complex verbal MWEs such as *kick the bucket* in English or *kroutit nad něčím hlavou* 'shake one's head (in disbelief) over something' in Czech) are annotated according to general rules (no specific information that the words belong to a MWE is assigned).

In Prague Dependency Treebank, the annotation on the surface syntactic level does not specifically deal with multiword expressions in general, only some special cases are treated separately: multiword prepositions and conjunctions, numbers, dates and multiword proper names. Multiword expressions are recognized in the PDT and marked in a separate standoff annotation [2].

Regardless of the selected annotation system, there are cases in which there is no point in trying to impose a structure on an expression and it is necessary to settle for a technical solution; for many MWEs, however, the structure is analogous to syntactic constructions in language in general, the only difference consists in the non-compositional meaning. And there are many cases in between. Most of the multiword expressions we analyzed do not show any syntactic anomalies, the only difference between such MWEs and other text consists in non-compositional meaning. For example, the saying *hodit flintu do žita* lit. 'to throw a gun into the rye', 'to give up' in the sentence *Kluci nehodili flintu do žita* 'the boys didn't give up' has exactly the same structure and relations between words as (compositional) *Nina hodila oblázek do moře* 'Nina threw a pebble into the sea'; the expression *Ariadnina nit* 'Ariadne's thread', i.e. a means to find one's way out of a labyrinth, is the same combination of an agreeing attribute (a possessive adjective) and a noun as in *Dianina smrt* 'Diana's death', with the difference in a non-compositional meaning of the MWE. In these cases, the syntactic structure and labels are the same as if the words did not belong to a MWE (as in UD or PDT), the information that the words belong to a MWE must be preserved, though.

In other MWEs, the structure is the same as in similar combinations of words in general language, but the syntactic relations change: in the expression *kroutit hlavou nad něčím* lit. 'twist one's head over something', 'shake one's head (in disbelief) over something', the prepositional phrase *nad něčím* is not a location as in *Tobogan se kroutí nad vodním areálem jako had* 'the water-slide twists over the water park like a snake'; in the MWE, it becomes an object (indirectly) affected by the action and this should be reflected in the dependency label[1]. Then there are multiword expressions which have a more or less unusual syntactic structure as in the abovementioned expression *být s to*: the verb *být* 'to be' does not usually govern an infinitive, but with the prepositional phrase *s to* it does. In the MWE *klesat na mysli* lit. 'to decline on mind', 'to lose hope', the verb *klesat* acquires an object with a valency it does not have in other uses.

For some multiword expressions, no meaningful syntactic structure can be constructed, the relations between words fall outside usual categories. In Czech, this happens in some fixed multiword adverbials as *křížem krážem* 'criss-cross' (where the second word is a phonetic variation of the first one and appears only in this MWE) or *(mlátit) hlava nehlava* lit. '(kick) head non-head', '(kick) without caring where the blows land' where the same noun appears twice, one in the usual, positive form, one negated. It is also difficult to find an appropriate dependency structure for expressions with ellipsis of the governing verb (or verbs) such as *já na bráchu, brácha na mě* lit. 'me to brother, brother to me', 'you scratch my back, I'll scratch yours', with two parallel groups of a noun or pronoun in nominative and a prepositional phrase, with supposedly the same verb omitted in each group. In such cases, a technical solution should be adopted, a more or less flat structure, with appropriate dependency labels reflecting the fact that the words belong to a MWE.[2]

4   The LEMUR Database

In order to register and describe Czech multiword expressions, a database LEMUR (**le**xicon of **mul**tiword expressions) has been created. It is designed to be both human and machine-readable. It contains more than 7000 multiword expressions of various types and uses: proverbs, sentence idioms, verbal idioms, light verb constructions, compound nominals, stereotyped comparisons, multiword prepositions and conjunctions etc. In the database, every MWE is assigned a lemma, a simple definition, a usage type (proverb, weather lore, stereotyped comparison, quotation, term, set phrase, multiword preposition/conjunction, other) and a syntactic type (nominal phrase, prepositional phrase, adjectival phrase, verbal phrase, clausal, light verb construction, other). If it displays morphologic, syntactic, lexical, semantic or pragmatic idiomaticity, it is described in

---

[1] The annotation manual of the PDT states: abstract or metaphorical meanings tend to be determined as **Obj** (see *zaplést se do intrik* 'to get involved in intrigues': this is not a location). https://ufal.mff.cuni.cz/pdt2.0/doc/manuals/en/a-layer/html/ch03s02x05.html.

[2] See the annotation manual of the PDT: There exist, however, collocations the syntactic structure of which is so doubtful and unclear that it is impossible to propose a reasonable syntactic representation. In such cases we take recourse to a technical representation. This is really the last resort, used only in cases when all other attempts at a meaningful representation fail. https://ufal.mff.cuni.cz/pdt2.0/doc/manuals/en/a-layer/html/ch03s06x23.html.

the database as well. Similarly, if an MWE exhibits variability on any of these levels (e.g. lexical variability), it is noted, too. The design of the database is described from the linguistic point of view in [10] and from a more technical point of view in [21], the description here will be briefer.

4.1   The Structure of the Database

The entries in the database are defined as slots (corresponding to the tokens) and fillers, the formalism allows for various types of a filler (lemma, morphological tag, the same lemma as in another slot etc.). The slots can be marked as obligatory or optional.

The MWE *já na bráchu, brácha na mě* 'you scratch my back, I'll scratch yours' has, for example, seven slots (six words and comma in the middle); for all the slots, morphological categories are defined (POS and/or case): nominative - preposition - accusative - comma - nominative - preposition - accusative; slots 2 and 6 have the same lemma: preposition *na* 'at/to'. Two alternative sub-entries are defined for this MWE: the first one describes the usual, canonic version *já na bráchu, brácha na mě* lit. 'me to brother, brother to me', the second sub-entry describes all possible lexical variants of the MWE such as *já na vládu, vláda na mě* lit. 'me to government, government to me' or *Klaus na Majora, Major na Klause* lit. 'Klaus to Major ...' (former Czech and British prime ministers). For both sub-entries, slot 7 has the same lemma as slot 1, slot 5 has the same lemma as slot 3. In the first sub-entry, the lemmas in slot 1 and 3 are defined (*já* 'me' and *brácha* 'brother'); in the second one, slots 1 and 3 can contain any lemma (it usually is a person or an institution, but such a restriction cannot be entered into the database).

4.2   Idiomaticity

A multiword expression is morphologically idiomatic when it contains word forms which are specific for this particular MWE, e.g. in *podle nosa poznáš kosa* lit. 'by the nose you recognize the blackbird', 'a person is recognizable by his/her appearence', the form *nosa* is a specific form of genitive singular of the noun *nos* 'nose' which appears only in this idiom (in order to rhyme with *kosa*). MWEs with lexical idiomaticity contain monocollocable (or near monocollocable) words such as the adjective *lvový* 'lion's', which is used almost exclusively in the biblical MWE *jáma lvová* 'lion's den'. Under syntactic idiomaticity, we describe any unusual syntactic behaviour of words, such as in *být s to*, unusual word order etc.

4.3   Variability

In the database entries, we also describe variability at several levels of language description. For example, in lexical variability, each token can be either invariable, partially variable (with a list of possible lexemes) or fully variable, sometimes with other limitations, eg. the MWE *Bůh dal, Bůh vzal* 'the Lord has given, the Lord has taken away' displays a more or less unrestricted variability of nouns, with the constraint that the same noun must be repeated (e.g. *stát dal, stát vzal* 'the state has given, the state has taken away'). In the domain of syntactic variability, we assume that all usual transformations and modifications are possible (word order changes, nominalization of verbal phrases, passivization etc.) unless stated otherwise in the database.

4.4 Syntactic Structure

Every MWE has a dependency and a constituency syntactic structure assigned. The dependency structure uses the formalism of the analytical layer of PDT. The constituency structure is based on HPSG grammar. Both syntactic structures are automatically generated and manually corrected.

5   Identification of MWEs in Texts

In order to link entries in the LEMUR database with texts (primarily in corpora), it is first necessary to identify MWEs. At this point, we are using the FRANTA system [12] and [13], an older software based on search for regular expressions manually entered in the fast lexical analyzer generator (FLEX), which is compiled and fast enough to process large texts. The system is based on word forms in the text and automatic lemmatization and morphological tagging. A large part of the multiword expressions originate from a printed lexicon of MWEs [3], other entries were added when identified in corpora. There are currently more than 36,000 different MWE variants in the FRANTA system (several variants may point to the same database entry). The variants are grouped by the last word in a given variant (used as a keyword in the text searches) entered in tables using combinations of lemmas (<l>) and parts of morphological tags (<t>) such as in the following entry for one variant of the MWE *hodit flintu do žita* lit. 'to throw a gun into the rye', 'to give up':

<l>**žito** <t>V<l>hodit <t>NNFS4<l>flinta <t>RR--2<l>do
<m><t>NNNS2 [<l2 >586_hodit_flintu_do_žita]

The keyword (last word) for this variant is *žito*. If this word is found in the text, the presence of other elements to the left of the keyword (*hodit, flinta, do*) is tested. If all elements with correct tags and in appropriate word order are found, all the elements are marked with one MWE lemma, the number (586) pointing to the corresponding entry in the LEMUR database.

A major drawback of this system, however, is its lack of transparency and the need to manually insert new entries to the LEMUR database also into the FRANTA system, including all documented or probable variants. Our long-term goal is to create an automated system that would work directly with the data exported from the LEMUR database (including data on variability, word order, etc.) and search for the multiword expressions in the texts.

5.1   Annotation of MWEs in Corpora

We plan to use the LEMUR database and the FRANTA system to annotate MWEs in written corpora of the Czech National Corpus of the SYN series [11][3], starting in 2020. The FRANTA system, expanded by some MWE variants automatically generated from the LEMUR database (for example, nominalizations of verbal MWEs) will be used to identify multiword expressions in texts. Each token that will be part of the MWE will be assigned a MWE lemma (identical to the lemma in the LEMUR database), a MWE tag that summarizes the basic characteristics of the MWE (usage type, syntactic properties, etc.) extracted from the LEMUR database. One token in each MWE will be tagged as the governing token of the whole MWE based on the syntactic structure (the first token for flat structures). One governing token is chosen for the purposes of statistics, in order to avoid counting MWEs according to the number of tokens, but only once per occurrence of the entire MWE.[4]

6   Parsing of Text Containing MWEs Using Data from the LEMUR Database

There are several principally different solutions in the area of dependency parsing of sentences containing MWEs: MWE can be identified and processed before parsing, along with parsing or after parsing (for a more detailed review of such approaches see Constant et al. [4]). Each solution has its advantages and disadvantages. For simple contiguous MWEs, the first approach, processing MWEs before parsing, seems to be the best one, as the MWE can be transformed into one token, parsed and, after parsing, restored with the dependency structure assigned by handcrafted rules (we process multiword prepositions and some multiword named entities in this way). For most of the MWEs, due to their variability and the possibility of individual tokens in the MWE to be modified by other, external words, this approach is inappropriate. As we can use manually verified internal syntactic structures of MWEs exported from the LEMUR database, we process most of the MWEs after parsing: for the MWEs identified by the FRANTA system, we verify and, if necessary, correct their syntactic structures.

6.1   Identification of Parsing Errors of MWEs

Using the manually checked dependency structures of the multiword expressions contained in the LEMUR database, errors in parsing of sentences containing MWEs can be identified. In order to test this approach, 700 MWEs containing verbs and prepositional phrases (e.g. *kroutit nad něčím hlavou* 'shake one's head over something') were exported with their syntactic structures. From the SYNv6 corpus [15], which is a large corpus of contemporary written Czech texts (mainly

---

[3] See also http://wiki.korpus.cz/doku.php/en:cnk:syn.
[4] See also http://wiki.korpus.cz/doku.php/en:cnk:syn.

journalistic) containing 4 billion words, we extracted sentences containing at least one MWE from the list, a total of 235,000 sentences. These sentences were parsed using the TurboParser [16] trained on PDT 3.0 training data.

We automatically verified to what extent the syntactic annotation of the selected MWEs is correct as compared to the structures extracted from the database. The parsing accuracy (unlabeled and labeled accuracy scores, UAS and LAS) is shown in Table 1. We compare the overall parser accuracy rates tested on the PDT e-test data (first line) and the parsing accuracy of tokens included in MWEs (second line), as measured by the automatic comparison of the parses and structures from the database, accounting for the manually detected error percentage in MWE identification.

Table 1. Parsing accuracy

	UAS	LAS
E-test	88.27	81.79
MWEs	95.96	79.98

The unlabeled accuracy score (UAS) of tokens included in MWEs is far higher than the overall one (95.96% vs 88.27%). According to our analysis this is because the sentences in which the selected MWEs appear are relatively simple sentences with fewer embedded sentences, coordination, apositions, ellipsis and other phenomena difficult to parse. Most (more than 90%) of the MWEs studied have, in addition, a structure and syntactic functions quite similar to those commonly found in Czech texts, so that MWE identification is not always necessary for correct parsing. The labeled accuracy score (LAS) of parsed MWEs is, however, lower than the overall score. This is because of frequent errors in dependency labels concerning MWEs with prepositional phrases such as *dát se do práce* lit. 'give oneself into work', 'start working', interpreted as objects in the database, but frequently labeled as adverbials by the parser (see below).

In order to better understand the differences between the parsing results and the structures exported from the databse, a sample of 500 cases was analyzed manually. According to this analysis, most errors in dependency (UAS), approx. 85%, consist in erroneous PP-attachment, for example in the MWE *sypat si popel na hlavu* lit. 'pour ashes over one's head', 'to regret', in which the parser repeatedly attaches the PP *na hlavu* to the noun *popel* instead of the verb *sypat*. The parser also frequently erroneously interprets the verb *být* as an auxiliary verb instead of a member of MWE (usually a predicate), as in *nebudu v pokušení číhat před jejím domem* 'I will not be tempted to lurk in front of her house', where the parser does not make the connection *nebudu v pokušení* and instead interprets the verb *nebudu* with the infinitive *číhat* as a compound future tense *nebudu číhat*, as shown in Fig. 2.

Most errors in dependency label assignment not related to errors in dependency relations involve prepositional phrases, with confusion between adverbial

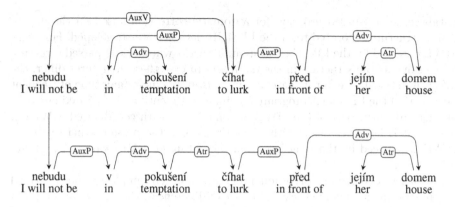

Fig. 2. Incorrect and correct parse of MWE *být v pokušení* (PDT style)

functions (obl, oblique in UD, Adv in PDT) and indirect object (iobj, Obj) such as *přivést do jiného stavu* lit. 'lead into a different state', 'make pregnant' or *dát se do hovoru* lit. 'give oneself into talk', 'start a conversation', in which prepositional phrases do not have the function of a local adverbial, but of an object indirectly affected by the action: in the database, we label these cases as objects (Obj), but the parser marks them as averbials.

In some cases (7% of differences in attachment), the system FRANTA incorrectly identifies MWEs leading to false flags (correct dependency structure marked as incorrect). This occurs mainly when two MWEs overlap or when two similar MWEs can be mapped to one sentence, such as in *půjde si sednout na osm měsíců do basy*, lit. 'he is going to sit for eight months in jail', where two possible MWEs overlap (*jít do basy* 'to go to jail' and *sednout si do basy* 'to sit in jail'). By incorrectly choosing the first one, the FRANTA system suggests that the prepositional phrase *do basy* should be attached to the verb *jít* 'go' instead of the verb *sednout* 'sit'. Some errors occur also when MWEs are coordinated, such as in *jsou zdraví a v kondici* 'they are healthy and in good condition', where the FRANTA system marks the MWE *jsou v kondici* 'they are in condition' and the identification tool than assumes that the PP *v kondici* 'in condition' should be attached directly to the verb *jsou* 'are'. Other errors are caused by the fact, that the system does not always take into account all the context of the (supposed) MWE, as in *Anička odešla s prázdnou miskou* 'Anička left with an empty bowl', in which the FRANTA system identifies the MWE *odejít s prázdnou* lit. 'leave with empty', 'go empty-handed', which is a stereotyped ellipsis, but in this case, a noun in the correct case *miskou* 'bowl' is present in the sentence, it is therefore not an instance of the marked MWE.

6.2   Correction of Parsing Errors of MWEs

Most of the identified MWE parsing errors can be corrected using the database by substituting the erroneous parsed structure with the structure from the database. A rule-based program for automatic correction based on the dependency structures exported from the LEMUR database was developed. For every MWE detected by the FRANTA system, it checks whether the parsed structure is the same as the structure in the database. In case these structures differ, the MWE is checked whether it matches any known weakness (any type of frequent false flag) of the FRANTA program, e.g. incorrect identification of auxiliar verbs as (not-auxiliary) part of the MWE or some issues with coordinated MWEs; if it does, it is left unchanged. Otherwise the part of the parsed structure of the MWE is replaced by the structure from the database, taking care to avoid creating cycles.

In order to test our correction program, another sample of 500 identified differences was manually checked. In 88% of differences, the correction program intervened (approx. 8% of the remaining 12% were incorrect identifications of MWEs by the FRANTA system; in 4%, the system was too cautious). Most of the corrections (90%) are reattachments of prepositional phrases in MWEs (usually from a noun to a verb). The majority of the remaining corrections concern the attachment of reflexive pronouns. The most complex corrections relate to stereotyped comparisons (e.g. *jako ryba ve vodě*, 'as a fish in water'[5], as shown in Fig. 3. No changes involving more than five tokens have been performed (in a single MWE, sometimes two MWEs in a sentence have been corrected).

As the correction program is more careful not to respond to typical false flags of the FRANTA system, it corrects only 88% of the identified differences between the parsing and the structure contained in the database, but 97% of these corrections are justified; in 1% an incorrect structure is inaccurately modified resulting in another incorrect structure, the remaining 2% are improper alternations of a correct structure, i.e. new errors caused by the correcting system. Most of these

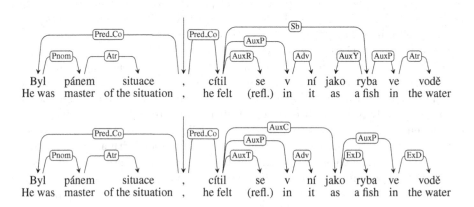

Fig. 3. Incorrect and corrected parse of MWE *cítit se jako ryba ve vodě* (PDT style)

---

[5] In PDT, the conjunction *jako* 'as' can be assigned two significantly different structures depending on its semantics, see https://ufal.mff.cuni.cz/pdt2.0/doc/manuals/en/a-layer/html/ch03s06x26.htm and https://ufal.mff.cuni.cz/pdt2.0/doc/manuals/en/a-layer/html/ch03s02x07.html\#auxyjakol. This is confusing for the parser.

errors are caused by erroneous identification of MWEs (system FRANTA), one error was due to incorrect structure stored in the database.

7   Conclusion

In this paper, we introduced a newly created database of Czech multiword expressions LEMUR, which aims to facilitate the handling of the complex phenomenon of MWEs for both NLP tools and linguists. We have shown one possible use of this database, namely automatic corrections of parsing of sentences containing MWEs. By using the syntax structures contained in the database, we are able to correct 92% of identified errors. We plan to further extend and refine the data contained in the LEMUR database, e.g. by adding typical translations (English, French, German) extracted from parallel corpora. The dependency structures in the database use the formalism of the analytical layer of the Prague Dependency Treebank to ensure their compatibility with other treebanks tagged in this formalism. However, we would like to add structures using the Universal Dependencies standard in order to increase usability of the database.

For dependency parsing in our experiments, we used TurboParser, which was state of the art a few years ago, and which we have used to automatically tag treebanks, but with the advent of deep learning methods, TurboParser has become obsolete, therefore we would like to train neural networks parsers such as one created by Nguyen and Verspoor [17] or Dozat and Manning [6].

In trying to understand the language system, we cannot do without understanding multiword expressions. For Czech, we are working on a database of such expressions that allows both linguists and computers to access a long list of MWEs along with detailed information about their properties. The work on the database and its use in NLP continues. Only by a thorough research can this complex phenomenon be resolved.

Acknowledgments. This paper, the creation of the database and the experiments on which the paper is based have been supported by the Ministry of Education of the Czech Republic, through the project Czech National Corpus, no. LM2015044 and by the Grant Agency of the Czech Republic through the grant 16-07473S (Between lexicon and grammar).

References

1. Baldwin, T., Kim, S.N.: Multiword expressions. In: Indurkhya, N., Damerau, F.J. (eds.) Handbook of Natural Language Processing, 2nd edn., pp. 267–292. Chapman and Hall/CRC (2010). http://www.crcnetbase.com/doi/abs/10.1201/9781420085938-c12

2. Bejček, E., Straňák, P.: Annotation of multiword expressions in the Prague dependency treebank. Lang. Resour. Eval. **44**(1–2), 7–21 (2010)

3. Čermák, F., et al.: Slovník české frazeologie a idiomatiky. Leda, Prague (2016)

4. Constant, M., et al.: Multiword expression processing: a survey. Comput. Linguist. **43**(4), 837–892 (2017). https://doi.org/10.1162/COLI_a_00302

5. Czerepowicka, M., Savary, A.: SEJF - a grammatical lexicon of polish multiword expressions. In: Vetulani, Z., Mariani, J., Kubis, M. (eds.) LTC 2015. LNCS (LNAI), vol. 10930, pp. 59–73. Springer, Cham (2018). https://doi.org/10.1007/978-3-319-93782-3_5. https://hal.archives-ouvertes.fr/hal-01223683

6. Dozat, T., Manning, C.D.: Deep biaffine attention for neural dependency parsing. CoRR abs/1611.01734 (2016). http://arxiv.org/abs/1611.01734

7. Geyken, A.: Bootstrapping a database of German multi-word expressions. In: Proceedings of the Fourth International Conference on Language Resources and Evaluation (LREC 2004). European Language Resources Association (ELRA), Lisbon, May 2004. http://www.lrec-conf.org/proceedings/lrec2004/pdf/595.pdf

8. Grégoire, N.: DuELME: a Dutch electronic lexicon of multiword expressions. Lang. Resour. Eval. **44**(1), 23–39 (2010). https://doi.org/10.1007/s10579-009-9094-z

9. Hajič, J., et al.: Prague dependency Treebank 3.5. LINDAT/CLARIN digital library at the Institute of Formal and Applied Linguistics (ÚFAL), Faculty of Mathematics and Physics, Charles University (2018). http://hdl.handle.net/11234/1-2621

10. Hnátková, M., et al.: Eye of a needle in a Haystack – multiword expressions in Czech: typology and lexicon. In: Mitkov, R. (ed.) EUROPHRAS 2017. LNCS (LNAI), vol. 10596, pp. 160–175. Springer, Cham (2017). https://doi.org/10.1007/978-3-319-69805-2_12

11. Hnátková, M., Křen, M., Procházka, P., Skoumalová, H.: The SYN-series corpora of written Czech. In: Proceedings of the Ninth International Conference on Language Resources and Evaluation (LREC 2014), pp. 160–164. European Language Resources Association (ELRA), Reykjavik, May 2014. http://www.lrec-conf.org/proceedings/lrec2014/pdf/294_Paper.pdf

12. Kopřivová, M., Hnátková, M.: Identification of idioms in spoken corpora. In: Gajdošová, K., Žáková, A. (eds.) Proceedings of the Seventh International Conference Slovko 2013, pp. 92–99. Slovak Academy of Sciences, Bratislava (2013)

13. Kopřivová, M., Hnátková, M.: From dictionary to corpus. In: Phraseology in Dictionaries and Corpora, Maribor, Slovenia, pp. 155–168 (2014)

14. Kordoni, V., Cholakov, K., Egg, M., Markantonatou, S., Nakov, P.: Proceedings of the 12th workshop on multiword expressions. In: Proceedings of the 12th Workshop on Multiword Expressions. Association for Computational Linguistics (2016). http://aclweb.org/anthology/W16-1800

15. Křen, M., et al.: Corpus SYN, version 6, 18 December 2017. http://kontext.korpus.cz

16. Martins, A., Almeida, M., Smith, N.A.: Turning on the turbo: fast third-order nonprojective turbo parsers. In: Annual Meeting of the Association for Computational Linguistics - ACL, pp. 617–622, August 2013

17. Nguyen, D.Q., Verspoor, K.: An improved neural network model for joint POS tagging and dependency parsing. CoRR abs/1807.03955 (2018). http://arxiv.org/abs/1807.03955

18. Nivre, J., et al.: Universal dependencies v1: a multilingual treebank collection. In: Calzolari, N., et al. (eds.) Proceedings of the Tenth International Conference on Language Resources and Evaluation (LREC 2016). European Language Resources Association (ELRA), Paris, May 2016

19. Sag, I.A., Baldwin, T., Bond, F., Copestake, A., Flickinger, D.: Multiword expressions: a pain in the neck for NLP. In: Gelbukh, A. (ed.) CICLing 2002. LNCS, vol. 2276, pp. 1–15. Springer, Heidelberg (2002). https://doi.org/10.1007/3-540-45715-1_1. http://dl.acm.org/citation.cfm?id=647344.724004

20. Savary, A., et al.: The PARSEME shared task on automatic identification of verbal multiword expressions. In: Proceedings of the 13th Workshop on Multiword Expressions (MWE 2017), pp. 31–47. Association for Computational Linguistics (2017). http://aclweb.org/anthology/W17-1704
21. Vondřička, P.: Design of a multiword expressions database. Prague Bull. Math. Linguist. **112**, 83–110 (2019)

Explicit Discourse Argument Extraction for German

Peter Bourgonje[(✉)] and Manfred Stede

Applied Computational Linguistics, Universität Potsdam, Potsdam, Germany
{bourgonje,stede}@uni-potsdam.de
http://angcl.ling.uni-potsdam.de

Abstract. We present an approach to the extraction of arguments for explicit discourse relations in German, as a sub-task of the larger task of shallow discourse parsing for German. Using the Potsdam Commentary Corpus, we evaluate two methods (one based on constituency trees, the other based on dependency trees) to extract both the internal and the external argument, for which our best results are 86.73 and 77.85 respectively. We demonstrate portability of this set of heuristics to another language and also put these scores into perspective by applying the same method to English and compare this to published results.

Keywords: Discourse processing · Shallow discourse parsing ·
Discourse argument extraction

1 Introduction

A central notion in the field of discourse processing is the uncovering of coherence relations contained in a piece of text. Typically, these relations are defined as two text spans that stand in a certain relation to each other, such as contrast, cause-reason, or concession. A relation can be signaled explicitly by the use of a discourse connective, or implicitly, in which case the relation and its sense must be inferred from the context. What constitutes a connective depends on the theory maintained. The same goes for how the two text spans -the arguments of the relation- are defined, and also for the sense assigned to the relation. On a high level, two different approaches can be distinguished; one where all discourse relations present in some text are connected in a tree-like hierarchy, to arrive at a single structure (usually a tree) to represent the entire text. An example of this approach is Rhetorical Structure Theory as proposed by [9]. Another approach, referred to as shallow discourse parsing, attempts to identify discourse relations without making any commitment to their higher-level ordering (e.g. how two discourse relations relate to each other). This approach has been popularized by the Penn Discourse TreeBank (PDTB) [11], a subset of the Penn TreeBank annotated for discourse relations. This latter approach is the one we follow. The task at hand then is to identify discourse relations, which are defined by two arguments, a connective (which can be implicit) and a relation sense. Within

© Springer Nature Switzerland AG 2019
K. Ekštein (Ed.): TSD 2019, LNAI 11697, pp. 32–44, 2019.
https://doi.org/10.1007/978-3-030-27947-9_3

this framework, the difference between explicit vs. implicit relations, referring to the presence or absence of an overt connective, is often reflected by a different strategy for the two, see [8,10,17] (a notable exception to this though is described in [2]). The experiments reported on in this paper focus on explicit relations only. Furthermore, the components described are to be understood as part of a larger architecture for shallow discourse parsing for German. In such a pipeline architecture (following [8]), connectives are identified and disambiguated first (see [3]), the two arguments are identified (the main contribution of this paper) and in subsequent steps a sense can be assigned. This paper addresses only the subtask of extracting the two arguments for explicit discourse relations. The rest is structured as follows: Sect. 2 reviews related work on this sub-task of discourse parsing. Section 3 described the data we used in our experiments. Section 4 explains the methods used to extract the arguments. Section 5 discusses the results and Sect. 6 concludes the main contributions.

2   Related Work

For related work on this sub-task of discourse parsing, we have to look to work on English, as to the best of our knowledge, no comparable approaches working on German exist. The shared tasks of the 2015 and 2016 CONLL conferences [20,21] sparked interest in this task, resulting in several approaches, most of which use a pipeline architecture of which explicit argument extraction is one component. For this particular task, [10] report f-scores of 52.0 and 76.2 for external and internal arguments, respectively. The figures for [8] are 47.7 and 70.3. [17] report the best scores, with 50.7 and 77.4. What makes it difficult to compare these scores to the German setting though is the size of the available training data. [10] present their scores over the training section of the 2016 shared task, comprising ca. 278k instances of relations. [8] and [17] use the training section of the PDTB, having a similar size.

Specifically focusing on the extraction of discourse arguments, [19] approach the issue by locating the lexical head of the argument in a dependency tree structure, side-stepping issues with discourse segmentation (which can to some extent be relatively arbitrary, for example with respect to whether or not to include unit-initial or unit-final punctuation marks). They report accuracy figures of 69.8 for external arguments and 90.8 for internal arguments in their best-scoring setup. [1] use the same approach and improve upon it by deploying specialized rankers for individual connectives or connectives grouped by syntactic type (as adverbials tend to have their arguments further away than conjunctions), boosting accuracy for both arguments by 9%. Due to the smaller size of training data available for German, we decided against experimenting with this setup, expecting the drawbacks of data sparsity to be too severe. Additionally, we like to point out that while [19] scores arguments based on lexical head matching, and we use precision and recall for all tokens that make up the arguments, the scores cannot directly be compared. More recently, an LSTM-based approach without any manual input (in the form of hand-crafted rules) is explored in [7]. While promising, their performance relies on the availability of training data and also for the English scenario does not improve on earlier work.

Since the PDTB is annotated over the same text as the Penn TreeBank, syntactic (gold) trees are available, making it possible to investigate alignment of discourse arguments with syntactic boundaries. [5] do exactly this, and find that a major source of dis-alignment is attribution (to someone other than the author of the text, usually a quote attributed to some speaker). While we acknowledge the impact of attribution on discourse segmentation, in the Potsdam Commentary Corpus we do not encounter any non-adjacent relation arguments where the intervening material is due to attribution.

3   Data

To investigate and experiment with discourse arguments in German, we use the Potsdam Commentary Corpus [15], henceforth PCC, which is a corpus of news commentary articles from a local German newspaper containing ca 33k words. It has been annotated for discourse relations and contains 1,110 instances of connectives and their arguments and is, to the best of our knowledge, the largest available resource for this task for German. A smaller corpus comprising a discourse annotation layer over the TÜBA-D/Z corpus is described in [16]. In our corpus, which is only annotated for explicit discourse relations (in contrast to the PDTB, which also includes implicit relations where no connective is present), a relation consists of the connective, an external and an internal argument. The connective is syntactically integrated with the internal argument. The external argument can precede or follow the internal argument and connective. In our corpus, external (or *ext*) and internal (or *int*) is used for the arguments, corresponding to *arg1* and *arg2* respectively in PDTB terminology. To accommodate readers familiar with the task, we will use the (more popular) PDTB terminology and refer to the external argument as *arg1* and the internal argument as *arg2* in the rest of this paper. A visual example of how this is reflected in the (XML) structure of the PCC is shown in Listing 1.1[1].

Listing 1.1. PCC discourse annotation excerpt

```
Und FDP–Luftikus Jürgen W. Möllemann bereist seinerseits
    schon jetzt eifrig den Nahen Osten , um
<unit type="ext" id="5">
    für diesen Fall gerüstet zu sein
</unit>
<unit type="int" id="5">
    <connective id="5" relation="addition">und</connective>
    sich als neuer liberaler Außenminister zu empfehlen .
</unit>
```

---

[1] For readability, only the relation with id 5 is shown in this excerpt. In the corpus, relations are also annotated for the connectives *Und* and *um...zu* in this sample text. Note that this example is not glossed, as its purpose is illustrating the structure of annotations in our corpus, not so much its actual content.

4   Method

The main contribution of this paper is to automatically classify the token spans that make up *arg2* and *arg1* of a connective, once the connective has already been identified. In an application scenario, the connective has to be located and disambiguated first (to establish whether it has discourse or sentential reading). In this contribution however, we will use the gold annotations from the PCC with regard to connectives, and we refer to [3] for more information on connective classification.

Since the task is split up in two parts, that of *arg2* and *arg1* extraction, the rest of this section and Sect. 5 will be split up accordingly. Because we are working toward a shallow discourse parser for German, with a focus on practical application, we use precision and recall of the tokens that make up the argument as a metric. While this makes it harder to compare our performance to other approaches ([1,18,19] use other metrics), we argue that it is more useful for potential downstream tasks to be able to pinpoint the exact token-based location. All numbers presented are the result of 10-fold cross-validation.

4.1   *arg2* Extraction

As mentioned in Sect. 3, the connective is always syntactically integrated with *arg2*. As a baseline, we extract all tokens from the sentence the connective appears in (excluding the connective itself, as the annotation guidelines state that the connective itself is not part of the internal argument). We make an important design decision (and also limiting factor) and only consider single, particular sentences when extracting tokens for the argument. That is, we do not consider the possibility of arguments spanning over multiple sentences. This is actually the case in 71 *arg1*s (6%) and in 26 *arg2*s (2%), so in these cases by design we can only expect to extract a part of the entire argument. Though it has more impact in the *arg1* case, because it is relatively rare in both cases, we consider it an acceptable shortcut. The results for our baseline method are included in Table 2.

To improve over this baseline, we experiment with both a dependency tree and a constituency tree based approach. The dependencies are generated using the German model from spaCy[2], which is trained on the TIGER and WikiNER corpora. We locate the connective in the dependency tree and recursively extract all the tokens under the head of the connective token. In case of multi-token connectives, we take the first token for this procedure. (In the entire corpus, we have 1.027 single token connectives and 83 multi token connectives, i.e. 7%) After that, we apply a set of rules resulting from error analysis on this output. First of all, similar to the baseline, we exclude the connective token(s) from the *arg2* token span. Next we include sentence-final punctuation, as this is typically not a dependency of the head of the connective token, but is part of *arg2* according to the annotation guidelines. Finally, if the connective is a conjunction, we only

---

[2] https://spacy.io/models/de.

take all tokens that, in the plain text, are to the right of the connective. The results for this setup are included in Table 2 under *dependency tree approach*.

The constituency trees are generated using NLTK's implementation of the Stanford parser with the German PCFG model [13]. We locate the connective in the constituency tree, find the first commanding node that is an *S*, *CS* or *VP* and extract all tokens of this sub-tree. Then we again exclude the connective token(s) from this token list, and similar to the dependency approach, take only tokens that are to the right of the connective if it is a conjunction (or in-between ones for discontinuous connectives). The results are shown in Table 2 under *constituency tree approach*.

4.2   *arg1* Extraction

Extracting *arg1* is more complicated than extracting *arg2*. As the connective is not syntactically integrated with it, the sentence containing *arg1* has to be found first. And once this sentence has been found, if the argument is not in the same sentence as the connective, there is little in terms of anchoring (i.e. position in sentence) that gives away the exact position of the token span containing the argument. The distribution of *arg1* positions relative to their connective sentence is shown in Table 1, where −9 means that *arg1* appeared 9 sentences before the connective, 0 means that *arg1* is in the same sentence and 1 means that *arg1* appeared in the sentence following the connective sentence. Note that this largely resembles the numbers reported in [11] (i.e. 60.9% same sentence, 39.1% previous sentence and less than 0.1% others), with the notable exception that the "other" category has a higher percentage in the PCC.

To first predict the sentence *arg1* is located in, a simple majority vote baseline, predicting the most popular class for every unique connective (differentiating between upper- and lower-case) already scores relatively high, with an accuracy of 86.59. To improve upon this, we train a classifier that uses the embedding of the connective itself, the part-of-speech embedding of the connective's part-of-speech and categorical values for sentence position and path to the root node (in a constituency tree). The word embeddings are trained on Common Crawl and Wikipedia [6]. We generated the part-of-speech embeddings from the TIGER corpus [4].

Table 1. Sentence position of *arg1* relative to the connective in the PCC

−9	1	<0.1%
−6	4	0.3%
−4	6	0.5%
−3	8	0.7%
−2	47	4.2%
−1	435	39.2%
0	603	54.3%
1	6	0.5%

We use a CNN with four fully connected layers. Training this on all classes from Table 1 results in an accuracy of 94.52. Since for multi-sentence arguments, we consider a prediction correct if the predicted sentence is in the set of actual sentences, the actual performance will be slightly lower. However, since multi-sentence arguments only make up a small portion of the data set (see Sect. 4.1) and because we are focusing on final, token-based precision and recall for the argument's tokens, we mention this somewhat inaccurate performance just as an indication. We use this position classifier throughout the rest of the experiments reported upon.

Once the position has been predicted, we proceed to extract the relevant token span. As a baseline, we extract all tokens in the predicted sentence if this is the preceding or following sentence, and all tokens up to the (first) connective token if the predicted sentence is the same sentence as the connective. The results are shown in Table 3.

Since the majority of *arg1* instances are in the same sentence, we again use both a constituency and dependency tree approach to improve on the baseline. For next or previous sentence cases, both approaches are equal to the baseline, since there is no anchoring in the tree possible if *arg1* is in another sentence than the connective.

For the dependency tree approach, we apply the following rules: If the connective is sentence-initial, all dependencies of the direct head of the connective are extracted. Since this would be *arg2*, we take the inverse of this set of tokens to be *arg1*. If the connective is not sentence-initial, we use a classifier to predict whether *arg1* will precede or follow the connective. If the classifier predicts *arg1* to the left of the connective, we find the first verb preceding the connective (traversing the sentence right to left, starting at the connective) and take all dependents of the head of this verb (including the head itself) to be *arg1*. If no verb was found, we take all tokens to the start of the sentence to be the argument. If the classifier predicts the argument to the right of the connective, we take the dependents of the head of the first verb to the right of the connective (including the head itself) as the argument (or all remaining tokens if no verb was found). The results for this setup are included in Table 3. To predict whether *arg1* precedes or succeeds the connective, we used a simple majority vote per connective (differentiating between upper- and lower-case), and obviously always assume *arg1* to be to the right of the connective if both are in the same sentence and the connective is sentence-initial. The accuracy of this within-sentence position prediction is 78.59.

An example of the dependency-based approach for both *arg2* and *arg1* is shown in Fig. 1, based on the example in (1). In the relevant part of the dependency tree, the connective (underlined) is "und" (*and*), *arg2* (bold) is extracted by taking all dependents of the head of the connective token "empfehlen" (*recommend*), and *arg1* (italics) is extracted by finding the first verb to the left of the connective (as per the same sentence classifier's prediction), taking the head of that (*sein*, as we exclude modals in search of the closest verb), and taking all dependents (including the head itself).

(1) "Und FDP-Luftikus Jürgen W. Möllemann bereist seinerseits schon jetzt
eifrig den Nahen Osten, um für diesen Fall gerüstet zu sein und sich als
neuer liberaler Außenminister zu empfehlen".
*And FDP-member Jürgen W. Mölleman is already eagerly visiting the east-
ern regions, to prepare for the scenario where he would be recommended as
the new liberal foreign minister.*

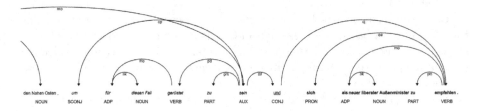

Fig. 1. Partial dependency tree example

For the constituency tree approach, we apply the following rules: If the connective is sentence-initial, we assume that *arg2* will follow first. Thus, the first
parent node of the connective that is either an S, CS or VP is extracted. We
select the right sibling(s) of this node, and take this to be *arg1*. If the connective
is not sentence-initial, we use the same-sentence predictor again. We extract the
first parent node of the connective that is either an S, CS or VP and depending
on the prediction of the classifier, we take the left sibling(s) or the right sibling(s)
of this node to be *arg1*. For discontinuous connectives (40 instances in total, i.e.
4% of all relations) we take the tokens in between the first part and the last
part, excluding the connective tokens themselves. The results for this setup are
included in Table 3.

5   Results and Evaluation

5.1   *arg2* Extraction

Table 2. *arg2* results

	Precision	Recall	f1-score
Baseline	58.87	96.88	73.23
Dependencies	87.31	85.52	86.41
Constituents	**87.53**	**85.94**	**86.73**

As mentioned earlier, and as also reflected by the scores, extracting *arg2* is a
significantly easier task than extracting *arg1*. Both approaches we tried improve

by over 13 points compared to the baseline, and perform very much comparable to each other. Upon error analysis, we found that for the dependency approach, a relatively common source of errors were a) cases where the dependency parser was not able to construct a correct tree. Most notably in the case of "aber" (*but/however*) as a connective, such as in (2) and (3). Or b) cases where the approach of selecting all dependents of the head of the connective does not suffice, as is the case for "auch" (*also*) in (4).

(2) "Die aber scheint nur bei zwei Standorten an der Berliner Straße garantiert:"
    However, this seems to be guaranteed only at two locations on the Berliner street:

(3) "Zu danken ist das Projekt vielen, in erster Linie aber der Eigeninitiative der Dorfbewohner".
    Much is thanks to the project, but first and foremost to the initiative of the villagers.

(4) "Mit der PR-Aktion wurde eben auch eine Hemmschwelle überwunden".
    With the PR campaign, an inhibition threshold was also overcome.

Furthermore, we found that sometimes punctuation marks were ignored by the dependency parser, but taken as cues by the annotator, as in (5), where the dependency approach extracted (for the connective "und" (*and*)) the complete phrase *wissen theoretisch Bescheid - in der Realität aber enden leider zu viele Fahrten aus den genannten Gründen verhängnisvoll.*, whereas the annotator selected only *wissen theoretisch Bescheid -*. Because accommodating to this tends to overfitting on the domain and data set, we decided against implementing an extra rule for these cases.

(5) "Sicher, wir haben das alles schon gehört und wissen theoretisch Bescheid - in der Realität aber enden leider zu viele Fahrten aus den genannten Gründen verhängnisvoll".
    Sure, we've heard all this before and theoretically know all about it - but in reality too many trips end fatally for the reasons mentioned.

For the constituency based approach, we also ran into the issue with punctuation, where in particular the hyphen is often used in the PCC to introduce some kind of related material which is not picked up on by the parser (i.e. interpreting this as an S-like structure would be more accurate, but of course would need domain-specific parser training). This issue sometimes lead to incorrectly including intervening material (which the annotator left out), or looking for the higher S-node and including the surrounding material as well (which the annotator deemed irrelevant for the relation). Something that had a negative impact on both approaches were inconsistencies with sentence-final punctuation. This has to be included as per the annotation guidelines, but is sometimes excluded; the tool that was used for annotation automatically suggests a piece of text as argument, but if this automatic suggestion was incorrect, the annotators had to manually select the relevant piece of text in the GUI, where initial or final punctuation characters are easily overlooked; we consider making the corpus more consistent with regard to this another aspect of future work.

To put these numbers into perspective, we applied the same combination of a position classifier and within-sentence heuristics to English, using the training section of the 2016 CoNLL shared task. Recall that this has ca. 278k relations, compared to the 1.110 in the PCC. However, because of the importance of the rule-based component, the data size does not necessarily have a large impact. The only changes in the set of rules is that while for German, clause-initial and/or clause-final punctuation is added to the argument (if this was not included in the sub-tree already), for English this is not done as a post-processing step (due to annotation guideline differences between the PCC and the PDTB). These numbers are to be compared to the numbers for *arg2* presented in Table 4 in [10]: 75.3 and 78.2 for the WSJ test set and the blind set respectively. As noted in Sect. 2, a direct comparison to other approaches is not straightforward either because of a different measure or the effect of error propagation from connective classification. Using the dependency approach (using the spaCy parser with the English model), we get an f1-score of 88.63 (compared to 86.41 for German/PCC) and using the constituency approach (also using the same (NLTK Stanford) parser but with English model), we get 82.58 (compared to 86.73 for German/PCC). One possible explanation for the considerable drop when using constituency trees could be the fact that both prepositions and subordinating conjunctions have the same part-of-speech tag (i.e *IN*). Although the PDTB, in contrast to the PCC, does not include prepositions as connectives, our heuristics were designed with the PCC in mind (which does include prepositions). This could lead certain rules to trigger in unwanted scenarios, although more investigation would be needed to clarify this. The much smaller difference for the dependency-based scenario could be due to more available training data and better models for the English dependency parser (though one would expect the same to be true for the constituency parser). Again, more research would be needed to verify this, but we consider it out of scope as we are focusing on German.

5.2   *arg1* Extraction

Table 3. *arg1* results

	Precision	Recall	f1-score
Baseline	55.46	85.75	67.26
Dependencies	76.25	**79.65**	**77.85**
Constituents	**82.43**	73.69	77.72

For *arg1* instances, the baseline performs lower and both approaches improve by a smaller margin compared to the *arg2* scenario. Moreover, precision and recall for dependencies and constituents show opposing images, with precision considerably higher than recall for constituents and the opposite scenario, though with a smaller difference, for dependencies. Upon error analysis we found several cases where conjunctions on S or VP-level were not treated correctly and again punctuation characters having a conjunction-like role, though in the *arg1* case this seems to be more problematic for the constituents approach (lower recall due to conjuncts being overlooked) than for the dependencies approach.

Looking at f1-score though, also in this setup both approaches perform very much comparable. This time the dependency-based approach outperforms the constituency-based one though by a small margin. Apart from the larger negative impact of punctuation and conjunction for the constituents approach, we generally encountered the same types of errors for the *arg2* scenario for both approaches. The lower performance can furthermore be explained by error propagation of the relative sentence position classifier; if the wrong sentence has been predicted, every token in that sentence contributes to the false positives and every token in the actual *arg1* to the false negatives. As illustrated in Table 1, the vast majority of discourse relations have their *arg1* either in the same sentence, the previous sentence, or the sentence before the previous sentence. In an attempt to increase accuracy of the sentence position classifier, we experimented with simplifying to a three-class classification problem accordingly. This however did not increase the final f-score. Due to the higher percentage of *arg1* cases being scattered over multiple sentences (see Sect. 4.1), our practical limitation of considering only single sentences also has more (negative) impact here. We consider the possibility of arguments being divided over multiple sentences an important piece of future work (6% for *arg1* and 2% for *arg2*, see Sect. 4.1).

To compare our results to English, we again applied the same procedure to the CoNLL 2016 shared task data. For the constituency approach, we obtained an f1-score of 59.32 (compared to our 77.72 for German) and for the dependency approach an f1-score of 59.35 (compared to our 77.85 for German). Again consulting Table 4 in [10], our scores should be compared to 57.2 and 58.6 for the WSJ test set and the blind set respectively. Given that in the *arg1* scenario, the position classifier plays a role, and more training data is likely to increase its performance, this significant drop in performance is not what we expect. Upon consulting the annotation manuals [12] and [14], we found no obvious cause for this discrepancy; both guidelines allow for nominalizations, VP-coordinates or other causes that may lead to annotated spans smaller than typical finite clauses[3] (both syntax-based approaches are biased toward typical finite clauses). Since our focus is on German, we consider a more detailed analysis of this difference an interesting piece of future work, but one that is out of scope for this paper.

Because the heuristics around selecting tokens once the position (i.e. sentence) of the *arg1* has been established are very much comparable to the ones for *arg2* (often times the same rules are applied, followed by tree subtraction to end up at *arg1*), the same sources of errors as in the *arg2* scenario occur here.

One considerable additional source of error for the *arg1* case though are ones where the wrong sentence has been predicted by the classifier, amounting to

---

[3] Note that while the PCC guidelines allow for these constructions, they contain no syntactic directives per se and instruct the annotator to select the minimal token span necessary to interpret the discourse relation without phrasing this in terms of syntactic units.

potentially many false negatives (every word of the actual *arg1*) and false positives (every word in the predicted sentence). To gain some insight into *arg1* instances that are not in the current or previous sentence (these cases occur relatively often compared to the PDTB, see Sect. 4.2), we looked at all relations where the *arg1* is not adjacent to *arg2* or the connective. Unlike [5], who study attribution as a source of discontinuous or non-adjacent arguments, we find no such cases (more precisely, we do find one case where attribution occurs, but it is not the main source of non-adjacency). After filtering for punctuation inconsistencies (as also reported in Sect. 5.1; where the token causing non-adjacency was just a single punctuation symbol), we are left with 15 cases where some related information or a fragment serving rhetorical purposes is intervening in between both arguments. A typical example is shown in (6), where again the *arg1* is displayed in italics, the connective underlined and *arg2* in bold face. The intervening material ("Warum sollten sie nicht noch einen guten Zweck erfüllen?" (*Why shouldn't it serve a good purpose?*)) here has the purpose of a rhetorical question which does not really contribute to the interpretation of the discourse relation.

(6) "*Wohin dann mit den vom Urlaub übrig gebliebenen Münzen, die bald sowieso nichts mehr wert sind?* Warum sollten sie nicht noch einen guten Zweck erfüllen können? <u>So</u> **wurde die Aktion "Euro-Cash for Kids" gestartet,** und sie fand speziell in Luckenwalde und Umgebung eine riesige Resonanz".
Where to then with the cash remaining from the vacation, which is soon worthless anyway? Why shouldn't it serve a good purpose? <u>Thus,</u> **the initiative "Euro-Cash for Kids" was started,** and it resonated very well especially in Luckenwalde and surroundings.

6   Conclusion and Outlook

We have presented a procedure to extract internal and external arguments (*arg2* and *arg1* in Penn Discourse TreeBank terminology) of explicit discourse relations in German, based on the annotation scheme of the Potsdam Commentary Corpus. Given gold connective information, we extract the internal argument (*arg2*) anchoring it in the connective's sentence using automatically generated constituency and dependency trees. Using a set of syntax-inspired rules, we achieve an f1-score (measuring token overlap) of 86.73. The external argument (*arg1*) is extracted based on a combination of a position classifier (which predicts the position relative to the connective) and a similar set of rules, again trying out both a constituency- and a dependency tree-based approach. We achieve an f1-score of 77.85 for this sub-task. Given the set of heuristics described in this paper, the availability of training data for the position classifier and an available parser, our approach can relatively easily be ported to another language. We demonstrate this by applying it to English and put our German scores into perspective. Furthermore, we note that the difference in performance for a constituency- or dependency tree-based approach is marginal in the German scenario. The work reported on is part of a larger project, working toward a shallow discourse parser for German. For the extraction of explicit discourse relation arguments specifically, we plan to look into multi-sentence arguments more closely, as in the algorithms presented here we only considered the possibility of single sentence arguments. This does not suffice and negatively impacts performance, already in the relatively small Potsdam Commentary Corpus. Because of the syntactic nature of our heuristics, evaluating how they perform in a different domain would be equally interesting (though to the best of our knowledge, only one other corpus, in the news domain, exists for German).

Next steps in the larger context of shallow discourse parsing for German will be the extraction of implicit relations and their arguments, and subsequently the classification of sense for particular discourse relations.

Acknowledgments. Funded by the Deutsche Forschungsgemeinschaft (DFG, German Research Foundation) - 323949969. We would like to thank the anonymous reviewers for their helpful comments on an earlier version of this manuscript.

References

1. Baldridge, J., Elwell, R.: Discourse connective argument identification with connective specific rankers. In: 2008 IEEE International Conference on Semantic Computing(ICSC), pp. 198–205, August 2008. https://doi.ieeecomputersociety.org/10.1109/ICSC.2008.50

2. Biran, O., McKeown, K.: PDTB discourse parsing as a tagging task: the two taggers approach. In: SIGDIAL Conference, pp. 96–104. The Association for Computer Linguistics (2015)

3. Bourgonje, P., Stede, M.: Identifying explicit discourse connectives in German. In: Proceedings of the 19th Annual SIGdial Meeting on Discourse and Dialogue, Melbourne, Australia (2018)

4. Brants, S., et al.: Tiger: linguistic interpretation of a german corpus. Res. Lang. Comput. **2**(4), 597–620 (2004). https://doi.org/10.1007/s11168-004-7431-3

5. Dinesh, N., Lee, A., Miltsakaki, E., Prasad, R., Joshi, A.K., Webber, B.L.: Attribution and the (non-)alignment of syntactic and discourse arguments of connectives. In: FCA@ACL, pp. 29–36. Association for Computational Linguistics (2005)

6. Grave, E., Bojanowski, P., Gupta, P., Joulin, A., Mikolov, T.: Learning word vectors for 157 languages. In: Proceedings of the International Conference on Language Resources and Evaluation (LREC 2018) (2018)

7. Hooda, S., Kosseim, L.: Argument labeling of explicit discourse relations using LSTM neural networks. CoRR abs/1708.03425 (2017). http://arxiv.org/abs/1708.03425

8. Lin, Z., Ng, H.T., Kan, M.Y.: A PDTB-styled end-to-end discourse parser. Nat. Lang. Eng. **20**, 151–184 (2014)

9. Mann, W., Thompson, S.: Rhetorical structure theory: towards a functional theory of text organization. TEXT **8**, 243–281 (1988)

10. Oepen, S., et al.: OPT: Oslo-Potsdam-Teesside–pipelining rules, rankers, and classifier ensembles for shallow discourse parsing. In: Proceedings of the CONLL 2016 Shared Task, Berlin (2016)

11. Prasad, R., et al.: The Penn discourse treebank 2.0. In: Proceedings of LREC (2008)
12. Prasad, R., Miltsakaki, E., Dinesh, N., Lee, A., Joshi, A.: The Penn discourse TreeBank 2.0 annotation manual, January 2007
13. Rafferty, A.N., Manning, C.D.: Parsing three German treebanks: lexicalized and unlexicalized baselines. In: Proceedings of the Workshop on Parsing German, PaGe 2008, pp. 40–46. Association for Computational Linguistics (2008)
14. Stede, M.: Das potsdamer kommentarkorpus. In: Lenk, H.E. (ed.) Persuasionsstile in Europa II. Olms, Hildesheim (2016)
15. Stede, M., Neumann, A.: Potsdam commentary corpus 2.0: annotation for discourse research. In: Proceedings of the Ninth International Conference on Language Resources and Evaluation (LREC 2014). European Language Resources Association (ELRA), Reykjavik, May 2014
16. Versley, Y., Gastel, A.: Linguistic tests for discourse relations in the TüBa-D/Z corpus of written German. Dialogue Discourse, pp. 1–24 (2012)
17. Wang, J., Lan, M.: A refined end-to-end discourse parser. In: Proceedings of the Nineteenth Conference on Computational Natural Language Learning - Shared Task, pp. 17–24. Association for Computational Linguistics (2015)
18. Wellner, B.: Sequence models and ranking methods for discourse parsing. Ph.D. thesis, Brandeis University, Waltham, MA, USA (2009)
19. Wellner, B., Pustejovsky, J.: Automatically identifying the arguments of discourse connectives. In: Proceedings of the 2007 Joint Conference on Empirical Methods in Natural Language Processing and Computational Natural Language Learning (EMNLP-CoNLL) (2007). http://www.aclweb.org/anthology/D07-1010
20. Xue, N., Ng, H.T., Pradhan, S., Prasad, R., Bryant, C., Rutherford, A.: The CoNLL-2015 shared task on shallow discourse parsing. In: Proceedings of the Nineteenth Conference on Computational Natural Language Learning - Shared Task. pp. 1–16. Association for Computational Linguistics, Beijing, China, July 2015. http://www.aclweb.org/anthology/K15-2001
21. Xue, N., et al.: CoNLL 2016 shared task on multilingual shallow discourse parsing. In: Proceedings of the CoNLL-16 Shared Task, pp. 1–19. Association for Computational Linguistics (2016). http://aclweb.org/anthology/K16-2001

Consonance as a Stylistic Feature for Authorship Attribution of Historical Texts

Lubomir Ivanov[✉] and Brandon Neilsen

Computer Science Department, Iona College,
715 North Ave., New Rochelle, NY 10801, USA
livanov@iona.edu

Abstract. We present an investigation of the usefulness of consonance as a stylistic feature for author attribution of historical texts. We describe an algorithm for extracting consonance from written text and a set of experiments using different classifiers to explore the accuracy of consonance-based attribution on a set of 18th-century documents and a collection of 19th-century literary works.

Keywords: Consonance · Authorship attribution · Machine learning · Prosody

1 Introduction

Author attribution is the task of identifying the writer of a text, whose authorship is either unknown or disputed. Modern attribution often blends a machine learning approach, which puts forth an attribution hypothesis, with the skills of a humanities researcher, who investigates this hypothesis in the context of the historical, political, and economic realities of the time period and the personal beliefs and idiosyncrasies of the potential authors. Machine learning has revolutionized authorship attribution by providing more objectivity and thoroughness, as well as the ability to uncover inconspicuous stylistic subtleties. Over the years, machine-learning based attribution has been used to re-examine the authorship of many important literary works [4–8, 14, 19, 20, 25, 26, 33] and to determine the authorship of historically significant documents [27, 30–32]. More recently, author attribution techniques have been adapted to modern applications such as digital copyright- and plagiarism detection, gender identification, forensic linguistics, and anti-terror investigation [1–3, 9, 11, 22, 23, 29, 34, 37].

Authorship attribution is based on three essential "ingredients":

- A set of stylistic features, which capture the intuitive notion of an author's style.
- One or more machine learning classifiers or an ensemble of classifiers.
- A corpus of attributed texts, which can be used to train the machine classifier(s).

K. Ekštein (Ed.): TSD 2019, LNAI 11697, pp. 45–57, 2019.
https://doi.org/10.1007/978-3-030-27947-9_4

The attribution process relies on extracting the frequencies of use of the selected stylistic features in attributed texts in order to train the machine learning classifiers to recognize each author's writing style. Once trained, the models can be applied to recognizing the style of a document of unknown or disputed authorship. For an overview of the field, the reader is referred to these surveys [21, 35, 36].

The proper selection of stylistic features is critical to the attribution process. Some traditionally used features, such as function words, character-/word-n-grams, and part-of-speech (PoS) tags have been demonstrated to consistently perform well in various literary styles - prose, fiction, poetry. Other stylistic features such as sentence length, vowel-initiated words, prefixes and suffixes can, at times, outperform the traditional features, but not consistently and not for all authors. The main contribution of such features is in ensemble classifiers, where they augment the power of traditional features and increase the overall accuracy of attribution. Recently, there has been interest in using prosodic features as stylistic markers for authorship. Lexical stress was considered in [10] and explored in more depth in [16,18]. In [15,17], the roles of assonance and alliteration for author attribution were investigated. These prosodic features are moderately successful, yielding strong results when the author pool is relatively small.

In this paper, we investigate the usefulness of consonance as a stylistic feature for author attribution. We begin by describing an algorithm for extracting consonance from written text. We then describe a set of machine learning author attribution experiments based on two historical corpora - a collection of 18th-century political texts and a corpus of 19th-century Victorian works [12]. The results of the experiments are compared to a set of baseline results obtained through the use of traditional stylistic features and employing the same machine classifier models on the same corpora. We conclude by making a few observations about facts uncovered by the experiments and about the usefulness of consonance in historical as well as in modern authorship attribution.

2 Consonance

2.1 Definition

Consonance is a prosodic literary technique, which involves the repeated use of a (combination of) consonant sound(s) to achieve a stronger effect on the listeners/readers. Consonance focuses the attention on a particular word or phrase to emphasize an idea or an emotion. Consider the following small example: "I have a craving for scrambled eggs". This short sentence contains multiple instances of consonance: The most prominent one is the combined "kr" sound repeated in "craving" and "scrambled". Additionally, the 'k' and the 'r' sounds constitute instances of consonance in their own right. The 'v' sounds in "have" and "craving" are also consonant.

One of the main difficulties in studying consonance (and other literary techniques) is that a precise definition is lacking. Several questions need to be addressed:

1. How far apart should consonant sounds be before they are no longer considered to belong to the same consonance sequence? The humanities literature gives only a vague answer - "close enough to be recognized as consonant". Such a (non-) definition is imprecise since it relies on the individual perception of the reader or listener: Some people may be more attuned to prosodic subtleties, while others may fail to recognize even close-by consonants as constituting an instance of consonance.

2. Are consonants in a consonant complex (e.g. "kr") consonant with single consonants (e.g. 'k')? For example, in the phrase "Craving for cookies", are the "kr" from "craving" and 'k's from "cookies" consonant?

3. Should multiple consonances be considered whenever close-by consonant complexes are encountered? For example, "strange story" has an "st"-based consonance ("st" from "strange" and from "story"), but should the 's' and the 't' be considered as separate instances of consonance, in addition to the "st" consonance? Note also that there is a consonance on 'r' in this example.

4. Deliberate vs. accidental consonance? A long sequence of nearby consonant sounds often indicates a deliberate use by the author. However, many authors rely on short, sometimes interwoven consonance sequences. Consider, for example, following excerpt from "Shall I Wasting in Despair" by George Wither:

> "Great, or good, or kind, or fair
> I will ne'er the more despair
> If she love me, this believe
> I will die ere she shall grieve"

In this case, multiple repetitions of 'g', 'd', 'r', 'l', and 'f' sounds create several interwoven consonant sequences. In this case, the use of these sounds is deliberate, but in many other cases identical consonant sounds may appear nearby circumstantially, simply as a result of the author using the words without conscious awareness of consonance. To the best of our knowledge, there has been no research into identifying accidental vs. deliberate use of consonance.

Exploring these questions in the existing literary and linguistic literature produced few, often conflicting answers. Therefore, we adopted the following convention:

1. We will perform multiple experiments, varying the maximum distance at which nearby identical consonant sounds are still considered consonant.

2. We will consider all possible combinations of nearby consonants and consonant complexes. For example, in the phrase "extremely strong" we will keep track of the "str" complex, the "st" and "tr" sub-complexes, and the 's', 't', and 'r' consonants.

3. We will consider all perceived instances of consonance - deliberate or accidental. We intend to eventually return to and explore this topic in more depth.

The above convention was adopted to achieve the broadest search for possible
consonance in texts. Part of our reasoning stemmed from the fact most authors
use consonance without a conscious thought, simply because particular combinations of words sound good to them. The number of authors who deliberately
employ consonance to achieve a literary effect is significantly smaller. While a
targeted study of such authors' styles will likely produce more definitive attribution results, it will be less useful in a typical attribution experiment, where
a varied collection of authors is usually encountered. Since, our primary goal is
to achieve a high accuracy of attribution under all circumstances, we are less
concerned with how closely we capture the intuitive literary notion of "consonance". That said, an in-depth study of consonance, investigating the questions
poised above, will likely not only serve authorship attribution purposes, but may
provide clarity to literary/linguistic researchers.

2.2   Extracting Consonance from Text

Our consonance extraction algorithm uses a modified version of the Carnegie
Mellon University (CMU) pronunciation dictionary. The CMU dictionary contains 133854 word-pronunciation pairs, which have been augmented with an
additional set of 1861 word-pronunciation pairs, extracted from our historical
corpus. The pronunciations of the additional historical words have been confirmed by experts in 18th-century American/English literature. The dictionary
specifies word pronunciations based on 39 phonemes. Vowels are marked with 0
(no stress), 1 (primary stress), or 2 (secondary stress).

The consonance algorithm takes as input a text and two parameters: the
maximum allowed inter-consonant-distance (maxICD) and the maximum number of tracked consonant-sound/frequency patterns (maxOut). The algorithm is
sketched out below:

```
Convert the text into a string of tokens, TxtStr: A token is
    a consonant, a vowel, or a consonant complex
Create a map, consMap, for <consonanceLabel, count, ICD>
    triples    // ICD means ''Inter-Consonant Distance''
Create a map, freqMap, for <<consonance,count>,freqCount>
    pairs
Create a consonance complex string, consComplexStr, for
    keeping track of consonant complexes
for (each token, t, in TxtStr) {
    if (t is a consonant) {
        if(consMap.containsKey(t)) {
            Increment count for entry with key t
            Set ICD = 0 for entry with key t
        }
        else {  Add <t, 1, 0> to consMap; }
        for (String k in consMap.keySet()) {
            if (k != t) {
```

```
            Increment ICD for entry with key k
            If (ICD > maxICD) {
                Remove entry <k, count, ICD> from consMap
                if (<k,count> does not exists in freqMap)
                    Add <<k,count>, 1> to freqMap
                else
                    Incr. freqCount of <k,count> in freqMap
            }
            Add t to consComplexStr;
            for (all suffixes Str of consComplexStr) {
                if (consMap.containsKey(Str)) {
                    Increment count for entry with key Str
                    Set ICD to 0 for entry with key Str
                }
                else { Add <Str, 1, 0> to consMap }
    } } }
    else { Reset consComplexStr to "" }
  }
  Set outputCount to 0;
  for (each key, k, in freqMap.keySet()) {
    if (outputCount++ < maxOut) {
        Compute the frequency of label k
        Write "k: frequency_of_k" to the output file
    } else break;
} }
```

As a brief example, consider how "strange story" is processed. First, the text string is converted into its corresponding pronunciation using the CMU dictionary: "S T R EY1 N JH S T AO1 R IY0". Then, the sounds are processed one-by-one as described in Table 1.

At the end, 'S', 'T', 'ST', and 'R' are selected as instances of consonance. While not illustrated in this brief example, if the ICD of any entry exceeds the user-specified maxICD parameter, the entry is removed from the consonance table and entered into the frequency table along with its recorded count. Any new instance of the same consonant or consonant complex is entered as a new entry in the consonance table. In the end, the entries in the frequency table are used to calculate the frequencies of consonant patterns, and are written out as vectors for the WEKA data mining software [13].

3   Consonance Experiments

3.1   The 18th-Century Corpus

Our 18th-century historical corpus consists of 224 documents authored by thirty-eight American and British political figures. The number of documents per author varies between 2 and 21 and the document sizes - between 959 and 19101 words (Table 2).

The baseline experiments were conducted using the JGAAP authorship attribution software [21]. We used the full set of historical documents and random

Table 1. Consonance extraction example

Iteration	Consonant	Count	ICD	Notes
1	S	1	0	S is processed as a new entry with a count = 1 and ICD = 0.
2	S	1	1	T and ST are processed as new entries with count = 1 and ICD = 0
	T	1	0	The ICD of S is incremented
	ST	1	0	
3	S	1	2	R, STR, and TR are processed as new entries with count = 1 and ICD = 0
	T	1	1	The ICDs of S, T, and ST are incremented
	ST	1	1	
	R	1	0	
	STR	1	0	
	TR	1	0	
4	S	1	3	N is processed as a new entry with a count = 1 and ICD = 0
	T	1	2	The ICDs of all other entries are incremented
	ST	1	2	
	R	1	1	
	STR	1	1	
	TR	1	1	
	N	1	0	
5	S	1	4	JH is processed as a new entry with a count = 1 and ICD = 0
	T	1	3	The ICDs of all other entries are incremented
	ST	1	3	
	R	1	2	
	STR	1	2	
	TR	1	2	
	N	1	1	
	JH	1	0	
6	S	2	0	A second S is encountered
	T	1	4	The count of S is set to 2, and the ICD of S is reset to 0
	ST	1	4	The ICDs of all other entries are incremented
	R	1	3	
	STR	1	3	
	TR	1	3	
	N	1	2	
	JH	1	1	
7	T	2	1	A second T is encountered
	T	2	0	The counts of T and ST are set to 2, their ICDs are reset to 0
	ST	2	0	The ICDs of all other entries are incremented...
	R	1	4	
	STR	1	4	
	TR	1	4	
	N	1	3	
	JH	1	2	
8	S	2	2	A second R is encountered
	T	2	1	The count of R is set to 2, and the ICD of R is reset to 0
	ST	2	1	The count of STR is not incremented
	R	2	0	... because the EY1 vowel terminates the STR complex
	STR	1	5	The counts of all entries except R are incremented
	TR	1	5	
	N	1	4	
	JH	1	3	

subsets of 15, 10, and 7 authors. The stylistic features used are described in Table 3. The classification was performed with JGAAP's WEKA support vector machines with sequential minimal optimization (SMO) and with WEKA multilayer perceptrons (MLP).

Table 2. Authors of attributed 18th-century texts

Author	Num. of docs	Author	Num. of docs
John Adams	10	James Mackintosh	7
Joel Barlow	4	William Moore	5
Anthony Benezet	5	William Ogilvie	4
James Boswell	5	Thomas Paine	11
James Burgh	7	Richard Price	4
Edmund Burke	6	Joseph Priestley	5
Charles Carroll	3	Benjamin Rush	6
John Cartwright	13	George Sackville	2
Cassandra (pseud. of J. Cannon)	4	Granville Sharp	8
Earl of Chatham (W. Pitt Sr.)	3	Earl of Shelburne (William Petty)	3
John Dickinson	4	Thomas Spence	6
Philip Francis	4	Charles Stanhope	2
Benjamin Franklin	9	Sir Richard Temple	2
George Grenville	3	John Horne Tooke	4
Samuel Hopkins	5	John Wesley	4
Francis Hopkinson	21	John Wilkes	5
Thomas Jefferson	7	John Witherspoon	8
Marquis de Lafayette	5	Mary Wollstonecraft	7
Thomas Macaulay	7	John Woolman	6

Table 3. Baseline accuracies (18th-century corpus)

Classifier/stylistic feature	38 authors	15 authors	10 authors	7 authors
MLP/Function Words	67.86%	85.86%	90.16%	92.31%
MLP/Char-2-Grams	70.09%	80/81%	82.25%	87.18%
MLP/FirstWordInSent	41.52%	64.65%	80.33%	89.74%
MLP/Prepositions	58.04%	69.70%	91.80%	97.44%
MLP/Suffices	58.93%	76.77%	86.89%	84.62%
MLP/VowelInitWords	64.73%	81.82%	86.72%	89.74%
SMO/FunctionWords	68.75%	85.86%	85.25%	92.31%
SMO/Char-2-Grams	61.16%	81.82%	90.16%	92.31%
SMO/FirstWordInSent	37.05%	65.66%	91.80%	97.44%
SMO/Prepositions	54.46%	79.80%	88.52%	89.74%
SMO/Suffices	56.25%	74.75%	85.25%	92.31%
SMO/VowelInitWords	60.27%	84.85%	96.72%	94.87%
Average (MLP):	60.20%	75.76%	86.36%	90.17%
Average (SMO):	56.32%	78.79%	89.62%	93.16%
AVERAGE:	58.26%	77.41%	87.99%	91.67%

We conducted a large number of experiments based on our historical corpus, varying the ICD parameter (5, 10, 15, 25). In all experiments we used maxOut set to 100 and a leave-one-out (L1O) document validation. Three different WEKA classification methods were employed - MLP, SMO, and Random Forest (RF).

The results of all experiments using the author sets from the baseline tests are summarized in Table 4.

Table 4. Consonance accuracies (18th-century corpus)

# of authors/learning method	Maximum accuracy
38 authors/SMO	45.87%
38 authors/MLP	46.79%
15 authors/SMO	74.00%
15 authors/MLP	77.00%
10 authors/SMO	82.67%
10 authors/MLP	88.00%
7 authors/SMO	85.48%
7 authors/MLP	91.94%

In all experiments, the maximum accuracy was obtained with maxICD set to 10. With maxICD either higher or lower than 10, the accuracy decreased, dropping off significantly past maxICD of 15. Thus, we only conducted a small set of experiments using maxICD of 25. The MLP classifiers consistently outperformed the SMO classifiers, and the performance gap increased as the number of authors was reduced. The MLP classifier, however, required a significantly longer time to train - over 16 h for each 38-author experiment. Compared to the baseline results, it is clear that the performance of consonance is fairly weak when a large number of authors is investigated. However, with fifteen or fewer authors the accuracy of consonance is at or above the baseline averages and, in fact, exceeds the accuracy of some traditional stylistic features.

3.2 The Victorian Corpus

The Victorian corpus [12] is a recently developed set of texts representing fifty 19th-century authors with at least five books each. The corpus was constructed from the Gdelt database and has been preprocessed specifically for use in authorship attribution experiments (see [21,38]). After preprocessing, the literary works have been broken up into 1000-word files. Table 5 summarizes the details of the Victorian corpus authorship.

Since processing all textual resources far exceeds the capacity of our available computational resources, we limited ourselves to selecting 20 authors at random and choosing 30 files at random for each author. The authors we selected for our experiments are 4, 8, 9, 11, 13, 17, 19, 24, 26, 27, 28, 32, 33, 34, 35, 39, 43, 44, 48, and 50 (see Table 5 for names). As before, we used JGAAP to conduct the baseline experiments. We performed tests with 20, 12, and 7 authors. Again, we used MLP and SMO classifiers and the same set of stylistic features used on the

Table 5. Authors of attributed 19th-century Victorian corpus texts

#	Author	# of docs	# of words	#	Author	# of docs	# of words
1	Arthur C. Doyle	16	1394980	26	Arlo Bates	15	1531925
2	Charles Darwin	10	513085	27	Bret Harte	64	6406984
3	Charles Dickens	7	368314	28	Catharine M. Sedgwick	18	1531925
4	Edith Wharton	27	2487978	29	Charles Reade	20	1170720
5	George Eliot	22	1064661	30	Edward Eggleston	6	806316
6	Horace Greeley	9	624680	31	Fergus Hume	20	1291603
7	Jack London	16	2216225	32	Frances H. Burnett	43	3464120
8	James Baldwin	16	10220446	33	George Moore	9	1174176
9	Jane Austen	12	1617346	34	George W. Curtis	19	2180926
10	John Muir	16	1162637	35	Helen Mathers	17	806600
11	Joseph Conrad	8	484102	36	Henry Rider Haggard	13	923255
12	Mark Twain	12	988713	37	Isabella L. Bird	20	1170895
13	Nathaniel Hawthorne	15	815377	38	Jacob Abbott	20	3316171
14	Ralph Emerson	28	3936896	39	James Grant	30	1620580
15	Robert L. Stevenson	21	1976693	40	James Payn	54	3667172
16	Rudyard Kipling	10	402301	41	John K. Bangs	12	665969
17	Sinclair Lewis	14	1051828	42	John P. Kennedy	14	1251338
18	Theodore Dreiser	16	1839202	43	John S. Winter	13	1358015
19	Thomas Hardy	22	2078753	44	Lucas Malet	12	1677565
20	Walt Whitman	10	839168	45	Marie Corelli	16	797761
21	Washington Irving	62	3426646	46	Oliver Optic	36	3484099
22	William Carleton	16	696567	47	Sarah O. Jewett	16	1105534
23	Albert Ross	16	844634	48	Sarah S. Ellis	74	5296691
24	Anne Manning	9	827145	49	Thomas A. Guthrie	30	2740952
25	Thomas N. Page	15	1217070	50	William Black	18	1597066

18th-century corpus. The baseline results are shown in Table 6. Notice that the averages are low due to the dismal performance of the First-Word-in-Sentence (FWiS) feature, the reason for which is the preprocessing of the Victorian corpus, which removes punctuation from all texts. Therefore, we also present the average without FWiS, and use it for comparison to the consonance results.

The consonance experiments with the 19th-century corpus were, once again, based on WEKA MLP and SMO classifiers and used a maxICD of 5, 10, and 15 and maxOut set to 100. The results are summarized in Table 7. Again, we observe that consonance is inferior to other stylistic features when the number of authors is large. However, for smaller author sets, consonance performs as well or better than other stylistic features. This is consistent with and confirms the findings from our 18th-century corpus study. Thus, we conclude that, for experiments with fewer than 15 authors, using consonance can enhance the accuracy of attribution. Considering that most actual attribution experiments conducted by our humanities colleagues involve no more than 13 authors (usually between 4 and 7), we are justified in adding consonance to our stylistic features set.

In the experiments with the 19th-century corpus the SMO classifiers outperformed the MLP classifiers by a wide margin. The disparity is due to the fact that the number of training documents used was relatively small compared to

Table 6. Baseline accuracies (19th-century corpus)

Classifier/stylistic feature	20 authors	12 authors	7 authors
MLP/Function Words	71.17%	84.72%	93.33%
MLP/Char-2-Grams	76.17%	91.94%	96.67%
MLP/FirstWordInSent	2.83%	9.72%	13.33%
MLP/Prepositions	44.50%	59.72%	81.90%
MLP/Suffices	54.50%	73.89%	89.05%
MLP/VowelInitWords	66.50%	78.33%	92.38%
MLP/Word-2-Grams	52.16%	69.44%	84.29%
SMO/FunctionWords	73.00%	86.94%	95.24%
SMO/Char-2-Grams	76.00%	89.17%	94.29%
SMO/FirstWordInSent	1.33%	4.72%	6.67%
SMO/Prepositions	49.17%	65.00%	83.81%
SMO/Suffices	57.33%	77.22%	90.00%
SMO/VowelInitWords	67.67%	81.11%	91.43%
SMO/Word-2-Grams	54.17%	71.11%	83.81%
AVERAGE (MLP):	55.48%	66.82%	78.70%
AVERAGE (SMO):	50.44%	67.90%	77.89%
Overall AVERAGE:	53.32%	67.36%	78.30%
Overall AVERAGE (no FWiS):	61.86%	77.38%	89.68%

the number of attributes. While the Victorian corpus provided us with sufficient data for larger scale experiments, we lacked the computational power to handle larger datasets in a reasonable time. We attempted an experiment 20 authors and 100 documents per author but abandoned it after the MLP classifier had completed only two folds after approximately 24 hours of computation. In the future, we intend to use dimensionality reduction techniques in order to address this issue. We also intend to develop a set of CUDA C based classifiers, which can be run on the NVIDIA GP-GPUs at our disposal.

3.3   Additional Observations

A closer examination of the individual author attribution accuracies reveals that some writing styles are more readily identifiable in terms of their use of consonance. In the 18th-century corpus experiments, the f-measure values for Ogilvie, Hopkins, Lafayette, Wollman, and Burgh are between 0.8 and 0.9, while several other authors (Paine, Wollstonecraft, Hopkinson, Adams, Sharp) have f-measure values between 0.65 and 0.7. On the other hand, authors like Witherspoon, Spence, Priestley, Rush, and Boswell exhibit an f-measure of 0. Similarly, in the 19th-century corpus experiments, the f-measures of the authors Hardy, Manning, and Guthrie are between 0.8 and 0.9, while other authors (Wharton, Austen, and

Table 7. Consonance accuracies (19th-century corpus)

# of authors/learning method	Maximum accuracy
20 authors/SMO	45.33%
20 authors/MLP	9.67%
12 authors/SMO	74.44%
12 authors/MLP	70.83%
7 authors/SMO	90.00%
7 authors/MLP	83.81%

Lewis) have an f-measure of 0.2 or less. The set of authors for whom consonance works well is fairly consistent throughout all experiments. Thus, we conjecture that some authors have integrated consonance (consciously or subconsciously) into their writing style, which allows the classifiers to correctly associate specific consonance patterns with these authors. On the other hand, the classifiers have difficulties with authors who do not employ consonance or use it in an indistinct fashion.

4   Conclusion and Future Work

We presented an algorithm for extracting consonance from written text and an experimental study of the use of consonance as a stylistic feature for authorship attribution of historical texts. The experiments indicate that consonance can be a valuable feature when the number of authors is less than fifteen. Consonance is particularly useful for distinguishing among authors who actively and distinctly use consonance in their writings. The experiments suggest that consonance can enhance the attribution results produced by traditional stylistic features and provide a greater confidence to the attribution expert in evaluating an authorship hypothesis. While not reported in this paper, we have conducted a number of additional consonance experiments based on the popular Reuters RCV1 corpus [24,28] and two small poetry corpora. The results are consistent with the ones presented in this paper. This implies that consonance can be useful in modern attribution applications as well.

As indicated earlier, we intend to explore in more depth the issue of accidental vs. deliberate use of consonance in literary works. This is a complex topic, in which machine learning will likely play a key role since crafting an explicit algorithm for recognizing deliberate use of consonance is exceedingly unlikely. We would also like to consider the use of other prosodic features such as intonation and speech rhythm. Finally, we are actively investigating the usefulness of various types of sentiment analysis for authorship attribution. The preliminary results appear promising.

References

1. Abbasi, A., Chen, H.: Applying authorship analysis to extremist group web forum messages. IEEE Intell. Syst. **20**(5), 67–75 (2005)
2. Addanki, K., Wu, D.: Unsupervised rhyme scheme identification in hip hop lyrics using hidden Markov models. In: Dediu, A.-H., Martín-Vide, C., Mitkov, R., Truthe, B. (eds.) SLSP 2013. LNCS (LNAI), vol. 7978, pp. 39–50. Springer, Heidelberg (2013). https://doi.org/10.1007/978-3-642-39593-2_3
3. Agrawal, M., Gonçalves, T.: Age and gender identification using stacking for classification. PAN at CLEF 2016. In: Balog, K., et al. (eds.) CLEF 2016 Eval. Labs and Workshop, 16 September, Evora, Portugal. CEUR-WS.org (2016). ISSN 1613–0073
4. Barquist, C., Shie, D.: Computer analysis of alliteration in Beowulf using distinctive feature theory. Literary Linguist. Comput. **6**(4), 274–280 (1991)
5. Binongo, J.N.G.: Who wrote the 15th book of Oz? An application of multivariate statistics to authorship attribution. Comput. Linguist. **16**(2), 9–17 (2003)
6. Burrows, J.: A second opinion on Shakespeare and authorship studies in the twenty-first century. Shakesp. Q. **63**(3), 355–92 (2012)
7. Burrows, J.: Computation into Criticism: A Study of Jane Austen's Novels and an Experiment in Method. Clarendon Press, Oxford (1987)
8. Craig, H., Kinney, A. (eds.): Shakespeare, Computers and the Mystery of Authorship. Cambridge University Press, Cambridge (2009)
9. deVel, O., Anderson, A., Corney, M., Mohay, G.M.: Mining e-mail content for author identification forensics. SIGMOD Rec. **30**(4), 55–64 (2001)
10. Dumalus, A., Fernandez, P.: Authorship attribution using writer's rhythm based on lexical stress. In: 11th Philippine Computing Science Congress, Naga City, Philippines (2011)
11. Ucelay, J.G., et al.: Profile-based approach for age and gender identification-PAN at CLEF 2016. In: Balog, K., et al. (eds.) CLEF 2016 Eval. Labs and Workshop, 16 September Evora, Portugal. CEUR-WS.org (2016). ISSN 1613–0073
12. Gungor, A.: Benchmarking authorship attribution techniques using over a thousand books by fifty victorian era novelists. Purdue Master of Thesis (2018)
13. Hall, M., Frank, E., Holmes, G., Pfahringer, B., Reutemann, P., Witten, I.: The WEKA data mining software: an update. SIGKDD Explor. **11**(1), 10–18 (2009)
14. Hoover, D.: Authorship attribution variables and victorian drama: words, word-ngrams, and character-ngrams. In: Proceedings of DH 2018, 18 June, Mexico City, Mexico, pp. 212–214 (2017)
15. Ivanov, L.: Learning patterns of assonance for authorship attribution of historical texts: FLAIRS-32, Sarasota, FL, USA, vol. 5, no. 19, pp. 191–196 (2019)
16. Ivanov, L., Aebig, A., Meerman, S.: Lexical stress-based authorship attribution with accurate pronunciation patterns selection. In: Sojka, P., Horák, A., Kopeček, I., Pala, K. (eds.) TSD 2018. LNCS (LNAI), vol. 11107, pp. 67–75. Springer, Cham (2018). https://doi.org/10.1007/978-3-030-00794-2_7
17. Ivanov, L.: Using alliteration in authorship attribution of historical texts. In: Sojka, P., Horák, A., Kopeček, I., Pala, K. (eds.) TSD 2016. LNCS (LNAI), vol. 9924, pp. 239–248. Springer, Cham (2016). https://doi.org/10.1007/978-3-319-45510-5_28
18. Ivanov, L., Petrovic, S.: Using lexical stress in authorship attribution of historical texts. In: Král, P., Matoušek, V. (eds.) TSD 2015. LNCS (LNAI), vol. 9302, pp. 105–113. Springer, Cham (2015). https://doi.org/10.1007/978-3-319-24033-6_12
19. Jackson, M.D.: Determining the Shakespeare Canon: Arden of Faversham and A Lover's Complaint. Oxford University Press, Oxford (2014)

20. Jackson, M.D.: New research on the dramatic canon of Thomas Kyd. Res. Oppor. Medieval Renaiss. Drama **47**, 107–127 (2008)
21. Juola, P.: JGAAP: a system for comparative evaluation of authorship attribution. J. Chicago Colloq. Digit. Hum. Comput. Sci. **1**(1), 1–5 (2009)
22. Kotzé, E.: Author identification from opposing perspectives in forensic linguistics. Southern Afr. Linguist. Appl. Lang. Stud. **28**(2), 185–197 (2010)
23. Kuznetsov, M., Motrenko, A., Kuznetsova, R., Strijov, V.: Methods for intrinsic plagiarism detection and author diarization-PAN at CLEF 2016. In Balog, K., et al. (eds.) CLEF 2016 Eval. Labs and Workshop, 16 September, Evora, Portugal. CEUR-WS.org (2016). ISSN 1613–0073
24. Lewis, D., Yang, Y., Rose, T., Li, F.: RCV1: a new benchmark collection for text categorization research. J. Mach. Learn. Res. **5**, 361–397 (2004)
25. Lowe, D., Matthews, R.: Shakespeare vs. Fletcher: a stylometric analysis by radial-basis functions. Comput. Hum. **29**, 449–461 (1995)
26. Morton, A.: The authorship of Greek prose. J. Roy. Stat. Soc. **128**, 169–233 (1965)
27. Mosteller, W.: Inference and Disputed Authorship: The Federalist. AWL, Reading (1964)
28. NIST. https://trec.nist.gov/data/reuters/reuters.html
29. Ogaltsov, A., Romanov, A.: Language variety and gender classification for author profiling in PAN 2017 - PAN at CLEF 2017. In: Cappellato, L., et al. (eds.) CLEF 2017 Eval. Labs and Workshop, 17 September, Dublin, Ireland. CEUR-WS.org (2017). ISSN 1613–0073
30. Petrovic, S., Berton, G., Campbell, S., Ivanov, L.: Attribution of 18th century political writings using machine learning. J. Technol. Soc. **11**(3), 1–13 (2015)
31. Petrovic, S., Berton, G., Schiaffino, R., Ivanov, L.: Examining the Thomas Paine corpus: automated computer author attribution methodology applied to Thomas Paine's writings. In: Cleary, S., Stabell, I. (eds.) New Directions in Thomas Paine Studies, edn. 1. Palgrave Macmillan, USA (2016). https://doi.org/10.1057/9781137589996_3
32. Petrovic, S., Berton, G., Schiaffino, R., Ivanov, L.: Authorship attribution of Thomas Paine works. In: Proceedings of the International Conference on Data Mining DMIN 2014, pp. 182–188 (2014). ISBN: 1-60132-267-4
33. Smith, M.W.A.: An investigation of Morton's method to distinguish Elizabethan playwrights. Comput. Hum. **19**, 3–21 (1985)
34. Sousa-Silva, R.: Detecting translingual plagiarism: a forensic linguistic contribution to computational processing (2016). http://www.uniweimar.de/medien/webis/events/pan-16
35. Stamatatos, E.: Authorship verification: a review of recent advances. Re. Comput. Sci. **123**, 9–25 (2016)
36. Stamatatos, E.: A survey of modern authorship attribution methods. J. Am. Soc. Inform. Sci. Technol. **60**(3), 538–556 (2009)
37. Tellez, E., Miranda-Jiménez, S., Graff, M., Moctezuma, D.: Gender and language-variety identification with MicroTC-PAN at CLEF 2017. In: Cappellato, L., et al. (eds.) CLEF 2017 Eval. Labs and Workshop, 17 September, Dublin, Ireland. CEUR-WS.org (2017). ISSN 1613–0073
38. University of California Irvine Machine Learning Repository. https://archive.ics.uci.edu/ml/datasets/Victorian+Era+Authorship+Attribution

Bidirectional LSTM Tagger for Latvian Grammatical Error Detection

Daiga Deksne[(✉)]

Tilde, Vienibas gatve 75a, Riga, Latvia
daiga.deksne@tilde.lv
https://www.tilde.com

Abstract. This paper reports on the development of a grammar error labeling system for the Latvian language. We choose to label six error types that are crucial for understanding a text as noted in a survey by native Latvian speakers. The error types are the following: an incorrect use of a preposition, an incorrect agreement in a phrase, an incorrect verb form, an incorrect noun form, an incorrect choice of the definite/indefinite ending of an adjective, and a missing comma. For neural network model training, a large amount of error-annotated training data is required. We generate artificial errors in a correct text to cope with the lack of manually annotated data. As a bidirectional Long Short-Term Memory neural network algorithm is considered the best for erroneous word detection by several authors, we chose this architecture. We train several models – models labeling a single type of error and models labeling all six types of errors. The precision for all types of errors reaches 94.61%, the recall – 94.08%.

Keywords: Grammar errors · Neural network · Word embeddings

1 Introduction

The task of assessing the grammaticality of a text is important in different areas. Existing NLP tools are designed to work well on a correct text but fail to produce a reliable result on a text containing grammatical errors. Errors in a text may interfere with the perception of the text's content, or an important part of the information may even be lost.

Automatic grammar checking systems have seen technological changes over the years. Dale [3] mentions three generations of grammar checking systems: (1) systems employing regular expressions, (2) rule based systems, and (3) systems using statistical language models. The grammar error correction solutions submitted to the shared task organized by the CoNLL-2014 [14] used different approaches: a statistical machine translation approach, a rule-based or machine-learning approach, or a combination of these approaches. However, none of these solutions employed neural network technologies.

In recent years, neural network technologies have gained popularity in many NLP areas including grammar error detection and grammar error correction.

© Springer Nature Switzerland AG 2019
K. Ekštein (Ed.): TSD 2019, LNAI 11697, pp. 58–68, 2019.
https://doi.org/10.1007/978-3-030-27947-9_5

The grammar error detection task is treated as a sequence labeling task [12,16, 17,20], while the grammar error correction task is handled as translation from an erroneous text into a correct text [2,8,11,19].

In this paper, we describe our experience in creating a neural network labeler that marks erroneous words in a sentence, signaling their error type for the Latvian language. Latvian belongs to the inflected language group, it has a complex morphological system. Nouns and adjectives have feminine and masculine gender forms and seven cases. Verbs have three simple tense forms and tree compound tenses. Word order is rather free but most typically it follows the pattern subject-verb-object.

2   Error Types in English and in Latvian Corpora

We compare the error types found in Latvian with the error types found in English as the Grammar Error Correction for English, especially for the texts created by language learners, is a widely studied area. Different mistakes are made by native language speakers and by language learners. Detection of errors in language learner writing is considered to be a different task. This is because universal grammar error correction systems for English typically deal with closed-class errors such as use of articles and prepositions and because content related errors are the third most common errors in language learner corpora, which are also often perceived subjectively by annotators [16]. There is some similarity in the error typology used by grammar correction tools in English and in Latvian. In older studies, article usage errors in English are tackled by machine-learning techniques such as maximum entropy models [10]; in recent years, neural network technologies are more popular [20]. This type of error in Latvian corresponds to a choice between a definite or an indefinite ending for an adjective.

In the CoNLL-2014 shared task [14], 28 error types were included, and the participants were expected to develop systems that detect and correct grammatical errors of all these types. Many types of errors are related to the morphological properties of different part-of-speech words: wrong verb tense, use of modal verbs, incorrect form of a verb, errors in subject-verb agreement, article errors, wrong noun number, erroneous noun and pronoun forms, and incorrect preposition usage. Other errors are more related to the syntax or semantics of text: wrong collocation, style error, incorrect word order, sentence fragment, ambiguous meaning, etc.

For Latvian, several taxonomies of errors are used. A rule-based grammar checker for Latvian is developed on the basis of an error-annotated corpus in which 22 types of errors are marked [5]. Errors are divided into five larger groups with subgroups:

- formatting errors;
- orthographic errors;
- morphology and syntax errors: case, number, or gender disagreement in an attributive phrase, subject-verb disagreement in person, number, or gender,

incorrect use of definite/indefinite ending of an adjective, incorrect noun case if verb is in debitive mood or if negation is used;
- punctuation errors: use of commas in compound or complex sentences, to separate a participial clause, or to separate equal parts of a sentence;
- style errors.

Additional types of errors have been identified while adding texts created by non-native language users to the corpus [6]. Non-native language users have difficulties in choosing the right pronoun, using reflexive verbs, choosing the correct number form for a singular or plural noun, choosing the appropriate prefix for a verb, or using the correct tense for a verb.

In the *Corpus of the Latvian Language Learners* [4], the taxonomy of six error types with up to six subtypes is used:

- spelling errors: capitalization, diacritics, missing or redundant letters, words written separately/together;
- punctuation errors: missing, redundant or incorrect punctuation;
- syntactic errors: word order, missing word, redundant word;
- grammatical errors: derivation, morphophonetic consonant alternation, incorrect word form;
- lexical errors: meaning, compliance, readability, collocation;
- unclear text errors.

In the *Corpus of the Learners of the Second Baltic Language* [23], a similar error taxonomy is used. There are five main error types:

- form (or spelling);
- morphology and word derivation;
- syntax;
- lexis;
- punctuation.

The severity of different types of errors varies. By conducting empirical studies using stimuli sentences from a natural language corpus and sentences generated by experts, Šķilters et al. [21] have identified types of syntactic constructions that are crucial for understanding a text and those that are not considered to be problematic by native Latvian speakers. Prepositional use and agreement errors and the incorrect choice of case and form of definiteness are regarded as the most problematic error types.

3   Error-Annotated Data and Artificial Error Generation

For neural network model training, a large amount of error-annotated or aligned training data is required. For the Grammar Error Correction (GEC) model training for English, several annotated language learner corpora are used with sizes varying from 1,500 text fragments up to 2.5M text fragments. A full review of the freely available error annotated corpora for English is given by Sakaguchi et al.

[18]. The weak aspect of the corpora available in English is a lack of versatility [18]. Most datasets contain texts created by language learners. It isn't clear how systems trained using such data will find errors in the texts of other genres.

For Latvian, there is no large error-annotated corpus available. The corpus developed by Deksne et al. [5] contains 20,877 sentences. The number of examples corresponding to each error type differs significantly. Only a few examples are provided for some types of errors, while a few hundred examples are given for other types of errors. Such a corpus is not suitable for training the neuron network model. The language learners corpora [4,23] are too small and errors made by language learners are very diverse.

Several authors have proposed different methods for generating artificial errors in correct text in order to cope with the lack of manually annotated data. The easiest way would be to replace a word in an arbitrary position with another word from the dictionary, but such examples would not reflect real text errors. It is therefore proposed to choose a linguistically related replacement, i.e., to replace a word with another word or word form made from the same root (e.g., *build, buildings, building*) or by a word with the same part-of-speech [13]. In this way, 16 of the 28 types of errors specified in CoNLL-2014 can be covered.

Rei et al. [15] suggest either translating correct text to incorrect text or inserting erroneous text fragments into correct text. The first method employs a statistical machine translation system that makes it possible to introduce errors in an arbitrary text. The second method identifies incorrect and correct pairs of phrases in a parallel corpus by taking into account the word that comes before and after the identified phrase. Such fragments of incorrect text are inserted elsewhere in a correct text.

To gather more error patterns and to solve the data sparsity problem, Ghosh et al. [9] analyze trigrams in a corrected Twitter corpus. Every erroneous word and its correction are extracted together with the previous and the next adjoining word. Erroneous patterns are introduced into the *OpenSubTitles* corpus [22].

For Latvian, we make linguistically motivated replacements while introducing errors in a correct text. We replace commonly mixed prepositions, we delete commas in some arbitrary positions, and we change endings of some word forms in phrases with a certain syntactic structure.

4   Neural Network Solutions Used for Grammaticality Testing

It is common to use neural network classifiers for grammaticality testing. There are two types of systems used - systems that recognize only one type of errors and those that recognize errors of different types.

The English article correction classifier [20] identifies which article *a/an*, *the*, or ϵ (marks the absence of an article) is appropriate for a given context. This classifier is a convolutional neural network that uses information about the context words before and after an article. Optimal results (precision: 30.15%, recall: 51.74%) are achieved if the six words before and after the location of an article are considered.

Rei and Yannakoudakis [16] train several models with different neural network architectures. Models receive strings of tokens and return the probability of correctness for each token in a context. The data is annotated with 77 types of errors. The best results (precision: 46.1%, recall: 28.5%) are achieved for a model that uses the bidirectional Long Short-term Memory (BiLSTM) neural network algorithm.

Liu and Liu [13] train a binary classifier that tags each word with a tag identifying whether it is grammatically correct. The study shows the shortcomings and benefits of different methods. For the Support Vector Machine (SVM) classifier, there are problems with choosing the properties of the word that are relevant for this task and should be used by the classifier. The convolutional neural network uses a fixed-size window (the n closest words) and does not learn a distant relationship in a sentence. The bidirectional LSTM neural network algorithm is considered the best; it recognizes a word as erroneous if it doesn't fit into context. It motivated as to choose BiLSTM for creation of the grammar error labeling system for the Latvian language.

5 Experiments

5.1 Preparation of Data

We overcome the lack of manually annotated data by introducing errors in a correct text.

We choose to cover error types that might most interfere with the comprehension of the content – agreement errors in a phrase, use of a preposition, incorrect verb forms, incorrect number and case forms of a noun, and incorrect use of the definite/indefinite ending of an adjective, as detected by Šķilters et al. [21].

We use the proprietary general corpus of Latvian texts compiled from different sources. The corpus is parsed using the in-house phrase structure parser. From the fragments of the parse trees, we manually create a list of regular expressions (see Fig. 1) that help to locate phrases with a certain structure and to change the specific words or the endings of the words included in the phrases; in such a way, these words become inappropriate for the context. The first regular expression (in Fig. 1) looks for a prepositional phrase PP consisting of the preposition *pēc* ("after") and the complimentary noun ending with -*uma* (the suffix -*um*- together with the ending -*a*). We create prepositional error by replacing the preposition *pēc* with the preposition *uz* ("on"). The second regular expression looks for a verbal phrase VP consisting of the negative auxiliary verb *nav* ("is not") and the complimentary noun with the ending -*ēja* (the suffix -*ēj*- together with the ending -*a*). In Latvian, noun after the negative auxiliary must be in the genitive case. We introduce the noun form error by changing the ending -*a* to the ending -*s* (the genitive form becomes the nominative form).

One, two, or three errors are introduced in the correct sentences. To guarantee that a source sentence is correct, we take only fully parsed sentences, and partially parsed sentences are skipped. Long sentences containing more than 50 words are also skipped.

```
\(advl\:PP\s+\(main:s\s+pēc\)\(pcomp\:n\s+([^\s]+\)uma\)\)
\(main\:VP\s+\(main\:v\s+(nav)\)\(comp\:n\s+\([^\s\)]+)ēja\)
```

Fig. 1. Samples of parse tree fragments converted to regular expressions

Since Latvian has rather free word order, an important part of the readability of a text depends on the proper use of punctuation marks. In Latvian, commas separate participial clauses, parts of a compound or a complex sentence, equal parts of a sentence, and group insertions. Missing comma errors are introduced in the corpus by deleting a comma in an arbitrary position and labeling the next word with the error type "missing comma".

The prepared corpus contains 2.3 million sentences. The corpus is split into three parts. The test set is formed by 115,000 sentences (or 5%), 1,000 sentences are used for validation, and the remaining sentences are used for training. The corpus also includes correct versions of "artificially damaged" sentences. Some experiments have been performed, including only "damaged" sentences in a corpus and creating separate corpora for each type of error.

5.2 Model Training

We train a neural network classifier based on a bidirectional LSTM algorithm. For model training, we use the neural network sequence labeling system *sequence-labeler* developed by Rei and Yannakoudakis [16]. The system uses the Adadelta optimization algorithm with learning rate 1.0, the size of hidden layers is 200, the batch size is 64, the dropout rate is 0.5, hyperbolic tangent function is used for activation. Training is stopped when the accuracy of the development data does not improve for 3 epochs or after 20 epochs. The models are trained using pre-trained word embeddings built with the *fastText* toolkit [1]. Experiments have been performed with a 100-dimensional word embeddings file that is trained on data with correct sentences from the proprietary general corpus and training data with artificially introduced errors (more than 18 million sentences in total). We have not conducted experiments with the contextual language representation model BERT [7] as multilingual BERT model was not yet released during the active development phase of the project. For the training, the data must be prepared in a CoNLL tab-separated format, i.e., every token and its tag are on a new line with an empty line separating sentences (see Fig. 2).

In our first experiments, we built small separate models for every type of error (see Table 1). In these experiments, each model labels only one type of error. In such a way, the labeler has to learn only five different labels – whether the word is correct (label "O"), whether the word signals the beginning of a wrong phrase (error label begins with "B–"), whether the word is in the middle

```
Atsavināts B-ADJENDING
ierocis E-ADJENDING
nogādāts O
ekspertīzē O
```

Fig. 2. Sample training sentence "Seized weapon delivered to an expert-examination" in CoNLL format

of a wrong phrase (error label begins with "I–"), whether the word is at the end of a wrong phrase (error label begins with "E–"), or whether the error is a single word (error label begins with "S–"). Only small part of prepared data is used for training and testing (the number of sentences used for training is shown in the second column of Table 1).

Table 1. Evaluation results (precision, recall, f-score) for models each labeling a single error type

Model for error type	Train sent.	P	R	F	Errors in test set	Found	Correct
Prepositions	10677	97.97	99.35	98.65	1069	1084	1062
Agreement	3411	91.31	87.81	89.52	3207	3084	2816
Verb form	8744	99.30	99.40	99.35	1000	1001	994
Noun form	1618	97.87	96.70	97.28	1000	988	967
Adjective ending	2965	95.33	95.90	95.61	1000	1006	959
Comma	90083	89.05	82.95	85.89	1167	1087	968

Since erroneous text might have different errors in reality, in the following experiments we build models covering six types of errors by a single model. For these models, the number of labels that the labeler must learn is much larger. We build three such systems differing by input data (see Table 2):

- For the first system M1, we merge training data sets used for the single-error systems (27,415 sentences in training data, 7,033 sentences with 7,276 errors in test data).
- For the second system M2, we randomly generate different errors in the corpus. 99 regular expressions are used for this task (1.15M sentences in training data, 57,500 sentences with 70,666 errors in test data).
- For the third system M3, we randomly generate different errors in the corpus (same as for M2), but we also include the correct sentences (2.3M sentences in training data, 115,000 sentences with 70,666 errors in test data).

Table 2. Evaluation results for models labeling all error types by a single model (precision, recall, and f-score)

Error type	M1			M2			M3		
	P	R	F	P	R	F	P	R	F
Prepositions	80.97	97.10	88.30	**98.54**	**98.86**	**98.70**	97.10	96.50	96.80
Agreement	90.30	83.29	86.65	**94.96**	**95.77**	**95.36**	92.09	93.25	92.67
Verb form	**96.42**	99.60	**97.98**	96.12	**99.74**	97.90	95.90	97.50	96.69
Noun form	**97.58**	**96.90**	**97.24**	96.59	96.74	96.66	93.09	96.28	94.66
Adj. ending	82.41	**95.60**	88.52	**86.30**	95.28	**90.57**	78.02	82.86	80.37
Comma	-	-	-	**96.45**	94.63	**95.53**	95.40	92.92	94.14
All errors	89.28	91.12	90.19	**96.45**	**96.54**	**96.49**	94.61	94.08	94.34

6   Results and Discussion

We start our experiments by building models that recognize a single error type. The best results are achieved by the model marking verb form errors (f-score – 99.35%) and the model marking preposition errors (f-score – 98.65%). Verb form errors introduced in text are related to the use of the imperative, indicative, and subjunctive mood of a verb. Only 7 regular expressions are used to introduce these errors. A common error in the prepositions class is the use of a certain postposition as a preposition. Other errors in this class are related to mistyping or dropping a single letter of a preposition. As a result, a different preposition is created. As errors in these groups are not very diverse, they are learned well by models. The worst results are shown by the model marking missing comma location (f-score – 85.89%) and by the model marking agreement errors (f-score – 89.52%). 27 different regular expressions are used to introduce agreement errors. In Latvian, the attribute and the noun must agree in case, number, and gender. It seems that the diversity of the comma error patterns has prevented them from being recognized at as high of a level as verb form and preposition errors are recognized. The model finds missing comma errors in front of conjunctions very well but not so well - missing commas between equal parts of a sentence.

We have three models recognizing several types of errors by a single model. For model M1, we merge the data created for the single error models. Results for this model are worse than for the separate single-error models. For model M2, we regenerate the training data by allowing different types of errors in a single sentence. The models are not directly comparable since the number of errors for the different error types in the prepared data is not equal. Nonetheless, the best results in model M2 are for verb form errors and for preposition errors.

To minimize the possibility that a model learns to mark correct words as erroneous, we also include the original correct sentences in the data set for our final experiment M3. The results are not as good as for model M2 but probably reflect a real situation more accurately. The worst performance is for the adjective ending error type (f-score of 80.37%). This error type often depends on a wider context or even on a few previous statements. Since the model's training data contains no information on the context outside of sentence boundaries, the model does not have the ability to learn such information. For example, the definiteness of the adjective in the phrase *speciālās īpašības* ("special features") (as expressed in Latvian by the ending of the adjective) depends on a wider context. But for the phrase *olimpiskās medaļas* ("Olympic medals"), the definite ending is used in any context.

7 Conclusion and Future Work

While analyzing the previous work done in the area of error detection, we have found that better results are achieved by error labeling systems built on the basis of the bidirectional LSTM neural network algorithm. We explore this approach for error detection in Latvian. LSTM models work well with the long distance dependencies. It is important for detection of agreement errors as well as missing comma errors. To increase the volume of training data, we artificially introduce errors in correct text. We cover the six types of errors that most obstruct comprehension of text as reported by Šķilters et al. [21]: agreement errors in a phrase, use of a preposition, verb forms, number and case forms of a noun, the definite/indefinite ending of an adjective, and missing commas.

Several models are trained including models labeling a single type of error and models labeling all six types of errors. The results are good. The precision for all types of errors reaches 94.61% and the recall reaches 94.08% for the model trained on correct and erroneous sentences. The lowest results are for the error types that depend on a wider context or on previous statements.

It can be concluded that the artificially introduced errors in the training data have been well mastered by the Bi-LSTM neural network labeler. But there are many other errors in real data that aren't as easy to replicate automatically. The next task for improving the model would be to complement the training data with a wider range of errors, and to try other deep learning algorithms, for example, convolutional neural network, that captures local structures and thus might work well for the languages with a rich morphological system.

Acknowledgment. The research has been supported by the European Regional Development Fund within the project "Neural Network Modelling for Inflected Natural Languages" No. 1.1.1.1/16/A/215.

References

1. Bojanowski, P., Grave, E., Joulin, A., Mikolov, T.: Enriching word vectors with subword information. Trans. Assoc. Comput. Linguist. **5**(1), 135–146 (2017)
2. Chollampatt, S., Ng, H.T.: A multilayer convolutional encoder-decoder neural network for grammatical error correction. In: Thirty-Second AAAI Conference on Artificial Intelligence (2018)
3. Dale, R.: Checking in on grammar checking. Nat. Lang. Eng. **22**(03), 491–495 (2016)

4. Dargis, R., Auziņa, I., Levāne-Petrova, K.: The use of text alignment in semi-automatic error analysis: use case in the development of the corpus of the Latvian language learners. In: Proceedings of the 11th International Conference on Language Resources and Evaluation (LREC), pp. 4111–4115 (2018)
5. Deksne, D., Skadina, I.: Error-annotated corpus of Latvian. In: Utka, A., et al. (eds.) Human Language Technologies - The Baltic Perspective. Proceedings of the sixth International Conference Baltic HLT 2014, FAIA, vol. 268, pp. 163–166. IOS Press, Amsterdam (2014)
6. Deksne, D.: A new phase in the development of a grammar checker for Latvian. In: Skadiņa, I., Rozis, R. (eds.) Human Language Technologies - The Baltic Perspective. Proceedings of the seventh International Conference Baltic HLT 2016, FAIA, vol. 289, pp. 147–152. IOS Press, Amsterdam (2016)
7. Devlin, J.; Chang, M.W.; Lee, K.; Toutanova, K.: Bert: pre-training of deep bidirectional transformers for language understanding. arXiv preprint arXiv:1810.04805 (2018)
8. Ge, T., Wei, F., Zhou, M.: Fluency boost learning and inference for neural grammatical error correction. In: Proceedings of the 56th Annual Meeting of the Association for Computational Linguistics (Volume 1: Long Papers), pp. 1055–1065 (2018)
9. Ghosh, S., Kristensson, P.O.: Neural networks for text correction and completion in keyboard decoding. arXiv preprint arXiv:1709.06429 (2017)
10. Han, N.R., Chodorow, M., Leacock, C.: Detecting errors in English article usage by non-native speakers. Nat. Lang. Eng. **12**(2), 115–129 (2006)
11. Junczys-Dowmunt, M., Grundkiewicz, R., Guha, S., Heafield, K.: Approaching neural grammatical error correction as a low-resource machine translation task. In: Proceedings of the 2018 Conference of the North American Chapter of the Association for Computational Linguistics: Human Language Technologies (Volume 1: Long Papers), pp. 595–606 (2018)
12. Kaneko, M., Sakaizawa, Y., Komachi, M.: Grammatical error detection using error-and grammaticality-specific word embeddings. In: Proceedings of the Eighth International Joint Conference on Natural Language Processing (Volume 1: Long Papers), pp. 40–48 (2017)
13. Liu, Z.R., Liu, Y.: Exploiting unlabeled data for neural grammatical error detection. J. Comput. Sci. Technol. **32**(4), 758–767 (2017)
14. Ng, H.T., Wu, S.M., Briscoe, T., Hadiwinoto, C., Susanto, R.H., Bryant, C.: The CoNLL-2014 shared task on grammatical error correction. In: CoNLL Shared Task, pp. 1–14 (2014)
15. Rei, M., Felice, M., Yuan, Z., Briscoe, T.: Artificial error generation with machine translation and syntactic patterns. In: Proceedings of the 12th Workshop on Innovative Use of NLP for Building Educational Applications, pp. 287–292. ACL, Copenhagen (2017)
16. Rei, M., Yannakoudakis., H.: Compositional sequence labeling models for error detection in learner writing. In: Proceedings of the 54th Annual Meeting of the Association for Computational Linguistics, pp. 1181–1191. ACL, Berlin (2016)
17. Rei, M., Yannakoudakis, H.: Auxiliary objectives for neural error detection models. In: Proceedings of the 12th Workshop on Innovative Use of NLP for Building Educational Applications, pp. 33–43. ACL, Copenhagen (2017)
18. Sakaguchi, K., Napoles, C., Tetreault, J.: GEC into the future: where are we going and how do we get there? In: Proceedings of the 12th Workshop on Innovative Use of NLP for Building Educational Applications, pp. 180–187. ACL, Copenhagen (2017)

19. Schmaltz, A., Kim, Y., Rush, A. and Shieber, S.: Adapting sequence models for sentence correction. In: Proceedings of the 2017 Conference on Empirical Methods in Natural Language Processing, pp. 2807–2813. ACL, Copenhagen (2017)
20. Sun, C., Jin, X., Lin, L., Zhao, Y., Wang, X.: Convolutional neural networks for correcting English article errors. In: Li, J., Ji, H., Zhao, D., Feng, Y. (eds.) National CCF Conference on Natural Language Processing and Chinese Computing. LNCS, vol. 9362, pp. 102–110. Springer, Cham (2015). https://doi.org/10.1007/978-3-319-25207-0_9
21. Šķilters, J., Zariņa, L., Žilinskaitė-Šinkūnienė, E., Skolmeistere, V.: Acceptability rating of ungrammatical colloquial Latvian: how native speakers judge different error types. Baltic J. Mod. Comput. **6**(2), 173–194 (2018)
22. Tiedemann, J.: News from OPUS - a collection of multilingual parallel corpora with tools and interfaces. In: Nicolov, N., Angelova, G., Mitkov, R. (eds.) Recent Advances in Natural Language Processing V. Selected papers from RANLP 2007, pp. 237–248. John Benjamins Publishing Company, Amsterdam/Philadelphia (2009)
23. Znotiņa, I.: Computer-aided error analysis for researching baltic interlanguage. Rural Environment, Education, Personality (REEP). In: Proceedings of the tenth International Scientific Conference, pp. 238–244. LLU, Jelgava (2017)

Methods for Assessing Theme Adherence in Student Thesis

Mikhail Tikhomirov$^{(\boxtimes)}$, Natalia Loukachevitch, and Boris Dobrov

Lomonosov Moscow State University, Moscow, Russia
tikhomirov.mm@gmail.com, louk_nat@mail.ru, dobrov_bv@mail.ru

Abstract. In this paper we study approaches to assessing the quality of student theses in pedagogics. We consider a specific subtask in thesis scoring of estimating its adherence to the thesis's theme. The special document (theme header) comprising the theme, aim, object, tasks of the thesis is formed. The theme adherence is calculated as the similarity value between the theme header and thesis segments. For evaluation we order theses in the increased value of the calculated theme adherence and compare the ordering with expert grades using the NDCG measure. We explore different methods, including probabilistic topic modeling, word embeddings and ontologies. The best configuration for theses ranking is based on the weighted averaged sum of word embeddings (word2vec) and keywords extracted from the theme header.

Keywords: Thesis assessment · Embeddings · Topic modeling · Cosine similarity · Ontology

1 Introduction

Automatic essay scoring can be considered as one of long-standing applications of natural language processing techniques [6,7,19]. But there exists another type of student works, which assessment is useful to be automated, namely student theses (bachelor or magister). Currently, in Russia the automated assessment of student theses exploits only so-called plagiarism detection systems (antiplagiat.ru, etxt.ru), which allow determining the percentage of borrowings in student works [11].

However, a student thesis should also meet such requirements as theoretical and practical significance, elements of novelty in the work, knowledge of the modern literature on the research topic, consistency in the presentation of the material, the scientific style of presentation, and others. Checking these requirements for a specific work could be automated in order to provide an expert with comprehensive information on the work characteristics.

One of important characteristics of a student thesis is its relatedness to the thesis theme. The proclaimed theme is usually concretized in the following terms: aim of the study, object of the study, and the tasks of the work. It is possible to gather all these information into so-called theme header. It is usually supposed

© Springer Nature Switzerland AG 2019
K. Ekštein (Ed.): TSD 2019, LNAI 11697, pp. 69–81, 2019.
https://doi.org/10.1007/978-3-030-27947-9_6

that a student should develop the theme and its details in the presented work. So, there is a subtask of thesis scoring to assess its adherence to the theme header. In the essay scoring, this subtask corresponds to the prompt relatedness subtask [7,16].

In this paper, we study approaches to determining the relatedness between the theme header and student thesis in pedagogics. To evaluate the methods, we have the collection of 40 thousand student theses, 120 student theses among them have double expert scores. The aim of the assessment is as follows: if low relatedness to the thesis theme is detected, then the problems should be visualized to experts and some penalties to the overall score for this work should be proposed by the system. We use several means for assessing relatedness including word embeddings, probabilistic topic modeling, and a thesaurus providing knowledge about domain term relations. As a thesaurus, we use the Ontology on natural sciences and technologies [5], where the pedagogics domain terms have been introduced.

2   Related Works

For assessing the quality of scientific works, Osipov et al. [15] discuss such characteristics as the presence of the necessary sections (introduction, problem statement, list of references, etc.); scientific and non-scientific vocabularies; the presence of logical and semantic defects in the text of a scientific publication; selecting author's terms – new concepts defined by the authors of publications; highlighting the results presented in publications etc. Some authors study methods for the recognition of artificially generated scientific papers [2,3,12].

Another task, which is similar to the thesis assessment task, is essay scoring [6,19]. In this task, one of the most significant approaches is dimension-reduction methods, which reduce initial space of vocabulary words to improve detection of incoherence and other text structure problems in student essays [10]. Such methods as latent semantic analysis [6,13], probabilistic LSA [13] and Latent Dirichlet allocation [4] are traditionally used in the essay grading task [10]. Recent approaches apply word embeddings for solving the same problem [1,14,19].

In the essay scoring, the most similar to our task is the task of prompt adherence that is assessing how the essay content corresponds to the announced essay topic [7,16]. In [7] the Relatedness to Prompt feature is studied. The text of a essay fragment and the prompt (text of the essay question) must be related. If this relationship does not exist, this is perhaps evidence that the student has written an off-topic essay. The assessment was made for each sentence. The quality of the assessment was evaluated using double expert annotation for specific sentences. Random Indexing (RI) is a vector-based semantic representation system similar to Latent Semantic Analysis. The RI similarity to prompt for a sentence measures to what extent the sentence contains terms in the same semantic domain as compared to those found in the prompt. The SVM-classifier is trained on the calculated features and labeled data.

Persing and Ng [16] continue the study of the prompt relatedness in essay scoring using more diverse features. They try to predict the prompt relatedness for the whole essay, not for a single sentence. The predicted score ranges from one to four points at half-point intervals. 830 argumentative essays were annotated using a numerical score from one to four. Persing and Ng consider the task as a regression problem. Seven types of features were utilized in prompt-specific regressors based on linear SVM. Besides the random indexing features from the previous work, the authors used lemmatized unigram, bigram, and trigram similarity; thesis clarity keywords, which are the subdivision of the initial prompt to logical parts; LDA statistically generated topics.

3   Task, Data and Preprocessing

For experiments we use the collection of 40 thousand theses in pedagogics from various universities defended in 2017–2018 (further FullCollection). 120 theses from this collection have double scores from two experts belonging to different institutions (further AnnotatedCollection).

The theses have similar structure. They include several parts: introduction, two-three chapters, sometimes recommendations, conclusion, appendices. In the introduction, a student introduces the theme of the thesis, the aim, the object, and the tasks of the work. The first chapter presents the survey of theoretical studies related to the theme of the work. The second and third chapters often describe practical experiments carried out by the student.

To have more information about the thesis' theme, we gather the above-mentioned structural elements (the theme, aim, object, and tasks of the thesis) into a specific document called theme header. The theme header conveys the main idea and direction of the thesis. It is clear that all parts of the thesis should correspond to the theme header in some extent. In this paper we assess how the first chapter of the thesis, survey, is related to the theme header. We extract the theme header and chapters of the thesis using a specialized vocabulary and patterns. An example of the theme header is as follows:

TITLE = "Safety and resilience of students of the Yaroslavl Town Planning College in the educational process"
GOAL = – Definition of safety and resilience of students of the Yaroslavl Town Planning College in the educational process.
OBJECT = – Resilience of YTPC students and safety of the educational process.
SUBJECT = – The dynamics of the characteristics of the resilience of students of the Yaroslavl Town Planning College. Safety of the educational process.
SIGNIFICANCE = The significance of the research topic lies in the fact that in the world around us there always existed and there are many dangers, but they were not sufficiently considered from the angle of influence on objects and the resulting security problems. Using a systematic approach, it

is necessary to deeply analyze and identify objects that are affected by hazards, as well as to offer solutions to safety problems and improve resilience. The solution of the problems of the modern complex of security problems can be obtained on the basis of the general theory of security.

TASKS = 1. On the basis of theoretical analysis to determine the criteria and conditions for the formation of the resilience of students and the safety of the educational process. 2. Choose methods aimed at identifying the severity of the components of the resilience and safety of the educational process. 3. Identify differences in the level and content of resilience of students 1 and 2 courses of specialties "Auto Mechanic" and "Mechanic on the repair of construction machines" during 2015–2017. 4. To analyze and draw conclusions.

The similarity between the theme header in a thesis and the prompt in essay writing can be seen. But the difference between two tasks: relatedness of a thesis to its theme header and an essay to the prompt is also significant. The authors of [20] enumerate the following distinctions: professionally formulated prompts in essays vs. student-written theme elements, uniqueness of the thesis' theme in contrast to prompts in essays, longer texts of theses (250 sentences on average in our case), and others.

In the current study, we do not have any manual annotation of the theme relatedness of the first chapters. For evaluation, we use the overall score given to a thesis by two professional experts according to 2–5 scale, where 5 is the maximum grade in the scale. We suppose that low-scored theses should also have some problems in its surveys that is such works usually have text fragments that do not correspond to the theme of the thesis. The following fragment is an example of nonrelevant fragment in the thesis "Safety and resilience of students of the Yaroslavl Town Planning College in the educational process". In fact, this segment is a direct plagiarism[1].

Forgetting about the spirituality of every thought and every action, about the spirituality of comprehending the values of the world, a human quickly rushes to a global catastrophe, armed to the teeth with the achievements of the scientific and technological progress of the last century. The pervasive utility and benefit, hopes for speedy new breakthroughs in further "curbing" and robbery of Nature make chronically untimely and difficult the formation of ideological alternatives. Science, like governance, dressed in official structures, handing out ranks and authorities, strictly follows the "protocol". Merging with power, it serves it faithfully, creating dozens of different directions of idealism and materialism in, but, ultimately, professing rationalism and, like all consumer societies, mercantilism. As a result, Nature was dragged apart in pieces into disciplinary niches, fenced in these niches of various sorts of taboos, created local languages.

We order all the theses according to the increase of the automatic scores of theme relatedness and evaluate methods of theme relatedness calculation using

---

[1] http://window.edu.ru/catalog/pdf2txt/200/58200/28147.

NDCG [9]. Table 1 shows the distribution of grades in AnnotatedCollection. Table 2 shows the deviation between grades of two experts.

We suppose that segments that are not relevant to the theme header are more likely in theses with low grades (2, 3), and less likely in those with high grades (4, 5). Therefore, we have selected the next scale for NDCG: 2 grade: 2.0, 3 grade: 1.0, 4 grade: 0.0, 5 grade: 0.0.

4   Preprocessing of Thesis Text

The preprocessing of the thesis collection includes the following steps.

Table 1. Distribution of marks in student theses

Mark	Number of theses with minimal grade	Number of theses with maximal grade
2	42	8
3	42	33
4	28	51
5	8	28

Table 2. Deviations between thesis marks

Points of difference	Number of works
0	49
1	51
2	16
3	4

First, the whole text was lemmatised and stop words were removed. The frequency characteristics of the words were calculated and the idf values were obtained.

Secondly, the procedure of extracting the concepts was carried out using the ontology [5]. Thus for each sentence there is a list of concepts contained in it. For concepts, idf was also counted.

Next, the word2vec model was trained on full collection of the theses, which contains 40 thousand documents (FullCollection). The parameters are: CBOW, vector length is 150, window size is 10. The training was conducted using the python gensim package[2].

Finally, we use the procedure of segmenting the whole chapter to thematic fragments with algorithm which based on TopicTilling [18], but using word2vec embeddings instead of topic modeling. For any block of text, such as a sentence, its vector representation is calculated by weighted averaging of the word embeddings with idf as weights [20].

Then we calculate similarity between specific segments and the theme header. The overall score of the theme relatedness of a chapter is based on averaging segment scores of this chapter.

---

[2] https://radimrehurek.com/gensim/index.html.

5   Methods of Assessing Theme Adherence

5.1   Baselines

The thesis chapter under analysis (further document) is presented in the form of N segments S and compared with the theme header H. Two baseline models were implemented to accomplish this task.

Baseline 1 (Tf-Idf). In this baseline model, the theme header and segments are represented as sparse vectors, where each vector's component corresponds to a word from the collection's vocabulary. The values of vector elements are calculated as tf-idf. Based on the cosine similarity between the theme header and the S_i segment vectors, the *adherence_score* with the theme is formed.

Baseline 2 (SegWord2Vec). Each segment, including the theme header, is converted into a vector using word2vec embeddings. This operation is performed by weighted averaging of the word vectors with idf as weights, as used in the segmentation procedure.

5.2   Probabilistic Topic Modeling

In addition to the baselines described above, probabilistic topic modeling was also used. Probabilistic topic modeling is a popular method of statistical text processing. This approach builds a topic model for a collection of documents, allowing you to determine which topics the document belongs to. Topics themselves are described by a discrete distribution of word probabilities. By its nature, the process of topic modeling decomposes the matrix of a term-document into two matrices: term-topic ϕ_{wt} and topic-document θ_{td}.

Popular approaches to topic modeling are PLSA [8] and LDA [4], which allows sparsing or smoothing the columns of the corresponding matrices by choosing hyperparameters α and β for dirichlet distributions.

As an implementation of the topic modeling module, the open source library BigARTM [21] was used. This package effectively implements the training of standard topic models, such as LDA and PLSA through the EM algorithm. When training models, the whole thesis was used as a document. Dividing the thesis into small segments of 100–500 words did not give any increase in quality for any of the models. The number of topics was chosen to be 100, the training took 20 iterations on FullCollection.

5.3   Features of Theme Adherence Assessment

The following features were implemented and combined with the baselines:

Concepts: As an additional source of information about the domain, we use the Ontology on natural sciences and technologies [5], which comprises terms of scientific fields (mathematics, physics, chemistry, geology, astronomy etc.) and terms of technological domains (oil and gas, power stations, cosmic technologies, aircrafts, etc.). Currently, about 6500 terms (including term variants) were added to the ontology to describe the pedagogics domain.

The main unit of the ontology is a concept, which has a unique name, the set of text entries, which express this concept in the text, and concept relations. For example, the concept *DEAF AND HARD OF HEARING EDUCATION* has the following text entries: *deaf education, deaf teaching, education of the deaf, teaching of the deaf* (translation from Russian).

We match the texts with the ontology and create concept index, which allow us to account for synonyms and multiword expressions. In such a way, each document can be represented as a vector of concepts. We can combine word and concept vectors using the following formula:

$$adherence\_score = \alpha * sim_{word} + (1 - \alpha) * sim_{conc} \qquad (1)$$

Keywords: For the theme header, the most significant k_w words and k_c concepts are determined according to tf-idf. When selecting keywords, verbs, adverbs and functional parts of speech were ignored. The set of keywords includes words and concepts whose tf-idf weights exceed the threshold. This threshold is calculated as 0.2 * average value to the 3 (2 for concepts) most significant (by tf-idf) words (or concepts). The weights of the keywords are multiplied by additional factors w_w and w_c, respectively.

Keywords for thesis "Safety and resilience of students of the Yaroslavl Town Planning College in the educational process" are as follow:

- *words*: resilience (1.00), safety (0.47), town-planning (0.42), Yaroslavl (0.30), college (0.21), ytpc (0.17), student (0.17);
- *concepts*: urban planning (1.00), safety (0.63), college (0.57), student (0.20), system approach (0.17);

EmbedExp: There is an expansion of keywords for the theme header, by adding most similar words to them using word2vec embeddings. To do this, for each of the k_w keywords, the n_{w2v} closest words are calculated using the word2vec representation. Those words that are present in the whole thesis are added to the theme header vector. In order to calculate the weight of new words in the vector, the following formula is used:

$$weight_{word_{ext}} = sim(word_{raw}, word_{ext}) * tf(word_{raw}) * idf(word_{ext}) \qquad (2)$$

Where $word_{raw}$ is a keyword on which the expansion is made, $word_{ext}$ is a new word. In addition, the weights of the new words are multiplied by the factor of w_{ext}. The set of expanded words for the thesis "Safety and resilience of students of the Yaroslavl Town Planning College in the educational process", includes:

- *new words* - hardiness (0.88), Maddy (0.76), tough (0.66), stories (0.62), coping (0.54), freshman (0.48), security (0.44), safe (0.41), highschool (0.14), scholar (0.13);

Regardless of a specific configuration, each segment and theme header are represented by a vector (or vectors) and *adherence_score* is calculated as cosine similarity between corresponding vectors. We calculate *adherence_score* for the whole chapter as following:

- *mean_worse*: The average value of *adherence_score*'s among the worst 20% of segments;

The *mean_worse* corresponds to the hypothesis that a thesis is characterized by its worst fragments. Further, theses are ranked in ascending order of their *adherence_score* values.

6   Evaluation and Results

The evaluation methodology is proposed as follows. The algorithm for each thesis forms the values of *adherence_score* (*mean_worse*), on the basis of which the reference collection is ranked so that the "worst" thesis was "above". As mentioned earlier, we have 2 expert grades for each thesis in AnnotatedCollection. The minimum value is considered as a reference grade (*min_grade*). We analyzed the difference between using *mean_worse* and the mean across the all segments in [20] and concluded that *mean_worse* gives the better results.

We use NDCG measure according to the next scale: 2 grade: 2.0, 3 grade: 1.0, 4 grade: 0.0, 5 grade: 0.0. More specifically, we calculate the $NDCG(n)$ for positions 12 (10% of AnnotatedCollection), 25 (20% of AnnotatedCollection) and average them, calling $NDCG_{mean}$.

$$DCG(n) = \sum_{i=1}^{n} \frac{rel_i}{log_2(i+1)} \tag{3}$$

$$NDCG(n) = \frac{DCG(n)}{IDCG(n)} \tag{4}$$

Where rel_i is a relevance weight for position i, $IDCG(n)$ is ideal DCG for position n.

The results of evaluating different topic models without additional features can be seen in Table 3. LDA ($\alpha = 0.1$, $\beta = 1.0$) was chosen as the best topic model (*TopicModel*) for this task and all subsequent modifications will be applied to it.

Table 3. Evaluation results on AnnotatedCollection

	$NDCG(12)$	$NDCG(25)$	$NDCG_{mean}$
PLSA	0.698	0.641	0.669
LDA ($\alpha = 0.1$, $\beta = 0.001$)	0.632	0.585	0.608
LDA ($\alpha = 0.1$, $\beta = 0.1$)	0.596	0.586	0.591
LDA ($\alpha = 0.1$, $\beta = 0.5$)	0.573	0.588	0.581
LDA ($\alpha = 0.1$, $\beta = 0.9$)	0.696	0.595	0.645
LDA ($\alpha = 0.1$, $\beta = 1.0$)	**0.756**	**0.674**	**0.715**
LDA ($\alpha = 0.1$, $\beta = 1.1$)	0.677	0.651	0.664
LDA ($\alpha = 0.1$, $\beta = 1.5$)	0.663	0.648	0.656

6.1 Configurations Evaluation

The results of the evaluation of the all configurations can be seen in Table 4.
Parameters tuning was carried out using the Random Search. It also presents the
result of random ordering (averaging 25000 random permutations). The results
of $NDCG$ measure are also shown in the Fig. 1.

For the best configuration (*SegWord2Vec + Keywords* was chosen as the
best, because adding *Concepts* does not improve results enough), the optimal
parameters were as follows:

– *SegWord2Vec + Keywords*: $k_w = 12$, $w_w = 1.25$
   Where k_w - number of word keywords, w_w - multiplier of word keywords;

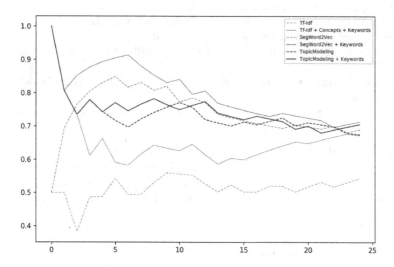

Fig. 1. NDCG graphs for different configurations

Table 4. Evaluation results on AnnotatedCollection

	$NDCG(12)$	$NDCG(25)$	$NDCG_{mean}$
Random	0.525	0.525	0.525
Tf-Idf	0.553	0.542	0.548
Tf-Idf + Concepts	0.591	0.580	0.586
Tf-Idf + Keywords	0.556	0.591	0.574
Tf-Idf + Concepts + Keywords	0.646	0.672	0.659
Tf-Idf + Keywords + EmbedExp	0.624	0.634	0.629
Tf-Idf + Concepts + Keywords + EmbedExp	0.640	0.640	0.640
SegWord2Vec	0.784	0.689	0.737
SegWord2Vec + Concepts	0.779	0.674	0.726
SegWord2Vec + Keywords	0.796	**0.712**	0.754
SegWord2Vec + Concepts + Keywords	**0.809**	0.708	**0.759**
TopicModel	0.756	0.674	0.715
TopicModel + Concepts	0.733	0.654	0.693
TopicModel + Keywords	0.762	0.705	0.733
TopicModel + Concepts + Keywords	0.765	0.675	0.720

Based on the results, we can conclude the following:

- A high level of values, even for *Random* configuration, follows from the fact that in the AnnotatedCollection there are 35% theses with minimum grade 2 and 35% theses with minimum grade 3;
- *SegWord2Vec* baseline is better than *Tf-Idf* and *TopicModel*;
- Use of *Keywords* mainly leads to better results;
- Use of *Concepts* is very useful for *Tf-Idf* especially in combination with *Keywords*;
- The use of concepts in the described way together with *TopicModel* brings only a negative result;
- Adding *Concepts* to the *SegWord2Vec + Keywords* configuration does not bring significant improvements.

Most likely, the *Concepts* do not improve the results for the *SegWord2Vec* and *TopicModeling* due to the fact that concepts bring semantic relatedness between different words, but in the basis of these approaches that problem was already solved in some maner. *Tf-Idf*, on the other hand, has no solution for this problem.

6.2   Hyperparameter Analysis

In addition to finding specific "best" configurations, it is also useful to evaluate the effect of each parameter separately. For this purpose, the technique proposed in [17] was used.

The approach is as follows:

- Some values of the target parameter are fixed;
- The remaining parameters are selected randomly, but in such a way that same randomly generated set of parameters is run with each selected value for the target parameter;
- By performing this procedure k times, there are a total of $k * p$ configurations, where p - number of fixed values;
- For each value of the target parameter, it is possible to calculate in how many cases the configuration with this value was better than the others;

According to the described scheme, the influence of the majority of features was analyzed. For each configuration, $k = 100$ runs were performed. The parameter grids were chosen meaningfully, based on the data already obtained at the early stages of the experiments. In the following tables you can see the result of the evaluation (Tables 5 and 6).

Table 5. Keywords feature (applied to words)

	Keywords count						Keywords multiplier			
	0	3	5	7	9	12	1.0	1.25	1.5	3.0
Tf-Idf	0.07	0.26	0.05	0.14	0.11	0.37	0.22	0.1	0.15	0.53
SegWord2Vec	0.02	0.11	0.38	0.03	0.06	0.4	0.03	0.22	0.28	0.47
TopicModeling	0.06	0.05	0.09	0.17	0.07	0.56	0.1	0.33	0.43	0.14

In addition, it was evaluated which segment representation model is better: *Tf-Idf*: 0.0, *SegWord2Vec*: 0.9, *TopicModeling*: 0.1. *EmbedExp* for *Tf-Idf* also gives positive results, the use of *EmbedExp* was better in 0.71 cases.

Table 6. Concepts feature

	Alpha			
	1.0	0.75	0.5	0.25
Tf-Idf	0.17	0.34	0.37	0.12
SegWord2Vec	0.31	0.55	0.14	0.0
TopicModeling	1.0	0.0	0.0	0.0

These data confirm the previously obtained results, at the same time such experiments are more robust. We again found that *Keywords* have a significant impact on all configurations, *Concepts* are useful for *Tf-Idf*, and completely useless for *TopicModeling*, and *EmbedExp* has a positive effect on *Tf-Idf*.

7 Conclusion

In this paper we studied approaches to assessing the quality of student theses in pedagogics. We considered a specific subtask in thesis scoring of estimating its adherence to the thesis's theme. The special document (theme header) comprising the theme, aim, object, tasks of the thesis is formed. The theme adherence is calculated as the similarity value between the theme header and thesis segments. We investigated different methods, including probabilistic topic modeling, embedding words and ontologies.

For evaluation we ordered theses in the increased value of the calculated theme adherence and compared the ordering with expert grades using the NDCG measure. The best configuration for theses ranking is based on the weighted averaged sum of word embeddings (word2vec) and keywords extracted from the theme header.

Acknowledgements. This article contains the results of the project "Developing new methods for analyzing large text data using linguistic and ontological resources, machine learning methods and neural networks", carried out as part of the Competence Center program of the National Technology Initiative "Center for Big Data Storage and Analysis", supported by the Ministry of Science and Higher Education of the Russian Federation under the Contract of Moscow State University with the Fund for Support of Projects of the National Technology Initiative No. 13/1251/2018 dated December 11, 2018.

References

1. Amorim, E., Cançado, M., Veloso, A.: Automated essay scoring in the presence of biased ratings. In: Proceedings of the 2018 Conference of the North American Chapter of the Association for Computational Linguistics: Human Language Technologies, Volume 1 (Long Papers), vol. 1, pp. 229–237 (2018)
2. Avros, R., Volkovich, Z.: Detection of computer-generated papers using one-class SVM and cluster approaches. In: Perner, P. (ed.) MLDM 2018. LNCS (LNAI), vol. 10935, pp. 42–55. Springer, Cham (2018). https://doi.org/10.1007/978-3-319-96133-0_4
3. Bakhteev, O., Kuznetsova, R., Romanov, A., Chekhovich, Y.: About one method of detecting artificial and unscientific texts in an extensive collection of documents. Electron. Libr. **20**(5), 298–304 (2017)
4. Blei, D.M., Ng, A.Y., Jordan, M.I.: Latent Dirichlet allocation. J. Mach. Learn. Res. **3**(Jan), 993–1022 (2003)
5. Dobrov, B.V., Loukachevitch, N.V.: Development of linguistic ontology on natural sciences and technology. In: LREC, pp. 1077–1082 (2006)
6. Foltz, P.W., Laham, D., Landauer, T.K.: Automated essay scoring: applications to educational technology. In: EdMedia+ Innovate Learning, pp. 939–944. Association for the Advancement of Computing in Education (AACE) (1999)
7. Higgins, D., Burstein, J., Marcu, D., Gentile, C.: Evaluating multiple aspects of coherence in student essays. In: Proceedings of the Human Language Technology Conference of the North American Chapter of the Association for Computational Linguistics: HLT-NAACL 2004 (2004)

8. Hofmann, T.: Probabilistic latent semantic analysis. In: Proceedings of the Fifteenth Conference on Uncertainty in Artificial Intelligence, pp. 289–296. Morgan Kaufmann Publishers Inc. (1999)

9. Järvelin, K., Kekäläinen, J.: Cumulated gain-based evaluation of ir techniques. ACM Trans. Inf. Syst. (TOIS) **20**(4), 422–446 (2002)

10. Kakkonen, T., Myller, N., Sutinen, E., Timonen, J.: Comparison of dimension reduction methods for automated essay grading. J. Educ. Technol. Soc. **11**(3), 275–288 (2008)

11. Khritankov, A., Botov, P., Surovenko, N., Tsarkov, S., Viuchnov, D., Chekhovich, Y.: Discovering text reuse in large collections of documents: a study of theses in history sciences. In: Artificial Intelligence and Natural Language and Information Extraction, Social Media and Web Search FRUCT Conference (AINL-ISMW FRUCT), pp. 26–32. IEEE (2015)

12. Labbé, C., Labbé, D.: Duplicate and fake publications in the scientific literature: how many scigen papers in computer science? Scientometrics **94**(1), 379–396 (2013)

13. Landauer, T.K., Foltz, P.W., Laham, D.: An introduction to latent semantic analysis. Discourse Process. **25**(2–3), 259–284 (1998)

14. Mikolov, T., Sutskever, I., Chen, K., Corrado, G.S., Dean, J.: Distributed representations of words and phrases and their compositionality. In: Advances in Neural Information Processing Systems, pp. 3111–3119 (2013)

15. Osipov, G., Smirnov, I., Tikhomirov, I., Vybornova, O.: Technologies for semantic analysis of scientific publications. In: 2012 6th IEEE International Conference Intelligent Systems, pp. 058–062. IEEE (2012)

16. Persing, I., Ng, V.: Modeling prompt adherence in student essays. In: Proceedings of the 52nd Annual Meeting of the Association for Computational Linguistics (Volume 1: Long Papers), vol. 1, pp. 1534–1543 (2014)

17. Reimers, N., Gurevych, I.: Optimal hyperparameters for deep LSTM-networks for sequence labeling tasks. arXiv preprint arXiv:1707.06799 (2017)

18. Riedl, M., Biemann, C.: TopicTiling: a text segmentation algorithm based on LDA. In: Proceedings of ACL 2012 Student Research Workshop, pp. 37–42. Association for Computational Linguistics (2012)

19. Taghipour, K., Ng, H.T.: A neural approach to automated essay scoring. In: Proceedings of the 2016 Conference on Empirical Methods in Natural Language Processing, pp. 1882–1891 (2016)

20. Tikhomirov, M., Loukachevitch, N., Dobrov, B.: Assessing theme adherence in student thesis. In: Computational Linguistics and Intellectual Technologies. Papers from the Annual International Conference "Dialogue" (2019), pp. 649–661 (2019)

21. Vorontsov, K., Potapenko, A.: Additive regularization of topic models. Mach. Learn. **101**(1–3), 303–323 (2015)

Natural Language Analysis to Detect Parkinson's Disease

P. A. Pérez-Toro[1], J. C. Vásquez-Correa[1,2(✉)], M. Strauss[2],
J. R. Orozco-Arroyave[1,2], and E. Nöth[2]

[1] Faculty of Engineering, University of Antioquia UdeA, Medellín, Colombia
{paula.perezt,jcamilo.vasquez,rafael.orozco}@udea.edu.co
[2] Pattern Recognition Lab, Friedrich-Alexander-Universität Erlangen-Nürnberg,
Erlangen, Germany
{juan.vasquez,martin.straauss,elmar.noeth}@fau.de

Abstract. Parkinson's disease (PD) is a neuro-degenerative disorder that produces motor and non-motor impairments. Non-motor impairments include communication and mood disorders. Most of the studies in the literature have been focused on the analysis of motor symptoms. However, non-motor signs are also present in most of the cases. This paper addresses the study of language production as a potential tool to diagnose and monitor the neurological state of PD patients. The study proposes the use of natural language processing methods to extract features from transcriptions obtained from spontaneous speech recordings to discriminate between healthy control people and PD patients. The analysis considered classical features such as Bag of Words and Term Frequency-Inverse Document Frequency, along with methods based on word-embeddings. Accuracies of up to 72% are obtained when discriminating between PD patients and healthy subjects, which confirms that there is information embedded in the language production that can be used for the assessment of the disease.

Keywords: Parkinson's disease · Natural language processing ·
Text processing · Language analysis · Classification

1 Introduction

Parkinson's disease (PD) is a neuro-degenerative disorder characterized by the progressive loss of dopaminergic neurons in the mid brain [1]. Communication problems and impairments in the grammar production appear in 90% of the patients due to the death of the dopaminergic neurons [2]. The standard scale to evaluate the neurological state of the patients is the Movement Disorder Society-Unified Parkinson's Disease Rating Scale (MDS-UPDRS-III) [3], which includes items related to the speech production, mental state, and body movements, and others. The third section (MDS-UPDRS-III) of the scale considers motor activities of patients. It has a total of 33 items, which range from 0 to 4, for a total

© Springer Nature Switzerland AG 2019
K. Ekštein (Ed.): TSD 2019, LNAI 11697, pp. 82–90, 2019.
https://doi.org/10.1007/978-3-030-27947-9_7

range from 0 (completely healthy) to 142 (completely impaired). Most of the studies in the literature have been more focused on the speech analysis rather than on the language comprehension. Several studies suggest that, besides articulatory problems, impairments in grammar, verbal fluency, and semantic are also present in most of the patients [4,5]. There are few studies analyzing language impairments due to PD. In [6] the authors analyzed different components of text on transcribed monologues produced by 51 PD patients and 50 healthy control (HC) subjects. The analysis was performed using latent semantic analysis, part-of-speech tagging and word-level repetitions via graph embedding tools. The authors considered several classifiers to discriminate between PD patients and HC subjects, including a support vector machine (SVM) with a radial basis function (RBF) kernel, a K-nearest neighbors, and an Adaboost algorithm. The authors reported accuracies of up to 66% using latent semantic analysis, 75% using part-of-speech tagging and 77% using graph embedding tools.

Cognitive deficits and behavioral disorders are more common in Alzheimer's disease (AD) than in PD. Thus, besides the studies on PD, there are several works on AD where the impact of language impairments is studied [7–9]. This opens more possibilities of finding frameworks and methodologies that could be adapted to address the problem of language modeling in PD. Recently in [9] the authors proposed an approach of counting word occurrences in transcriptions via Bag of Words (BoW) vectors. English transcriptions from the Pitt Corpus of the Dementia Bank [10] (168 AD patients and 94 HC subjects), were considered. The participants were asked to describe the cookie theft image [11]. BoW features were used to classify the AD patients and HC subjects using an artificial neural network. The authors followed a Leave-One-Speaker-Out (LOSO) cross-validation strategy, and reported accuracies of up to 84.4%.

Although acoustic analysis has shown to be a suitable tool to study symptoms of PD patients, there are components related to language production that are not modeled with that approach. With the aim to model language deficits exhibited by PD patients, this study considers the use of several Natural Language Processing (NLP) methods including classical approaches such as BoW and Term Frequency-Inverse Document Frequency (TF-IDF), along with novel methods based on word-embeddings like word2vec (W2V). Experiments with recordings of spontaneous speech produced by 50 PD patients and 50 healthy subjects are considered. Accuracies of up to 72% are obtained, which confirms the results reported in similar studies.

2   Data

Recordings of spontaneous speech of 50 PD patients and 50 HC subjects are manually transcribed. The speech recordings are part of the PC-GITA corpus [12]. For this paper only recordings of monologues are considered. The task consisted on asking the participants to talk about their daily routines. The average duration of the monologues is 48 ± 29 s for the patients and 45 ± 24 for the healthy subjects. The transcriptions were produced following the verbatim protocol, using headphones to maximize the transcription accuracy and to minimize possible human errors. The whole vocabulary of the transcriptions without stop-words (e.g., the, of, in, on, etc.) consists of 1182 words. The patients were evaluated by an expert neurologist and labeled according to the MDS-UPDRS-III score. Table 1 shows additional information of the subjects.

Table 1. General information of the subjects. Time since diagnosis, age and education are given in years. [a]p calculated through Chi-square test. [b]p calculated through t test.

	PD patients	Healthy controls	Patients vs. controls
Gender [F/M]	25/25	25/25	$p = 1.00$[a]
Age [F/M]	60.7(7.3)/61.3(11.7)	61.4(7.1)/60.5(11.6)	$p = 0.98$[b]
Education [F/M]	11.5(4.1)/10.9(4.5)	11.5(5.2)/10.6(4.4)	$p = 0.88$[b]
Time since diagnosis [F/M]	12.6(11.5)/8.7(5.8)		
MDS-UPDRS-III [F/M]	37.6(14.0)/37.8(22.1)		

3   Methods

NLP approaches are considered to process information from the texts resulting from the transcription process. Figure 1 shows the main steps followed in this study to perform the text analysis. Details of the processes performed on each stage are included in the following subsections.

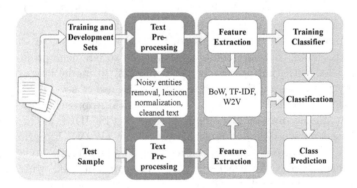

Fig. 1. Scheme of the general methodology addressed in this study.

3.1   Train, Development, and Test Data Distribution

The data is distributed following a LOSO strategy as it is shown in Fig. 2. There is always a test subject and the remaining data is used for the process of training and development which is performed following a 10-fold cross validation strategy to optimize the meta-parameters of the classifier. The optimization criterion is the accuracy obtained in development. This process can be seen as a set of independent experiments over the training data. We are aware about the fact that this process might be slightly optimistic since we have a different set of meta-parameters for each test sample; however, the results show that the distribution of the meta-parameters is stable across the different test sets.

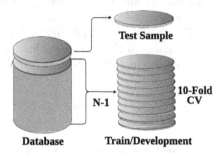

Fig. 2. Database distribution. **CV:** cross-validation. **N:** number of samples.

3.2 Pre-processing

The data is cleaned and standardized, making it noise-free and ready for analysis as it is shown in Fig. 1. The following two steps are implemented for this purpose:

- *Noise removal:* non relevant information for the context, such as stopwords, accents or punctuation, are removed from the text. We considered a Spanish dictionary of noise entities from the Natural Language Toolkit (NLTK) [13] to remove the noise words from the transcriptions.
- *Lexicon normalization:* there are multiple representation for a single word. To standardize the words in an equal representation, all words were transformed via stemming to remove the suffixes. Another implemented method was lemmatization, which transforms the words into their root form.

3.3 Feature Extraction

Bag of Words-BoW
This method creates a vocabulary of all words that appear in the whole document, i.e., it is a collection of words that will be represented into a feature vector with fixed size. The process to extract the BoW feature vector includes the following steps: (1) the sentences are represented as a collection of words. (2) Each sentence is pre-processed and tokenized. (3) The vocabulary is created, and multiple occurrences of the same word are removed. (4) The words of the entire corpus are counted and stored in a vector with a length of 1182 words (the total number of words in the corpus). A more realistic feature set could be formed only with the words from the training set, by considering the words from the test set that are not in the vocabulary as out-of-vocabulary words.

Term Frequency-Inverse Document Frequency

Term frequency (TF) gives the relative frequency of a specific term, word or combination of words. This value is compared to the relative frequency of other terms in a text or document. Inverse Document Frequency (IDF) compares the number of all available documents and the number of documents that contain the target word. IDF determines the relevance of the text with respect to a specific word. Finally, TF-IDF features are expressed by Eq. 1 for the word $W_{i,j}$. $TF_{i,j}$ is the number of occurrences of the term i in the document j, d_{f_i} is the number of documents containing i, and N is the total number of documents.

$$W_{i,j} = TF_{i,j} \log \left(\frac{N}{d_{f_i}} \right) \tag{1}$$

Word2Vec-W2V

The aim of W2V is to represent the words as a vector in a multidimensional space, where similar or related words are represented by nearby points. The model consists of a Neural Network (NN) with one hidden layer. The activations of the hidden layer are stored, being those "the word vectors". The input words are represented as one-hot encodings, i.e., as binary vectors. Neighbor words in this representation are considered to train the NN. The selection of the neighbor words depends on the "window size", which is necessary to model the temporal context of each word. For our experiments, the NN was trained using the Spanish WikiCorpus, which contains 120 million of words [14]. The window size was fixed in 7, because it was the average number of words per sentence in the transcripts. The length for the word-embedding vector was defined in 100. Then, four statistical functionals were computed: mean, standard deviation, skewness, and kurtosis, forming a 400-dimensional feature vector per transcription.

3.4   Classification

Kruskal-Wallis tests were performed to assess whether there is a significant difference between the median of the features computed for PD patients and HC subjects. The null hypothesis of the medians coming from the same distribution was rejected ($p \ll 0.05$) in all cases. The discrimination capability of the extracted features is evaluated using two classifiers, RBF-SVM and Random Forest (RF). The criterion for the meta-parameters optimization is based on the accuracy obtained in the development data. Optimal parameters are found through a grid search where $C \in \{10^{-4}, 10^{-3}, ...10^4\}$ and $\gamma \in \{10^{-4}, 10^{-3}, ...10^4\}$ for the RBF-SVM, and number of trees $N \in \{5, 10, 20, 30, 50, 100\}$ and $D \in \{2, 5, 10, 20, 30, 50, 100\}$ for the RF. The performance of the classifiers is evaluated considering the accuracy, sensitivity, specificity, and the area under the receiving operating characteristic curve (AUC).

4   Results and Discussion

In order to visualize linguistic differences between PD and HC subjects, Fig. 3 shows a word cloud representation Note words as "casa" (house) or "ver televisión" (watch television) are more frequently used for the patients, while words as "trabajar" (work) or "salir" (go out) appear more frequently in HC subjects. In addition to the words related to the daily activities of the subjects, in PD patient appears more frequently a Colombian crutch "pues", denoting a lack of fluency in the speech of the patients.

Fig. 3. Word cloud representation: (A) PD patient. (B) HC subject.

Results considering the three feature sets individually and their combination in an early fusion strategy are shown in Table 2. Note that in general sensitivity is higher than specificity, which indicates that PD patients were better discriminated in most of the cases. This difference between specificity and sensitivity suggests that AUC is a better statistic to compare the approaches. The highest AUC is observed with the BoW features classified with the RF (0.76). Note also that the fusion strategy did not improve the results indicating that the considered features are not complementary and further research is required to find an optimal strategy to merge such information.

Table 2. Classification results.

Features	RBF-SVM						RF					
	Acc (%)	Sens (%)	Spe (%)	AUC	C	γ	Acc (%)	Sens (%)	Spe (%)	AUC	N	D
BoW	62.0	70.0	54.0	0.60	10^{10}	10^0	70.0	74.0	66.0	0.76	100	20
TF-IDF	58.0	58.0	56.0	0.60	10^1	10^0	67.0	68.0	66.0	0.71	100	100
W2V	72.0	92.0	52.0	0.66	10^0	10^0	67.0	74.0	60.0	0.71	5	5
Fusion	60.0	62.0	58.0	0.62	10^1	10^0	66.0	68.0	64.0	0.71	100	5

Notes: Acc: accuracy. Sens: sensitivity. Spe: specificity. AUC: Area under the ROC curve. C and γ are the optimal meta-parameters obtained in development for RBF-SVM. N and D are the optimal meta-parameters obtained in development for RF.

With the aim to compare the approaches that provided better AUC values, the distribution of the scores obtained with the RF classifier for the two classes considering the BoW and TF-IDF features are shown in Fig. 4A and B, respectively. The dark gray bars correspond to the scores for HC subjects, the white

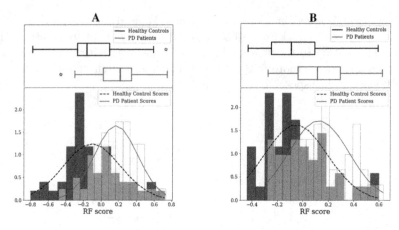

Fig. 4. Scores obtained for the RF classifier for: (A) BoW. (B) TF-IDF.

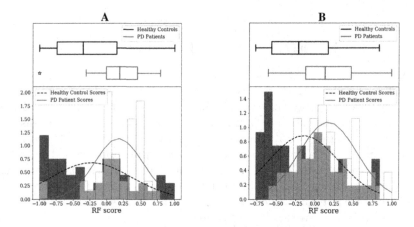

Fig. 5. Scores obtained for the RF classifier for: (A) W2V. (B) Fusion.

bars are the scores computed for the PD patients, and the light gray bars correspond to the intersection between both sets, and reflect the classification errors. Note that the scores of the PD patients are less sparse than those obtained for the HC subjects, additionally the scores for the TF-IDF features are more overlapped. Figure 5A and B show the score distributions obtained also with the RF classifier when considering W2V features and the fusion, respectively. Note that these scores are more overlapped and sparse, especially for HC subjects, were a higher variance is observed.

The results found here are similar to others reported in the state-of-the-art, and show to be complementary to those reported previously, where we performed an acoustic analysis of the daily routine monologues performed by the patients [15]. We believe that they could improve if the participants were evaluated in conversational speech samples or in recordings while describing a scene or a story (retelling tasks). Further research with these kinds of experiments is required to find more discriminant approaches.

5 Conclusion

Several NLP techniques were considered in this paper to discriminate between HC subjects and PD patients. The feature sets included classical methods such as BoW and TF-IDF along with other techniques based on word-embeddings like W2V. The main aim was to analyze the suitability of NLP methods to discriminate PD vs. HC subjects. The proposed approach allows the study of different communication disorders that cannot be observed in motor activities. Thus this is a step forward in the evaluation of language impairments that affect the communication capabilities of PD patients. The proposed models are relatively accurate to classify PD patients and HC subjects. As it was also observed in previous studies, the results obtained here suggest that there is information that reflects language impairments in PD patients and it can be used to discriminate between PD and HC subjects and also to evaluate the neurological state of the patients.

Although we think that the results reported here are a step towards the automatic evaluation of language impairments in PD patients, the main limitation is related to the restricted task performed by the participants. They were asked to describe their daily routines. According to our observations, it seems like this task does not reflect communication deficits of PD patients properly because there is an implicit bias in the recorded task. Healthy subjects tend to do more active activities than PD patients who do mainly passive activities like reading, thinking, and taking their medication. Our team is currently collecting more recordings with the aim of evaluating the suitability of other tasks like image description. Further experiments will explore more robust word embedding methods such as ELMo or BERT to improve the performance of the system. Additionally, we are also working on the fusion of acoustic and language information to see whether the results can be improved.

References

1. Hornykiewicz, O.: Biochemical aspects of Parkinson's disease. Neurology **51**(2 Suppl 2), S2–S9 (1998)
2. Smith, K.M., Caplan, D.N.: Communication impairment in Parkinson's disease: impact of motor and cognitive symptoms on speech and language. Brain Lang. **185**, 38–46 (2018)
3. Goetz, C.G., et al.: Movement disorder society-sponsored revision of the unified Parkinson's disease rating scale (MDS-UPDRS): scale presentation and clinimetric testing results. Mov. Disord. **23**(15), 2129–2170 (2008)
4. Murray, L.L., Lenz, L.P.: Productive syntax abilities in Huntington's and Parkinson's diseases. Brain Cogn. **46**(1–2), 213–219 (2001)

5. Vanhoutte, S., De Letter, M., Corthals, P., et al.: Quantitative analysis of language production in Parkinson's disease using a cued sentence generation task. Clin. linguist. Phonetics **26**(10), 863–881 (2012)

6. García, A.M., Carrillo, F., Orozco-Arroyave, J.R., Trujillo, N., et al.: How language flows when movements don't: an automated analysis of spontaneous discourse in Parkinson's disease. Brain Lang. **162**, 19–28 (2016)

7. Fraser, K.C., Meltzer, J.A., Rudzicz, F.: Linguistic features identify Alzheimer's disease in narrative speech. J. Alzheimers Dis. **49**(2), 407–422 (2016)

8. Wankerl, S., Nöth, E., Evert, S.: An N-gram based approach to the automatic diagnosis of Alzheimer's disease from spoken language. In: Proceedings of the Annual Conference of the International Speech Communication Association, INTERSPEECH (2017)

9. Klumpp, P., Fritsch, J., Noeth, E.: ANN-based Alzheimer's disease classification from bag of words. In: 13th ITG-Symposium on Speech Communication, pp. 1–4. VDE (2018)

10. Becker, J.T., et al.: The natural history of Alzheimer's disease: description of study cohort and accuracy of diagnosis. Arch. Neurol. **51**(6), 585–594 (1994)

11. Goodglass, H., Kaplan, E.: Boston Naming Test: Scoring Booklet. Lea & Febiger, Philadelphia (1983)

12. Orozco-Arroyave, J.R., Arias-Londoño, J.D., Vargas-Bonilla, J.F., et al.: New Spanish speech corpus database for the analysis of people suffering from Parkinson's disease. In: LREC, pp. 342–347 (2014)

13. Bird, S., Loper, E.: NLTK: the natural language toolkit. In: Proceedings of the ACL 2004 on Interactive Poster and Demonstration Sessions, pp. 31. Association for Computational Linguistics (2004)

14. Reese, S., Boleda, G., Cuadros, M., et al.: Wikicorpus: a word-sense disambiguated multilingual wikipedia corpus (2010)

15. Vásquez-Correa, J.C., Orozco-Arroyave, J.R., Nöth, E.: Convolutional neural network to model articulation impairments in patients with Parkinson's disease. In: Proceedings of INTERSPEECH, pp. 314–318 (2017)

Using Auto-Encoder BiLSTM Neural Network for Czech Grapheme-to-Phoneme Conversion

Markéta Jůzová$^{(\boxtimes)}$ and Jakub Vít

Department of Cybernetics and New Technologies for the Information Society,
Faculty of Applied Sciences, University of West Bohemia, Pilsen, Czech Republic
{juzova,jvit}@kky.zcu.cz

Abstract. The crucial part of almost all current TTS systems is a grapheme-to-phoneme (G2P) conversion, i.e. the transcription of any input grapheme sequence into the correct sequence of phonemes in the given language. Unfortunately, the preparation of transcription rules and pronunciation dictionaries is not an easy process for new languages in TTS systems. For that reason, in the presented paper, we focus on the creation of an automatic G2P model, based on neural networks (NN). But, contrary to the majority of related works in G2P field, using only separate words as an input, we consider a whole phrase the input of our proposed NN model. That approach should, in our opinion, lead to more precise phonetic transcription output because the pronunciation of a word can depend on the surrounding words. The results of the trained G2P model are presented on the Czech language where the cross-word-boundary phenomena occur quite often, and they are compared to the rule-based approach.

Keywords: Grapheme-to-phoneme · Sequence-to-sequence ·
Neural networks · Encoder-decoder model · Czech phonetic transcription

1 Introduction

The text-to-speech (TTS) systems, in general, besides some end-to-end systems [24] from recent years transforming the raw text directly into generated speech, rely on steady grapheme-to-phoneme (G2P) modules which are able to ensure a high-quality phonetic transcription of any input text sentence. The output sequence of units is then used in the TTS itself, no matter the synthesis method used (unit selection, statistical parametric synthesis, neural network synthesis) and potential errors in the predicted phonemes can lead to unintelligible or incomprehensible speech. And it has also been showed that some of the annotation errors in large speech corpora are caused by an incorrect automatic phonetic transcription [10, 11], and the errors of the G2P module can negatively affect the results of the segmentation process [4, 12] – which of course causes errors in the synthesis itself. To avoid that, the phonetic transcription should be dealt with very carefully to achieve as high phoneme/word accuracy as possible.

Unfortunately, for many different languages, the grapheme-to-phoneme mapping is not a simple one-to-one mapping – the problem is much more complex. Having large

© Springer Nature Switzerland AG 2019
K. Ekštein (Ed.): TSD 2019, LNAI 11697, pp. 91–102, 2019.
https://doi.org/10.1007/978-3-030-27947-9_8

pronunciation dictionaries, the transcription can be solved for common words by a simple (but huge) look-up table. However, new words appear in the language every year (completely new terms and names, loanwords, etc.) so it is impossible to cover all of them. On the other hand, people are able to predict the pronunciation of a new word (unknown for them) in their native language with very high accuracy (very close to 100%) because of some (less or more) pronunciation patterns they have learned before. And people are also able to guess the "irregular" pronunciation of unknown foreign-like words based on their knowledge and experience with other similar words. Based on that, the experts supposed that a neural network (or other types of models) would also be able to learn these patterns in the grapheme-to-phoneme mapping from large corpora and could be used instead of rules and look-up dictionaries. Some of these approaches are mentioned in Sect. 1.1.

Slavic languages, the Czech being one of them, belong to the group of inflected languages so the dictionaries would be huge (when containing all word forms). Fortunately, their fundamental phonetic transcription can be easily described by a set of rules [13, 15, 16], see Sect. 2.1, which are usually designed by a phonetic expert. The paper presents a neural network (NN) model which could replace the hand-written Czech phonetic rules with the exception dictionary in the TTS system.

1.1 Related Work

Besides large pronunciation dictionaries and hand-crafted transcription rules, or automatically trained sets of rules from dictionaries, there are many approaches to the automatic G2P. The popular traditional models for grapheme-to-phoneme conversion include joint-sequence alignments using n-grams [2], some studies represented the models as weighted finite state transducers [17]. There are also studies of using different classifiers, conditional random fields [23] and HMM [6]. In recent years, different types of neural networks have been applied on the G2P problem, e.g. [20, 27].

As explained in [20], the great advantage of using (LSTM [5]) neural networks for G2P problem lies in the avoiding of the need for explicit grapheme-to-phoneme alignment which is not usually straightforward – although there is a one-to-one mapping of some graphemes to phonemes in different languages, many graphemes are not pronounced or, on the other hand, a grapheme may be rendered into a sequence of more phonemes. Such a NN model is able to make contextually-dependent decisions.

The majority of all G2P studies use the pronunciation dictionary as an input and the authors of them train their model to be able to predict the phonetic transcription word by word. Contrary to that, we decided to use phrases (short sequences of words) for training our model since the word context is, based on our knowledge, as important as the phoneme context within a word (as will be explained in Sect. 2). That assumption drives us closer to the machine translation approaches where the need of using the word sequences in the training data is unquestionable – the correct translation from one language to another in a word-by-word manner is infeasible. The neural machine translation approaches usually use the encoder-decoder architecture of the NN model, e.g. [3, 21, 26], where the encoder extracts the representation from an input sentence and the decoder generates a correct translation from this representation.

2 Specifics of Czech Phonetic Transcription

The Czech language is, compared e.g. to English, quite straightforward concerning the G2P conversion – for the first view, the text is read almost the same as written. However, there are some specifics [7,8,18] in Czech which are very important to be dealt with when realizing the phonetic transcription, see the examples below (the SAMPA [25] phonetic alphabet is used in all the examples of the phonetic transcription in this paper):

- the written Czech has two graphemes *i* and *y* (and their long variants *í* and *ý*) while the spoken Czech has only one phoneme i (and its long variant i:)
- the Czech grapheme *ě* is transcribed as je or Je[1], depending on the preceding consonant
- diphthongs – some groups of 2 vowels are pronounced as one phoneme o_u, a_u, e_u
- assimilation of the place of articulation – Czech nasals *m/n* before particular consonants are realized by articulators further back in the human vocal tract
- final devoicing – the voiced obstruents are realized voiceless before a pause (at the end of a phrase)
- voice assimilation – it concerns a group of consonants, all the consonants (obstruents) in the group are either voiced or unvoiced, depending mostly on the last one

The last item mentioned is realized both within the words and across the word boundaries – the last graphemes-consonants [1] become voiceless if the following word starts with a voiced consonant and vice-versa, as demonstrated by the examples of transcriptions of the Czech preposition *bez* (*EN: without*):

bez práce	[b e **s** p r a: t_s e]	(*EN: without job*)
bez oběda	[b e **s** ? o b j e d a]	(*EN: without lunch*)
bez zranění	[b e **z** z r a J e J i:]	(*EN: without injury*)
bez dluhů	[b e **z** d l u h u:]	(*EN: without debt*)

2.1 Czech Phonetic Hand-Crafted Rules

In our TTS system *ARTIC* [22], we use a set of hand-written rules for the phonetic transcription (explained in [9]) which are automatically applied on the input text to get the phoneme sequence. As defined in [15,19], the rules can be written in the form of production rules:

IF the sequence of graphemes *A* is preceded by the sequence of graphemes *C* and is followed by the sequence of graphemes *D*,
THEN the sequence of graphemes *A* is transcribed to the sequence of phonemes *B*.

The created set of phonetic rules used includes all the Czech specifics mentioned above (voice assimilation, final devoicing, etc.) and they are able to transform almost any Czech text in its correct phonetic form. More specifically, the TTS system *ARTIC* uses

---

[1] In SAMPA [25], the symbol J corresponds to the palatal nasal.

a set of 164 phonetic rules providing the expected pronunciation. designed manually by phonetic experts. And since Czech is our native language, the G2P module is very well tuned.

Unfortunately, the Czech phonetic rules do not work correctly for the number of words of foreign origin which also appear in Czech texts. These exceptions mostly concern no softening in words containing syllables *di, ti, ni* and the phonetic transcription of *s* to z in some words, e.g.:

technický	[t e x **n i** t_s k i:]	(*EN: technical*)
	not [t e x ɟ i t_s k i:]	
diskuse	[**d i** s k u **z** e]	(*EN: discussion*)
	not [ɟ\i s k u s e]	

For that reason, a large exception dictionary is used in our TTS (containing almost 200 thousands of items), besides the hand-written rules. Due to that, the system is able to transcribe common words in the correct phonetic form. But the dictionary has been still being expanded, all the time we find out another exception. And it is unfeasible to create an exception dictionary which will completely cover all these words, especially for inflected languages, Czech being one of them, where all these words should be included in the dictionary in all possible word forms. And there are also some problems with Czech (not foreign-like) words – e.g. the simple rule-based phonetic transcription is not able to distinguish whether the group of 2 graphemes *au, eu, ou* should be transcribed as a diphthong a_u/e_u/o_u or two separate vowels with a glottal stop between (in Czech, a glottal stop occurs at the beginning of a word starting with a vowel and it is also inserted before an initial vowel of the second part of compound words, i.e. between prefix and stem, [14]), e.g.:

poutník	[p **o_u** t n i: k]	(*EN: pilgrim*)
použití	[p **o ? u** Z i c i:]	(*EN: usage*)

3   Experiment Setting

The main goal of the presented experiment is the effort to verify the possibility of using *encoder-decoder* NN-based G2P model, trained on phrases from a large-scale text corpus, instead of using the manual hand-written rules. The corpus used contains approx. 770 thousands of Czech phrases with phonetic transcriptions (these proprietary data were created automatically and checked by phonetic experts). The texts consist of 40 graphemes (for the lowercase text inputs) and the phonetic transcriptions contain 48 phonemes (including the # symbol for a pause between phrases) [19]. We randomly selected 10% of phrases for evaluation steps during the training and the other phrases were used for the training itself.

3.1   Auto-Encoder BiLSTM Neural Network for G2P Problem

For the experiment, we designed a special structure of our NN-based model, which is shown in Fig. 1. First of all, the words w_i in the input phrases (and also the corresponding transcriptions) are transformed to the sequences of symbols with the same length

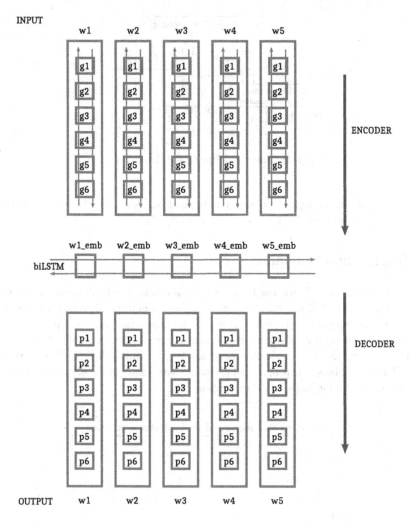

Fig. 1. The structure of our Auto-Encoder BiLSTM Neural Network for G2P.

using a padding symbol –. The first layer of our model is the *embedding* layer which transforms each symbol/grapheme to a vector representation g_i (of the length of 8), and the outputs of the *embedding* layer are forced to the second, bidirectional LSTM layer with 64 units in each direction – that is illustrated in the first part of the Fig. 1. This layer should, according to our assumption, learn within-word phonetic relations since the model is able to learn from past and future states simultaneously. After that, the LSTM *encoder* layer creates the word embeddings w_i_emb whose are used as an input of another bidirectional LSTM layer with 64 units working, therefore, on the word level (the middle part of the scheme) so it could be able to learn cross-word-boundary relations. Finally, the LSTM decoder followed by a linear projection with *softmax* activation generates the sequences of phoneme posteriors p_i from the word representations

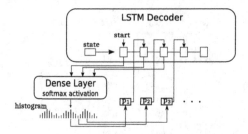

Fig. 2. The structure of the LSTM-decoder layer.

(the bottom part of the figure). It employs the feedback loop, in which the previously generated phoneme is fed back to the next input (Fig. 2).

4   Training and Evaluation

As mentioned in Sect. 3, we used our proprietary data provided to us by phonetic experts. The model itself was trained to minimize cross-entropy of phoneme posteriors. During the training phrase, in each step, the model received a batch of 4 phrases (word sequences containing 5 words) randomly selected from the training data. With the best parameter setting, the best evaluation accuracy 99.95% was achieved after 1,000,000 steps[2]. The Fig. 3 shows the progress of phoneme, word and phrase accuracy during the first 1,000,000 training steps on the evaluation data.

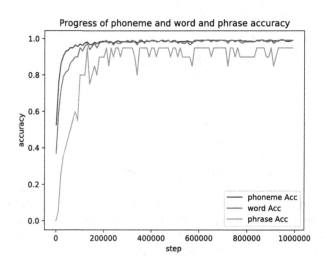

Fig. 3. The progress of phoneme and word accuracy during training the NN model (first 1,000,000 training steps).

---

[2] Note: This accuracy was counted on phoneme level and includes the padding symbols ' - ' and the <break> words, too.

Before presenting the final results on the testing data, let us focus on the progress of learning the G2P issue. It is obvious that the model first learns the transcriptions of the padding symbol –, as can be seen in the extract of the evaluation data after the first 1,000 steps in Fig. 4 (i.e. only 1,000 batches of four phrases were shown to the network). The word length is converted correctly, but the regular phonemes do not correspond the correct transcription at all – in fact, those belong to the most common phonemes in the training data.

word	correct	predicted	is_ok?
až--------	? a S - - - - - - -	? e e - - - - - - -	False
nás-------	n a: z - - - - - - -	? e e - - - - - - -	False
znudí-----	z n u J\ i: - - - - -	p o e e e - - - - -	False
i---------	? i - - - - - - - -	? e - - - - - - - -	False
městský---	m J e s t_s k i: - - -	p o o e e e i: - - -	False
ruch------	r u x - - - - - - -	? e e - - - - - - -	False

Fig. 4. The extract of the evaluation data after first 1,000 steps.

After 100,000 steps, the predicted output is much more similar to the correct phonetic transcription of the transcribed phrases, but still containing a lot of errors (see Fig. 5). However, the incorrect predicted phoneme sequence for the second word is one of two possible transcriptions of the word *nás* (these are [n a: s] and [n a: z], depending on the following word; see Sect. 2).

word	correct	predicted	is_ok?
až--------	? a S - - - - - - -	? a S - - - - - - -	True
nás-------	n a: z - - - - - - -	n a: s - - - - - - -	False
znudí-----	z n u J\ i: - - - - -	z J i d i: - - - - -	False
i---------	? i - - - - - - - -	? i - - - - - - - -	True
městský---	m J e s t_s k i: - - -	m J e s t_s k i: - - -	True
ruch------	r u x - - - - - - -	r u x - - - - - - -	True

Fig. 5. The extract of the evaluation data after 100,000 steps.

And the output after first 1,000,000 steps is in Fig. 6 – as can be seen, the model was able to learn the cross-word-boundary assimilation (the last grapheme *s* in *nás* was correctly predicted as phoneme z because of the voiced consonant *z* at the beginning of the following word *znudí*).

word	correct	predicted	is_ok?
až--------	? a S - - - - - - -	? a S - - - - - - -	True
nás-------	n a: z - - - - - - -	n a: z - - - - - - -	True
znudí-----	z n u J\ i: - - - - -	z n u J\ i: - - - - -	True
i---------	? i - - - - - - - -	? i - - - - - - - -	True
městský---	m J e s t_s k i: - - -	m J e s t_s k i: - - -	True
ruch------	r u x - - - - - - -	r u x - - - - - - -	True

Fig. 6. The extract of the evaluation data after 1,000,000 steps.

4.1 Results

In this paper, the G2P problem is evaluated on 3 levels – *phoneme accuracy, word accuracy* and *phrase accuracy*. The testing data consist of 20,000 phrases with approx. 143 thousand of words. The average word length is 5 phonemes, a maximum 19 phonemes. Comparing the best NN model to the rule-based approach and the combined rules-dictionary approach used in our TTS *ARTIC* [22] (see Sect. 2.1), we get the Table 1.

Table 1. Comparison of phoneme, word and phrase accuracy on 20,000 testing phrases.

	phoneme Acc	word Acc	phrase Acc
Only hand-crafted rules	95.08%	96.75%	82.13%
Rules + exception dictionary	98.72%	99.16%	97.86%
Proposed NN-based approach	99.69%	98.92%	92.83%

The phoneme accuracy of the fully trained G2P transcription for Czech is 99.69% which is higher compared to the phoneme accuracy of the hand-crafted rules and the approach using both the rules and the exception dictionary[3]. On the other hand, the combined approach (rules + dictionary) still outperforms our NN model in word and phrase accuracy. The detailed analysis of the predicted output evinces more frequent errors in longer words.

The graph in Fig. 8 shows the word accuracy on the word length – the longer the word, the lower the accuracy of our new G2P model. If the word length exceeds 12 phonemes, the word accuracy decreases below 80%, but that concerns only approx. 1.2% of all words in the corpus. The incorrect transcriptions of long words are demonstrated in Fig. 7 on randomly chosen long words from the testing data with wrong predicted output. Those errors are, unfortunately, senseless (and the rules would never make such errors). Probably, the NN-based model is not always able to remember the whole input word correctly if too long. This needs more investigations in our future research. In any case, despite increasing encoder/decoder capacity, the model did not yield better results and the accuracy on longer words was still significantly lower compared to shorter words.

```
šéfredaktorkou   S e: f r e d a k t o r k o_u –   S e: f r e d a s t o r k o_u –
organizátorek–   ! o r g a n i z a: t o r e k     ! o r g a n i z a: t a: t e k
přibývajícími–   p Q i b i: v a j i: c i: m i –    p Q i b i: v a j i: c i: m i: –
```

Fig. 7. The examples of long wrongly transcribed words.

As described in Sect. 2.1, the traditional rule-based G2P has to be supported by a large exceptions dictionary to work satisfactory in the TTS system with a general text

---

[3] This time, the accuracies were counted only for regular phonemes and words, without padding symbol "-" and without phrase-break words.

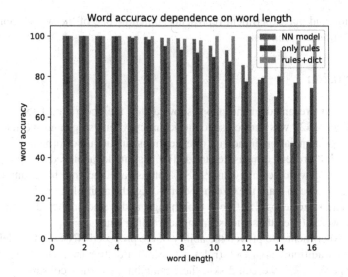

Fig. 8. Word accuracy dependence on word length.

input. Based on that, we wanted to find out the G2P model accuracy on the problematic sentences which contain these foreign-like words. And we supposed the NN model may be able to learn the specifics of loan words transcription. So the second testing set of 1,000 phrases was prepared so that every phrase contains at least one foreign-like word with non-Czech pronunciation; 8,242 words in total. Our assumption proved to be correct because some words with a specific pronunciation were really transcribed correctly by the model. And it was proved that the proposed NN model was able to outperform the only-rules approach both in word and phoneme accuracy (and, of course, in the phrase accuracy, too). The results are shown in Table 2. However, the combined approach is still better in word and phrase accuracy.

Table 2. Comparison of phoneme, word and phrase accuracy on 1,000 phrases, containing at least one foreign-like word.

	phoneme Acc	word Acc	phrase Acc
Only hand-crafted rules	95.02%	86.22%	0.00%
Rules + exception dictionary	98.82%	99.40%	98.41%
Proposed NN-based approach	99.35%	98.61%	84.27%

It can be objected the previous experiment is not fair for the rule-based approach, given that the testing data were intentionally selected so that each sentence contained words where the rules were useless (and it was clear that the phrase accuracy would be 0%). Nevertheless, we have carried out that experiment because nowadays Czech texts contain a great amount of foreign-like words and loanwords with non-standard pronunciation and our experiment represents somehow one of the worst scenarios for the phonetic transcription task.

5 Conclusion

The experiment presented in the paper showed that the accuracy of the trained NN model for Czech G2P was very close to the accuracy when using hand-written phonetic rules and the pronunciation dictionary of exceptions, and it outperformed the only-rules approach in all 3 presented measures used. The best model achieved 99.69% phoneme accuracy, 98.92% word accuracy and 92.83% phrase accuracy on the testing data. The model was also able to learn the Czech specifics, e.g. the assimilation of voice (even on word boundaries), to recognize Czech diphthongs, and it also predicted correctly some foreign-like words (even those not seen in the training data).

By this experiment, we proved the ability of the proposed NN-based model to compete with the traditional approach (rules + exception dictionary). Therefore, having a new language for TTS, we could skip the demanding and time-consuming works on phonetic rules and the dictionary extending and we can simply train a G2P model for that language from a large (transcribed) text corpus (if available). In our opinion, our idea of taking the whole phrases as an input (contrary to the dictionary approaches applied to G2P, Sect. 1.1) could be an inspiration for other researches since the model is able to learn and interpret the cross-words relations. However, the main disadvantages of the presented model are the need for a large amount of training data and, as shown in Fig. 8, the error rate for long words.

As future work, we will experiment with more NN structures and settings for improving the model accuracy, especially regarding longer words. We also plan to enrich the input data with part-of-speech tags since the pronunciation can, in some cases in Czech, depend on the morphological categories of the particular word. And, since we are also preparing a similar experiment for other languages we have text corpora for (English, Russian, Slovak, etc.), this idea could be also helpful for those; e.g. in English where the different pronunciation of a word (if it is a noun or a verb) is quite often.

Acknowledgement. This research was supported by the Czech Science Foundation (GA CR), project No. GA19-19324S, and by the grant of the University of West Bohemia, project No. SGS-2019-027.

References

1. Bičan, A.: Distribution and combinations of Czech consonants. Zeitschrift für Slawistik **56**, 153–171 (2011)
2. Bisani, M., Ney, H.: Joint-sequence models for grapheme-to-phoneme conversion. Speech Commun. **50**(5), 434–451 (2008)
3. Cho, K., et al.: Learning phrase representations using RNN encoder-decoder for statistical machine translation. In: Moschitti, A., Pang, B., Daelemans, W. (eds.) EMNLP, pp. 1724–1734. ACL (2014)

4. Hanzlíček, Z., Vít, J., Tihelka, D.: LSTM-based speech segmentation for TTS synthesis. In: Ekštein, K. (ed.) TSD 2019. LNAI, vol. 11697, pp. 361–372. Springer, Heidelberg (2019)
5. Hochreiter, S., Schmidhuber, J.: Long short-term memory. Neural Comput. 9(8), 1735–1780 (1997)
6. Jiampojamarn, S., Cherry, C., Kondrak, G.: Joint processing and discriminative training for letter-to-phoneme conversion. In: Proceedings of ACL-08: HLT, pp. 905–913. Association for Computational Linguistics, Columbus (2008)
7. Kučera, H.: The phonology of Czech, Slavistic printings and reprintings, vol. 30, 's-Gravenhage, Mouton (1961)
8. Machač, P., Skarnitzl, R.: Principles of phonetic segmentation. Edition erudica, Epocha (2009)
9. Matoušek, J.: Building a New Czech text-to-speech system using triphone-based speech units. In: Sojka, P., Kopeček, I., Pala, K. (eds.) TSD 2000. LNCS (LNAI), vol. 1902, pp. 223–228. Springer, Heidelberg (2000). https://doi.org/10.1007/3-540-45323-7_38
10. Matoušek, J., Tihelka, D.: Annotation errors detection in TTS corpora. In: Proceedings of INTERSPEECH 2013, Lyon, France, pp. 1511–1515 (2013)
11. Matoušek, J., Tihelka, D., Šmídl, L.: On the impact of annotation errors on unit-selection speech synthesis. In: Sojka, P., Horák, A., Kopeček, I., Pala, K. (eds.) TSD 2012. LNCS (LNAI), vol. 7499, pp. 456–463. Springer, Heidelberg (2012). https://doi.org/10.1007/978-3-642-32790-2_55
12. Matoušek, J., Tihelka, D., Psutka, J.: Experiments with automatic segmentation for Czech speech synthesis. In: Matoušek, V., Mautner, P. (eds.) TSD 2003. LNCS (LNAI), vol. 2807, pp. 287–294. Springer, Heidelberg (2003). https://doi.org/10.1007/978-3-540-39398-6_41
13. Matoušek, J., Tihelka, D., Romportl, J., Psutka, J.: Slovak unit-selection speech synthesis: creating a new Slovak voice within a Czech TTS system ARTIC. IAENG Int. J. Comput. Sci. 39, 147–154 (2012)
14. Matoušek, J., Kala, J.: On modelling glottal stop in Czech text-to-speech synthesis. In: Matoušek, V., Mautner, P., Pavelka, T. (eds.) TSD 2005. LNCS (LNAI), vol. 3658, pp. 257–264. Springer, Heidelberg (2005). https://doi.org/10.1007/11551874_33
15. Matoušek, J., Psutka, J.: ARTIC: a new czech text-to-speech system using statistical approach to speech segment database construction. In: Interspeech 2000 - ICSLP, Beijing, China, vol. 4, pp. 612–615 (2000)
16. Matoušek, J., Tihelka, D.: Slovak text-to-speech synthesis in ARTIC system. In: Sojka, P., Kopeček, I., Pala, K. (eds.) TSD 2004. LNCS (LNAI), vol. 3206, pp. 155–162. Springer, Heidelberg (2004). https://doi.org/10.1007/978-3-540-30120-2_20
17. Novak, J.R., Minamatsu, N., Hirose, K.: Phonetisaurus: exploring grapheme-to-phoneme conversion with joint n-gram models in the WFST framework. Natural Lang. Eng. 22(6), 907–938 (2016)
18. Palková, Z.: Fonetika a fonologie češtiny [Phonetics and phonology of Czech], 1st edn. Univerzita Karlova, Nakladatelství Karolinum, Praha (1994)
19. Psutka, J., Müller, L., Matoušek, J., Radová, V.: Mluvíme s počítačem česky [Talking with Computer in Czech]. Academia, Praha (2006)
20. Rao, K., Peng, F., Sak, H., Beaufays, F.: Grapheme-to-phoneme conversion using long short-term memory recurrent neural networks. In: 2015 IEEE International Conference on Acoustics, Speech and Signal Processing (ICASSP), pp. 4225–4229 (2015)
21. Sutskever, I., Vinyals, O., Le, Q.V.: Sequence to sequence learning with neural networks. In: Proceedings NIPS, Montreal, Canada, pp. 3104–3112 (2014)
22. Tihelka, D., Hanzlíček, Z., Jůzová, M., Vít, J., Matoušek, J., Grůber, M.: Current state of text-to-speech system ARTIC: a decade of research on the field of speech technologies. In: Sojka, P., Horák, A., Kopeček, I., Pala, K. (eds.) TSD 2018. LNCS (LNAI), vol. 11107, pp. 369–378. Springer, Cham (2018). https://doi.org/10.1007/978-3-030-00794-2_40

23. Wang, D., King, S.: Letter-to-sound pronunciation prediction using conditional random fields. IEEE Signal Process. Lett. **18**(2), 122–125 (2011)
24. Wang, Y., et al.: Tacotron: towards end-to-end speech synthesis (2017). https://arxiv.org/abs/1703.10135
25. Wells, J.C.: SAMPA computer readable phonetic alphabet. In: Gibbon, D., Moore, R., Winski, R. (eds.) Handbook of Standards and Resources for Spoken Language Systems. Mouton de Gruyter, Berlin (1997)
26. Wu, Y., et al.: Google's neural machine translation system: bridging the gap between human and machine translation. CoRR abs/1609.08144 (2016). http://arxiv.org/abs/1609.08144
27. Yao, K., Zweig, G.: Sequence-to-sequence neural net models for grapheme-to-phoneme conversion. CoRR abs/1506.00196 (2015)

The FRENK Datasets of Socially Unacceptable Discourse in Slovene and English

Nikola Ljubešić[1]([✉])(iD), Darja Fišer[1,2](iD), and Tomaž Erjavec[1](iD)

[1] Department of Knowledge Technologies, Jožef Stefan Institute, Ljubljana, Slovenia
{nikola.ljubesic,tomaz.erjavec}@ijs.si
[2] Department of Translation, Faculty of Arts,
University of Ljubljana, Ljubljana, Slovenia
darja.fiser@ff.uni-lj.si

Abstract. In this paper we present datasets of Facebook comment threads to mainstream media posts in Slovene and English developed inside the Slovene national project FRENK (the acronym FRENK stands for "FRENK - Raziskave Elektronske Nespodobne Komunikacije" (engl. "Research on Electronic Inappropriate Communication")) which cover two topics, migrants and LGBT, and are manually annotated for different types of socially unacceptable discourse (SUD). The main advantages of these datasets compared to the existing ones are identical sampling procedures, producing comparable data across languages and an annotation schema that takes into account six types of SUD and five targets at which SUD is directed. We describe the sampling and annotation procedures, and analyze the annotation distributions and inter-annotator agreements. We consider this dataset to be an important milestone in understanding and combating SUD for both languages.

Keywords: Socially unacceptable discourse · Slovene language ·
English language · Manually annotated dataset

1 Introduction

With the transformative role of social media in public communication and opinion, there is increased pressure to understand and manage inappropriate online content. The research community is by now generally aware of the complexity of the inappropriateness in on-line communication, and there is an overall agreement that annotating real-world datasets with these phenomena, both for understanding the phenomenon via statistical analysis, as well as for (semi-)automation via machine learning is the way forward in combating this major downside of the social media [4,5].

The currently available datasets of inappropriate on-line communication are primarily compiled for English, such as the Twitter dataset annotated for racist

© Springer Nature Switzerland AG 2019
K. Ekštein (Ed.): TSD 2019, LNAI 11697, pp. 103–114, 2019.
https://doi.org/10.1007/978-3-030-27947-9_9

and sexist hate speech [7][1], the Wikimedia Toxicity Data Set [8][2], the Hate Speech Identification dataset [1][3], the SFU Opinion and Comment Corpus [4], and the Offensive Language Identification Dataset (OLID) [9][5]. Datasets in other languages have recently started to emerge as well, with a German Twitter dataset on the topic of refugees in Germany [6][6], a Greek Sport News Comment dataset [5][7] and two large datasets of Slovene and Croatian online news comments manually moderated by the site administrators [4][8,9].

The annotation schemas used in these datasets are very different, ranging from encoding multiple toxicity levels, covert vs. overt aggressiveness, the target of the inappropriateness only etc. The first two pieces of work to take into account both the type of SUD and its target are the annotation schema presented in [2] (which is used in the dataset presented in this paper) and the OLID dataset [9].

In this paper we present datasets of Facebook posts and comments of mainstream news media from Slovenia and Great Britain, covering the topics of migrants and LGBT. Each comment is annotated with a two-dimensional annotation schema for SUD, covering both the type and the target of SUD. The main contributions of this paper are the following: (1) we offer a selection of Facebook pages aimed at representativeness and comparability for a specific country/language, (2) we apply an identical formalism on comparable data in two languages, making this the first multilingual dataset annotated for SUD we are aware of, (3) we annotate for a very broad phenomenon of SUD, covering most phenomena various datasets cover in isolation, (4) we annotate full discussion (comment) threads, not isolated short utterances, ensuring both that (a) the annotators are as informed of the context as possible while making their decisions (e.g., annotating tweets in isolation, not knowing their context, is a questionable, but regular practice) and (b) that the context of the comment is available either for analyzing the dataset or using the dataset for (semi)automating the identification of SUD, and (5) we perform a first analysis of this rich dataset, observing interesting phenomena both across topics and across languages.

2   Dataset Construction

By selecting the Facebook pages of mainstream media that would constitute our dataset, we were aiming at criteria that would make the datasets as comparable

---

[1] https://github.com/ZeerakW/hatespeech.

[2] https://figshare.com/projects/Wikipedia_Talk/16731.

[3] https://data.world/crowdflower/hate-speech-identification.

[4] https://github.com/sfu-discourse-lab/SOCC.

[5] https://scholar.harvard.edu/malmasi/olid.

[6] https://github.com/UCSM-DUE/IWG_hatespeech_public.

[7] https://straintek.wediacloud.net/static/gazzetta-comments-dataset/gazzetta-comments-dataset.tar.gz.

[8] http://hdl.handle.net/11356/1201.

[9] http://hdl.handle.net/11356/1202.

as possible across languages.[10] We opted for the most visited web sites of mainstream media according to the Alexa service[11] that have popular Facebook pages. For Slovene, this procedure yielded 24urcom,[12] SiOL.net.Novice[13] and Nova24TV[14], while for English we selected bbcnews,[15] DailyMail [16] and theguardian.[17] The only intervention into the list obtained from the Alexa service was the removal of the Slovene public broadcast RTV Slovenija, as its Facebook page RTV.SLOVENIJA is not very active since this medium has a very good in-house solution to news commenting.

Once we harvested all the available posts and comments from these pages via the public Graph API[18,19], we started the process of identifying posts covering our two topics: migrants and LGBT. Topic identification was performed in the following way: (1) we manually identified a selection of around 100 posts per topic (including a category for covering *other* news, i.e., not migrants and not LGBT) via keywords, (2) we trained a simple word- and character-ngram-based linear SVM classifier on these posts, (3) we classified the whole collection of Facebook posts with that classifier, (4) we manually corrected classifications of 100 random posts per topic (including the *other* category), (5) we added these posts to our dataset of manually-annotated posts and retrained the classifier, and (6) we performed a final classification of the posts. For the final annotation we discarded the posts annotated as *other* and selected the posts annotated with the two remaining topics with the highest confidence score.

With this process which included two rounds of (quick) manual annotation we wanted to produce a training set representative of the two topics, and not of the keywords used in the initial topic identification.

In early stages of the development of the topic identification process, we experimented with (1) merging all Facebook pages together vs. classifying each Facebook page separately and (2) representing each post either through the post text only vs. representing it with the post text as well as the text of the first ten comments. These experiments showed that better results are achieved if (1) all Facebook posts were classified together (having three times the amount of training data, but greater variety of post and comment styles) and (2) each post was represented through the text of the post and the first ten comments (having

---

[10] While in this paper we describe the annotation results of Slovene and English only, an annotation campaign over Croatian data is already under way and plans exist to annotate Dutch and French data as well.

[11] https://www.alexa.com/topsites/countries.

[12] https://www.facebook.com/24urcom.

[13] https://www.facebook.com/SiOL.net.Novice.

[14] https://www.facebook.com/Nova24TV.

[15] https://www.facebook.com/bbcnews.

[16] https://www.facebook.com/DailyMail.

[17] https://www.facebook.com/theguardian.

[18] https://developers.facebook.com/docs/graph-api/.

[19] To use this service from May 2018 onwards, users have to go through a screening process that would quite likely not be successful for harvesting purposes, but our collection was performed in October 2017, before this restrictive change in policy.

more text per post at classifier's disposal, but combining the text of the post together with the users' responses, which might be less informative of the topic).

3   Dataset Annotation

For annotating the datasets, we used a two-dimensional annotation schema an early version of which was presented in [2], covering both the type of potentially socially unacceptable discourse and the target this discourse is aimed at. The annotation was performed in PyBossa,[20] a web-based crowdsourcing tool.

3.1   Annotation Schema

While annotating for the type of SUD, annotators used the decision tree sketched in Fig. 1. This decision tree has six leaves, representing the six types of SUD we discriminate between. The main distinctions regarding the type of SUD are made whether SUD is aimed at the background of a person (e.g., religion, sexual orientation), whether the SUD is aimed at other groups or an individual (vs. just being unacceptable in terms of swearing), and whether there are elements of violence in SUD or not.

```
Is this SUD aimed at someone's background?
    YES: Are there elements of violence?
        YES: background, violence
        NO:  background, offensive speech
    NO:  Is this SUD aimed towards individuals or other groups?
        YES: Are there elements of violence?
            YES: other, threat
            NO:  other, offensive speech
        NO:  Is the speech unacceptable?
            YES: inappropriate speech
            NO:  acceptable speech
```

Fig. 1. Decision tree used for identifying the type of socially unacceptable discourse

As for the target of SUD, we discriminate between (1) SUD aimed at migrants or LGBT (2) SUD aimed at individuals or groups related to migrants or LGBT (such as NGOs, public bodies etc.), (3) SUD aimed at journalists and media, (4) SUD aimed at other commenters in the discussion thread and (5) SUD aimed at someone else.

We consider this annotation schema to be the most comprehensive schema of SUD-related phenomena applied to this day on any dataset.

---

[20] https://pybossa.com.

3.2   Annotation Procedure

The annotation campaign was divided into tasks, where each task consisted of the post text (published by the medium) and all the comments (written by their readers) in the discussion thread. For each task the post either had to be annotated as irrelevant (in case of incorrect topic classification presented in Sect. 2), or each comment in the task had to be annotated with the corresponding SUD type and target via two drop-down menus. Going back to tasks that were already submitted was not possible as PyBossa does not offer such an option. Furthermore, discussion threads that were longer than 20 comments were split into multiple tasks as annotating more than 20 comments before submitting a task would easily become too cumbersome for the annotators. The tasks continuing the annotation of a discussion thread also contained the five last comments from the previous task to give the annotators some discussion context. Whole discussion threads were annotated regardless of their length as such an approach was considered to be the least problematic regarding sampling decisions (e.g., what part of the discussion thread to annotate). An example screenshot of the annotation interface is depicted in Fig. 2.

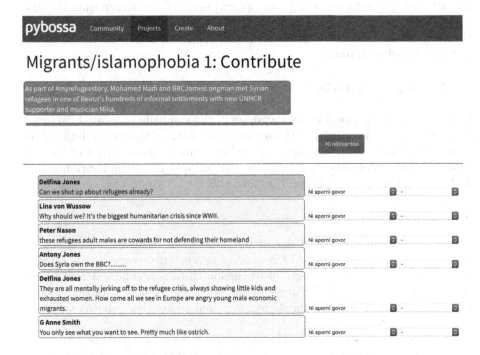

Fig. 2. The PyBossa interface used for annotating the datasets.

The annotators performing the annotation were master students from the Faculty of Arts and the Faculty of Social Sciences from the University of Ljubljana. They all attended an initial half-day annotator training which was followed by an initial annotation round where all of the 32 annotators annotated the same data and discussions about the problematic cases were held via a mailing list. After the initial training, the annotators were randomly assigned to one of the two topics (migrants or LGBT). The same split by topic was then retained throughout the entire annotation campaign. In the first annotation campaign, Slovene data were annotated by approximately eight annotators per comment. The overall decision to gather around eight annotations per comment was based on the awareness of the complexity of the annotation schema and the phenomenon itself, as well as initial calculations of inter-annotator (dis)agreement. After the annotation campaign of Slovene data, roughly half of the annotators signed up for the annotation of the English data, depending both on their previous performance and their self-assessed skill of the English language. To keep the number of annotations per comment similar to Slovene data, the English annotation campaign took twice as long as the Slovene annotation campaign.

After finishing each PyBossa project, the annotations were downloaded from the PyBossa instance and analyzed, measuring the agreement inside each comment as the entropy of the annotation distribution. Comments with the highest entropy were then manually analyzed by an expert (social scientist working at the national centre for reporting hate speech) in order to communicate the disagreement issues via a mailing list with all the annotators, regardless of the topic they covered in order to fine-tune annotation guidelines and avoid similar issues in future annotation rounds.

4   Dataset Analysis

In this section we perform various analyses of the manually annotated datasets. We start with the description of the size of the dataset, continue with the analysis of the distribution of annotations and the inter-annotator agreement of the two dimensions of annotation, and wrap up with an analysis of the distribution of SUD among the users producing the comments.

4.1   Size of the Datasets

We first report on the overall size of the datasets in terms of the number of posts, number of comments and the number of annotator responses in Table 1. The results show that the length of discussion threads is similar across topics and languages, with the LGBT topic in Slovene being the only strong deviation, where the average discussion thread length is four to five times shorter than the rest of the topics and languages.

Regarding the distribution of the sources (Facebook pages) of the posts that were annotated, they are all rather evenly distributed, except for the topic of LBGT in the Slovene dataset, where the number of posts from the Nova24TV is significantly higher than is the case for the other two sources. The Nova24TV source, is associated with the extreme right of the political spectrum, discussing LGBT issues, especially the Slovene referendum on same-sex marriage, more fervently than the remaining sources.

Table 1. Size of the datasets by language and topic.

	Slovene		English	
	Migrants	LGBT	Migrants	LGBT
Number of posts	30	93	16	14
Number of comments	6545	4571	5855	5906
Average thread length	218	49	366	422
Number of annotations	56211	41433	44969	49978
Average number of annotations	8.59	9.06	7.68	8.46

4.2 Annotation Distribution

In this subsection we perform an analysis of the distribution of all the annotations by topic and language. Given that there is a large number of possible combinations regarding the type and target of the SUD that we annotate for, Table 2 lists only the five most frequently assigned annotation combinations in both languages, treating the two topics as portions of the annotation probability distributions of all the annotation combinations.

Table 2. Probability distribution of the most frequent annotations by language and topic.

Type	Target	Slovene		English	
		Migrants	LGBT	Migrants	LGBT
Acceptable	No target	0.42	0.54	0.50	0.67
Background, violence	Target	0.07	0.02	0.02	0.00
Background, offensive	Target	0.23	0.17	0.21	0.12
Other, offensive	Commenter	0.08	0.08	0.06	0.11
Other, offensive	Related to	0.04	0.02	0.02	0.01

The results show that about half of the annotated comments are socially acceptable, which is a surprisingly low result. It is true that the topics where chosen with the expectation of high SUD occurrence, but we consider the amount of SUD in roughly half of the comments to be rather striking, especially given the fact that some of the most unacceptable comments might have been removed from Facebook prior to our data harvesting.

In Slovene there seems to be less socially acceptable content on these topics, which is observed more frequently on the topic of LGBT than migrants in both languages. The difference between the two languages is especially visible on the

LGBT topic where there is an absolute difference of 13% between Slovene and English, pointing towards greater acceptance of LGBT in the British society.[21]

The four most frequently occurring category combinations of SUD in both languages and topics are, in decreasing order: (1) SUD directed at migrants or LGBT people, being offensive, (2) SUD directed at other commenters, being offensive (3) SUD directed at migrants or LGBT people, inciting violence and (4) SUD directed at people or organisations related to migrants and LGBT people, being offensive.

The most worrisome result among these is that the most problematic category, SUD inciting violence towards migrants or LGBT people, is present in the top five categories, covering between 7 and below 1% of the annotations, depending on the language and topic. It follows the overall trend of observing higher numbers for Slovene compared to English, and for migrants compared to LGBT. The overall good side of these results is that in the English dataset on the topic of LGBT the percentage of such annotations is below 1%, but the percentage of such annotations in Slovene related to migrants is at very high 7%.

Regarding the SUD directed at fellow commenters, in Slovene it is similarly present on both topics, while in English data it is similarly frequent on the topic of migrants, but almost as twice as high on the topic of LGBT. This suggests that the SUD generated on the LGBT topic in English data is often generated due to disagreement with the remaining commenters, not directed at LGBT people directly. This result also explains the lower percentage of more problematic types of SUD for this language and topic. It seems that British people (or, to be more precise, commenters on British online media) are not directly intolerant towards LGBT people *per se*, but are intolerant towards related issues, such as same-sex marriage, same-sex partners adopting children etc.

4.3   Inter-annotator Agreement

To measure the complexity of the annotation task as well as the level up to which we should trust single annotations performed in this dataset, we calculated the Krippendorff's α inter-annotator agreement score presented in Table 3. This score is suitable for annotation campaigns with more than two annotators, as well as spotty annotations, taking also into account agreement by chance [3]. Given that the type of SUD can be considered both a nominal as well as an ordinal variable, we perform calculations of inter-annotator agreement for both cases. For the target of the SUD, no order can be established, therefore we consider this variable to be nominal only.

---

[21] As always, these results have to be taken with caution and not as final, as other factors might have produced this difference, such as (1) the fact that in Slovenia the referendum regarding same-sex marriages was carried out during the period these Facebook posts cover and (2) the fact that most of the LGBT-related content comes from Nova24TV, which is, as already mentioned, a medium on the right side of the political spectrum. The latter has proven to have an impact as this source has socially acceptable comments in 42% of cases, while the other two have 57% and 62% of non-SUD comments on this topic. Both other sources still have, however, a higher percentage of SUD comments than the English average.

Table 3. Krippendorff's α inter-annotator agreement by language and topic.

Dimension	Variable type	Slovene		English	
		Migrants	LGBT	Migrants	LGBT
Type	Nominal	0.499	0.500	0.436	0.357
Type	Ordinal	0.595	0.590	0.516	0.444
Target	Nominal	0.528	0.507	0.445	0.380

The measured agreement between the annotators is considered low by social science standards, i.e., not good enough to draw even tentative conclusions. This is why we have decided to gather multiple annotations from the beginning, with the goal of combining them into single high-quality annotations. Some initial experiments on collecting professional annotations for a subset of Slovene comments and comparing those to the mode of all non-professional annotations, i.e., the most frequent annotation, show that collecting multiple non-professional annotations is a reasonable approach, with the Krippendorff's α for the type of SUD as a nominal variable being 0.731, for the type of SUD as an interval variable 0.795, and for the target of SUD as a nominal variable the Krippendorff's α being 0.733. Thereby, all the agreements are above 0.66, which is the lower threshold for useful annotations by social science standards. Obtaining high-quality annotations from the non-professional annotations is, however, not the focus of this work and will be performed in more detail in future experiments.

Regarding the difference in the observed agreements, it tends to be higher on Slovene than on English which can be due to the fact that the annotators were native speakers of Slovene, living in Slovenia, with better linguistic but also contextual knowledge. As expected, if we consider the type of SUD to be an ordinal, and not a nominal variable, the agreement increases, which shows that the type of SUD does indeed have properties of an ordinal variable. Annotating the type and target of SUD seem to be similarly complex tasks for the annotators. The only deviation in agreement within a language seems to be on English data, where we observe a ten-point lower result for the LGBT topic than for migrants. A tentative hypothesis for such a result is the distribution of the annotations, with the three most frequent annotation combinations making 91% of the annotations, while in the remaining three cases these cover between 75 and 81% of the annotations only. Thereby the agreement by chance in the LGBT topic on English data is higher, making the Krippendorff's α with the same observed agreement lower than for the remaining cases.

As already briefly discussed, future work is planned in increasing the quality of the annotations by exploiting the fact that we have around 8 annotations available per comment which can be used to calculate some statistic, e.g., the mode (most frequent case) of the annotations, which has preliminarily showed to significantly improve the quality of annotations, or to learn to extract the optimal annotation from the multiple annotations by using a small subset of expert annotations in a supervised machine learning setting.

4.4 Distribution of SUD Among Users

While this dataset enables a myriad of analyses of the occurrence of various forms of SUD due to metadata richness, we have chosen one of the most pressing questions for the first analysis of this dataset: Who produces most of SUD? Is this a small number of users, or is SUD generated in a similar intensity by most users?

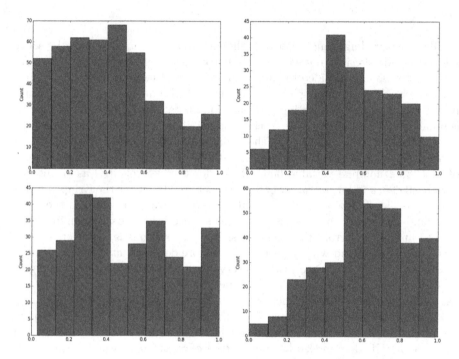

Fig. 3. Distribution of percentage of non-SUD comments among users of Slovene (left) and English (right) datasets on topics of migrants (up) and LGBT (down).

We operationalise the amount of SUD produced by specific users as the percentage of non-SUD comments for each user who has posted 3 or more comments in a specific topic and language. We present the results via histograms of percentages of non-SUD comments per user presented in Fig. 3, where the left histograms show the results for Slovene, right for English, upper for the topic of migrants and lower for the topic of LGBT.

When reading these plots, one has to bear in mind the percentage of non-SUD annotations from Sect. 4.2, which was the lowest for the topic of migrants in Slovene (upper left histogram) and highest for the topic of LGBT in English (lower right histogram). What these plots are primarily informative for is their shape, i.e., whether they are (1) bell-shaped, which points to the conclusion that the majority of users produces a medium amount of SUD, while just a smaller portion produces very little or a lot of SUD, (2) U-shaped, which means that there are users producing either large or small quantities of SUD or (3) rather evenly-distributed, which indicates that users produce various quantities of SUD. The regularity, which can be observed in Fig. 3 is that in the English dataset, regardless of the amount of SUD produced, the distributions are rather bell-shaped, meaning that most users are average producers of SUD, while in the Slovene dataset the distributions are rather even, suggesting that users are producing various amounts of SUD.

The results of this analysis point towards the conclusion that English users are more mainstream-oriented regarding the production of SUD, while among the Slovene users there are both extreme, medium and non-producers of SUD. A possible explanation would be for the British media to show a more mature community of commenters than is the case for the Slovene media. Another explanation for the differing distributions between Slovene and English might be a more responsible policy of British media, removing regularly a significant portion of unacceptable content. This phenomenon will have to be investigated in more detail in future work.

5   Conclusion

In this paper we have presented a dataset of Facebook comments on posts from mainstream media in Slovenia and Great Britain covering the topics of migrants and LGBT, which were manually annotated with the type and target of socially unacceptable discourse. We have described the data sampling, topic identification and manual annotation of the dataset.

We have performed an initial analysis of the manually annotated dataset, showing that more SUD is produced in Slovene than in English media, and that more SUD is produced on the topic of migrants than LGBT.

Our analysis of the inter-annotator agreement shows that both type and target are similarly complex for the annotators, with a medium agreement below the expected quality in social science. Initial experiments on comparing professional annotations with the modes (most frequent annotations) of the non-professional annotations show to improve agreement significantly, moving it to the area of useful annotations for social sciences. The fact that we have collected around eight annotations per comment will be exploited further in future work on extracting annotations of highest quality possible.

Finally, we have performed an initial analysis of the distribution of SUD among different users, showing that there is a trend of a similar number of users who produce large, medium and low quantities of SUD in Slovene, while the English users tend to produce mostly an average amount of SUD, with just small numbers of users on the extremes of the (non)production of SUD.

Future work on this dataset will focus primarily on the two envisaged usages of the dataset: (1) further analysis of the phenomenon of SUD and (2) (semi-)automation of SUD identification.

Acknowledgement. The work described in this paper was funded by the Slovenian Research Agency within the national basic research project "Resources, methods and tools for the understanding, identification and classification of various forms of socially unacceptable discourse in the information society" (J7-8280, 2017–2020) and the Slovenian-Flemish bilateral basic research project "Linguistic landscape of hate speech on social media" (N06-0099, 2019–2023).

References

1. Davidson, T., Warmsley, D., Macy, M.W., Weber, I.: Automated hate speech detection and the problem of offensive language. CoRR abs/1703.04009 (2017). http://arxiv.org/abs/1703.04009

2. Fišer, D., Erjavec, T., Ljubešić, N.: Legal framework, dataset and annotation schema for socially unacceptable online discourse practices in Slovene. In: Proceedings of the First Workshop on Abusive Language Online, pp. 46–51 (2017)

3. Krippendorff, K.: Content Analysis: An Introduction to Its Methodology, 2nd edn. Sage Publications, Thousand Oaks (2004)

4. Ljubešić, N., Erjavec, T., Fišer, D.: Datasets of slovene and croatian moderated news comments. In: Proceedings of the 2nd Workshop on Abusive Language Online (ALW2), pp. 124–131 (2018)

5. Pavlopoulos, J., Malakasiotis, P., Androutsopoulos, I.: Deeper attention to abusive user content moderation. In: Proceedings of the 2017 Conference on Empirical Methods in Natural Language Processing, EMNLP 2017, Copenhagen, Denmark, 9–11 September 2017, pp. 1125–1135 (2017). https://aclanthology.info/papers/D17-1117/d17-1117

6. Ross, B., Rist, M., Carbonell, G., Cabrera, B., Kurowsky, N., Wojatzki, M.: Measuring the reliability of hate speech annotations: the case of the European refugee crisis. CoRR abs/1701.08118 (2017). http://arxiv.org/abs/1701.08118

7. Waseem, Z., Hovy, D.: Hateful symbols or hateful people? Predictive features for hate speech detection on Twitter. In: Proceedings of the Student Research Workshop, SRW@HLT-NAACL 2016, The 2016 Conference of the North American Chapter of the Association for Computational Linguistics: Human Language Technologies, San Diego California, USA, 12–17 June 2016, pp. 88–93 (2016). http://aclweb.org/anthology/N/N16/N16-2013.pdf

8. Wulczyn, E., Thain, N., Dixon, L.: Ex Machina: personal attacks seen at scale. In: Proceedings of the 26th International Conference on World Wide Web, WWW 2017, International World Wide Web Conferences Steering Committee, Republic and Canton of Geneva, Switzerland, pp. 1391–1399 (2017). https://doi.org/10.1145/3038912.3052591

9. Zampieri, M., Malmasi, S., Nakov, P., Rosenthal, S., Farra, N., Kumar, R.: Predicting the type and target of offensive posts in social media. In: Proceedings of NAACL (2019)

KAS-term: Extracting Slovene Terms from Doctoral Theses via Supervised Machine Learning

Nikola Ljubešić[1]([✉]) [iD], Darja Fišer[1,2] [iD], and Tomaž Erjavec[1] [iD]

[1] Department of Knowledge Technologies, Jožef Stefan Institute, Ljubljana, Slovenia
{nikola.ljubesic,tomaz.erjavec}@ijs.si
[2] Department of Translation, Faculty of Arts,
University of Ljubljana, Ljubljana, Slovenia
darja.fiser@ff.uni-lj.si

Abstract. This paper presents a dataset and supervised learning experiments for term extraction from Slovene academic texts. Term candidates in the dataset were extracted via morphosyntactic patterns and annotated for their termness by four annotators. Experiments on the dataset show that most co-occurrence statistics, applied after morphosyntactic patterns and a frequency threshold, perform close to random and that the results can be significantly improved by combining, with supervised machine learning, all the seven statistic measures included in the dataset. On multi-word terms the model using all statistics obtains an AUC of 0.736 while the best single statistic produces only AUC 0.590. Among many additional candidate features, only adding multi-word morphosyntactic pattern information and length of the single-word term candidates achieves further improvements of the results.

Keywords: Terminology extraction · Supervised machine learning · Slovene language

1 Introduction

One of the cornerstones of academic language is its terminology, but for small languages, such as Slovene, it is unrealistic to expect that professional terminologists will be able to fill the gaps for all the scientific fields still lacking a terminological dictionary and keep up with the rapid advancement of sciences and the new terms that are regularly coined in the process. The only viable solution is to enable the scientific communities to manage their own terminologies collaboratively, with a common infrastructure and some technical and linguistic support, by taking advantage of the growing number of scientific works available on-line in order to automatically extract terminologies and offer them as a starting point towards their consolidation by the community. In this paper we report on the first steps in this process for Slovene, by describing a manually annotated

© Springer Nature Switzerland AG 2019
K. Ekštein (Ed.): TSD 2019, LNAI 11697, pp. 115–126, 2019.
https://doi.org/10.1007/978-3-030-27947-9_10

dataset of term candidates extracted via morphosyntactic patterns, performing analyses on the dataset and running a set of experiments on supervised learning of terminology extraction.

The rest of the this paper is structured as follows. Section 3 describes the corpus used for the dataset construction, the dataset annotation procedure and its encoding. Section 4 analyses annotator agreement. Section 5 gives the baseline experiments on predicting whether a term candidate is indeed a term, and Sect. 6 gives conclusions and directions for further research.

2   Related Work

A broad overview of linguistic, statistical and hybrid approaches to automatic terminology extraction (ATE) is given in [13]. Contemporary term recognition tasks are usually performed in two steps [8]: (1) candidate term extraction and (2) term scoring and ranking, which we follow in this paper as well. For scoring and ranking, we combine various statistical predictors in a supervised learning setting, inspired by [11] who combine 16 features with logistic regression, which improves the best single result by removing 30–50% of errors depending on the domain. Similarly, [3] show on three domain corpora of Portuguese that combinations of 19 features significantly outperform well-known statistics for ATE.

Such approaches require ATE datasets, several of which are already available, most notably the ACL RD-TEC [9], a dataset for evaluating the extraction and classification of computational linguistics terms. Reference datasets for terminology extraction in the biomedical domain are the GENIA corpus [10] and the CRAFT corpus [1], where terms in the abstracts or scientific articles annotated with concepts from well-defined ontologies. In a reference dataset for the domain of automotive engineering [2] the authors also apply annotation in running text, but allow for evaluation of extracted lists of term candidates. [16] report surprisingly high inter-annotator agreement given the overall vagueness of the task of automatic term extraction without relying on an ontology. The authors generate a reference dataset on German DIY instructions and report a Fleiss κ agreement among three annotators for multi-word terms of 0.59 and single-word terms of 0.61.

3   The KAS-term Dataset

3.1   The Corpus

The dataset was extracted from the KAS corpus of Slovene academic writing [4] which was collected via the Open Science Slovenia aggregator [12] harvesting the metadata of digital libraries of all Slovene universities, as well as other academic institutions. The KAS corpus contains, inter alia, 700 PhD theses (40 million tokens) from a large range of disciplines.[1] For the term extraction experiments

---

[1] The complete KAS corpus and the KAS-Dr corpus of PhDs are available for exploring through the CLARIN.SI concordancers, http://www.clarin.si/info/concordances/.

presented in this paper we focused on PhD theses from three fields: Chemistry, Computer Science, and Political Science, which we selected by matching them with their CERIF (Common European Research Information Format) keywords, thus obtaining 48 PhDs form Chemistry, 105 from Computer Science, and 23 from Political Science. We sampled 5 PhD theses per field for manual annotation, yielding all together 15 theses for further processing.

3.2   Term Candidate Extraction

From these three 15 PhD theses we first automatically extracted term candidates, using the CollTerm tool [15] given a set of manually defined term patterns. These patterns were originally developed for the Sketch Engine terminology extraction module [6]. For the present experiments we used only 31 nominal patterns, from unigrams and up to 4-grams, e.g. Nc.*,S.*,Nc.*,Nc.*g.*. The identified term candidates were extracted in the form of lemma sequences and the most frequent inflected phrases, keeping those that appear at least three times in the corpus. The candidates were alphabetically sorted to remove bias stemming from frequency or statistical significance of co-occurrence, both provided by the CollTerm tool.

3.3   Annotation Procedure

We produced separate lists of term candidates for each doctoral thesis. Each of these lists was then annotated by four annotators. Annotators, who were graduate students of the three fields in focus, were asked to choose among one of the 5 labels:

- in-domain term: words and phrases that represent a term from the field in focus
- out-of-domain term: words and phrases that represent a term from a field other than the one in focus
- academic vocabulary: vocabulary that is typical of academic discourse
- irrelevant sequence: words and phrases that belong to general vocabulary, foreign-language expressions, definitions, fragments of terminology
- to be discussed: borderline cases that need to be discussed

Annotators were also given instructions how to deal with difficult cases, such as how to distinguish between terms and general or academic vocabulary, in- and out-of domain terms, term boundaries etc. To ensure maximum consistency of the annotations, annotation was performed in several cycles, each cycle covering candidates from a single thesis. At the end of each cycle the referee examined and discussed all the discrepancies among the annotators, as well as resolved the borderline cases (the cases annotated with the *discuss* label).

3.4   Dataset Encoding

We constructed the final dataset with term candidates being our data instances, along with their metadata, manual annotations and some basic statistics. The final dataset consists of 22,950 instances. The metadata we encode are the thesis identifier, scientific field, annotation round, lemma and most frequent surface form sequence, morphosyntactic pattern and length in words. We encode all the four manual annotations in the dataset, preserving the information about the annotator (anonymized, 1–4) who performed a specific annotation. Finally, we encode seven statistics calculated with the CollTerm tool during the term candidate extraction. These statistics are the frequency of the term candidate, and its tf-idf, chi-square, dice, pointwise mutual information, and t-score values. We distribute the final dataset in comma-separated-value and json formats via the CLARIN.SI repository [5].[2]

4   Dataset Analysis

4.1   Overall Analysis

The dataset consists of 22,950 instances (15,110 unique, 34% duplicates), each covering a term candidate extracted from one of the 15 doctoral theses, 5 per each of the three areas covered. The two plots in Fig. 1 show the distribution of term candidate through the three areas and the distribution of the annotations in each area, both on an absolute (left) and a relative scale (right). In that figure we can observe that most of the term candidates come from the area of political sciences, followed by computer science, which can be followed back to the length of the dissertations in each area. Regarding the term productivity of the three areas, computer science seems to have the highest percentage of irrelevant term candidates, while chemistry has the lowest. It is quite striking that out of the extracted term candidates, between 65 and 80% of term candidates can not be considered terms.

4.2   Annotator Agreement

Table 1 shows the observed agreements to be similar across all three areas, ranging from 72 to 78%. However, Fleiss κ suggests that the lowest agreement is in Computer science, followed by Political Science and Chemistry. The only area in which moderate agreement (> 0.4) is achieved is in Chemistry.

5   Term Prediction

In this section we perform experiments on predicting whether a candidate is a term or not given the variables available in the prepared dataset. We perform all our experiments with `scikit-learn` [14].

---

[2] http://hdl.handle.net/11356/1198.

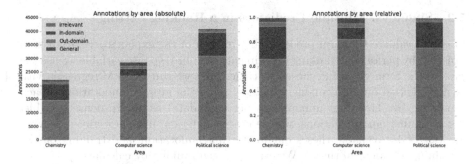

Fig. 1. Distribution of labels given the length of the term candidate (in tokens)

Table 1. Inter-annotator agreement in three areas, measured with Fleiss κ and the average, minimum and maximum pairwise observed agreement.

Area	κ	Avg	Min	Max
Chemistry	0.425	0.72	0.652	0.781
Computer science	0.282	0.781	0.744	0.835
Political science	0.341	0.748	0.658	0.832
Overall	0.366	0.752	0.684	0.807

5.1 Experimental Setup

To be able to calculate a single, discrete gold label per instance in this dataset, we first map the four available categories to a binary schema. We consider two options: (1) considering only the *in-domain* category as positive and the remaining as negative, we call this mapping *exclusive* or (2) considering only the *irrelevant* category as negative and the remaining as positive, calling this mapping *inclusive.* While the exclusive mapping can be considered precision-oriented, the inclusive is more focused on recall. To inform our decision on which option to use in the remaining experiments, we calculate the overall Fleiss κ for both. While the exclusive mapping obtains a κ of 0.414 and an average observed agreement of 0.820, the inclusive mapping reaches a κ of 0.369 and average observed agreement of 0.767. Given that we observe a higher agreement for the exclusive mapping, in the following ranking experiments presented in Sect. 5.2 we will primarily exploit that mapping, while for the final classification experiments between terms and non-terms presented in Sect. 5.3, we will investigate both of the mappings.

The explanatory variables we have at our disposal are frequency (*freq*) and six co-occurrence statistics: chi-square (*chisq*), Dice (*dice*), pointwise mutual information (*mi*), t-score (*tscore*) and tf-idf (*tfidf*). Due to its popularity, *C-value* [7] has been added to these experiments as well, although it uses information beyond frequency, such as intersection to other term candidates. We separate the prediction of multi-word terms (MWT) and single-word terms (SWT) as for single-word terms the only available variables are the frequency and the tf-idf statistic. For MWTs of all lengths all the seven variables are available.

5.2   Single vs. Multiple Predictors in a Ranking Setting

We first evaluate the term predictability of each of the explanatory variables in isolation by performing ranking experiments. As our response variable we use the rank of the term given the chosen statistic. Next we run an SVM regressor with an RBF kernel on all available variables, using the average annotation of each candidate (we have four annotations per candidate) as our response variable. For obtaining our predictions, we use cross-validation, in each iteration leaving one out of 15 available theses out for testing/annotation, and training on the remaining 14 doctoral theses. We evaluate each ranking by calculating the area under the curve (AUC) score which is a very convenient estimate as it does not require any decision on a threshold, i.e., the precision and recall trade-off. In Table 2 we give AUC scores for multi-word terms (MWT) and single-word terms (SWT) by each of the three areas for each of the statistics, as well for all statistics combined via the regressor, with the C-value (*all+cv*) and without it (*all*). In Fig. 2 we plot ROC curves for MWT for each statistic separately, as well as for the regressor combining all the available statistics (*all*).

While performing experiments on MWT ranking via single variables, all the statistics seem to be similarly good rankers except for t-score which is almost at the level of random ranking (AUC of 0.5). It should be noted that the remaining statistics are also not that far from this random baseline, ranging from 0.52 to 0.59. When we combine the available variables into the regression model, leave-one-thesis-out-folding over the available data, we obtain single best results in all areas, as well as overall, the AUC climbing up to 0.736. Interestingly, the results are lowest in the Computer science area, and highest in Chemistry, i.e., they have the same order as in the Fleiss κ inter-annotator agreement. It is hard to say whether the ranker has problems with specific areas due to the intrinsic complexity of the specific areas, or the lower annotation quality in these areas.

We further analyze the differences between specific statistics in the MWT setting via the ROC curves in Fig. 2. These show the statistics to be easily divided into two groups: gradually peaking statistics (*frequency*, *dice* and *mi*) and late peaking statistics (*chisq*, *ll* and *tfidf*). While the gradually peaking statistics obtain best results in low true positive rates (TPRs) and false positive rates (FPRs), which is preferable in a precision-high setting, the late peaking ones take over at the bottom of the candidate list, i.e., in higher TPR and FPR values, therefore are more preferable in recall-oriented settings. However, the combination of the seven available statistics shows to obtain better results on the whole scale of TPR and FPR except for the final part of the ranking (FPR $>= 0.8$ where late peakers *ll* and *tfidf* obtain slightly better results. This setting is, however, quite non-useful as it would require human inspection (or usage) of more than 80% of the term candidates.

For single word terms (SWT), tf-idf is a much better ranker than frequency, the latter being very close to the random baseline. Combining the two available variables for SWTs, frequency and tf-idf, does not yield any improvements over ranking term candidates by the tf-idf statistic only, except for a similar result on the Chemistry area. Again, as with MWTs, the same order in the various

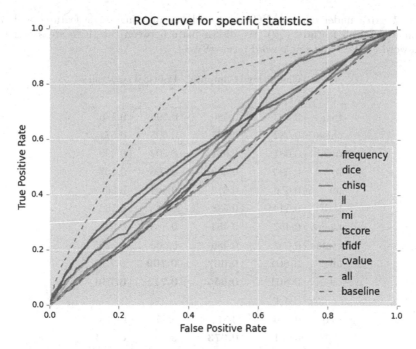

Fig. 2. Receiver-operator-characteristic (ROC) curves for each of the variables, and for their combination *all*. The *baseline* is a random baseline.

ranking results between areas was obtained as is the Fleiss κ inter-annotator agreement on the manual annotations.

5.3   Classification Experiments

We move from ranking experiments to classification as this is our realistic final setting where, based on the content of each doctoral thesis, or any other scientific writing, we generate a manageable list of terms. During the classification experiments we continue differentiating between multi-word terms (MWTs) and single-word terms (SWTs) as the two cases have a very different amount of explanatory information available. While we have 7 statistics available for MWTs, there are only two available in the SWT case.

Mapping Comparison. Our first experiment on MWTs uses an SVM classifier with an RBF kernel, reporting precision, recall and F1 on the term class obtained via leave-one-thesis-out cross-validation, on each area separately, and all together. We perform an experiment on each of the response variable mappings discussed at the beginning of the section, the exclusive mapping (where only the *in-domain* label is considered to be positive) and the inclusive one (where only the *irrelevant* label is considered to be negative). The results are reported in Table 3. Again, the results per area depict that on both mappings

Table 2. Area under curve (AUC) results when exploiting single features and the combination of all features (*all*). We discriminate between the three areas and the multi-word (MWT) and single-word terms (SWT).

	Chemistry	Computer	Political	Overall
	MWT			
freq	0.593	0.580	0.596	0.586
chisq	0.582	0.537	0.605	0.571
dice	0.681	0.631	0.503	0.590
ll	0.590	0.560	0.566	0.557
mi	0.656	0.612	0.464	0.56
tfidf	0.544	0.538	0.613	0.582
tscore	0.457	0.454	0.585	0.505
cvalue	0.502	0.536	0.535	0.520
all	**0.801**	**0.667**	**0.709**	**0.736**
all+cv	**0.801**	**0.655**	**0.711**	**0.736**
	SWT			
freq	0.496	0.512	0.551	0.523
tfidf	0.791	**0.673**	**0.71**	**0.703**
all	**0.8**	0.509	0.687	0.613

the classification is the simplest in Chemistry where annotators agree among themselves best, followed by Political Science and Computer Science.

Interestingly, the inclusive mapping gives more precise results, with a small loss in recall, obtaining an overall significantly better F1 of five points. Given that the annotator agreement was better on the exclusive than the inclusive mapping, the only explanation for this difference in performance is to be sought in our explanatory variables, i.e., the corpus co-occurrence statistics. It seems that these statistics differentiate better between non-terms (*irrelevant label*) and any kind of terms, being in the same (*in-domain*), another (*out-domain*), or general science domain (*general*), than between in-domain terms and the rest. Given these results, the experiments on improving the classifier will be focused on the inclusive mapping as (1) we consider the output of both mappings to be different, but equally relevant for terminologists and (2) we seek to obtain overall best possible classification performance for an as-clean-as-possible output to be given to terminologists and other interested parties. On the inclusive mapping the results in Chemistry are very encouraging, with 56% of the positive labeled candidates being terms, and among those, 79% of all terms being present. Overall these numbers are lower, with 41% of candidates in the positive class being terms, and two out of three terms being labeled with the positive class.

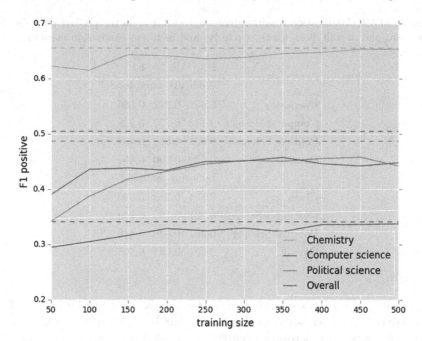

Fig. 3. Learning curves per area. The reported results are average F1 on positive class. The label mapping is inclusive. The dashed lines represent the result obtained on full datasets.

Sensitivity to Amount of Training Data. To measure the sensitivity of the task to the amount of training data, we calculated learning curves for MWTs only while applying the inclusive mapping. The resulting learning curves are presented in Fig. 3. They show for the learning to be quite steady with rather flat learning curves already at the level of having just a few hundred annotated term candidates. The only area for which more annotations are useful, regardless of the rather flat learning curve, is Political science.

Additional Features. We wrap up our classification experiments by investigating additional features that are easily extractable from the KAS-term dataset. We also investigate whether any useful information from the context of terms and non-terms can be obtained from the full texts of doctoral theses. We first investigate whether *Oversampling* instances for which the annotators were in agreement boosts our performance. We next add the *Candidate length* in form of one-hot encodings, investigating whether features behave differently depending on the length of the candidate. Next we add *Average token length* of the candidate with the intuition that very short tokens probably do not form good term candidates. We continue with the most promising feature, the morphosyntactic *Pattern* the candidate satisfies. It is to expect that some patterns produce better candidates than other. We finish with the *Context* feature which presents

Table 3. MWT classification results (precision, recall, F1) on the positive class for the three areas and overall, both for the exclusive and inclusive annotation mappings.

	P	R	F1
	Exclusive mapping		
Chemistry	0.453	0.827	0.586
Computer Science	0.148	0.777	0.249
Political Science	0.361	0.651	0.464
Overall	0.339	0.690	0.455
	Inclusive mapping		
Chemistry	0.564	0.783	0.656
Computer Science	0.221	0.752	0.342
Political Science	0.391	0.649	0.488
Overall	0.409	0.661	0.505

the certainty of a context-based classifier for the candidate to be a term. The context-based classifier is an SVM with a linear kernel, features of the classifier being frequencies of tokens occurring in a 3-token window around all the occurrences of a term candidate in the respective doctoral thesis.

The results on MWT candidate classification are presented in Table 4 showing that none of the examined features improves the overall results except the pattern feature as, naturally, some patterns produce better term candidates than others. This information yields a 2-point improvement on the overall F1 score.

Table 4. MWT classification results (precision, recall, F1) on the positive class as additional features are added.

	P	R	F1
Original	0.406	0.660	0.503
Oversampling	0.417	0.635	0.503
Candidate length	0.407	0.646	0.500
Average token length	0.375	0.742	0.498
Pattern	0.392	0.776	**0.521**
Context	0.399	0.688	0.505

Our SWT experiments are based on using *tf-idf* as our only feature and, to double-check the negative ranking result for frequency from Sect. 5.2, we add *Frequency* as our first additional feature to be examined. We follow with adding the remaining features as with MWTs, except that we omit *Candidate length* and *Patterns*, as SWTs are all of same length and based on one single pattern.

As expected, the results in Table 5 show that the *Frequency* feature deteriorates the results, similarly as in the ranking task, while *Oversampling* has a similar impact as with MWTs, improving precision and lowering recall, with no significant difference in F1. The *Context* feature does not change the result significantly, similar as in the MWT setting. Finally, the feature that we expected to improve results, *Average token length*, did actually improve F1 by 2.5 points.

Table 5. SWT classification results (precision, recall, F1) on the positive class as additional features are added.

	P	R	F1
Original	0.405	0.563	0.471
Frequency	0.417	0.522	0.463
Oversampling	0.408	0.557	0.471
Average token length	0.422	0.601	**0.496**
Context	0.427	0.510	0.465

6 Conclusion

In this paper we presented the dataset and a machine-learning approach for automatic terminology extraction from Slovene academic texts from three different scientific areas. The obtained Fleiss κ coefficient classifies the agreement between annotators to be only fair, depicting the high complexity of the annotation task. We then analysed term predictability of various statistics included in the dataset, showing that when combining all the available statistics, we obtain a significant improvement on multiword terms, with a relative improvement of AUC of 25% over the single best-performing statistic. We further improve our multi-word term predictor by adding the information on the morphosyntactic pattern and our single-word term predictor via the character length of the term candidate. Interestingly, adding the context information does not improve our results on either of the problems.

Acknowledgements. The work described in this paper was funded by the Slovenian Research Agency within the national basic research project "Slovene scientific texts: resources and description" (J6-7094, 2016–2019).

References

1. Bada, M., et al.: Concept annotation in the CRAFT corpus. BMC Bioinformatics **13**, 161 (2012)
2. Bernier-Colborne, G., Drouin, P.: Creating a test corpus for term extractors through term annotation. Terminology **20**, 50–73 (2014)
3. Conrado, M., Pardo, T., Rezende, S.: A machine learning approach to automatic term extraction using a rich feature set. In: Proceedings of the 2013 NAACL HLT Student Research Workshop, pp. 16–23 (2013)

4. Erjavec, T., Fišer, D., Ljubešić, N., Logar, N., Ojsteršek, M.: Slovenska znanstvena besedila: prototipni korpus in načrt analiz, Slovene scientific texts: prototype corpus and research plan. In: Proceedings of the Conference on Language Technologies and Digital Humanities. Ljubljana University Press (2016)
5. Erjavec, T., et al.: Terminology identification dataset KAS-term 1.0, slovenian language resource repository CLARIN.SI (2018). http://hdl.handle.net/11356/1198
6. Fišer, D., Suchomel, V., Jakubíček, M.: Terminology extraction for academic Slovene using sketch engine. In: RASLAN 2016: Recent Advances in Slavonic Natural Language Processing, pp. 135–141 (2016)
7. Frantzi, K., Ananiadou, S., Mima, H.: Automatic recognition of multi-word terms: the C-value/NC-value method. Int. J. Digit. Libr. **3**(2), 115–130 (2000). https://doi.org/10.1007/s007999900023
8. Nakagawa, H., Mori, T.: Automatic term recognition based on statistics of compound nouns and their components. Terminology **9**(2), 201–219 (2003)
9. Handschuh, S., QasemiZadeh, B.: The ACL RD-TEC: a dataset for benchmarking terminology extraction and classification in computational linguistics. In: COLING 2014: 4th International Workshop on Computational Terminology (2014)
10. Kim, J.D., Ohta, T., Tateisi, Y., Ichi Tsujii, J.: GENIA corpus - a semantically annotated corpus for bio-textmining. In: ISMB (Supplement of Bioinformatics), pp. 180–182 (2003)
11. Loukachevitch, N.V.: Automatic term recognition needs multiple evidence. In: LREC, pp. 2401–2407 (2012)
12. Ojsteršek, M., et al.: Vzpostavitev repozitorijev slovenskih univerz in nacionalnega portala odprte znanosti (the set-up of the repository of slovene universities and the national portal of open science). Knjižnica **58**(3) (2014)
13. Pazienza, M., Pennacchiotti, M., Zanzotto, F.: Terminology extraction: an analysis of linguistic and statistical approaches. In: Sirmakessis, S. (ed.) Knowledge Mining. Studies in Fuzziness and Soft Computing, vol. 185, pp. 255–279. Springer, Heidelberg (2005). https://doi.org/10.1007/3-540-32394-5_20
14. Pedregosa, F., et al.: Scikit-learn: machine learning in Python. J. Mach. Learn. Res. **12**, 2825–2830 (2011)
15. Pinnis, M., Ljubešić, N., Ştefănescu, D., Skadiņa, I., Tadić, M., Gornostay, T.: Term extraction, tagging, and mapping tools for under-resourced languages. In: Proceedings of the Terminology and Knowledge Engineering (TKE2012) Conference (2012)
16. Schäfer, J., Rösiger, I., Heid, U., Dorna, M.: Evaluating noise reduction strategies for terminology extraction. In: TIA, pp. 123–131 (2015)

A Self-organizing Feature Map for Arabic Word Extraction

Hassina Bouressace[(✉)] and János Csirik[(✉)]

University of Szeged, 13 Dugonics Square, Szeged 6720, Hungary
bouressacehassina@hotmail.fr, jcsirik@gmail.com

Abstract. Arabic word spotting is a key step for Arabic NLP and the text recognition task. Many recent studies have addressed segmentation problems in the Arabic language. However, many issues still have to be overcome. In this paper, we propose a new approach for segmenting an image Arabic text into its constituent words. Our approach consists of two main steps. In the first step, a set of features is extracted from connected components using the Run-length smoothing algorithm (RLSA). In the second step, spatially close connected components that are likely to belong to the same word component are grouped together. This is done via a learning technique called the self-organizing feature map (Kohonen map). We evaluated our approach on 300 images with different sizes and fonts for handwritten text using AHDB. Our results suggest that our approach can efficiently segments lines. Moreover, as our approach is based on a straightforward machine learning model, it should be possible to adapt it to other languages as well.

Keywords: Handwriting documents · Word segmentation · Neural network · Connected components

1 Introduction

Natural language processing (NLP) is the basic phase in most language searches of the world, where the programs for searching are generated in such a way that they can readily comprehend and manipulate human language text. Segmenting Arabic sentences is the most crucial step for Arabic recognition as it is used in many natural language processing technologies such as parsing and machine translation. Unlike English texts, in Arabic texts, there is no explicit space between all the words. For example, (العمل واهميته means: Work and its importance) is composed of three words (العمل، و ، اهميته), while in another sentence (العمل واجبنا means: work is our duty) it is composed of just two words, not three (العمل، واجبنا) as we can see the same structure, but the result is different because of the non-uniform spacing of words.

Arabic writing starts from right to left in a cursive style and includes 28 letters, and most letters have contextual letterforms and are cursive in handwritten form (Fig. 1).

© Springer Nature Switzerland AG 2019
K. Ekštein (Ed.): TSD 2019, LNAI 11697, pp. 127–136, 2019.
https://doi.org/10.1007/978-3-030-27947-9_11

ص ش س ز ر ذ د خ ح ج ث ت ب ا
ṣ sh s z r dh d kh ḥ j th t b ā

ض ط ظ ع غ ف ق ك ل م ن ه و ي
y w h n m l k q f gh ʿ ẓ ṭ ḍ

Fig. 1. Arabic alphabet with Common pronunciation order.

Many concentrated on the segmentation phase using various solutions and aspects for a line or page segmentation. However, this is not used much in text segmentation. The methods used produce good results in the case of English and Latin texts as bottom-up methods based on connected components [1], structural features [2], or both of them [3], but it fails in some text cases due to the type of structure, overlapping words, large sets of different writing style, punctuation marks, dots, and diacritics. In handwritten texts, Arabic text writing has many features that make handwriting somewhat hard to process, which is shown by unique shapes at the letter level, and it may vary over time even it is done by the same person. For this, there is no stable and fixed segmentation that can be applied. Here, we introduce a new flexible segmented approach of a text document which efficiently distinguishes inter-word distances. From the input-output point of view, our approach receives connected component features and outputs a vector with binary values corresponding to the gaps between components.

The rest of the paper is organized as follows. In Sect. 2, we go through related studies. In Sect. 3, we outline the methodology used to segment words. In Sect. 4, we present the experimental results and lastly, in Sect. 5, we present our conclusions and future work.

2   Related Works

Several methods of the text segmentation phase have been resolved and reported in the literature. Many previous studies on word spotting focused on CCs (connected components), got by extracting the distances between adjacent CCs using a metric such as the Euclidean distance, the bounding box distance or the convex hull metric [4–6], and then classifying these distances to determine whether they are inter-word or inter-character gaps. In [7], Belabiod et al. proposed a method using a CNN (Convolutional Neural Network) [8] to extract the input features, then they applied a bidirectional LSTM (100 neurons for each LSTM), which was followed by a CTC function (Connectionist Temporal Classification) [9] where the CTC decoder output was a sequence of "word-spaces". This method tested on the KHATT Arabic database achieved a word segmentation rate of 80.1%. Al-Dmour et al. [12] calculated the CC length and the distance between them. The lengths are used to classify the CCs into sub-words or words, where the purpose of a metric distance is to decide whether to classify them as separation gaps or not. Lengths and gaps are then clustered to identify an optimal threshold for word content and distinguish between "between-words" or "within-words". This method was tested on the AHDB dataset [13] and it attained a spotting rate of 86.3%.

3   The Proposed Approach

As we mentioned in the Introduction, many letters are not joined to the adjacent letter, even in the middle of a word. Each letter has up to four distinct forms, based on its position (beginning, middle, end, or isolated) within a word or between the words. The figure below shows a sample of numerous letter shapes in different positions in Arabic text (Fig. 2).

Isolated	Beginning	Middle	End
ل	ل	ـل	ـل
ق	ق	ـق	ـق
أل	أ	ﻷ	أل
ه	ه	ـهـ	ـه
ت/ة	ت	ـتـ	ت/ة

Fig. 2. Handwritten Arabic letters.

Next, we shall describe our proposed method for the word spotting. Some well-known techniques developed for other languages would have to be modified for Arabic text words extraction. The method is outlined in Fig. 3 below. The input of the schema is a handwritten Arabic text image that consists of one line of text and the output is its segmentation result given by a vector of 0s and 1s. The sections, later on, will explain how the proposed method works.

3.1   Pre-processing

The pre-processing step actually consists of two parts. In the first part, images are binarized to enhance the image for better performance. For this, we used the well-known Otsu's method [15]. The second part involves noise removal using a median filter [16] to delete the very small items (noise) caused by the acquisition process with a scanner.

3.2   Segmentation

The dataset images that were used contain several lines. We made us of our previous results [17] for line segmentation which is based on the application of a horizontal projection, local minima, and conflict resolution. Now the new images

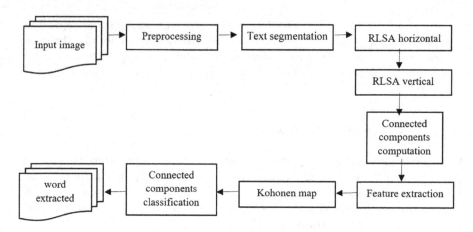

Fig. 3. Outline of the method proposed for word extraction.

will have only one line of text. Then, every resulting image will be normalized to a height of 45 and a width proportional to the height modification. So we will have a standard height in the later steps. For CC (connected component) extraction, we used the RLSA [11] algorithm beforehand in order to reduce the number of CCs. Doing this, we can delete dots and diacritics where they exist. This will then enhance the results of the later steps. So rather than having two CCs where they cover one letter with its dots, there will be just one CC (see Fig. 4). We start from the horizontal RLSA with threshold = 1 to the vertical RLSA with threshold = 30. These thresholds were chosen by testing many values on 50 images. As a result, we have found these values suitable for most normalized Arabic text images.

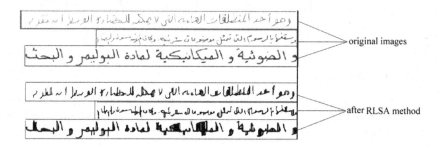

Fig. 4. Text image after RLSA method.

In this phase, the connected components will be determined and then the features will be extracted. Each connected component represents a region that exists in the image: it may be a letter, a half word or a word. In [12], the authors categorize CCs to isolate words, sub-word particles or words based on

CC lengths. However, it is not clear how they categorized these lengths because every writer has different word structure. A word-length for one writer may be a sub-word particle and a word for another writer.

In our study, we utilized feature information for the classification. To classify these connected components of the Arabic text, we extracted six features from each component. To do this, we assigned geometric information to the connected components according to their corresponding position in the text. Here, we will use the following geometric features related to the size and the shape of the CCs:

- Height: The height of the connected component bounding box;
- Width: The width of the connected component bounding box;
- Aspect Ratio: The width divided by the height;
- Distance: The gap between two adjacent connected components;
- Area: The number of pixels in the connected component;
- Position: Horizontal connected component coordinate using the bounding box, taking the center of the left and right lines of the box.

Connected component features are then used as the input for SOM clustering, which is also known as Kohonen Neural Networks [10]. The features of the connected components are fed into the input neurons. Since there is one input for each feature for every connected component, the number of the input will be six times the number of CCs for each segmented text. The number of output neurons will be the number of 2^{CCs-1} as we have to make a decision on each space. We will represent the output by 0s and 1s with 0 for inter-words and 1 for between-words spaces (see Fig. 5). Hence if the text contains ten words, the output will be 2^9 neurons.

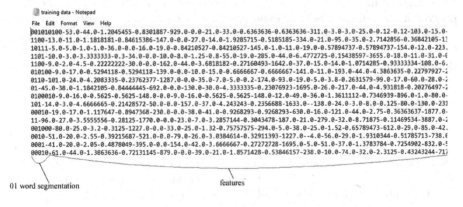

Fig. 5. Training data file sample

In addition to the input and output neurons, there are also connections between the neurons represented as weights, which are the substrate of this network and the main elements for determining what the network will output based on the input data. The total number of connections is related to the number of input and output neurons. The competitive learning rule defines the change Δw_{ij} applied to the synaptic weight w_{ij}, where x_i is the input signal and α is the learning rate parameter.

$$\Delta w_{ij} = \begin{cases} \alpha\,(x_i - w_{ij})\,, & \text{if neuron } j \text{ wins the competition} \\ 0, & \text{if neuron } j \text{ loses the competition} \end{cases}$$

A Kohonen neural network learns by evaluating and optimizing a weight matrix in a regular way. Beginning with an initial random weight matrix, the training will start and evaluate the weight matrix to get the error estimate. If it is under 10% the training will be finished; otherwise, it will go on optimizing until the error falls within the desired accuracy (see Fig. 6).

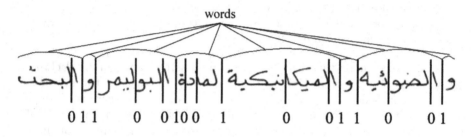

Fig. 6. Word segmentation example (1: between-word; 0: inter-word)

4   Experimental Results

The proposed method was implemented in Eclipse Java oxygen.2 using the Java programming language. Several experiments were conducted to verify the performance of the proposed method. Our method can be used in two modes; namely, the application returns the cropped words, or it returns a vector of 0s and 1s. Both demonstrate the segmentation phase in a clear way.

4.1   Database

We tested our approach on 300 images extracted from the AHDB database (300 images after line segmentation) with many different handwritten Arabic documents, with 7356 images (after line segmentation) for training. In both sets, we start with feature data extraction. Then, we divide up images with more than nine CCs into two parts. The details for this procedure are given below.

4.2   Training and Error Analysis

A long text means ten or more of connected components which must be covered by thousands of training images to give good results. To handle this problem we will use the following method: if there are more than nine CCs, the text will be divided up into two parts automatically at the maximum extracted space between connected components, so the number of images will be 10,245 along with 95,030 CCs rather than 7356 training images. In the figure below, we have plotted the distribution for the Arabic text image proportion along with the number of connected components (Fig. 7).

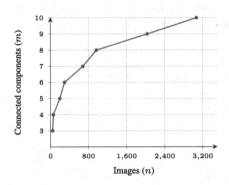

Fig. 7. Number of training images corresponding its CCs numbers.

The evaluation process was performed using two types of errors; namely the spacing and overlapping error.

4.2.1 Spacing and Overlapping

A lot of Arabic text in handwritten form has two problems called spacing and overlapping problems. The spaces between adjacent words are present at random so there are no fixed thresholds that can be determined as separators between the words, and this is the spacing problem. With the overlapping problem, two letters or characters have a zero or negative space between them even though they belong to different words, not the same one. Figure 8 shows an example of outliers, where spaces between words and letters are either the same or the inter-space is larger than the between-space.

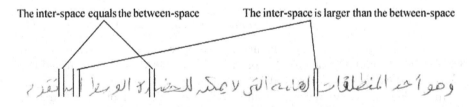

Fig. 8. Example of randomly spacing in an Arabic text image.

4.2.2 Method Validity

We used the Kohonen map to classify the spaces. With this method, we partially solved the spacing problems due to the large size of information in the training data file which contains connected components features taken from a wide variety of text word positions and writing shapes. However, this method will not be effective when the two words have no distance between each other either in a horizontal or vertical segmentation and it will be treated as one word. In the figure below we give examples of an inaccurate segmentation (Fig. 9).

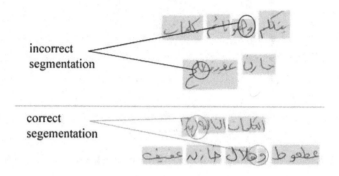

Fig. 9. Examples of overlapping problem in Arabic text.

4.3 Results

To evaluate our proposed method, we used several criteria for the segmentation accuracy relating to spacing and overlapping errors in percentage terms. Here, we defined the following error types:

(1) If two words are treated as one word;
(2) If one word is treated as two words;
(3) If part-word and word are treated as two words;
(4) If part-word is treated as one word.

We denoted the total number of errors by E and we used the following formula to compute the accuracy:

$$Accuracy\% = 100 - (E/Totalnumberwords) * 100 \qquad (1)$$

Some results obtained using this method are listed in Table 1. We processed 300 test images and attained a score of 87.54%. The best results shown had the correct word extraction rate of 100%.

In Table 2, we compared our results with the results of other researchers working on handwritten Arabic text processing. We got their results from previously published studies using the same dataset (AHDB). We notice here that our results seem to be better: Al-Dmour et al. [12] achieved a score of 85%, while Belabiod et al. [7] achieved a score of 80.1%.

Table 1. Test results

Image no.	No. words in the line	No. wrong seg. words	Correct seg. rate
1	14	4	71.42%
2	15	1	93.34%
3	14	0	100.00%
4	19	5	73.48%
5	13	0	100.00%
6	20	4	80.00%
7	18	2	88.89%
.	.	.	.
.	.	.	.
300	17	1	94.11 %
Total	5400	672	87.54%

Table 2. Rates of correct word extraction.

Our work	Belabiod et al.	Al-Dmour et al.
87.45%	80.1%	86.3%

5   Conclusions and Future Work

In this paper, a new robust and flexible approach based on a machine learning model was presented for word spotting. The segmentation system commenced by preprocessing a text using Otsu binarization and the Median filter, then we applied vertical and horizontal RLSA to eliminate dots and diacritics, so as to compute connected components as building blocks. The latter is used for extracting the most important features that will provide the input for the Kohonen map. To evaluate the potential of the method, we used 300 images extracted from the AHDB database. In the future, we plan to extract words from images that have many strange shapes and lines along with actual words hastily written as scribble.

References

1. Louloudis, G., Gatos, B., Pratikakis, I., Halatsis, C.: Text line and word segmentation of handwritten documents. Pattern Recogn. **42**, 3169–3183 (2009)
2. Aouadi, N., Kacem-Echi, A.: Word extraction and recognition in Arabic handwritten text. Int. J. Comput. Inf. Sci. **12**, 17–23 (2016)
3. Elzobi, M., Al-Hamadi, A., Aghbari, Z.A.: Off-line handwritten Arabic words segmentation based on structural features and connected components analysis. In: WSCG 2011: Communication Papers Proceedings: The 19th International Conference in Central Europe on Computer Graphics, Visualization, and Computer Vision, pp. 135–142 (2011)

4. Mahadevan, U., Nagabushnam, R.C.: Gap metrics for word separation in handwritten lines. In: Third International Conference on Document Analysis and Recognition, Montreal, Canada, pp. 124–127 (1995)

5. Marti, U.V., Bunke, H.: Text line segmentation and word recognition in a system for general writer independent handwriting recognition. In: Sixth International Conference on Document Analysis and Recognition, Seattle, WA, USA, pp. 159–163 (2001)

6. Seni, G., Cohen, E.: External word segmentation of offline handwritten text lines. Pattern Recogn. **27**(1), 41–52 (1994)

7. Belabiod, A., Belaïd, A.: Line and word segmentation of Arabic handwritten documents using neural networks, LORIA - University of Lorraine (2018)

8. Simard, P.Y., Steinkraus, D., Platt, J.C.: Best practices for convolutional neural networks applied to visual document analysis. In: Proceedings of the Seventh International Conference on Document Analysis and Recognition, vol. 2, pp. 958–962 (2003)

9. Graves, A., Fernández, S., Gomez, F., Schmidhuber, J.: Connectionist temporal classification: labelling unsegmented sequence data with recurrent neural networks. In: International Conference on Machine learning, pp. 369–376 (2006)

10. Kohonen, T.: The self-organizing map. Proc. IEEE **78**(9), 1464–1480 (1990)

11. O'Gorman, L., Kasturi, R.: Executive Briefing: Document Image Analysis. IEEE Computer Society Press, Los Alamitos (1997)

12. Al-Dmour, A., Zitar, R.A.: Word extraction from Arabic handwritten documents based on statistical measures. Int. Rev. Comput. Soft. (IRECOS) **11**, 436–444 (2016)

13. Al-Ma'adeed, S., Elliman, D., Higgins, C.A.: A database for Arabic handwritten text recognition research. In: Proceedings of the Eighth International Workshop on Frontiers in Handwriting Recognition, pp. 485–489 (2002)

14. AlKhateeb, J.H., Jiang, J., Ren, J., Ipson, S.: Interactive knowledge discovery for baseline estimation and word segmentation in handwritten Arabic text. In: Strangio, M.A. (ed.) Recent Advances in Technologies. IntechOpen, London (2009)

15. Zeki, A.M., Zakaria, M.S., Liong, C.-Y.: Segmentation of Arabic characters: a comprehensive survey. Int. J. Technol. Diffus. **2**(4), 48–82 (2011)

16. Wang, J.-H., Lin, L.-D.: Improved median filter using min-max algorithm for image processing. Electron. Lett. **33**(16), 1362–1363 (1997)

17. Bouressace, H., Csirik, J.: Recognition of the logical structure of Arabic newspaper pages. In: Sojka, P., Horák, A., Kopeček, I., Pala, K. (eds.) TSD 2018. LNCS (LNAI), vol. 11107, pp. 251–258. Springer, Cham (2018). https://doi.org/10.1007/978-3-030-00794-2_27

Czech Text Processing with Contextual Embeddings: POS Tagging, Lemmatization, Parsing and NER

Milan Straka[✉], Jana Straková, and Jan Hajič

Faculty of Mathematics and Physics, Institute of Formal and Applied Linguistics,
Charles University, Prague, Czechia
{straka,strakova,hajic}@ufal.mff.cuni.cz
http://ufal.mff.cuni.cz

Abstract. Contextualized embeddings, which capture appropriate word meaning depending on context, have recently been proposed. We evaluate two methods for precomputing such embeddings, BERT and Flair, on four Czech text processing tasks: part-of-speech (POS) tagging, lemmatization, dependency parsing and named entity recognition (NER). The first three tasks, POS tagging, lemmatization and dependency parsing, are evaluated on two corpora: the Prague Dependency Treebank 3.5 and the Universal Dependencies 2.3. The named entity recognition (NER) is evaluated on the Czech Named Entity Corpus 1.1 and 2.0. We report state-of-the-art results for the above mentioned tasks and corpora.

Keywords: Contextualized embeddings · BERT · Flair ·
POS tagging · Lemmatization · Dependency parsing ·
Named entity recognition · Czech

1 Introduction

Recently, a novel way of computing word embeddings has been proposed. Instead of computing one word embedding for each word which sums over all its occurrences, ignoring the appropriate word meaning in various contexts, the *contextualized embeddings* are computed for each word occurrence, taking into account the whole sentence. Three ways of computing such contextualized embeddings have been proposed: ELMo [27], BERT [5] and Flair [1], along with precomputed models.

Peters et al. [27] obtain the proposed embeddings, called *ELMo*, from internal states of deep bidirectional language model, pretrained on a large corpus. Akbik et al. [1] introduced *Flair*, contextualized word embeddings obtained from internal states of a character-level bidirectional language model, thus significantly increasing state of the art of POS tagging, chunking and NER tasks. Last, but not least, Devlin et al. [5] employ a Transformer [38] to compute contextualized embeddings from preceding and following context at the same time, at the cost of

© Springer Nature Switzerland AG 2019
K. Ekštein (Ed.): TSD 2019, LNAI 11697, pp. 137–150, 2019.
https://doi.org/10.1007/978-3-030-27947-9_12

increased processing costs. The new *BERT* embeddings achieved state-of-the-art results in eleven natural language tasks.

Using two of these methods, for which precomputed models for Czech are available, namely BERT and Flair, we present our models for four NLP tasks: part-of-speech (POS) tagging, lemmatization, dependency parsing and named entity recognition (NER). Adding the contextualized embeddings as optional inputs in strong artificial neural network baselines, we report state-of-the-art results in these four tasks.

2   Related Work

As for the Prague Dependency Treebank (PDT) [13], most of the previous works are non-neural systems with one exception of [19] who hold the state of the art for Czech POS tagging and lemmatization, achieved with the recurrent neural network (RNN) using end-to-end trainable word embeddings and character-level word embeddings. Otherwise, Spoustová et al. [31] used an averaged perceptron for POS tagging. For parsing the PDT, Holan and Zabokrtský [16] and Novák and Žabokrtský [26] used a combination of non-neural parsing techniques.

In the multilingual shared task *CoNLL 2018 Shared Task: Multilingual Parsing from Raw Text to Universal Dependencies* [40], raw text is processed and the POS tagging, lemmatization and dependency parsing are evaluated on the Universal Dependencies (UD) [24]. Czech is one of the 57 evaluated languages. Interestingly, all 26 participant systems employed the artificial neural networks in some way. Of these, 3 participant systems used (a slightly modified variant of) the only newly presented contextualized embeddings called ELMo [27], most notably one of the shared task winners [3]. BERT and Flair were not available at the time.

For the Czech NER, Straková et al. [36] use an artificial neural network with word- and character-level word embeddings to perform NER on the Czech Named Entity Corpus (CNEC) [28–30].

3   Datasets

Prague Dependency Treebank 3.5. The *Prague Dependency Treebank 3.5* [13] is a 2018 edition of the core *Prague Dependency Treebank*. The Prague Dependency Treebank 3.5 contains the same texts as the previous versions since 2.0, and is divided into `train`, `dtest`, and `etest` subparts, where `dtest` is used as a development set and `etest` as a test set. The dataset consists of several layers – the morphological m-layer is the largest and contains morphological annotations (POS tags and lemmas), the analytical a-layer contains labeled dependency trees, and the t-layer is the smallest and contains tectogrammatical trees. The statistics of PDT 3.5 sizes is presented in Table 1.

A detailed description of the morphological system can be found in [11], a specification of the syntactic annotations has been presented in [10]. We note that in PDT, lemmas with the same word form are disambiguated using a number suffix – for example, English lemmas for the word forms `can` (noun) and `can` (verb) would be annotated as `can-1` and `can-2`.

In evaluation, we compute:

– POS tagging accuracy,
– lemmatization accuracy,
– unlabeled attachment score (UAS),
– labeled attachment score (LAS).

Table 1. Size of morphological and analytical annotations of PDT 3.5 train/development/test sets.

Part	Morphological m-layer		Analytical a-layer	
	Words	Sentences	Words	Sentences
Train	1 535 826	90 828	1 171 190	68 495
Development	201 651	11 880	158 962	9 270
Test	219 765	13 136	173 586	10 148

Universal Dependencies. The *Universal Dependencies* project [24] seeks to develop cross-linguistically consistent treebank annotation of morphology and syntax for many languages. We evaluate the Czech PDT treebank of UD 2.3 [25], which is an automated conversion of PDT 3.5 a-layer to Universal Dependencies annotation. The original POS tags are used to generate **UPOS** (universal POS tags), **XPOS** (language-specific POS tags, in this case the original PDT tags), and **Feats** (universal morphological features). The UD lemmas are the raw textual lemmas, so the discriminative numeric suffix of PDT is dropped. The dependency trees are converted according to the UD guidelines, adapting both the unlabeled trees and the dependency labels.

To compute the evaluation scores, we use the official *CoNLL 2018 Shared Task: Multilingual Parsing from Raw Text to Universal Dependencies* [40] evaluation script, which produces the following metrics:

– **UPOS** – universal POS tags accuracy,
– **XPOS** – language-specific POS tags accuracy,
– **UFeats** – universal subset of morphological features accuracy,
– **Lemmas** – lemmatization accuracy,
– **UAS** – unlabeled attachment score, **LAS** – labeled attachment score,
– **MLAS** – morphology-aware LAS, **BLEX** – bi-lexical dependency score.

Czech Named Entity Corpus. The *Czech Named Entity Corpus 1.1* [28,29] is a corpus of 5 868 Czech sentences with manually annotated 33 662 Czech named entities, classified according to a two-level hierarchy of 62 named entities.

The *Czech Named Entity Corpus 2.0* [30] contains 8 993 Czech sentences with manually annotated 35 220 Czech named entities, classified according to a two-level hierarchy of 46 named entities.

We evaluate the NER task with the official CNEC evaluation script. Similarly to previous literature [28,36] etc., the script only evaluates the first round annotation classes for the CNEC 1.1. For the CNEC 2.0, the script evaluates all annotated classes.

4   Neural Architectures

All our neural architectures are recurrent neural networks (RNNs). The POS tagging, lemmatization and dependency parsing is performed with the *UDPipe 2.0* (Sect. 4.1) and NER is performed with our new sequence-to-sequence model (Sect. 4.2).

4.1   POS Tagging, Lemmatization, and Dependency Parsing

We perform POS tagging, lemmatization and dependency parsing using *UDPipe 2.0* [32], one of the three winning systems of the *CoNLL 2018 Shared Task: Multilingual Parsing from Raw Text to Universal Dependencies* [40] and an overall winner of *The 2018 Shared Task on Extrinsic Parser Evaluation* [7]. An overview of this architecture is presented in Fig. 1 and the full details of the architecture and the training procedure are available in [32].

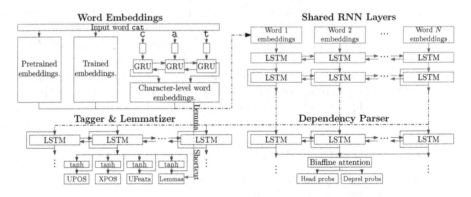

Fig. 1. UDPipe 2.0 architecture overview.

POS Tagging and Lemmatization. The tagger employs a standard bi-LSTM architecture. After embedding input words, three bidirectional LSTM [15] layers are performed, followed by a softmax output layers for POS tags and lemmas. While a classification output layer is natural for POS tags, we also apply it to lemmatization and generate lemmas by classifying the input words into lemma generation rules, therefore considering lemmatization as another tagging task.

We construct a lemma generation rule from a given form and lemma as follows:

- We start by finding the longest continuous substring of the form and the lemma. If it is empty, we use the lemma itself as the class.
- If there is a common substring of the form and the lemma, we compute the shortest edit script converting the prefix of the form into the prefix of the lemma, and the shortest edit script converting the suffix of the form to the suffix of the lemma. The edit scripts permit the operations `delete_current_char` and `insert_char(c)`.
- All above operations are performed case insensitively. To indicate correct casing of the lemma, we consider the lemma to be a concatenation of segments, where each segment is composed of either a sequence of lowercase characters, or a sequence of uppercase characters. We represent the lemma casing by encoding the beginning of every such segment, where the offsets in the first half of the lemma are computed relatively to the start of the lemma, and the offsets in the second half of the lemma are computed relatively to the end of the lemma.

Dependency Parsing. The dependency parsing is again predicted using *UDPipe 2.0* architecture. After embedding input words, three bidirectional LSTM [15] layers are again performed, followed by a biaffine attention layer [6] producing labeled dependency trees.

In our evaluation we do not utilize gold POS tags and lemmas on the test set for dependency parsing. Instead, we consider three ways of employing them during parsing:

- not using them at all;
- adding predicted POS tags and lemmas on input;
- perform joint training of POS tags, lemmatization, and dependency parsing. In this case, we share first two bidirectional LSTM layers between the tagger and the parser.

Input Embeddings. In our **baseline** model, we use the end-to-end word embeddings and also character-level word embeddings (bidirectional GRUs, [4,9,22] of dimension 256) trained specifically for the task.

Our architecture can optionally employ the following additional inputs

- **pretrained word embeddings (WE):** For the PDT experiments, we generate the word embeddings with `word2vec`[1] on a concatenation of large raw Czech corpora[2] available from the LINDAT/CLARIN repository.[3] For UD

---

[1] With options `-size 300 -window 5 -negative 5 -iter 1 -cbow 0`.
[2] The concatenated corpus has approximately 4G words, two thirds of them from SYN v3 [14].
[3] https://lindat.cz.

Czech, we use FastText word embeddings [2] of dimension 300, which we pre-train on Czech Wikipedia using segmentation and tokenization trained from the UD data.[4]

- **BERT** [5]: Pretrained contextual word embeddings of dimension 768 from the Base model.[5] We average the last four layers of the BERT model to produce the embeddings. Because BERT utilizes word pieces, we decompose UD words into appropriate subwords and then average the generated embeddings over subwords belonging to the same word.
- **Flair** [1]: Pretrained contextual word embeddings of dimension 4096.

POS Tags and Lemmas Decoding. Optionally, we employ a morphological dictionary MorfFlex [12] during decoding. If the morphological dictionary is used, it may produce analyses for an input word as *(POS tag, lemma)* pairs. If any are generated, we choose the pair with maximum likelihood given by both the POS tag and lemmatization model.

4.2 Named Entity Recognition

We use a novel approach [37] for nested named entity recognition (NER) to capture the nested entities in the Czech Named Entity Corpus. The nested entities are encoded in a sequence and the problem of nested NER is then viewed as a sequence-to-sequence (seq2seq) problem, in which the input sequence consists of the input tokens (forms) and the output sequence of the linearized entity labels.

The system is a encoder-decoder architecture. The encoder is a bi-directional LSTM and the decoder is a LSTM. The encoded labels are predicted one by one by the decoder, until the decoder outputs the "`<eow>`" (end of word) label and moves to the next token. We use a hard attention on the word whose label(s) is being predicted.

We train the network using the lazy variant of the Adam optimizer [18], which only updates accumulators for variables that appear in the current batch,[6] with parameters $\beta_1 = 0.9$ and $\beta_2 = 0.98$. We use mini-batches of size 8. As a regularization, we apply dropout with rate 0.5 and the word dropout replaces 20% of words by the unknown token to force the network to rely more on context. We did not perform any complex hyperparameter search.

In this model, we use the following word- and character-level word embeddings:

- **pretrained word embeddings:** We use the FastText [2] word embeddings of dimension 300 from the publicly available Czech model.[7]

---

[4] We use `-minCount 5 -epoch 10 -neg 10` options to generate the embeddings.

[5] We use the BERT-Base Multilingual Uncased model from https://github.com/google-research/bert.

[6] `tf.contrib.opt.lazyadamoptimizer` from www.tensorflow.org.

[7] https://fasttext.cc/docs/en/crawl-vectors.html.

- **end-to-end word embeddings:** We embed the input forms and lemmas (256 dimensions) and POS tags (one-hot).[8]
- **end-to-end character-level word embeddings:** We use bidirectional GRUs [4,9] of dimension 128 in line with [22]: we represent every Unicode character with a vector of dimension 128, and concatenate GRU outputs for forward and reversed word characters.

Optionally, we add the **BERT** [5] and the **Flair** [1] contextualized embeddings in the same way as in the UDPipe 2.0 (Sect. 4.1).

5   Results

5.1   POS Tagging and Lemmatization on PDT 3.5

The POS tagging and lemmatization results are presented in Table 2. The word2vec word embeddings (WE) considerably increase performance compared to the baseline, especially in POS tagging. When only Flair embeddings are added to the baseline, we also observe an improvement, but not as high. We hypothesise that the lower performance (in contrast with the results reported in [1]) is caused by the size of the training data, because we train the word2vec WE on considerably larger dataset than the Czech Flair model. However, when WE and Flair embeddings are combined, performance moderately increases, demonstrating that the two embedding methods produce at least partially complementary representations.

The BERT embeddings alone bring highest improvement in performance. Furthermore, combination with WE or Flair again yields performance increase. The best results are achieved by exploiting all three embedding methods, substantially exceeding state-of-the-art results.

Utilization of morphological dictionary improves prediction accuracy. However, as the performance of a model itself increases, the gains obtained by the morphological dictionary diminishes – for a model without any pretrained embeddings, morphological dictionary improves POS tagging by and lemmatization by 0.43% and 0.45%, while the best performing model gains only 0.11% and 0.23%.

5.2   Dependency Parsing on PDT 3.5

The evaluation of the contextualized embeddings methods as well as various ways of POS tag utilization is presented in Table 3. Without POS tags and lemmas, the Flair embeddings bring only a slight improvement in dependency parsing when added to WE. In contrast, BERT embeddings employment results in substantial gains, increasing UAS and LAS by 1.6% and 2.1%. A combination

---

[8] POS tagging and lemmatization done with MorphoDiTa [34], http://ufal.mff.cuni.cz/morphodita.

Table 2. POS tagging and lemmatization results (accuracy) on PDT 3.5. **Bold** indicates the best result, *italics* related work. [†]Reported on PDT 2.0, which has the same underlying corpus, with minor changes in morphological annotation (our model results differ at 0.1% on PDT 2.0).

WE	BERT	Flair	Without dictionary			With dictionary		
			POS Tags	Lemmas	Both	POS Tags	Lemmas	Both
✗	✗	✗	96.88%	98.35%	96.21%	97.31%	98.80%	96.89%
✓	✗	✗	97.43%	98.55%	96.77%	97.59%	98.82%	97.18%
✗	✗	✓	97.24%	98.49%	96.61%	97.54%	98.86%	97.14%
✓	✗	✓	97.53%	98.63%	96.91%	97.69%	98.88%	97.28%
✗	✓	✗	97.67%	98.63%	97.02%	97.91%	98.94%	97.51%
✓	✓	✗	97.86%	98.69%	97.21%	98.00%	98.96%	97.59%
✗	✓	✓	97.80%	98.67%	97.16%	98.00%	98.96%	97.59%
✓	✓	✓	**97.94%**	**98.75%**	**97.31%**	**98.05%**	**98.98%**	**97.65%**
Morče (2009) [31]			—	—	—	*95.67%*[†]	—	—
MorphoDiTa (2016) [35]			—	—	—	*95.55%*	*97.85%*	*95.06%*
LemmaTag (2018) [19]			*96.90%*	*98.37%*	—	—	—	—

Table 3. Dependency tree parsing results on PDT 3.5 a-layer. **Bold** indicates the best result, *italics* POS tagging and lemmatization results. For comparison, we report results of a parser trained using gold POS tags and lemmas, and of a tagger trained on a-layer (both also in *italics*).

POS Tags, Lemmas	BERT	Flair	UAS (unlabeled attachment score)	LAS (labeled attachment score)	POS Tags	Lemmas
✗	✗	✗	91.16%	87.35%	—	—
✗	✗	✓	91.38%	87.69%	—	—
✗	✓	✗	92.75%	89.46%	—	—
✗	✓	✓	92.76%	89.47%	—	—
Predicted on input	✓	✓	92.84%	89.62%	—	—
Joint prediction	✗	✗	91.69%	88.16%	*97.33%*	*98.42%*
Joint prediction	✗	✓	91.89%	88.42%	*97.48%*	*98.42%*
Joint prediction	✓	✗	93.01%	89.74%	*97.62%*	*98.49%*
Joint prediction	✓	✓	**93.07%**	**89.89%**	*97.72%*	*98.51%*
Gold on input	✓	✓	*92.95%*	*89.89%*	—	—
POS tagger trained on 3.5 a-layer			—	—	*97.82%*	*98.66%*

of BERT and Flair embeddings does not result in any performance improvement, demonstrating that BERT syntactic representations encompass the Flair embeddings.

Table 4. Dependency tree parsing results on PDT 2.0 a-layer. **Bold** indicates the best result, *italics* related work. [†]Possibly using gold POS tags. [‡]Results as of 23 Mar 2019.

System	UAS (unlabeled attachment score)	LAS (labeled attachment score)
Our best system (joint prediction, BERT, Flair)	**93.10%**	**89.93%**
Holan and Žabokrtský [16]	*85.84%*	—
Novák and Žabokrtský [26]	*84.69%*	—
Koo et al. [21][†]	*87.32%*	—
Treex framework (using MST parser& manual rules) [39][‡]	*83.93%*	*77.04%*
PDT 2.0 subset in CoNLL 2007 shared task; manually annotated POS tags available.		
Nakagawa [23]	*86.28%*	*80.19%*
PDT 2.0 subset in CoNLL 2009 shared task; manually annotated POS tags available.		
Gesmundo et al. [8]	—	*80.38%*

When introducing POS tags and lemmas predicted by the best model from Sect. 5.1 as inputs for dependency parsing, the performance increases only slightly. A better way of POS tags and lemmas exploitation is achieved in a joint model, which predicts POS tags, lemmas, and dependency trees simultaneously. Again, BERT embeddings bring significant improvements, but in contrast to syntax parsing only, adding Flair embeddings to BERT results in moderate gain – we hypothesise that the increase is due to the complementary morphological information present in Flair embeddings (cf. Sect. 5.1). Note that the joint model achieves better parsing accuracy than the one given gold POS tags and lemmas on input. However, the POS tags and lemmas predicted by the joint model are of slightly lower quality compared to a standalone tagger of the best configuration from Sect. 5.1.

Table 4 compares our best model with state-of-the-art results on PDT 2.0 (note that some of the related work used only a subset of PDT 2.0 and/or utilized gold morphological annotation). To our best knowledge, research on PDT parsing was performed mostly in the first decade of this century, therefore even our baseline model substantially surpasses previous works. Our best model with contextualized embeddings achieves nearly 50% error reduction both in UAS and LAS.

5.3 POS Tagging, Lemmatization and Dependency Parsing on Universal Dependencies

Table 5 shows the performance of analyzed embedding methods in a joint model performing POS tagging, lemmatization, and dependency parsing on Czech PDT UD 2.3 treebank. This treebank is derived from PDT 3.5 a-layer, with original POS tags kept in XPOS, and the dependency trees and lemmas modified according to UD guidelines.

We observe that the word2vec WEs perform similarly to Flair embeddings in this setting. Our hypothesis is that the word2vec WEs performance loss (compared to WEs in Sect. 5.1) is caused by using a considerably smaller raw corpus to pretrain the WEs (Czech Wikipedia with 785M words, compared to 4G words used in Sect. 5.1), due to licensing reasons. BERT embeddings once more deliver the highest improvement, especially in dependency parsing, and our best model employs all three embedding methods.

In the previous ablation experiments, we used the gold segmentation and tokenization in the Czech PDT UD 2.3 treebank. For comparison with state of the art, Czech PDT UD 2.2 treebank without gold segmentation and tokenization is used in evaluation, according to the CoNLL 2018 shared task training and evaluation protocol. Our system reuses segmentation and tokenization produced

Table 5. Czech PDT UD 2.3 results for POS tagging (UPOS: universal POS, XPOS: language-specific POS, UFeats: universal morphological features), lemmatization and dependency parsing (UAS, LAS, MLAS, and BLEX scores). **Bold** indicates the best result, *italics* related work.

WE	BERT	Flair	UPOS	XPOS	UFeats	Lemmas	UAS	LAS	MLAS	BLEX
✗	✗	✗	99.06	96.73	96.69	98.80	92.93	90.75	84.99	87.68
✓	✗	✗	99.18	97.28	97.23	99.02	93.33	91.31	86.15	88.60
✗	✗	✓	99.16	97.17	97.13	98.93	93.33	91.33	86.19	88.56
✓	✗	✓	99.22	97.41	97.36	99.07	93.48	91.49	86.62	88.89
✗	✓	✗	99.25	97.46	97.41	99.00	94.26	92.34	87.53	89.79
✓	✓	✗	99.31	97.61	97.55	99.06	94.27	92.34	87.75	89.91
✓	✓	✓	**99.34**	**97.71**	**97.67**	**99.12**	**94.43**	**92.56**	**88.09**	**90.22**

CoNLL 2018 Shared Task results on Czech PDT UD 2.2 treebank, from raw text (without gold segmentation and tokenization).

Our best system			**99.24**	**97.63**	**97.62**	**99.08**	**93.69**	**91.82**	**87.57**	**89.60**
HIT-SCIR (2018) [3]			*99.05*	*96.92*	*92.40*	*97.78*	*93.44*	*91.68*	*80.57*	*87.91*
TurkuNLP (2018) [17]			*98.74*	*95.44*	*95.22*	*98.50*	*92.57*	*90.57*	*83.16*	*87.63*

Table 6. Named entity recognition results (F1) on the Czech Named Entity Corpus. **Bold** indicates the best result, *italics* related work.

BERT	Flair	CNEC 1.1		CNEC 2.0	
		Types	Supertypes	Types	Supertypes
✗	✗	82.96	86.80	80.47	85.15
✗	✓	83.55	87.62	81.65	85.96
✓	✗	86.73	89.85	**86.23**	**89.37**
✓	✓	**86.88**	**89.91**	85.52	89.01
Konkol et al. [20]		–	*79.00*	–	–
Straková et al. [33]		*79.23*	*82.82*	–	–
Straková et al. [36]		*81.20*	*84.68*	*79.23*	*82.78*

by UDPipe 2.0 in the CoNLL 2018 shared task and surpasses previous works substantially in all metrics (bottom part of Table 5).

Comparing the results with a joint tagging and parsing PDT 3.5 model from Table 1, we observe that the XPOS results are nearly identical as expected. Lemmatization on the UD treebank is performed without the discriminative numeric suffixes (see Sect. 3) and therefore reaches better performance. Both UAS and LAS are also better on the UD treebank, which we assume is caused by the different annotation scheme.

5.4   Named Entity Recognition

Table 6 shows NER results (F1 score) on CNEC 1.1 and CNEC 2.0. Our sequence-to-sequence (seq2seq) model which captures the nested entities, clearly surpasses the current Czech NER state of the art. Furthermore, significant improvement is gained when adding the contextualized word embeddings (BERT and Flair) as optional input to the LSTM encoder. The strongest model is a combination of the sequence-to-sequence architecture with both BERT and Flair contextual word embeddings.

6   Conclusion

We have presented an evaluation of two contextualized embeddings methods, namely BERT and Flair. By utilizing these embeddings as input to deep neural networks, we have achieved state-of-the-art results in several Czech text processing tasks, namely in POS tagging, lemmatization, dependency parsing and named entity recognition.

Acknowledgements. The work described herein has been supported by OP VVV VI LINDAT/CLARIN project (CZ.02.1.01/0.0/0.0/16_013/0001781) and it has been supported and has been using language resources developed by the LINDAT/CLARIN project (LM2015071) of the Ministry of Education, Youth and Sports of the Czech Republic.

References

1. Akbik, A., Blythe, D., Vollgraf, R.: Contextual string embeddings for sequence labeling. In: Proceedings of the 27th International Conference on Computational Linguistics, pp. 1638–1649. Association for Computational Linguistics (2018)
2. Bojanowski, P., Grave, E., Joulin, A., Mikolov, T.: Enriching word vectors with subword information. Trans. Assoc. Comput. Linguist. **5**, 135–146 (2017)
3. Che, W., Liu, Y., Wang, Y., Zheng, B., Liu, T.: Towards better UD parsing: deep contextualized word embeddings, ensemble, and treebank concatenation. In: Proceedings of the CoNLL 2018 Shared Task: Multilingual Parsing from Raw Text to Universal Dependencies, pp. 55–64. Association for Computational Linguistics (2018)

4. Cho, K., van Merrienboer, B., Bahdanau, D., Bengio, Y.: On the properties of neural machine translation: encoder-decoder approaches. CoRR (2014)
5. Devlin, J., Chang, M.W., Lee, K., Toutanova, K.: BERT: pre-training of deep bidirectional transformers for language understanding. CoRR abs/1810.04805 (2018)
6. Dozat, T., Manning, C.D.: Deep biaffine attention for neural dependency parsing. CoRR abs/1611.01734 (2016)
7. Fares, M., Oepen, S., Øvrelid, L., Björne, J., Johansson, R.: The 2018 shared task on extrinsic parser evaluation: on the downstream utility of English Universal Dependency Parsers. In: Proceedings of the CoNLL 2018 Shared Task: Multilingual Parsing from Raw Text to Universal Dependencies, pp. 22–33. Association for Computational Linguistics (2018)
8. Gesmundo, A., Henderson, J., Merlo, P., Titov, I.: A latent variable model of synchronous syntactic-semantic parsing for multiple languages. In: Proceedings of the Thirteenth Conference on Computational Natural Language Learning (CoNLL 2009): Shared Task, Boulder, pp. 37–42. Association for Computational Linguistics, June 2009
9. Graves, A., Schmidhuber, J.: Framewise phoneme classification with bidirectional LSTM and other neural network architectures. Neural Netw. **18**(5–6), 602–610 (2005)
10. Hajič, J.: Building a syntactically annotated corpus: the Prague dependency treebank. In: Hajičová, E. (ed.) Issues of Valency and Meaning. Studies in Honour of Jarmila Panevová, pp. 106–132. Karolinum, Charles University Press, Prague (1998)
11. Hajič, J.: Disambiguation of Rich Inflection: Computational Morphology of Czech. Karolinum Press, Prague (2004)
12. Hajič, J., Hlaváčová, J.: MorfFlex CZ 161115 (2016). LINDAT/CLARIN digital library at the Institute of Formal and Applied Linguistics (ÚFAL), aculty of Mathematics and Physics, Charles University. http://hdl.handle.net/11234/1-1834
13. Hajič, J., et al.: Prague dependency treebank 3.5 (2018). LINDAT/CLARIN digital library at the Institute of Formal and Applied Linguistics (ÚFAL), Faculty of Mathematics and Physics, Charles University. http://hdl.handle.net/11234/1-2621
14. Hnátková, M., Křen, M., Procházka, P., Skoumalová, H.: The SYN-series corpora of written Czech. In: Proceedings of the Ninth International Conference on Language Resources and Evaluation, LREC 2014, Reykjavik, Iceland, pp. 160–164. European Language Resources Association (ELRA), May 2014
15. Hochreiter, S., Schmidhuber, J.: Long short-term memory. Neural Comput. **9**(8), 1735–1780 (1997)
16. Holan, T., Žabokrtský, Z.: Combining Czech dependency parsers. In: Sojka, P., Kopeček, I., Pala, K. (eds.) TSD 2006. LNCS (LNAI), vol. 4188, pp. 95–102. Springer, Heidelberg (2006). https://doi.org/10.1007/11846406_12
17. Kanerva, J., Ginter, F., Miekka, N., Leino, A., Salakoski, T.: Turku neural parser pipeline: an end-to-end system for the CoNLL 2018 shared task. In: Proceedings of the CoNLL 2018 Shared Task: Multilingual Parsing from Raw Text to Universal Dependencies, Brussels, Belgium, pp. 133–142. Association for Computational Linguistics, October 2018
18. Kingma, D., Ba, J.: Adam: a method for stochastic optimization. In: International Conference on Learning Representations, December 2014
19. Kondratyuk, D., Gavenčiak, T., Straka, M., Hajič, J.: LemmaTag: jointly tagging and lemmatizing for morphologically rich languages with BRNNs. In: Proceedings of the 2018 Conference on Empirical Methods in Natural Language Processing, pp. 4921–4928. Association for Computational Linguistics (2018)

20. Konkol, M., Konopík, M.: CRF-based Czech named entity recognizer and consolidation of Czech NER Research. In: Habernal, I., Matoušek, V. (eds.) TSD 2013. LNCS (LNAI), vol. 8082, pp. 153–160. Springer, Heidelberg (2013). https://doi.org/10.1007/978-3-642-40585-3_20

21. Koo, T., Rush, A.M., Collins, M., Jaakkola, T., Sontag, D.: Dual decomposition for parsing with non-projective head automata. In: Proceedings of the 2010 Conference on Empirical Methods in Natural Language Processing, Cambridge, MA, pp. 1288–1298. Association for Computational Linguistics, October 2010

22. Ling, W., et al.: Finding function in form: compositional character models for open vocabulary word representation. CoRR (2015)

23. Nakagawa, T.: Multilingual dependency parsing using global features. In: Proceedings of the CoNLL Shared Task Session of EMNLP-CoNLL 2007, Prague, Czech Republic, pp. 952–956. Association for Computational Linguistics, June 2007

24. Nivre, J., et al.: Universal dependencies v1: a multilingual treebank collection. In: Proceedings of the 10th International Conference on Language Resources and Evaluation (LREC 2016), Portorož, Slovenia, pp. 1659–1666. European Language Resources Association (2016)

25. Nivre, J., et al.: Universal dependencies 2.3 (2018). LINDAT/CLARIN digital library at the Institute of Formal and Applied Linguistics (ÚFAL), Faculty of Mathematics and Physics, Charles University. http://hdl.handle.net/11234/1-2895

26. Novák, V., Žabokrtský, Z.: Feature engineering in maximum spanning tree dependency parser. In: Matoušek, V., Mautner, P. (eds.) TSD 2007. LNCS (LNAI), vol. 4629, pp. 92–98. Springer, Heidelberg (2007). https://doi.org/10.1007/978-3-540-74628-7_14

27. Peters, M., et al.: Deep contextualized word representations. In: Proceedings of the 2018 Conference of the North American Chapter of the Association for Computational Linguistics: Human Language Technologies, Volume 1 (Long Papers), pp. 2227–2237. Association for Computational Linguistics (2018)

28. Ševčíková, M., Žabokrtský, Z., Krůza, O.: Named entities in Czech: annotating data and developing NE tagger. In: Matoušek, V., Mautner, P. (eds.) TSD 2007. LNCS (LNAI), vol. 4629, pp. 188–195. Springer, Heidelberg (2007). https://doi.org/10.1007/978-3-540-74628-7_26

29. Ševčíková, M., Žabokrtský, Z., Straková, J., Straka, M.: Czech named entity corpus 1.1 (2014). LINDAT/CLARIN digital library at the Institute of Formal and Applied Linguistics (ÚFAL), Faculty of Mathematics and Physics, Charles University. http://hdl.handle.net/11858/00-097C-0000-0023-1B04-C

30. Ševčíková, M., Žabokrtský, Z., Straková, J., Straka, M.: Czech named entity corpus 2.0 (2014). LINDAT/CLARIN digital library at the Institute of Formal and Applied Linguistics (ÚFAL), Faculty of Mathematics and Physics, Charles University. http://hdl.handle.net/11858/00-097C-0000-0023-1B22-8

31. Spoustová, D.J., Hajič, J., Raab, J., Spousta, M.: Semi-supervised training for the averaged perceptron POS tagger. In: Proceedings of the 12th Conference of the European Chapter of the ACL (EACL 2009), pp. 763–771. Association for Computational Linguistics, March 2009

32. Straka, M.: UDPipe 2.0 prototype at CoNLL 2018 UD shared task. In: Proceedings of CoNLL 2018: The SIGNLL Conference on Computational Natural Language Learning, Stroudsburg, PA, USA, pp. 197–207. Association for Computational Linguistics (2018)

33. Straková, J., Straka, M., Hajič, J.: A new state-of-the-art Czech named entity recognizer. In: Habernal, I., Matoušek, V. (eds.) TSD 2013. LNCS (LNAI), vol.

8082, pp. 68–75. Springer, Heidelberg (2013). https://doi.org/10.1007/978-3-642-40585-3_10

34. Straková, J., Straka, M., Hajič, J.: Open-source tools for morphology, lemmatization, POS tagging and named entity recognition. In: Proceedings of 52nd Annual Meeting of the Association for Computational Linguistics: System Demonstrations, Stroudsburg, PA, USA, pp. 13–18. Johns Hopkins University, USA, Association for Computational Linguistics (2014)

35. Straková, J., Straka, M., Hajič, J.: Open-source tools for morphology, lemmatization, POS tagging and named entity recognition. In: Proceedings of 52nd Annual Meeting of the Association for Computational Linguistics: System Demonstrations, Baltimore, MD, USA, pp. 13–18. Johns Hopkins University, Association for Computational Linguistics (2014)

36. Straková, J., Straka, M., Hajič, J.: Neural networks for featureless named entity recognition in Czech. In: Sojka, P., Horák, A., Kopeček, I., Pala, K. (eds.) TSD 2016. LNCS (LNAI), vol. 9924, pp. 173–181. Springer, Cham (2016). https://doi.org/10.1007/978-3-319-45510-5_20

37. Straková, J., Straka, M., Hajič, J.: Neural architectures for nested NER through linearization. In: Proceedings of the 57th Annual Meeting of the Association for Computational Linguistics (Volume 2: Short Papers). Association for Computational Linguistics (2019)

38. Vaswani, A., et al.: Attention is all you need. CoRR abs/1706.03762 (2017)

39. Žabokrtský, Z.: Treex - an open-source framework for natural language processing. In: Lopatková, M. (ed.) Information Technologies - Applications and Theory, vol. 788, pp. 7–14. Univerzita Pavla Jozefa Šafárika v Košiciach, Slovakia (2011)

40. Zeman, D., Ginter, F., Hajič, J., Nivre, J., Popel, M., Straka, M.: CoNLL 2018 shared task: multilingual parsing from raw text to universal dependencies. In: Proceedings of the CoNLL 2018 Shared Task: Multilingual Parsing from Raw Text to Universal Dependencies, Brussels, Belgium. Association for Computational Linguistics (2018)

On GDPR Compliance of Companies' Privacy Policies

Nicolas M. Müller[✉], Daniel Kowatsch, Pascal Debus, Donika Mirdita, and Konstantin Böttinger

Fraunhofer AISEC, Parkring 4, 85748 Garching near Munich, Germany
{nicolas.mueller,daniel.kowatsch,pascal.debus,
donika.mirdita,konstantin.boettinger}@aisec.fraunhofer.de

Abstract. We introduce a data set of privacy policies containing more than 18,300 sentence snippets, labeled in accordance to five General Data Protection Regulation (GDPR) privacy policy core requirements. We hope that this data set will enable practitioners to analyze and detect policy compliance with the GDPR legislation in various documents. In order to evaluate our data set, we apply a number of NLP and other classification algorithms and achieve an F_1 score between 0.52 and 0.71 across the five requirements. We apply our trained models to over 1200 real privacy policies which we crawled from companies' websites, and find that over 76% do not contain all of the requirements, thus potentially not fully complying with GDPR.

Keywords: GDPR data set · GDPR compliance · Natural language processing

1 Introduction

In May 2018, the European Union implemented the General Data Protection Regulation, a new data and privacy protection piece of legislation that applies to everyone within the EU and EEA. This new legislation aims to unify the definition of data protection and privacy related to individuals and forces all the companies that operate in the EU and EEA to provide all the rights, disclaimers and precautions, as defined in the legislation, to every individual in Europe that uses their services and platforms. As a result, companies and businesses from all over the world, large and small, need to update their privacy policies to reflect the GDPR requirements, or shut down their operations in the EU/EEA if they disagree with the legislation. Failure to comply can result in hefty fines.

The GDPR was written and passed in 2016 but it was officially implemented only in May 2018 in order to give businesses a grace period to familiarize themselves with the legislation and make the appropriate changes and adaptations in their own policies. However, not every business entity has made the appropriate changes and a non-negligible fraction of those who have tried to adapt, fall short

© Springer Nature Switzerland AG 2019
K. Ekštein (Ed.): TSD 2019, LNAI 11697, pp. 151–159, 2019.
https://doi.org/10.1007/978-3-030-27947-9_13

on reflecting the necessary policy changes and are thus open to potential fines and/or lawsuits [4,11].

In this paper, we address this situation on several levels, and make the following contribution.

- We present a new labeled data set[1] containing over 18,300 sentence snippets, each labeled with respect to its compliance with five GDPR core privacy policy requirements.
- We show the validity of our data set by designing classifiers which achieve 0.52–0.71 F_1 score between the five classification tasks.
- We evaluate the state of compliance with GDPR 'in the wild': We check over 1200 privacy policies crawled from real companies' websites against our five requirements, and find that at least 76% do not comply with at least one of our core requirements.

Section 2 briefly describes related work. In Sect. 3, we introduce the policy data set in detail and explain its format, class labels and characteristics. Section 4 will introduce the methods we use to generate and rate our policy embeddings and in Sect. 5, we describe our experiments and results. In Sect. 6, we analyze the goodness of our data set and present our conclusions as well as our ideas for further research on this topic.

2   Related Work

There is a considerable amount of research in the area of legal text processing using NLP techniques. However, most of the work is focused on methodologies for doing legal text analysis, automatic rule extraction and summarization [5, 7,10]. Other projects have looked at creating annotating tools for extracting complex document rules, regulations, rights and obligations. One of these tools is "Gaius-T", whose performance is satisfactory but it does not provide statistically relevant improvements compared to a human annotator [9]. To the best of our knowledge there is no prior work that analyzes legal compliance on massive user generated policies, and no other work that uses the GDPR legislation as legal text of interest.

3   Privacy Policy Data Set

In this section we introduce our data set. We provide a detailed description and an overview of its characteristics. We also describe the generation and labeling process.

---

[1] Obtainable at: http://git.aisec.fraunhofer.de/projects/GDPRCOM/repos/on-gdpr-compliance.

3.1   Data Set Generation and Labeling

We obtain our seed data by automatically crawling and storing over 1200 policies in the English language. This set of policies is used for a twofold purpose. First, we use it to train word embeddings (for motivation and details, see Sect. 4). Second, we create our labeled data set for policy compliance rating by manually analyzing and labeling a subset of these policies. This manually labeled set comprises 250 individual policies, containing over 18,300 natural sentences. For legal reasons, we have anonymized the data set, e.g. we have scrambled all numbers and substituted names, email addresses, companies and URLs with generic replacements (e.g. 'company_42645').

We measure policy compliance using five handpicked policy requirements as described in Table 1. Every sentence is assigned a binary score for each class: 0 if the sentence contains no information related to the label, 1 if the sentence discloses class-relevant information. We choose the five requirements in Table 1 because we feel that they represent core requirements of GDPR: They are generic and easily identifiable, which is why we feel that they provide a good overview of how GDPR-compliant a given policy is.

Table 1. The five GDPR requirements we chose to evaluate privacy policy compliance.

No.	Category	Required content in privacy policy	Source
1	DPO	Contact details for the data protection officer or equivalent	[6] 2b/a
2	Purpose	Disclosure of the purpose for which personal data is or is not used for	[6] 2b/b
3	Acquired data	Disclosure that personal data is or is not collected, and/or which data is collected	[6] 2a
4	Data sharing	Disclosure if 3rd parties can or cannot access a user's personal data	[6] 2b/c, d
5	Rights	Disclosure of the user's right to rectify or erase personal data	[6] 2b/f

We use the following set of guidelines.

1. For the **DPO** class, we define a sentence as compliant (assigned the class 1) if the Data Protection Officer or an equivalent authority is named, or contact details of a similar authority are provided.
2. The requirement **Purpose** is considered fulfilled if purpose for processing is stated. Generic purposes such as 'we may use your personal data for any purpose allowed by the law' do not count.
3. The requirement **Acquired data** is considered fulfilled if the sentence informs on the data collected (phone number, first and last name, address, ...), but also if the sentence informs the reader *that* personal data is collected (for more, see [6] 2a).

4. When analyzing **Data sharing**, we label sentences positive that state either of the following: Personal data is shared (a) with other companies, (b) is shared (or not shared) with the public, (c) is transferred to a third country.
5. When labeling for **Rights**, we narrow our threshold down to two GDPR specific definitions: the rights of a user to have his information rectified or deleted. The disclosure of other rights such as transferability is not counted here!

Note the following caveats: First, for classes **Purpose**, **Acquired Data** and **Data Sharing**, the data in question has to be explicitly marked as personal data (e.g. 'your information', 'your data'). Anonymized information and cookies are not considered personal data.

Second, for all requirements except **DPO**, we label sentences positive if they provide any information related to the class in question, which also includes 'negative' information. For example, if a sentence clearly states that data would *not* be shared with some entity or would not be used for specific purposes, we consider this a proper disclosure and assign a positive label.

Third, note that we label sentences as positive if they refer to some list or enumeration of information relevant to the class in question. For example, the sentence 'We use you data for the following purposes:' is compliant, even though the sentence itself does not contain the purposes.

3.2   Data Set Statistics

In this section, we provide detailed information on the labeled data set. Table 2 shows the number of sentences with a positive label for each of the GDPR requirements, as well as the total number of sentences and documents. Duplicates have already been removed, even if they originate from different documents. Considerable class imbalance can be observed, which is due to the nature of privacy policies. Section 3.3 will detail this issue.

Table 3 provides insight into the GDPR compliance of the set of policies that make up our labeled data set. About 37% of our policies are fully compliant over our five core requirements, 27% comply to four out of five requirements and 1.6% of our policies do not fulfill any of the five core requirements. This analysis foreshadows the results of Sect. 5, where we generalize to all of our 1200 crawled policies and find that a significant percentage does not cover all five of our core requirements.

Table 4 provides more information regarding the occurrence of the different classes in our labeled data set. The *Coverage* column gives the percentage of documents where the individual classes occur. The *Sentences per Doc* column shows the average number of sentences per class per document.

3.3   Class Imbalance

As we can see from Table 2, the classes are considerably imbalanced. For example, for every sentence compliant with the class **DPO**, the data set contains 50 non-compliant sentences. However, this imbalance is to be expected. Privacy policies

Table 2. Data point counts.

No. of labeled documents	250
No. of sentences	18397
DPO	363
Purpose	971
Acquired data	558
Data sharing	904
Rights	299

Table 3. Compliance ratios.

Compliance	Ratio
No class	1.6%
One class	5.2%
Two classes	10.0%
Three classes	19.6%
Four classes	26.8%
Full compliance	36.8%

Table 4. Average frequencies.

Label	Coverage	Sentences per Doc
DPO	63.2%	1.54
Purpose	88.8%	4.52
Acquired data	77.6%	2.57
Data sharing	84.8%	4.19
Rights	60.8%	1.50

are supposed to contain a multitude of information, which is why individual requirements will be represented by a few sentences only.

High class imbalance can be a problem in machine learning [8], which is why we take the following measures. First, instead of accuracy, we use F_1 score as evaluation metric for model selection and evaluation. Second, we use class weights during training, where classes that have a smaller representation get a higher weight in order to even out the representation. Third, we use data up-sampling.

4   Methods

In this section, we introduce the algorithms we use to learn from our data set. Our learning pipeline is as follows. First, we generate sentence embeddings and map the privacy policies under test to numerical vector representation. Second, we use supervised learning algorithms to classify a given sentence as either compliant to a given class, or not. We train and evaluate our classifiers for each class individually, resulting in five independent classifiers.

4.1   Sentence Embeddings

In this section, we detail how we map textual data to vector representation. To this end, we use Word2Vec [12], FastText [1], and ELMo [14], three highly popular word embedding techniques. We experiment with both pre-trained models as well as with training our own embeddings, using 1.200 privacy policies crawled of the web as training data. However, we find pre-trained models to yield superior performance compared to the models we train ourselves. Thus, we exclusively use pre-trained embeddings, whose results we report in the following sections. Specifically, we use the Google News Negative 300 Slim embeddings[2], Facebook's official FastText weights[3] and ELMo embeddings from Tensorflow Hub[4].

4.2   Classification Models

In this section, we introduce the classifiers we use for rating policy compliance. We evaluate Support Vector Machines, Logistic regression and Neural Networks. In order to counter the heavy class imbalance, we use SMOTE up-sampling [2] in conjunction with neural networks. For Logistic regression and SVM, we use balanced class weights to counter the class imbalance.

We train all of the classification models using 3-fold cross-validated grid search to find the optimal set of hyperparameters. Each class is trained and evaluated independently. As evaluation metric, we use the F_1 score, which is the harmonic mean of precision and recall. We use *sklearn*'s implementation [13] of SVM and Logistic Regression, and *keras* [3] to implement the Neural Networks.

5   Experiments

In this section we report the performance of our supervised classifiers on our labeled data set. We then apply the best performing classifiers on a large set of previously unseen privacy policies and evaluate GDPR compliance.

5.1   Classifier Evaluation

Table 5 provides a performance breakdown over all classes, algorithms, and embedding models. We report the test F_1 score of the classifiers with the hyper parameters found via cross-validated grid-search on the train set. We highlight the table cells which show the best classifier per class. Based these results, we find a clear dominance of ELMo embeddings over FastText over Word2Vec. We observe that for most classes, SVM and Neural Networks yield the same performance.

The best hyper parameters for SVM always include the following *sklearn* parameters: *gamma : scale* and *class_weights : balanced*, and either *rbf* or *poly* kernel. The best performing neural networks contain two hidden layers with 40 Neurons each, 10% dropout and *relu* activations.

---

[2] https://github.com/eyaler/word2vec-slim.

[3] https://dl.fbaipublicfiles.com/fasttext/vectors-crawl/cc.en.300.bin.gz.

[4] https://tfhub.dev/google/elmo/2.

Table 5. F_1 test score for all models and embeddings, using the best hyper parameters found via grid search.

	ElMo			FT			W2V		
	LR	NN	SVM	LR	NN	SVM	LR	NN	SVM
Acquired data	0.47	0.52	0.51	0.31	0.49	0.46	0.27	0.48	0.48
DPO	0.59	0.61	0.64	0.38	0.60	0.60	0.37	0.51	0.60
Data sharing	0.55	0.63	0.63	0.44	0.58	0.58	0.42	0.57	0.58
Purpose	0.46	0.54	0.54	0.32	0.46	0.48	0.31	0.48	0.46
Rights	0.61	0.67	0.67	0.31	0.57	0.57	0.35	0.65	0.71

5.2 Experimental Analysis of Unseen Privacy Policies

In this section, we present and interpret the results we obtain when classifying unseen privacy policies from real companies' websites for GDPR-compliance according to our five requirements. Our test data set contains 1,200 documents. For each document, we estimate whether each of our requirements is fulfilled. To this end, we use ELMo embeddings and SVM classifiers, which provided the best or close to best results according to Table 5.

Table 6. Coverage for unseen policies.

Class	Coverage
DPO	68.07%
Purpose	74.72%
Acquired data	62.01%
Data sharing	76.39%
Rights	39.48%

Table 7. Compliance ratios.

Compliance	Ratio
No class	9.56%
One class	8.98%
Two classes	9.81%
Three classes	18.04%
Four classes	30.09%
Full compliance	23.25%

Table 6 provides an estimate of how many of the privacy policies fulfill each of the classes. Our models appear to have good generalization capabilities. A comparison to Table 4 shows a lack of overfitting and overall proportionate results. We observe a difference in coverage values between less than 5% for class **DPO** and about 20% for class **Rights**.

Table 7 shows the compliance rate of our test data set of 1,200 unseen policies. We can see that about 76% are not fully compliant with our requirements, whereas 9.5% do not cover any requirement at all.

6 Conclusion

In this paper, we introduced a novel labeled data set of privacy policies for the purpose of studying GDPR compliance. This data set contains 250 privacy policies and a total of over 18,300 sentences labeled over the five classes **DPO, Purpose, Acquired Data, Data Sharing, Rights** as described in Table 1. We apply a comprehensive set of NLP algorithms in combination with supervised learning to analyze the soundness of our data set and build a framework that can rate GDPR compliance of privacy policies. We achieve an F_1 score of 0.52–0.71 between the five classes, indicating that while there is room for improvement with respect to the classification algorithms, our data set may be useful in real-word tasks.

7   Future Work

Future work in this project includes the growth of our labeled data set. Adding more data should boost the performance of our classifiers, and allow for the use of more advanced networks such as RNNs. In addition to this, other classifiers such as Label Propagation could be evaluated. Finally, we would also like to expand our set of legal requirements for compliance, which would make our compliance rating more comprehensive and expressive.

References

1. Bojanowski, P., Grave, E., Joulin, A., Mikolov, T.: Enriching word vectors with subword information. Trans. Assoc. Comput. Linguist. **5**, 135–146 (2017)
2. Bowyer, K.W., Chawla, N.V., Hall, L.O., Kegelmeyer, W.P.: SMOTE: synthetic minority over-sampling technique. CoRR abs/1106.1813 (2011). http://arxiv.org/abs/1106.1813
3. Chollet, F.: Keras (2015). https://github.com/fchollet/keras
4. Deloitte: Deloitte general data protection regulation benchmarking survey (2018). https://www2.deloitte.com/content/dam/Deloitte/be/Documents/risk/emea-gdpr-benchmarking-survey.pdf
5. Dragoni, M., Villata, S., Rizzi, W., Governatori, G.: Combining NLP approaches for rule extraction from legal documents. In: 1st Workshop on MIning and REasoning with Legal Texts (MIREL 2016) (2016)
6. Gowling WLG: Checklist for tasks needed in order to comply with GDPR. https://gowlingwlg.com/GowlingWLG/media/UK/pdf/170630-gdpr-checklist-for-compliance.pdf. Accessed 31 Mar 2019
7. Hachey, B., Grover, C.: Extractive summarisation of legal texts. Artif. Intell. Law **14**(4), 305–345 (2006)
8. Japkowicz, N., Stephen, S.: The class imbalance problem: a systematic study. Intell. Data Anal. **6**, 429–449 (2002)
9. Kiyavitskaya, N., et al.: Automating the extraction of rights and obligations for regulatory compliance. In: Li, Q., Spaccapietra, S., Yu, E., Olivé, A. (eds.) ER 2008. LNCS, vol. 5231, pp. 154–168. Springer, Heidelberg (2008). https://doi.org/10.1007/978-3-540-87877-3_13
10. Lame, G.: Using NLP techniques to identify legal ontology components: concepts and relations. In: Benjamins, V.R., Casanovas, P., Breuker, J., Gangemi, A. (eds.) Law and the Semantic Web. LNCS (LNAI), vol. 3369, pp. 169–184. Springer, Heidelberg (2005). https://doi.org/10.1007/978-3-540-32253-5_11

11. Law.Com: Over half of companies are far from GDPR compliance, report finds (2018). https://www.law.com/corpcounsel/2018/10/19/over-half-of-companies-are-far-from-gdpr-compliance-report-finds/
12. Mikolov, T., Sutskever, I., Chen, K., Corrado, G.S., Dean, J.: Distributed representations of words and phrases and their compositionality. In: Advances in Neural Information Processing Systems, pp. 3111–3119 (2013)
13. Pedregosa, F., et al.: Scikit-learn: machine learning in Python. J. Mach. Learn. Res. **12**, 2825–2830 (2011)
14. Peters, M.E., et al.: Deep contextualized word representations. CoRR abs/1802.05365 (2018). http://arxiv.org/abs/1802.05365

A Semi-automatic Structure Learning Method for Language Modeling

Vitor Pera[(✉)]

Faculdade de Engenharia da Universidade do Porto,
Rua Dr Roberto Frias, s/n, 4200-465 Porto, Portugal
vcp@fe.up.pt
http://www.fe.up.pt

Abstract. This paper presents a semi-automatic method for statistical language modeling. The method addresses the structure learning problem of the linguistic classes prediction model (LCPM) in class-dependent N-grams supporting multiple linguistic classes per word. The structure of the LCPM is designed, within the Factorial Language Model framework, combining a knowledge-based approach with a data-driven technique. First, simple linguistic knowledge is used to define a set with linguistic features appropriate to the application, and to sketch the LCPM main structure. Next an automatic algorithm selects, based on Information Theory solid concepts, the relevant factors associated to the selected features and establishes the LCPM definitive structure. This approach is based on the so called Buried Markov Models [1]. Although only preliminary results were obtained, they afford great confidence on the method's ability to learn from the data, LCPM structures that represent accurately the application's real dependencies and also favor the training robustness.

Keywords: Language modeling · Structure learning ·
Class-dependent N-gram

1 Introduction

The ability of the language model (LM) to represent with enough accuracy the real linguistic structure and redundancy patterns present in an application, reducing properly and as much as possible the task perplexity, is in general crucial for the performance of the system using the LM. N-grams continue to be quite common, at least in automatic speech recognition (ASR), given their effectiveness in many applications and also because linguistic expertise is dispensed [5]. Nevertheless, when the vocabulary is very large the sparse data estimation problem usually becomes critical. Statistical modeling techniques based on data sharing or smoothing principles, e.g. back-off strategies or interpolation methods, have been developed to mitigate over-fitting effects [3,4]. Another proposed approach has been the class-dependent N-grams. These are at the basis of this

© Springer Nature Switzerland AG 2019
K. Ekštein (Ed.): TSD 2019, LNAI 11697, pp. 160–170, 2019.
https://doi.org/10.1007/978-3-030-27947-9_14

work. It has been recognized that in the case of some applications exhibiting relatively complex linguistic patterns involving multiple linguistic features, new and better approaches to exploit those patterns are needed [6,7]. This work addresses this particular issue, proposing a method to optimize according to some criteria, based on solid Information Theory principles, the structure of the linguistic classes prediction model.

The structure of the paper is as follows. Section 2 presents a brief analysis of the class-dependent N-grams modeling ability. Section 3 begins with some discussion on the application's properties motivating the proposed method, and then presents its two main steps. Preliminary results obtained using this method are presented in Sect. 4. The main conclusions of this work are pointed-out in Sect. 5.

2 The Class-Dependent N-Grams

Given a sequence of words $\omega_{1:T}$, the Language Model estimates the probability $P(\omega_{1:T})$, which can be factorized as $\prod_t P(\omega_t|\omega_{1:t-1})$. Let assume that each word, ω, in the vocabulary, $\mathcal{V}$, is associated to some subset, $C(\omega)$, eventually a singleton, of the linguistic classes set, $\mathcal{C}$. Then

$$P(\omega_t|\omega_{1:t-1}) = \sum_{c_t \in C(\omega_t)} P(\omega_t|c_t, \omega_{1:t-1})P(c_t|\omega_{1:t-1}). \tag{1}$$

Two assumptions are made that approximate this conditional probability: (1) it depends almost entirely of the recent history, so N and M values are set for ω and c depths, respectively; (2) the linguistic classes prediction can be adequately modeled discarding the word terminals information. Accordingly,

$$P(\omega_t|\omega_{1:t-1}) \approx \sum_{c_t \in C(\omega_t)} P(\omega_t|c_t, \omega_{t-N+1:t-1})P(c_t|c_{t-M+1:t-1}). \tag{2}$$

In general $M > N$, typical ranges are $N = 2, ..., 5$ and $M = 3, ..., 7$ (and $|\mathcal{C}| << |\mathcal{V}|$).

Let now make a brief analysis of the class-dependent N-grams modeling ability, comparing it with standard N-grams. Let consider $|C(\omega)| = 1$, $\forall \omega \in \mathcal{V}$, which is accurate for many words, in order to simplify the following analysis. Accordingly,

$$P(\omega_t|\omega_{1:t-1}) \approx P(\omega_t|c_t, \omega_{t-N+1:t-1})P(c_t|c_{t-M+1:t-1}), \tag{3}$$

where $c_t = f(\omega_t)$ for some known function f. Then, the conditional probability expected log-value $\mathcal{E} = E[log(P(\omega_t|\omega_{1:t-1}))]$, over a representative data set $\{\omega_{1:T_l}\}_{l=1}^L$, can be approximated as follows (assuming $M > N$):

$$\sum_{\omega_{t-M+1:t}} P(\omega_{t-M+1:t})log(P(\omega_t|c_t,\omega_{t-N+1:t-1})P(c_t|c_{t-M+1:t-1}))$$

$$= \sum_{\omega_{t-M+1:t}} P(\omega_{t-M+1:t})log\Big(\frac{P(\omega_t,c_t|\omega_{t-N+1:t-1})}{P(c_t|\omega_{t-N+1:t-1})}P(c_t|c_{t-M+1:t-1})\Big)$$

$$= \sum_{\omega_{t-N+1:t}} P(\omega_{t-N+1:t})logP(\omega_t|\omega_{t-N+1:t-1})$$

$$+ \sum_{\omega_{t-M+1:t}} P(\omega_{t-M+1:t})log\frac{P(c_t|c_{t-M+1:t-1})}{P(c_t|\omega_{t-N+1:t-1})}$$

The first term expresses the conditional probability expected log-value corresponding to a standard N-gram. Continuing to assume that c is uniquely determined by ω, the second term can be written:

$$\sum_{\omega_{t-M+1:t}} P(\omega_{t-M+1:t})log\frac{P(c_t|c_{t-M+1:t-N},c_{t-N+1:t-1})}{P(c_t|c_{t-N+1:t-1})}$$

$$= \sum_{\omega_{t-M+1:t}} P(\omega_{t-M+1:t})log\frac{P(c_t,c_{t-M+1:t-N}|c_{t-N+1:t-1})}{P(c_t|c_{t-N+1:t-1})P(c_{t-M+1:t-N}|c_{t-N+1:t1})}$$

It is clear that the second term represents the conditional mutual information between c_t and $c_{t-M+1:t-N}$ given $c_{t-N+1:t-1}$, i.e., $I(c_t;c_{t-M+1:t-N}|c_{t-N+1:t-1})$. Comparing with a standard N-gram, is fair to expect that the descriptive power of this model is substantially larger, iff $c_{t-M+1:t-N}$ conveys relevant information about the outcome of c_t, not present in $c_{t-N+1:t-1}$. Some quite common circumstances favor this potential improvement: (1) the value of N is in general severely limited by the data resources, therefore not allowing to capture important past cues; (2) the contrary occurs in relation to M, which value in general can be made large enough to model early cues that can be useful; (3) in many real applications the entropy associated to the conditionals $P(c_t|c_{1:t-1})$ is small, which favors the linguistic classes information as an aid to predict the sentence words.

3 The Linguistic Classes Prediction Model

3.1 A Factorial Language Model Approach

The linguistic classes prediction model (LCPM) design follows the factorial language model (FLM) formalism. In terms of notation, the linguistic classes variable c becomes a vector with K components (factors), $f^{1:K}$; accordingly, hereafter, $c_{t_1:t_2}$ is replaced by $f_{t_1:t_2}^{1:K}$. It is well known that in general statistical models may improve greatly when structural changes, even mild though well-aimed, are made to model relevant statistical dependencies, or pruning unimportant and wasteful ones.

Just to illustrate the initial step of the proposed method, let consider a very simple example. Based on common linguistic knowledge let suppose that the

LCPM for an application requires only two linguistic features, the thematic tag (sports, fruits, etc.) and the gender inflection (masculine, feminine or neuter) associated to any word, corresponding respectively to the factors f_t^1 and f_t^2 for the present word, ω_t. The goal is to build a model able to deliver good estimates for $P(f_t^{1:2}|f_{t-M+1:t-1}^{1:2})$. If these features were mutually independent then a simple factorization would lead to $\prod_{i=1}^{2} P(f_t^i|f_{t-M+1:t-1}^i)$ to compute these estimates. Let now make the two following assumptions (very reasonable in the Portuguese language): (1) the outcome of f_t^1 is conditionally independent of $f_{1:t}^2$, given its own history, i.e., $f_t^1 \perp\!\!\!\perp f_{1:t}^2|f_{1:t-1}^1$; and (2) f_t^2 depends strongly of f_t^1, even knowing its own history, i.e., $f_t^2 \not\perp\!\!\!\perp f_{1:t}^1|f_{1:t-1}^2$. Now, a statistical structure corresponding to $P(f_t^1|f_{t-M+1:t-1}^1)P(f_t^2|f_{t-M+1:t}^1, f_{t-M+1:t-1}^2)$ should be considered to compute the intended estimates. Such as just illustrated, the method's initial step (formalized in Sect. 3.2) consists of selecting manually the linguistic features at the basis of the set of factors and establishing a baseline structure.

Prolonging the example above, in order to illustrate the second step of the method, let suppose that the data had shown using appropriate measures that the gender instantiated two words preceding the present word (ω_t) is dominant to help predicting the gender of ω_t, when the theme of ω_t is known. In that case, $P(f_t^2|f_{t-M+1:t}^1, f_{t-M+1:t-1}^{1:2}) \approx P(f_t^2|f_t^1, f_{t-2}^2)$ seems a good approximation. Indeed, the method's second step, which is performed automatically based on a data-driven approach, selects criteriously factors corresponding to past instantiations of the previously selected features and establishes the definitive structure of the model, ultimately pursuing a good compromise between descriptive ability and robustness. The selection criterion essentially uses an information utility measure [2], applying it to the candidate factors in different contexts, such as explained in Sect. 3.3, which may bring special advantages in some applications.

3.2   The Baseline Structure

Jointly, the selected linguistic features must satisfy two main requisites: (1) to convey information that effectively contributes to predict correctly the words in the sentence; and (2) the available data resources fit up the requirements to get robust models. The linguistic features are selected based on common linguistic knowledge relevant for the application, which in general is a relatively simple task that yields a suitable set $f^{1:K}$.[1] Having in mind the need to achieve a good statistical structure, it follows a procedure to split $f^{1:K}$ into two subsets based on the assumption that some features are conditionally independent of the other ones given its own history. For instance, in the illustrative example in the previous section, $f_t^1 \perp\!\!\!\perp f_{1:t}^2|f_{1:t-1}^1$ but the conditional independence assumption does not verifies in relation to f_t^2, i.e., $f_t^2 \not\perp\!\!\!\perp f_{1:t}^1|f_{1:t-1}^2$. This splitting operation is performed non-automatically, once again common linguistic knowledge is in

---

[1] The lighter notation $f^{1:K}$ is used to express the features set $\{f^1, f^2, \ldots, f^K\}$. The same convention is used, from now on, with $f_{i:j}^{m:n}$ representing a factors set (where $f_\tau^\nu, \tau = i, \ldots, j \quad \nu = m, \ldots, n$ represents the factor corresponding to the linguistic feature f^ν at time τ).

general sufficient to achieve the intended result (in this work was not developed an automatic data-driven method to split $f^{1:K}$, but that is very well feasible). The following conventions are used hereafter: it is assumed that any feature in $f^{1:J}$, with $J < K$, is conditionally independent of any other feature, present or past instantiations, given its own history, i.e., $f_t^i \perp\!\!\!\perp f_{1:t}^j | f_{1:t-1}^i$, $\forall i \neq j$, $1 \leq i \leq J$, $1 \leq j \leq K$; and $f^{J+1:K}$ correspond to the remaining features, not satisfying the conditional independence assumption. Accordingly, the baseline LCPM computes the estimates:

$$P(c_t|c_{t-M+1:t-1}) \approx P(f_t^{J+1:K}|f_t^{1:J}, f_{t-M+1:t-1}^{1:K}) \prod_{i=1}^{J} P(f_t^i|f_{t-M+1:t-1}^i) \qquad (4)$$

The product-operator factors can be computed by standard N-grams. The conditional probability corresponding to the "non-independent" features is addressed in the next section.

3.3   The Structure Optimization

In general it is not trivial to train robustly a model able to generate accurate estimates for $P(f_t^{J+1:K}|f_t^{1:J}, f_{t-M+1:t-1}^{1:K})$. Even if M is only a few units and J and K are in the order of the dozens, a fully connected statistical structure is not practicable. Some structural optimization, based on proper criteria, is essential. Follows the presentation of an automatic method that selects only the factors in $f_{t-M+1:t-1}^{1:K}$ satisfying a criteria adapted from the work [1] that lead to the so called Buried Markov Models. In order to simplify the exposition, let introduce the following notation: X, Y and W stand for the sets $f_t^{1:J}$, $f_t^{J+1:K}$ and $f_{t-M+1:t-1}^{1:K}$, respectively; and Z denotes a subset of W. Accordingly, the goal is to find $Z \subset W$ such that robust estimates $P(Y|X,Z)$ approximate well enough $P(Y|X,W)$. Using an Information Theory formulation, any factor $f_\tau^\nu \in W$ candidate to be an element of Z must be selected only if it conveys new information, not provided by those factors already selected or by X, i.e., it must exhibit high score for the conditional mutual information (CMI) $I(Y; f_\tau^\nu|X, Z \setminus f_\tau^\nu)$. This criterion should lead to $|Z|$ factors that, as a whole, exhibit the larger score for the CMI $I(Y; Z|X)$ measured on a sufficiently large and representative data set, so reinforcing the model descriptive power [9]. An extended criterion was introduced in order to favor the selection of factors that increase the difference between the CMI scores measured in different contexts established by X.

Before formalizing the method, the following example illustrates the idea. Keeping the example as simple as possible, let consider that both random variables X and Y are scalars (each represents a single feature): $X \in \{F, S\}$ and $Y \in \{A, B, U\}$. Let suppose that $Y = U$ corresponds to "undefined" category (or simply means unlabeled data) and let also admit that this value, U, brings very little information to the LCPM. Let confront two possible sets for the variable Z, also scalar: $Z^{(1)} \in \{C, D, V\}$ and $Z^{(2)} \in \{E, F, W\}$. In the performed simulation $P(X = F) = 0.6$ (so $P(X = S) = 0.4$) and the conditionals $P(y, z^{(i)}|x)$, $i = 1, 2$ are shown in Fig. 1. According to the criterion referred above, $Z^{(1)}$ is selected instead of $Z^{(2)}$ ($I(Y; Z^{(1)}|X) = 0.177 > I(Y; Z^{(2)}|X) = 0.009$). Indeed, the results in the Fig. 1 show that in both contexts, $X = F$ or $X = S$, $Z^{(1)}$ is clearly more informative than $Z^{(2)}$ about the outcome of Y. Let suppose now that another data set is used. Running again the simulation are obtained the distributions shown in Fig. 2. Applying the same criterion as above, now $Z^{(2)}$ is selected instead of $Z^{(1)}$ ($I(Y; Z^{(1)}|X) = 0.208 < I(Y; Z^{(2)}|X) = 0.471$). At first, this result seems acceptable, given the peak $P(y = U, z^{(2)} = W|X)$, on both contexts of X, which does not happens in the case of $Z^{(1)}$. But considering the supposition made that $Y = U$ brings very little information to the LCPM, then this result becomes very unfortunate, since with any of the data sets $Z^{(1)}$ is much more informative than $Z^{(2)}$ about the outcome of Y if not considering $Y = U$. A very interesting evidence provided by the Fig. 2 is that in the case of $Z^{(2)}$ the results are very similar when comparing both contexts, $X = F$ or $X = S$. And very important too, that similarity does not happens at all in the case of $Z^{(1)}$. It worth's to notice that the same evidence is provided by the results in the Fig. 1. This illustrative example suggests that a selection criterion based on some measure able to account for the CMI scores estimated in different contexts established by the variable X, should be considered.

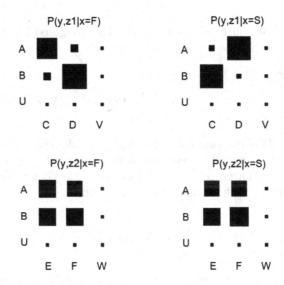

Fig. 1. Probabilistic distributions corresponding to the first data set (Y and Z variables in the vertical and horizontal axis, respectively).

Let begin invoking the cross-context conditional mutual information (CCCMI)

$$I_{X_m}(Y; Z|X = X_n) = \sum_Y \sum_Z P(Y, Z|X_m) \log \frac{P(Y, Z|X_n)}{P(Y|X_n)P(Z|X_n)} \qquad (5)$$

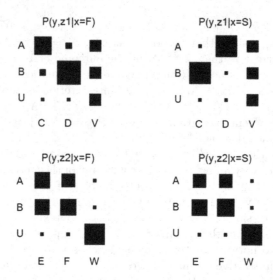

Fig. 2. Probabilistic distributions corresponding to the second data set (Y and Z variables in the vertical and horizontal axis, respectively).

If $X_m = X_n$ then obviously results the CMI. The Weighted Utility (WU) measure [1] is defined as follows

$$M_{(\lambda)}(Y; Z|X = X_n) = I(Y; Z|X = X_n) - $$
$$-\lambda \sum_{X_m \neq X_n} P(X_m) I_{X_m}(Y; Z|X = X_n) \qquad (6)$$

where $\lambda \in [0, 1]$. This measure could be used to implement a criterion so that new components of Z should increase the difference between the CMI and some fraction of the CCCMI average. Finally, let introduce the Global Weighted Utility (GWU) measure [1], that averages the WU based on the distribution of the variable X.

$$N_{(\lambda)}(Y; Z|X) = \sum_{X_m} P(X_m) M_{(\lambda)}(Y; Z|X = X_m) \qquad (7)$$

Revisiting the illustrative example above, using the GWU measure with $\lambda = 1$, now for both data sets the variable $Z^{(1)}$ is selected instead of $Z^{(2)}$. In the case o the second data set the GWU scores are: $N_{(1.0)}(Y; Z^1|X) = 0.427 > N_{(1.0)}(Y; Z^2|X) = 0.223$. A secure margin separates the scores for the comparing variables, as a consequence of the ability of the GWU measure to capture the variables informativeness differences depending on the context (established by X).

Using the GWU measure, the selection of certain number of factors in W should be relatively straight. Often though the available data is scarce in relation to the dimensions of X, Y and Z, preventing reliable estimates of the defined measures. The proposed algorithm (see "Algorithm 1") follows an iterative app-roach, eventually finding a sub-optimal solution though more reliable and surely less costly [2]. The strategy is simple, begin with an empty Z and, at each new iteration, add criteriously a component to it. The parameters γ and η must be tuned empirically. Lines 1 to 5 eliminate from the initial candidates set, the lin-guistic factors that do not convey enough information, using as threshold some fraction of the entropy associated to $f_t^{J+1:K}$ conditioned on $f_t^{1:J}$. Line 6 sorts the remaining factors, placing those with higher GWU scores on the top. Lines 7 to 13 begin with an empty Z, then at each new iteration the factor at the top of the queue sorted in 6 is pulled out and is added to Z if is not redundant in relation to the factors already selected. The process stops when the required dimension of Z, D_z, is reached.

Algorithm 1 Factors selection (definition of Z)

Require: $f_{t-M+1:t}^{1:K}$, J, K, M, D_Z, λ, γ, η,*Data*
Ensure: Structure of the vector Z
1: **for each** $z \in f_{t-M+1:t-1}^{1:K}$ **do**
2:    **if** $I(f_t^{J+1:K}; z|f_t^{1:J}) < \gamma H(f_t^{J+1:K}|f_t^{1:J})$ **then**
3:        Remove z from $f_{t-M+1:t-1}^{1:K}$
4:    **end if**
5: **end for**
6: Sort $f_{t-M+1:t-1}^{1:K}$ by descending order of $N_{(\lambda)}(f_t^{J+1:K}; z|f_t^{1:J})$
7: $Z \Leftarrow \emptyset$
8: **repeat**
9:    $z \Leftarrow$ next non-processed element in $f_{t-M+1:t-1}^{1:K}$
10:    **if** $I(f_t^{J+1:K}; z|f_t^{1:J}) > \eta I(z; r|f_t^{1:J}), \forall r \in Z$ **then**
11:        Add z to Z
12:    **end if**
13: **until** $|Z| = D_Z$ or all elements of $f_{t-M+1:t-1}^{1:K}$ are processed
14: **return** Z

---

4   Results

The results here presented were obtained from two experiments, kept as simple as possible, though still allowing to en-light key aspects of the proposed method. The data used, extracted from the corpus "CETEMPublico" [10], has a vocab-ulary with $200K$ words. Just $K = 3$ linguistic features were used, which factors span a window with length $M = 3$. The available data allowed the robust estima-tion of the used measures. The linguistic factors associated to each word are the morpho-syntactic tag (or *part-of-speech*) [8], the gender inflection and the num-ber inflection, denoted respectively by the symbols m, g and n. The features can take the values: $m_t \in \{\text{ADJ}, \text{ADV}, \text{CONJ}, \text{DET}, \text{NOM}, \text{P}, \text{PR}, \text{PRP}, \text{PRP+DET}, \text{V}, \text{other}\}$; $g \in G2$ or $g \in G3$, where $G2 = \{\text{MASC}, \text{FEM}\}$ and $G3 = \{\text{MASC}, \text{FEM}, \text{NEUT}\}$; $n \in G2$ or $n \in G3$, where $N2 = \{\text{SING}, \text{PLUR}\}$ and $N3 = \{\text{SING}, \text{PLUR}, \text{UNDEF}\}$. Only the feature m is assumed to be independent of the other ones, so $J = 1$

and $f^1_{t-2:t} = m_{t-2:t}$. Likewise, $f^2_{t-2:t} = g_{t-2:t}$ and $f^3_{t-2:t} = n_{t-2:t}$. In order to make clear the results from the two experiments, an adaptation of the algorithm presented in Sect. 3.3 was used, computing separately the factors set Z for each factor in $f^{J+1:K}_t$. Consequently, the joint conditional in Eq. 4 is approximated considering the factors in $f^{J+1:K}_t$ conditionally independent each other, which does not harms the conclusions of this experiment. Let denote by Z_g and Z_n the subsets of W corresponding, respectively, to the features g and n.

In the initial experiment $g \in G2$ and $n \in N2$. Table 1 presents the factors selection ranking for g and n. In the case of g, such as expected both for $\lambda = 0$ (GWU parameter) or $\lambda = 1$, g_{t-1} is the most informative factor concerning the outcome of g_t. The following rank positions are different depending on λ, but must be noticed that the three first places coincide, g_{t-2} and m_{t-1} are selected the most relevant factors after g_{t-1}. These results seem very reasonable, such as those referring to n, with the past instantiations of n, and then of m and g, by this order, selected as relevant cues for n_t.

In the second experiment $g \in G3$ and $n \in N3$, i.e., are also considered the "neuter" and "undefined" categories for g and n, respectively. Table 2 presents the factors selection ranking for g and n. The results are very surprising, either for n or g, when $\lambda = 0$: n_t is selected as the most relevant factor to inform about the g_t outcome, and vice-verso! Only in the second place stand the expected choices: g_{t-1} for g_t and n_{t-1} for n_t. Contrarily, when $\lambda = 1$ the factors selected as the most relevant are precisely the expected ones. It is important to find the explanation for these differences, depending on the value of λ. In large part the explanation is the following. Even for categories of m having no gender inflection, such as verbs for instance, in many data samples of the second data set, $g = \texttt{NEUT}$ and $n = \texttt{UNDEF}$, therefore g and n become quite informative each other (similarly to the illustrative example presented in Sect. 3.3) and consequently when $\lambda = 0$ are obtained unexpected results. When $\lambda = 1$, the GWU measure is able to capture the g and n informativeness differences depending on the context established by m, leading to selections that agree with basic linguistic knowledge. It worth's to emphasize the ability of the method to circumvent this "unfavorable" annotation circumstance, which is not uncommon. Eventually, the method is also able to deal properly with some other "flaws" affecting the corpus. Such as pointed out before, just preliminary experiments were already performed. Further experiments have been planed for comparing the method with other approaches on standard tasks. Nevertheless, the obtained results afford confidence on the method's ability to learn, from the data, good statistical structures for the LCPM in practical applications.

Table 1. Results of experiment 1.

Rank	Z_g		Z_n	
	$\lambda = 0$	$\lambda = 1$	$\lambda = 0$	$\lambda = 1$
1	g_{t-1}	g_{t-1}	n_{t-1}	n_{t-1}
2	g_{t-2}	m_{t-1}	n_{t-2}	n_{t-2}
3	m_{t-1}	g_{t-2}	m_{t-1}	m_{t-1}
4	n_t	m_{t-2}	m_{t-2}	m_{t-2}
5	m_{t-2}	n_{t-1}	g_t	g_{t-1}
6	n_{t-1}	n_t	g_{t-1}	g_{t-2}
7	n_{t-2}	n_{t-2}	g_{t-2}	g_t

Table 2. Results of experiment 2.

Rank	Z_g		Z_n	
	$\lambda = 0$	$\lambda = 1$	$\lambda = 0$	$\lambda = 1$
1	n_t	g_{t-1}	g_t	n_{t-1}
2	g_{t-1}	m_{t-2}	n_{t-1}	m_{t-2}
3	m_{t-1}	g_{t-2}	m_{t-1}	n_{t-2}
4	m_{t-2}	n_{t-2}	n_{t-2}	g_{t-2}
5	g_{t-2}	n_{t-1}	m_{t-2}	g_{t-1}
6	n_{t-1}	m_{t-1}	g_{t-2}	m_{t-1}
7	n_{t-2}	n_t	g_{t-1}	g_t

5   Conclusions

In this paper was presented a method for statistical language modeling, designed
for an application that satisfies the following conditions: (1) the vocabulary is
large, typically at least a few hundred thousand words, in general making difficult to build accurate and robust models; (2) the redundancy patterns inherent
to the application can be exploited more efficiently selecting, based on proper
criteria and common linguistic knowledge, some set of linguistic features that
can be associated to the vocabulary words, following an approach such as the
class-dependent N-grams; (3) at least part of these features cannot be modeled
independently and the data resources are too scarce to allow building a robust
linguistic classes prediction model (LCPM) with fully connected structure. The
designed method deals precisely with the problem of optimizing the LCPM structure (the implementation and training problems are not addressed), and complies
with two general principles: (1) the overall performance of a statistical model
is strongly related to the ability of its structure to represent the application's
real dependencies; (2) parsimony favors structures modeling just the relevant
statistical dependencies according to some appropriate criterion. The proposed

method follows a semi-automatic structure learning approach: after the basic structure being set manually, then a data-driven algorithm, using Information Theory measures, refines the model structure. Although only preliminary experiments were performed, the obtained results show that the method is able to deliver LCPM structures that represent the application's real dependencies and also favor the robustness requirement. Besides, the method presents a remarkable ability to deal with some unfavorable circumstances, or even some flaws, which are not uncommon, affecting the annotation information of the data used to build the models.

References

1. Bilmes, J.: Natural statistical models for automatic speech recognition. Ph.D. thesis, U.C. Berkeley, Department of EECS, CS Division (1999)
2. Bilmes, J.: Natural statistical models for automatic speech recognition. Technical report, International Computer Science Institute, October 1999
3. Bilmes, J., Kirchhoff, K.: Factored language models and generalized parallel backoff. In: Proceedings of the 2003 Human Language Technology Conference of the North American Chapter of the Association for Computational Linguistics, pp. 4–6, May 2003. https://www.aclweb.org/anthology/N03-2002
4. Federico, M.: Language models. Presented at the Fourth Machine Translation Marathon - Open Source Tools for Machine Translation, January 2010
5. Federico, M., Cettolo, M.: Efficient handling of n-gram language models for statistical machine translation. In: Proceedings of the Second Workshop on Statistical Machine Translation, pp. 88–95. Association for Computational Linguistics, Prague, June 2007. https://www.aclweb.org/anthology/W07-0712
6. Kirchhoff, K., Bilmes, J., Duh, K.: Factored language model tutorial. Technical report, University of Washington, Department of EE, February 2008
7. Kirchhoff, K., Yang, M.: Improved language modeling for statistical machine translation. In: Proceedings of the ACL Workshop on Building and Using Parallel Texts, ParaText 2005, pp. 125–128. Association for Computational Linguistics, Stroudsburg (2005). http://dl.acm.org/citation.cfm?id=1654449.1654476
8. Mateus, M., Brito, A., Duarte, I., Faria, I.: Gramática da Língua Portuguesa. Editorial Caminho, S.A., Rua Cidade de Córdova n°2, 2610–038 Alfragide, Portugal (2003)
9. Peng, H., Long, F., Ding, C.: Feature selection based on mutual information: criteria of max-dependency, max-relevance, and min-redundancy. IEEE Trans. Pattern Anal. Mach. Intell. **27**, 1226–1238 (2005)
10. Santos, D., Rocha, P.: Evaluating cetempúblico, a free resource for Portuguese. In: Proceedings of the 39th Annual Meeting of the Association for Computational Linguistics, pp. 450–457. Association for Computational Linguistics, Stroudsburg, July 2001. http://www.linguateca.pt/superb/busca_publ.pl?idi=1141122240

Coreference in English OntoNotes: Properties and Genre Differences

Berfin Aktaş[✉], Tatjana Scheffler, and Manfred Stede

SFB1287, Research Focus Cognitive Sciences,
University of Potsdam, Potsdam, Germany
{berfinaktas,tatjana.scheffler,stede}@uni-potsdam.de

Abstract. The OntoNotes corpus is widely used for training and testing coreference resolution systems, but only little attention has so far been given to the differences between the different genres of language that the corpus is composed of. We are primarily interested in the contrast between spoken and written language, and thus we conducted in-depth analyses of various reference-related properties of the sub-corpora of OntoNotes, which yield several statistically significant differences. We compare these to predictions made in the Linguistics literature, and draw some conclusions for potential genre-specific implementations of coreference resolution.

Keywords: Ontonotes · Coreference · Genre · Spoken · Written

1 Introduction

The OntoNotes corpus [21] has been widely used for training and testing coreference resolution systems for the English language, and thereby its annotation scheme has become a quasi-standard for the field. One interesting aspect of the corpus is that its text documents come from different genres[1] (see Sect. 3); this is in contrast with many other data-oriented tasks in computational linguistics, which tend to address quite homogeneous corpora.

At the same time, not much is known about the potential differences between the OntoNotes sub-corpora so far. Our concern in this paper is predominantly with the question whether *spoken* and *written* language – in different forms – pose different challenges to automated resolution systems (or, for that matter, to the human reader). In linguistics, this question of a spoken/written contrast for coreference phenomena has received some attention, as we will outline in Sect. 2. In brief, the results are somewhat mixed, and our aim here is to gather empirical evidence that can contribute to clarifying the picture.

---

[1] For the purposes of this paper, we use the term *genre* in a broad sense of text variety, and *text* in the sense of "any passage (of language), spoken or written, of whatever length, that does form a unified whole" [11].

© Springer Nature Switzerland AG 2019
K. Ekštein (Ed.): TSD 2019, LNAI 11697, pp. 171–184, 2019.
https://doi.org/10.1007/978-3-030-27947-9_15

Besides this primary motivation for our study, we also expect that any difference in the coreference phenomenon between spoken and written language can have ramifications for automatic coreference resolution, when it is applied to language data from different modes. One indication for the relevance of genres are the experiments by [1], who tested an off-the-shelf coreference resolution system for English (which was trained on OntoNotes) on Twitter data. We compared their results to results of the same system on the portion of OntoNotes used as CoNLL 2012 Shared Task data[2] and found a performance decrease of 14% for the Twitter data. This indicates that the same off-the-shelf coreference system performs very differently on the spoken-like and nonstandard language in Twitter conversations than on other text genres.

In order to get further insights into such performance differences, in this paper, we systematically compare the various sections of the OntoNotes corpus in terms of properties of the referring expressions (henceforth also called *mentions*) and the chains they form. We show that in particular the sections corresponding to spoken versus written language can be differentiated by properties of their referring expressions. The main contribution of the paper thus is to draw attention to these phenomena, explore them quantitatively, and thereby prepare for follow-up work that aims at adapting automatic coreference resolution to the needs of specific language modalities or genres. Furthermore, in future work it can be tested whether the differences we encountered can be utilized as additional features for systems doing automatic genre identification, insofar as they address a spoken/written contrast.

The paper is structured as follows: Sect. 2 discusses previous related work on coreference in spoken versus written language, or on genre differences. Then, in Sect. 3, we explain the structure of the OntoNotes corpus, and in Sect. 4 we present our methods for analyzing relevant aspects of coreference and show our results. Section 5 discusses the findings from the perspective of genre differentiation, and Sect. 6 draws some conclusions.

2   Related Work

A number of studies use quantitative corpus-based methods to examine the variation of coreference phenomena in terms of linguistically-motivated features. Variation is explored in different domains such as across languages [8,13–15], regional language varieties [16], production media (spoken, written, web) [2,4,9] and across genres in these domains. As for features, distance and frequency-based statistics are widely used for comparative purposes. Distance based measures are computed by taking the average of distance between referring expressions and their antecedents[3]. Different distance metrics are used in different studies, which yield partly incompatible results:

---

[2] We calculated this by taking the average of MUC, BCUBED and CEAF F1 scores in Table 4 in [1] as explained in http://conll.cemantix.org/2011/faq.html and comparing it with the CoNLL value in Table 3 in [6].

[3] The closest previous mention of the same referent.

- [5] and [14] measure the distance in terms of number of tokens. The findings of these studies are similar to each other: Average distance is longer in spoken texts than in written texts.
- [9] measures the distance in terms of number of clauses and argues that average distance is longer in spoken texts than in written texts.
- [2] measures the distance in terms of sentences and argue that the average distance is longer in written texts than in spoken texts.
- [4] measures the distance in terms of number of interfering references and concludes that the average distance is longer in written texts than in spoken texts.

The differences in the distance comparisons indicate that textual distance metrics are not always comparable. For instance, the distance in terms of tokens may not always correspond to distance in terms of clauses or sentences. This is one of the aspects we will address in this paper.

In the literature, we also find studies of the distribution of referring expressions in terms of their syntactic categories (i.e., pronouns vs. NPs) as a feature of the referential characteristics of texts. [9] argues that referential NPs are more frequent in written texts than in spoken conversations (47% in written texts vs. 22% in conversations), whereas [2,5] found different characteristics. On the one hand, [2,5] confirm the finding of [9] that NPs are more frequently used than pronouns in the written medium than in the spoken medium. But in written text, NPs are more frequent than pronouns as well (63% NPs vs. 29 % pronouns in written texts, reported in [2]), which is different from what [9] describes. An interesting finding regarding the distribution of syntactic categories, which is observed by [2,4,5,15,16], is that narrative genres (fiction) show spoken-like characteristics in terms of the usage of pronouns as referring expressions.

The other quantitative metrics for the investigation of coreference phenomena used in the literature are as follows: Number of referring expressions [4], number of referents [4,14], chain length [2,4,14]. We did not examine these features in this study because in the OntoNotes data some documents are artificially split into smaller parts and singletons are not annotated (see in Sect. 3); therefore, these metrics may create misleading results.

To our knowledge, although it is one of the largest resources of coreference, the OntoNotes corpus has not been extensively examined for quantitative comparison of genres in terms of their general coreference phenomena. However, there are some studies on OntoNotes that focus on the differences in genres in terms of certain specific coreference-related features. [12] investigated how organisational named entities are being referred to in English OntoNotes, and found that there is a correlation between the preferred reference type and the genre type (e.g., pronouns are more common in telephone conversations than newswire and broadcast news). [22] used OntoNotes as the empirical data for the prediction of the 'notional anaphora' task and found a correlation between genre and notional agreement (notional agreement is more common in broadcast conversations than in newswire). Zeldes used 20 features including PoS tags, semantic classes, and genre/medium for the classification task, and among these features, genre emerges as the third-most important one, which indicates that observed differences between genres can have a strong impact on the automatic classification task.

There is little work that specifically addresses the performance difference of coreference systems across genres. [17] reported the results of automatic coreference resolution for the various sections of OntoNotes. The tested system shows better performance on telephone conversations (64%) than news texts (56%) and broadcast news (59%). They evaluated these results and noted which sections turned out to be the "easiest" but did not assess the possible reasons. Beyond this result, we are aware of only one study that looks in detail at performance differences in OntoNotes (and also in two other corpora): [20] compared the performance of "domain-specific" and "generic" models, for both knowledge-poor statistical systems and for implementations using hand-crafted linguistic features.

We performed experiments with the Berkeley coreference resolution system [7] on the data that we are dealing with and observed similar performance differences according to genre. After dividing the dataset described in Sect. 3 into train and test sets, we trained the Berkeley resolver on the train set and test the system performance for the different genre sections of the data. The scores[4] according to genre are as follows: broadcast conversations 56%, broadcast news 63%, newswire 60%, telephone conversations 63%, and web texts 56%. Although the data size for each of the genres varies considerably, we still consider these numbers as possible indicators of variation in the coreference properties of different genres.

3   The OntoNotes Corpus

The OntoNotes corpus is composed of multi-language data (English, Arabic and Chinese) from a range of different sources and contains gold annotations at different linguistic layers such as part of speech tags, syntactic constituent parses and coreference chains. We conducted a variety of quantitative analyses on the coreference annotations of the English part of the OntoNotes corpus. This part of the corpus contains translations from Arabic and Chinese to English, as well as texts originally produced in English. For the purposes of this paper, we only considered the original English data, in order to avoid effects from potential translation divergences. The portion of the data we worked on contains texts from both the spoken and the written medium. Spoken data includes telephone conversations, broadcast conversations, and broadcast news, whereas written data contains newswire texts and web data. More specifically, the portions are:

---

[4] The performance rates are calculated with the CONLL scorer as explained in http://conll.cemantix.org/2011/faq.html.

telephone conversations (tc): transcripts of informal conversations from the
  CallHome corpus
broadcast conversations (bc): transcripts of conversations in TV talk shows
  from CNN and MSNBC
broadcast news (bn): transcripts of broadcast news from ABC, CNN, NBC,
  MNB, Public Radio International and Voice of America
newswire (nw): texts from the Wall Street Journal
web data (wb): texts from web blogs and news groups

We used the CoNLL-formatted OntoNotes data [17] and processed it by
using the open source library AllenNLP [10]. The data is organized into CoNLL
2011/2012-formatted *files*. Since some texts belonging to *bc*, *tc* and *wb* genres
were considered too long for coreference annotation in OntoNotes, they have
been split into smaller parts (i.e. *documents* in CoNLL terminology) during the
annotation process [18]. Therefore, there are some *files* in the data which contain
more than one *document*.

The general statistics on the final sub-corpus we used is shown in Table 1. The
corpus contains 903K *tokens* distributed across 2040 *documents*. The proportion
of the data according to genre in terms of sentences, clauses and tokens is also
presented in the table. We counted the clauses by applying the criteria introduced
in Sect. 4.1 below. A visual representation of the proportion of different genres in
the data is shown in Fig. 1 in terms of tokens and clauses. The figure shows that
measuring the data size in terms of different units result in different proportions.
For instance, in the token-based division of data in Fig. 1, *tc* covers 11.5% and
nw covers 39.4% of the data, whereas the proportion of the *tc* genre becomes
16.5% and the size of the *nw* decreases to 32% of the whole data in clause-based
comparison of genre sizes. This difference is caused by the difference in average
lengths of clauses in *tc* and *nw* data, which is also given in Table 1.

Descriptive statistics on the coreference chains computed from the data are
presented in Table 1 as well. These chain and mention statistics give a good
overview of the data that we are dealing with, but they should be interpreted
carefully by considering the specifications in the OntoNotes annotation guidelines. For instance, non-referential pronouns (e.g., expletives) and singleton mentions are not annotated in OntoNotes [3]. In addition to that, as stated in [17],
coreference annotation only covers document-level chains. As pointed out above,
however, the texts belonging to *tc*, *bc* and *nw* genres are divided into different
documents. Therefore, a more precise quantitative description of the genres in
terms of referring expressions and chains could be computed only by providing
the missing inter-document annotation of coreference, and by also marking the
singletons; these steps would require substantial effort, though.

Table 1. General statistics on the dataset

	Entire dataset	tc	bc	bn	nw	wb
# of files	1625	46	17	947	597	18
# of documents	2040	142	274	947	597	80
# of tokens	903467	103587	147118	225657	355641	71464
# of sentences	55570	14162	10798	12147	14786	3677
# of clauses	110680	18242	21719	27219	35428	8072
# of coreference chains	25872	2461	4518	8042	9328	1523
# of mentions	103625	15345	20235	28103	34115	5827
# of ignored non-nominal mentions	2248	278	523	676	664	107
# of utterances not counted as clauses	3933	3266	334	262	12	59
Average document length (token)	442.9	729.5	537.0	238.3	595.7	893.3
Average document length (sentence)	27.2	99.7	39.4	12.8	24.8	46.0
Average document length (clause)	54.3	128.5	79.3	28.7	59.3	101.0
Average sentence length (token)	16.3	7.3	13.6	18.6	24.1	19.4
Average sentence length (clause)	2.1	1.7	2.1	2.3	2.4	2.2
Average clause length (token)	8.2	5.4	6.7	8.3	10	8.8

4 Methods and Results

We used distance- and frequency-based metrics in the quantitative comparison of texts according to the genre they belong to and the medium they are produced in (i.e., spoken or written). First, we computed the linear distances between anaphoric third-person pronouns and their antecedents. As specified in Sect. 2, distance-based metrics are commonly used for quantitative description and comparison of coreference features across different genres. In those studies, distance is computed in terms of different units, which are, however, often not specified in detail. This concerns questions such as how the text is tokenized, and

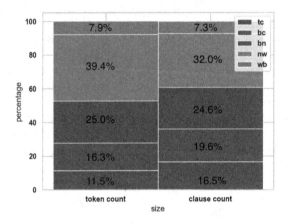

Fig. 1. Data size distribution in terms of token count and clause count

which syntactic units are being considered as clauses. We consider a definition of those units as important for interpreting the differences and similarities in the results of different studies. In the following subsection, we thus give a detailed description of the distance measures and relevant procedures used in our study.

In addition to distance-based comparison, we also examined the relative frequency distribution of mentions according to their syntactic categories (i.e., NP vs. pronoun) and for pronouns according to first, second and third person. For details, see Sect. 4.2. Considering these comparative metrics with the descriptive statistics of gold data in Table 1, such as the average sentence length (in terms of tokens and clauses), the average document size (in terms of different units) in the genres, etc., can provide a solid basis for comparing our findings with the relevant work in the literature.

4.1   Distance Metrics

As Table 1 shows, the average length of clauses differs across genres. Therefore, we calculated the distance in terms of both tokens and clauses to describe the data from different perspectives.

We do not consider the usage of reflexive pronouns as anaphoric when they are used for emphasis, as in "He himself would bring.." or "It was the evacuation itself that proved the..". In these constructions, the reflexive pronouns immediately follow the phrase they are coreferring with. We did not take these constructions into account in distance-based comparison of texts.

As specified in [3], verbs are annotated as mentions in the OntoNotes corpus when they refer to the same entity as a nominal mention. An example chain containing a verbal entity is "chain_meeting=[met, the meeting, the APEC meeting, it]". Since we want to focus on nominal coreference (which is also in line with the majority of work in coreference resolution), we excluded these non-nominal mentions (such as *met* in "chain_meeting") in our analyses. As it can be seen in Table 1, the portion of excluded non-nominal mentions is relatively small compared to the total number of mentions ($\approx 2\%$ for the whole dataset), and 95% of them are located either in chain-initial or in chain-final position. Therefore, we do not expect a significant impact of excluding these non-nominal mentions in our distance-based and categorical distribution analyses.

Clause-Based Distance. The first step in measuring the clause-based distance (CBD) between two mentions is determining the clause boundaries in the texts. For this purpose, we used the constituent syntactic parse trees of the sentences provided in the OntoNotes annotations. We marked the first token of each clause as an indicator of a new clause and counted the number of clause indicators between two mentions for calculating the CBD. The labels indicating complete clauses in the data are S, SBAR, SQ, SINV, and SBARQ; incomplete clause labels are RRC and FRAG. We took these labels as potential indicators of the beginning of new clauses. Some examples regarding how we deal with different cases in the data are presented in Table 2.

Table 2. Examples on the computation of clause boundaries

Pseudo-parse[a]	# of clauses
SBARQ(**What** kind of memory?)	1
S(S(**This** is him), S(**thank** you all for watching).)	2
S(S(**He** threatened her) she said.)	2
SBARQ(**Well**, what exactly SQ(was this incident)?)	1
S(**and** she said SBAR(**that** um S(she feels S(**she** was brainwashed)))).)	3
S(SBAR(**What** S(**you** are interested in) is SBAR(**exactly** what S(we will be focusing on))).)	3
FRAG(**For** instance perhaps the chapter seven resolution.)	1

[a] The token which is signalling the start of a new clause according to our procedure is marked with **bold** case.

There exist some utterance parses in the corpus that do not have a clausal label. These utterances are considered as clauses in our calculations if they contain a nominal tag, such as in "The first time?", "Question for you.", "The look in her eyes", and "Pat Fitzgerald", and/or a verbal tag as in "Go in not go in or go in with greater strength", "Look", "Paid or unpaid?" and "be over". We excluded utterances with no clause marker and without a nominal or verbal tag, such as "Hello", "Absolutely", "Hopeless and angry", "No longer", and "Ouch". The distribution of utterances that we do not consider as clauses is presented in Table 1. The biggest portion of these utterances are encountered in the *tc* data (83%). We calculated the CBD means for all the genres both for the case where we didn't count these utterances as clauses and for the case where we counted them as clauses, in order to see the impact of ignoring them in CBD measurements. The results are shown in Table 3.

Table 3. Distance-based comparison of pronoun-antecedent pairs across genres

Genre	CBD 1[a]	CBD 2[b]	TBD
Entire dataset	1.94	2.04	14.62
tc	2.97	3.49	16.90
bc	2.44	2.47	16.21
bn	1.65	1.66	13.01
nw	1.45	1.45	14.07
wb	1.42	1.42	13.23

[a] Utterances with no clausal label, no NP or VP are ignored.
[b] Utterances with no clausal label, no NP or VP are counted as a clause.

As expected, the biggest difference between "CBD 1" and "CBD 2" is observed for the *tc* genre. We computed the statistical significance of the results and verified that ignoring the clauses with no clause label, no NP and no VP does not have an impact on the statistical significance of differences between genres in terms of CBD mean values. Therefore, we henceforth only consider the "CBD 1" values in our analysis.

Token-Based Distance. In the OntoNotes corpus, the texts are tokenized by following the Penn TreeBank tokenization scheme[5] [21]. The main principles of this scheme are as follows:

- Words and punctuation marks are considered as separate tokens.
- Verb contractions and genitive morphemes are separated from the root (e.g. children's → children,'s; I'm → I,'m).

We count the number of tokens between the initial tokens of two mentions to calculate the linear token-based distance (TBD) between them. Some examples regarding how we deal with different cases in the data are shown in Table 4. The quantitative comparison of different genres in terms of TBD mean values is shown in Table 3. We discuss the implications of these distance values in Sect. 5.

Table 4. Examples on the computation of token-based distances

String[a]	Token-based distance
[**The** manager]$_i$ is being treated in the hospital, but [**his**]$_i$ life..	10
I had [**one** client who said that [**he**]$_i$'d pay me]$_j$..	5
When I saw [**him**]$_i$ talking about [**himself**]$_i$..	3
He threatened [**her**]$_i$ [**she**]$_i$ said.	1
He threatened her [**she**]$_i$ said. He threatened to kill [**her**]$_i$..	7
Er, [**they**]$_i$ [**themselves**]$_i$ claim that..	Ignored

[a] We use subscripts to mark the coreferent mentions, and **boldface** for the beginnings of mentions.

4.2 NP and Pronoun Distributions

As a third metric for the genre/medium comparison, we computed the relative distribution of mentions according to their syntactic categories (pronoun vs. full NP). We encountered the following personal pronoun varieties in the corpus: "i", "you", "he", "she", "it", "we", "they", "me", "mine", "him", "her", "us", "them", "myself", "yourself", "himself", "herself", "itself", "ourselves", "yourselves", "themselves", "yours", "his", "hers", "its", "ours", "theirs", "'s", "y'all". We computed the relative frequencies of these personal pronouns and other nominal mentions for the elements of coreference chains; the comparative results are given in Fig. 2. In addition to the distribution of syntactic categories, we also computed the frequency distribution of personal pronouns according to their "person" type (fist, second, third). The representative chart for the pronoun distribution is shown in Fig. 3.

---

[5] ftp://ftp.cis.upenn.edu/pub/treebank/public_html/tokenization.html.

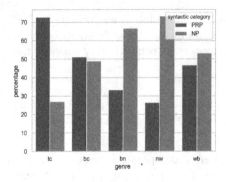
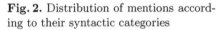
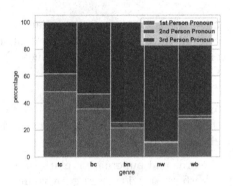

Fig. 2. Distribution of mentions according to their syntactic categories

Fig. 3. Distribution of personal pronouns per genre

5   Genre Differentiation

As shown in Sect. 2, in the literature certain quantitative features of coreference chains are correlated with genres and production medium. Our own results in the previous section confirm this, and we now revisit them from the perspective of genre/medium.

First, the application of one-way ANOVA to the mean distances in Table 3 indicates differences between the genres. Since we have five genres in our dataset, we run Tukey's HSD as a post-hoc test to check for statistical significance between the genres. The test yields the p-value results shown in Table 5.

We found that spoken genres allow longer pronominal CBD mean values which is compatible with the results of [9]. There is a clear distinction between *bc*, *tc* on the one hand, and *nw*, *wb* on the other hand in this regard. Although the *bn* genre also allows longer average CBD values than the written genres, the statistical tests do not indicate significant differences between them. We also observe intra-medium variation for spoken genres. The results indicate that informal *tc* texts allow longer CBD values than *bc* texts, which are probably less spontaneous.

The TBD metric suggests slightly different findings. Again, the two spoken genres *tc* and *bc* allow longer average distance than written texts, as it is argued in [5,14]. Further, *bn* is closer to written texts, which makes sense as the *bn* genre mostly contains prepared speeches (i.e., edited language). In contrast to the CBD case, we do not observe intra-medium variability for spoken data (i.e., no statistically significant difference is found between *bc* and *tc*). We conclude that both CBD and TBD can be useful for differentiating the medium of the text; while CBD can show fine-grained differences for intra- and inter-medium comparisons, TBD can be used only for more coarse-grained classification of genres according to medium.

The second type of comparison depends on the distribution of mentions in terms of their syntactic categories. We applied the Chi-square test to the values in Fig. 2, which indicates that the observed differences between the genres are

Table 5. Statistical significance of pairwise pronominal distance differences between genres ('***' = p < 0.05)

Genre pair	CBD	TBD
tc-bc	***	n.s.[a]
tc-bn	***	***
tc-nw	***	***
tc-wb	***	***
bc-bn	***	***
bc-nw	***	***
bc-wb	***	***
bn-nw	***	n.s
bn-wb	n.s	n.s
nw-wb	n.s	n.s

[a] Not significant.

not due to chance (p-value < 2.2e–16). The pairwise Fisher Test confirms that the differences are significant for all genre pairs. Our results confirm the findings of [2,5] that pronouns are more common than full NPs in conversational spoken genres (*bc* and *tc*). In written genres, NPs are more common, and the *bn* genre shows written-like characteristics in this sense.

Finally, we computed the relative frequency distribution of personal pronouns for all genres as represented in Fig. 3, and verified the statistical significance of the differences with the Chi-square test (p-value < 2.2e–16). The pairwise tests indicate that the differences between genre pairs in terms of the relative frequency of personal pronouns are not due to chance. The frequency of second person pronoun is very small ($\approx$0.5%) in the *nw* data; therefore it is not clearly visible in the chart. The minimal usage of second person pronouns in *nw* data, and slightly higher usage in *bn* and *wb* data indicates the more "interactive" nature of *bn* and *wb* genres in comparison to *nw*. The higher usage of first person pronouns in *tc* and *bc* genres comparing to written genres (including *bn*) can be considered another distinguishing characteristic of conversational spoken texts. Given the speaker information, it is not a challenging task to construct the coreference chains composed of first and second person pronouns. Therefore, this distinguishing feature of spoken medium can be one reason of relatively high performance rates of automated resolvers on conversational data reported in Sect. 2.

6   Conclusion and Outlook

Our analysis of distance-based metrics shown in Table 3 shows that both in terms of token-based as well as clause-based distance, the spoken sub-corpora of OntoNotes exhibit a significantly longer distance between mentions of a referring entity. However, this observation excludes the broadcast news (bn) section, which instead matches the written corpora in terms of token distance. The frequency-based metrics shown in Figs. 2 and 3 show similar tendencies: While *bc* and *tc* are grouped together, *bn* is closer to the written genres in terms of these features. This indicates that the spoken medium might not be the critical factor for the distance, but rather the conversational nature of two of the genres. We plan to investigate this further by analyzing written conversations, as in chat or microblogs.

We also plan to extend our study from OntoNotes to another corpus, such as ARRAU [19], especially because the annotation scheme of OntoNotes has some disadvantages for our purposes (no singletons, artificial division of larger texts into smaller documents). In addition, we want to investigate the average length and/or syntactic complexity of noun phrases as another feature for the comparison.

Finally, as indicated earlier, we intend to examine the effects of genre differences for automatic coreference resolution: The previous findings on performance differences need to be explained, and possibilities for factoring the genre information into the resolution process are to be explored.

Acknowledgments. This work was funded by the Deutsche Forschungsgemeinschaft (DFG, German Research Foundation), Projektnummer 317633480, SFB 1287, Project A03. We thank the anonymous reviewers for their comments.

References

1. Aktaş, B., Scheffler, T., Stede, M.: Anaphora resolution for twitter conversations: an exploratory study. In: Proceedings of the First Workshop on Computational Models of Reference, Anaphora and Coreference, New Orleans, Louisiana, pp. 1–10. Association for Computational Linguistics, June 2018
2. Amoia, M., Kunz, K., Lapshinova-Koltunski, E.: Coreference in spoken vs. written texts: a corpus-based analysis. In: Chair, N.C.C., et al. (eds.) Proceedings of the Eight International Conference on Language Resources and Evaluation (LREC 2012), Istanbul, Turkey. European Language Resources Association (ELRA), May 2012
3. BBN Technologies: Co-reference Guidelines for English OntoNotes Version 7.0 (2007)
4. Biber, D.: Using computer-based text corpora to analyze the referential strategies of spoken and written texts. In: Svartvik, J. (ed.) Directions in Corpus Linguistics: Proceedings of Nobel Symposium 82, Stockholm, 4–8 August 1991, pp. 213–252. Berlin, Mouton (1992)
5. Biber, D., Finegan, E., Johansson, S., Conrad, S., Leech, G.: Longman Grammar of Spoken and Written English, 1st edn. Longman, Harlow (1999)
6. Clark, K., Manning, C.D.: Entity-centric coreference resolution with model stacking. In: Proceedings of the 53rd Annual Meeting of the Association for Computational Linguistics and the 7th International Joint Conference on Natural Language Processing (Volume 1: Long Papers), Beijing, China, pp. 1405–1415. Association for Computational Linguistics, July 2015

7. Durrett, G., Klein, D.: Easy victories and uphill battles in coreference resolution. In: Proceedings of the 2013 Conference on Empirical Methods in Natural Language Processing, Seattle, Washington, USA, pp. 1971–1982. Association for Computational Linguistics, October 2013

8. Engell, S.: Coreference in English and German: A Theoretical Framework and Its Application in a Study of Court Decisions. Logos Verlag, Berlin (2016)

9. Fox, B.A.: Discourse Structure and Anaphora: Written and Conversational English. Cambridge University Press, Cambridge (1987)

10. Gardner, M., et al.: Allennlp: a deep semantic natural language processing platform. In: Proceedings of Workshop for NLP Open Source Software (NLP-OSS) (2017)

11. Halliday, M., Hasan, R.: Cohesion in English. Longman, London (1976)

12. Hardmeier, C., Bevacqua, L., Loáiciga, S., Rohde, H.: Forms of anaphoric reference to organisational named entities: hoping to widen appeal, they diversified. In: Proceedings of the Seventh Named Entities Workshop, Melbourne, Australia, pp. 36–40. Association for Computational Linguistics, July 2018

13. Kunz, K., Lapshinova-Koltunski, E.: Cross-linguistic analysis of discourse variation across registers. cross-linguistic studies at the interface between lexis and grammar. Nord. J. Eng. Stud. **14**, 258–288 (2015)

14. Kunz, K., Lapshinova-Koltunski, E., Martínez, J.M.: Beyond identity coreference: contrasting indicators of textual coherence in English and German. In: Proceedings of the Workshop on Coreference Resolution Beyond OntoNotes (CORBON 2016), pp. 23–31. Association for Computational Linguistics (2016)

15. Lapshinova-Koltunski, E.: Exploration of inter- and intralingual variation of discourse phenomena. In: Proceedings of the Second Workshop on Discourse in Machine Translation, DiscoMT@EMNLP 2015, Lisbon, Portugal, pp. 158–167, 17 September 2015

16. Neumann, S., Fest, J.: Cohesive devices across registers and varieties: the role of medium in English. In: Schubert, C., Sanchez-Stockhammer, C. (ed.) Variational Text Linguistics: Revisiting Register in English, Topics in English Linguistics, Berlin, Boston, vol. 90, pp. 195–220. DeGruyter (2016)

17. Pradhan, S., et al.: Towards robust linguistic analysis using ontonotes. In: Proceedings of the Seventeenth Conference on Computational Natural Language Learning, pp. 143–152. Association for Computational Linguistics (2013)

18. Pradhan, S., Moschitti, A., Xue, N., Uryupina, O., Zhang, Y.: ConLL-2012 shared task: modeling multilingual unrestricted coreference in ontonotes. In: Joint Conference on EMNLP and CoNLL - Shared Task, pp. 1–40. Association for Computational Linguistics (2012)

19. Uryupina, O., Artstein, R., Bristot, A., Cavicchio, F., Rodríguez, K.J., Poesio, M.: ARRAU: linguistically-motivated annotation of anaphoric descriptions. In: Proceedings of the Tenth International Conference on Language Resources and Evaluation LREC 2016, Portorož, Slovenia, 23–28 May 2016

20. Uryupina, O., Poesio, M.: Domain-specific vs. uniform modeling for coreference resolution. In: Proceedings of the Eighth International Conference on Language Resources and Evaluation (LREC-2012), Istanbul, Turkey, pp. 187–191. European Language Resources Association (ELRA), May 2012

21. Weischedel, R., et al.: Ontonotes release 5.0 ldc2013t19. Web Download. Linguistic Data Consortium, Philadelphia, PA (2013)
22. Zeldes, A.: A predictive model for notional anaphora in English. In: Proceedings of the First Workshop on Computational Models of Reference, Anaphora and Coreference, New Orleans, Louisiana, pp. 34–43. Association for Computational Linguistics, June 2018

The TransBank Aligner: Cross-Sentence Alignment with Deep Neural Networks

Ahmad Aghaebrahimian[1,2(✉)], Michael Ustaszewski[1], and Andy Stauder[1]

[1] Department of Translation Studies, University of Innsbruck, Innsbruck, Austria
[2] Institute of Applied Information Technology,
Zurich University of Applied Sciences, Winterthur, Switzerland
{Ahmad.Aghaebrahimian,Michael.Ustaszewski,Andy.Stauder}@uibk.ac.at

Abstract. Sentence-aligned parallel bilingual corpora are the main and sometimes the only required resource for training Statistical and Neural Machine Translation systems. We propose an end-to-end deep neural architecture for sentence alignment. In addition to one-to-one alignment, our aligner can perform cross alignment as well. We used three language pairs from Europarl corpus and an English-Persian corpus to generate an alignment dataset. Using this dataset, we tested our system both in isolation and in an SMT system. In both settings, we obtained significantly better results compared to two competitive baselines.

Keywords: Sentence alignment · Parallel corpora ·
Deep neural network

1 Introduction

Sentence alignment is useful in many Natural Language Processing (NLP) tasks, including word-sense disambiguation, bilingual lexicography, and especially Statistical and Neural Machine Translation (SMT, NMT). Due to recent advances in Deep Neural Networks (DNN), NMT [7,15] has advanced rapidly in a few past years. A typical NMT system requires millions of source sentences aligned with their translations to be adequately trained. In some state-of-the-art NMT systems [26] sentence-aligned parallel corpora are the only required resource for training.

Although large quantities of parallel documents can be obtained easily [23], they are of limited value without transformation into sentence-aligned text pairs. Parallel sentence extraction from a document-aligned text is not a trivial task for mainly two reasons.

First, the pairs of aligned sentences may arrange in different beads[1] with different fertility rate. Although, one-to-one beads constitute the majority of the beads, two-to-one, one-to-two, etc. can be found in parallel texts too.

---

[1] A bead specifies how many source sentences are aligned with how many target ones.

© Springer Nature Switzerland AG 2019
K. Ekštein (Ed.): TSD 2019, LNAI 11697, pp. 185–196, 2019.
https://doi.org/10.1007/978-3-030-27947-9_16

Second, although the source and target sentences of a parallel pair are in near positional proximity, they are not always in the exact same order. It means that the source sentence in the nth position of a source text could change to the mth position in the target text as a result of so-called translation shifts [12] employed by the translator. Therefore, there is not an easy or systematic way to recognize cross-alignment in parallel texts.

Failure in cross-alignment detection is a big concern in linguistic and contrastive studies where the data quality is the primary concern. Even in applied studies like Machine Translation (MT) where large quantities of data compensate for the slight decrease in data quality caused by the inability to identify cross-alignment, new accurate cross-alignment methods may extend the capacity of the algorithms beyond sentence boundary and lead to more coherent and naturally structured translations by capturing inter-sentence relations.

To address these issues we designed and implemented *TransBank Aligner*, a deep neural architecture enhanced by an attention mechanism which extracts one-to-one and cross-alignments in parallel texts. We hypothesize that the use of deep neural networks equipped with the attention mechanism enhances the quality of sentence alignment significantly. We confirmed the validity of this hypothesis using the results obtained from our intrinsic and extrinsic experiments.

The contribution of our work are, first, designing an end-to-end architecture for sentence alignment with a complexity of $O(n)$ with n being the length of the document and second, showing experimentally that the aligner works well.

2   Related Work

Sentence alignment has a history as long as the history of MT. Statistical analysis of sentence length, either character-wise [11] or word-wise [6] is the first successful method for sentence alignment. These two approaches, combined with some other techniques like dynamic programming or vocabulary matching, were used by many researchers [3–5,8,9,29] for sentence alignment.

Some open-source or commercial implementations of these methods are already available on the market. They include but not limited to Bleualign [25], which uses BLEU scores [20] for alignment; Hunalign which uses a length-based approach based on Gale and Church method [11]; the commercial ABBYY Aligner; and Unitex Aligner, which works based on a character-length algorithm. Many of these aligners does not support cross alignment. Moreover, some aligners based on dynamic programming assume specific formatting in input texts, such as having paragraph delimiters, without which the alignment of long passages becomes infeasible.

Other successful approaches for sentence alignment are beam searching [27] and classifier-based methods (e.g. Maxent classifier [19]). One way of training a classifier-based model is to train a word alignment model, such as IBM Model 1 [5] or HMM-based word alignment [30] and to use it to generate features for training a binary classifier. The other possibility is to use a Siamese deep neural network to extract the features automatically [13]. The classifier is applied on all or, using a pruning heuristic, on some fractions of all Cartesian products between the source and target sentences to identify parallel ones.

Classifier-based aligners are more robust and less dependent on language-specific characteristics of language pairs. However, they suffer from the imbalance between positive and negative samples. In a parallel document, positive and negative sentences are in the order of $O(n)$ and $O(n^2)$ respectively, which makes such systems not very scalable.

In our system, by defining a windowing mechanism, we keep the complexity of both correct and wrong alignments at $O(n)$. In this approach at training time, given each source sentence, we only need one correct and one wrong alignment to train the system. At testing time, given a source sentence, we estimate a probability distribution on a limited number of sentences around the target sentence with the same position as the source sentence and take the target sentence with the highest probability as the correct alignment. Compared to many open-source aligners, this approach is fast enough already. Still, using some heuristics like length disparity pruning, which defines a Poisson distribution over the length of source and target sentences and prunes those which fall under some threshold [18], we can significantly improve the speed.

TransBank Aligner is designed to work in two modes namely online and offline. In the online mode, we use the Google Translate API as a part of our system. Some recent studies successfully integrated Google or other translation services into their aligners [31]. To enhance these models, we show that using a DNN architecture over translated sentences to project them into a vector space achieves better results [1]. In the offline mode, we propose an approach which removes the need for external translation or any other third party services.

3 Training Data

To train our system, we used Europarl parallel corpus [16] and the English-Persian (EN-FA) corpus TEP [22] as a non-European language pair. The Europarl corpus is a collection of sentence-aligned texts in twenty one European languages. It is compiled from the proceedings of the European Parliament for training MT systems. TEP is collected by aligning movies subtitles.

In addition to (EN-FA) from TEP, we selected English-German (EN-DE), English-French (EN-FR), and English-Italian (EN-IT) from Europarl for our study. From each pair, we extracted the first 200 K sentences to retain the original passage structure. Then, we divided each dataset into 90%, 5%, and 5% for training, validation, and testing respectively making sure that there is neither duplicate nor overlap in any set.

Europarl was originally aligned using the Gale-and-Church algorithm [16]. Although it is acceptable to use these semi-perfect data for training, for testing we need perfect data. Therefore, we modified the validation and test data to make sure they are aligned perfectly. We ran the algorithm on validation and test data again and removed alignments with less than 95% confidence. This process removed around 1500 pairs from both sets. Then we randomly extracted

1000 pairs from the remaining and asked two annotators to decide if they are parallel. With 80% Cohen's kappa inter-rater agreement, both annotators agreed that more than 99% of the remaining sentence pairs in both sets are parallel. We used these remaining pairs (around 18500) for validation and evaluation in equal shares.

In our model, we need to project both source and target sentences into a shared multidimensional space and then try to compute the distance between them to get the nearest ones as parallel sentences. To project the target sentences, we need to translate them into the source language first.

Although having a perfect translation helps to obtain an accurate distance between the source and target sentences, having an approximation of the distance is sufficient to give us competitive results. Through initial prototyping, we observed that replacing the words in target sentences with their literal translation in the source language, does not affect the system performance significantly. The reason is that in this model, we do not need a perfect vector representation of the sentences. What we need is to estimate a relative distance between sentences hence, as long as the same mechanism translates all sentences, our need is already satisfied. To confirm this claim, we designed two modes for our system titled the online and the offline modes.

In the online mode, target sentences are translated into English using Google translation API in real-time, while in the offline mode, they are translated by replacing the words with their English equivalents using a dictionary. The system in the online mode, as we will see in Sect. 5, obtains slightly better results; however, it is dependent on an external service. In contrast, the offline mode is stand-alone, considerably faster (i.e., linear to the number of questions) and highly scalable (i.e., highly parallelizable).

In the offline mode, we need a dictionary which is representative enough of the target language. Replacing the words in target sentences with their English equivalents using this dictionary yields pseudo-translated texts which approximate the location of target sentences in vector space. To decide whether a dictionary is representative enough, we devised a metric called the replacement rate which measures how many words in target sentences are replaced with the entries of the dictionary. The replacement rate for each language pair in addition to dictionary size and the number of sentences are mentioned in Table 1.

We compiled the required dictionaries by extracting unique word types from the language-pair corpora and translating them using Google translation API. Any externally available dictionary with roughly the same replacement rate as in Table 1 will do the same job.

To provide the model with its inputs, we need to transform train, development and test sets each into three matrices of source, correctly aligned, and wrongly aligned target sentences. In these matrices, each row is a sentence and columns are the tokens in sentences. For the train set, the source sentences and the correctly aligned target sentences are directly retrieved from the pre-processed dataset as described above. The matrix of wrongly aligned target sentences is generated by randomly picking target sentences.

Table 1. Number of sentences in respective corpora, number of sampled sentences, number of English words, their dictionary size and the rate of word replacement in target sentences for four language pairs. The dictionaries are generated simply by extracting the unique word types from each corpus.

Language pair	Sentences	Sampled sentences	English words	Dictionary size	Replacement ratio
English-German	1,920,209	200,000	47,818,827	149,227	87.64%
English-French	2,007,723	200,000	50,196,035	95,589	82.86%
English-Italian	1,909,115	200,000	49,666,692	119,536	88.42%
English-Persian	612,086	200,000	4,499,928	132,193	81.19%

The matrices of the development and test set are compiled by taking and shuffling an n-sized window of target sentences given each source sentence. Now that the inputs are ready we can describe the details of the model.

4   Model

In this section, we describe the details of our model. In this model, we run a Recurrent Neural Network (RNN) over tokens of sentences to train their vector representations. An attention mechanism enriches the representation by attending to the source sentence. For RNN we used multi-layer Long Short-Term Memory (LSTM) [14] neural cells to encode textual strings into fixed-length vectors. Equations 1 to 3 and Eqs. 4 to 8 mathematically describe our source and target sentence encoding units respectively.

$W_{i,t}$ in Eq. 1 is the words in the ith training sentence each in time step t. $W_{i,t}$ is embedded using an embedding matrix which is already trained on billions of textual tokens. $W_{i,t}$ is fed into LSTM cells in Eqs. 1 and 2 to have a forward and backward pass over sentences. Then, the resulting vectors are concatenated (Eq. 3) to form a joint representation of the forward and backward LSTMs.

$$\overrightarrow{S}_{i,t} = LSTM(\overrightarrow{S}_{i,t-1}, W_{i,t}) \tag{1}$$

$$\overleftarrow{S}_{i,t} = LSTM(\overleftarrow{S}_{i,t+1}, W_{i,t})\} \tag{2}$$

$$S_i = [\overrightarrow{S}_{i,N}; \overleftarrow{S}_{i,1}] \tag{3}$$

Target sentences should be encoded into two categories: correct and wrong. The correct category includes correct alignments of source sentences while the wrong category comprises wrong random sentences with no connection to source sentences. The target encoding unit is similar to our source encoding unit, with the difference that it is equipped with an attention mechanism which helps to detect relevant and essential features in target sentences concerning source sentences.

In the target encoding unit, the input to LSTM cells are again word embeddings generated by the lookup table. An attention layer similar to the mechanism proposed in [24] (Eqs. 5 and 7) in this unit is added on top of the LSTM layers to update the output sequence of forward and backward LSTM cells with a focus on source sentences.

$$\overrightarrow{T}_{i,t} = LSTM(\overrightarrow{T}_{i,t-1}, W_{i,t}) \tag{4}$$

$$\overrightarrow{T}_{i,t} = ATT(\overrightarrow{T}_{i,t}, S_i) \tag{5}$$

$$\overleftarrow{T}_{i,t} = LSTM(\overleftarrow{T}_{i,t+1}, W_{i,t}) \tag{6}$$

$$\overleftarrow{T}_{i,t} = ATT(\overleftarrow{T}_{i,t}, S_i) \tag{7}$$

$$T_i = [\overrightarrow{T}_{i,N}; \overleftarrow{T}_{i,1}] \tag{8}$$

The correct and wrong categories are passed through the target encoding unit (Eqs. 4 to 8) to generate correct and wrong alignments. These alignments, in addition to source sentences, are fed into a Hinge loss function. This function increases the loss by any decrease in the distance between source sentences and wrong alignments and vice versa. The idea is to increase the loss when the vectors of the source and wrongly aligned target sentences get similar to each other.

The most straightforward way to measure the distance between two vectors is to use Cosine or Euclidean measures. However, we obtained better results using the Geometric mean of Euclidean and Sigmoid Dot product (GESD) proposed by Feng et al. [10]. Similar behaviour is reported in [2] too. In Sect. 5 we included the results on using both Cosine and GESD for this task.

GESD (Eq. 9) is a linear combination of L2-norm and the inner product of two vectors. The inner product measures the angle between two vectors and L2-norm is the forward-line semantic distance between two vectors.

$$GESD(V1, V2) = \frac{1}{1+exp(-(V1 \cdot V2))} * \frac{1}{1+||V1-V2||} \tag{9}$$

Now we can train the model by providing the loss function with its arguments. S_i in Eq. 10 denotes source sentences for which T_i^+ and T_i^- are generated as correct and wrong alignments, respectively. Parameter m is the margin between correct and wrong alignments. As we expect, the loss increases when the distance between a source language sentence and a correct alignment increases and viceversa. An illustration of the model is depicted in Fig. 1.

$$\mathcal{L} = \sum_i \max(0, m - GESD(S_i, T_i^-) + GESD(S_i, T_i^+)) \tag{10}$$

At testing time, we pass the logits generated by the model to a softmax function which transforms them into probabilities. Finally, we apply an argmax function over the probabilities to return the id of the predicted correct alignment given each source sentence.

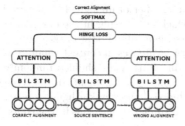

Fig. 1. Symbolic model of the system. Correct and wrong alignment modules estimate a source-sentence-aware vector representation for correctly and wrongly aligned target sentences. Hinge function estimates the loss by contrasting source sentence/wrong alignment and source sentence/correct alignment.

5   Results

We generated an embedding matrix by integrating the 300-dimensional pre-trained word vectors Glove[2] [21] into our lookup table. We kept the word vectors updated through training. We used 128-dimensional LSTM cells and used 'Adam' with parameters learning rate $= 0.001$, $\beta_1 = 0.9$, $\beta_2 = 0.999$ to optimize the network parameters. The recurrent and last-layer dropout ratios of the LSTMs are set to 0.5 and 0.2, respectively.

We used the Bleualign open source alignment tool [25] as the first baseline. We provide it with the same translations as we used for our aligner (i.e., Google translate service). As the second baseline, we implemented the Siamese architecture proposed by Gregoire and Langlais [13].

To make use of the full potential of our model, we designed two different test settings. In test setting A, we fed the algorithm with a source sentence and a window of n target sentences. The order of the sentences in this window is kept unchanged. In setting B, we shuffled the order of these sentences. In this setting, we provide a mean for checking the system performance on doing cross-alignment.

In both settings, our system needs to compute the vectors of a source sentence and all n target sentences and to find the nearest one to the source sentence. Therefore the performance of our system in both settings is the same. However, we observed that feeding the test data in setting B into Bleualign severely decreases the accuracy and increases the number of lost lines (Setting B in Table 2) which makes sense due to the fact that Bleualign is not designed to take care of cross-alignment[3].

Although the impact of GESD is already demonstrated in [10], to make a comparison between its results with another common similarity measure, we ran

---

[2] The vectors are publicly available at https://nlp.stanford.edu/projects/glove/.

[3] For a more detailed account of the performance of Bleualign on a regular test where the source and target sentences are mostly in the same order, and a comparative analysis of its performance with respect to other commonly available aligners, please refer to [31].

Table 2. Loss refers to the number of unaligned sentences, i.e., neither correctly nor incorrectly aligned ones, which are missing in the output text of Bleualign. Setting A and B refers to different arrangements of data in the target window provided for each source sentence. In setting A, sentences in context windows are in the same order as in the original dataset. In setting B, they are shuffled randomly. Setting B is a means to estimate model performance on cross-alignment. In the results reported for Bleualign, the lost sentences are excluded. TransBank Aligner-1 uses Cosine while TransBank Aligner-2 uses GESD as the similarity measure in their models. All the statistics are reported in percent.

Models	Offline (%)				Online (%)			
	EN-DE	EN-FR	EN-IT	EN-FA	EN-DE	EN-FR	EN-IT	EN-FA
Bleualign - Setting A	93.05	91.80	93.41	-	-	-	-	-
Bleualign Loss - Setting A	603	584	465	-	-	-	-	-
Bleualign - Setting B	62.34	67.19	64.73	-	-	-	-	-
Bleualign Loss - Setting B	3416	3257	3382	-	-	-	-	-
Gregoire and Langlais [13]	95.49	94.95	95.81	94.85	-	-	-	-
TransBank Aligner-1 - Setting A,B	96.73	96.15	96.47	95.16	97.68	96.73	97.19	96.84
TransBank Aligner-2 - Setting A,B	**97.12**	**96.53**	**97.13**	**96.71**	**98.43**	**97.89**	**98.61**	**97.29**
TransBank Aligner Loss	0	0	0	0	0	0	0	0

our experiments using both Cosine and GESD and obtained the best results using the latter.

Since the cross-aligned sentences are not annotated in the Europarl corpus, we manually extracted 300 cases of cross alignments generated by our model and asked our two annotators to check their accuracy. The result of their analysis showed only six examples of wrong alignments. For measuring the system performance on one-to-one alignments, we used automatic evaluation using the accuracy metric just on the first best-aligned sentences given each source sentence. The overall results of the system are presented in Table 2.

To check how robust the system is against window sizes we did an ablation study on the window size parameter for the EN-DE model. We observed that although reviewing more neighboring sentences means more computation and more overall testing time, the performance does not change significantly with larger or smaller windows. As indicated in Table 3, with $p > 0.95$ and sample size 10,000, there is no statistically significant difference among the performances of the system with different window sizes.

We also analyzed the learning curve of the system and the number of required sentences to train it in the online mode. The curve is illustrated in Fig. 2. As the graph shows, the system converges after around 150k samples. It seems the system begins to overfit at this point since from this point on getting any higher accuracy is difficult. This is in line with our observation in test data preparation, where we observed that there is a disagreement between humans annotators on whether some sentences are parallel or not.

By contrasting the replacement rate and the achieved system accuracy, we obtain a threshold for deciding which language pair requires a more

Table 3. System performance analysis on the first best alignment. The differences among the reported accuracies are not statistically significant.

Window size	Accuracy(%)	Time
5	96.98	≈480 sentences per minute
10	97.24	≈400 sentences per minute
15	97.36	≈340 sentences per minute

representative dictionary or extra preprocessing. Since all target languages are translated to English, and that setting for English-German had 98% accuracy, we can argue any other language pair with less than that accuracy requires more preprocessing or a more comprehensive dictionary.

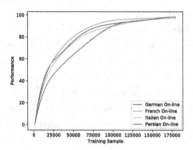

Fig. 2. The learning curve

Sentence alignment models are not themselves a means to an end, and their output is used for some downstream tasks, typically MT. To check how much our aligner improves the performance of a typical MT system, we trained an SMT model using the sentences aligned by our aligner and two other baselines. For preprocessing, we followed the same procedure as described above. We used the Moses toolkit to train an SMT model and utilized the Moses decoder [17] to decode the translations. Then, we computed their BLEU scores using the original sentences in the test set as reference sentences. The results of these two experiments reported in Table 4 show significant differences in the quality of system outputs compared to the other two aligners.

The error analysis performed on the aligned dataset and the MT-translated sentences shows that nested sentences, unknown words, overlapping sentences, and semantically similar sentences are the primary source of errors in the system. Another source of error is nested sentences when they are aligned to target sentences which are equivalent to only one clause of the source sentence. This is also the case for some of the overlapping sentences which contain several clauses. Finally, the last dominant class of errors is caused by sentences with similar contents, but different word orders or additional information not contained in the corresponding source/target sentence.

Table 4. SMT System performance on the aligned data generated by different systems.

Aligner	Dataset	Performance (BLEU)
Bleualign	Europarl (De-En)	24.2
Gregoire and Langlais [13]	Europarl (De-En)	24.9
TransBank Aligner	Europarl (De-En)	**25.6**

6   Conclusion

Sentence alignment is a crucial step in MT and some other NLP tasks, including word sense disambiguation and bi-lingual lexicography. Different information structure, topic development, translation shifts and some other linguistic phenomena in different languages may lead to nonlinear alignments such as cross-alignments in parallel documents.

In regular alignment tasks, the assumption is that the sentences of the source and target texts are close to each other. However, this assumption is not always valid. For instance, in a partial parallel passage where one document contains some more sentences which are absent in the other one, this assumption drops the accuracy of aligners sharply and leads to sentence loss (i.e., sentences for which no alignment from source or target sentences is found). Available alignment systems usually suffer from one or more shortcomings such as lack of support of nonlinear (e.g. cross-) alignment or losing sentences in the alignment process.

We proposed TransBank Aligner, a fast, accurate, and end-to-end neural architecture for sentence alignment. Compared to two state-of-the-art baseline aligners, our system obtained significantly better results in the system performance both as a stand-alone aligner and in a pipeline for an SMT system.

Due to its improved cross-alignment capability, the proposed aligner is suitable, among other things, for sentence alignment of literary and creative texts, in which non-linear and crossing relations are arguably more common. In this way, TransBank Aligner also contributes to the emerging line of research on computer-assisted translation and MT for creative texts [28].

We observed that the difference in the system performance for different language pairs is only due to the gap in their dictionary coverage because in all language pairs, source and target sentences are in English. Therefore, as long as there is access to a sufficiently representative dictionary suitable for literal translation, we can get competitive performance.

Acknowledgments. This work is part of the project "TransBank: A Meta-Corpus for Translation Research", funded by the Austrian Academy of Sciences (grant number GD 2016/56). The computational results presented in this work have been achieved (in part) using the HPC infrastructure LEO of the University of Innsbruck.

References

1. Aghaebrahimian, A.: Deep neural networks at the service of multilingual parallel sentence extraction. In: Proceedings of the 27th International Conference on Computational Linguistics (CoLing), Santa Fe, New Mexico, USA, pp. 1372–1383. Association for Computational Linguistics, August 2018
2. Aghaebrahimian, A.: Linguistically-based deep unstructured question answering. In: Proceedings of the 22nd Conference on Computational Natural Language Learning (CoNLL), Brussels, Belgium, pp. 433–443. Association for Computational Linguistics, October 2018
3. Braune, F., Fraser, A.: Improved unsupervised sentence alignment for symmetrical and asymmetrical parallel corpora. In: Proceedings of the 23rd International Conference on Computational Linguistics (CoLing): Posters, Stroudsburg, PA, USA, pp. 81–89. Association for Computational Linguistics (2010)
4. Brown, P.F., et al.: A statistical approach to machine translation. Comput. Linguist. **16**(2), 79–85 (1990)
5. Brown, P.F., Della Pietra, S.A., Della Pietra, V.J., Mercer, R.L.: The mathematics of statistical machine translation: parameter estimation. Comput. Linguist. **19**(2), 263–311 (1993)
6. Brown, P.F., Lai, J.C., Mercer, R.L.: Aligning sentences in parallel corpora. In: Proceedings of the 29th Annual Meeting on Association for Computational Linguistics ACL 1991, Stroudsburg, PA, USA, pp. 169–176. Association for Computational Linguistics (1991)
7. Cho, K., et al.: Learning phrase representations using RNN encoder-decoder for statistical machine translation. In: Proceedings of the 2014 Conference on Empirical Methods in Natural Language Processing (EMNLP), Doha, Qatar, pp. 1724–1734. Association for Computational Linguistics, October 2014
8. Church, K.W.: Char-align a program for aligning parallel texts at the character level. In: Proceedings of the Association for Computational Linguistics (ACL) (1993)
9. Church, K.W., Dagan, I., Gale, W.A., Fung, P., Helfman, J., Satish, B.M.: Aligning parallel texts: Do methods developed for English-French generalize to Asian languages? (1993)
10. Feng, M., Xiang, B., Glass, M.R., Wang, L., Zhou, B.: Applying deep learning to answer selection: a study and an open task. In: 2015 IEEE Workshop on Automatic Speech Recognition and Understanding (ASRU), pp. 813–820, December 2015
11. Gale, W.A., Church, K.W.: A program for aligning sentences in bilingual corpora. Comput. Linguist. **19**(1), 75–102 (1993)
12. Gambier, Y.: Translation Strategies and Tactics. Handbook of Translation Studies, vol. 1, pp. 412–418 (2010)
13. Grégoire, F., Langlais, P.: Extracting parallel sentences with bidirectional recurrent neural networks to improve machine translation. In: Proceedings of the 27th International Conference on Computational Linguistics, Santa Fe, New Mexico, USA, pp. 1442–1453. Association for Computational Linguistics, August 2018
14. Hochreiter, S., Schmidhuber, J.: Long short-term memory. Neural Comput. **9**(8), 1735–1780 (1997)
15. Kalchbrenner, N., Blunsom, P.: Recurrent continuous translation models. In: Proceedings of the Conference on Empirical Methods in Natural Language Processing (EMNLP) (2013)

16. Koehn, P.: Europarl: a parallel corpus for statistical machine translation. In: Conference Proceedings: The Tenth Machine Translation Summit, Phuket, Thailand, pp. 79–86. AAMT (2005)
17. Koehn, P., et al.: Moses: open source toolkit for statistical machine translation. In: Proceedings of the 45th Annual Meeting of the Association for Computational Linguistics Companion Volume Proceedings of the Demo and Poster Sessions, pp. 177–180. Prague, Czech Republic, June 2007
18. Moore, R.C.: Fast and accurate sentence alignment of bilingual corpora. In: Richardson, S.D. (ed.) AMTA 2002. LNCS (LNAI), vol. 2499, pp. 135–144. Springer, Heidelberg (2002). https://doi.org/10.1007/3-540-45820-4_14
19. Munteanu, D.S., Marcu, D.: Improving machine translation performance by exploiting non-parallel corpora. Comput. Linguist. **31**(4), 477–504 (2005)
20. Papineni, K., Roukos, S., Ward, T., Zhu, W.J.: Bleu: a method for automatic evaluation of machine translation. In: Proceedings of the 40th Annual Meeting on Association for Computational Linguistics ACL 2002, Stroudsburg, PA, USA, pp. 311–318. Association for Computational Linguistics (2002)
21. Pennington, J., Socher, R., Manning, C.: Glove: global vectors for word representation. In: Proceedings of the 2014 Conference on Empirical Methods in Natural Language Processing (EMNLP), Doha, Qatar, pp. 1532–1543. Association for Computational Linguistics, October 2014
22. Pilevar, M.T., Faili, H., Pilevar, A.H.: TEP: Tehran english-persian parallel corpus. In: Gelbukh, A. (ed.) CICLing 2011. LNCS, vol. 6609, pp. 68–79. Springer, Heidelberg (2011). https://doi.org/10.1007/978-3-642-19437-5_6
23. Resnik, P., Smith, N.A.: The web as a parallel corpus. Comput. Linguist. **29**(3), 349–380 (2003)
24. dos Santos, C.N., Tan, M., Xiang, B., Zhou, B.: Attentive pooling networks. CoRR abs/1602.03609 (2016)
25. Sennrich, R., Volk, M.: Iterative, MT-based sentence alignment of parallel texts. In: Proceedings of the 18th Nordic Conference of Computational Linguistics (NODALIDA 2011), Riga, Latvia, pp. 175–182. Northern European Association for Language Technology (NEALT), May 2011
26. Sutskever, I., Vinyals, O., Le, Q.V.: Sequence to sequence learning with neural networks. In: Ghahramani, Z., Welling, M., Cortes, C., Lawrence, N.D., Weinberger, K.Q. (eds.) Advances in Neural Information Processing Systems, vol. 27, pp. 3104–3112. Curran Associates, Inc. (2014)
27. Tillmann, C.: A beam-search extraction algorithm for comparable data. In: Proceedings of the ACL-IJCNLP 2009 Conference Short Papers ACLShort 2009, Stroudsburg, PA, USA, pp. 225–228. Association for Computational Linguistics (2009)
28. Toral, A., Wieling, M., Way, A.: Post-editing effort of a novel with statistical and neural machine translation. Front. Digital Humanit. **5**, 1–11 (2018)
29. Varga, D., et al.: Parallel corpora for medium density languages. In: Proceedings of the RANLP, pp. 590–596 (2007)
30. Vogea, S., Ney, H., Tillmann, C.: HMM-based word alignment in statistical translation. In: Proceedings of the 16th Conference on Computational Linguistics, pp. 836–841 (1996)
31. Wołk, K., Marasek, K.: A sentence meaning based alignment method for parallel text corpora preparation. In: Rocha, Á., Correia, A.M., Tan, F.B., Stroetmann, K.A. (eds.) New Perspectives in Information Systems and Technologies, Volume 1. AISC, vol. 275, pp. 229–237. Springer, Cham (2014). https://doi.org/10.1007/978-3-319-05951-8_22

Exploiting Large Unlabeled Data in Automatic Evaluation of Coherence in Czech

Michal Novák[✉], Jiří Mírovský, Kateřina Rysová, and Magdaléna Rysová

Faculty of Mathematics and Physics, Institute of Formal and Applied Linguistics,
Charles University, Malostranské nám. 25, 118 00 Prague 1, Czech Republic
{mnovak,mirovsky,rysova,magdalena.rysova}@ufal.mff.cuni.cz

Abstract. The paper contributes to the research on automatic evaluation of surface coherence in student essays. We look into possibilities of using large unlabeled data to improve quality of such evaluation. Particularly, we propose two approaches to benefit from the large data: (i) n-gram language model, and (ii) density estimates of features used by the evaluation system. In our experiments, we integrate these approaches that exploit data from the Czech National Corpus into the evaluator of surface coherence for Czech, the EVALD system, and test its performance on two datasets: essays written by native speakers (L1) as well as foreign learners of Czech (L2). The system implementing these approaches together with other new features significantly outperforms the original EVALD system, especially on L1 with a large margin.

Keywords: Text coherence · Automated essay scoring ·
Machine learning · Large data

1 Introduction

Essay scoring is a task important not only in education (both for students of a language as L1 – their native language – and L2 – second/foreign language), but often also in legal proceedings (e.g. L2 for immigration policy or university admissions). The evaluation of an essay often consists of the overall grade and several grades for various other aspects such as clarity, coherence, and topical relevance. Such scoring, when performed by humans, is a task which is time-consuming, expensive, and prone to bias. Automated essay scoring attempts to overcome all these drawbacks of human raters: it aims to be fast, cheap, and fair.

We focus on automatic evaluation of surface coherence in Czech essays, both in L1 and L2. Previously published works about this topic [23,24,28] have only used labeled data, i.e. corpora of essays manually annotated with coherence grades. Nevertheless, datasets for Czech with such annotation are very small, comprising around 1,000 essays.

© Springer Nature Switzerland AG 2019
K. Ekštein (Ed.): TSD 2019, LNAI 11697, pp. 197–210, 2019.
https://doi.org/10.1007/978-3-030-27947-9_17

We study possible ways to leverage also unlabeled texts, which are naturally available in much larger volume. Particularly, we work with the SYN collection of the Czech National Corpus [11], which consists mainly of journalistic texts, i.e. the texts assumed to be of high language quality. However, among the possible inputs of a system for evaluation, high quality language represents only one end of the scale. The effect of such data, if applied directly for training the system in a weakly supervised manner, would be questionable. Instead, we opt for an indirect approach. Information from the unlabeled data is represented as probability estimates and it flows to the system through some specific features.

We propose two approaches how to incorporate unlabeled data to the EVALD system [23] – a supervised evaluator of surface coherence in Czech. First, we build an n-gram language model and use it to estimate probabilities for entire texts. And second, we look at the data through the features that EVALD employs, building their probability density functions and then returning the probability estimates of the particular feature values.

In addition to exploiting unlabeled data, we designed a set of various additional features and examine the importance of the choice of the machine learning method and its hyperparameters. The reason for the latter is that almost all of the presented extensions lead to a substantial increase in a number of features, effect of which does not have to be evident unless the learning settings are optimized.

The subsequent text is structured into the following parts. Section 2 describes related work from several points of view relevant to the topics of the paper and Sect. 3 introduces the EVALD system. The following two sections present newly implemented features. Section 4 gives an overview of various new features that do not use unlabeled data, while Sect. 5 introduces two approaches to exploit unlabeled data. Section 6 gives details about labeled and unlabeled datasets used in the experiments, which are subsequently described in Sect. 7, along with the results. Section 8 offers several final remarks.

2   Related Work

Automatic assessment of quality of essays is a well-established field of research both for L1 and L2, and in a variety of languages. Most of the works focus on evaluating the overall grade (i.e. not specifically text coherence or other qualities of the text). They differ in several important aspects, most importantly in (i) size of training/test data, (ii) granularity of evaluation grades (for L2, various subsets of CEFR levels are often used), (iii) levels of language description they draw their features from (from phonetics to morphology, to syntax, and to higher levels), (iv) evaluation methods (classification, text ordering ranking,[1] etc.), and – last but not least – (v) usage of labeled and/or unlabeled data. Most of the works

---

[1] In the task of text ordering ranking, the original text is compared with a text created from the original one by a random permutation of its sentences; it is assumed that the original text is always more coherent than the shuffled one. This allows using raw data with no annotation of grades for training and testing the models.

(but not all) avoid using meta features such as text length or native language of the essay author.

Hancke and Meurers [9] use 1 027 German learner texts from the MERLIN corpus divided into a training set (721 texts) and a test set (302 texts), both sets unbalanced, with classes A1–C1. They process the texts up to the surface syntax layer, extract several groups of features (morphological, lexical and syntactic), and use the sequential minimal optimization classifier from the WEKA toolkit to predict the overall CEFR level grade of each text (i.e. not a grade for coherence).

Volodina et al. [34] predict the overall CEFR grade on the same scale of A1–C1 in 339 Swedish L2 texts. Their feature set consists of 61 features (lexical, morphological, syntactic and semantic features). Vajjala and Lõo [33] perform experiments on 879 Estonian learner texts, predicting the overall CEFR level of the texts. They restrict only to predicting four CEFR levels: A2–C1.

Vajjala later [32] investigates the role of various linguistic features on the performance of automatic scoring of English L2 essays, testing on a balanced sample of 3 thousand essays from the TOEFL11 Corpus (marked with the overall score low, medium and high) and an unbalanced sample from the First Certificate of English corpus (1248 texts with scores on a large scale of 1–40). In the experiments, the texts were automatically tagged, parsed and marked with coreference links. The 116 features cover word level, part of speech, syntactic characteristics, discourse properties, errors and other phenomena such as the prompt (the question for which the learners responded with answers) and the native language of the learner.

Zesch et al. [35] present result of experiments with a set of 96 essays of L2 learners of German, predicting one of three grades (good, fair, poor) as an overall evaluation of the essays. Their system uses a large set of lexical and morphological features (961 features in total).

For English, there are also works that focus directly on evaluation of text coherence (mostly in L1 texts). Lin et al. [15] use a discourse parser that automatically annotates a text with discourse relations, i.e. a framework similar to our approach that captures local coherence of the text. Their system further studies and evaluates a sequence of discourse relations in the text and their transitions, thus assessing global coherence of the text. Feng et al. [7], on the other hand, base their representation of discourse on the Rhetorical Structure Theory [16], which aims from the beginning at a representation of global coherence of a text. They use a parser that annotates the full hierarchical tree-like representation of coherence relations in the text.

Within the scope of similar tasks (evaluation of the overall essay score, text coherence, clarity, prompt adherence/topical relevance, etc.), there have also been attempts to use unlabeled data. Chen et al. [2] use an unsupervised machine learning method for automated essay scoring in Chinese. The authors use a voting algorithm based on initial scores and similarities between essays to iteratively train the system to score the essays.

Persing and Ng [26] use both labeled and unlabeled data for modeling prompt adherence in student L2 essays in English. In order to construct Latent Dirichlet

Allocation features, they collect all essays from a large International Corpus of Learner English written in response to each prompt (i.e. not just those in much smaller annotated dataset). Unsupervised modeling of topical relevance in English L2 learner texts has also been studied by Cummings et al. [5]. Via pseudo-relevance modeling, they expand (often short) prompts with topically related words.

Ostling et al. [25] developed a system for grading high school L1 essays in Swedish with one of four overall grades. It is based on a linear discriminant analysis classifier and incorporates lexical and morphological features. Some of their features use cross entropy with n-grams of part-of-speech tags and n-grams of words extracted from large amount of unlabeled data.

Some recent works utilize deep learning methods, trying to overcome a limitation of other approaches and distinguish texts that are only coherent formally from those that are coherent also semantically. These methods have been successfully applied, for example, to the sentence ordering task [6], automated essay scoring [4], and readability assessment [20].

3   EVALD

EVALD is a system for automatic evaluation of surface coherence in Czech essays [29], available in two variants. The first variant targeting texts written by native speakers (L1) automatically assigns to a text a grade on the scale 1–5 (excellent–fail). The second variant targeting texts written by foreign speakers (L2) estimates a CEFR proficiency level of the essay author on the scale A1–C2 (beginner–mastery). The system is freely downloadable under the Creative Commons license from the Lindat/Clarin digital repository,[2] available for usage and further development [21,22].

Decision making of EVALD is based on standard supervised learning. It thus must be trained on a set of documents that have been manually labeled with grades of surface coherence. The system first processes the documents and augments them with rich linguistic annotation. The annotated text is then described by a set of manually designed features, which are fed along with the labels into the machine learning method.

Text processing from the plain text to the deep syntactic layer and further to phenomena crossing the sentence boundary is performed withing a modular system for natural language processing Treex [27]. The analysis up to the deep syntactic layer uses a predefined Treex scenario: it comprises of numerous steps including tokenization, sentence segmentation, morphological tagging, and finally surface-syntax and deep-syntax parsing.

Additional modules have been implemented for the purposes of EVALD: automatic annotation of discourse relations (as reported in [28]), coreference relations (reported in [24]) and information structure (topic–focus articulation) of the sentences (see details in [23]).

---

[2] http://lindat.cz.

Feature Extraction. From the pre-processed texts, the EVALD system extracts a list of features divided into several sets according to various levels of language description. In the last published version of EVALD, i.e. EVALD 3.0 [23], it was altogether 180 features divided into the following feature sets: spelling (2 features), vocabulary (4 features), morphology (26 features), syntax (19 features), discourse (24 features), coreference (94 features), and topic–focus articulation (TFA; 11 features).

Table 1 gives an overview of types of features in the individual feature sets. Apart from feature sets and features already implemented in EVALD 3.0 (and reported in [23]), the table also presents newly designed features and new feature sets, which will be described in the following text. The original features are typeset in a regular font, while the new additions are highlighted in bold.

Table 1. Overview of feature sets in the EVALD systems, including the new features presented in this paper (new features are typeset in bold). Please note that all absolute numbers are normalized to the length of the text.

Feature set	Overview of features in the set
Spelling	Number of typos, punctuation marks, **accented characters and diphthongs**, etc.
Vocabulary	Richness of vocabulary expressed by several measures, average length of words, **percentage of lemmas být [to be], mít [to have] and the most frequent lemma**
Morphology syntax	Percentage of individual cases, parts of speech, degrees of comparison, verb tenses, moods, etc.
Syntax	Average sentence length, percentage of sentences without a predicate, number and types of dependent clauses, structural complexity of the dependency tree (number of levels, numbers of branches at various levels), **distributions of functors and part-of-speech tags at the first and second positions in the sentences**, etc.
Discourse	Quantity and variety of discourse connectives (intra-sentential, inter-sentential, coordinating, subordinating), percentages of four basic classes of types of discourse relations (temporal, contingency, contrast, expansion) and numbers of most frequent connectives, etc.
Coreference	Proportion of 21 different pronoun subtypes, variety of pronouns, percentage of null subjects and several concrete (most commonly used) pronouns, number of coreference chains (intra-sentential, inter-sentential) and distribution of their lengths, etc.
TFA	Variety of rhematizers (focalizers), number of sentences with a predicate on the first or second position, percentage of (contrastive-) contextually bound and non-bound words (more precisely: nodes in the tectogrammatical tree), percentage of SVO and OVS sentences, position of enclitics, percentage of coreference links going from a topic part of one sentence to the focus part of the previous sentence, etc.
Readability	**Various readability measures combining number of characters, syllables, polysyllables and sentences (Flesch-Kincaid Grade Level Formula, SMOG index, Coleman–Liau index, etc.)**
Language model	**Prob. estimates of the texts with respect to an n-gram language model**
Density estimates	**Prob. estimates of all the other features with respect to large unlabeled data**

4   Miscellaneous New Features

Various new features (51 in total) have been implemented in comparison with the previously reported version 3.0 of EVALD [23]. Some of them belong to previously existing sets of features – new features have been added to spelling (3 features: relative numbers of accented characters, diphthongs and capital characters after final punctuation), vocabulary (3 features: percentage of lemmas *být* [*to be*], *mít* [*to have*] and the most frequent lemma), and syntax (40 features: distributions of functors and part-of-speech tags at the first and second positions in the sentences). A new set of readability features has been introduced, consisting of 5 features that compare number of characters, syllables, polysyllables and sentences (Flesch-Kincaid Grade Level Formula [13], SMOG index [17], Coleman–Liau index [3], and their variations).

5   Exploiting Unlabeled Data

One of the main ideas in this paper is utilization of unlabeled data to improve the evaluation of surface coherence. That is, we want to benefit from the texts that are not assigned a grade describing their level of surface coherence. In the following sections, we propose two methods to achieve this goal: (i) n-gram language modeling, and (ii) density estimation of the feature values. The common feature shared by both methods is that they provide us with probability estimates of the input text, given a large corpus of high quality texts.

5.1   N-Gram Language Model

The problem of language modeling is to predict the next word given the previous words In *n-gram language models*, such prediction is based only on specified number of $n - 1$ previous words.[3] The probability of the next word is thus represented as $P(w_n|w_1...w_{n-1})$. Using a chain rule, one can then estimate probability of any text. Thanks to this property, the n-gram models have been largely used in machine translation. We also wish to take advantage of it in this work.

Training. We use the KenLM tool [10] to build a 5-gram language model of Czech. For robustness purposes, the tool employs modified Kneser-Ney smoothing and pruning of singleton n-grams. The model yielded by KenLM returns log probabilities with base 10.

---

[3] Unlike n-gram models, word-based [18,19] or character-based [12] recurrent neural language models are able to handle longer dependencies. However, we leave their incorporation in this task for the future work.

Querying and Feature Extraction. Given an essay, we calculate four log probability scores using our n-gram model based on two possible options of the following two parameters:

- *Whole text/sentence-by-sentence.* A log probability can be estimated for the whole text. Another option is to calculate it for each sentence separately and then average over all sentences of the text. In addition, we normalize the log probabilities by the number of words in the text or sentence.
- *Treated as a sentence?* If a query is desired to be treated as a sentence, it must be surrounded by special symbols representing the start and the end of the sentence.

Results of exponentiating each of the four scores form the individual features.

5.2   Density Estimates of Feature Values

The large unlabeled data may also serve as a source for estimating probability densities of all the features incorporated in our system. These density estimates would then be queried to find out to what extent the feature values describing an essay resemble the features describing the large corpus.

Training. To build density estimates for any feature, we first need to create a sufficiently big sample of documents from the unlabeled corpus. The corpus should be either inherently structured as a set of documents, or we need to split the corpus to documents on our own. Each document then must be processed with the same pre-processing pipeline as the one that has been applied to labeled essays (see Sect. 3). Subsequently, the same set of features as EVALD uses is extracted from a pre-processed document. Documents sampled from the corpus can then be understood as data points in a vector space and the extracted features as individual dimensions of the vector space.

We wish to find a probability distribution from which the set of data points could have been drawn. Moreover, we seek for a probability density function of a distribution that can then estimate probability of any data point in the vector space. We utilize the technique of *kernel density estimation* for this purpose. The principle of the technique lies in a smoothing kernel function $\kappa_h(x, x_i)$, which can be treated as a similarity function anchored in a specified data point x_i. The farther another data point x lies from x_i, the lower values the smoothing kernel returns. The width of the kernel (i.e. the degree of smoothing) is controlled by the bandwidth parameter h. In our system we employ Gaussian kernel,[4] which has the following form:

$$\kappa_h(\mathbf{x}, \mathbf{x_i}) = \exp \frac{\|\mathbf{x} - \mathbf{x_i}\|^2}{2h^2}$$

---

[4] Gaussian smoothing kernel corresponds to the *radial basis function* kernel frequently used in Support Vector Machines (SVM).

By averaging the kernels based in all data points seen in the data, we finally arrive at the desired density function.

Due to the curse of dimensionality, the need for support data points rises exponentially with rising number of features. The time complexity also rises as a result. Therefore, we decided to build density estimators for every feature independently on the others.

Querying and Feature Extraction. Having a density function modeled for every feature originally used by the system, we are able to yield probability estimates of features describing the training and testing documents. For each original feature, we represent its probability estimate as a new separate feature. As a result, the system that employs density estimates takes advantage of twice as much features than the original system.

6   Datasets

Our system mainly benefits from the labeled data, the collection of essays with grades of surface coherence level manually annotated. However, the presented feature extensions require also unlabeled data to be processed. The overall statistics of the datasets used in this work are shown in Table 2.

Labeled Data. EVALD is a system adopting mainly supervised learning methods. It thus relies on labeled datasets, namely the two described in detail in [24]. One dataset comprises texts written by Czech native speakers (L1), the other one by non-native speakers (learners) of Czech (L2). The datasets have been compiled from several language acquisition corpora available for Czech: the MERLIN corpus [1], CzeSL-SGT/AKCES 5 [30], and Skript2012/AKCES 1 [31].

The datasets are too small to provide reliable results if we performed evaluation in a standard fashion of splitting the data to train and test portions. Furthermore, the density estimation component doubles the number of features, which could harm the quality of grading unless the learning methods and their hyperparameters were tuned on a development test set. We thus adopt a nested 5-fold cross-validation, where in each fold the test partition is split into two halves, the development set for tuning the learning setting and the evaluation set for measuring the final scores. The learning setting that performs the best in average on development sets is then selected for building models to be evaluated. Finally, we take an average performance of the models over corresponding evaluation sets as a score reported in the results.

Table 2. Basic statistics on the labeled and unlabeled datasets, in total and for individual grades.

L1 dataset	1	2	3	4	5		Total
# documents	484	149	121	239	125		1,118
# sentences	20,986	4,449	2,913	3,382	939		32,669
# tokens	301,238	65,684	40,054	43,797	11,379		462,152
L2 dataset	**A1**	**A2**	**B1**	**B2**	**C1**	**C2**	**Total**
# documents	174	176	171	157	105	162	945
# sentences	1,802	2,179	2,930	2,302	1,498	10,870	21,581
# tokens	15,555	21,750	27,223	37,717	21,959	143,845	268,049
SYN dataset							**Total**
# macro-documents							87,653
# sentences							275,349,473
# tokens							4,351,945,964

Unlabeled Data. We use the SYN collection (version 4) of the Czech National Corpus [11] as a source of unlabeled data in both approaches proposed in Sect. 5. A language model was trained on the entire dataset, which comprises about 275 million sentences.

On the other hand, density estimation required some data preparation. The complete SYN data is a collection of stand-alone macro-documents representing full books, journals, and newspapers. Since the macro-documents are too long to be efficiently manipulated by our preprocessing stage, we partitioned them uniformly so that each micro-document contains at most 100 sentences. Although the uniform cuts may worsen some of the coherence properties, we believe their effect is marginal. Density functions were estimated from 200,000 micro-documents, which accounts for 7% of full SYN data.

7   Experiments

In our experiments, we extend the EVALD 3.0 system with the three new feature sets presented in the previous sections: (i) miscellaneous new hand-crafted features (MISC), (ii) language model features (LM), and (iii) density estimation features (DE). We exploit texts from the SYN corpus in order to build LM and DE features. On both L1 and L2 datasets, we evaluate seven possible combinations[5] of new feature sets using the evaluation procedure described in Sect. 6. The evaluation procedure includes tuning of the learning method and its hyperparameters in a cross-validation fashion. We carried out an automatic

---

[5] Note that anytime we combine LM and DE features, density estimates are calculated from all but the LM features.

Table 3. The results of evaluation of the baseline EVALD system extended with all the combinations of the three new feature sets: miscellaneous (MISC), language model (LM), and density estimation (DE) features. Performance of the system is measured on both labeled datasets using accuracy and macro-averaged F-score. The scores in gray and typeset in bold indicate the configurations that are significantly better than EVALD 3.0 in its baseline setting and with tuning, respectively.

System	L1 dataset		L2 dataset	
	Macro-F	Acc (%)	Macro-F	Acc (%)
EVALD 3.0	47.0	66.1	61.4	66.3
EVALD 3.0, tuned	53.9	64.3	63.7	65.3
+ MISC	53.8	66.1	63.3	64.7
+ LM	54.8	58.2	63.4	64.9
+ DE	54.2	65.0	59.8	63.2
+ MISC + LM	53.5	65.2	63.3	64.9
+ MISC + DE	58.4	67.0	65.7	68.1
+ DE + LM	56.5	65.4	63.8	65.5
+ MISC + DE + LM	**59.9**	**67.9**	65.6	68.3

randomized search of hyperparameters of multiple classification and regression[6] methods, e.g. random forests, linear models optimized by stochastic gradient descent and SVMs with various kernels.

Evaluation Measures. Results of the experiments are reported by two scores: accuracy and macro-averaged F-score. Being easy to interpret, accuracy may be biased by an uneven distribution of the grades in our datasets, though. F-score is thus our main metrics used for hyperparameter tuning as well as for the final evaluation. Macro-averaging ensures that performance on every grade is weighed equally.

Baseline System. We employ the EVALD 3.0 system as described in Sect. 3 as our baseline. The system has been trained by random forests[7] with no hyperparameter tuning.

Results. The results in Table 3 show that inclusion of the new hand-crafted features and the features based on unlabeled data as well as tuning of learning settings lead to a substantial improvement. The best configurations of the extended system significantly[8] outperform the baseline by almost 13 and more

---

[6] Regression models require the labels in the L2 dataset (CEFR proficiency levels) to be converted to numbers. Furthermore, all (possibly non-integer) predictions must be discretized.

[7] Implemented in the Weka toolkit [8].

[8] Statistical significance was calculated by paired bootstrap resampling [14] at p-level $p \leq 0.05$.

than 4 F-score points on the L1 and the L2 dataset, respectively.[9] Originally a huge gap of more than 14 F-score points between performance of EVALD on the two datasets thus shrunk to only less than 6 points. Despite its secondary role, the new extensions show some improvement also in terms of accuracy. The three following main observations stand out from the results.

First, it is apparent that proper selection of the learning methods and their hyperparameters is essential. Solely by tuning, we were able to outperform the baseline EVALD system [23] by almost 7 and 2 points on the L1 and the L2, respectively. Tuning of learning settings is thus responsible for reducing a half of a difference between the best scores on the two datasets. The most successful models utilize an SVM classifier with a radial basis function kernel, preceded by feature normalization.

Next, the newly presented feature sets heavily contribute to the final performance. The combination of MISC and DE features achieves one of the highest scores on both datasets. On the L1 dataset, it is surpassed only by the combination of all three feature sets. Interestingly, individual effect of any of the feature sets seems to be marginal.

Last, the positive impact of new features is higher on the L1 dataset than on the L2 dataset. Whereas the improvement of 6 F-score points is statistically significant on the former, it does not hold for the 2-point improvement on the latter. The disproportion may be caused by the origin of the SYN corpus, which we use as unlabeled data. The majority of the texts it comprises were written by native speakers of Czech (journalists, writers, translators, etc.). The language used in these texts are thus more similar to the texts from the L1 dataset, which consists of essays also written by native speakers of Czech.

8   Conclusion

The presented work focused on leveraging unlabeled data in automatic evaluation of surface coherence in student essays. We proposed two approaches that use unlabeled data: (i) n-gram language models, and (ii) density estimates of features employed by the evaluation system. In addition, we designed multiple various features that are not related to unlabeled data.

The results show that the proposed features have a substantial impact on quality of evaluation, especially if used in combination. Furthermore, tuning the learning method and its hyperparameters turns out to be crucial, as many new features were introduced. Although the improvements are apparent in evaluation of both L1 and L2 essays, the increase in F-score is much bigger for L1. We suppose that it can be justified by higher similarity of the unlabeled data to the L1 texts.

---

[9] Note that the scores of EVALD 3.0 presented here slightly differ from those reported in [23] due to the modification in cross-validation procedure (see Sect. 6).

Acknowledgment. The authors acknowledge support from the Ministry of Culture of the Czech Republic (project No. DG16P02B016 *Automatic Evaluation of Text Coherence in Czech*). This work has been using language resources developed, stored and distributed by the LINDAT/CLARIN project of the Ministry of Education, Youth and Sports of the Czech Republic (project LM2015071). Many thanks to our colleagues Milan Straka and Jakub Náplava for providing us with a pre-trained n-gram model.

References

1. Boyd, A., et al.: The MERLIN corpus: learner language and the CEFR. In: Proceedings of LREC 2014, Reykjavík, Iceland, pp. 1281–1288. ELRA (2014)
2. Chen, Y.Y., Liu, C.L., Lee, C.H., Chang, T.H., et al.: An unsupervised automated essay-scoring system. IEEE Intell. Syst. **25**(5), 61–67 (2010)
3. Coleman, M., Liau, T.L.: A computer readability formula designed for machine scoring. J. Appl. Psychol. **60**(2), 283–284 (1975)
4. Cui, B., Li, Y., Zhang, Y., Zhang, Z.: Text coherence analysis based on deep neural network. In: Proceedings of CIKM 2017, pp. 2027–2030. ACM (2017)
5. Cummins, R., Yannakoudakis, H., Briscoe, T.: Unsupervised modeling of topical relevance in L2 learner text. In: Proceedings of the 11th Workshop on Innovative Use of NLP for Building Educational Applications, San Diego, CA, pp. 95–104. ACL (2016)
6. Farag, Y., Yannakoudakis, H., Briscoe, T.: Neural automated essay scoring and coherence modeling for adversarially crafted input. In: Proceedings of the NAACL:HLT 2018, New Orleans, Louisiana, Volume 1 (Long Papers), pp. 263–271. ACL (2018)
7. Feng, V.W., Lin, Z., Hirst, G.: The impact of deep hierarchical discourse structures in the evaluation of text coherence. In: Proceedings of COLING 2014: Technical Papers, Dublin, Ireland, pp. 940–949. Dublin City University and ACL (2014)
8. Hall, M., Frank, E., Holmes, G., Pfahringer, B., Reutemann, P., Witten, I.H.: The WEKA data mining software: an update. ACM SIGKDD Explor. Newsl. **11**(1), 10–18 (2009)
9. Hancke, J., Meurers, D.: Exploring CEFR classification for German based on rich linguistic modeling. In: Learner Corpus Research 2013. Book of Abstracts, pp. 54–56. Bergen, Norway (2013)
10. Heafield, K.: KenLM: faster and smaller language model queries. In: Proceedings of WMT 2011, Edinburgh, Scotland, pp. 187–197. ACL (2011)
11. Hnátková, M., Křen, M., Procházka, P., Skoumalová, H.: The SYN-series corpora of written Czech. In: Proceedings of LREC 2014, Reykjavik, Iceland, pp. 160–164. ELRA (2014)
12. Kim, Y., Jernite, Y., Sontag, D., Rush, A.M.: Character-aware neural language models. In: Proceedings of AAAI 2016, pp. 2741–2749. AAAI Press, Phoenix (2016)
13. Kincaid, J.P., Fishburne, Jr., R.P., Rogers, R.L., Chissom, B.S.: Derivation of New Readability Formulas (Automated Readability Index, Fog Count and Flesch Reading Ease Formula) for Navy Enlisted Personnel. Technical report, pp. 8–75, Institute for Simulation and Training (1975)
14. Koehn, P.: Statistical significance tests for machine translation evaluation. In: Proceedings of EMNLP 2004, Barcelona, Spain. ACL (2004)
15. Lin, Z., Ng, H.T., Kan, M.Y.: Automatically evaluating text coherence using discourse relations. In: Proceedings of ACL:HLT 2011, Portland, OR, vol. 1, pp. 997–1006. ACL (2011)

16. Mann, W.C., Thompson, S.A.: Rhetorical structure theory: toward a functional theory of text organization. Text-Interdisc. J. Study Discourse **8**(3), 243–281 (1988)

17. McLaughlin, H.G.: SMOG grading - a new readability formula. J. Reading **12**(8), 639–646 (1969)

18. Melis, G., Dyer, C., Blunsom, P.: On the state of the art of evaluation in neural language models. In: Proceedings of ICLR 2018. Vancouver, Canada (2018)

19. Merity, S., Keskar, N.S., Socher, R.: Regularizing and optimizing LSTM language models. In: Proceedings of ICLR 2018. Vancouver, Canada (2018)

20. Mesgar, M., Strube, M.: A neural local coherence model for text quality assessment. In: Proceedings of EMNLP 2018, Brussels, Belgium, pp. 4328–4339. ACL (2018)

21. Mírovský, J., Novák, M., Rysová, K., Rysová, M., Hajičová, E.: EVALD 3.0 – Evaluator of Discourse, Charles University, Prague, Czech Republic (2018)

22. Mírovský, J., Novák, M., Rysová, K., Rysová, M., Hajičová, E.: EVALD 3.0 for Foreigners - Evaluator of Discourse, Charles University. Czech Republic, Prague (2018)

23. Novák, M., Mírovský, J., Rysová, K., Rysová, M.: Topic–focus articulation: a third pillar of automatic evaluation of text coherence. In: Batyrshin, I., Martínez-Villaseñor, M.L., Ponce Espinosa, H.E. (eds.) MICAI 2018. LNCS (LNAI), vol. 11289, pp. 96–108. Springer, Cham (2018). https://doi.org/10.1007/978-3-030-04497-8_8

24. Novák, M., Rysová, K., Rysová, M., Mírovský, J.: Incorporating coreference to automatic evaluation of coherence in essays. In: Camelin, N., Estève, Y., Martín-Vide, C. (eds.) SLSP 2017. LNCS (LNAI), vol. 10583, pp. 58–69. Springer, Cham (2017). https://doi.org/10.1007/978-3-319-68456-7_5

25. Östling, R., Smolentzov, A., Hinnerich, B.T., Höglin, E.: Automated essay scoring for Swedish. In: Proceedings of the 8th Workshop on Innovative Use of NLP for Building Educational Applications, Atlanta, GA, pp. 42–47. ACL (2013)

26. Persing, I., Ng, V.: Modeling prompt adherence in student essays. In: Proceedings of ACL 2014, Baltimore, MD, (Volume 1: Long Papers), pp. 1534–1543. ACL (2014)

27. Popel, M., Žabokrtský, Z.: TectoMT: modular NLP framework. In: Loftsson, H., Rögnvaldsson, E., Helgadóttir, S. (eds.) NLP 2010. LNCS (LNAI), vol. 6233, pp. 293–304. Springer, Heidelberg (2010). https://doi.org/10.1007/978-3-642-14770-8_33

28. Rysová, K., Rysová, M., Mírovský, J.: Automatic evaluation of surface coherence in L2 texts in czech. In: Proceedings of ROCLING 2016, Taipei, Taiwan, pp. 214–228. ACLCLP (2016)

29. Rysová, K., Rysová, M., Mírovský, J., Novák, M.: Introducing EVALD - software applications for automatic evaluation of discourse in czech. In: Proceedings of RANLP 2017, Varna, Bulgaria, pp. 634–641. INCOMA Ltd. (2017)

30. Šebesta, K., Bedřichová, Z., Šormová, K., et al.: AKCES 5 (CzeSL-SGT) data/software, LINDAT/CLARIN digital library at ÚFAL MFF UK, Prague, Czech Republic (2014)

31. Šebesta, K., Goláňová, H., Letafková, J., et al.: AKCES 1, data/software, LINDAT/CLARIN digital library at ÚFAL MFF UK, Prague, Czech Republic (2016)

32. Vajjala, S.: Automated assessment of non-native learner essays: investigating the role of linguistic features. Int. J. Artif. Intell. Educ. **28**(1), 79–105 (2018)

33. Vajjala, S., Lõo, K.: Automatic CEFR level prediction for estonian learner text. In: Proceedings of the Third Workshop on NLP for Computer-assisted Language Learning, no. 107, pp. 113–127. Linköping University Electronic Press, Linköping (2014)

34. Volodina, E., Pilán, I., Alfter, D.: Classification of Swedish learner essays by CEFR levels. In: Proceedings of EuroCALL 2016, Limassol, Cyprus, pp. 456–461. Research-publishing.net (2016)

35. Zesch, T., Wojatzki, M., Scholten-Akoun, D.: Task-independent features for automated essay grading. In: Proceedings of the 10th Workshop on Innovative Use of NLP for Building Educational Applications, Denver, CO, pp. 224–232. ACL (2015)

Examining Structure of Word Embeddings with PCA

Tomáš Musil[✉]

Faculty of Mathematics and Physics, Institute of Formal and Applied Linguistics,
Charles University, Malostranské náměstí 25, 118 00 Prague, Czech Republic
musil@ufal.mff.cuni.cz
http://ufal.mff.cuni.cz/tomas-musil

Abstract. In this paper we compare structure of Czech word embeddings for English-Czech neural machine translation (NMT), word2vec and sentiment analysis. We show that although it is possible to successfully predict part of speech (POS) tags from word embeddings of word2vec and various translation models, not all of the embedding spaces show the same structure. The information about POS is present in word2vec embeddings, but the high degree of organization by POS in the NMT decoder suggests that this information is more important for machine translation and therefore the NMT model represents it in more direct way. Our method is based on correlation of principal component analysis (PCA) dimensions with categorical linguistic data. We also show that further examining histograms of classes along the principal component is important to understand the structure of representation of information in embeddings.

Keywords: Word embeddings · Part of speech · Sentiment analysis

1 Introduction

Embeddings of linguistic units (sentences, words, subwords, characters, ...) are mappings from the discrete and sparse space of individual units into a continuous and dense vector space. Since neural networks became the dominant machine learning method in NLP, embeddings are used in majority of NLP tasks.

Embeddings can be either learned together with the rest of the neural network for the specific task, or pretrained in a neural network for different task, typically language modelling. Because different information is useful in various tasks, the embeddings may vary with respect to the information they represent.

In this paper, we examine the structure of word embeddings for Czech words. We compare the word2vec model embeddings with embeddings from three different neural machine translation architectures (for translation between Czech and English) and embeddings from a convolutional neural network for sentiment analysis. We show how these models differ in the structure of information represented in the embeddings.

© Springer Nature Switzerland AG 2019
K. Ekštein (Ed.): TSD 2019, LNAI 11697, pp. 211–223, 2019.
https://doi.org/10.1007/978-3-030-27947-9_18

In Sect. 2 we discuss related work. In Sect. 3 we describe the tasks and the models that we are solving them with. To compare the embeddings from different tasks, we show what information is contained in embeddings in Sect. 4. In Sect. 5 we examine the structure of the vector space with respect to the represented information. We summarize the findings in the concluding Sect. 6.

2   Related Work

A comprehensive survey of word embeddings evaluation methods was compiled by Bakarov [2]. An overview can also be found in the survey of methodology for analysis of deep learning models for NLP by Belinkov [4].

Hollis and Westbury [13] extracted semantic dimensions from the word2vec embeddings. They used principal component analysis as candidate dimensions and measured their correlation with various psycholinguistic quantities. Our approach is different in that we examine categorical discrete information in word embeddings.

Quian et al. [17] investigate properties (including POS and sentiment score) of embeddings from 3 different language model architectures for more than 20 languages including Czech. They use a multilayer perceptron classifier trained on a part of the vocabulary and evaluated on the rest.

Saphra and Lopez [18] show that language models learn POS first. They use singular vector canonical correlation analysis to "demonstrate that different aspects of linguistic structure are learned at different rates, with part of speech tagging acquired early and global topic information learned continuously".

Belinkov et al. [3,5] evaluate what NMT models learn about morphology and semantics by training POS, morphological, and semantic taggers on representations from the models. Chen et al. [8] propose several tasks that will help us better understand the information encoded in word embeddings, one of them being sentiment polarity. Our approach differs from these in that we are examining the structure of the embeddings, not only predicting the information from them.

3   Tasks, Models and Data

In this section we describe the tasks for which the examined models were trained, the models themselves and the data we used to train them.

3.1   Neural Machine Translation

Neural machine translation (NMT) started with the sequence-to-sequence recurrent neural network architecture [19]. The first model to significantly surpass the previous paradigm of statistical MT introduced the attention mechanism [1]. Further development proved that attention is all you need [20].

We trained our NMT models on the CzEng [7] Czech-English parallel corpus, the *c-fiction* section. The models were trained with the *Neural Monkey* toolkit

[12]. The embedding size was 512, vocabulary size 25k. The embeddings were taken from the Czech part of the MT system, that is from the *cs-en* encoder and *en-cs* decoder. We compare three different models:

The RNN MODEL is a LSTM encoder and decoder with a hidden state of size 1024.

The ATTENTION MODEL is bidirectional conditional GRU [9] with attention [1].

The TRANSFORMER MODEL is the *Neural Monkey* implementation of the transformer architecture [20], with 6 layers and 16 attention heads in each layer.

3.2 Neural Language Models

Neural language models used word embeddings before machine translation and other applications [6]. Eventually they inspired the word2vec/Skip-gram approach [15,16], which can be thought of as an inverted language model: it is trained by predicting the context words from a word that is given.

For the word2vec embeddings to be comparable with the ones from NMT models, we trained the word2vec model on the Czech side of the parallel corpus that we used for the translation models. We used the Skip-gram model with embedding size 512, window size 11, and negative sampling with 10 samples.

3.3 Sentiment Analysis

Sentiment analysis is a task of deciding whether a given text is positive, negative, or neutral in its emotional charge. It find applications in marketing and public relations. Comments of products or services accompanied by a rating are a valuable data resource for this task.

For training the sentiment analysis models we used the CSFD CZ dataset [10], where data were obtained from user comments in the ČSFD film database.[1] The model is a convolutional neural network based on [14] with embedding size 300, kernels of size 3, 4 and 5 with output dimension 100, dropout 0.8, and a classifier with 100 hidden units. The model was trained with batch size 500, for 40 epochs.

3.4 Part of Speech Tagging

Part of speech tags for Czech words were obtained from MorfFlex [11]. It contains morphologically analyzed wordlist for Czech. The POS is the first position in MorfFlex morphological tag and there are 10 possible values for Czech POS (and two possible values for special cases that we did not use): Adjective (A), Numeral (C), Adverb (D), Interjection (I), Conjunction (J), Noun (N), Pronoun (P), Verb (V), Preposition (R), and Particle (T). Some word forms are homonymous with other words with different POS. In that case, we mark that word as multivalent.

---

[1] https://www.csfd.cz/.

4 What Information is Represented in Word Embeddings

To show that some information is represented in word embeddings, we can train a model to predict that information an embedding alone (with no context). If the model correctly predicts the information for previously unseen embeddings, then the information must be inferable from the embeddings.

We evaluate the model's ability to learn to predict the information by cross-validation. We divide the vocabulary randomly into 10 bins and train the model 10 times, each time leaving 1 bin for evaluation and training on the remaining 9.

4.1 Part of Speech Classification

We use an intersection of the vocabulary of our translation models (25k word forms) with the MorfFlex dictionary and discard word forms occuring with more than one different POS tags in the dictionary. We are left with 21 882 forms.

For predicting the POS tags, we use a simple multilayer perceptron classifier, with one hidden layer of size 100 and a softmax classification layer.

Table 1. Accuracy of predicting POS classes from word embeddings taken from various models. The number in parenthesis is twice the standard deviation, covering the 95% confidence interval.

Model	Accuracy
RNN NMT ENCODER	94.69% (±0.93%)
RNN NMT DECODER	**97.77%** (±1.16%)
ATTENTION MODEL ENCODER	96.17% (±1.39%)
ATTENTION MODEL DECODER	96.12% (±1.27%)
TRANSFORMER MODEL ENCODER	96.37% (±1.49%)
TRANSFORMER MODEL DECODER	93.36% (±3.86%)
WORD2VEC	95.01% (±1.94%)

In Table 1, we compare classification accuracies of POS tag predictions from word embeddings learned in different network architectures described in Sect. 3. For each NMT architecture we have trained models for both translation directions. We are examining the embeddings from the Czech side of the model, that is encoder for Czech-English translation and decoder for English-Czech translation.

We observe that in case of RNN MODEL without attention mechanism, POS tags can be significantly better predicted from decoder embeddings than from the encoder embeddings. The reason may be the fact that the decoder is trained to produce grammatically correct sentences and therefore needs to store this kind of information about words. The encoder, on the other hand, only needs to be aware of POS tags to the extent of its contribution to meaning disambiguation.

The ATTENTION MODEL performs slightly worse, which may be because this model has additional parameters in the attention mechanism to store information in and therefore does not need to represent it in the embeddings.

The information may be even more scattered in case of the TRANSFORMER MODEL, which uses multiple attention layers. That may explain why the results for the decoder have the highest variance. The lower performance compared to encoder embeddings classifier may seem to contradict our previous hypothesis (that decoder needs more information about morphology), but due to the high variance this difference is not significant.

The WORD2VEC model is trained on the Czech side of the parallel data on which the NMT models were trained.

There are no major differences in the classifier performance on embeddings from different models. Since it performs well on all of these embeddings, it may seem that POS is of roughly same importance for all of the models. However, in the next section we will show there are significant differences.

5   Structure of the Vector Space

In Sect. 4 we have seen that there is not much difference in the amount of the examined information represented in embeddings from different models. However, there may be difference in the structure of the representation.

One major obstacle in examining the structure of the embedding space is the random initialization, which means that two runs of the same experiment may render completely different embedding spaces and a single dimension or direction in the embedding space has no fixed interpretation.

Inspired by [13], we use principal component analysis and examine the correlation of the information in question with individual components. This helps us to establish invariants and visualise the differences in the structure. Principal component analysis (PCA) is a transformation that is defined in a way that the first component has the highest variance. The next component is the direction that has the highest variance and is ortogonal to the first component, and so on.

When we find a principal component that higly correlates with information that interests us, we can further examine the structure of the representation by plotting the information along the principal component.

5.1   Emebedding Space and Part of Speech

We measure a correlation between the principal components of the embeddings and binary vectors indicating whether a word belongs to a given POS category. For each of the POS categories, we generate an indication vector with a position for each word from the vocabulary, containing 1 if that word falls under the particular category and 0 otherwise. We then measure correlation between these vectors and principal components of the embeddings.

For example, in the correlation matrix for embeddings from the NMT RNN encoder in Fig. 1 we see a strong correlation between the first principal component and verbs. This correlation is negative, but that does not matter, because the direction of the principal components is arbitrary. We also see a strong correlation between the first principal component and nouns. In this case, the correlation is positive. That by itself is again arbitrary, but it is important that the correlation with verbs has the opposite sign. It means that in the direction of the first principal component verbs are concentrating on one side of the embedding space and nouns on the other. And indeed when we plot a histogram of the POS categories along the first principal component in Fig. 3, we see that is the case.

As we have demonstrated in Sect. 4, the NMT RNN architecture without attention stores more information about POS categories in the embeddings than architectures with attention, so we will examine the structure of its embedding space.

There is an obvious difference in POS representation between encoder and decoder. This is not an artifact of random initialization. After we apply the PCA, we see the same structure across models with different random seeds, as in Fig. 2.

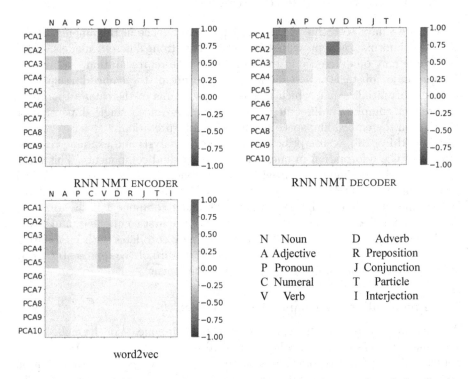

Fig. 1. Correlations of POS and PCA dimensions from the encoder of the Czech-English RNN NMT model (top left), the decoder of the English-Czech RNN NMT model (top right) and the word2vec model (bottom). The direction of the PCA dimensions is arbitrary, so the sign of the correlation is not important in itself, only if there are values with opposite signs in the same row we know that they are negatively correlated.

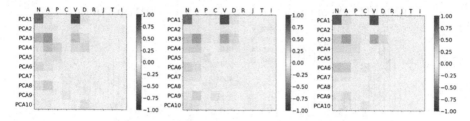

Fig. 2. Correlations of POS and PCA dimensions of the RNN NMT ENCODER embeddings from three runs of the Czech-English RNN NMT ENCODER with different random initialization. The direction of the PCA dimensions is arbitrary, so inversion of the first PCA dimension in the third matrix does not matter (see Fig. 1 for more information).

When we compare the correlation matrices for the encoder and the decoder embeddings in Fig. 1, we see that in the encoder:

- verbs and nouns are strongly distinguished in the first dimension of the PCA,
- there are adjectives (and adverbs to a lesser extent) on one side and nouns with verbs on the other in the third dimension,

whereas in the decoder:

- the first dimension of the PCA distinguishes adjectives from nouns,
- the second dimension distinguishes verbs from nouns and adjectives,
- the seventh dimension correlates with adverbs,
- and overall the correlation with POS classes seems to be more pronounced than in the encoder.

To better understand the structure of the POS representation in the embedding space we can look at the histograms of the four most important POS classes along the dimensions of the PCA of the embeddings. The histogram for the first dimension of the RNN NMT ENCODER embeddings is plotted in Fig. 3. It demonstrates in this dimension verbs are separated from the rest of the POS categories.

For the first PCA dimension of the RNN NMT DECODER embeddings in Fig. 3 we see that nouns are concentrated on one side, adjectives on the other side and verbs with adverbs are in the middle.

For the second PCA dimension of the RNN NMT DECODER embeddings in Fig. 3 we see that verbs are concentrated on one side and all other categories on the other side.

The second PCA dimension shows interesting distribution of nouns in Fig. 3. There is a separate cluster of nouns, which is even more apparent if we plot the distribution along two PCA dimensions in a planar graph in Fig. 4. When we take a sample of words from this cluster, it contains almost exclusively named entities: *Fang, Eliáši, Još, Aenea, Bush, Eddie, Zlatoluna, Gordon, Bellondová, and Hermiona.*

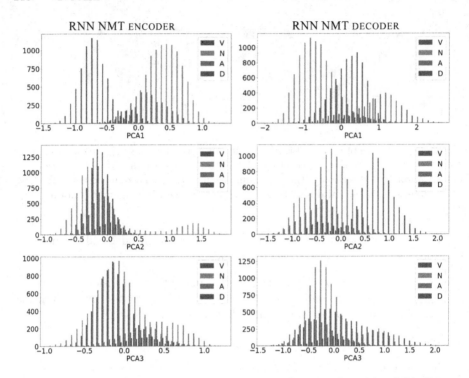

Fig. 3. Histograms of the four largest POS classes along the first three PCA dimensions of the embeddings from the NMT RNN MODEL. The Czech-English RNN NMT ENCODER is on the left and the English-Czech RNN NMT DECODER on the right. V = verbs, N = nouns, A = adjectives, D = adverbs.

There is a similar distribution of nouns in the third PCA dimension of the RNN NMT DECODER embeddings. The smaller group again consists of named entities.

As we can already tell from Fig. 1, the analysis of the WORD2VEC embeddings is different. With respect to POS, the embeddings look normally distributed in the first dimensions of the PCA (see also the left part of Fig. 5). There is a correlation with nouns and an inverse correlation with verbs in dimension three to five. In the middle and right parts of Fig. 5, we see that verbs are composed of several clusters. When we take a sample from the cluster that is in the top left of the PCA3/PCA4 plot or in the top right of the PCA4/PCA5 plot, it concains almost exclusively infinitive verb forms: *odpovědět, přenést, zabránit, získat, říct, předvídat, přiznat, opřít, přemoci, setřást.* The other protrusion of verbs in the lower right of the PCA3/PCA4 plot and lower left of the PCA4/PCA5 plot contains modal verbs: *mohli, mohl, lze, nemohla, měla, musel, museli, musí, dokázala, podařilo.*

This is a stronger result than just being able to predict these categories with a classifier: not only can the POS (named entities, verb forms and possibly

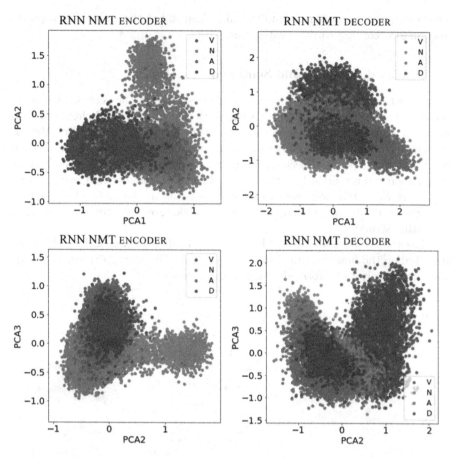

Fig. 4. Distribution of the four largest POS classes along the first/second and second/third PCA dimensions of the embeddings from the the NMT RNN MODEL. The Czech-English RNN NMT ENCODER is on the left and the English-Czech RNN NMT DECODER on the right. V = verbs, N = nouns, A = adjectives, D = adverbs.

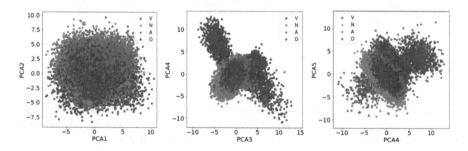

Fig. 5. Distribution of the four largest POS classes along the first/second (left), the third/fourth (middle), and the fourth/fifth PCA dimensions of the embeddings from the word2vec model. V = verbs, N = nouns, A = adjectives, D = adverbs.

other categories) be inferred from the embeddings, but the embeddings space is structured according to these categories.

5.2   Embedding Space and Sentiment

In this section, we examine the word embeddings from the sentiment analysis model. When we computed the PCA correlation matrix for POS classes just like in the previous section, we found that there is no significant correlation (the correlation coefficient with the largest absolute value is 0.0680, more than 10 times lower than in the previous section, although the vocabulary is different, therefore the numbers are not directly comparable). The same classifier that predicts POS with more than 93% accuracy from the translation model embeddings did not converge at all at the embeddings from this task. However, there is a different interesting structure.

The subplot in the top right of Fig. 6 shows the distribution of the embbedings projected on the first two dimensions of the PCA. They form a triangular shape which is unlikely to be formed by a random distribution.

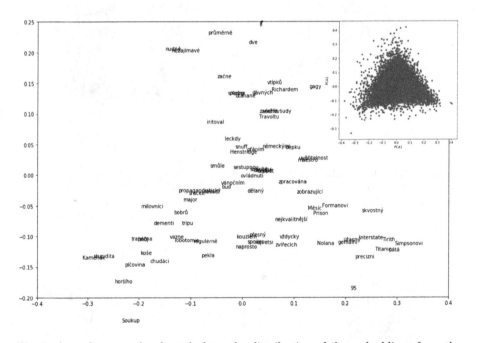

Fig. 6. A random sample of words from the distribution of the embeddings from the sentiment analysis CNN model along the first (horizontal) and second (vertical) PCA dimension. The top right subplot shows the complete distribution.

To examine the distribution further, we plotted a sample of the words in Fig. 6. The plot shows that in the bottom right corner there are words like "skvostný" (*magnificent*), "precizní" (*precise*), "geniální" (*brilliant*) and also "Titanic" and "Simpsonovi" (*the Simpsons*). These are positive words or film works that are generally regarded as epitome of quality (indicated also by their high ranking in the ČSFD database). There is also the number "95" in the bottom right. The perceived positiveness of this number is due to users expressing their rating of the film as percentage in the comments. In the bottom left there are words such as "stupidita" (*stupidity*), "horšího" (*worse*), "píčovina" (obscene word sometimes translated as *bullshit*) and "Kameňák" (a Czech comedy). These are obviously negative words, with Kameňák being a film which while being relatively well known has a low score in the database (29%), making it a suitable film to use as a negative comparison. This suggests that the first dimension of the PCA corresponds to valence or polarity of the word.

In the top of the figure, we see words such as "průměrné" (*average, mediocre*) and "nezajímavé" (*uninteresting*). These are neutral and not very intense. On the opposite side, in the middle near the bottom, we have words like "naprosto" (*absolutely, completely*) and "největší" (*biggest*) that are also neutral by themselves, but intensify the next word. Therefore, the second dimension corresponds to intensity. This also explains the triangular shape of the distribution: the words that are highly positive or highly negative are also intense, therefore there are words far right and left in the bottom part of the figure and not in the top part.

This is a stronger result than just being able to predict the emotional characteristics of the word from its embedding, because it shows that the embedding space of the sentiment analysis model is in the first place organised by these characteristics.

6   Conclusion

We examined the structure of Czech word embedding spaces with respect to POS and sentiment information. Our method is based on correlating PCA dimension to categorical linguistic data.

We have demonstrated that although it is possible to successfully predict POS tags from embedding from various translation models and word2vec, not all of them show the same structure. Even though the information about POS is present in word2vec embeddings, the high degree of organization by POS in the NMT decoder suggests, that this information is important for machine translation and therefore the NMT model represents it in more direct way.

We have demonstrated that examining histograms of classes along the principal component is important to understand the structure of representation of information in embeddings. We have also demonstrated that NMT models represent named entities separately in the embedding space, word2vec distinguishes infinitive forms and modal verbs from the rest of the verbs, and CNN sentiment analysis models emotional properties of words in the shape of the embedding space. This shows that the embedding space of a neural network is literally shaped by the task for which it is trained.

The presented method of examining the representation can be extended to other languages, tasks and linguistic and non-linguistic information and may tell us a lot about the way that neural networks in NLP represent language.

Acknowledgements. This work has been supported by the grant 18-02196S of the Czech Science Foundation. This research was partially supported by SVV project number 260 453.

References

1. Bahdanau, D., Cho, K., Bengio, Y.: Neural machine translation by jointly learning to align and translate. In: 3rd International Conference on Learning Representations ICLR 2015, San Diego (2015). http://arxiv.org/abs/1409.0473
2. Bakarov, A.: A survey of word embeddings evaluation methods (2018). https://arxiv.org/abs/1801.09536
3. Belinkov, Y., Durrani, N., Dalvi, F., Sajjad, H., Glass, J.: What do neural machine translation models learn about morphology? In: Proceedings of the 55th Annual Meeting of the Association for Computational Linguistics, pp. 861–872 (2017). https://www.aclweb.org/anthology/P17-1080
4. Belinkov, Y., Glass, J.: Analysis methods in neural language processing: a survey. Trans. Assoc. Comput. Linguist. **7**, 49–72 (2019)
5. Belinkov, Y., Màrquez, L., Sajjad, H., Durrani, N., Dalvi, F., Glass, J.: Evaluating layers of representation in neural machine translation on part-of-speech and semantic tagging tasks. In: Proceedings of the Eighth International Joint Conference on Natural Language Processing, pp. 1–10 (2017). https://www.aclweb.org/anthology/I17-1001
6. Bengio, Y., Ducharme, R., Vincent, P., Jauvin, C.: A neural probabilistic language model. J. Mach. Learn. Res. **3**, 1137–1155 (2003)
7. Bojar, O., et al.: CzEng 1.6: enlarged czech-english parallel corpus with processing tools dockered. In: Sojka, P., Horák, A., Kopeček, I., Pala, K. (eds.) TSD 2016. LNCS (LNAI), vol. 9924, pp. 231–238. Springer, Cham (2016). https://doi.org/10.1007/978-3-319-45510-5_27
8. Chen, Y., Perozzi, B., Al-Rfou, R., Skiena, S.: The expressive power of word embeddings. arXiv preprint arXiv:1301.3226 (2013)
9. Firat, O., Cho, K.: Conditional gated recurrent unit with attention mechanism, May 2016. https://github.com/nyu-dl/dl4mt-tutorial/blob/master/docs/cgru.pdf. Published online, version adbaeea
10. Habernal, I., Ptáček, T., Steinberger, J.: Sentiment analysis in czech social media using supervised machine learning. In: Proceedings of the 4th Workshop on Computational Approaches to Subjectivity, Sentiment and Social Media Analysis, pp. 65–74 (2013)
11. Hajič, J., Hlaváčová, J.: MorfFlex CZ 160310, LINDAT/CLARIN digital library at the Institute of Formal and Applied Linguistics (ÚFAL), Faculty of Mathematics and Physics, Charles University (2016). http://hdl.handle.net/11234/1-1673
12. Helcl, J., Libovický, J.: Neural monkey: an open-source tool for sequence learning. Prague Bull. Math. Linguist. **107**, 5–17 (2017). http://ufal.mff.cuni.cz/pbml/107/art-helcl-libovicky.pdf
13. Hollis, G., Westbury, C.: The principals of meaning: extracting semantic dimensions from co-occurrence models of semantics. Psychon. Bull. Rev. **23**(6), 1744–1756 (2016)

14. Kim, Y.: Convolutional neural networks for sentence classification. In: Proceedings of the 2014 Conference on Empirical Methods in Natural Language Processing (EMNLP), pp. 1746–1751 (2014). http://dx.doi.org/10.3115/v1/d14-1181

15. Mikolov, T., Chen, K., Corrado, G., Dean, J.: Efficient estimation of word representations in vector space. CoRR abs/1301.3781 (2013). http://arxiv.org/abs/1301.3781

16. Mikolov, T., Sutskever, I., Chen, K., Corrado, G.S., Dean, J.: Distributed representations of words and phrases and their compositionality. In: Advances in Neural Information Processing Systems, pp. 3111–3119 (2013)

17. Qian, P., Qiu, X., Huang, X.: Investigating language universal and specific properties in word embeddings. In: Proceedings of the 54th Annual Meeting of the Association for Computational Linguistics (Volume 1: Long Papers), vol. 1, pp. 1478–1488 (2016)

18. Saphra, N., Lopez, A.: Language models learn pos first. In: Proceedings of the 2018 EMNLP Workshop BlackboxNLP: Analyzing and Interpreting Neural Networks for NLP, pp. 328–330 (2018). http://aclweb.org/anthology/W18-5438

19. Sutskever, I., Vinyals, O., Le, Q.V.: Sequence to sequence learning with neural networks. In: Advances in Neural Information Processing Systems, pp. 3104–3112 (2014)

20. Vaswani, A., et al.: Attention is all you need. In: Advances in Neural Information Processing Systems, pp. 5998–6008 (2017)

Semantic Structure of Russian Prepositional Constructions

Victor Zakharov[(✉)] and Irina Azarova

Saint-Petersburg State University,
Universitetskaya Emb. 7-9, 199034 Saint-Petersburg, Russia
v.zakharov@spbu.ru

Abstract. The paper represents a part of a research project which is aimed at the development of corpus-driven semantic-grammatical description of Russian prepositional constructions. In this paper we investigate the structure of synonymous and quasi-synonymous semantic relations for primary and secondary prepositions in the Russian language. The metalanguage for prepositional meaning identification is described. The methodology for processing corpus data and calculating frequency characteristics of prepositional constructions in modern Russian texts is presented. We demonstrate results of our methodology on semantics rubrics of temporative and locative syntaxemes. The semantic description of preposition governors and governees and its usage is shown.

Keywords: Russian prepositional constructions · Preposition meaning · Corpus statistics · Locative constructions · Temporal constructions · Semantic rubrics

1 Introduction

The paper represents a part of a research project which is aimed at the development of corpus-driven semantic-grammatical description of Russian prepositional constructions. To achieve this goal we carry out four interdependent tasks: (1) the integral description of Russian prepositional system as an interconnected structure in terms of the sense metalanguage specified according to prepositional meanings; (2) the collection of corpus statistics for pairs "preposition-its meaning" from this structure; (3) the sense representation of prepositional constructions as a function expressed by prepositions from this structure over the unity of their governors and governees; (4) the exposition of prepositional semantics as a part of syntactic links between classes of content words, some sort of the prepositional ontology.

These tasks are challenging due to the prepositional ambiguity, which is manifested in selectional preferences of particular prepositions expressing synonymic relations between similar content words. We couldn't rely on abstract scholastic presentation of prepositional meanings. Therefore, all elements of our description are based on the corpus data: the enumeration of prepositional constructions, variance of their grammatical features, synonymic and near synonimic prepositional constructions, and so on. This corpus-based semantic and grammatical description of Russian prepositional constructions uses empiric data from various contemporary Russian corpora in order to

K. Ekštein (Ed.): TSD 2019, LNAI 11697, pp. 224–235, 2019.
https://doi.org/10.1007/978-3-030-27947-9_19

identify and then formalize the basic ontologic semantic patterns of "prepositional grammar". We foresee the results of our research to be a useful part of NLP resources because prepositions have not been getting much attention by the specialists in this sphere.

The semantics of Russian prepositions was a matter of a large number of works which are mentioned in [12] by Solonitsky and [5] by Filipenko though they follow mainly more traditional methodology and investigate several specific aspects of prepositional constructions. Anyway, the linguistic prerequisites of prepositional construction analyses are the vital part of our method (see below).

2 Prepositions Inventory

Preposition is a part of speech whose frequency in Russian is extraordinary large. In the Russian National Corpus (RNC), prepositions hold more than 10% of tokens. There are 3 prepositions among the first ten most frequent words (в 'in', на 'on', с 'with') and 18 prepositions among the first hundred ones. Primary Russian prepositions are highly polysemous (Fig. 1).

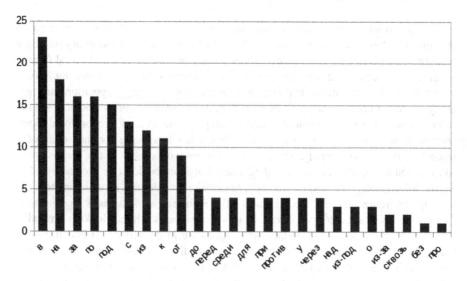

Fig. 1. A number of meanings of primary Russian prepositions according to Zolotova's syntaxeme [16]. The listed primary prepositions are as follows: в 'in', на 'on', за 'behind', по 'along, by', под 'under', с 'with', из 'from', к 'to', от 'from', до 'to', перед 'before', среди 'among', для 'for', при 'near', против 'against', у 'near', через 'through', над 'above', из-под 'from under', о 'about', из-за 'from behind', сквозь 'through', без 'without', про 'about'.

However, meanings of a particular preposition are distributed in corpus texts statistically. For instance, the preposition "в" ('in') has 23 or more meanings in the explanatory dictionaries, and their corpus frequencies are arranged according to the Gauss law. The majority of them is quite rare as may be seen in Fig. 2.

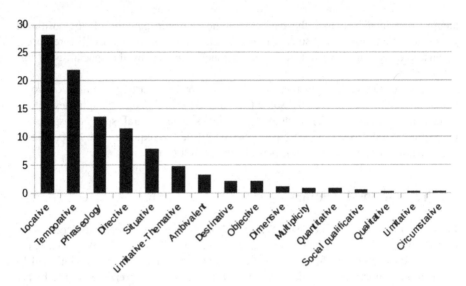

Fig. 2. The percentage ratio of meanings for the preposition "в" ('in') in the random sample from the Newspaper subcorpus of the RNC

The prepositions in Russian are heterogeneous and diverse. There is a small group of primary prepositions (approximately 25) and a large number of secondary ones, the latter being motivated by the content parts of speech (nouns, adverbs and verbal forms), which may be combined with the primary prepositions forming complex multiword expressions. This fact shows that corpus frequencies of primary prepositions are regularly overrated because they may be used as parts of secondary prepositions. Even the strict division between secondary multiword prepositions and prepositional noun phrases is not specified. There are some ideas what is specific for the status of a secondary preposition. Firstly, the nouns and other words used in the prepositional construction are abstract. Secondly, their linear sequence couldn't be broken by other words, for instance, *в течение* ('during'), *несмотря на* ('despite'), etc. Ultimately the spelling differences fix the special status of the phrase, as *несмотря на непогоду* ('despite the bad weather') vs *не смотря по сторонам* ('without looking around'). However, many supposed secondary prepositions are in the process of becoming the "accepted" ones. The most significant evidence of the "prepositional" nature of the multiword expression is its full or partial synonymy to the meaning of some primary preposition, bearing in mind that secondary prepositions with modified spelling or highly frequent ones gained the confirmed status before. In order to compile the full list of secondary prepositions it is possible to look through existing inventories, however, they are only partially overlap. The large list of 315 secondary prepositions is presented in [4]. Other lists with additional complex prepositions can be found in [8] and [14]. Our main focus in identifying and describing secondary prepositions will be corpus analyses and corpus statistics.

In our project, we will consider prepositions to be a stereotypical way for clarifying case meanings of nouns expressing valencies of content words (fist of all, verbs and verbal derivatives) and/or different circumstantial qualifiers in a sentence. The stereotype in our method should be proven by high corpus frequency of prepositional expressions with a particular meaning. The synonymy or partial synonymy between primary and secondary prepositions will be based on the semantic class specification for governors and governees. This point of view allows us to outline the corpus strategy for picking up secondary prepositions. We may use some frequent noun that is used recurrently in a prepositional construction with some primary one as a "prepositional pattern", then we may specify roughly or finely its meaning. After that we may find repeated multiword expressions in the corpus sample expressing a similar sense, for example: *в войне* ('during the war'), *во время войны* ('during the war'), *в годы войны* ('during the war'), *в период войны* ('during the war'), etc.

3   The Metalanguage for Prepositional Meaning Description

The meaning of prepositions in explanatory dictionaries are usually expressed by primary or secondary synonyms, it is not uncommon that they are not interchangeable with the prepositions in question. For example in Russian Wiktionary (https://ru. wiktionary.org/) the first meaning of preposition *через* (through) is described by secondaries *сквозь, поперек* and a gloss *Он помог женщине перейти через дорогу* ('He helped the woman cross the road'), in which it is impossible to insert equivalents from the definition. Prepositions from the dictionary interpretation may be defines by the primary one, forming "a vicious circle". The translation dictionaries demonstrate a number of phrasal examples which may be extrapolated by a user for other cases, but it is not unusual that this is done wrongly.

That is the reason why it is very important to provide a special semantic metalanguage for description of prepositional meanings. The notions of this language may be very coarse as in Russian grammar [10] description (objective, subjective, attributive, adverbial), more detailed as semantic argument (objective, addressee, instrumental, spatial, temporal, etc.) [9] or specially invented for description of prepositional constructions, such as syntaxemes proposed by Zolotova [16].

The syntaxeme is characterized by a morphological arrangement (a preposition plus a noun case form) which has a unity of the form and the sense that functions as a constructive and significant component of a phrase or a sentence. The syntaxeme is a minimal grammatical construction which could not be split further into meaningful elements. The syntaxeme types look like semantic roles or argument specification [2]: direction, destination, correlation, quantification, qualification, location, mediation, temporative, etc. The designation of syntaxemes in original Zolotova's version is formed according to pattern of semantic roles: directive, destinative, correlative, quantitative, qualitative, locative, mediative, temporative [16: 383]. We use these nomenclature forms as a starting point for our metalanguage due to its particular trait – specification of items according to their use in prepositional phrases.

For the sake of quantitative grammar of prepositional constructions, we use the term "semantic rubric" as a generic name for the group of meanings of prepositions. It is often the case that these rubrics correspond to several Zolotova's syntaxemes, minor variations of the major prepositional sense forming the structure within the syntaxemes.

4   Methodology for Selection Pairs "Preposition - Its Meaning"

To solve this task, we need appropriate corpora. We carry out our research on the basis of morphologically annotated corpora. We have chosen 2 corpora of Russian texts: Russian National Corpus (http://ruscorpora.ru/en/index.html), consisting of different genre subcorpora, and Russian corpora of the Aranea corpus family created by the wacky technology [1] (http://unesco.uniba.sk). Also we use our own corpora. For the moment, these are Mathematical Linguistics Department's balanced corpus Bokryonok (25 mln. tokens) and Law corpus (1.5 mln. tokens).

It is worth noting that prepositional meaning frequencies obtained on the basis of various corpora differ due to different reasons. In order to receive comparable frequencies from corpora of different sizes we use IPM normalized measure, that is the corpus frequency of a token divided to the number token millions in the corpus.

The crucial point of our methodology is a compilation of a random sample of contexts with prepositional constructions from the chosen corpora. The contexts are annotated loosely by a linguist. Propositional meanings are ranked according the percentage of a particular meaning of some preposition. The upmost ranks demonstrate the regular use of prepositional constructions, and the bottom ranks show the irregular use. The meanings from the top ranks are extrapolated according the total frequency of a preposition in the corpus and normalized to a number of token millions presented in the corpus processed as an IPM frequency measure of prepositional meanings. They may be used for aligning of pairs "preposition-its meaning" according to the similar meaning, that is, the rubric or syntaxeme.

5   Examples of Corpus-Based Analyses of Prepositional Constructions

We demonstrate results of our methodology on several rubrics. Two of them – temporative and locative syntaxemes – are supposed to be representatives of so called circonstants [13], that is, adverbial characteristics which may be attached to any predicative phrase. Due to this absence of selectional preferences they have the highest corpus frequencies.

5.1   Locative Prepositional Constructions

The local specification of a predicate has 2 basic groups of syntaxemes (location and trajectory) and several peripheral ones.

1. The locative syntaxeme is the most frequent one among them. We can see versatile types of governing verbs (*stand, breathe, see*, etc.) as well as non-verbal governors. The most frequent Russian prepositions "в" ('in') and "на" ('on') are combined with a prepositional case of the noun in a prepositional phrase: *в городе* ('in the town'), *на улице* ('in the street'), *в комнате* ('in the room'), *на окне* ('on the window'), etc. Sometimes this case is called 'locative' due to the standard meaning of this construction.

The preposition "в" ('in') has the maximal corpus frequency 4000 IPM with the meaning of location of an event or object, the next position is occupied by the preposition "на" ('on') with 2500 IPM (data given in this article are obtained on the base of balanced Bokryonok corpus). The other locative prepositions have frequencies 10 or 20 times less than these ones. The opposition of meanings between "в" ('in') and "на" ('on') is usually described by the three-dimensional type of the concrete object designated by the dependent noun and the idea of possible inclusion into its inner space for the former, and the idea of contiguity and support for the latter [10]. Some objects designated in the locative construction may be specified by both prepositions: *в столе/ на столе* ('in/inside the table'/'on [the surface of] the table'), but very often there is the only one possibility: *в городе* ('in the town'), *на полу* ('on the floor'). In some cases, we see controversial object specification in different languages: *на дереве* ('in the tree'), *на улице* ('in the street', Czech 'v ulici') and suchlike. These constructions don't follow logical way of locative interpretation. We look at this particularity as an evidence of the grammatical nature of prepositional constructions. Moreover, the frequency drop-off of other prepositions shows the increase of the grammatical burden which may be expressed by latent oppositions of Jakobson's type.

Less frequent locative prepositions usually combined with a genitive noun case. They form several cluster groups unified by the corpus frequency rank: "у" ('at'), "около" ('near'), "вокруг" ('around') and "под" ('under') – 250 ± 75 IPM; "за" ('behind'), "над" ('above') – 150 ± 50 IPM; "перед" ('before'), "от" ('from'), "до" ('to') – 50 ± 25 IPM. The last group includes secondary multiword prepositions: "рядом с" ('next to'), "близко/вблизи от" ('close to'), "вдалеке/вдали от" ('far from'), "далеко от" ('far off'), "недалеко/неподалеку от" ('not far from'), "справа/ слева от" ('to the right/left of'), "спереди от" ('in front of'), "сзади от" ('from behind'), "посредине/посреди" ('in the middle') and suchlike – 2–10 IPM. We use a corpus statistics threshold 2 IPM. The last group of locative prepositions shows the lexical variability of item representation that may be considered to be an evidence of non-grammatical nature of these combinations. There are regular oppositions inside the locative group:

– the basic opposition "inclusion" versus "contiguity/support": "в" vs "на";
– the "point-wise" localization of the object versus "intersection of two points/lines" [10]: "в"/"на" vs "у"—"в городе" ('in the town'), "у города" ('near the town');
– "location" of the object versus vertical localization without specification of the "support" of the object: "на" vs "под"/"над"—"на столе" ('on the table'), "под столом" ('under the table'), "над столом" ('above the table') without precise coincidence of the object borders;
– "location" of the object versus visual location of the object as it is seen by a speaker: "на"/"в" vs "за"/"перед"—"на столе" ('on the table') vs "перед/за столом" ('before/behind the table') without precise coincidence of the object borders;
– the deictic reference to the closeness or remoteness of object localization: "близко/ вблизи от" ('close to'), "вдалеке/вдали от" ('far from'), "далеко от" ('far off'), "недалеко/неподалеку от" ('not far from');
– object positioning according to the limits of some area: "посредине/посреди" ('in the middle'), "на границе" ('on the border of').

The location of several objects in relation to each other is not frequent (total 500 IPM). Usually "inclusion" or "exclusion" of objects ("внутри" ('inside'), "вне" ('beyond'), "спереди" ('in front of'), "снаружи" ('outside of')), space configuration of objects ("напротив" ('opposite')) and spatial area ("от ... до" ('from ... to'), "между" ('between'), "с ... до" ('from ... to')) are specified.

2. The next type of locative prepositional groups reflects **the trajectory of object or subject movement** which is compatible with travel verbs and verbs denoting the change of object location. Three aspects of this trajectory are usually specified in the corpus texts (sorting to their frequency rank): (a) the end point of trajectory, that is, the goal; (b) the initial or starting point of the trajectory; (c) the space traversed. Zolotova proposes 3 different syntaxemes, directive, destinative, and transitive instead of one. Here we can speak about hierarchy in preposition meanings similar to preposition supersenses (hierarchically organized unlexicalized classes) in [11].

As in the locative syntaxeme two prepositions are the most frequent: "в" ('in') and "на" ('on') designating the end point of the trajectory but they are attached to the accusative noun form. So, the difference in their meaning from the locative construction in Russian is quite clear as opposed to languages without case forms though preferences of usage for the former or the latter are just the same as in locative one: *выйти на улицу* ('get out on the street'), *выйти во двор* ('go out into the yard'). The directive frequency of the preposition "в" ('in') is lesser than in locative construction 2500 IPM, that is explained by the reduction of context types with governing verbs.

There is an important peculiarity of prefix verbs of mentioned types: regularly the prefix is duplicated by the same preposition or the preposition with the same locative meaning: *вбежать в комнату* ('run into the room'), *выбежать из комнаты* ('run out of the room'), *наступить на щель* ('step on the gap'), *перепрыгнуть через щель* ('jump over the gap'), etc.

The important issue is what syntaxemes are used with the verbs of mental activity which are usually the metaphoric transformation of the source travel verbs or verbs of other types: *прийти в голову* (take into one's head), *вылететь из головы* ('slipped one's mind'), *прийти на ум* ('come to mind'), *сойти с ума* ('go out of one's head'). The trajectory analogy is looking a bit straightforward for such construction, though Zolotova's description of them follows the pattern of literal ones. The reason for this position is lesser frequency of figurative constructions (about 25% of contexts), thus smaller part of the quantitative score of the propositional construction. However, examples of figurative use of locative constructions show that the whole group, that is, predicate with a prepositional phrase may construct the set expression, in which a prepositional meaning is removed from an idiom: *сойти с ума* = 'go mad'. It is not the case for every figurative use, e.g. *вылететь из головы* ('slipped one's mind') and others, though we are to look for cues in their structure to pick up those prepositional constructions that have lost their specificity. The next vital issue – the validation of directive and locative syntaxemes in metaphoric usage – will be the subject of a separate article.

The problem of variation of the argument semantic roles in corpus texts is well known, the idea of role clustering [7] is seemed to be productive. Thus we will split a semantic rubric into syntaxemes, which, in their turn, may be divided into the detailed subtypes as was done with a different versions of the locative prepositional construction.

5.2   Temporative Prepositional Constructions

The "circonstant" status of temporal constructions means that it may be attached to any predicate. The temporal preposition with the highest rank "в" ('in') has corpus frequency 1850 IPM, that is two times less than the locative prepositional construction. It is usually explained by the fact that "time is structured on the model of space". Anyway, the corpus frequency decrease is an evidence of its grammatical markedness in comparison with the locative one. The case form in this construction is the same as in the locative one: prepositional or locative (*в 1999 году* ('in 1999'), *в августе* ('in August')). The usual nouns in the temporal constructions are words denoting such time periods as a year or a month. The accusative form in the prepositional temporal construction is less frequent in the same manner as we see in the locatives, it leads to their quantitative decrease to 985 IPM. In this construction time periods denoting day of the week or the time of day are used: *в пятницу* ('on Friday'), *в 10 часов* ('at 10 o'clock'). If numerals stand in the position of a noun, the case form is applied to them and specification of time is expressed by coordinated noun (*в 1999 году* ('in 1999'), *в третьем часу* ('at three o'clock')) or a special "counting" noun case form (*в три часа* ('at three o'clock'), *в восемь часов* ('at eight o'clock')). Sometimes the time period is described by the phrase: *в зимнее время* ('in winter time'), *в этом месяце* ('this month'), *в свое время* ('in due time'). Several lexemes, *время, период, момент* ('time', 'period', 'moment') form the secondary multiword prepositions in combination with the primary "в" ('in'): *во время* [170 IPM], *в период* [30 IPM], *в момент* [21 IPM], *во времена* [15 IPM], the dependent nouns in these secondary prepositions denote actions, states or events: *во время войны* ('during war'), *в период беременности* ('during pregnancy'), *в момент опасности* ('at the moment of danger'), во времена крестовых походов ('during the crusades'). Occasionally preposition "в" ('in') with an accusative case may attach nouns denoting atmospheric phenomena implying the time period of their duration: *в бурю* ('in a thunderstorm'), *в жару* ('in the heat'), *в дождь* ('in the rain'). Combination of "в" ('in') with a prepositional case indicates the period of human life: *в детстве* ('in childhood'), *в зрелости* ('in adulthood').

The next frequency group (850 IPM) is formed by the preposition "до" ('until') which indicates the end of time period: *до пятого марта* ('until March 5'), *до зимы* ('before winter'), *до 1917 года* ('before 1917'), *до поезда* ('before train [departure]'), *до появления заболеваний* ('before the onset of disease'). The logical extension of this point is specification of the beginning and the end of time interval: "от… до" [40 IPM], "с… до" [12 IPM]: *от 12 до 15 лет/с 12 до 15 лет* ('from 12 to 15 years'), *с 5 часов утра до 7 часов вечера* ('from 5 am to 7 pm'). The first construction is specified further by multiword secondaries: на срок от… до [20 IPM], "за период от… до" ('for a/the period from… to') [10 IPM], "[с] продолжительностью от… до" ('[with] duration from… to'). The duration of time interval may be shown as well: *за [день] до [встречи]* ('[a day] before [meeting]'). The primary "до" ('until') is productive for formation of secondaries: "задолго до" [10 IPM] ('long before'), "незадолго до" [10 IPM] ('just before'), "до момента" [2 IPM] ('until the moment'), "примерно до" [1 IPM] ('until about'). The primary "перед" [75 IPM] is synonymous to "до" ('until') in combination with event designation: *перед боем* ('before the fight'), *перед встречей с министром* ('before meeting with the minister').

The next frequency rank is formed by primary "при" ('at') [675 IPM] and secondary "после" ('after') [500 IPM] which is used on corpus texts predominantly as a preposition (99,9%). Both prepositions are used for the deictic reference: the first one signaled the simultaneity with some event: *при оказании помощи* ('in assisting'), *при обыске на квартире* ('during a search of the apartment'), and the second – the precedence to some: *после оказания помощи* ('after helping'), *после обыска на квартире* ('after searching the apartment').

The next group consists of two prepositions: "с" ('from') [320 IPM] и "через" ('through') [300 IPM]. The first preposition in combination with time intervals denotes the starting point of time: *с прошлого года* ('since last year'), *с двух часов дня* ('from two o'clock in the afternoon'). The secondary preposition on the base of "с" ('from') is *с момента* [10 IPM] *ареста* ('since arrest'). The preposition "через" ('through') means after a certain period of time. It depends little on the expressed proposition, regularly occurs as a determinant at the beginning of the sentence and attaches the nouns that denote time intervals modified by numerals: *через день* ('in one day'), *через столетие* ('after a century'), *через 2 дня* ('in 2 days'). The equivalent secondary preposition is "спустя" ('later'). It can appear after a noun phrase as a postposition as well: *спустя несколько лет/несколько лет спустя* ('a few years later'). The secondary preposition "по истечении" ('upon expiration') [3 IPM] combines with the nouns of the *"через"* ('through') model: *по истечении года* ('after a year'), *по истечении месяца* ('at the end of the month'), *по истечении двух лет* ('after two years'). The secondary "по окончании" ('at the end') [9 IPM] follows the model of "после" ('after'): *по окончании месяца* ('at the end of the month'). The secondary "вслед за" ('after') [2 IPM] is used mainly to indicate a non-independent movement and only in some cases similarly to *"после"* ('after') indicates the completion of an event: *вслед за заключением мира* ('following the conclusion of peace').

The next group includes three prepositions: primary "за" ('after') [260 IPM], secondary "во время" [170 IPM] and "в течение" ('during') [120 IPM]. The primary "за" is combined with time intervals as well as event designation: *за годы реформ* ('over the years of reform'), *за 2 недели* ('in 2 weeks'). Secondary prepositions "во время" and "в течение" are interchangeable with "за" in some contexts but without time interval specification: *в течение реформ* ('during the reforms'), *во время реформ* ('during reform'), *во время войны* ('during the war').

The next frequency rank is reserved to primary "к" ('to') [155 IPM] synonymous to "до" ('until'): *к 9 часам утра* ('by 9 am'), *к 1917 году* ('by 1917'), *к вылету самолета* ('to the flight'). The secondary "к моменту" ('to the moment') [5 IPM] governs the designation of events: *к моменту ареста* ('by the time of arrest').

The temporal secondary prepositions with frequency less than 50 IPM show some position in the time interval: "в начале" ('at the beginning'), "в конце" ('in the end'), "в ходе" ('in progress'), "в период" ('during the period'), "в процессе" ('in the process'). They attach nouns denoting time intervals or events: *в начале года* ('at the beginning of the year'), *в начале строительства* ('at the beginning of construction'), *в конце дня* ('at the end of the day'), *в ходе строительства* ('during construction'), *в процессе строительства* ('in process of construction').

6   Semantic Distribution of Governors and Governees

We are going to use the BC semantic nomenclature, that is, the Base Concepts in Wordnets (http://www.globalwordnet.org/gwa/ewn_to_bc/corebcs.html) which were adopted to Russian wordnet (RussNet). This structure seems to us the most reliable because it was tested by several national wordnets during EuroWordNet project. The attractive feature of this structure is the level hierarchy. There are 4 concepts at the top: ENTITY: concrete things (1st Order Entity); CONCEPT: concepts, ideas in mind (3rd Order Entity); EVENT: happenings involving change (Dynamic 2nd Order Entity); STATE: static situations (Static 2nd Order Entity). Each of these is further subdivided, in some cases 4 levels deep (http://globalwordnet.org/gwa/ewn_to_bc/ewnTopOntology. htm). The Russian semantic groups assigned to the lowest category of the taxonomy are listed at http://ct05647.tmweb.ru/russnet/?page=synsets.

The procedure for gathering the semantic distribution for prepositional construction assigned to the syntaxeme or some specified syntaxeme subdivision consists of the following actions:

(1) to fix the appropriate semantic groups from the Russian list for the governees in the marked up context random sample mentioned above;
(2) if there is some semantic group with more than 60% governee examples, it is nominated to be the prototypical label for this prepositional meaning, in other case the more abstract level of the BC hierarchy should be taken as a nominee, and so on up the utmost level;
(3) to fix the appropriate semantic groups from the Russian list for the governors in the marked up context random sample mentioned above;
(4) to repeat calculation described in (2) for the prototypical semantic type of governors.

The description of prepositional locative and temporal meanings above include mentioning of these labels. Moreover, semantic labels may be used for making decision in difficult and ambivalent cases of syntaxeme usage.

For instance, the mediative syntaxeme in Zolotova's description is "a method or means of action". There is also an instrumentive syntaxeme implying an instrument of action. The difference between them is seen in contexts when the instrument is used along with a means: *гладить утюгом через ткань* ('to crease by an iron through a cloth'). One of the mediative prepositions in Zolotova's list is "через" ('through') from the example above. This preposition is included into the list for the transitive syntaxeme (i.e. the movement path) as well as "сквозь" ('through'): *виден через/сквозь щель* ('visible through the gap'). The definite decision concerning a syntaxeme type is not obvious for contexts: *пропустить мясо через мясорубку* (to mince meat = to skip the meat through a meat grinder), *протереть творог сквозь/через сито* (to wipe cottage cheese through a sieve). According to Zolotova, the first example is mediative or/and transitive, the second is transitive. The semantic group for a *meat grinder* ('a mill for grinding meat') is a "appliance_type", for a *sieve* ('a strainer for separating lumps from powdered material or grading particles') is a "utensils_type". The next level of nomenclature for both is "1.4.9 Instrument", so they are *instrumentive* syntaxemes notwithstanding Zolotova's assignment. The next context *фильтровать через/сквозь вату* ('to filter through cotton') may be identified as a mediative due to the semantic class of *cotton* ('soft silky fibers from cotton plants in their raw state'), that is, "material_stuff" with a higher label "1.2.3 Substance". However, the governor type of *filter* ('to remove by passing through a filter') is "change_integrity" which implies the use of an instrument. So this is the *instrumentive* syntaxeme as well.

Zolotova mentioned two types of syntaxemes: bound or free ones. We started from the point that all preposition constructions are bound, that is, have a governor. However, some of the described locative and temporative prepositions may be attached to dummy centre of the sentence: *в лесу много снега* ('there is a lot of snow in the forest'). In Russian this construction is very natural, the locative at the beginning describes the situation in which the proposition is fulfilled or exists. In this case there is no predicate at all. We don't want to insert unreal predicates in such cases, though we will consider them to belong to the highest level of our semantic taxonomy.

7   Conclusion and Further Work

The semantic rubrics presented in our approach help to organize rather vague prepositional meanings. Their affinity and difference may be explicated through the overlap of semantic classes of governing and subordinate words. The whole structure of prepositional frequencies that so far have not been in any study and neighbor semantic distributions are resources for the compilation of the quantitative prepositional grammar for Russian.

We are going to compile the first version of essential semantic rubrics to proceed in the outlined direction and to grasp the dispersion for primary prepositional meanings. Then we'll assign the secondary prepositions to these sets: the particular semantic rubric plus variants of primary prepositional meanings. Thus we'll check the initial hypothesis that the granularity of prepositional meanings are restricted by the diversity of secondary prepositions.

Further stages of investigation include:

- to finalize the set of syntaxemes for prepositional constructions referring to governers and governees semantic types;
- to compile sets of prepositional constructions from corpora of different genres in order to discover the significant variation of statistical parameters;
- to describe prepositional constructions with heterogeneous stylistic statistical characteristics according to their distribution of IPMs and percentage ratios; lists of predominant semantic classes and/or lexemes used as "governors"; lists of predominant semantic classes and/or lexemes used as "governees";
- to compile rules of the hybrid generative grammar showing the use of prepositional phrases for expressing the comprehensive set of syntaxemes.

Acknowledgements. This paper has been supported by the Russian Foundation for Basic Research, project No. 17-29-09159, and partly (Sects. 2 and 3) project 17-04-00552-ОГН-А.

References

1. Benko, V.: Aranea: yet another family of (comparable) web corpora. In: Sojka, P., Horák, A., Kopeček, I., Pala, K. (eds.) TSD 2014. LNCS (LNAI), vol. 8655, pp. 247–256. Springer, Cham (2014). https://doi.org/10.1007/978-3-319-10816-2_31
2. Bonial, C., Corvey, W., Palmer, M., Petukhova, V.V., Bunt, H.: A hierarchical unification of LIRICS and VerbNet semantic roles. In: IEEE Fifth International Conference on Semantic Computing (2011). http://verbs.colorado.edu/~mpalmer/Ling7800/SACL-ICSC2011.pdf
3. Dictionary of the Russian Language, 3rd edn, vol. 1–4. Moscow (1985)
4. Efremova, T.F.: Explanatory Dictionary of the Service Parts of the Speech of the Russian Language [Tolkovyy slovar' sluzhebnykh chastey rechi russkogo yazyka]. Moscow (2001). (in Russian)
5. Filipenko, M.V.: Problems of the description of prepositions in modern linguistic theories [Problemy opisaniya predlogov v sovremennykh lingvisticheskikh teoriyakh]. In: Research on the semantics of prepositions. Russkie Slovari, Moscow pp. 12–54 (2000)
6. Herskovits, A.: Semantics and pragmatics of locative expressions. Cogn. Sci. **9**, 341–378 (1985)
7. Lyashevskaya, O.N., Kashkin, E.V.: Evaluation of frame-semantic role labeling in a case-marking language. In: Computational Linguistics and Intellectual Technologies Papers from the Annual International Conference "Dialogue", Moscow, no. 13, pp. 363–379 (2014)
8. Morkovkin, V.V., et al.: Dictionary of structural words of the Russian language [Slovar' strukturnykh slov russkogo yazyka]. Moscow (1997)
9. Mustajoki, A.: Theory of Functional Syntax [Teorija funtsionalnogo sintaksisa]. Moscow (2006)
10. Russian grammar in 2 volumes. Moscow (1980)
11. Schneider, N., Hwang, J.D., Srikumar, V., et al.: A corpus of preposition supersenses. In: Proceedings of the 10th Linguistic Annotation Workshop (2016)
12. Slolonitskiy, A.V.: Problems of semantics of Russian primitive prepositions [Problemy semantiki russkikh pervoobraznykh predlogov]. Vladivostok (2003)
13. Tesnière, L.: Éléments de syntaxe structurale. Klincksieck, Paris (1959)
14. Vsevolodova, M.V., Kukushkina, O.V., Polikarpov, A.A.: Russian Prepositions and means of prepositional type. Materials for functional grammar description of real use. Book 1. Introduction to the time grammar and lexicography of Russian prepositional units [Russkie predlogi i sredstva predlozhnogo tipa. Materialy k funktsional'no-grammaticheskomu opisaniju real'nogo upotreblenija. Kn. 1: Vvedenije v objektivnuju grammatiku i leksiko-grafiju russkikh predlozhnykh jedinits]. URSS, Moscow (2013)
15. Vsevolodova, M.V., Potapova, G.V.: Ways of expressing temporal relations in modern Russian [Sposoby vyrazheniya vremennykh otnosheniy v sovremennom russkom yazyke]. Moscow (1975)
16. Zolotova, G.A.: Syntactical Dictionary: A Set of Elementary Units of Russian Syntax [Sintaksicheskiy slovar': repertuar elementarnykh edinits russkogo sintaksisa], 4th edn. Moscow (2011)

Explicit and Implicit Discourse Relations in the Prague Discourse Treebank

Šárka Zikánová$^{(\boxtimes)}$, Jiří Mírovský, and Pavlína Synková

Faculty of Mathematics and Physics, Institute of Formal and Applied Linguistics,
Charles University, Prague, Czechia
{zikanova,mirovsky,synkova}@ufal.mff.cuni.cz

Abstract. Coherence of a text is provided by various language means, including discourse connectives (coordinating and subordinating conjunctions, adverbs etc.). However, semantic relations between text segments can be deduced without an explicit discourse connective, too (the so called implicit discourse relations, cf. *He missed his train. 0 He had to take a taxi.*). In our paper, we introduce a corpus of Czech annotated for implicit discourse relations (*Enriched Discourse Annotation of Prague Discourse Treebank Subset 1.0*) and we analyze some of the factors influencing the explicitness/implicitness of discourse relations, such as the text genre, semantic type of the discourse relation and the presence of negation in discourse arguments.

Keywords: Implicit discourse relations · Text genre · Negation

1 Some Explicit Questions About Implicitness

Text coherence is often provided by various language means, such as information structure, anaphoric chains, bridging (associative) anaphora or discourse relations. In our analysis, we deal with discourse relations: they can be either signaled by a discourse connective (typically coordinating and subordinating conjunctions, discourse adverbs etc.) or there is no connective device signaling the relation (so called implicit discourse relations, cf. Example 1).

(1)   He did not come. **0** He was ill.

Our general research question is, how can we understand a text if some signals of coherence (discourse markers) are omitted? How do we deduce the meaning of such a relation between text segments? To get more insight into this general research question, we have split it into several subtopics that we describe in this paper. First, we want to know how often implicit discourse relations occur in Czech in general, since it may be just a peripheral phenomenon. Second, we want to see some conditions or correlations of implicitness and explicitness, connected with other language phenomena. Is the implicitness of a discourse relation influenced by text genre [12,13]? Are there any semantic types of discourse relations

© Springer Nature Switzerland AG 2019
K. Ekštein (Ed.): TSD 2019, LNAI 11697, pp. 236–248, 2019.
https://doi.org/10.1007/978-3-030-27947-9_20

more prone to be implicit than other [5]? Or, in other words, are there any semantic types of discourse relations which must be expressed explicitly, as they are not deducible from the context? And, last but not least, can the implicitness/explicitness of discourse relations be influenced by such phenomenon as a sentence negation?

2 Data

To formulate hypotheses about the questions raised in Sect. 1 and to test them reliably, we needed manually annotated data. We had at our disposal the already published annotation of discourse relations in the Prague Discourse Treebank 2.0 (PDiT 2.0; [11]). It is a corpus of 50 thousand sentences of Czech journalistic texts from the 1990's, manually annotated on morphological, surface syntax and deep syntax (tectogrammatical) layer. Additional annotations (performed on top of the tectogrammatical layer) include coreference, bridging anaphora and discourse relations.

The annotation of discourse relations in the PDiT was inspired by the annotation scenario of the Penn Discourse Treebank 2.0 [8], which follows a lexically-grounded approach [15]: A discourse connective is a lexical anchor of a discourse relation that holds between two text spans called discourse arguments. The connective signals the sense of the discourse relation (Table 1 gives a list of possible senses). See Example 2 for a temporal discourse relation of *synchrony* expressed by the connective *when*. If the connective is absent (like in Example 1), the relation is called "implicit".

(2)   **When** I was young, the winters were much colder.

However, annotation of discourse relations in the PDiT only covers explicit relations. To be able to study also other types of cohesive means (and having only limited resources), we have selected a subcorpus (approx. 5%) from the PDiT and enriched[1] the original annotation of explicit discourse relations by the annotation of implicit relations, entity-based relations, question–answer relations and other discourse-structuring phenomena (see Table 2 for overall numbers of the relations). Our aim was to mark all local connections between discourse arguments and to present a text as a continuous chain of discourse segments, with the following possible types of connections:

- explicit discourse relations expressed by primary discourse connectives (expressions such as *because, if, but* etc.)
- explicit discourse relations expressed by secondary discourse connectives (e.g. *the reason is that*)
- implicit discourse relations (without a discourse connective)
- entity-based relations (relations based on the coreferential connections between discourse arguments)

---

[1] Using an adapted environment for annotation of discourse relations on top of the deep syntax (tectogrammatical) layer implemented in tree editor TrEd [3,4].

Table 1. Semantic types of discourse relations in the PDiT-EDA

CONTRAST	EXPANSION
Confrontation	Conjunction
Opposition	Conjunctive alternative
Restrictive opposition	Disjunctive alternative
Pragmatic contrast	Instantiation
Concession	Specification
Correction	Equivalence
Gradation	Generalization
	Empty relation
CONTINGENCY	TEMPORAL
Reason–result	Synchrony
Pragmatic reason–result	Precedence–succession
Explication	
Condition	
Pragmatic condition	
Purpose	

- questions (question–answer relation and also a relation between the previous context and the question)
- lists (e.g. *First, … Second, …*)
- coherence gaps (no relation to the preceding context can be found)
- specific parts of a text (author, location, heading, caption, etc.)
- attribution (relation between the author speech and the reported speech)
- macrostructure (relation between large segments of the text related to the text as a whole)

The data was annotated by two annotators with an overlap for inter-annotator agreement measurements. Newly we measured agreement on the implicit relations; for numbers of agreement on several other types of relations, see a paper about the underlying PDiT corpus [7]. The agreement on the recognition of the presence of an implicit relation was 0.54 (F1-measure). Agreement on discourse types (senses) of implicit discourse relations recognized by both annotators was 57.7% (agreement ratio), with Cohen's κ 47.4%.[2]

The enriched subcorpus contains 2 592 sentences in 100 documents and covers 15 genres (see Table 4 for the list of genres). It is available to download under the Creative Commons license from the LINDAT/CLARIN repository as the Enriched Discourse Annotation of PDiT Subset 1.0 (PDiT-EDA 1.0; [17]).

---

[2] For a comparison, a measurement of inter-annotator agreement for implicit relations in the Turkish Discourse Treebank reports chance-corrected κ values of 0.52 for the class level, 0.43 for the type level and 0.34 for the subtype level [16]. The measurement at the subtype level corresponds to our measurement of agreement on discourse types.

3   Results

The first question of our analysis is, what is the distribution of explicit and implicit discourse relations in our data. As presented in Table 2, the occurrence of explicit and implicit discourse relations is comparable, implicit discourse relations are slightly more common than explicit ones. (In the table, relations expressed with secondary discourse connectives, so called AltLexes, such as *the reason is,* are counted as a subset of explicit discourse relations.)

Let us compare these results with the annotation in the Penn Discourse Treebank 3.0 (PDTB 3.0; [10]), as presented in [14, p. 5]. In the PDTB 3.0, the amount of explicit and implicit discourse relations is comparable (25 865 explicit discourse relations, together with AltLexes, 21 731 implicit discourse relations), but in contrast with the PDiT-EDA, the explicit discourse relations are prevalent. The proportion of implicit discourse relations in the PDiT-EDA is comparable with the results of the Penn Discourse Treebank 2.0, too, where they present an amount of 40% of the whole set of annotated discourse relations [9]. The occurrence of implicit discourse relations in the Prague Discourse Treebank data is slightly higher (it must be accounted that the number for the implicit discourse relations covers inter-sentential as well as intra-sentential ones).

Table 2. Overall numbers of relations in the PDiT-EDA 1.0

Total on 2 592 sentences	3 149
Explicit discourse relations	1 288
Implicit discourse relations	1 427
Entity-based relations	264
Lists	105
Questions	65

To test the validity of the annotation of implicit discourse relations in the PDiT-EDA 1.0, a part of the data was annotated in parallel (12 documents containing 233 sentences). The inter-annotator agreement was measured according to the three following values: (a) agreement on the presence of an implicit discourse relation (the same pair of a starting and target nodes in the tree is connected with a discourse arrow by both annotators, disregarding its semantic label); (b) agreement on a semantic type of a discourse relation (in cases where both annotators agree on the presence of a discourse relation); (c) Cohen's κ for the second type of agreement.

In Table 3, the inter-annotator agreement on the annotation of implicit discourse relations in the PDiT-EDA 1.0 is compared to annotation of other kinds of text relations in the data, namely explicit discourse relations, textual coreference (i.e. mostly inter-sentential coreference in cases where the coreference cannot be directly deduced by grammatical rules), and bridging anaphora (such as *a room – the door* etc.), as they were annotated in the PDiT and reported in [7].

Table 3. Inter-annotator agreement in different types of the text annotation.

	Discourse implicit	Discourse explicit	Textual coreference	Bridging anaphora
F1 – presence of a relation	0.54	0.84	0.72	0.46
Agreement on types	0.58	0.77	0.90	0.92
Cohen's κ on types	0.47	0.71	0.73	0.89

3.1   Implicit Discourse Relations and Text Genres

Our data enables us to test the hypothesis that the proportion of implicitness and explicitness of discourse relations varies depending on text genre. We had supposed that in some text genres, the understanding is based rather on the recipient's genre-based expectations than on explicit lexical discourse signals. E.g., in a letter, an address and a date can be expected at the beginning of a text; a weather forecast provides the recipient with information about different aspects of the weather, structured as an additive chain without specific discourse markers. On the other hand, we assumed that narrative texts tend to express discourse relations rather explicitly, as they usually describe more complicated plots with unexpected nets of relations (additive, contrastive, temporal etc.).

Table 4 presents the distribution of implicit and explicit discourse relations among text genres in the PDiT-EDA. The relations between implicit and explicit discourse relations in different text genres were compared in Fig. 1, converted to percentages.

According to the Chi-square test, the differences in the distribution of implicit and explicit discourse relations among text genres are significant. Text genres with a typical prevalence of implicit discourse relations (weather, overview, invitation) describe simple events or more of them in a row, usually in a present or future tense, cf. Example 3 (overview):

(3)   (1) Jak na koncert Pink Floyd_HEADING
...
(9) Na pražské hlavní nádraží bude vypraven mimořádný rychlík z Bohumína (odjezd v 8.30 hod.), který zastavuje na hlavním nádraží v Ostravě, Ostravě-Svinově, Studénce, Suchdole nad Odrou, Hranicích na Moravě a Olomouci._IMPLICIT CONJUNCTION WITH (10)
(10) Další posilový rychlík (odjezd v 15.18 hod.) z Českých Budějovic zastavuje v Hluboké nad Vltavou-Zámostí, Veselí nad Lužnicí, Soběslavi, Táboře, Olbramovicích a Benešově u Prahy._IMPLICIT CONJUNCTION WITH (11)
(11) O další vozy budou rozšířeny pravidelné rychlíkové spoje Brno – Praha (odjezd ve 14.06 hod.) a Břeclav – Brno – Praha (odjezd ve 14.40 hod.)

(1) How to get to the Pink Floyd concert. HEADING

...

(9) A special express train from Bohumín (departure at 8.30 am) will be dispatched to Prague Main Station, which stops at the main railway station in Ostrava, Ostrava-Svinov, Studénka, Suchdol nad Odrou, Hranice na Moravě and Olomouc. IMPLICIT CONJUNCTION WITH (10)

(10) Another support train (departure at 15.18) from České Budějovice stops in Hluboká nad Vltavou-Zámostí, Veselí nad Lužnicí, Soběslav, Tábor, Olbramovice and Benešov u Prahy. IMPLICIT CONJUNCTION WITH (11)

(11) Regular express trains Brno – Prague (departure at 14.06) and Břeclav - Brno - Prague (departure at 2.40 pm) will be extended with additional wagons.

Table 4. Numbers of occurrences of implicit and explicit discourse relations among text genres in the PDiT-EDA.

Genre	Implicit	Explicit	Total
Sports news	126	108	234
Topical interview	112	121	233
Overview	111	36	147
Invitation	110	60	170
Reflective essay	107	106	213
Critical review	102	96	198
Letters from readers	101	126	227
Advice column	97	105	202
Weather forecast	96	13	109
Comment	92	105	197
News report	89	77	166
Readers' survey	89	81	170
Description	88	91	179
Collection	72	92	164
Personality-focused interview	35	71	106
Total	1 427	1 288	2 715

On the other hand, high explicitness of discourse relations is typical for other genres, such as personality-focused interview or letters from readers. In these cases, explicitness can be connected with a higher complexity of the situations/events described, typically argumentation in letters from readers or various inter-personal reactions and argumentation in dialogue personality-focused interviews (see Example 4, personality-focused interview).

(4) (1) Do té doby se aparát [Československé] konfederace [sportovních a tě-
lovýchovných svazů] vystěhuje?_QUESTION
(2) "Nikdo z nás si nedovolí zbytečně zabírat nějaké prostory._OPPOS-
ITION TO (3), EXPRESSED BY **ovšem** IN (3)
(3) Nejdříve se **ovšem** musí rozdělit majetek konfederace._CONJU-
NCTION WITH (4), EXPRESSED BY **a** IN (4)
(4) **A** jestli v této budově tělovýchova zůstane i nadále, bude záležet na
tom, zda české svazy budou mít ve svých dosavadních kancelářích na Stra-
hově dost prostoru, **či**_INTRA-SENTENTIAL DISJUNCTIVE ALTER-
NATIVE, EXPRESSED BY **či**_ vzhledem ke svým novým rozšířeným
kompetencím budou mít zájem i o kanceláře tady Na Poříčí."

(1) Until then, the apparatus of the [Czechoslovak] confederation [of sport
associations] will move out?_QUESTION
(2) "None of us will dare to occupy any space unnecessarily._OPPOS-
ITION TO (3), EXPRESSED BY **however** IN (3)
(3) **However**, the property of the confederation has to be divided
first._CONJUNCTION WITH (4), EXPRESSED BY **and** IN (4)
(4) **And** whether the sport association stays in the building will depend
on whether the Czech unions will have enough space in their existing
offices at Strahov, or_INTRA-SENTENTIAL DISJUNCTIVE ALTER-
NATIVE, EXPRESSED BY **or**_ due to their new extended competencies
will also be interested in offices here in Na Poříčí."

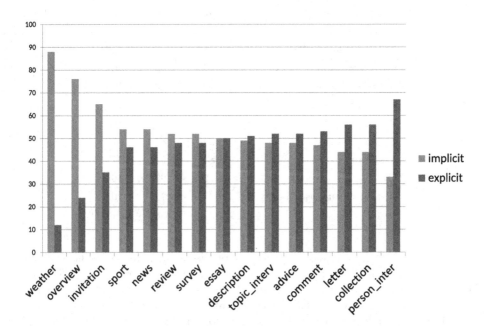

Fig. 1. Implicitness of discourse relations according to the text genre. The graph shows
relative frequencies of implicit (left column) and explicit relations (right column) in
individual genres.

3.2   Which Senses Are More Likely to Be Implicit?

The semantics of discourse relations differs in the specificity of the meaning: some relations have a very clear and narrow semantics with specific features which can be easily recognized (e.g. correction, with a typical discourse connective *not X - but rather Y*), whereas meaning of the others can be wide and rather free (conjunction).

Based on this observation, we assumed that discourse relations with more specific meaning would be more likely expressed by explicit devices while relations with "wider" semantics would be more often implicit.

Further, we assumed that implicit discourse relations cannot cover the whole range of semantic categories introduced for explicit discourse relations, because some discourse connectives have specific lexical semantics which cannot be deduced from the context.

The distribution of implicitness and explicitness across semantic types of discourse relations is presented in Table 5 and in relative frequencies in Fig. 2. As

Table 5. Numbers of occurrences of implicit and explicit discourse relations according to the semantic type of the discourse relation in the PDiT-EDA.

	Implicit	Explicit	Total
Conjunction	446	462	908
Specification	236	60	296
Empty relation	196	8	204
Reason–result	125	169	294
Explication	104	29	133
Opposition	67	178	245
Confrontation	66	31	97
Precedence–succession	55	47	102
Generalization	25	8	33
Instantiation	23	10	33
Equivalence	19	4	23
Gradation	12	22	34
Conjunctive alternative	12	8	20
Concession	11	44	55
Correction	10	15	25
Restrictive opposition	6	24	30
Synchrony	5	12	17
Condition	4	109	113
Purpose	3	26	29
Disjunctive alternative	1	12	13
Total	1 426	1 278	2 704

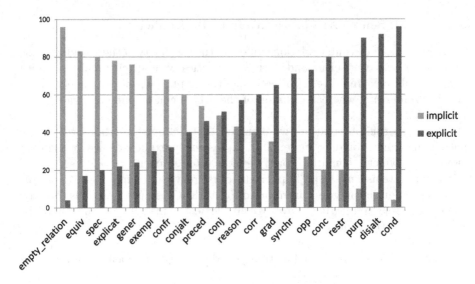

Fig. 2. Implicitness of discourse relations according to their semantic type. The graph shows relative frequencies of implicit (left column) and explicit relations (right column) for individual semantic types.

can be seen from these figures, there is a wide range of semantic types of discourse relations which can be realized implicitly. Contrary to our assumptions, implicit discourse relations cover almost all semantic categories of discourse relations.

Based on our annotation experience with explicit discourse relations, we did not expect specific groups of relations to be realized predominantly implicitly. However, there is a quite high occurrence of implicit *equivalence, specification, generalization* and *instantiation* in our data, i.e. relations from the general group of expansion. On the other hand, relations with a narrow semantics based on the links between events are rather explicit (*condition, purpose, concession*) [1].

There are interesting differences in implicitness/explicitness among relations which seem to be semantically close to each other. Within the class of temporal relations, the relation of *precedence–succession* is more often implicit, while *synchrony* tends to be expressed explicitly. Similarly, there is a big difference between two types of alternatives: *conjunctive alternative* is more often implicit, while *disjunctive alternative* is expressed with a discourse connective almost obligatorily.

3.3   Implicit Discourse Relations and Negation

We can assume that relations with an explicit discourse connective are easier to understand than implicit relations; there is no need to deduce the meaning of the relations from other linguistic signals or from world knowledge, the connective is a strong semantic signal. Intuitively, we assume that implicit discourse relations are more complex structures for the semantic decoding than the explicit ones.

A question arises then, whether this kind of complexity is in a certain interplay with other complexity features of discourse structure. Another such complexity feature could be e.g. sentence negation. A negative sentence requires one more cognitive operation of the recipient than an affirmative one. Is it possible that discourse arguments with sentence negation are connected rather explicitly than implicitly, in order to facilitate the understanding, or, in other words, to compensate the complexity of negation with the simplicity in the discourse structure.

We have observed that there is a relation between sentence negation and implicitness/explicitness in our data, see Table 6 and Fig. 3 with relative frequencies of implicit and explicit discourse relations depending on the presence of sentence negation in none, one or the other, or both arguments.

Table 6. Numbers of occurrences of implicit and explicit discourse relations according to presence of sentence negation in the two arguments in the PDiT-EDA (the arguments are referred to as start and target; "-" marks presence of negation).

Negation	Implicit	Explicit	Total
start −, target −	10	29	39
start +, target +	1 234	1 008	2 242
start −, target +	89	130	219
start +, target −	94	121	215
Total	1 427	1 288	2 715

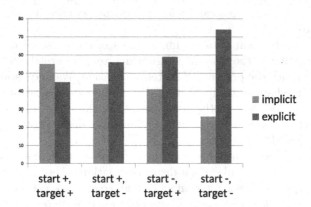

Fig. 3. Implicitness of discourse relations according to the sentence negation of the two arguments. The graph shows relative frequencies of implicit (left column) and explicit relations (right column) for various combinations of presence of sentence negation in the two arguments (the arguments are referred to as start and target; "-" marks presence of negation).

We find significant differences in implicitness/explicitness of discourse relations in structures with affirmative and negative discourse arguments, confirmed by a Chi-square test. Disregarding semantic types of discourse relations, we can say that the higher occurrence of negation correlates with the higher occurrence of explicit discourse relations. Thus, the complexity on the axis of affirmation and negation is compensated with the relative non-ambiguity of the meaning of the discourse relation.

4   Conclusion

The analysis of implicit and explicit discourse relations in Czech led to results and further observations on more levels then just one. First, we got a description of data presenting the distribution of implicitness and explicitness of discourse relations in the analyzed texts. Generally, the amount of implicit and explicit discourse relations is comparable, with a prevalent occurrence of implicit discourse relations. The implicitness/explicitness of discourse relations is connected with further features of texts and the surrounding language context. E.g. a text genre determines the measure of explicitness: the genres with easy and predictable (formal) structure describing simple events without argumentation tend to more implicit way of expressing discourse relations than text genres reporting about complex plots or containing argumentation and subjectivity.

Semantics of the discourse relation is another decisive feature for its implicitness/explicitness. Some discourse relations with a very specific, narrow semantics are predominantly explicit (purpose, condition, concession); these relations hold typically between events as wholes. On the other hand, many relations from the expansion group (exemplification, specification, equivalence, generalization) are usually implicit; it is characteristic for these relations that their underlying semantic concepts can be identified when connecting units like nominal phrases, too.

We tested the relation between implicitness of discourse relations and the presence of negation in the discourse arguments, too. It turned out that implicitness decreases with the presence of sentence negation. We understand this phenomenon as a mechanism compensating the complexity of a negative discourse argument for the recipient in the communication: the more complex the internal structure of the discourse arguments, the simpler orientation in the external structure between the arguments.

Second, more general insights and questions arise from this analysis of the relation between implicit and explicit discourse relations. The further we get from the surface forms, the lower inter-annotator agreement we get. Although some cases of disagreement always come from a vague annotation scenario and from annotators' mistakes, we dare to say – having certain experience in annotation, and in agreement with other works such as [2,6] – that with higher structures in the language, we may come to a limit of a reliable annotation.

Acknowledgments. This work has been supported by project "Implicit relations in text coherence" GA17-03461S of the Czech Science Foundation. The research team has been using language resources and tools distributed by the LINDAT/CLARIN project of the Ministry of Education, Youth and Sports of the Czech Republic (projects LM2015071 and OP VVV VI CZ.02.1.01/0.0/0.0/16 013/0001781).

References

1. Jínová, P., Poláková, L., Mírovský, J.: Sentence Structure and Discourse Structure (Possible Parallels), Linguistics Today, vol. 215, pp. 53–74. John Benjamins Publishing Company, Amsterdam (2014)
2. Mírovský, J., Hajičová, E.: What can linguists learn from some simple statistics on annotated treebanks. In: Henrich, V., Hinrichs, E., de Kok, D., Osenova, P., Przepiórkowski, A. (eds.) Proceedings of 13th International Workshop on Treebanks and Linguistic Theories (TLT13). pp. 279–284. University of Tübingen, University of Tübingen, Tübingen (2014)
3. Mírovský, J., Mladová, L., Žabokrtský, Z.: Annotation tool for discourse in PDT. In: Huang, C.R., Jurafsky, D. (eds.) Proceedings of the 23rd International Conference on Computational Linguistics (Coling 2010). vol. 1, pp. 9–12. Chinese Information Processing Society of China, Tsinghua University Press, Beijing (2010)
4. Pajas, P., Štěpánek, J.: Recent advances in a feature-rich framework for treebank annotation. In: Scott, D., Uszkoreit, H. (eds.) The 22nd International Conference on Computational Linguistics - Proceedings of the Conference. vol. 2, pp. 673–680. The Coling 2008 Organizing Committee, Manchester (2008)
5. Pitler, E., Louis, A., Nenkova, A.: Automatic sense prediction for implicit discourse relations in text. In: Proceedings of the Joint Conference of the 47th Annual Meeting of the ACL and the 4th International Joint Conference on Natural Language Processing of the AFNLP, vol. 2, pp. 683–691. Association for Computational Linguistics (2009)
6. Poláková, L.: K možnostem korpusového zpracování nadvětných jevů [on the possibilities of a corpus-based approach to discourse phenomena]. Naše řeč 4-5/2014, pp. 241–258 (2014)
7. Poláková, L., Mírovský, J., Nedoluzhko, A., Jínová, P., Zikánová, Š., Hajičová, E.: Introducing the prague discourse treebank 1.0. In: Proceedings of the 6th International Joint Conference on Natural Language Processing, pp. 91–99. Asian Federation of Natural Language Processing, Asian Federation of Natural Language Processing, Nagoya (2013)
8. Prasad, R., et al.: Penn Discourse Treebank Version 2.0. Data/software (2008). lDC2008T05
9. Prasad, R., et al.: The Penn Discourse Treebank 2.0 Annotation Manual. Technical Report IRCS-08-01. Institute for Research in Cognitive Science, University of Pennsylvania (2007)
10. Prasad, R., Webber, B., Lee, A., Joshi, A.: Penn Discourse Treebank Version 3.0. Data/software (2019). lDC2019T05
11. Rysová, M., et al.: Prague discourse treebank 2.0. Data/Software. LINDAT/CLARIN digital library at the Institute of Formal and Applied Linguistics (ÚFAL), Faculty of Mathematics and Physics, Charles University (2016). http://hdl.handle.net/11234/1-1905

12. Taboada, M., Brooke, J., Stede, M.: Genre-based paragraph classification for sentiment analysis. In: Healey, P., Pieraccini, R., Byron, D., Young, S., Purver, M. (eds.) Proceedings of the SIGDIAL 2009 Conference. The 10th Annual Meeting of the Special Interest Group on Discourse and Dialogue, pp. 62–70. Association for Computational Linguistics, Stroudsburg (2009)

13. Webber, B.: Genre distinctions for discourse in the Penn TreeBank. In: Su, K.Y., Su, J., Wiebe, J., Li, H. (eds.) Proceedings of the Joint Conference of the 47th Annual Meeting of the ACL and the 4th International Joint Conference on Natural Language Processing of the AFNLP. pp. 674–682. Association for Computational Linguistics, Suntec (2009)

14. Webber, B., Prasad, R., Lee, A., Joshi, A.: The Penn Discourse Treebank 3.0 Annotation Manual. Technical report, University of Edinburgh (2019)

15. Webber, B., Stone, M., Joshi, A., Knott, A.: Anaphora and discourse structure. Comput. Linguist. **29**(4), 545–587 (2003)

16. Zeyrek, D., Demirşahin, I., Çallı, A.B.S., Kurfalı, M.: Annotating implicit discourse relations in Turkish & the challenge of annotating corrective discourse relations. Oral presentation. In: IPrA Conference 2015, Antverp, Belgium (2016)

17. Zikánová, Š., Synková, P., Mírovský, J.: Enriched Discourse Annotation of PDiT Subset 1.0 (PDiT-EDA 1.0). Data/Software. LINDAT/CLARIN digital library at the Institute of Formal and Applied Linguistics (ÚFAL), Faculty of Mathematics and Physics, Charles University (2018). http://hdl.handle.net/11234/1-2906

Speech

On Practical Aspects of Multi-condition Training Based on Augmentation for Reverberation-/Noise-Robust Speech Recognition

Jiri Malek$^{(\boxtimes)}$ and Jindrich Zdansky

Institute of Information Technologies and Electronics,
Technical University of Liberec, Studentská 2, 46010 Liberec, Czech Republic
{jiri.malek,jindrich.zdansky}@tul.cz

Abstract. Multi-condition training achieved through data augmentation belongs to the most successful techniques for noise/reverberation-robust automatic speech recognition (ASR). Its basic principle, i.e., generation of artificially distorted speech signals, is well documented in the literature. However, the specific choice of hyper-parameters for the generation process and its influence on the results of the subsequent ASR is usually not discussed in detail. Often, it is simply assumed that the augmentation should include as many acoustic conditions as possible. When designed in this broad manner, the computational/storage demands of the augmentation process grow rapidly.

In this paper, we rather aim for careful selection of a limited number of acoustic conditions that are highly relevant with respect to the target environment. In this manner, we keep the computational requirements feasible, while retaining the improved accuracy of the augmented models. We experimentally analyze two augmentation scenarios and draw conclusions regarding suitable setup choices. The first case concerns augmentation for reverberation-robust ASR. We propose to exploit Clarity C_{50} as a feature for selection of Room Impulse Responses (RIRs) crucial for the augmentation. We show that mismatches in other RIR-related parameters, such as Reverberation Time T_{60} or the room dimension, have small influence on ASR accuracy, as long as the training-test conditions are matched from the C_{50} perspective. Subsequently, we investigate the augmentation for noise-reverberation-robust ASR. We discuss selection of Signal-to-Noise Ratio (SNR), the type of noise and reverberation level of speech. We observe the influence of mismatches in these parameters on the ASR accuracy.

Keywords: Multi-condition training · Data augmentation · Noisy speech recognition · Far speech recognition

K. Ekštein (Ed.): TSD 2019, LNAI 11697, pp. 251–263, 2019.
https://doi.org/10.1007/978-3-030-27947-9_21

1　Introduction

Robustness against detrimental distortions is a key topic of the research in the area of Automatic Speech Recognition [29]. Owing to this fact, the ASR is able to operate in real-world applications, such as subtitle production for audio-visual broadcast, smart home control or transcription of telephone conversations. In all of these scenarios, the reverberation and the presence of background noise are the major sources of deteriorated ASR results.

The robustness of an ASR system against these two distortions can be improved in various parts of the transcription chain [29]. In the front-end, the signal/feature enhancement techniques are often employed. These can be most notably divided by the number of available input channels. Classical single-channel methods are focused on removal of stationary noise only and rely on the knowledge of noise spectrum. This concerns techniques such as Noise Subtraction [1] or Minimum-Mean Square-Error Spectral Estimator [6]. Modern methods are based on supervised deep learning principles [26]. The multi-channel approaches are often based either on Beamforming [8] or Blind Source Separation (BSS) [18]. Beamformers exploit known parameters of the signal mixture (such as locations of the sources or signal's spatial covariance matrices), which, however, need to be estimated in practice. The BSS methods try to enhance speech based on its statistical independence from the background noise.

Methods increasing the robustness within the back-end usually modify the Acoustic Model (AM). Nowadays, the most often encountered type is the hybrid Hidden Markov Model-Deep Neural Network (HMM-DNN) type. One approach is the adaptation of an existing non-distorted speech AM for recognition of distorted utterances [21]. Another approach constitutes the environment-aware AM training. Here, the DNN input vector is extended by additional features that carry explicit information about the acoustic environment or present background noise. The reverberation can be described, e.g., by T_{60} parameter or Direct-to-Reverberant-Ratio as in [9]. The stationary noise can be represented by features computed on noise-only frames [24]. Environment-aware training for non-stationary noise was presented in [27]; the required noise representation was provided by a DNN trained in a supervised manner.

One of the most successful approaches to robust ASR is the multi-condition training [24], where the speech distorted by various noise-types and reverberation-levels is directly added to the training dataset, in order to reduce the often encountered training-test mismatch. Since large amount of real data can be difficult to collect and both noise and reverberation can be reasonably well simulated, the training set is often extended by artificially created data. This process is called augmentation by label preserving transformations; the clean speech is convolved with a set of room impulse responses and summed with noise from selected acoustical environments [7,13,15,23].

Usually, the data to be augmented need to be labeled; the labels are unchanged in the process and serve as targets during the AM training. An alternative approach, which alleviates the need of labeled data, represents the "student-teacher" training [17]. Here, an unlabeled corpus of parallel data (i.e., pairs of undistorted and distorted speech) and an AM trained on undistorted speech are required. The targets for the training of the robust AM are given as the outputs of the existing model processing the undistorted utterances.

The augmentation can be used to mitigate other distortions beyond noise and reverberation. The simulation of various compression schemes were discussed in [7,19]. The effects in speaking style were addressed through Vocal Tract Length Perturbation (VTLP) in [12] and Stochastic Feature Mapping in [3].

The contribution of the current paper lies in the analysis of the setup for the augmentation process and its influence on ASR accuracy. We aim to include only a limited number of highly relevant acoustic conditions (with respect to the target scenario), rather than to plainly incorporate all possible options (which is discussed, e.g., in [13]). In this manner, we keep the amount of generated data feasible from computational and/or storage point of view, while maintaining the robustness of the augmented models.

Two augmentation scenarios are discussed; the first one concerns reverberation robustness. In contrast to papers mentioned above, we propose to utilize the Clarity C_{50} parameter as a feature for selection of room impulse responses (RIRs) crucial for the augmentation. Clarity is a RIR-derived measure; a ratio of energy of the early part of the RIR and the energy of the late counterpart (see Sect. 2.2). It was used as a feature describing the amount of reverberation for ASR purposes in [22]. We propose to include in the augmentation only such RIRs that have C_{50} roughly comparable to the RIRs of the target environment. We show that for this purpose, C_{50} represents the reverberation in a more meaningful manner than other related measures, such as T_{60} or room dimension. Further, we compare the utilization of genuine and artificial RIRs within the augmentation.

During finalization of this paper, we found that a measure related to Clarity called Early-to-Late Reverberation Ratio (ELR) was independently suggested in [2] to control the augmentation (denoted there as data contamination). The ELR parameter can be seen as a generalization of the widely used Clarity. The findings from both papers, achieved on completely different simulated datasets, are in agreement and corroborate the proposed use of Clarity (and ELR). The current paper extends the analysis from [2]. We validate the proposition on real-world noiseless test sets and especially datasets with background noise, which was not performed in [2].

Second part of the paper is dedicated to noise-reverberation robustness. The selection of noise-type, noise-level and reverberation-level (from the C_{50} perspective) is discussed. We train several acoustic models that exhibit training-test mismatch in one or more of these parameters and analyze the influence of this mismatch on ASR accuracy. The results indicate that a closely matched noise-type is the most important parameter for successful noise-robust ASR.

The paper is organized as follows. Section 2 describes utilized training/test sets and our concept of the augmentation process. Section 3 concerns the ASR system we utilize. Section 4 presents and discusses the achieved experimental results. Section 5 concludes the paper and presents recommendations for the setup of the augmentation process.

2   Augmentation Process

2.1   Training and Test Datasets

Due to the availability of training/test datasets, the recognition of Czech speech is discussed (without any loss of generality to the topic). We utilize single training dataset that consists of 132 h of clean speech from broadcast news and dictated utterances (sampled at 16 kHz).

The following test sets are considered: (1) The real-world dataset denoted as **Test:Real** contains 2.2 h of speech dictated in a room with T_{60} about 700 ms on four microphones. One microphone is close-talk, the other have distance 1, 2 and 3 m. The estimated Clarity values corresponding to these distances are 9.33, 5.89 and 6.44 dB, respectively. In total, this gives $4 \times 2.2 = 8.8$ h of speech. Computer fan noise with estimated SNR about 15 dB is present in the background.

(2) The simulated dataset labeled as **Test:Simu** contains 2.1 h of undistorted speech convolved with RIRs from two rooms. For the first room, $T_{60} = 610$ ms; the impulse responses originate from database [11]. The second set of RIRs was measured in a classroom with $T_{60} = 1070$ ms. Two source-microphone distances $(1, 2$ m) are considered. The detailed C_{50} values are given in Table 1. The dataset comprises of $2.1 \times (2 \times 2 + 1) = 10.5$ h of speech.

(3) The real-world dataset referred to as **Test:Shop** contains 15 m of dialog between shopkeepers and customers recorded on a microphone in an approximate distance of 1 m. There is a (rather non-stationary) background noise originated from the shop traffic, music and babble noise from concurrent speakers. We estimated that the SNR is ranging approximately between 8–12 dB.

(4) The simulated dataset denoted as **Test:Mall** was created by adding background noise from several shopping centers (as available in the Task 1 and th development dataset from the DCASE2018 challenge [5]) to the Test:Real dataset. We created two dataset instances with respective SNR values 3 and 8 dB, i.e., $2.2 \times 4 \times 2 = 17.6$ h of speech.

2.2   Reverberation-Robust Augmentation

The reverberation is a distortion encountered in enclosed acoustic spaces, such as rooms. The sound propagating through the air is reflected off the objects in the environment. It is modeled through Room Impulse Responses, i.e., finite impulse response filters. The RIRs depend on enclosure properties (geometry, material, temperature etc.) as well as source-sensor distance/location.

The augmentation with respect to reverberation thus proceeds through convolution of the clean speech recordings with a set of RIRs corresponding to desired environments and locations. The potential number of RIRs (and the generated speech samples) can be enormous in complex environments. The measurement of real-world RIRs is time consuming. To mitigate these effects, we setup the augmentation process based on the following two propositions.

(1) Along with parameters mentioned above, other RIR properties are crucial from the ASR perspective. These are measures that quantify the amount of reverberation, such as Clarity C_{50} [16] given by

$$C_{50} = 10 \log \left(\frac{\sum_{n=0}^{N} h^2[n]}{\sum_{n=N+1}^{\infty} h^2[n]} \right) \text{ [dB]}, \tag{1}$$

where $h[n]$ denotes the room impulse response and N is the index of the sample corresponding to 50 ms after the arrival of the direct path. Clarity was presented as a feature quantifying the amount of reverberation for the ASR purposes in [22].

Based on experimental results presented in Sect. 4.1, we propose to include in the augmentation process only such RIRs that correspond to C_{50} values expected for the test scenario. Section 4.1 indicates that these C_{50} expectations can be very approximate. We selected RIRs with $C_{50} \in (6, 12)$ dB to represent moderately reverberant rooms and $C_{50} \in (2, 12)$ dB for highly reverberant environments. RIRs with $C_{50} > 12$ dB indicate very low reverberation that does not deteriorate the ASR accuracy.

We show that the C_{50} is a more suitable measure of reverberation for augmentation purposes than other RIR-related parameters, such as reverberation time T_{60}, size of the room or source-microphone distance. The augmented models retain high accuracy, when the training-test conditions are matched from the C_{50} perspective and mismatches occur in the other mentioned parameters.

(2) The RIRs utilized within the augmentation process can be genuine (measured in a real-world room) or artificially simulated through RIR generator. The latter is an effortless computational process. In our experiments, we compare both approaches using the RIR generator from [10]. We show that the accuracy achieved through utilization of the artificial RIRs is only slightly lower compared to the genuine ones. Thus the artificial RIRs are suitable to be used within the augmentation process.

All reverberation robust models are trained on one instance of the training dataset, i.e. 132 h of speech. The training set is divided into $N + 1$ parts, where N is the number of considered T_{60} cases × the number of distances. These N parts are distorted by a different sets of RIRs and the remaining part is left undistorted.

2.3   Reverberation-and-Noise-Robust Augmentation

Real-world speech recording contain various kinds of additive noise in the background. In can be environmental noise, music or even concurrent speech. For single channel ASR, only the spectral content and the loudness of the noise are relevant.

The augmentation proceeds by addition of a specific noise signal to a (reverberated) noiseless utterance with a predefined SNR level. The number of potentially generated artificial signals grows rapidly, as the speech should be augmented by all combinations of considered noise-types, noise-levels and amounts of reverberation.

To constrain the size of the generated dataset, we investigate to what extend the mismatch in the above mentioned parameters deteriorates the accuracy of the augmented model. We show that augmentation approaching (but not necessarily identical) to the test conditions is able to significantly improve the accuracy compared to AM trained on undistorted data. We also show that a mismatch in noise-type deteriorates the accuracy the most from the above mentioned parameters.

All augmented AMs are trained on two instances of training dataset, i.e., $2 \times 132 = 264$ h.; one instance is kept undistorted and the other is augmented. The augmented part is divided into N parts, where N is the number of considered T_{60} cases $\times$ the number of SNR levels.

3   Recognition System

We use our own ASR system based on a one-pass speech decoder performing a time-synchronous Viterbi search. The system consists of an acoustic and language model. The former varies according to the augmented training sets we consider, the latter remains the same in all the experiments.

3.1   Acoustic Models

Utilized models have Hidden Markov Model-Deep Neural Network (HMM-DNN) hybrid architecture [4]. The DNN input layer corresponds to 11 consecutive feature vectors, 5 preceding and 5 following the current frame. It is followed by five fully-connected hidden layers consisting of 768 units; the activation function is ReLU. The output layer corresponds to 2219 senones. These hyper-parameters correspond to the best performance in preliminary experiments with undistorted data.

The feature vectors contain 39 filter bank coefficients [28], computed using 25-ms frames with frame shift of 10 ms. We employ the Mean Subtraction [20] normalization with a floating window of 1 s.

The DNN parameters are trained by minimization of the negative log-likelihood criterion via the stochastic gradient descent. The training ends after 50 epochs or when the criterion does not improve on a small validation dataset. The training is implemented in the Torch library [25].

3.2   Linguistic Part

The utilized lexicon contains 550k entries. These represent the most frequently observed items in a 10 GB large corpus that covers newspaper texts and broadcast program transcripts. Due to very large vocabulary size, the Language Model (LM) is based on bigrams. This allows good recognition performance with reasonable computational costs. The unseen bigrams are backed-off by the Kneser-Ney smoothing technique [14].

4   Experimental Results

In the following experiments, we will denote by an identical name both the specific dataset and the acoustic model trained on this dataset. The AM trained without any augmentation is denoted as **Baseline**. The results are given in the terms of Accuracy [%] or Correctness [%] (number of hits divided by number of all words).

4.1   Reverberation: Clarity (C_{50})

As stated in Sect. 2.2, we aim to use C_{50} as a feature for selection of RIRs that should be included in the augmentation process. The validity of this proposition is experimentally demonstrated using **Test:Simu** dataset. The parameters of RIRs used to create both train and test data are summarized in Table 1. Each instance of the test set was created using RIRs corresponding to a specific room/distance that corresponds to a specific value of C_{50}. The RIRs of the three augmented training sets cover a certain interval of C_{50} values that is shown in the last column of Table 1.

The results presented in Table 2 show the the Baseline AM achieves the best performance on the close-talk instance of the Test:Simu dataset (88.90%). Here, the augmented AMs achieve comparable accuracy, i.e., the augmentation does not deteriorate the performance on undistorted data. The performance of Baseline AM deteriorates on datasets with reverberation.

The bold numbers in Table 2 correspond to scenarios, where the interval of C_{50} covered by the augmented AM also contains the C_{50} value corresponding to the specific test set. In these cases, the achieved accuracy approaches the result achieved on close-talk data and is always higher than 85.7%. From the perspective of the C_{50}, these can be regarded as matched training-test conditions. However, this does not necessarily mean that the exact acoustic conditions corresponding to the test set are are present within the training set. For example, the Room 2 does have high $T_{60} = 1070$ ms. For the distance of 1 m, the Rev:Gen-1 model still achieves high accuracy, although its training data does not contain signals with such a high reverberation time T_{60}.

In the remaining cases, where C_{50} of the test set lies outside the interval of the corresponding training set, the performance deteriorates. The accuracy ranges from 69.0–84.8%. Still, the augmented AMs achieve higher accuracy than the Baseline AM.

4.2   Reverberation: Comparison of Genuine and Artificial RIRs

This section compares accuracy of AMs trained on data augmented either by genuine RIRs or artificial RIRs with similar C_{50}. We utilize both simulated test data of the **Test:Simu** dataset and real-world **Test:Real** utterances.

The AMs augmented with genuine data (Rev:Gen) are the same as in the previous section (see Table 1). The RIRs for AMs augmented with artificial data were created using RIR generator [10], such that they exhibit similar C_{50} value

Table 1. Parameters of genuine RIRs used to simulate both training and test data. Each setting corresponds to a set of RIRs that differ by the angle (-45 to $45°$) of the sound source from the axis of the recording microphone. N denotes the number parts within training set; each part corresponds to one of the acoustic conditions (see Sect. 2.2).

Name	Train/Test	T_{60} [ms]	Distance [m]	C_{50} [dB]
Test:Simu (Room 1)	Test	610	1;2	11.81; 7.44
Test:Simu (Room 2)	Test	1070	1;2;3	7.76; 4.49; 2.42
Rev:Gen-1 ($N = 6$)	Train	160; 310; 610	1;2	7.44–32.39
Rev:Gen-2 ($N = 4$)	Train	1330; 1590	1;2	2.72–10.79
Rev:Gen-3 ($N = 2$)	Train	1330	1;2	6.33–10.79

Table 2. Accuracy [%] of augmented systems (rows) for various instances of the Test:Simu dataset. The "C_{50}-Test" parameter corresponds to Clarity of the RIRs utilized to simulate the test utterances. **The bold values** correspond to the cases, where interval of C_{50} corresponding to the augmented training set contains the C_{50} value corresponding to the test set (i.e., matched training-test condition from the C_{50} perspective). See Table 1 for the detailed configuration of the training sets.

	Close-talk	Room 1 1 m	Room 1 2 m	Room 2 1 m	Room 2 2 m	Room 2 3 m	C_{50} interval (Train) [dB]
C_{50}-Test [dB]	-	11.81	7.44	7.76	4.49	2.42	
Baseline	**88.90**	85.87	76.86	80.89	18.31	7.48	-
Rev:Gen-1	**88.66**	**88.18**	**87.62**	**86.73**	77.81	69.04	7.44–32.39
Rev:Gen-2	**88.59**	**87.43**	**85.61**	**87.65**	**85.66**	82.54	2.72–10.79
Rev:Gen-3	**88.67**	**87.84**	**85.91**	**87.73**	84.83	79.31	6.33–10.79

compared the genuine RIRs. The artificial RIRs originate from a shoe-box room of size $8 \times 7 \times 3$ m with T_{60} ranging from 175–650 ms. The angle of the source from the microphone direction was -45 to $45°$, the source-microphone distance was 1–2 m.

The results summarized in the Table 3 indicate that both AM types achieve comparable results. The AMs trained using the genuine RIRs achieve on average slightly higher accuracy, but the largest absolute difference in accuracy is lower than 2.5%. This means that the easily acquired generated RIRs can be used successfully for the creation of the augmented training sets instead of genuine RIRs.

4.3   Reverberation: Artificial RIRs and Importance of Room Setup

This section continues the discussion from Sect. 4.1 about the importance of C_{50} parameter. We aim to show that room setup parameters used to produce the artificial RIRs, such as room size and T_{60}, do not influence ASR accuracy much, as long as the training-test conditions are matched from the C_{50} perspective.

Table 3. Comparison of accuracy [%] yielded by AMs augmented by genuine (Rev:Gen) or artificial (Rev:Art) RIRs on Test:Simu and Test:Real datasets. **The bold values** indicate higher accuracy between a pair of comparable systems. See Section 4.2 for the detailed configuration of the training sets.

Model name	C_{50} interval [dB]	Simu Close-talk	Simu Room 1 1 m	Simu Room 1 2 m	Simu Room 2 1 m	Simu Room 2 2 m	Simu Room 2 3 m	Real Close-talk	Real 1 m	Real 2 m	Real 3 m
Baseline	-	88.90	85.87	76.86	80.89	18.31	7.48	90.19	71.08	39.51	26.17
Rev:Gen-1 ($N = 6$)	7.44–32.39	**88.66**	**88.18**	**87.62**	**86.73**	**77.81**	**69.04**	**90.07**	**83.50**	72.63	**67.53**
Rev:Art-1 ($N = 6$)	7.43–33.01	88.58	87.70	86.88	85.87	76.47	67.91	89.97	82.52	**74.56**	67.16
Rev:Gen-2 ($N = 4$)	2.72–10.79	**88.59**	87.43	85.61	**87.65**	**85.66**	**82.54**	**89.67**	**84.17**	76.82	**75.46**
Rev:Art-2 ($N = 4$)	2.36–10.36	88.48	**87.82**	**87.10**	86.64	83.25	79.97	89.51	84.13	**78.51**	74.54

We compare two AMs that were generated from two different RIR groups. Both groups contain RIRs with similar C_{50} values (i.e. around 2–10 dB), but the room dimensions and T_{60} differ significantly. (1) The model Rev:Art-2 from Sect. 4.2 was generated using RIRs originating from a room with fixed dimensions ($8 \times 7 \times 3$ m), source-microphone distance 1–2 m and T_{60} ranging from 175 to 650 ms.

(2) The model designated as Rev:Art-3 was generated from RIRs originating in rooms with varying dimensions (square floor of size 4–7 m and height 3 m), source-microphone distance 1–2 m and T_{60} from interval 400–700 ms.

The results in Table 4 seem to confirm the given assumption; both model achieve comparable accuracy. The highest absolute difference in performance is lower than 0.5%.

Table 4. Influence of room setup: Accuracy [%] yielded by AMs augmented by artificial RIRs; RIR groups for both models share similar C_{50} values but differ with respect to room size and T_{60}. See Sect. 4.3 for the detailed configuration of the training sets.

Model name	C_{50} interval [dB]	Simu Close-talk	Simu Room 1 1 m	Simu Room 1 2 m	Simu Room 2 1 m	Simu Room 2 2 m	Simu Room 2 3 m	Real Close-talk	Real 1 m	Real 2 m	Real 3 m
Rev:Art-2 ($N = 4$)	2.36–10.36	88.48	87.82	87.10	86.64	83.25	79.97	89.51	84.13	78.51	74.54
Rev:Art-3 ($N = 4$)	2.43–12.25	88.50	87.72	87.01	86.41	83.14	80.34	89.85	84.34	78.79	74.07

4.4 Noise-Robust Augmentation

This section describes a set of experiments conducted on two noisy test sets: artificial **Test:Mall** (Test:Real with added noise) and real-world **Test:Shop**. The parameters of the augmentation for the considered AMs are summarized in Table 5. The utilized RIRs are identical to the Rev:Art-2 model. The background noise "Mall" originates from the Task 1 of the DCASE2018 challenge (development dataset, [5]); there is no overlap with the recordings utilized to generate Test:Mall test set. The noise type "Shop" was recorded in the same environment (at a different time) as Test:Shop dataset.

The results presented in Table 6 indicate that the performance of the Baseline AM deteriorates significantly for these noisy and reverberant conditions. Observing the simulated datasets, all the augmented models are able to improve over the accuracy of the Baseline model. Unsurprisingly, the highest accuracy is achieved for the matched training-test conditions (bold values in Table 6). However, the improvement over Baseline remains even in situations, where the training-test condition mismatch arises (non-bold values). This indicates that augmentation setting need to approach the test conditions, but need not be identical.

However, this tolerance to augmentation setup is not entirely valid for the real-world Test:Shop. For example, the conditions for model Noi:Mall2 can be considered matched from the perspective of SNR and the distance and mismatched due to noise-type. However, the model is able to improve only the achieved correctness (by about 9.5%), but the accuracy deteriorates. This is caused by an increased number of insertions as the model attempts to recognize some words from the background babble. The Noi:Shop-2 model corresponds to matched conditions with respect to Test:Shop dataset. It achieves the highest accuracy and improves the accuracy by about 4% over the Baseline.

The results indicate that a closely matched noise-type is the most important parameter for successful augmentation. Although the "Mall" and "Shop" noises are of similar nature, the models with matched noise-type (even when mismatches in SNR and Clarity occur) achieve practically always higher accuracy compared to models with mismatched noise-type (even when SNR and Clarity are matched). This holds for both simulated Test:Mall and real-world Test:Shop datasets.

Concerning the utilization of C_{50} for the selection of relevant reverberant conditions, the Table 6 indicates validity of the proposition for both real-world and noisy datasets. For instance, model Noi:Mall3 (matched from a C_{50} perspective, see Sect. 2.1 for details) achieves higher accuracy for Test:Real and Test:Mall (8 dB) and distances 2 and 3 m than the mismatched Noi:Mall-1 and Noi:Mall-2 models. Again, this does not mean that the train set of the Noi:Mall-3 model contains all acoustic conditions corresponding to the Test:Real dataset; for example, the source-sensor distance 3 m and $T_{60} = 700$ ms are not included.

Table 5. Description of the augmentation settings for the considered noise-robust AMs. N denotes the number parts within training set; each part corresponds to one of the acoustic conditions (see Sect. 2.3).

Name	C_{50} [dB]	T_{60} [ms]	Distance [m]	Noise Type	SNR [dB]
Noi:Mall-1 ($N = 6$)	6.51–10.36	400;550	1	Mall	3;8,∞
Noi:Shop-1 ($N = 6$)				Shop	
Noi:Mall-2 ($N = 6$)	6.51–10.36	400;550	1	Mall	8;13;∞
Noi:Shop-2 ($N = 6$)				Shop	
Noi:Mall-3 ($N = 12$)	2.36–10.36	400;550 (1m)	1;2	Mall	8;13;∞
Noi:Shop-3 ($N = 12$)		450;650 (2m)		Shop	

Table 6. Accuracy (Acc.) [%] yielded on noisy datasets Test:Mall and Test:Shop. For the Test:Shop, the Correctness [%] (column Corr.) is stated as well. **The bold values** indicate matched training-test conditions (by the Clarity value, noise type and SNR level). The Test:Real dataset is a noiseless version of the Test:Mall datasets, see Sect. 2.1 for details. See Table 5 for the detailed configuration of the training sets.

Model name	Test Real Close	Test Real 1 m	Test Real 2 m	Test Real 3 m	Mall 8 dB Close	Mall 8 dB 1 m	Mall 8 dB 2 m	Mall 8 dB 3 m	Mall 3 dB Close	Mall 3 dB 1 m	Mall 3 dB 2 m	Mall 3 dB 3 m	Shop Acc.	Shop Corr.
Baseline	**90.19**	71.08	39.51	26.17	51.56	10.09	1.61	1.31	11.67	1.28	0.10	0.13	26.94	28.92
Noi:Mall-1	**90.46**	**84.56**	76.81	71.03	**82.58**	**73.38**	58.55	53.36	**69.99**	**56.47**	37.90	34.21	21.53	39.53
Noi:Mall-2	**90.64**	**84.95**	78.78	70.91	**82.34**	**72.48**	56.51	51.14	66.72	49.22	29.40	27.32	24.77	39.46
Noi:Mall-3	**90.31**	**84.67**	**78.61**	**73.35**	**81.00**	**71.91**	60.05	**55.54**	64.44	50.93	34.87	31.82	19.37	39.46
Noi:Shop-1	**90.54**	**84.44**	77.16	72.46	80.57	69.42	55.61	52.04	65.09	46.54	29.86	29.84	25.10	40.78
Noi:Shop-2	**90.58**	**85.00**	77.92	72.90	80.18	66.27	49.65	48.11	59.05	34.78	18.23	19.73	**30.83**	**40.78**
Noi:Shop-3	**90.39**	**84.73**	**78.58**	**73.88**	78.75	67.11	54.67	51.77	55.20	38.73	25.44	23.91	25.89	41.30

5 Conclusion

This paper studied a selection of acoustic conditions that should be included in the augmentation process, in order to preserve reasonable size of the output training set. We draw the following conclusions regarding the setup in reverberant scenarios. (1) The value of Clarity C_{50} estimated in the target test environment can be used as threshold indicating which RIRs are crucial for the augmentation. It is beneficial to augment data with RIRs corresponding to C_{50} approximately equal or higher than this value; RIRs with lower Clarity (that is more reverberant) can be omitted. (2) Utilization of genuine RIRs leads to slightly higher accuracy (up to 2.5%) compared to their artificial counterparts. (3) When utilizing RIRs with appropriate C_{50} value, mismatch in other room setup parameters, such as T_{60} or room dimensions, does not deteriorate the ASR accuracy significantly. Concerning the augmentation for noise-robustness: (4) The augmented AMs achieve higher accuracy in noisy conditions compared to baseline model without augmentation, even when the augmentation parameters are not entirely identical to test conditions. However, the results achieved on artificial test set indicate higher tolerance to this mismatch than the results yielded on the real-world dataset. (5) A closely matched noise-type appears to be the most important parameter of the noise-focused augmentation. Other parameters such as SNR or reverberation-level influence the accuracy to a lesser extend.

Acknowledgments. This work was supported by the Technology Agency of the Czech Republic (Project No. TH03010018).

References

1. Boll, S.: Suppression of acoustic noise in speech using spectral subtraction. IEEE Trans. Acoust. Speech Signal Process. **27**(2), 113–120 (1979)
2. Brutti, A., Matassoni, M.: On the relationship between early-to-late ratio of room impulse responses and asr performance in reverberant environments. Speech Commun. **76**, 170–185 (2016)

3. Cui, X., Goel, V., Kingsbury, B.: Data augmentation for deep neural network acoustic modeling. IEEE/ACM Trans. Audio Speech Lang. Process. (TASLP) **23**(9), 1469–1477 (2015)
4. Dahl, G., Yu, D., Deng, L., Acero, A.: Context-dependent pre-trained deep neural networks for large-vocabulary speech recognition. IEEE/ACM Trans. Audio Speech Lang. Process. **20**(1), 30–42 (2012)
5. DCASE Community: DCASE 2018 challenge. http://dcase.community/challenge2018/index. Accessed 5 December 2018
6. Ephraim, Y., Malah, D.: Speech enhancement using a minimum-mean square error short-time spectral amplitude estimator. IEEE Trans. Acoust. Speech Signal Process. **32**(6), 1109–1121 (1984)
7. Ferras, M., Madikeri, S., Motlicek, P., Dey, S., Bourlard, H.: A large-scale open-source acoustic simulator for speaker recognition. IEEE Signal Process. Lett. **23**(4), 527–531 (2016)
8. Gannot, S., Vincent, E., Markovich-Golan, S., Ozerov, A.: A consolidated perspective on multimicrophone speech enhancement and source separation. IEEE/ACM Trans. Audio Speech Lang. Process. **25**(4), 692–730 (2017)
9. Giri, R., Seltzer, M.L., Droppo, J., Yu, D.: Improving speech recognition in reverberation using a room-aware deep neural network and multi-task learning. In: 2015 IEEE International Conference on Acoustics, Speech and Signal Processing (ICASSP), pp. 5014–5018. IEEE (2015)
10. Habets, E.A.: Room impulse response generator. Technische Universiteit Eindhoven, Technical Report 2(2.4), 1 (2006)
11. Hadad, E., Heese, F., Vary, P., Gannot, S.: Multichannel audio database in various acoustic environments. In: 2014 14th International Workshop on Acoustic Signal Enhancement (IWAENC), pp. 313–317. IEEE (2014)
12. Jaitly, N., Hinton, G.E.: Vocal tract length perturbation (VTLP) improves speech recognition. In: Proceedings of ICML Workshop on Deep Learning for Audio, Speech and Language, pp. 625–660 (2013)
13. Kim, C., et al.: Generation of large-scale simulated utterances in virtual rooms to train deep-neural networks for far-field speech recognition in Google home. In: Proceedings of INTERSPEECH, ISCA (2017)
14. Kneser, R., Ney, H.: Improved backing-off for m-gram language modeling. In: 1995 International Conference on Acoustics, Speech, and Signal Processing, ICASSP-1995, vol. 1, pp. 181–184. IEEE (1995)
15. Ko, T., Peddinti, V., Povey, D., Seltzer, M.L., Khudanpur, S.: A study on data augmentation of reverberant speech for robust speech recognition. In: 2017 IEEE International Conference on Acoustics, Speech and Signal Processing (ICASSP), pp. 5220–5224. IEEE (2017)
16. Kuttruff, H.: Room Acoustics. CRC Press, Boca Raton (2016)
17. Li, J., Seltzer, M.L., Wang, X., Zhao, R., Gong, Y.: Large-scale domain adaptation via teacher-student learning. arXiv preprint arXiv:1708.05466 (2017)
18. Makino, S., Lee, T.W., Sawada, H.: Blind Speech Separation, vol. 615. Springer, Switzerland (2007). https://doi.org/10.1007/978-1-4020-6479-1
19. Málek, J., Ždánský, J., Červa, P.: Robust recognition of conversational telephone speech via multi-condition training and data augmentation. In: Sojka, P., Horák, A., Kopeček, I., Pala, K. (eds.) TSD 2018. LNCS (LNAI), vol. 11107, pp. 324–333. Springer, Cham (2018). https://doi.org/10.1007/978-3-030-00794-2_35
20. Mammone, R.J., Zhang, X., Ramachandran, R.P.: Robust speaker recognition: a feature-based approach. IEEE Signal Process. Mag. **13**(5), 58 (1996)

21. Mirsamadi, S., Hansen, J.H.: A study on deep neural network acoustic model adaptation for robust far-field speech recognition. In: Sixteenth Annual Conference of the International Speech Communication Association (2015)
22. Parada, P.P., Sharma, D., Lainez, J., Barreda, D., van Waterschoot, T., Naylor, P.A.: A single-channel non-intrusive c50 estimator correlated with speech recognition performance. IEEE/ACM Trans. Audio Speech Lang. Process. (TASLP) **24**(4), 719–732 (2016)
23. Prisyach, T., Mendelev, V., Ubskiy, D.: Data augmentation for training of noise robust acoustic models. In: Ignatov, D.I., et al. (eds.) AIST 2016. CCIS, vol. 661, pp. 17–25. Springer, Cham (2017). https://doi.org/10.1007/978-3-319-52920-2_2
24. Seltzer, M.L., Yu, D., Wang, Y.: An investigation of deep neural networks for noise robust speech recognition. In: 2013 IEEE International Conference on Acoustics, Speech and Signal Processing (ICASSP), pp. 7398–7402. IEEE (2013)
25. Torch team: torch - a scientific computing framework for luajit. http://torch.ch. Accessed 5 December 2018
26. Wang, D., Chen, J.: Supervised speech separation based on deep learning: an overview. IEEE/ACM Trans. Audio Speech Lang. Process. **26**, 1702–1726 (2018)
27. Xu, Y., Du, J., Dai, L.R., Lee, C.H.: Dynamic noise aware training for speech enhancement based on deep neural networks. In: Fifteenth Annual Conference of the International Speech Communication Association (2014)
28. Young, S., Young, S.: The HTK hidden Markov model toolkit: design and philosophy. Entropic Cambridge Research Laboratory, Ltd. vol. 2, pp. 2–44 (1994)
29. Zhang, Z., Geiger, J., Pohjalainen, J., Mousa, A.E.D., Jin, W., Schuller, B.: Deep learning for environmentally robust speech recognition: an overview of recent developments. ACM Trans. Intell. Syst. Technol. (TIST) **9**(5), 49 (2018)

Evaluation of Synthetic Speech by GMM-Based Continuous Detection of Emotional States

Jiří Přibil[1]([⊠]), Anna Přibilová[2], and Jindřich Matoušek[1]

[1] Faculty of Applied Sciences, Department of Cybernetics, UWB,
Pilsen, Czech Republic
umerprib@savba.sk, jmatouse@kky.zcu.cz
[2] FEE & IT, Institute of Electronics and Photonics, SUT in Bratislava,
Bratislava, Slovakia
pribilova@stuba.sk

Abstract. The paper describes a system for automatic evaluation of synthetic speech quality based on continuous detection of emotional states throughout the spoken sentence using a Gaussian mixture model (GMM) classification. The final evaluation decision is made by statistical analysis of the results of emotional class differences between the sentences of original male or female voices and the speech synthesized by various methods with different parameters, approaches to prosody manipulation, etc. The basic experiments confirm the functionality of the developed system producing results comparable with those obtained by the standard listening test method. Additional investigations have shown that a number of mixtures, types of speech features, and a speech database used for creation and training of GMMs have a relatively great influence on continuous emotional style detection and the final quality evaluation of the tested synthetic speech.

Keywords: GMM classification · Statistical analysis ·
Synthetic speech evaluation · Text-to-speech system

1 Introduction

Different methods implemented in text-to-speech (TTS) synthesis can be evaluated by various objective or subjective criteria. The subjective ones are usually based on a perceptual rating of intelligibility, naturalness, or similarity by a mean opinion score scale [1,2], a preference test [3], a comparison category rating [4,5], etc. The objective measures include various approaches to speech spectrum comparison, evaluation of pitch and voicing errors [6,7], etc. The final decision may

This work was supported by the Ministry of Education, Youth and Sports of the Czech Republic, project No. LO1506, and by the Ministry of Education, Science, Research, and Sports of the Slovak Republic VEGA 1/0854/16 (A. Přibilová).

K. Ekštein (Ed.): TSD 2019, LNAI 11697, pp. 264–273, 2019.
https://doi.org/10.1007/978-3-030-27947-9_22

be obtained by a score-level fusion of different features [8] with the predominant use of Gaussian mixture models (GMM) [9].

In general, for proper operation of the automated classification and evaluation systems based on statistical approaches, a greater number of sentences must be processed to build databases of speech features. The basic condition of statistical differentiability between groups of speech features determined from the original and the evaluated synthetic speech corpus must be fulfilled for the principal function of this method. It is important for the successfulness of the training process of the GMMs as well as for the classification phase of this system. The process of collecting larger databases is very time-consuming and it is also very difficult to get a homogenous distribution of classified speech properties (emotional styles, etc.). For these reasons, we try to design, realize, and test the designed system which could become a fully-fledged alternative to the standard subjective listening test and which can solve or eliminate the mentioned problems with statistically-based systems for evaluation of the synthetic speech quality.

The paper describes experiments with using the GMM-based classifier for continuous detection of the speaker's emotional state and subsequent automatic evaluation of the synthetic speech quality. The sentences used for testing were produced by a TTS system based on the unit selection (USEL) synthesis method [10] in the Czech language with male and female voices. The proposed system works on the principle of determination of similarity between the synthesized and original sentence uttered by the speaker. Three databases of expressive speech were used for creation and training of the GMMs: the German speech database Emo-DB [11], the Czech and Slovak speech material (CZ&SK) extracted from the stories performed by professional actors [12], and the English emotional speech from the acted audiovisual database MSP-IMPROV [13]. In this way, both two principal requirements mentioned in the previous paragraph are fulfilled at the same time: differentiability between features of neutral and emotional speech styles, and a larger size of available databases. Influence of a number of mixture components, types of speech features, and used speech databases on continuous emotion detection and on the final evaluation of the synthetic speech quality is analyzed, too. Finally, the objective results are compared with the subjective ratings of human evaluators.

2   Description of Proposed Automatic Evaluation System

In GMMs, an input data vector specified by a covariance matrix, a vector of means, and weights is modeled as a linear combination of multiple Gaussian probability distribution functions. An expectation-maximization (EM) iteration algorithm is used for the maximum likelihood parameter estimation [9]. The EM algorithm is first initialized by the number of mixtures N_{MIX} and the number of iterations. The classifier returns the probability score that the tested speech belongs to this GMM.

In the preprocessing phase of the proposed evaluation method, the GMMs are created and trained on the emotional speech databases that differ from the speech material used in the classification phase. In GMM-based speaker as well as emotion recognition, the resulting class is given by the maximum overall probability of the obtained scores calculated for the total number of processed speech frames, so only one value of an accumulated score is finally obtained for the whole sentence. The designed evaluation system uses normalized scores corresponding to N_{EMOT} emotions calculated and processed in each speech frame. Consequently, a speech of a native speaker (further called $Orig$) and two types of speech synthesis $(Synt1, 2)$ are processed in such a way – see Fig. 1. The GMM scores are statistically analyzed for each of the classified emotions: designation of changes in the determined emotional classes is followed by the construction of histograms of class distribution, analysis of variance (ANOVA), and comparison of group means [14]. Three output measures for comparison of the values between $Orig$ and $Synt1, 2$ are calculated: Abs_{DIFF} – absolute differences for every emotional class, Dh_{RMS} – RMS distances between histograms, and Da_{GRP} – distances between group means of ANOVA, as documented in Fig. 2a–e.

Partial results are determined together with the percentage of the proximity of two tested syntheses to the original voice for each of the mentioned measures – see the last but one row in a demonstration example in Fig. 2f. The output value "1" ("2") means $Synt1$ ($Synt2$) close to the original and "0" denotes similarity due to differences below the set threshold. The final decision about better synthesis is determined using the majority function of the partial results. The percentage of the final decision is calculated as the mean of the percentage values corresponding to the measures with the majority. If there is no majority (each of the used measures produces different partial decision), the one with the highest percentage is taken as a winner and the final percentage value is set to the maximum of this measure divided by a mean of all three measures.

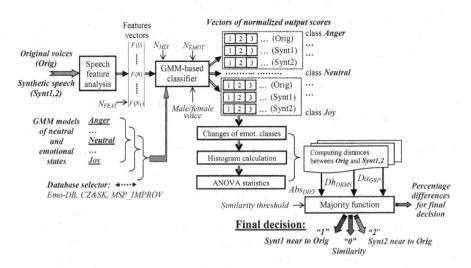

Fig. 1. Block diagram of the proposed automatic evaluation system.

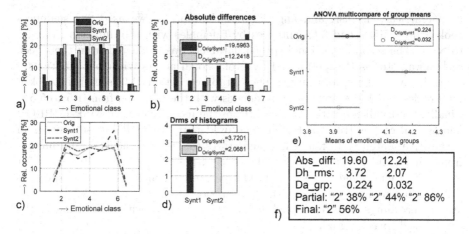

Fig. 2. Visualization of statistical processing of detected emotional classes and comparison of differences between original voice ($Orig$) and two types of synthetic speech ($Synt1, 2$): bar-graph of class relative occurrence in [%] (a), bar-graph of absolute differences (b), histograms of classes (c), RMS distances from histograms (d), ANOVA multi-compare of group means (e), numerical results of evaluation (f).

Unlike the standard speaker recognition tasks with mostly used mel frequency cepstral coefficients [15], this experiment utilizes the following three types of speech features: prosodic parameters, basic, and supplementary spectral properties. First, the fundamental frequency F_0 is determined from the segmented and weighted input speech signal. Its values are used to calculate a micro-intonation component of speech melody represented by differential fundamental frequency F_{0DIFF}, zero-crossing frequency F_{0ZCR}, absolute jitter J_{abs}, and relative peak-to-peak amplitude (shimmer) AP_{rel}. Subsequently, the smoothed spectral envelope and the power spectral density are determined to calculate spectral properties. The basic ones are the first two formants (F_1, F_2), their ratio (F_1/F_2), spectral tilt (S_{tilt}), etc. The supplementary ones are harmonics-to-noise ratio (HNR), spectral centroid (S_{centr}), entropy (SE), and flatness (S_{flat}). The first four cepstral coefficients $(c_1 - c_4)$ are also used together with statistical parameters of spectral description: spectral spread (S_{spread}), skewness (S_{skew}), and kurtosis (S_{kurt}). Every processed speech feature vector is used to calculate N_{FEAT} representative statistical values of mean, median, relative min/max, etc. These are further used for training of the GMMs as well as for the classification phase. The choice of these parameters was justified by the experiments described in [16].

3   Material, Experiments, and Results

For the creation and training of the GMMs, three databases were used: the first speech corpus was taken from the Berlin Database of Emotional Speech Emo-DB [11] in the German language. This speech database consists of a set of sentences with the same contents expressing seven emotional states: neutral, joy, sadness, boredom, fear, disgust, and anger. From this corpus, we used 233 sentences spoken by 5 males and 302 sentences by 5 females with the duration from 1.5 to 8.5 s. The second emotional speech database was extracted from the Czech and Slovak stories [12] performed by professional actors with four emotions – neutral, joy, sadness, and anger. The database contains 143 sentences spoken by 9 males and 140 sentences by 9 females with the duration from 1.5 to 5.5 s. Finally, the English emotional speech from the recently created MSP-IMPROV audiovisual corpus [13] was tested. The used part of this database consists of declarative sentences in four emotional states (angry, sad, neutral, and happy) from 3 male and 3 female speakers. For the purpose of this work, 60 records for each of four emotional states were used separately for male and female speakers – 2×240 sentences in total with the duration from 0.5 to 6.5 s. All original speech recordings were resampled at 16 kHz to comply with the format of the synthesized speech signal.

For continuous detection of emotional states, a separate speech corpus was collected consisting of three subsets: the original speech uttered by real speakers and two variations of speech synthesis produced by a Czech TTS system using the USEL method [10] with voices based on the corresponding original speakers. Two methods of prosody manipulation were applied: the rule-based method (assigned to $Synt1$) and the modified version reflecting the final syllable status (assigned to $Synt2$) [17]. Native as well as synthetic speech originates from four professional speakers – 2 males (M1, M2) and 2 females (F1, F2). Only declarative sentences were used for each of four original speakers (140 in total). As regards the synthesis, there were totally 124 sentences with two synthesis types from each of four voices. The processed speech signals were sampled at 16 kHz and their duration was from 2.5 to 5 s.

Three sets of speech features were selected for use in the classification process – see their detailed description in Table 1. In correspondence with the work [12], the length of the input feature vector was set to $N_{FEAT} = 16$. The GMM with a diagonal covariance matrix was used due to its lower computational complexity. The described analysis and speech signal processing were currently realized in the Matlab ver. 2016b environment and the Ian T. Nabney "Netlab" pattern analysis toolbox [18] was used for the implementation of the basic functions in the designed GMM classifier.

Table 1. Structure of the used speech feature sets.

Set	Feature type	Representative statistical value
SF0	$\{S_{tilt}, S_{centr}, S_{flat}, HNR, F_{0DIFF}, F_{0ZCR}, J_{abs}, AP_{rel}\}$	{min, max, rel. max, mean, median, std}
SF2	$\{F_1, F_2, F_1/F_2, S_{tilt}, HNR, SE, F_{0DIFF}, J_{abs}, AP_{rel}\}$	{skewness, kurtosis, std, mean, rel. max}
SF4	$\{c_1 - c_4, S_{spread}, S_{skew}, S_{kurt}, F_{0DIFF}, J_{abs}, AP_{rel}\}$	{skewness, kurtosis, mean, median, std}

The basic performed experiments were aimed at testing the functionality, stability, and precision of the proposed GMM-based continuous emotional class detector. The following impacts were next investigated in order to find the appropriate setting of control parameters in the phases of GMM creation, training, and classification:

1. influence of the number of applied Gaussian mixtures on continuous emotional style detection and partial decision about the evaluated quality of the tested synthetic speech for $N_{MIX} = \{16, 32, 64, 128, 256,$ and $512\}$ – see the visualization of partial decision trajectories for the voices M1 and F1 in Fig. 3,
2. influence of different types of speech features in the input vector on percentage differences between the sets SF0, SF2, and SF4 using three difference/distance measures (Abs_{DIFF}, Dh_{RMS}, and Da_{GRP}) – see the graphical comparison for the voices M1 and F1 in Fig. 4,
3. influence of different databases for creation/training of the GMMs corresponding to the emotional states on the evaluated quality of two speech synthesis types for the voices M1 and F1 – see the numerical comparison in Table 2.

Finally, the summary results for all four speakers were compared with the ones obtained by the standard listening test (see a bar-graph in Fig. 5) published in [17]. Here two synthesized versions of the same utterance were evaluated by the choice from among "*A sounds better*", "*A sounds similar to B*", or "*B sounds better*".

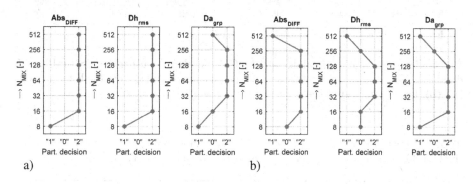

Fig. 3. Visualization of the partial decision trajectories showing the influence of a number of applied Gaussian mixtures on synthetic speech quality for male M1 (a), and female F1 (b); GMMs trained on Emo-DB with 7 emotions, feature set SF4, "1" = *Synt1* is better, "2" = *Synt2* is better, and "0" = similarity.

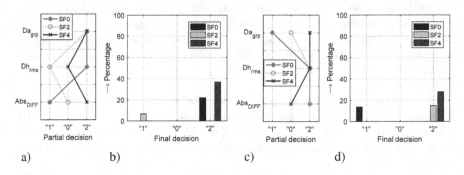

Fig. 4. Comparison of the impact of different speech feature sets {SF0, SF2, SF4} on partial decisions for each of three used difference/distance measures (a), (c), a final decision together with its percentage (b), (d); used male M1 (left two graphs), and female F1 (right graphs) voices, $N_{MIX} = 32$, CZ&SK with 4 emotional styles, "1" = $Synt1$ is better, "2" = $Synt2$ is better, and "0" = similarity.

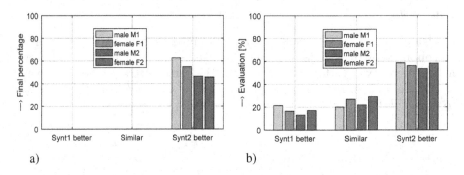

Fig. 5. Comparison of the final decision by GMM evaluation using the MSP-IMPROV database, $N_{MIX} = 32$, and feature set SF4 (a), results obtained from the listening test [17] (b), for all four tested speakers.

Table 2. Partial evaluation results for different emotional speech databases used in the GMM creation/training phase – comparison for speakers M1 and F1.

Speech database [A]	M1 – partial decision results and difference percentage [B]			F1 – partial decision results and difference percentage [B]		
	Abs_{DIFF}	Dh_{RMS}	Da_{GRP}	Abs_{DIFF}	Dh_{RMS}	Da_{GRP}
Emo-DB	"**2**" 8.6 %	"**2**" 13.3 %	"**2**" 87.9 %	"**2**" 9.0 %	"**2**" 5.4 %	"**2**" 42.8 %
CZ&SK	"**2**" 35.1 %	"**0**" 1.8 %	"**2**" 46.9 %	"**0**" 1.2 %	"**2**" 25.4 %	"**2**" 29.7 %
MSP-IMPROV	"**2**" 62.7 %	"**2**" 54.7 %	"**2**" 58.4 %	"**2**" 60 %	"**2**" 45.2 %	"**2**" 35.6 %

[A] used the best settings of parameters: N_{MIX}=32, feature set SF4.
[B] partial results: "1"= $Synt1$ better, "0"= Similar, "2"= $Synt2$ better.

4   Discussion and Conclusion

The obtained results confirm that the proposed GMM-based evaluation system is functional and can be used for automatic evaluation of synthetic speech quality. This system produces results comparable with the standard listening test method as documented by a bar-graph of all four tested speakers in Fig. 5. The listening test results have shown that the modified version of prosody manipulation (*Synt2*) is evaluated significantly better than the synthesis with the rule-based method (*Synt1*) for all four voices [17]. The designed system has an advantage over the previous methods of synthetic speech quality evaluation in processing only sentences of the originals and the tested ones. The speech features for the training of the GMMs are determined from other corpora without any relation to the tested speech material.

Decision making by the majority of three statistical parameters is in principle good, however, practical realization brings about a problem with the determination of the final winner and its percentage. The wrong decision can be made with a high percentage and the correct one with a low percentage – see the graphical comparison in Fig. 4. Therefore, in the near future, we will try to find another method for the determination of statistical differences to produce homogenous results.

The detailed analysis of the partial results shows principal importance of the correct choice of the number of mixture components as well as the used speech feature set for the stability of the final decision. The situation is different for male and female voices: while the lowest values of $N_{MIX} = 8/16$ give the wrong decision practically in all cases, an increase of N_{MIX} up to 512 mixtures has a negative impact, mainly for female voices, as documented by the partial output class trajectories in Fig. 3b. It is safe and stable to initialize the algorithm with 32 GMM components as their increase to 128 or 256 mixtures brings only higher computational complexity. Therefore, the setting of $N_{MIX} = 32$ was finally applied in further experiments. The best result and stability were achieved for the feature set SF4 (containing the first four cepstral coefficients and the mix of spectral and prosodic speech properties), so it was chosen in the next analysis. Comparison of different speech corpora used for GMM creation/training has shown worse results in the case of female voices. A larger speech corpus and/or a higher number of contained emotions (7 in Emo-DB vs. 4 in CZ&SK and MSP-IMPROV) result in the correct final decision and its higher percentage but the language seems to have no observable influence as can be seen in Table 2. Additional experiments using other databases with a higher number of emotions will be necessary to confirm or reject this hypothesis.

In the near future, we would also like to test this evaluation system on the synthetic speech produced by more different synthesis methods as statistical parametric synthesis (SPS) and neutral network based ones [10]. Another task will be to analyze whether in our case the GMM with a full matrix outperforms that with a simpler diagonal one. Finally, the system is currently realized in the Matlab environment, so optimization and implementation in a higher programming language are necessary for real-time processing of the evaluation phase.

References

1. Biagetti, G., Crippa, P., Falaschetti, L., Turchetti, N.: HMM speech synthesis based on MDCT representation. Int. J. Speech Technol. **21**(4), 1045–1055 (2018)
2. Zhao, Y., Takaki, S., Luong, H.T., Yamagishi, J., Saito, D., Minematsu, N.: Wasserstein GAN and waveform loss-based acoustic model training for multi-speaker text-to-speech synthesis systems using a WaveNet vocoder. IEEE Access **6**, 60478–60488 (2018)
3. Saito, Y., Takamichi, S., Saruwatari, H.: Statistical parametric speech synthesis incorporating generative adversarial networks. IEEE/ACM Trans. Audio Speech Lang. Process. **26**(1), 84–96 (2018)
4. Vít, J., Matoušek, J.: Unit-selection speech synthesis adjustments for audiobook-based voices. In: Sojka, P., Horák, A., Kopeček, I., Pala, K. (eds.) TSD 2016. LNCS (LNAI), vol. 9924, pp. 335–342. Springer, Cham (2016). https://doi.org/10.1007/978-3-319-45510-5_38
5. Tihelka, D., Grůber, M., Hanzlíček, Z.: Robust methodology for TTS enhancement evaluation. In: Habernal, I., Matoušek, V. (eds.) TSD 2013. LNCS (LNAI), vol. 8082, pp. 442–449. Springer, Heidelberg (2013). https://doi.org/10.1007/978-3-642-40585-3_56
6. Adiga, N., Khonglah, B.K., Prasanna, S.R.M.: Improved voicing decision using glottal activity features for statistical parametric speech synthesis. Digital Signal Process. **71**, 131–143 (2017)
7. Achanta, S., Gangashetty, S.V.: Deep Elman recurrent neural networks for statistical parametric speech synthesis. Speech Commun. **93**, 31–42 (2017)
8. Pal, M., Paul, D., Saha, G.: Synthetic speech detection using fundamental frequency variation and spectral features. Comput. Speech Lang. **48**, 31–50 (2018)
9. Reynolds, D.A., Rose, R.C.: Robust text-independent speaker identification using Gaussian mixture speaker models. IEEE Trans. Speech Audio Process. **3**, 72–83 (1995)
10. Tihelka, D., Hanzlíček, Z., Jůzová, M., Vít, J., Matoušek, J., Grůber, M.: Current state of text-to-speech system ARTIC: a decade of research on the field of speech technologies. In: Sojka, P., Horák, A., Kopeček, I., Pala, K. (eds.) TSD 2018. LNCS (LNAI), vol. 11107, pp. 369–378. Springer, Cham (2018). https://doi.org/10.1007/978-3-030-00794-2_40
11. Burkhardt, F., Paeschke, A., Rolfes, M., Sendlmeier, W., Weiss, B.: A database of german emotional speech. In: Proceedings of INTERSPEECH 2005, ISCA, Lisbon, Portugal, pp. 1517–1520 (2005)
12. Přibil, J., Přibilová, A.: Evaluation of influence of spectral and prosodic features on GMM classification of Czech and Slovak emotional speech. EURASIP J. Audio Speech Music Process. **2013**, 8 (2013)
13. Busso, C., Parthasarathy, S., Burmania, A., AbdelWahab, M., Sadoughi, N., Provost, E.M.: MSP-IMPROV: an acted corpus of dyadic interactions to study emotion perception. IEEE Trans. Affect. Comput. **8**(1), 67–80 (2017)
14. Rencher, A.C., Schaalje, G.B.: Linear Models in Statistics, 2nd edn. Wiley, Hoboken (2008)
15. Jokinen, E., Saeidi, R., Kinnunen, T., Alku, P.: Vocal effort compensation for MFCC feature extraction in a shouted versus normal speaker recognition task. Comput. Speech Lang. **53**, 1–11 (2019)
16. Přibil, J., Přibilová, A., Matoušek, J.: Automatic text-independent artifact detection, localization, and classification in the synthetic speech. Radioengineering **26**(4), 1151–1160 (2017)

17. Jůzová, M., Tihelka, D., Skarnitzl, R.: Last syllable unit penalization in unit selection TTS. In: Ekštein, K., Matoušek, V. (eds.) TSD 2017. LNCS (LNAI), vol. 10415, pp. 317–325. Springer, Cham (2017). https://doi.org/10.1007/978-3-319-64206-2_36

18. Nabney, I.T.: Netlab Pattern Analysis Toolbox, Release 3.3. http://www.aston.ac.uk/eas/research/groups/ncrg/resources/netlab/downloads. Accessed 2 Oct 2015

Deep Representation Learning for Orca Call Type Classification

Christian Bergler[1](✉), Manuel Schmitt[1], Rachael Xi Cheng[2],
Hendrik Schröter[1], Andreas Maier[1], Volker Barth[3], Michael Weber[3],
and Elmar Nöth[1](✉)

[1] Department of Computer Science – Pattern Recognition Lab,
Friedrich-Alexander-University Erlangen-Nuremberg, Martensstr. 3,
91058 Erlangen, Germany
{christian.bergler,elmar.noeth}@fau.de
[2] Leibniz Institute for Zoo and Wildlife Research (IZW) in the Forschungsverbund
Berlin e.V., Alfred-Kowalke-Str. 17, 10315 Berlin, Germany
[3] Anthro-Media, Nansenstr. 19, 12047 Berlin, Germany
https://www5.cs.fau.de

Abstract. Marine mammals produce a wide variety of vocalizations. There is a growing need for robust automatic classification methods especially in noisy underwater environments in order to access large amounts of bioacoustic signals and to replace tedious and error prone human perceptual classification. In case of the northern resident killer whale *(Orcinus orca)*, echolocation clicks, whistles, and pulsed calls make up its vocal repertoire. Pulsed calls are the most intensively studied type of vocalization. In this study we propose a hybrid call type classification approach outperforming our previous work on supervised call type classification consisting of two components: (1) deep representation learning of killer whale sounds by investigating various autoencoder architectures and data corpora and (2) subsequent supervised training of a ResNet18 call type classifier on a much smaller dataset by using the pre-trained representations. The best semi-supervised trained classification model achieved a test accuracy of 96% and a mean test accuracy of 94% outperforming our previous work by 7% points.

Keywords: Deep learning · Classification · Representation learning · Bioacoustics · Orca · Killer whale · Call type

1 Introduction

An increasing use of passive acoustic monitoring of various animal species result in massive quantity of bioacoustic data. For example, the Orcalab [20] has collected

The authors would like to thank Helena Symonds and Paul Spong from Orcalab, and Steven Ness, formerly UVIC, for giving us permission to use the raw data and annotations from orcalab.org, and the Paul G. Allen Frontiers Group for their initial grant for the pilot research.

K. Ekštein (Ed.): TSD 2019, LNAI 11697, pp. 274–286, 2019.
https://doi.org/10.1007/978-3-030-27947-9_23

underwater recordings on killer whales for 23 years resulting in about 20,000 h. There is a growing need for effective methods of automatic classification of bioacoustic signals. It offers significant advantages as in assessing large datasets, frees humans from time-consuming and labor intensive work, and offers rigorous and consistent results. Killer whales *(Orcinus orca)*, the largest member of the dolphin family, are one of several species with relatively well-studied and complex vocal cultures [7]. Extensive research on killer whale acoustic behavior has been conducted on the resident fish-eating killer whales in the northeast Pacific. Resident killer whales live in stable matrilineal units [2]. Those matrilines, that often travel together to socialize on a regular basis, form subpods and pods [2,8,9,15]. Apart from echolocation clicks and whistles, killer whales produce a number of social sounds with distinct frequency contours which are group specific. Those pulsed calls, the most common and excessively studied type of killer whale vocalization, are classified into discrete, variable, and aberrant calls. It typically shows sudden and patterned shifts in frequency, according to the pulse repetition rate, which is normally between 250 and 2000 Hz [10]. Acoustically related animals are assigned to a so-called clan, an acoustic grouping of pods that have one or more discrete calls in common [2]. Basically, all pods of a clan have a common repertoire of calls, with slight vocal distinctions in between [11]. Due to the resulting variety of call variants, group-specific dialects arise [11]. Those pod-specific dialects consist of up to 20 types of discrete calls each, and in total the northern residents' vocal repertoire of discrete calls consists of more than 40 types [9,11] (examples in Fig. 1). Call structure variations can be observed in various shared call types [18]. Group-specific vocal signals are believed to play an important role in maintaining contact among members or coordinate group activities, especially when the group is dispersed and when visual signals can only be used in short-distance communication [10]. The current study builds on the previously achieved deep learning-based segmentation [22] and tries to improve our previous supervised call type classification result [22]. Unsupervised deep representation learning and subsequent classification could also be very helpful improving language or even speaker

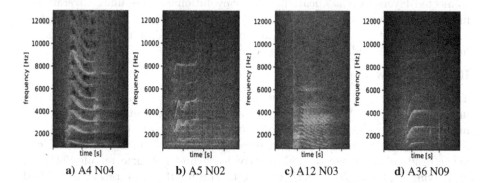

Fig. 1. Pod-specific (A4, A5, A12, A36) killer whale call type (N04, N02, N03, N09) spectrograms (sample rate = 44.1 khZ, FFT–size = 4096 samples (∼100 ms), hop–size = 441 samples (∼10 ms))

dependent classification/identification models. Moreover, unsupervised deep representation learning of (compressed) bottleneck features can support to identify and examine indigenous languages.

1.1 Related Work

Brown et al. [3] used dynamic time warping to compare the melodic contours of 57 captive killer whale vocalizations and k-means to cluster into 9 call types. Furthermore, Brown et al. [4] classified 75 killer whale calls into 7 call types using hidden Markov models and Gaussian mixture models resulting in more than 90% agreement. Ness [19] classified between 12 various killer whale call types achieving an average accuracy of 76% by using an SVM with a Radial Basis Function kernel. Brown et al. [5] did killer whale individual identification by distinguishing within four diverse animals via differentiating between one specific call type. Deecke et al. [6] introduced a method for dolphin and killer whale sound categorization via dynamic time warping and an adaptive resonance theory neural network. Mercado et al. [17] classified 242 humpback whale vocalizations via a combination of a source-filter model and an artificial neural network. Garland et al. [12] classified 1,019 Beluga whale sounds into 34 different call types using non-parametric classification tree analysis and random forest analysis achieving an accuracy of 83%.

2 Methodology

Convolutional Neural Network (CNN)

Convolutional neural network (CNN) is a state-of-the-art end-to-end deep learning concept first used by LeCun et al. [16] for handwritten letter recognition. CNNs facilitate to efficiently handle 2-D input data (e.g. spectrograms). CNNs are designed after the traditional principle of pattern recognition, implementing covolutional layers for feature learning/extraction and subsequent fully-connected layers for classification [16]. Convolutional layers unite several very important architectural approaches: (1) local receptive fields, (2) shared weights, and (3) spatial/temporal sub-sampling (pooling) [16]. For a more detailed explanation of a CNN and its underlying concepts, see [16].

Residual Network (ResNet)

Training very deep neural networks in order to learn higher-level and more discriminative features results in various optimization problems (vanishing/exploding gradients, degradation problem) [14]. He et al. [14] introduced a residual learning framework in an architecture called residual network (ResNet), using residual mappings to not directly learn and optimize an unreferenced underlying mapping $H(x)$ with respect to the input x but rather a residual mapping $F(x) = H(x) - x$, in order to counteract the degradation problem. Moreover, He et al. [14] present different and typical ResNet architectures based on their number of concatenated layers which have proven successful in practice. For a more detailed explanation about deep residual learning, see [14].

Autoencoder

An autoencoder is a (deep) neural network architecture, trying to map a given input x to an output/reconstruction r via a hidden representation h [13]. This architecture consists of two basic components: (1) an encoder e acting as a function, mapping the input x to the hidden layer representation h via $h = e(x)$, (2) a decoder d officiating as a function which maps the hidden layer latent code h to the output/reconstruction r via $r = d(h)$ [13]. In this work we used various *residual-based convolutional undercomplete autoencoders* constraining h to a smaller dimension than the input x [13] in order to learn an embedding h comprising the most prominent features via minimizing the loss $L(x, d(e(x)))$, penalizing the dissimilarity between x and $d(e(x))$ [13].

Deep Representation Learning

Representation learning is a way of learning useful data representations (features), directly on the given input data, rather than performing a labor-intensive feature extraction/selection based on handcrafted features (feature engineering), in order to utilize them for a subsequent classification task [1]. Usually the amount of unlabeled data is much higher than the one of labeled data. Consequently, a pure supervised training on limited labeled data mostly results in overfitting [13] and a lack of robustness/generalization towards unseen real-world data especially in case of extremely heterogeneous data corpora. Representation learning provides an opportunity of combining unsupervised and supervised learning by using the unsupervised learned task-related representations as initialization of the original supervised task in order to produce a more accurate and robust semi-supervised trained classification model [13]. In this study deep learning techniques were used to derive adequate feature representations.

3 Datasets and Data Distribution

3.1 Datasets

Orchive Annotation Catalog (OAC)

Ness [19] published the OAC dataset in cooperation with the Orcalab [20], comprising 15,480 labeled underwater events (stereo, sampling rate: 44.1 kHz) extracted from the Orchive [19]. The annotations include various killer whale sounds and several noise samples [22]. For later killer whale specific representation learning, we extracted all valid killer whale signals (killer whale calls, whistles, echolocations) from the OAC containing 7,903 killer whale samples with a total annotated time of 9.96 h.

Automatic Extracted Orchive Tape Data (AEOTD)

In order to provide further killer whale signals for representation learning, we filtered all killer whale sounds from the AEOTD dataset described in [22]. The entire dataset includes 1,667 killer whale sounds with an annotation time of 1.4 h.

DeepAL Fieldwork Data 2017/2018 (DLFD)

During our research expedition in northern British Columbia (2017/2018) we have collected additional multi-channel killer whale and noise data via a 15-meter research trimaran using underwater microphone arrays [22]. According to [22] we selected four different channels out of the multi-channel labeled killer whale sound events to furthermore increase our overall killer whale data for representation learning. The DLFD comprises 3,331 killer whale signals and an overall annotation time of 3.40 h.

Orca Segmented Data (OSD)

The OSD corpus is a result of a fully automatic segmentation using our trained ResNet18 classifier [22], distinguishing between killer whale and noise sound events. To enlarge the existing database even further, we automatically extracted killer whale signals detected by our segmenter. The resulting OSD corpus comprises 19,211 killer whale signals and an overall annotated time of 34.47 h. Thus, according to [22], there should be about 4% false positives within the OSD corpus.

Call Type Catalogs

For training, validation and testing of the call type classifier we used the same data pool as described in [22], consisting of two different call type catalogs – Orcalab catalog (CCS) with 138 killer whale sounds containing 7 various call type classes, Ness catalog (CCN) with 286 killer whale signals including 6 different call types – plus an extension catalog (EXT) including 30 echolocations, 30 whistles, and 30 noise files manually selected from the Orchive data [22] in order to simulate a real-world scenario. In total this results in 12 classes, consisting of 9 various call types, echolocations, whistles, and noise samples summing up to 514 samples (see Table 1).

Table 1. Orca call type, echolocation, whistle, and noise label distribution of the CCS, CCN, and EXT data corpus

Orca call type/corpus	N01	N02	N03	N04	N05	N07	N09	N12	N47	Echo	Whistles	Noise	SUM
CCS	33	10	—	21	14	18	26	16	—	—	—	—	138
CCN	36	—	56	60	—	31	70	—	33	—	—	—	286
EXT	—	—	—	—	—	—	—	—	—	30	30	30	90
SUM	69	10	56	81	14	49	96	16	33	30	30	30	514

3.2   Data Distribution

In Table 2 the data distribution of the entire representation learning and whole call type classification data corpus is described. The representation learning data listed in Table 2a consists of the aforementioned OAC, AEOTD, DLFD, and OSD corpus summing up to a total amount of 32,112 killer whale sounds. The call type classification dataset in Table 2b includes the previously illustrated CCS,

CCN, and EXT dataset summing up to an overall amount of 514 signals [22]. For the entire representation learning data corpus every file was removed which belonged to the same tape as one of the signals from the call type classification dataset. Consequently, the training, validation and test signals of the representation learning corpus are completely independent of those from the call type classification dataset.

Table 2. Training, validation, and test distribution for representation learning and call type classification

Split/ Datasets	train		val		test	
	smp	%	smp	%	smp	%
OAC	**7,903**	5,832	73.8	1,171	14.8	900	11.4
AEOTD	**1,667**	1,172	70.3	260	15.6	235	14.1
DLFD	**3,331**	1,384	41.5	1,171	35.2	776	23.3
OSD	**19,211**	13,493	70.2	2,863	14.9	2,855	14.8
SUM	**32,112**	21,881	68.1	5,465	17.0	4,766	14.8

a) Representation learning data distribution

Split/ Datasets	train		val		test	
	smp	%	smp	%	smp	%
CCS	**138**	102	73.9	19	13.8	17	12.3
CCN	**286**	198	69.2	41	14.4	47	16.4
EXT	**90**	63	70.0	12	13.3	15	16.7
SUM	**514**	363	70.6	72	14.0	79	15.4

b) Call type data distribution

4 Experimental Setup

4.1 ResNet18 Autoencoder

In this work we used an undercomplete autoencoder based on the ResNet18 [14] architecture. Figure 2 visualizes the utilized network architecture. For the bottleneck layer, various layer types were investigated: (1) convolutional layer (1×1 convolution without stride to compress 512 channels to $4 \times 16 \times 8$ and back to $512 \times 16 \times 8$) and (2) fully-connected layer (max-pooling of $512 \times 16 \times 8$ to a 512-D latent layer and subsequent max-unpooling back to $512 \times 16 \times 8$).

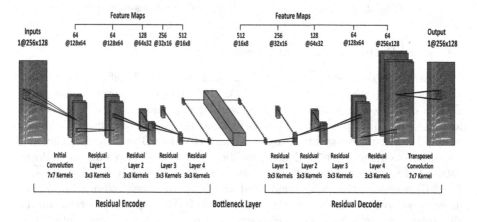

Fig. 2. Architecture of the ResNet18 autoencoder with a parametric bottleneck layer

The ResNet18 encoder architecture was slightly modified in terms of removing the 3 × 3 (stride 2) max-pooling from the first residual layer in order to keep higher frequency resolutions within the early stages [22]. The decoder utilized transposed convolutions for upsampling and slightly differs from the encoder. In order to avoid artifacts in our last layer, potentially caused by transposed convolutions with stride 2, we already upsampled to 256 × 128 in the penultimate layer and processed a final transposed convolution (stride 1) to compensate such errors.

4.2 ResNet18 Call Type Classifier

Our call type classifier [22] is based on a ResNet18 architecture (feature extraction part) combined with a 512-D fully connected hidden layer and a subsequent 12-D output layer (classification part) in order to distinguish between 12 classes (see Table 1). Figure 3 visualizes the network architecture of our call type classifier [22].

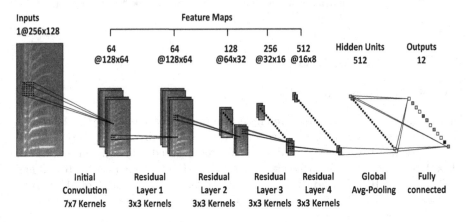

Fig. 3. Architecture of the ResNet18 call type classifier [22]

4.3 Data Preprocessing and Augmentation

The ResNet18 based autoencoder (Fig. 2) and call type classifier (Fig. 3) used the same data preprocessing toolchain. As described in [22] every audio sample was converted to a 44.1 kHz mono wav signal, followed by a STFT (window size = 4,096, hop size = 441) transforming the audio to a power spectrogram [22]. The power spectrogram was converted to dB and further changed via various sequential ordered augmentation techniques, all using an uniform distributed random scaling [22]. Intensity (−6−+3 dB), pitch (0.5–1.5), and time (0.5–2.0) augmentation were conducted first [22]. In a next step a linear frequency compression (fmin = 500 Hz, fmax = 10 kHz) was processed resulting in 256 frequency bins. Afterwards characteristic pitch and time augmented, frequency compressed noise files of the segmenter train set in [22] were added using a randomly chosen SNR between -3 and $+12\,dB$ [22]. Noise augmentation was only activated while training the classifier. A subsequent dB-normalization within $-100\,dB$ (minimum level) and $+20\,dB$ (reference level) was performed. To provide training clips of equal size we randomly chose a $1.28\,s$ segment (if applicable zero-padding) of the final spectrogram resulting in a 256×128 large training sample [22].

4.4   Training, Validation, and Testing

All our trained models, implemented in PyTorch [21], used an Adam optimizer together with an initial learning rate of 10^{-5}, $\beta_1 = 0.5$, and $\beta_2 = 0.999$ [22]. The learning rate was decayed by $1/2$ after 4 epochs, and the entire training was stopped after 10 epochs without having any improvements on the validation set [22]. For deep representation learning, we utilized a batch size of 32 together with a weighted mean squared error (MSE) loss. For call type classification a batch size of 4 in combination with a 12-class cross entropy loss was used [22]. The lowest validation loss was selected as criterion for the best autoencoder model, whereas the highest validation accuracy was picked in case of finding the best call type classifier. The autoencoder was trained on the entire or portions of the data listed in Table 2a. The call type classifier was trained on the same data as in [22], listed in Table 2b. Furthermore, we computed a 10-fold cross-validation on the entire call type dataset in order to get a better impression about the overall model robustness.

4.5   Experiments

Our experimental setup is divided into three major parts: (1) investigations regarding the best ResNet18 autoencoder architecture trained on the entire or various data portions of Table 2a, (2) evaluating the impact of representation learning by training, validating, and testing our pretrained call type classifier on the given data corpus illustrated in Table 2b, and (3) analyzing the pretrained ResNet18 classifiers models by performing a 10-fold cross validation using the entire call type classification corpus in Table 2b. In (1) we examined two bottleneck architectures; linear versus convolutional architectures (see Sect. 4.1) of our ResNet18 autoencoder (Fig. 2) together with different data combinations: semi-automatic labeled data (entire representation corpora), fully hand-labeled data (only OAC corpus), and automatic labeled data (only OSD dataset), listed in Table 2a. In (2) we evaluated the call type classifier (Fig. 3) by using the pre-trained autoencoder weights and calculating the accuracy based on 10 training/evaluation runs (Fig. 5a). Moreover, in experiment (3), a 10-fold cross validation was conducted on the entire call type dataset listed in Table 2b in order to give an impression about the overall classifier robustness. Here we only evaluated the best pre-trained classifiers with respect to the trained data combinations (semi-automatic labeled, hand-labeled, automatic labeled; see Fig. 5b).

5   Results

In this study six different ResNet18-based autoencoders were trained and analyzed utilizing linear or convolutional bottleneck layers for semi-automatic labeled, hand-labeled, and automatic labeled data corpora: (1) linear/convolutional autoencoder on the entire dataset listed in Table 2a (semi-automatic labeled data), (2) linear/convolutional autoencoder on the OAC dataset (hand-labeled data), and (3) linear/convolutional autoencoder on the OSD dataset (automatic machine-labeled data). Figure 4 shows the autoencoder signal reconstruction results based on the three different killer whale sound types taken from the call type test set listed in Table 2b. None of the reconstructed files was part of the training or validation. With respect to each trained dataset we only visualized the reconstructions of the autoencoders using the convolutional bottleneck layer, since they provided better results.

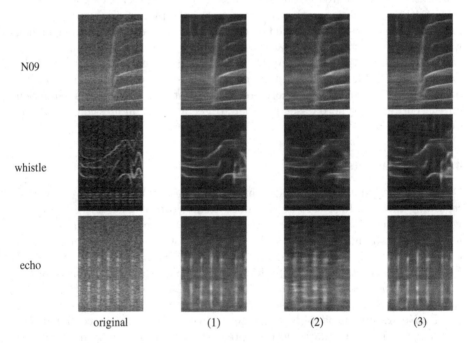

Fig. 4. Autoencoder (AE) reconstructions of killer whale sound types from the call type test set **(1)** AE (convolutional bottleneck) trained on the entire data listed in Table 2a (semi-automatic labeled data), **(2)** AE (convolutional bottleneck) trained on the OAC corpus (hand-labeled data) **(3)** AE (convolutional bottleneck) trained on the OSD dataset (automatic machine-labeled data)

All of our six pretrained autoencoder encoder parts were separately used for weight initialization of the call type classifier which was trained on the data listed in Table 2b. Therefore we removed bottleneck layer and decoder part in order to only use the encoder part combined with a global average pooling and subsequent fully-connected layer followed by a 12-dimensional output layer in order to classify between the different sound events (see Fig. 3). Deeper layers learn more specific and high-level features. In the case of representation learning, the last residual layer learns to provide a good basis for a successful reconstruction rather than an accurate classification. Hence, we randomly initialized the last residual layer and did not use the pretrained weights in that case. Figure 5 visualizes the impact of deep representation learning with respect to the call type classification accuracy. All six pretrained autoencoders and their classification results are illustrated. The notation used for the various autoencoder variants consists of a number (1, 2, 3) illustrating the entire dataset (1), OAC dataset (2), and the OSD dataset (3) as well as a letter (c, l) describing if a convolutional (c) or linear (l) bottleneck layer was used (e.g. 3-c describes an autoencoder with a linear bottleneck layer trained on the OSD dataset). In addition a result without any pretraining (Figure 5a, row 4) was added. The statistics about the accuracy were based on 10 training/evaluation runs. Furthermore, we also put the mean test accuracy of our previous work [22] to the graph which corresponds to only 5 runs (Figure 5a, row 5). The average accuracy for every pretrained classifier was better than without pretraining. According to Fig. 5a, the best test performance on average (94%), smallest variance/stdv, and the best single model accuracy (96%) was achieved by the pretrained classifier using the convolutional autoencoder (3-c) trained on the fully automatic machine-segmented OSD dataset. Figure 6 visualizes the confusion matrix of our best model (3-c, 96% accuracy) compared to the matrix illustrated in our previous work [22]. In order to compute the overall classifier accuracy with respect to the entire call type dataset (Table 2b) we conducted a 10-fold cross validation. For each dataset we selected the pretrained autoencoder version which led to a better subsequent classification accuracy. In all cases the autoencoder with the convolutional bottleneck

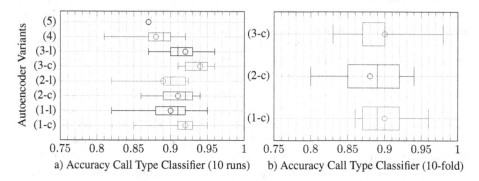

Fig. 5. (a) Mean test accuracy of 10 train/evaluation runs: (1-c) convolutional, (1-l) linear AE on the entire data listed in Table 2a, (2-c) convolutional, (2-l) linear AE on the OAC corpus, (3-c) convolutional, (3-l) linear AE on the OSD dataset, (4) no pretrain (5) mean test accuracy of [22]. (b) Classifier accuracy in a 10-fold cross validation (Table 2b) for the top 3 AEs (1-c), (2-c), (3-c)

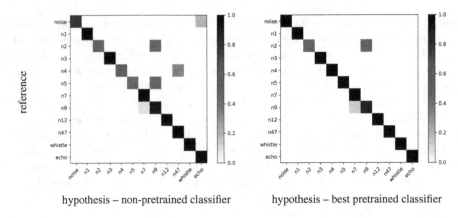

Fig. 6. Confusion matrix (12-classes) – non-pretrained call type classifier (ACC = 87%) [22] vs. best pretrained call type classifier (ACC = 96%))

layer outperformed the linear variant. Consequently, we used autoencoder 1-c, 2-c, and 3-c for weight initialization of the different classifiers to run the 10-fold cross validation. The classification results about the 10-fold cross validation are shown in Fig. 5b. The best semi-supervised trained call type classifier (Fig. 5b, 3-c) used the machine-segmented OSD dataset and achieved the highest mean test accuracy of 90% whereas one test fold reached up to 98%.

6   Conclusion

In summary, deep representation learning has a significant positive influence on killer whale call type classification. Particularly important is the fact that regardless of the autoencoder architecture, as well as from the utilized data corpora, any form of representation learning has led to an improvement referring to the mean test classification accuracy. Moreover, pretraining on our fully automatic machine-labeled OSD corpus led to the best performance being a great indicator of having a robust and reliable segmentation process [22]. In future work we will segment the entire 20,000 h of underwater recordings for further killer whale representation learning. Moreover, we plan to investigate the huge variety of machine-segmented killer whale call types by using various feature learning techniques combined with subsequent clustering methods in order to establish a fully unsupervised pipeline for killer whale call type identification/classification. On the one hand, this allows us to explore finer, more significant and potential undiscovered killer whale call types. On the other hand, the entire call type classification can be performed completely independent from human perception. Furthermore, the unsupervised identified call types and possible sub-call types can be also used for subsequent supervised learning approaches.

References

1. Bengio, Y., Courville, A.C., Vincent, P.: Representation learning: a review and new perspectives. IEEE Trans. Pattern Anal. Mach. Intell. **35**, 1798–1828 (2013)
2. Bigg, M.A., Olesiuk, P.F., Ellis, G.M., Ford, J.K.B., Balcomb, K.C.: Organization and genealogy of resident killer whales (Orcinus orca) in the coastal waters of British Columbia and Washington State. Int. Whaling Comm. **12**, 383–405 (1990)
3. Brown, J., Hodgins-Davis, A., Miller, P.: Classification of vocalizations of killer whales using dynamic time warping. JASA Express Lett. **119**(3), 617–628 (2006)
4. Brown, J.C., Smaragdis, P.: Hidden Markov and Gaussian mixture models for automatic call classification. J. Acoust. Soc. Am. **125**, 221–224 (2009)
5. Brown, J.C., Smaragdis, P., Nousek-McGregor, A.: Automatic identification of individual killer whales. J. Acoust. Soc. Am. **128**, 93–98 (2010)
6. Deecke, V.B., Janik, V.M.: Automated categorization of bioacoustic signals: avoiding perceptual pitfalls. J. Acoust. Soc. Am. **119**, 645–653 (2006)
7. Filatova, O.A., Samarra, F.I., Deecke, V.B., Ford, J.K., Miller, P.J., Yurk, H.: Cultural evolution of killer whale calls: background, mechanisms and consequences. Behaviour **152**, 2001–2038 (2015)
8. Ford, J., Ellis, G., Balcomb, K.: Killer Whales: The Natural History and Genealogy of Orcinus Orca in British Columbia and Washington. UBC Press, Vancouver (2000)
9. Ford, J.K.B.: A catalogue of underwater calls produced by killer whales (Orcinus orca) in British Columbia. Canadian Data Report of Fisheries and Aquatic Science (633), p. 165 (1987)
10. Ford, J.K.B.: Acoustic behaviour of resident killer whales (Orcinus orca) off Vancouver Island, British Columbia. Can. J. Zool. **67**, 727–745 (1989)
11. Ford, J.K.B.: Vocal traditions among resident killer whales (Orcinus orca) in coastal waters of British Columbia. Can. J. Zool. **69**, 1454–1483 (1991)
12. Garland, E., Castellote, M., Berchok, C.: Beluga whale (Delphinapterus leucas) vocalizations and call classification from the eastern Beaufort sea population. J. Acoust. Soc. of Am. **137**, 3054–3067 (2015)
13. Goodfellow, I., Bengio, Y., Courville, A.: Deep Learning. MIT Press, Cambridge (2016)
14. He, K., Zhang, X., Ren, S., Sun, J.: Deep residual learning for image recognition. In: 2016 IEEE Conference on Computer Vision and Pattern Recognition (CVPR), pp. 770–778 (2016)
15. Ivkovich, T., Filatova, O., Burdin, A., Sato, H., Hoyt, E.: The social organization of resident-type killer whales (Orcinus orca) in Avacha Gulf, Northwest Pacific, as revealed through association patterns and acoustic similarity. Mamm. Biol. **75**, 198–210 (2010)
16. LeCun, Y., Bottou, L., Bengio, Y., Haffner, P.: Gradient-based learning applied to document recognition. Proc. IEEE **86**, 2278–2324 (1998)
17. Mercado, E., Kuh, A.: Classification of humpback whale vocalizations using a self-organizing neural network. In: IEEE International Conference on Neural Networks - Conference Proceedings, pp. 1584–1589, June 1998
18. Miller, P., Bain, D.: Within-pod variation in the sound production of a pod of killer whales, Orcinus orca. Anim. Behav. **60**, 617–628 (2000)
19. Ness, S.: The Orchive: a system for semi-automatic annotation and analysis of a large collection of bioacoustic recordings. Ph.D. thesis (2013)

20. ORCALAB: a whale research station on Hanson Island. http://orcalab.org. Accessed May 2019

21. Paszke, A., et al.: Automatic differentiation in PyTorch. In: NIPS 2017 Workshop, October 2017

22. Schröter, H., Nöth, E., Maier, A., Cheng, R., Barth, V., Bergler, C.: Segmentation, classification, and visualization of orca calls using deep learning. In: International Conference on Acoustics, Speech, and Signal Processing, Proceedings (ICASSP), May 2019

On Using Stateful LSTM Networks
for Key-Phrase Detection

Martin Bulín[1]([⊠]), Luboš Šmídl[2], and Jan Švec[1]

[1] NTIS - New Technologies for Information Society, Faculty of Applied Sciences,
University of West Bohemia, Pilsen, Czech Republic
{bulinm,honzas}@ntis.zcu.cz
[2] Department of Cybernetics, Faculty of Applied Sciences,
University of West Bohemia, Pilsen, Czech Republic
smidl@kky.zcu.cz

Abstract. In this paper, we focus on LSTM (Long Short-Term Memory) networks and their implementation in a popular framework called Keras. The goal is to show how to take advantage of their ability to pass the context by holding the state and to clear up what the stateful property of LSTM Recurrent Neural Network implemented in Keras actually means. The main outcome of the work is then a general algorithm for packing arbitrary context-dependent data, capable of 1/ packing the data to fit the stateful models; 2/ making the training process efficient by supplying multiple frames together; 3/ on-the-fly (frame-by-frame) prediction by the trained model. Two training methods are presented, a window-based approach is compared with a fully-stateful approach. The analysis is performed on the Speech commands dataset. Finally, we give guidance on how to use stateful LSTMs to create a key-phrase detection system.

Keywords: LSTM · Stateful · Context modeling ·
Key-phrase detection · ASR

1 Introduction

As well as human thoughts have persistence and our reasoning at a single point of time is highly dependent on what happened a moment ago, there is a call for artificial models that would imitate this behavior and allow information persist over time. These models are believed to target that type of data where we need to know the past in order to predict the future, generally known as context-dependent or sequence data. One example for all is language in general, either in its textual or the speech form. The meaning of a single word may significantly change with the change of its context as well as the meaning of a whole sentence could vary depending on what had been said right before it. The key feature we need these models to be capable of is working with time dependencies.

Recurrent neural networks (RNNs) have loops in them and hence they are a good candidate to address this issue. In addition to the network input, these

K. Ekštein (Ed.): TSD 2019, LNAI 11697, pp. 287–298, 2019.
https://doi.org/10.1007/978-3-030-27947-9_24

loops make single cells see their output and state at the previous point of time. Besides the default RNN version (known as Vanilla RNN), there are two more well-known RNN designs - GRU (Gated Recurrent Unit) [2] and LSTM (Long Short-Term Memory) [5]. These two deals with the main shortcoming of the default version, which is the inability to learn long-term dependencies caused by the vanishing gradient problem [8].

In this work, we focus on the LSTM RNN design. The main goal is to give guidance on how to use its internal state properly in a popular framework called Keras [3]. Apart from the GRU design, there is one extra feature the LSTM design has - each cell computes and holds a value of its internal state. The implementation and usage of this state in Keras can be tricky, especially because of its special property called the *stateful* flag. As in principle all LSTM models are stateful [1], one of the main objectives of this work is to clear up what the *stateful* flag in Keras actually means. There are several design choices we encounter when building an LSTM model in Keras and this work will help set up the model optimally and understand what all the parameters are responsible for.

As a baseline, we take a window-based approach, a powerful tool when using samples of the same (or relatively similar) length. This scenario is quite rare in practice though, hence we describe a second approach called a fully-stateful model. This method is capable of dealing with samples of various numbers of frames, like for example speech usually has - the number of frames depends on the length of a word or a sentence.

In practice, when training some kind of sequence data in Keras, the crucial issue lies in a proper arrangement of the samples we want to fit the model with. As long as we want to use a reasonable batch size for training, we need to respect the rules of how the flow of sequence data is being read in Keras. The novelty of this work is in a data packing algorithm capable of taking arbitrary context-dependent data and organizing them correctly to fit a stateful LSTM model in Keras.

Moreover, the fully-stateful approach opens the possibility of on-the-fly prediction. We show how a model can be efficiently trained by feeding a model by multiple frames at the same time, while the prediction is then being done frame-by-frame. This idea complies with the theoretical idea of how LSTM RNNs are aimed to be used and, furthermore, the frame-by-frame prediction provides a model output at every single point of time and ensures that no frame is processed more than once. This feature is perfectly suited for online prediction as well as for a deployment to low-resource devices.

1.1 Objectives of this Work

1. to give an overview about the theory behind the LSTM RNN model and to explain its implementation hitches in Keras;
2. to clear up the stateful property of the LSTM RNN model implemented in Keras and to compare the window-based approach with the fully-stateful approach;

3. to design a general data packing algorithm for arbitrary sequence data for Keras;
4. to give guidance on how to use LSTM models for the key-phrase detection task

1.2 Notation

- L_i: number of frames of sample i
- B: batch size
- T: number of frames (timesteps) processed at once
- F: number of features
- S_t/S_v: number of training/validation samples
- M: number of classes

2 Theoretical Background

In general, the concept of recurrent neural networks (RNNs) together with the Backpropagation through time (BPTT) algorithm [4] is a great tool for sequence data learning, however, the default version suffers from so-called short-term memory. To make the model capable of learning long-term dependencies as well, we use Long Short-Term Memory (LSTM) networks [5] based on the idea of internal gates (see Fig. 1).

The functionality of a single LSTM cell including the background math is well explained in [7]. The core idea lies in the presence of an internal state c_t connected to three gates:

1. a *forget* gate deciding on what information we keep or throw away;
2. an *input* gate saying what new information we want to store in the state;
3. an *output* gate responsible for final output.

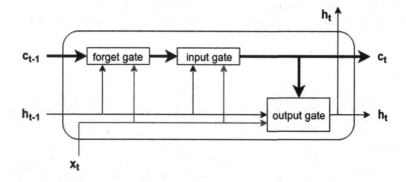

Fig. 1. Three gates in the LSTM cell controlling state c_t and output h_t.

The internal state c_t is what makes the model capable of learning the dependencies and memorize. Now, we give some details on how this state is implemented and used in a popular framework called Keras.

First of all, we need to understand the principle of so-called *timesteps* (see Fig. 2). With no loss of generality, we take speech as the sequence data for this example. Let $X = [x_1, x_2, ..., x_L]$ be a sequence of frames (feature vectors) in a single utterance over time. The number of timesteps T in Keras is given by the number of frames sent to the model together in one batch.

From Fig. 1 we see that the cell output h_t is always dependent on the previous output of the same cell h_{t-1}, previous cell's state c_{t-1} and current cell's input x_t, where $h_0 = [0]$ and $c_0 = [0]$ (zero vectors of appropriate dimensions).

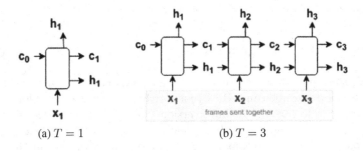

(a) $T = 1$ (b) $T = 3$

Fig. 2. Meaning of the T (*timesteps*) parameter.

Figure 2 shows that frame x_t is always combined with the information (state c_{t-1} and output h_{t-1}) from the previous frame x_{t-1} in case those two frames are sent to the model together in the same batch. However, if two consecutive frames are divided into two separate batches (or in case of $T = 1$, when no two frames share a batch), in Keras, we have to switch the stateful mode on in order to make the state and output of the first frame visible for the second one and to make c_t and h_t retain between batches. Otherwise, if the stateful flag is set to false, the state and the output of a cell are both reset to zeros after every batch (after sending T frames to the model). The difference is graphically illustrated in Fig. 3.

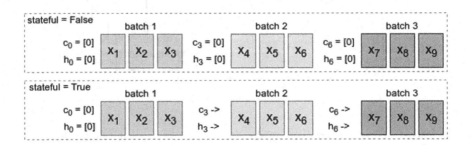

Fig. 3. Influence of the stateful flag in Keras ($T = 3$, $L = 9$).

In theory, all LSTMs are stateful and hold the state even between batches, which is a logical way of how to use LSTMs correctly for several reasons. Primarily, it allows us to set $T = 1$ for the prediction phase and so to process sequence data on-the-fly (frame-by-frame). Secondly, if we have a stream of sequence data or samples of various lengths in the training phase, we do not have to worry about breaking any dependencies as the states are not being reset.

One of the main objectives of this work is to show the influence of the stateful flag in Keras and so to compare a window-based approach (the stateful flag set to false) to a fully-stateful approach (the stateful flag set to true).

2.1   Window-Based LSTM Approach

When the stateful flag is set to false in Keras, the state and output of each cell are reset to zeros every time a batch is processed (see Fig. 3). It can be very effective in the training phase, when we have samples of a fixed length and so there is no risk in breaking any dependencies by resetting the states after a complete sample is processed. The length of the samples L equals the number of timesteps T and so all frames of one sample are sent together. A one-hot vector is commonly used as a target (see targets in Sect. 3.2) for each sample, where one sample is given by $L = T$ frames.

The training is comparatively fast in this case and we can get a relatively good performance as the task is categorical. On the other hand, difficulties arise when we have samples of various lengths - apart from a fully-stateful LSTM model.

2.2   Fully Stateful LSTM Approach

In case of a fully-stateful LSTM model (see Fig. 3 - stateful set to true), we know the state is forwarded between two consecutive batches, which is the key feature of this approach. It allows the model to use samples of various lengths for training. We do that by connecting the samples one by one together into a stream of sequence data and then generate batches of T frames alongside this stream. A detailed explanation of the data generation process is given in the following section. When the stream is cut into batches of T frames, dependencies are never broken as the information always persist between the batches in this approach.

Another advantage here is taken in the prediction phase. The state persistence between frames allows us to make the prediction on-the-fly by setting $T = 1$ and so get the output from a model at every single point of time (for each frame).

2.3   Data Packing Algorithm

In order to make context-dependent samples of an arbitrary length suitable for an LSTM model, firstly we need to represent it correctly. We implemented an algorithm for packing frames into training batches. The generation of the batches is being done on-the-fly using CPU, while the network training is performed using GPU.

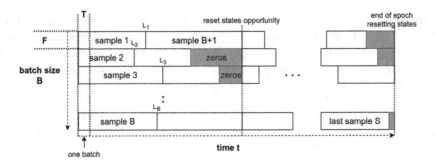

Fig. 4. The generated stream of context-dependent data.

First of all, we determine three parameters:

- F: number of features in a single frame (fixed in data preprocessing)
- T: number of timesteps (frames) of one sample sent together in one batch
- B: batch size - number of independent samples sent together in one batch

Figure 4 shows the desired composition of samples into a stream. Putting parts of B samples together within one batch is a common approach that speeds up the training phase as well as, to some extent, it helps the gradient learning method (more samples are shown together).

Then we choose the T parameter, saying how many frames we put together into one batch. Choosing T can influence the training phase a lot. Even though the fully-stateful model ensures that the previous cell's state and output are always seen between batches, the gradients are computed separately for every batch. Therefore, if $T = 1$ (or is relatively small), learning the context cannot work properly. An analysis of choosing the optimal T is performed in Sect. 4.

Having the parameters fixed and samples concatenated in a stream as shown in Fig. 4, there is one more issue worth considering before we start the training. The fully-stateful model does not reset states automatically between batches, but we can do that manually. Samples are picked up and put into the stream in a random manner, so it makes sense to reset the states at the end of one sample as it is generally not related to the following one. On top of that, reinitialization of the states at the right moment may possibly help the algorithm get out of a wrong way and so learn better.

However, we need to make sure the reset is not being done in the middle of any of the samples across a batch. We set a reset interval to our data packing algorithm, at which all samples in a batch are aligned by padding the shorter ones with zeros (see the gray boxes in Fig. 4) and then the states can be blithely reset. In this work, we do the reset at the end of each epoch only.

After every epoch, the stream is shuffled as the samples are picked up randomly each time. The number of batches per epoch Z can be estimated by:

$$Z = \frac{L \cdot S}{B \cdot T} \tag{1}$$

where L is the mean sample length and S is the number of samples in the stream.

3   Experimental Dataset

As we discuss the usage of the internal state of LSTM cells and the ability
to keep information over time, we need the demonstration data to be context-
dependent, like for example speech is. This requirement is met by the Speech
commands dataset [9], which is also suitable in terms of size, availability and
credibility. Therefore, we based on it all our experiments in this work.

The dataset consists of 65 K one-second-long audio clips recorded by thousands of different people. As shown in Fig. 5, we have samples of 30 English
words plus clips representing silence - a combination of different kinds of noise
like doing the dishes, miaowing or an artificially made white noise. The validation
and testing lists of samples are provided with the data, ensuring a reasonable
data split ratio (80:10:10) and keeping utterances of the same person in one set.

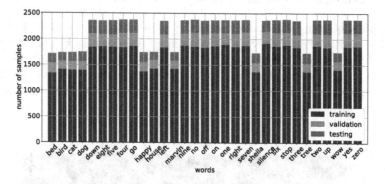

Fig. 5. Distribution of the speech commands dataset. [9]

3.1   Sample Preprocessing

The sampling rate of the audio clips is 16 kHz. We use the standard parametrization approach with 40 frequency filters, the window size of 512 (32 ms) and the
window shift of 160 (10 ms). This setting gives 100 frames for a one-second long
audio clip. Not all of the clips are precisely one second long, the length in frames
over the dataset varies from 33 to 124, however, this issue is exactly what we do
deal with by using the stateful cells. Hence, no additional padding or aligning is
needed.

Finally, for each frame we compute 13 Mel-Frequency Cepstral Coefficients
(MFCCs) out of the 40 frequency filters and add deltas. This way each sample
in the dataset turns into a $L_i \times F$ feature matrix E shown in Eq. 2. We can
see that $F = 26$ is fixed, while L_i differs sample from sample depending on the
audio length.

$$E_i = \begin{bmatrix} f_{11} & \cdots & f_{1F} \\ \vdots & \ddots & \\ f_{L_i1} & & f_{L_iF} \end{bmatrix} \tag{2}$$

3.2 Target Functions

In this work, we define two target types.

1. *A categorical target* represented by a one-hot vector and used together with the window-based approach. All frames of one sample share one scalar value only (zero or one). For example, we would have a target vector $Y = [0, 1, 0]$ for a 3-class classification problem.
2. *A frame-based target* defining a target value for every single frame x_t and being used together with the fully-stateful approach (see Fig. 6).

The idea of using the frame-based target function allows us to tailor the desired network output for every single sample. As shown in Fig. 6, we use the energy of the first MFCC to detect the speech signal in the recording. Once the utterance position is found in the sample, the target is set to one for the last 15 frames of the word. This makes sense, as we can only say a word was pronounced after it was or at the very end of it.

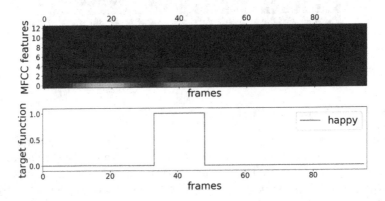

Fig. 6. An example of a frame-based target function for keyword "happy".

3.3 Evaluation Metrics

Each of the specified target types from the previous section needs its evaluation metric. In case of the categorical target, we use the standard categorical accuracy (Eq. 3) giving the proportion of correctly labeled samples to all samples.

$$ACC_{cat} = \frac{n_{correct}}{n_{correct} + n_{fail}} \tag{3}$$

Using ACC_{cat} (Eq. 3) for frame-based targets is possible, but not optimal. In this case, we do not insist on a correct prediction of every single frame, but rather we want to know if the key sequence consisting of several frames was found in a stream or not. For a sequence of data we have a ground truth information about the position of single words (samples) in the sequence. The goal is to hit the right class at these positions with a trained model.

Therefore, we define three more evaluation metrics for the frame-based targets. All of them are graphically illustrated in Fig. 7.

1. *M1 - max.* This metric takes the class whose prediction curve reaches the maximal value across the sample window (Eq. 4).

$$k^* = \operatorname*{argmax}_{k,t=0,1,...,L} y_t^{(k)} \tag{4}$$

2. *M2 - sum.* This metric computes the sum of all values across the sample window for all classes and takes the class with the greatest area under its prediction curve.

$$k^* = \operatorname*{argmax}_{k} \sum_{t=0}^{L} y_t^{(k)} \tag{5}$$

3. *M3 - window-max.* In this case, we use a floating window of length $N = 15$ and shift it over the sample and compute the sum for each t (frame) and each k (class). The predicted class k^* is then the one having the floating window with the maximal value.

$$k^* = \operatorname*{argmax}_{k,t=0,1,...,L-N} \sum_{i=t}^{t+N} y^{(k)}(i) \tag{6}$$

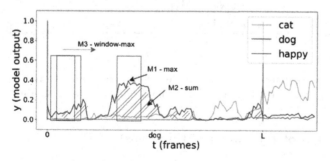

Fig. 7. Illustration of the evaluation metrics on one sample in a stream.

4   Results

In this section, we show how LSTM RNNs can be used for an online prediction of a sequence data stream on the key-phrase detection task. Then an analysis of the influence of the T parameter is performed.

4.1   Key-Phrase Detection

The key-phrase detection task is a well-fitting application for the on-the-fly prediction ability of LSTM RNNs. The model takes a real-time sequence data and produces the output for every single frame, while the previous context is considered using the model's state. We used only 10 classes (the same as in [6]) from all the 31 labelled classes in the Speech command database (see Sect. 3). The experimental setup is as follows. A model of two LSTM layers of 256 and 128 cells is trained for 50 epochs. The product $T \cdot B$ was held constant to maintain the constant number of frame samples in the batch.

Figure 8 shows model's predictions on a stream of 5 randomly chosen testing samples, where the dashed lines represent the ground truth targets. The value true is assigned for N (N = 15) last frames from the end of the word position in the sample. The prediction is being done on-the-fly ($T = 1$).

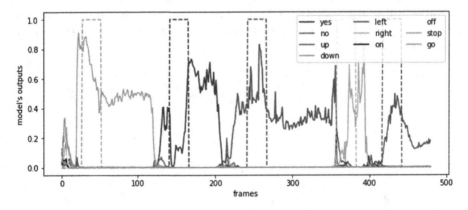

Fig. 8. Key-phrase detection – performance illustration on random testing samples for stateful model and on-the-fly prediction without resetting states after each test file.

4.2   Influence of T (number of timesteps)

Finally, we make an analysis of the influence of the T parameter on the training of a fully-stateful model and compare it to the performance of a window-based model. We use the evaluation metrics defined in Sect. 3.3 to compare the results.

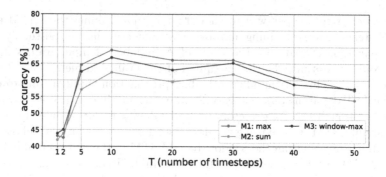

Fig. 9. Influence of the T parameter on training a fully-stateful model.

Figure 9 shows the maximal possible accuracy achieved in training for different settings of the T parameter in case of the fully-stateful models. As expected, choosing a small value ($T < 5$) breaks the context dependencies and therefore is not suggested for training. The experiments show that the values of T between 10 and 30 optimize the evaluated metrics for the Speech commands dataset.

Even though the accuracy of the window-based model seems promising, using the categorical target function makes the window-based model unable of frame-by-frame prediction, like the fully-stateful models are capable of.

Table 1. Comparison of different types of models on two tasks – keyword classification implies state reset at the beginning of a keyword. On-the-fly prediction processes the stream of concatenated samples without the state reset and therefore without the knowledge about the keyword boundaries. The table shows the values of $M1$ metric.

	Keyword classification	On-the-fly prediction
Window-based LSTM	85.4%	49.3%
Fully-stateful LSTM	84.5%	**69.1%**

5   Conclusion

This paper is devoted to the usage of LSTM RNN models for learning context-dependent data. Although the LSTM RNNs could be used as a simple classifier in the window-based mode, its use in the on-the-fly prediction is questionable - to achieve robust predictions the keyword boundaries are necessary. If we focus on the on-the-fly prediction [10] (especially on the real-time online keyword detection on low resourced hardware) without the knowledge of keyword boundaries, the window-based LSTM is useless. The reasons are (1) the windows for classification must be overlapping and therefore for $T = 100$ any single frame is taken 100 times into the computation (when no decimation is used) and (2) the keyword boundaries are not known in the online problem and therefore the performance of the model is degraded (compare the first and second column of Table 1).

The goal of this paper was to show that by maintaining the LSTM state across batches during training improves the accuracy in the on-the-fly prediction scenario. In addition, the value of T (number of input frames in one batch) could be optimized - the maximum of the evaluated metrics is achieved around $T = 10$. This setting allows the backpropagation through time to optimize the LSTM parameters not only for the current time step but also backpropagate through the state vectors (c_t and h_t) into previous time steps. The fully-stateful LSTM trained using the described data generation method perform better ($M1 = 69.1\%$) than the window-based LSTM in the on-the-fly prediction ($M1 = 49.3\%$). At the same time the fully-stateful LSTM allows frame-by-frame computation – each frame is passed through the network only once. If we supply the network with information about the keyword boundaries, the prediction accuracy reaches the accuracy of the window-based LSTM.

Acknowledgement. This work was supported by The Ministry of Education, Youth and Sports of the Czech Republic project No. LO1506.

References

1. Bosch, R.: Stateful LSTM model training in keras (2018). https://fairyonice.github.io/Stateful-LSTM-model-training-in-Keras.html
2. Cho, K., et al.: Learning phrase representations using RNN encoder-decoder for statistical machine translation. In: Proceedings of the 2014 Conference on Empirical Methods in Natural Language Processing (EMNLP), Doha, Qatar, pp. 1724–1734. Association for Computational Linguistics, October 2014. https://www.aclweb.org/anthology/D14-1179
3. Chollet, F., et al.: Keras (2015). https://keras.io
4. De Jesus, O., Hagan, M.T.: Backpropagation algorithms for a broad class of dynamic networks. IEEE Trans. Neural Networks **18**(1), 14–27 (2007)
5. Hochreiter, S., Schmidhuber, J.: Long short-term memory. Neural Comput. **9**(8), 1735–1780 (1997). https://doi.org/10.1162/neco.1997.9.8.1735
6. Kaggle: Tensorflow speech recognition challenge (2017). https://www.kaggle.com/c/tensorflow-speech-recognition-challenge
7. Olah, C.: Understanding LSTM networks (2015). http://colah.github.io/posts/2015-08-Understanding-LSTMs/
8. Pascanu, R., Mikolov, T., Bengio, Y.: On the difficulty of training recurrent neural networks. In: Proceedings of the 30th International Conference on International Conference on Machine Learning - Volume 28, ICML 2013, pp. III-1310–III-1318, JMLR.org (2013). http://dl.acm.org/citation.cfm?id=3042817.3043083
9. Warden, P.: Speech commands: a dataset for limited-vocabulary speech recognition. CoRR abs/1804.03209 (2018). http://arxiv.org/abs/1804.03209
10. Zhang, Y., Suda, N., Lai, L., Chandra, V.: Hello edge: keyword spotting on microcontrollers. CoRR abs/1711.07128 (2017). http://arxiv.org/abs/1711.07128

Consonant-to-Vowel/Vowel-to-Consonant Transitions to Analyze the Speech of Cochlear Implant Users

T. Arias-Vergara[1,2,3]([✉]), J. R. Orozco-Arroyave[1,2], S. Gollwitzer[3], M. Schuster[3], and E. Nöth[2]

[1] Faculty of Engineering, Universidad de Antioquia UdeA, Calle 70 No. 52-21, Medellín, Colombia
[2] Pattern Recognition Lab, Friedrich-Alexander University, Erlangen-Nürnberg, Erlangen, Germany
[3] Department of Otorhinolaryngology, Head and Neck Surgery, Ludwig-Maximilians University, Munich, Germany
tomas.ariasvergara@lmu.de

Abstract. People with postlingual onset of deafness often present speech production problems even after hearing rehabilitation by cochlear implantation. In this paper, the speech of 20 postlingual (aged between 33 and 78 years old) and 20 healthy control (aged between 31 and 62 years old) German native speakers is analyzed considering acoustic features extracted from Consonant-to-Vowel (CV) and Vowel-to-Consonant (VC) transitions. The transitions are analyzed with reference to the manner of articulation of consonants according to 5 groups: nasals, sibilants, fricatives, voiced stops, and voiceless stops. Automatic classification between cochlear implant (CI) users and healthy speakers shows accuracies of up to 93%. Considering CV transitions, it is possible to detect specific features of altered speech of CI users. More features are to be evaluated in the future. A comprehensive evaluation of speech changes of CI users will help in the rehabilitation after deafening.

Keywords: Hearing loss · Acoustic analysis · Automatic classification · Cochlear implant

1 Introduction

Hearing loss can affect speech production in both adults and children. People suffering from severe to profound deafness may experience different speech disorders such as decreased intelligibility, changes in terms of articulation, increased or decreased nasality, slower speaking rate, and decreased variability in fundamental frequency (F0) [4,8,10]. Furthermore, speech disorders vary depending on the age of occurrence of deafness. When hearing loss occurs after speech acquisition (postlingual onset of deafness), speech impairments are caused by the lack

© Springer Nature Switzerland AG 2019
K. Ekštein (Ed.): TSD 2019, LNAI 11697, pp. 299–306, 2019.
https://doi.org/10.1007/978-3-030-27947-9_25

of sufficient and stable auditory feedback [9]. Currently, there are different treatments available for different types and degrees of hearing loss. Cochlear Implants (CI) are the most suitable devices for severe and profound deafness when hearing aids do not improve sufficiently speech perception. CI consists of an outer part, the speech processor, where acoustic information is transformed into electrical stimuli that are forwarded through the skin to the implanted part that goes into the cochlea. Due to the frequency distribution along the cochlear length, the electric stimuli can provide frequency information. However, CI users often present altered speech production and limited understanding even after hearing rehabilitation. If the deficits of speech would be known the rehabilitation might be adequately addressed. Previous studies have analyzed speech disorders in postlingual CI users. In [3], a study was presented to evaluate hypernasality considering speech recordings of 25 postlingual CI users and 25 age-matched Healthy Controls (HC). Nasometric measures were obtained using two sentences uttered by patients and controls. The authors reported higher nasalance scores in the CI users compared to the healthy speakers. In [18], a study was presented considering speech recordings of 40 postlingual CI users and 12 HC speakers. Acoustic analysis was performed computing the fundamental frequency ($F0$) from the sustained phonation of vowel /a/. The authors reported a reduction of $F0$ in the CI users compared to the control group. In [6], a study was presented to evaluate speech deterioration in 3 postlingually deafened adults. Additionally, speech recordings of 3 HC speakers were considered for comparison. The authors reported greater $F0$ variability in the CI users compared with the control group. Furthermore, the patients showed less differentiation of place of articulation in fricative and plosive consonants.

This paper investigates the use of Consonant-to-Vowel (CV) and Vowel-to-Consonant (VC) transitions to detect speech problems in postlingual deafened CI users. Furthermore, the consonants are labeled as nasals, sibilants, fricatives, voiced stops, and voiceless stops. The reason is that the articulatory settings necessary to produce certain speech sounds may be altered in the hearing impaired people. As described in [7], after cochlear implantation, the user may notice differences between the sounds perceived and the sounds produced. If this is the case, then the CI user will move the articulators in order to produce a speech sound similar to the sound perceived. Such changes may be captured with the transitions. Previous work has considered voiced-to-voiceless/voiceless-to-voiced transitions to evaluate altered articulatory motor control in neurological diseases such as Parkinson's disease [13]. In the present study, the transitions are extracted considering different phoneme groups in order to detect speech production problems in CI users. In the neural model of speech production (DIVA model) proposed in [2], speech movements are planned considering phoneme-specific and speaker-specific mappings, which are acquired and maintained with the use of auditory feedback. With ongoing hearing loss the speech sound map can slightly change, but moreover, the sensory-motor control is decreasing as one tends to use only as much force and effort for all movements as necessary. Therewith articulation looses its precision. The use of transitions in this study is also motivated by previous findings related to speech motor control. As proposed in [14], the production of speech sound sequences is based on acoustic goals. For example, for many consonants one goal is the abrupt acoustic transition to surrounding vowels associated with a diminution of sound level. According to [14], an internal model is used by the brain to control the necessary articulatory movements to achieve different acoustic goals. Such an internal model is acquired and maintained with the use of auditory feedback. Thus, speech disorders occur when there is no sufficient speech perception. For instance, note that voiceless-stop-to-vowel transitions might be correlated with the voice onset time, which is defined as the time between the release of the oral constriction for any plosive sound and the beginning of vocal fold vibrations [11] and has been considered in other studies to evaluate voicing contrast in CI users [7]. On the other hand, previous work suggests that fricative and sibilant production differs between CI users and HC speakers. Particularly for sibilants, these changes are produced because the spectral resolution of the CIs is lower in higher frequencies, thus, CI users shift the production of the sibilant sounds into the frequency range perceived by them [12]. We caution that it is not the aim of our study to find acoustic goals (as described in [14]), but to detect speech problems in CI users by extracting different acoustic features from the CV/VC transitions. We believe that such an approach will lead to the development of computational tools that will help to adapt hearing rehabilitation and speech therapy to the specific needs of CI users.

The rest of the paper is organized as follows: Sect. 2 includes details of the data and methods. Section 3 describes the experiments and results. Section 4 provides conclusions derived from this work.

2   Materials and Methods

Fig. 1 shows the methodology proposed in this work. First, forced alignment is performed over the speech recordings uttered by each speaker. Then, the phonemes are labeled as vowels, nasals, sibilants, fricatives, voiced stops, and voiceless stops. Then, the CV/VC transitions are extracted and assigned to their corresponding phoneme group. In the next step, acoustic features are extracted for each group of CV/VC transitions and then a Support Vector Machine (SVM) is considered to classify between CI users and healthy controls (HC). Each stage of the methodology is described in more detail in the following sections.

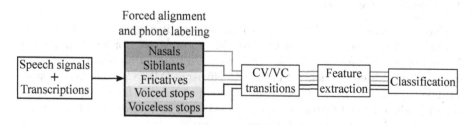

Fig. 1. Methodology implemented in this study.

2.1 Data

Standardized speech recordings of 20 postlingual deafened CI users (4 men) and 20 healthy controls (11 men) German native speakers were considered for the tests. The speech signals were captured in noise-controlled conditions at the Clinic of the Ludwig-Maximilians University in Munich, with a sampling frequency of 44.1 kHz and a 16 bit resolution. The speech signals were re-sampled to 16 kHz. All of the patients were asked to read 97 words [1], which contain every phoneme of the German language in different positions within the words. The age of the CI users ranges from 33 up to 78 years old (57.2 ± 12.2). The age of the healthy speakers ranges from 31 up to 62 years old (44.2 ± 9.3).

2.2 Segmentation

The speech of the CI users is evaluated considering acoustic features extracted from CV/VC transitions formed with different phoneme groups of the standard German consonant system (Table 1). In order to obtain the time stamps of the

Table 1. Phoneme groups considered in this study.

Group	IPA transcription
Nasals	/n/, /m/, /ŋ/
Sibilants	/s/, /ʃ/, /z/, /ʒ/
Fricatives	/f/, /v/, /j/, /ç/, /h/
Voiced stops	/b/, /d/, /g/
Voiceless stops	/p/, /t/, /k/

phonemes in the recordings, the BAS CLARIN web service is used [5]. This web service provides a forced alignment tool based on the Munich Automatic Segmentation system presented in [15]. The speech recordings are uploaded with their corresponding orthographic transcription to obtain the time stamps of the phonemes represented in SAMPA format. Then, the SAMPA segments are labeled according to Table 1. Additionally, short vowels, long vowels, and vowels that occur in unstressed position are labeled into one group. In the final step, the CV/VC transitions are extracted and grouped individually according to their phoneme label. Figure 2 summarizes this process.

2.3 Feature Extraction

A Hamming window of 25 ms with a time step of 10 ms are applied from the beginning of the consonant (for CV transitions) or vowel (for VC transitions). The set of acoustic features includes 9 Perceptual Linear Predictive (PLP) coefficients and 13 Mel-Frequency Cepstral Coefficients (MFCCs). The mean, standard deviation, skewness, and kurtosis are computed from the descriptors, forming an 88-dimensional feature vector per speaker. Thus, there are 5 feature vectors per transition, one for each phoneme group.

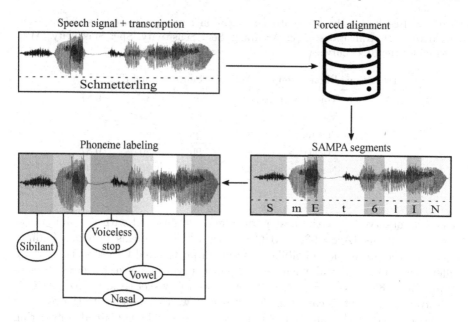

Fig. 2. Phoneme labeling procedure. In the figure, the German word "Schmetterling" contains two VC transitions (vowel-voiceless stop, vowel-nasal) and two CV transitions (voiceless stop-vowel, nasal-vowel)

2.4 Automatic Classification

The automatic classification of postlingual CI users and HC is performed with a radial basis SVM with margin parameter C and a Gaussian kernel with parameter γ. C and γ are optimized through a grid search with $10^{-4} < C < 10^4$ and $10^{-6} < \gamma < 10^3$. The selection criterion is based on the performance obtained in the training stage. The SVM is tested following a 10-fold cross validation strategy. The performance of the system is evaluated by means of the accuracy (Acc), which measures the proportion of speakers that were assigned to the correct group by the system, the sensitivity (Sen), which measures the proportion of speakers correctly assigned to the CI users group, and the specificity (Spe), which measures the proportion of speakers correctly assigned to the HC group. Additionally, the Area Under the ROC Curve (AUC) is considered. The values of the AUC range from 0.0 up to 1.0, were 1.0 means a perfect system. The AUC is interpreted as follows: AUC < 0.70 indicates poor performance, $0.70 \leq$ AUC < 0.80 is fair, $0.80 \leq$ AUC < 0.90 is good, and $0.90 \leq$ AUC < 1 is excellent [16].

3 Experiments and Results

Table 2 shows the obtained results for the classification of CI users and HC speakers when only features extracted from CV transitions are considered for training.

Table 2. Results for the automatic classification between CI users vs HC speakers, considering CV transitions. Acc: Accuracy. Sen: Sensitivity. Spe: Specificity. AUC: Area under the ROC curve.

Transition	Phone group	Acc (%)	Sen (%)	Spe (%)	AUC
CV	Voiceless stops	83	80	85	0.87
	Voiced stops	70	65	75	0.73
	Sibilants	93	95	90	0.94
	Fricatives	85	90	80	0.87
	Nasals	88	85	90	0.90

It can be observed that the best performance is obtained with the sibilant-to-vowel transitions (Acc = 93%, AUC = 0.94), which confirms previous findings regarding the production of sibilant sounds in postlingual CI users [12]. Also, a difference can be observed when comparing the performance of voiceless-stop-to-vowel (Acc = 83%, AUC = 0.87) and voiced-stop-to-vowel (Acc = 70%, AUC = 0.73) transitions. In this case, the highest results were obtained with the voiceless stops compared to the voiced stops. These results can be explained considering the study presented in [17]. The authors suggest that voiceless stop consonants require a more complex timing in coordinating the upper and laryngeal articulators than voiced stop consonants, which may be produced by simultaneous action of these articulators. Additionally, good results were also achieved for nasal-to-vowel (Acc = 88%, AUC = 0.90) and fricative-to-vowel (Acc = 85%, AUC = 0.87) transitions. Table 3 shows the obtained results for the classification of CI users and HC speakers when only features extracted from VC transitions are considered for training. In general, it can be observed that the classification results are lower than those presented in Table 2. For VC transitions, the highest results were obtained with fricative-to-vowel (Acc = 80%, AUC = 0.84) and sibilant-to-vowel (Acc = 78%, AUC = 0.85) transitions. Fair results were also obtained with voiced-stop-to-vowel transitions, however, from the sensitivity measure we can observe that the system is not able to identify postlingually deafened CI users properly (Sen = 60%).

Table 3. Results for the automatic classification between CI users vs HC speakers, considering VC transitions. Acc: Accuracy. Sen: Sensitivity. Spe: Specificity. AUC: Area under the ROC curve.

Transition	Phone group	Acc (%)	Sen (%)	Spe (%)	AUC
VC	Voiceless stops	68	70	65	0.74
	Voiced stops	75	60	90	0.71
	Sibilants	78	85	70	0.85
	Fricatives	80	80	80	0.84
	Nasals	63	65	60	0.63

4 Conclusions

In this paper we presented a study to investigate the use of acoustic features extracted from CV/VC transitions to detect speech problems in postlingually deafened CI users. In order to do this, the transitions were grouped individually according to the manner of articulation of the consonants, i.e, voiceless stops, voiced stops, sibilants, fricatives, and nasals. According to the results, CV transitions prove to be more suitable than the VC transitions to detect changes in the speech of the patients in comparison to a group of HC speakers. Furthermore, the obtained results were similar to previous findings which are related to consonant production problems in CI users. The highest classification accuracy was obtained with features extracted from sibilant-to-vowel transitions (Acc = 93%), which indicates that there are differences between the production by CI users and HC controls. Additionally, good classification results were obtained with features from fricative-to-vowel (Acc = 85%), nasal-to-vowel (Acc = 88%), and voiceless-stop-to-vowel transitions (Acc = 93%). These results motivate us to implement this approach for the longitudinal monitoring of CI users. We are aware of a mismatch regarding the age and sex in CI and HC. Currently, we are collecting more HC. However, we don't expect the outcome of the experiments to change, i.e., that CV are better than VC and that sibilant-to-vowel transitions provide the best discrimination. The long term goal of this study is to provide to the expert clinicians with additional information that could be used to help the patients with their speech therapy. Future work will include more speech tasks such as text reading, rapid repetition of syllables, and sentence reading.

Acknowledgments. The authors acknowledge to the Training Network on Automatic Processing of PAthological Speech (TAPAS) funded by the Horizon 2020 programme of the European Commission. Tomás Arias-Vergara is under grants of Convocatoria Doctorado Nacional-785 financed by COLCIENCIAS.

References

1. Fox-Boyer, A.: PLAKSS: Psycholinguistische Analyse kindlicher Sprechstörungen. Swets Test Services (2002)
2. Guenther, F.H., Perkell, J.S.: A neural model of speech production and its application to studies of the role of auditory feedback in speech. In: Maassen, B., Kent, R., Peters, H., van Lieshout, P., Hulstijn, W. (eds.) Speech Motor Control Normal and Disordered Speech, chap. 2, pp. 29–49. Oxford University Press, Oxford (2004)
3. Hassan, S.M., Malki, K.H., Mesallam, T.A., Farahat, M., Bukhari, M., Murry, T.: The effect of cochlear implantation on nasalance of speech in postlingually hearing-impaired adults. J. Voice **26**(5), 669.e17–669.e22 (2012)
4. Hudgins, C.V., Numbers, F.C.: An investigation of the intelligibility of the speech of the deaf. Genet. Psychol. Monogr. **25**, 289–392 (1942)
5. Kisler, T., Reichel, U., Schiel, F.: Multilingual processing of speech via web services. Comput. Speech Lang. **45**, 326–347 (2017)
6. Lane, H., Webster, J.W.: Speech deterioration in postlingually deafened adults. J. Acoust. Soc. Am. **89**(2), 859–866 (1991)

7. Lane, H., Wozniak, J., Matthies, M., Svirsky, M., Perkell, J.: Phonemic resetting versus postural adjustments in the speech of cochlear implant users: an exploration of voice-onset time. J. Acoust. Soc. Am. **98**(6), 3096–3106 (1995)

8. Langereis, M., Dejonckere, P., Van Olphen, A., Smoorenburg, G.: Effect of cochlear implantation on nasality in post-lingually deafened adults. Folia phoniatrica et logopaedica **49**(6), 308–314 (1997)

9. Leder, S.B., Spitzer, J.B.: A perceptual evaluation of the speech of adventitiously deaf adult males. Ear Hear. **11**(3), 169–175 (1990)

10. Leder, S.B., Spitzer, J.B., Kirchner, J.C.: Speaking fundamental frequency of postlingually profoundly deaf adult men. Ann. Otol. Rhinol. Laryngol. **96**(3), 322–324 (1987)

11. Liberman, A., et al.: Some cues for the distinction between voiced and voiceless stops in initial position. Lang. Speech **1**(3), 153–167 (1958)

12. Neumeyer, V., Schiel, F., Hoole, P.: Speech of cochlear implant patients: an acoustic analysis of sibilant production. In: ICPhS (2015)

13. Orozco-Arroyave, J.: Analysis of Speech of People with Parkinson's Disease. Logos-Verlag, Berlin (2016)

14. Perkell, J.S., et al.: A theory of speech motor control and supporting data from speakers with normal hearing and with profound hearing loss. J. Phon. **28**(3), 233–272 (2000)

15. Schiel, F.: Automatic phonetic transcription of non-prompted speech. In: Proceedings of ICPhS, pp. 607–610 (1999)

16. Swets, J.A., et al.: Psychological science can improve diagnostic decisions. Psychol. Sci. Public Interest **1**(1), 1–26 (2000)

17. Tobey, E.A., Pancamo, S., Staller, S.J., Brimacombe, J.A., Beiter, A.L.: Consonant production in children receiving a multichannel cochlear implant. Ear Hear. **12**(1), 23–31 (1991)

18. Ubrig, M.T., et al.: Voice analysis of postlingually deaf adults pre- and postcochlear implantation. J. Voice **25**(6), 692–699 (2011)

Czech Speech Synthesis with Generative Neural Vocoder

Jakub Vít[(⊠)], Zdeněk Hanzlíček, and Jindřich Matoušek

NTIS - New Technology for the Information Society, Faculty of Applied Sciences,
University of West Bohemia, Univerzitní 22, 306 14 Plzeň, Czech Republic
{jvit,zhanzlic,jmatouse}@ntis.zcu.cz
http://www.ntis.zcu.cz/en

Abstract. In recent years, new neural architectures for generating high-quality synthetic speech on a per-sample basis were introduced. We describe our application of statistical parametric speech synthesis based on LSTM neural networks combined with a generative neural vocoder for the Czech language. We used a traditional LSTM architecture for generating vocoder parametrization from linguistic features. We replaced a standard vocoder with a WaveRNN neural network. We conducted a MUSHRA listening test to compare the proposed approach with the unit selection and LSTM-based parametric speech synthesis utilizing a standard vocoder. In contrast with our previous work, we managed to outperform a well-tuned unit selection TTS system by a great margin on both professional and amateur voices.

Keywords: Speech synthesis · LSTM-based speech synthesis ·
WaveRNN · Neural vocoder · Unit selection

1 Introduction

Recently, traditional source-filter model based vocoders in statistical parametric speech synthesis have been replaced with new autoregressive neural network models. These data-driven models are able to recover much more original waveform quality than a traditional vocoder can.

For a long time, parametric speech synthesis offered many great features, like speech stability, modifiability, and low data requirements. However, it suffered from buzziness and over-smoothness. This was the main reason why a concatenative unit selection algorithm [3] with all its problems (possible sudden quality drops at unit boundaries) was still being preferred in real-word text-to-speech (TTS) applications, especially for Indo-European languages. With WaveNet [12] and other similar models, this has changed in favor of parametric speech synthesis.

In this paper, we describe our TTS framework for the Czech language based on long short-term memory (LSTM) based parametric speech synthesis with a neural WaveRNN vocoder. The vocoding part was the main bottleneck of parametric methods since it introduced speech quality degradation. By replacing the

© Springer Nature Switzerland AG 2019
K. Ekštein (Ed.): TSD 2019, LNAI 11697, pp. 307–315, 2019.
https://doi.org/10.1007/978-3-030-27947-9_26

vocoder with a WaveRNN neural network, the gap between generated and natural speech is reduced greatly. Since the WaveRNN is trained only as a vocoder (converting acoustic representation to speech samples) and not as a full TTS (in which linguistic-to-acoustic mapping must be also trained), its job is much easier and straightforward. Converting linguistic features to acoustic features is still left for LSTM neural network which can handle this part well.

LSTM parametric speech synthesis is very easy to train. It is also not sensitive to annotation and segmentation errors like the unit selection. It requires fewer data and there are many ways of controlling speech properties like tempo, phrasing, and intonation. These properties make this method ideal for cases where amateur voices are used. In such cases, the consistency of the data is reduced which degrades to a large extent the quality of concatenative methods [5]. Since LSTM training is not sensitive to this problem and the neural vocoder is trained only on acoustic data, our approach is able to train well even for these scenarios.

2   Related Work

In our previous work [1], we used WaveNet architecture working in a full TTS mode (conditioned on linguistic features, without the use of any other neural networks) to generate speech from linguistic features. However, according to a listening test, we were not able to outperform our baseline system (a well-tuned unit selection [14]) on our voice corpora. In this paper, we used WaveNet/WaveRNN architecture working only as a neural vocoder leaving the speech modeling part to traditional LSTM statistical parametric speech synthesis.

In the original paper [12], WaveNet was used in a full TTS mode, i.e., it was conditioned on linguistic features. The ability to work as a vocoder was also mentioned. The same setup was used in WaveRNN [6]. In paper [13], the authors described the WaveNet architecture working as a speaker-dependent vocoder. They compared this method to other traditional well-established vocoders. Similarly, we use a generative network for the same task, also as a speaker-dependent vocoder. In [8], the authors present a WaveRNN-inspired universal neural vocoder which is speaker-independent.

2.1   End-to-End Models

Many fully end-to-end approaches exist today. They are based on a sophisticated neural network architectures that learn text-to-waveform mapping completely unsupervised. Among other things, they do not require training data to be segmented to phone (or some other phonetic units) and can deal with grapheme-to-phoneme transcription internally. End-to-end systems are a great choice for new languages or for a quick expansion of voice portfolio.

But in situations, where well-annotated data, phonetic rules and/or pronunciation dictionaries, and complete TTS pipeline is present, standard parametric speech synthesis can offer few advantages like a better control and adjustment of the synthesized speech. In a traditional pipeline, duration and F0 contour can be analyzed and modified easily just by changing the outputs of a duration/F0 model.

3   TTS Implementation

Our implementation of a TTS system is a modification of a standard LSTM parametric speech synthesis architecture (e.g. [15]). It consists of two parts: a model for the mapping of input linguistic information to acoustic parameters (F0, voicing, and spectral envelope) and a *vocoder* for the conversion of the acoustic parameters into a speech waveform signal.

The linguistic-to-acoustic mapping is realized with the use of multi-layer bi-directional LSTM neural networks. For the generation of resulting speech, a traditional rule-based vocoder (e.g. WORD [11] or STRAIGHT [7]) was replaced by a trainable WaveRNN [6] neural network. Alternatively, WaveNet [12] could also be used as a trainable neural vocoder as it achieves the same quality of generated speech as WaveRNN [6].

3.1   Linguistic Features

The statistical parametric speech synthesis uses linguistic features as input. These features are extracted from input text representation. We used commonly used features such as phone identity, word position, phrase position, and phone position (for frame-aligned versions).

3.2   Speech Synthesis Architecture

The scheme of our speech synthesis system with the WaveRNN-based vocoder is shown in Fig. 1. The individual components will be described further in the next subsections.

3.3   Parametric Speech Synthesis

Duration Model. In order to build frame-aligned linguistic features, duration of each phone has to be predicted. This is done by a two-layer bi-directional LSTM network. For each phone, the network infers duration, which is then rounded to the nearest multiple of 5 ms and converted to a number of frames. At this stage, the duration of each phone (i.e. the tempo of the generated speech) can be adjusted by changing the number of frames for each phone.

F0 Model. The second model is the F0 model. It predicts F0 contour (i.e. the course of intonation throughout each phrase). Its inputs are linguistics features aligned into 5 ms frames. In fact, the F0 model could be part of the acoustic model; however, we keep this model separate because it allows us to modify F0

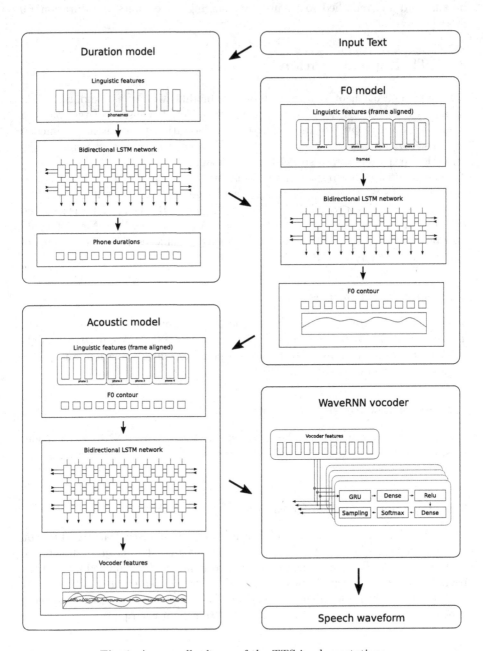

Fig. 1. An overall scheme of the TTS implementation.

contour externally which is useful for intonation and voice-style modifications. Since the outputs are normalized for the neural network training (zero mean and unit variance), it is possible to reuse the F0 model from a different speaker (e.g., in the case when speech is generated from data of an amateur speaker with poor prosody characteristics or of a speech-impaired person).

Acoustic Model. The acoustic model generates acoustic features (40 MFC coefficients, aperiodicity and voicing) suitable for the use in a vocoder from linguistic features and from the generated F0 contour. We use a three-layer bi-directional LSTM neural network for this task. Multi-speaker training is used, meaning that global conditioning in the form of a speaker embedding vector is added to the input of the network. The model is then trained on data from all speakers jointly.

3.4 Neural Generative Vocoder

The neural vocoder's role is to convert frame-aligned acoustic features into a speech waveform. We employed WaveRNN architecture [6] for this task. Unlike WaveNet, it uses recurrent gated recurrent unit (GRU) network to manage its state instead of a stack of convolutional layers from previous samples. It achieves the same quality as a WaveNet structure, but it is easier to implement and has a faster generation [6]. Our network contains 1024 GRU units and is conditioned with vocoder features for each 5ms frame and speaker identity as a global condition.

4 Experiments and Results

4.1 Experimental Speech Data

For our experiments, we utilized the following speech data

- 2 large speech corpora recorded by professional voice talents (male Mp and female Fp) for the purposes of unit selection speech synthesis [10];
- 2 smaller speech corpora recorded by amateur speakers (male Ma and female Fa) recorded for various experiments with speech synthesis [5].

Speech data is supplemented by a phonetic segmentation created by an HMM-based segmentation procedure with various correction procedures [9]. Since the professional voices are utilized for many years in a TTS system [14] and lots of additional manual corrections have been made over time, their phonetic representation and segmentation can be considered as near to perfect (Table 1).

Table 1. Description of experimental speech data. The total speech duration [hh:mm:ss] is without utterance leading and trailing pauses.

Speaker	Duration	#Utterances	#Words	#Pauses	#Phones
Mp	14:43:50	12,129	156,607	13,684	624,592
Fp	15:22:20	12,050	145,509	3,568	621,397
Ma	1:54:17	1,962	18,063	1,039	73,277
Fa	1:29:22	1,801	16,445	841	67,019

4.2 Listening Test

To evaluate and compare speech synthesis systems under consideration, we conducted a MUltiple Stimuli with Hidden Reference and Anchor (MUSHRA) listening test [4]. Three speech synthesis systems were compared:

- unit selection based TTS system [14]
- LSTM based system with the conventional WORLD vocoder [11]
- LSTM based system with the WaveRNN vocoder

The test contained 10 sets of utterances for each speaker. Each set included 4 utterances for evaluation: natural speech (which serves as an upper anchor) and 3 utterances synthesized by the compared systems. The overall quality of particular utterances was rated on a scale between 0 (very poor) and 100 (like natural). The lower quality anchor was not used since its definition is not clear when rating synthetic speech [2].

18 listeners participated in the test, 8 of them had background in speech synthesis. They all evaluated the same utterances. The overall results of the listening test are presented in Table 2 and Fig. 2. The system combining LSTM and WaveRNN as a neural vocoder was rated as the best, unit selection synthesizer was placed second and the combination of LSTM and the conventional WORLD vocoder took the last place.

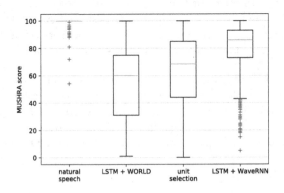

Fig. 2. MUSHRA listening test: the overall results.

4.3   Results and Discussion

A detailed analysis for particular voices in Table 2 and Fig. 3 shows that results for both LSTM-based systems are consistent for all speakers, whereas the performance of the unit selection system is noticeably worse for amateur voices. This is not surprising since amateur voices have considerably smaller training data which is (besides the speech quality and inconsistency) an important factor for the unit selection method. For these voices, the unit selection system was evaluated similarly as the LSTM-based system with the conventional WORLD vocoder.

Table 2. Results of the MUSHRA listening test.

Speaker	LSTM + WORLD		Unit selection		LSTM + WaveRNN	
	mean ± std	median	mean ± std	median	mean ± std	median
Mp	59.8 ± 25.2	67	67.1 ± 24.8	75	85.1 ± 15.0	90
Fp	51.2 ± 25.1	56	74.7 ± 20.2	80	81.7 ± 18.4	88
Ma	52.1 ± 25.8	58	58.9 ± 27.3	64	76.9 ± 18.5	82
Fa	48.5 ± 25.0	50	48.9 ± 27.1	50	75.7 ± 20.6	81
all	52.9 ± 25.6	60	62.4 ± 26.8	68	79.8 ± 18.6	86

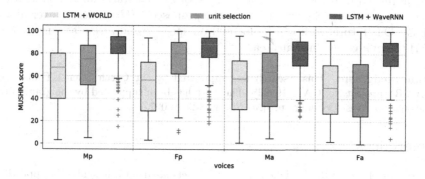

Fig. 3. MUSHRA listening test: results for particular speakers.

Considerable variability in evaluation by individual listeners is evident in Fig. 4. As a consequence of the missing lower quality anchor in the MUSHRA test, particular listeners used various parts of the evaluation scale. The large variability among listeners explains also the large variance and number of outliers in Figs. 2 and 3.

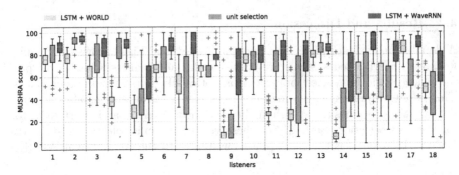

Fig. 4. MUSHRA listening test: evaluation of particular listeners.

5 Conclusion

This paper has presented a Czech parametric speech synthesis system with a neural vocoder. In our experiments, we compared the proposed system with two other speech synthesis methods: unit selection (which can be considered a quality benchmark) and parametric speech synthesis with a conventional vocoder. It was shown that the proposed system outperformed the unit selection method which is in line with the conclusions of other studies [12]. More concretely, the proposed system proved to be better on both large professional voices and small amateur voices. Hence, these conclusions make the proposed method more universal and robust. Our future work will be focused on speed optimization as currently no efforts were invested in that area.

Acknowledgment. This research was supported by the Czech Science Foundation (GA CR), project No. GA19-19324S. The work has been supported by the grant of the University of West Bohemia, project No. SGS-2019-027.

References

1. Hanzlíček, Z., Vít, J., Tihelka, D.: Wavenet-based speech synthesis applied to Czech. In: Sojka, P., Horák, A., Kopeček, I., Pala, K. (eds.) TSD 2018. LNCS (LNAI), vol. 11107, pp. 445–452. Springer, Cham (2018). https://doi.org/10.1007/978-3-030-00794-2_48
2. Henter, G.E., Merritt, T., Shannon, M., Mayo, C., King, S.: Measuring the perceptual effects of modelling assumptions in speech synthesis using stimuli constructed from repeated natural speech. In: Proceedings of Interspeech, pp. 1504–1508 (2014)
3. Hunt, A.J., Black, A.W.: Unit selection in a concatenative speech synthesis system using a large speech database. In: Proceedings of ICASSP 1996, pp. 373–376 (1996)
4. International Telecommunications Union: Method for the subjective assessment of intermediate quality level of coding systems. ITU Recommendation ITU-R BS.1534-2 (2014)
5. Jůzová, M., Tihelka, D., Matoušek, J., Hanzlíček, Z.: Voice conservation and TTS system for people facing total laryngectomy. In: Proceedings Interspeech 2017, pp. 3425–3426 (2017)

6. Kalchbrenner, N., et al.: Efficient neural audio synthesis. Proc. Mach. Learn. Res. **80**, 2410–2419 (2018)
7. Kawahara, H., Morise, M., Toda, T., Banno, H., Nisimura, R., Irino, T.: Excitation source analysis for high-quality speech manipulation systems based on an interference-free representation of group delay with minimum phase response compensation. In: Proceedings of Interspeech, pp. 2243–2247 (2014)
8. Lorenzo-Trueba, J., Drugman, T., Latorre, J., Merritt, T., Putrycz, B., Barra-Chicote, R.: Robust universal neural vocoding. CoRR abs/1811.06292, submitted to ICASSP 2019 (2018)
9. Matoušek, J., Tihelka, D., Psutka, J.: Automatic segmentation for Czech concatenative speech synthesis using statistical approach with boundary-specific correction. In: Proceedings of Eurospeech, pp. 301–304 (2003)
10. Matoušek, J., Tihelka, D., Romportl, J.: Building of a speech corpus optimised for unit selection TTS synthesis. In: Proceedings of LREC (2008)
11. Morise, M.: D4C, a band-aperiodicity estimator for high-quality speech synthesis. Speech Commun. **84**, 57–65 (2016)
12. van den Oord, A., et al.: WaveNet: a generative model for raw audio. CoRR abs/1609.03499 (2016). http://arxiv.org/abs/1609.03499
13. Tamamori, A., Hayashi, T., Kobayashi, K., Takeda, K., Toda, T.: Speaker-dependent WaveNet vocoder. In: Proceedings of Interspeech, pp. 1118–1122 (2017)
14. Tihelka, D., Hanzlíček, Z., Jůzová, M., Vít, J., Matoušek, J., Grůber, M.: Current state of text-to-speech system ARTIC: a decade of research on the field of speech technologies. In: Sojka, P., Horák, A., Kopeček, I., Pala, K. (eds.) TSD 2018. LNCS (LNAI), vol. 11107, pp. 369–378. Springer, Cham (2018). https://doi.org/10.1007/978-3-030-00794-2_40
15. Zen, H.: Acoustic modeling in statistical parametric speech synthesis - from HMM to LSTM-RNN. In: Proceedings of MLSLP (2015)

Linguistic Resources Construction: Towards Disfluency Processing in Spontaneous Tunisian Dialect Speech

Emna Boughariou[1]($\boxtimes$), Younès Bahou[2], and Lamia Hadrich Bleguith[1]

[1] Faculty of Economics and Management of Sfax, University of Sfax, Sfax, Tunisia
emnaboughariou@gmail.com, lamia.belguith@gmail.com
[2] Hail University, Hail, Kingdom of Saudi Arabia
bahou.younes@gmail.com

Abstract. The Tunisian Dialect (TD) is an under-resourced language which lacks both corpora and Natural Language Processing (NLP) tools despite being increasingly used in spoken and written forms. In this paper, we presented our endeavour to build linguistic resources for TD in order to process disfluencies. First, we created the Disfluencies Corpus from Tunisian Arabic Transcriptions (DisCoTAT), which is a set of manual transcriptions with several disfluency phenomena. Also, we constructed the Tunisian Dialect Wordnet (TD-WordNet) from existing TD lexicons to annotate words with morpho-syntactic tags. Then, we developed the Disfluency Annotation Tool (DisAnT) in order to annotate DisCoTAT. DisAnT provides two levels of annotation: morpho-syntactic tagging and disfluency annotation.

Keywords: Tunisian Dialect · Linguistic resources · Corpus · Annotation tool · Disfluency processing

1 Introduction

A characteristic of spontaneous speech, that makes it different from a written text, is the presence of disfluencies. Disfluencies are frequent in all forms of spontaneous speech, whether casual discussions or formal arguments [23]. They present significant challenges for some NLP tasks on spoken transcripts, such as parsing and machine translation. Indeed, the automatic processing of dialectal Arabic has taken off in recent years. On its side, TD has sparked increased interest in the NLP community. Increasing efforts are being made to catch up the lack of linguistic resources and tools developed, particularly those dealing with dialect identification, speech recognition and comprehension and morpho-syntactic tagging, among others. This work is part of the disfluency processing task in spontaneous spoken TD. We described in details the DisCoTAT corpus, the TD-WordNet and the DisAnT tool, which are designed in order to process disfluencies.

© Springer Nature Switzerland AG 2019
K. Ekštein (Ed.): TSD 2019, LNAI 11697, pp. 316–328, 2019.
https://doi.org/10.1007/978-3-030-27947-9_27

The remainder of this paper is organized as follows: Sect. 2 provided an overview of disfluency types. Section 3, introduces the background of some existing linguistic resources and tools that deal with the spontaneous spoken TD. Our linguistic resources and tools created for disfluency processing dealing with TD are detailed in Sect. 4, before drawing our major conclusions in Sect. 5.

2 Disfluency Overview

Detecting disfluencies in spontaneous speech has been widely studied by researchers in different communities including NLP, speech processing and psycholinguistics. Disfluencies are additional noises that are corrected by the speaker during the utterance. Although disfluent words present only an average of 10% of the utterance, they make it much harder for speech processing systems to predict the correct structure of the utterance [21].

According to Shriberg, [22], speech disfluencies can be divided into three intervals, the reparandum, the editing term and the repair. The reparandum is the disfluent portion of the utterance that is corrected or abandoned. The editing term (also called interregnum) is the optional portion of the utterance; it could include speech words (i.e., specific words to spontaneous speech). The repair is the portion of the utterance that corrects the reparandum, and is in some cases optional.

For the following example: "ماشي بعد غدوة اه لا نقصد ماشي غدوة غدوة" [mA$y bEd gdwp Ah lA nqSd mA$y gdwp gdwp] (I will go after tomorrow to Tunis ah no I mean I will go tomorrow tomorrow)"[1], "ماشي بعد غدوة" [mA$y bEd gdwp] (I will go after tomorrow) is the reparandum, "اه لا نقصد" [Ah lA nqSd] (ah no I mean) is the interregnum and "ماشي غدوة غدوة" [mA$y gdwp gdwp] (I will go tomorrow tomorrow) is the repair.

Among all types of disfluencies, we are interested in the following phenomena:

- Syllabic elongations: are abnormal vowel lengthening of a syllable lasting more than 1 second. The elongations appear essentially at the final position of the word.
- Speech words: are words used only in spontaneous speech. They include filler words (e.g., 'uh', 'um') and discourse markers (e.g., 'I mean', 'you know').
- Word-fragments: are words started and interrupted by the same speaker. These truncated words may be dropped, taken up or replaced.
- Repetitions: are syntagms of one or more words that are repeated by the same speaker in exactly the same form. It happens that a repetition is not the exact form of the initial term but one of its derivatives. Repetitions do not serve grammatical or emphatic purposes.
- Self-corrections: are the corrections made by the speaker himself in order to correct his utterance. They include the correction of syllables, words, groups of words, or even the entire utterance. There are three cases of self-corrections: these can be either insertions (the speaker adds tokens without changing the

---

[1] We used the Buckwalter transliteration.

syntactic structure), or substitutions (the speaker modifies some tokens without changing the syntactic structure) or also deletions (the speaker abandons some tokens and starts a new syntactic structure).

According to its complexity in the running time, we adopt the following taxonomy for disfluencies [5]:

- Simple Disfluencies (SD): these affect only one minimal token [9]. They include syllabic elongations, speech words, word-fragments and simple repetitions (i.e., the successive repetition of one token).
- Complex Disfluencies (CD): they follow the reparandum-interregnum-repair pattern and include complex repetitions (i.e., the repetition of more than one token) and self-corrections.

A quick glance at the art-of-state studies reveals a huge body of the literature that deals with disfluencies in dotted languages like English, compared to a relative scarcity of studies for the standard or dialectal Arabic language like in [1,15,19]. This scarcity can be due to the fact that they were conceived for a restricted domain (e.g. railway information) where the lexicons are relatively small and there are no annotation tools and guidelines to annotate the disfluencies.

3   Tunisian Dialect Linguistic Resources and Tools for Speech Processing

In this section, we provide a critical description of some of the linguistic resources for TD that deal with speech processing.

3.1   Lexicons and Dictionaries

The MSA-DT bilingual lexicon [7] contains around 2.550 words of Modern Standard Arabic (MSA) and their translations into TD. The construction of this lexicon is based on a manual translation of MSA to TD using the Penn Arabic Treebank [16] and conversion rules based on differences between MSA and TD.

The Railway Information Ontology (RIO) [14] is created to semantically label TD utterances for the railway domain from the TUDICOI corpus [10]. The authors used a hybrid method for extracting concepts using a statistical method, and for the identification of semantic relations using a linguistic method. RIO consists of 14 concepts, 387 concept instances and 25 semantic relations.

The Tunisian Dialect WordNet (TunDiaWN) [4] is made up of around 32.848 words from the Multi-source Tunisian Dialect corpus issued from social networks (Twitter, Facebook, etc.), dictionaries, recorded dialogs, etc. The authors applied a clustering method (i.e., using a k-mode algorithm) that aims to group the extracted TD words into meaningful clusters.

The aebWordNet wordnet [18] covers 18.209 synsets for TD words. It was modelled from the bilingual dictionary Peace Corps Dictionary (5.133 words), and was enriched by a derivational lexicon based on 1.507 roots.

In addition, several bilingual dictionaries were constructed for TD such as the Tunisian-French dictionary Karmous[2] (3.800 words, proverbs and expressions), the Tunisian-French online dictionary[3] (4.000 words), the Peace Corps Dictionary[4] (5.133 words), the language survival kits[5], etc.

3.2   Corpora

The TUnisian DIalect COrpus Interlocutor (TUDICOI) [10] consists of 52 hours of audio recording, and is made up of 1.825 dialogs of 1.831 users asking for railway information services. TUDICOI is transcribed according to the OTTA orthographic convention [26].

The Tunisian Arabic Railway Interaction Corpus, abbreviated TARIC [17], consists of 20 hours of transcribed speech using the Transcriber tool in accordance with the transcription convention CODA-TUN [24]. It contains 4.662 dialogs with 18.657 utterances and 71.684 words.

In another study, Boujelbane et al. in [6] transcribed 5 hours and 20 min of recordings coming mainly from a Tunisian TV channel (TV News program, political debate broadcasts). The transcription is made using the Transcriber tool. This corpus consists of 37.964 words while the TD words represent approximately only 32.1% of this corpus.

The Spoken Tunisian Arabic Corpus, abbreviated STAC [27], is made up of 4 hours and 50 min of audio recordings (42.388 words) collected from different TV channels and radio stations. This corpus is transcribed and annotated according to the OTTA [26] and the CODA-TUN [24] conventions. STAC includes morphosyntactic tagging and disfluency annotations.

To observe the multiplicity of the future used in speech, Ben Ahmed et al. in [2] built a Tunisian Arabic corpus of Tunisian speakers living in Orléans in face-to-face interview conditions. It consists of 17 h divided into 37 recordings transcribed using the Latin alphabet. This corpus includes annotation of future appearances.

3.3   Automatic Transcription Tools

Ben Ltaief et al. in [3] built an automatic speech recognition system for TD using Kaldi Recognition toolkit [20]. Several acoustic models have been trained using HMM-GMM and HMM-DNN system. The language model was built using a 3-gram model and the TARIC corpus [17]. The best results were achieved by DNN models, with an overall WER of 25% for the training set 36.8% for the testing set.

Happy Scribe[6] is a transcription-as-a-service platform for the research and media communities founded in 2017. It can transcribe from speech to text almost

---

[2] https://www.fichier-pdf.fr/2010/08/31/m14401m/dico-karmous.pdf.
[3] http://www.arabetunisien.com/.
[4] https://files.eric.ed.gov/fulltext/ED183017.pdf.
[5] https://fieldsupport.dliflc.edu/productList.aspx?v=lsk.
[6] https://www.happyscribe.co/.

all types of audio and video formats, for more than 119 languages including TD. Happy Scribe uses state-of-the-art machine-learning models to transcribe audio files uploaded by users automatically.

3.4 Orthographic Analysis Tools

Zribi et al. in [26] have proposed a convention of Orthographic Transcription of Tunisian Arabic (OTTA). They used the spelling rules of MSA to define new rules that would allow the transcription of the words in TD based on their phonology. OTTA includes 27 conventions for the words' annotation and for the annotation of typographic phenomena (e.g., numbers, abbreviations, etc.), noise and non-linguistic events, laughter and disfluencies.

Another convention was developed by [24] adapting the CODA map (Conventional Orthography for Dialectal Arabic) [11] to TD. The authors proposed a set of guidelines for writing TD words. CODA-TUN follows the same spelling rules as MSA with some phonological, phonolexical, morphological, and lexical exceptions and extensions. Later, Boujelbane et al. in [8] developed COTA (Conventionalized Orthography for Tunisian Arabic), an automatic normalization system of TD. This system is based on a hybrid approach combining methods based on CODA-TUN rules and statistical methods.

For detecting the sentence boundary of transcriptions, Zrini et al. in [25] proposed three different methods. The first uses contextual rules based on punctuation, lexical elements and simple prosodic features. The second is based on the PART classifier, which classifies words into four classes according to their position in the utterance. The third mixes the results of the linguistic and statistical methods.

3.5 Morpho-Syntactic Analysis Taggers

Zribi et al. in [28] built TAMDAS, the Tunisian Arabic Morphological DisAmbiguation System. TAMDAS uses the output of a TD morphological analyzer Al-Khalil-TUN [26] to morphologically disambiguate annotated transcriptions. The system tests three different classifiers and combines their results with a bigram module in failure cases.

Hamdi et al. in [13] proposed a morpho-syntactic analyzer for TD. They convert TD sentences into an MSA lattice by analyzing them morphologically using MAGEAD-DT [12] to generate further analysis for each word by exploiting its proximity to MSA. The labeling process is based on HMM models.

Boujelbane et al. in [6] retrained the POS tagger Stanford. They used the translated corpus from MSA to TD, which is generated from an automatic translation of ATB. Nouns, verbs and tool words issued from TD were translated into MSA and then they were labelled with POS tags using the POS tagger Stanford.

4   Proposed Language Resources for Disfluency Processing in TD

In this section, we described our own method to create linguistic resources of TD, with the aim of disfluency processing.

4.1   Disfluencies Corpus from Tunisian Arabic Transcriptions (DisCoTAT)

The corpora presented in Sect. 3.2 are inadequate for disfluency processing. The main weakness of TARIC [17] and TUDICOI [10] lies in their restricted domain (i.e., railway interaction). They provide a limited portion of the TD vocabulary. Nevertheless, STAC [27] is the only corpus for TD that includes disfluency annotation; however, it covers only three types of disfluencies annotation (word-fragments, filled pauses and simple repetitions). Hereby, we sought to build DisCoTAT, which would be used as our study corpus for disfluency processing.

The building process consists of two basic steps. The first one is to provide transcribed data in order to be annotated later. The second step consists in its annotation using the annotation tool DisAnT (see Sect. 4.3).

4.1.1   Data Collection

We have collected raw transcriptions from three existing corpora: STAC [27], TARIC [17] and TUDICOI [10] (see Sect. 3.2). Table 1 summarizes the characteristics of the collected corpora.

Table 1. Characteristics of collected corpora

	STAC	TARIC	TUDICOI
Recorded hours	4 h and 50 min	20 h	52 h
Utterances	7.788	18.657	12.182
Words	42.388	71.684	21.682
Domain	TV channels and radio stations	Tunisian railway information	Tunisian railway information
Transcription conventions	OTTA and CODA-TUN	OTTA	CODA-TUN

STAC includes 97.20% of TD words, while the MSA words and the foreign words (i.e., French and English words) represent respectively 0.37% and 2.43%. TARIC and TUDICOI include, respectively, about 20% and 11.81% of foreign words, specifically French. The disfluency rate in STAC, TARIC and TUDICOI represents, respectively, 27,42%, 21.13% and 21.41%. This means that more than 20% of 38.657 utterances contain at least one phenomenon among the disfluency types presented in Sect. 2. DisCoTAT disfluency rates can be specified as: 56%

for repetitions, 33% for word-fragments, 5% for syllabic elongations, 4% for self-corrections and 2% for speech words.

Similar to STAC, we have been transcribing two hours of recordings collected from different TV channels and radio stations to enrich the DisCoTAT corpus with more occurrences of disfluency phenomena. Since there is no speech transcription system available for TD, the transcription was achieved manually according to the OTTA and CODA-TUN conventions [27]. It is worth noting that we transcribed 20 min of recordings through the automatic transcription system Happy Scribe presented in Sect. 3.3. Unfortunately, the word error rate (WER) was about less than 30%.

The DisCo'TAT vocabulary includes MSA words, TD words and foreign words (especially French and English). All the words, including the foreign ones, are written using the Arabic alphabet without diacritics.

4.1.2 Corpus Annotation

Many linguistic annotations could be added to a spoken corpus. Indeed, texts contain lexical particularities specific to speech; spoken texts are full of disfluencies [27]. Therefore, we enriched our corpus with two types of annotation: morpho-syntactic annotation and disfluencies annotation.

Mophosyntactic Annotation. The morpho-syntactic annotation consists in marking up a word in a corpus as corresponding to a particular part of speech, based on both its definition, and its context [27]. The disfluency processing based on morpho-syntactic tags (POS) has achieved high performance in several studies. Words in an utterance are labelled according 44 POS tags already specified when building TD-WordNet, a large TD lexicon that includes nouns, verbs, tool words, etc. enriched by their morpho-syntactic information (see Sect. 4.2).

Disfluencies Annotation. Spoken corpus annotation must take into consideration the specificities of the spontaneous speech, particularly, disfluencies. The disfluency annotation process allows to identify the boundaries of the Disfluent Segment (DS) in an utterance. It consists of a word classification task based on the four classes: Begin (i.e, the current word is the beginning of the DS), Inside (i.e, the current word is inside the DS), End (i.e, the current word is the end of the DS), and Out (i.e, the current word does not belong to the DS). To this end, we created an annotation guide that contains 8 rules of disfluency annotation (see Sect. 4.3).

However, the annotation of the corpus in a manual way is very difficult and time consuming. We developed the DisAnT, a semi-automatic annotation tool. DisAnT enables two types of annotation namely, mopho-syntactic annotation and disfluency annotation.

4.2 Tunisian-Dialect WordNet (TD-WordNet)

The state-of-the-art methods based on morpho-syntactic information, have achieved a high performance, leading to an absolute detection of disfluencies in the utterance. However, the main weakness of the lexicons presented in Sect. 3.1 lies in their limited size: they present only a small part of the TD vocabulary that makes them inadequate for TD processing.

In this context, we opted to build TD-WordNet, a simplified WordNet for TD, through the combination of three lexicons: the MSA-DT bilingual lexicon [7], the aebWordNet [18] and the TD lexicon [25].

- The MSA-DT bilingual lexicon [7] contains approximately 2.550 words of MSA and their translations into TD. This lexicon consists of 1.050 names, 1.500 verbs and 197 tool words (i.e., adverbs, conjunctions, interjections, etc.).
- The aebWordNet [18] includes about 8.279 lemmas and consists of 3.502 verbs, 3.025 nouns, 483 adverbs and 1.269 adjectives. These words are from TD, MSA and foreign languages.
- The TD lexicon of [25] was created in order to predict sentence boundaries and morpho-syntactic analysis. It includes 6.618 words divided into 365 words, 2.654 proper nouns, 10 exceptional words, 259 nouns, 1.738 adjectives, 1.476 verbs and 117 foreign words written in the Arabic alphabet.

We extracted, for all the collected words, their following morpho-syntactic information (i.e., POS tags), has been organized in an ad-hoc way in two main levels: a grammatical category (i.e., verbs, nouns, pronouns, interjections, adverbs, particles, adjectives, conjunctions and speech words) and the syntactical function (i.e., number and gender) of verbs, nouns, pronouns and adjectives. Figure 1 presents the full tag-sets for POS.

Nouns	N_Prop	Proper noun	Adverbs	Adv	Adverb
	N_MS	Masculin Singular Noun		Adv_Time	Adverb of time
	N_MP	Masculin Plural Noun		Adv_Place	Adverb of place
	N_FS	Feminine Singular Noun		Adv_Neg	Adverb of negation
	N_FP	Feminine Plural Noun		Adv_Interg	Interrogative Adverb
Pronouns	P_MS	Masculin Singular Pronoun		Adv_Rel	Relative Adverb
	P_MP	Masculin Plural Pronoun	Particles	Locution	Locution
	P_FS	Feminine Singular Pronoun		Part_Rest	Restriction Particle
	P_FP	Feminine Plural Pronoun		Part_Futur	Particle of future
	P_Dem	Demonstrative Pronoun		Part_Verb	Particle of Verb
	P_Rel	Relative Pronoun		Part_Cond	Particle of condition
Possessive pronouns	PP_MS	Masculin Singular Possessive Pronoun	Adjectives	Adj_NCard	Numeral Cardinal Adjective
	PP_MP	Masculin Plural Possessive Pronoun		Adj_NOrd	Numeral Ordinal Adjective
	PP_FS	Feminine Singular Possessive Pronoun		Adj_MS	Masculin Singular Adjective
	PP_FP	Feminine Plural Possessive Pronoun		Adj_MP	Masculin Plural Adjective
Verbs	V_MS	Masculin Singular Verb		Adj_FS	Feminine Singular Adjective
	V_MP	Masculin Plural Verb		Adj_FP	Feminine Plural Adjective
	V_FS	Feminine Singular Verb		Prep	Preposition
	V_FP	Feminine Plural Verb	Conjunctions	Conj_Sub	Subordinating conjunction
	V_S	Singular neutral Verb		Conj_Coord	Coordinating conjunction
	V_P	Plural neutral Verb	Speech words	Marq_Disc	Discourse marker
Interjections	Interj	Interjection		Marq_Hesit	Hesitation marker

Fig. 1. Full tag-sets for POS.

In addition, we created a lexicon of compound words under TD-WordNet containing about 430 compound word. Each lexical unit consists of all of its words and is followed by its morpho-syntactic tag. For example,"منزل [mnzl] (Manzel)" and "بوزيان [bwzyAn] (Bouzayen)" constitute one lexical unit "منزل-بوزيان[7]"(proper noun). In addition, we have been enriching our TD-WordNet by other TD words, using the DisAnT annotation tool that was presented in the next section.

4.3 Disfluency Annotation Tool (DisAnT)

The annotation of corpora proves to be a complex and expensive process. Thus, annotation tools allow human annotators to optimize the annotation process in terms of time and effort required. This section introduced the first version of DisAnT, a semi-automatic annotation tool for spoken transcribed corpora that integrates POS tagging with basic disfluency annotation.

DisAnT accepts orthographic corpora, basically transcribed using the Arabic alphabet. The input formats may be a (.txt) file or an (.xml) file that contains a set of utterances. Annotated utterances can be output in (.xml) files, and (.csv) files. The system architecture is not tied to a particular language; it can support other languages. However, the lexical resources have to be adapted to a specific language. DisAnT follows a cascade of annotation steps in which each step depends on the results of the previous one. Figure 2 shows the annotation steps of DisAnT.

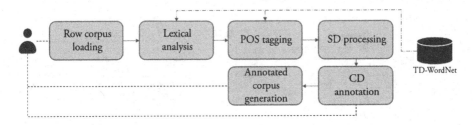

Fig. 2. Architecture of DisAnT.

Lexical Analysis. It consists of two complementary tasks: normalization and morpho-syntactic tagging. The normalization process led to tokenize lexical units including, compound words, using the lexicon of compound words under TD-WordNet. It also allows tokenizing agglutinated words. In this case, affixes and suffixes are separated from the main words, like in the following example: "للدار [lldAr] (to the house)" is recognized as a set of: "ل" (preposition) and "الدار" (noun).

POS Tagging. Words are automatically tagged by the POS tags presented above through the use of the TD-WordNet.

---

[7] A city located in the center of Tunisia.

Simple Disfluencies Processing. This step aims to detect SD phenomena, including syllabic elongations; speech words; word-fragments and simple repetitions. SD present about 71% of the overall number of disfluencies in DisCoTAT. Their detection can improve the performance of the CD processing process. They are processed based on simple regular expressions inspired from the following rules.

Rule 1	**Syllabic elongations**	
	Vowel lengthening of the final syllable in a word	
	Example: عناIII تران برك [EnAAAA trAn brk] (we only have one train)	
Rule 2	**Speech words**	
	Filler words and discourse markers	
	Example: نعرفش ما II [||] mA nErf$] (I do not know)	
Rule 3	**Word-fragments**	
	Word interrupted and taken up	
	Example: شـنوة اللـ- الفرق [$nwp All- Alfrq] (what is the difference)	
Rule 4	**Simple repetitions**	
	Case 1	Two identical words that are successively repeated
		Example: من من بنزرت [mn mn bnzrt] (de de Bizerte)
	Case 2	Two identical words that are successively repeated with a speech word in the middle
		Example: اليوم II اليوم [Alywm || Alywm] (today uuh today)

Syllabic elongations; word-fragments and simple repetitions and automatically removed from the utterance. Nevertheless, we decided not to remove speech words during this step since several related studies prove that they contribute to better predict CD.

Complex Disfluencies Annotation. CD (i.e., complex repetitions and self-corrections) are identified in a manual way. An annotation expert should label words according to the four classes described in Sect. 4.1.2 (i.e, Begin, Inside, End and Out) in order to identify the boundaries of the DS. We created four rules that may help the annotation expert to identify the DS. It is worth noting that the annotation expert can check and update the morpho-syntactic annotation. Also, he can add lexical entries into the TD-WordNet.

		Complex repetitions	
Rule 5	Case 1	Two identical words that are repeated after 1 / + words	
		Example: عشرين دينار عشرين [E$ryn dynAr E$ryn] (twenty dinars twenty)	
	Case 2	Two identical group of words that are repeated	
		Example: من هنا من هنا [mn hnA mn hnA] (this way this way)	

		Self-corrections (Insertions)
Rule 6	A word is inserted in the repair part	
	Example: موش أنا موش ليا انا [mw$ OnA mw$ lyA AnA] (it's not me it's not for me)	

		Self-corrections (Substitutions)
Rule 7	A word is replaced in the repair part	
	Example: من تونس من صفاقس [mn twns mn SfAqs] (from Tunis from Sfax)	

		Self-corrections (Deletions)
Rule 8	A word is abandoned in the repair part	
	Example: الاي روتور كنفور الاي روتور [AlAy rwtwr knfwr AlAy rwtwr] (goings and comings comfort goings and comings)	

DisAnT is written in the Java programming language. Thus, the TD-WordNet and the list of compound words are stored as (.xml) files.

5   Conclusion

Disfluency detection is the task of detecting the infelicities in spoken language transcripts. This work is a part of the disfluency processing task in spontaneous spoken TD. We presented our language resources developed for TD to build a system that extracts the disfluencies phenomena (i.e., syllabic elongations, speech words, word-fragments, repetitions and self-corrections) from transcribed utterances. First, we constructed DisCoTAT, a speech transcribed data corpus collected from three existing corpora. This corpus was enriched with a two-hour transcription. Then, we created the TD-WordNet by collecting all the possible TD words from several existing lexicons. TD-WordNet is a large TD lexicon that includes nouns, verbs, tool words, etc. tagged by their morpho-syntactic information. Finally, we developed the first version of DisAnT, a semi-automatic annotation tool. It supports POS tagging and disfluency annotation. The next step of our work consists basically in proposing a new method for disfluency processing in TD, and this is based on the linguistic resources presented in this paper.

References

1. Abbassi, H., Bahou, Y., Maaloul, M.H.: L'apport d'une approche hybride dans la compréhension de l'oral arabe spontané. In: 29th of Proceedings of International Business Information Management Association, pp. 2145–2157. Vienna, Austria, May 2017

2. Ben Ahmed, Y.: Constitution d'un corpus d'arabe tunisien parlé à orléans. In: Actes des 9éme Journées Internationales de la Linguistique de corpus, p. 173 (2017)
3. Ben Ltaief, A., Estève, Y., Graja, M., Belguith Hadrich, L.: Automatic speech recognition for Tunisian Dialect. In: Proceedings of the First Conference on Language Processing and Knowledge Management, LPKM 2017. Kerkennah (Sfax), Tunisia, September 2017
4. Bouchlaghem, R., Elkhlifi, A., Faiz, R.: Tunisian dialect wordnet creation and enrichment using web resources and other wordnets. In: Proceedings of the EMNLP 2014 Workshop on Arabic Natural Language Processing, pp. 104–113 (2014)
5. Boughariou, E., Bahou, Y., Maaloul, M.H.: Application d'une méthode numérique à base d'apprentissage pour la segmentation conceptuelle de l'oral arabe spontané. In: 29th of Proceedings of International Business Information Management Association, pp. 2820–2835. Vienna, Austria, May 2017
6. Boujelbane, R., Khemekhem Ellouze, M., Béchet, F., Belguith Hadrich, L.: De l'arabe standard vers l'arabe dialectal: projection de corpus et ressources linguistiques en vue du traitement automatique de l'oral dans les médias tunisiens. In: Revue TAL (2015)
7. Boujelbane, R., Khemekhem Ellouze, M., Ben Ayed, S., Belguith Hadrich, L.: Building bilingual lexicon to create Dialect Tunisian corpora and adapt language model. In: Proceedings of the Second Workshop on Hybrid Approaches to Translation, pp. 88–93 (2013)
8. Boujelbane, R., Zribi, I., Kharroubi, S., Khemekhem Ellouze, M.: An automatic process for Tunisian Arabic orthography normalization (2016)
9. Christodoulides, G., Avanzi, M., Goldman, J.P.: DisMo: a morphosyntactic, disfluency and multi-word unit annotator. an evaluation on a corpus of french spontaneous and read speech. arXiv preprint. arXiv:1802.02926 (2018)
10. Graja, M., Jaoua, M., Belguith Hadrich, L.: Lexical study of a spoken dialogue corpus in Tunisian dialect. In: The International Arab Conference on Information Technology. Benghazi, Libya (2010)
11. Habash, N., Diab, M.T., Rambow, O.: Conventional orthography for dialectal Arabic. In: LREC, pp. 711–718 (2012)
12. Hamdi, A., Boujelbane, R., Habash, N., Nasr, A.: Un système de traduction de verbes entre arabe standard et arabe dialectal par analyse morphologique profonde. In: Traitement Automatique des Langues Naturelles, pp. 396–406 (2013)
13. Hamdi, A., Nasr, A., Habash, N., Gala, N.: POS-tagging of tunisian dialect using standard Arabic resources and tools. In: Workshop on Arabic Natural Language Processing, pp. 59–68 (2015)
14. Karoui, J., Graja, M., Boudabous, M.M., Belguith Hadrich, L.: Domain ontology construction from a Tunisian spoken dialogue corpus. In: International Conference on Web and Information Technologies (2013)
15. Labiadh, M., Bahou, Y., Maaloul, M.H.: Complex disfluencies processing in spontaneous Arabic speech. In: Language Processing and Knowledge Management International Conference, LPKM 2018 (2018)
16. Maamouri, M., Bies, A., Buckwalter, T., Mekki, W.: The penn Arabic treebank: building a large-scale annotated Arabic corpus. In: NEMLAR Conference on Arabic Language Resources and Tools, vol. 27, Cairo, Egypt. pp. 466–467 (2004)
17. Masmoudi, A., Khmekhem, M.E., Esteve, Y., Belguith Hadrich, L., Habash, N.: A corpus and phonetic dictionary for Tunisian Arabic speech recognition. In: LREC. pp. 306–310 (2014)

18. Moussa, N.K.B., Soussou, H., Alimi, Adel, M.: Tunisian arabic aeb wordnet: current state and future extensions. In: First International Conference on Arabic Computational Linguistics (ACLing), pp. 3–8 (2015)

19. Neifar, W., Bahou, Y., Graja, M., Jaoua, M.: Implementation of a symbolic method for the Tunisian dialect understanding. In: Proceedings of 5th International Conference on Arabic Language Processing. Oujda, Maroc, November 2014

20. Povey, D., Ghoshal, A., Boulianne, G., Burget, L., Glembek, O., Goel, N., Hannemann, M., Motlicek, P., Qian, Y., Schwarz, P., et al.: The kaldi speech recognition toolkit, Tech. rep. IEEE Signal Processing Society (2011)

21. Rasooli, M.S., Tetreault, J.: Joint parsing and disfluency detection in linear time. In: Proceedings of the 2013 Conference on Empirical Methods in Natural Language Processing, pp. 124–129 (2013)

22. Shriberg, E.E.: Preliminaries to a theory of speech disfluencies. Ph.D. thesis, University of California, Berkeley (1994)

23. Zayats, V., Ostendorf, M., Hajishirzi, H.: Disfluency detection using a bidirectional LSTM. arXiv preprint. arXiv:1604.03209 (2016)

24. Zribi, I., Boujelbane, R., Masmoudi, A., Khemekhem Ellouze, M., Belguith Hadrich, L., Habash, N.: A conventional orthography for Tunisian Arabic. In: LREC, pp. 2355–2361 (2014)

25. Zribi, I., Kammoun, I., Khemekhem Ellouze, M., Belguith Hadrich, L., Blache, P.: Sentence boundary detection for transcribed Tunisian Arabic. In: Bochumer Linguistische Arbeitsberichte, pp. 223–231 (2016)

26. Zribi, I., Khemekhem Ellouze, M., Belguith Hadrich, L.: Morphological analysis of Tunisian dialect. In: Proceedings of the Sixth International Joint Conference on Natural Language Processing, pp. 992–996 (2013)

27. Zribi, I., Khemekhem Ellouze, M., Belguith Hadrich, L., Blache, P.: Spoken Tunisian Arabic corpus "STAC": transcription and annotation. Res. Comput. Sci. **90**, 123–135 (2015)

28. Zribi, I., Khemekhem Ellouze, M., Belguith Hadrich, L., Blache, P.: Morphological disambiguation of Tunisian dialect, pp. 147–155 (2017)

Comparing Front-End Enhancement Techniques and Multiconditioned Training for Robust Automatic Speech Recognition

Meet H. Soni[✉], Sonal Joshi, and Ashish Panda

TCS Innovation Labs, Mumbai, India
{meet.soni,sonals.joshi,ashish.panda}@tcs.com

Abstract. We present comparison of various front-end enhancement techniques and multiconditioned training for robust Automatic Speech Recognition (ASR) for additive noise. We compare De-noising Autoencoders (DAEs) based on Deep Neural Network (DNN), Time-Delay Neural Network (TDNN) architecture, and Time-Frequency (T-F) masking based DNN based front-ends. We train these front-ends and evaluate their performance on various seen/unseen noise conditions. In multiconditioned training, we train acoustic model on various noise conditions and test on seen/unseen noises along with Noise Aware Training (NAT). The results suggest that all front-ends provide performance improvement for seen noise conditions while degrading performance for unseen noise conditions. TDNN-DAE provides the most improvement for seen conditions while giving the most degradation for unseen conditions. We use a method to improve performance of TDNN-DAE in unseen conditions by training it on features enhanced using Vector Taylor Series with Acoustic Masking (VTS-AM) and Spectral Subtraction (SS). We show that these enhancement techniques improve the efficacy of the TDNN-DAE significantly in unseen noise conditions. Overall we observed that multiconditioned training still gives better performance in case of both seen/unseen noise conditions, although the enhanced TDNN-DAE comes closest among all the front-ends to the performance of multiconditioned training.

Keywords: Speech recognition · Noise robustness ·
Front-end processing · Multiconditioned training

1 Introduction

The superiority of Deep Neural Network (DNN) based Automatic Speech Recognition (ASR) systems over traditional Gaussian Mixture Models (GMMs) based systems has been well established in the literature. However, the performance of such systems under various degradation conditions such as channel distortion,

© Springer Nature Switzerland AG 2019
K. Ekštein (Ed.): TSD 2019, LNAI 11697, pp. 329–340, 2019.
https://doi.org/10.1007/978-3-030-27947-9_28

presence of additive noise, reverberation etc. is still sub-par when compared to performance of such systems evaluated on clean data [16]. Such degradation in performance limits the use of these systems in real-world scenarios. Various studies have tried to tackle this problem either by employing enhancement front-ends or various model adaptation techniques to achieve robustness. Model adaptation techniques include computing an entropy measure over a short window on the given hidden layer's neuron's activation [14], Hybrid Convolutional Neural Network (HCNN) [17], using Noise Aware Training (NAT) by giving noise estimate to the model while training/decoding [25], and employing very deep CNN architecture obtained by choosing the best configuration for the sizes of filters, pooling, and input feature maps [23]. Front-end techniques can be broadly classified into three categories. First, extracting robust features like combined binaural and cortical features [26], denoised bottleneck features using deep autoencoders [9], and a constrained Multichannel Wiener Filter for reduction of noise [30]. Second, feature transformation techniques, such as cepstral mean and variance normalization, speaker adaptation like feature-space Maximum Likelihood Linear Regression (fMLLR) transform [22] or Bottleneck (BN) features extracted from deep autoencoder [15]. Third, using speech enhancement techniques such as Spectral Subtraction (SS) [2] and De-noising Autoencoder (DAE). DAEs based on different types of networks like Recurrent Neural Network (RNN) [12,13], and Time delay neural network (TDNN) [6] have been investigated to improve robustness against noise. Other techniques like Vector Taylor Series (VTS) [11] and VTS-Acoustic Modelling (AM) [4] feature enhancement have also been used to good effect. These front-end enhancement techniques are general purpose and can be used for many applications such as speaker recognition or verification to achieve robustness.

Study reported in [7] presents the effectiveness of such front-end using DNN for feature enhancement to improve ASR performance in presence of channel and additive noise. It also compares the performance of such approach with acoustic model trained on noisy database. The authors reported that if such front-end is trained independent of application, it can degrade the performance on unseen noise conditions. To overcome this limitation, application specific enhancement techniques are proposed in [18,24,29] to adapt the enhancement process for improving ASR performance. In [18,29], Time-Frequency (T-F) masking based enhancement front-end was used that was trained separately on clean-noisy feature pairs and then jointly fine-tuned using pre-trained DNN acoustic model. All these studies report performance improvement with tuning the enhancement front-end along with acoustic model to improve ASR accuracy. However, very few studies have reported the performance improvement in unseen noise conditions without fine-tuning it along with acoustic model. One such study reports the improvement in unseen noise conditions by training DAE with features enhanced using some other enhancement techniques such as SS and VTS-AM [10]. Such study is important since many times in real application it is not possible to have the luxury of training an acoustic model for various conditions, especially when off-the-shelf acoustic models are used. Employing enhancement front-end trained in isolation of the acoustic model is the only option in such scenarios.

In this paper, we consider single channel speech input and additive noise as we examine the performance of DNN-DAE [7], TDNN-DAE [6], and T-F masking based DNN [18] in seen and unseen conditions on a DNN-based ASR task. The seen noise condition is where noise type does not change between training the model, either DAE or acoustic model, and testing/decoding phases. While unseen condition is the one where noise types differ between training and testing/decoding. The unavailability of apriori knowledge of all the noise types that can be encountered in real world scenario makes this study vital. We first compare various DNN architectures used as enhancement front-ends. We show that TDNN-DAE gives best performance in the case of seen noise conditions. However, it also gives the most degradation in case of unseen conditions. Second, we show that a TDNN-DAE trained using enhanced features (enhanced TDNN-DAE) performs very well in unseen conditions, while slightly reducing the performance in seen conditions. This can be tackled by using a simple algorithm proposed in [10] that automatically uses the TDNN-DAE for seen conditions and the enhanced TDNN-DAE for unseen conditions, thereby improving the performance in both seen and unseen conditions. And finally, we compare the results of enhancement front-ends with multiconditioned training and multiconditioned training with NAT. We show that multiconditioned training works best in the case of both seen and unseen noise conditions. However, it is possible to achieve significant improvement in unseen noise conditions by using enhancement front-ends and acoustic model trained on clean data. The main contribution of this paper lies in providing the relative performance of all these methods under similar experimental set-up.

The remainder of the paper is organized as follows. Section 2 briefly describes various front-ends used for comparison in this work along with details of NAT, Sect. 3 contains details of the experimental setup and results, while Sect. 4 concludes this paper.

2 Front-End Techniques and Noise Aware Training

2.1 Deep Neural Network Based Denoising Autoencoder (DNN-DAE)

DNN based DAEs are very effective as an enhancement front-end for ASR task [7]. In the training of DNN-DAE, the input features are noisy speech Mel-Frequency Cepstral Coefficients (MFCCs) and target features are the corresponding clean speech MFCCs. Back propagation training is used to calculate network parameters to capture feature enhancement mapping. After the DNN-DAE has learned the mapping, it can be used to enhance MFCCs of noisy utterances. We have used a DNN with 4 hidden layers and 1024 units in each layer. The hidden layers had ReLU activation function and output layer had linear activation. We use 9 neighbouring frames (1 central frame, and 4 left and right frame context) of noisy features as input and central frame of clean features as output to train the DNN-DAE.

2.2   Time Delay Neural Network Based Denoising Autoencoder (TDNN-DAE)

The TDNN architecture [28] has a narrow context for initial layers and wider context for deeper layers. This enables the TDNN to learn the features and the temporal relationships in a long term temporal context. Thus the TDNN architecture is employed in DAE so that it can model temporal evolution of speech and noise [6]. We have followed the TDNN-DAE network architecture used in [20]. This TDNN-DAE network has 4 hidden layers and each hidden layer consists of 1024 ReLU activation nodes. As with the DNN-DAE, once trained, TDNN-DAE can be used to enhance MFCCs of a noisy utterance. Since TDNN architecture has a long temporal context in time-domain, we expect it can give improved enhancement capabilities compared to DNN-DAE.

2.3   Time-Frequency Masking Based DNN

T-F masking approaches are state-of-the-art in case of speech separation problems. In many cases, single channel speech enhancement is posed as a speech separation problem with the aim of separating clean speech from its noisy counterpart [18,29]. We have trained an Ideal Ratio Mask (IRM) estimator as proposed in [18]. The only difference being we used 4 hidden layers instead of 3 for consistency with other experiments. The input-output pairs to train the T-F mask DNN were same in the case of DNN-DAE.

2.4   Spectral Subtraction (SS) Enhanced TDNN-DAE (SS Enhanced-TDNN-DAE)

To improve the performance of the TDNN-DAE, we train a TDNN-DAE with some preprocessing. Spectral subtraction is carried out on the noisy utterances and MFCCs extracted from such files are given as inputs to the TDNN-DAE. The target features are the corresponding clean speech MFCCs. We have denoted the TDNN-DAE, such trained, as SS enhanced-TDNN-DAE.

Spectral Subtraction (SS). SS estimates the noise spectrum from the power spectrum of the noisy speech utterance, subtracts the noise energy from the noisy speech energy, and then recombines the new spectrum with the original phase to reconstruct the time domain signal [1]. The main advantage of SS is that it is computationally simple as only an noise spectrum is to be found. We have used the VoiceBox Toolbox's specsub function [3] to perform spectral subtraction on noisy files.

2.5   Vector Taylor Series - Acoustic Modelling (VTS-AM) Enhanced TDNN-DAE (VTS-AM Enhanced-TDNN-DAE)

Vector Taylor Series - Acoustic Modelling (VTS-AM) is a feature enhancement technique that has been shown to be more effective than the VTS [4]. VTS-AM enhanced-TDNN-DAE is similar SS enhanced-TDNN-DAE except for that VTS-AM is carried out on the noisy utterance MFCCs and the enhanced MFCCs are used as inputs for the TDNN-DAE training.

2.6 SNR Based Scheme

If the TDNN-DAE fails to enhance the noisy features, then it is reasonable to expect that the SNR of TDNN-DAE output will be low. Thus the SNR of the output will be a reliable indicator as to whether the TDNN-DAE has succeeded or failed in enhancing he signal. The challenge lies, however, in estimating the SNR of TDNN-DAE output, since neither the clean signal nor the noise signal is available. We use SNR estimation technique proposed in [10] for this task. We use this SNR as a measure to decide whether the TDNN-DAE has failed to work. If the SNR value is greater than the threshold, then we assume that the TDNN-DAE enhanced features are clean enough to get a good output from the ASR. Otherwise, the test utterance is too noisy for the ASR and needs more enhancement. So we enhance the test utterances using either SS enhances TDNN-DAE or VTS-AM enhanced TDNN-DAE as discussed in Sects. 2.4 and 2.5 and then the enhanced output is provided to the decoding module.

2.7 Multiconditioned Training and Noise Aware Training

We also train various acoustic model with multiconditioned data for performance comparison. These models are trained using different combination of train and test noise conditions to verify their performances on different seen/unseen conditions. We also train acoustic model with Noise Aware Training (NAT) proposed in [25] to give additional information to acoustic model. We give noise estimate calculated by averaging feature values of first and last 10 frames of an utterance to the acoustic model to help it adapt to various noise conditions.

3 Experiments

3.1 Experimental Setup

To compare performance of various approaches we have performed experiments on LibriSpeech [19] database. DNN-based ASR system was implemented using the Kaldi speech recognition toolkit [21]. To prepare the noisy data, we have added three types of noise from the NOISEX-92 database [27] viz. hf channel (HF), F-16 (F16) and babble (BAB) at four SNR levels 0 dB, 5 dB, 10 dB and 15 dB using the Filtering and Noise Adding Tool (FaNT) [8] to the utterances of the database. One more noisy dataset was prepared by adding 4 more types of noise, namely, cafe, car, home, and street from QUT noise corpus [5]. Using the DNN framework (nnet2 from Kaldi) for speech recognition, we have trained clean acoustic models using the clean training speech. MFCCs with 23 coefficients are used in all the experiments. We have used a subset of the LibriSpeech database, the train set comprised of 10,000 utterances and test set is comprised of 614 utterances. The acoustic model trained using clean data achieves 14.18% Word Error Rate (WER). We have also trained multiconditioned acoustic models by adding noise to the training utterances at various SNRs.

TDNN-DAE architecture is the same as in [20]. Contexts for the DAE network with four hidden layers is organized as $(-2,-1,0,1,2)$ $(-1,2)$ $(-3,3)$ $(-7,2)$ (0) and the input temporal context to $[-13,9]$. It can be observed that narrow context is selected for initial hidden layers whereas higher contexts for deeper layers as per TDNN architecture. For VTS-AM, clean training data LibriSpeech database is used to train GMM with 128 components.

To simulate the *seen* and *unseen* conditions, we have used two types of noise for training and all three noise type for testing. For example, if the TDNN-DAE is trained using train set corrupted with hf + bab (all noise levels), then the each test set corrupted with hf(0 dB), hf (5 dB), hf (10 dB), hf (15 dB), bab (0 dB), bab (5 dB), bab (10 dB), bab (15 dB) will fall under the *seen* condition category while the test set corrupted with f16 (0 dB), f16 (5 dB), f16 (10 dB), f16 (15 dB) will fall under the *unseen* condition category. Similarly, the other two train sets will be all noise levels of hf+f16 and bab+f16. The average performance in case of seen conditions is reported. Moreover, we have also prepared one more dataset to further verify the results of unseen condition by adding totally different types of noise from QUT database [5].

For multiconditioned training experiments, same datasets having different seen/unseen conditions were used for acoustic model training. A full multiconditioned model was also trained by adding all 3 noises (hf, f16, and bab) in the clean set. One more multiconditioned acoustic model was trained by using dataset that had QUT noises for verifying performance on unseen conditions.

3.2 Results

Results of Multiconditioned Training. Table 1 shows the results of the multiconditioned training in % WER. The results are reported for acoustic models trained using various train/test noises and tested on various seen/unseen conditions.

The average WER of 52.43% is achieved across all the noisy test conditions using the model trained on clean data. Multiconditioned training using seen/unseen conditions gave relative reduction of 42.59% (30.10% WER) in seen conditions and 31.05% (36.15% WER) on unseen conditions over testing using acoustic model trained on clean data (52.43 % WER). The relative improvement is calculated on the average performance (last row of the table) across all the conditions. In case of full multiconditioned training, the relative improvement over clean acoustic model was 30.90% (36.21% WER). This result is a bit surprising since all the noise conditions were seen during acoustic model training. It suggests that there are other factors involved in effectiveness of multiconditioned training other than simply adding noise in acoustic model training. Some of these factors can be distribution of noise conditions in entire data, number of samples per noise condition, etc. In case of multiconditioned training using QUT noises, the performance improvement over clean training was 27.84% (37.83% WER). In this case, all noise conditions in test dataset were unseen. This experiment suggests that good performance can be achieved by multiconditioned training even with totally different noise types.

These results clearly show that training acoustic model with noisy data greatly improves the performance on noisy test data, even in the case of unseen noise conditions. We trained one more acoustic model using Noise Aware Training (NAT) proposed in [25]. Multiconditioned training with NAT of acoustic model gave similar performance as multiconditioned training. Unlike the results reported in [25], we did not get any performance improvement using NAT. One reason for this can be the less number of noise used to train the acoustic model.

Results of Enhancement Front-End Experiments. Table 2 shows results using different enhancement front-ends to enhance the noisy speech features. These front-ends were trained and evaluated using seen/unseen conditions on acoustic model trained on clean data. DNN-DAE gave 32.00% (35.65% WER) relative improvement over noisy testing in case of seen noises, while it degraded performance by 3.36% (54.19% WER) relative on unseen noises. The relative improvement and degradation is calculated on the average performance (last row of the table) across all the conditions. In case of TDNN-DAE, relative improvement of 39.29% (31.83% WER) over noisy testing was observed in case of seen noises, while relative degradation of 16.21% (60.93% WER) was observed

Table 1. Results (WER%) for multi-conditioned training for seen/unseen conditions (Multi), multiconditioned training using all noise conditions (Full Multi), and multi-conditioned training using QUT noises (Unseen Multi).

Test noise	SNR	Noisy testing	Multi		NAT-Multi		Full Multi	QUT Multi
			Seen	Unseen	Seen	Unseen		
f16	0 dB	89.16	55.46	62.91	54.96	63.70	65.42	65.13
	5 dB	70.72	32.70	36.49	32.31	37.79	38.96	41.22
	10 dB	41.52	22.60	23.94	22.53	24.89	25.29	27.83
	15 dB	23.69	18.62	19.12	18.64	20.13	20.21	22.16
hf	0 dB	83.33	40.36	49.98	40.61	49.27	52.94	56.24
	5 dB	61.11	26.07	31.01	26.59	30.58	32.85	36.75
	10 dB	34.73	20.19	23.22	20.65	22.65	23.83	26.91
	15 dB	22.86	17.89	19.51	18.2	19.27	19.91	22.23
bab	0 dB	85.54	55.06	72.24	56.84	72.98	68.91	65.24
	5 dB	60.35	32.58	45.55	33.62	43.81	42.54	41.19
	10 dB	34.28	21.73	28.46	22.98	27.33	23.13	27.45
	15 dB	21.88	17.99	21.36	19.21	20.78	20.51	21.66
Average		52.43	30.10	36.15	30.59	36.10	36.21	37.83

on unseen noises. T-F masking based DNN enhancement gave 25.97% (38.81% WER) relative improvement in case of seen noises, while degradation in performance by 4.97% (55.04% WER) relative was observed in case of unseen noises.

The results suggest that all the front-ends improve performance over noisy testing in seen noise conditions. TDNN-DAE gave the highest improvement in performance on seen conditions. However, it also gave the most degradation in performance for unseen conditions. These observations suggest that there is a need for performance improvement of enhancement front-ends in case of unseen noise conditions.

Improving Results of Enhancement Front-End in Case of Unseen Conditions. Since TDNN-DAE gave the best performance in case of seen conditions, we have used it for performance improvement in unseen conditions. We trained TDNN-DAE with SS enhanced and VTS-AM enhanced features. Table 3 shows results of these experiments. The SS enhanced TDNN-DAE and the VTS-AM enhanced TDNN-DAE improve the average performance significantly for unseen noise conditions by 16.99% (50.34% WER) and 26.64% (42.46% WER) respectively over the TDNN-DAE (60.93% WER). The relative improvement is calculated on the average performance (last row of the table) across all the conditions. On the other hand, they both underperform the TDNN-DAE in case of seen noise conditions by 3.99% (33.44% WER) and 8.05% (34.81% WER) on average as compared to TDNN-DAE (31.83% WER). The VTS-AM enhanced TDNN-DAE provides the best performance for unseen noise conditions. One

Table 2. Results (WER%) of enhancing noisy data using DNN-DAE, TDNN-DAE, and T-F masking DNN front-ends.

Noise type	SNR	DNN-DAE		TDNN-DAE		TF-Masking	
		Seen	Unseen	Seen	Unseen	Seen	Unseen
f16	0 dB	62.59	86.51	55.12	87.85	66.86	87.57
	5 dB	38.63	65.04	33.60	67.41	42.60	67.04
	10 dB	24.86	40.20	22.98	38.96	26.42	41.03
	15 dB	18.96	24.61	18.48	24.43	19.91	25.92
hf	0 dB	66.60	88.47	45.34	88.59	70.39	87.53
	5 dB	42.33	65.42	29.70	74.27	45.20	65.82
	10 dB	26.79	39.00	21.84	52.94	28.26	40.21
	15 dB	19.59	25.40	18.38	39.01	20.11	26.16
bab	0 dB	52.30	85.41	58.56	91.13	59.38	85.41
	5 dB	33.16	63.84	35.73	73.46	39.15	63.84
	10 dB	23.19	39.95	23.54	52.44	26.67	42.47
	15 dB	18.84	26.45	18.67	40.67	20.81	27.46
Average		35.65	54.19	31.83	60.93	38.81	55.04

interesting observation we had was that, although the enhanced speech improved performance of the TDNN-DAE, it did not improve the performance of the multiconditioned training. This maybe due to the nature of the residual noise left behind by the enhancement methods. For example, the residual noise of the VTS-AM enhancement may be preferable to the residual noise of TDNN-DAE, but it may not be preferable to multiconditioning with actual noise.

Next, we examine the SNRs of the TDNN-DAE output signal. We found that average SNR in case of seen noise conditions was 175.51 dB while in case of unseen noise conditions it was 38.28 dB [10]. It clearly shows that for the SNRs for the unseen noise conditions are quite low compared to the seen noise conditions and it is possible to set a threshold value which can reliably indicate the failure of the TDNN-DAE. These values validates the hypothesis put forth in Sect. 2.6 that the SNRs of TDNN-DAE output will be lower for unseen noise conditions as compared to those for the seen noise conditions. For our purpose, the threshold was set at 105 dB, meaning if the SNR of the output of the TDNN-DAE was below 105 dB, we fall back on the enhanced TDNN-DAE to improve the performance of the ASR. This is not a hard threshold and increasing or decreasing the threshold by 5 to 10 dB did not change the results significantly.

Table 3 also shows the results of ASR performance using the method presented in [10] to improve performance of TDNN-DAE in unseen conditions. It can be seen from Table 3 that the front-end technique proposed in [10] results in better performance in case of unseen noise conditions (SS enhanced TDNN-

Table 3. Results in WER(%) for TDNN-DAE trained using enhanced features using SS and VTS-AM with and without SNR estimation.

Test noise	SNR	SS enhanced TDNN-DAE		VTS-AM enhanced TDNN-DAE		SS enhanced TDNN-DAE with SNR		VTS-AM enhanced TDNN-DAE with SNR	
		Seen	Unseen	Seen	Unseen	Seen	Unseen	Seen	Unseen
f16	0 dB	57.01	75.41	59.06	66.44	54.87	75.39	54.87	66.42
	5 dB	35.5	47.55	36.74	41.18	33.57	47.57	33.58	41.18
	10 dB	23.41	27.97	24.86	27.33	23.02	27.97	23.03	27.32
	15 dB	18.7	20.21	19.4	20.54	18.46	20.21	18.52	20.54
hf	0 dB	48.19	75.62	48.83	57.87	45.36	75.61	45.39	57.88
	5 dB	31.44	51.83	32.58	39.4	29.7	51.83	29.77	39.4
	10 dB	22.85	35.34	23.83	27.59	21.88	35.34	22.04	27.59
	15 dB	18.63	25.65	19.64	20.84	18.36	25.65	18.57	20.84
bab	0 dB	62.63	90.89	65.39	84.67	58.58	90.88	58.57	84.68
	5 dB	38.55	69.18	41.36	61.11	35.78	69.17	35.83	61.08
	10 dB	24.91	47.66	26.13	37.4	23.57	47.65	23.69	37.39
	15 dB	19.42	36.78	19.88	25.18	18.69	36.78	18.84	25.18
Average		33.44	50.34	34.81	42.46	31.82	50.34	31.89	42.46

DAE performance improves by absolute 10.59% while VTS enhanced TDNN-DAE improves by absolute 18.47% over the TDNN-DAE) while matching the performance of the TDNN-DAE in case of seen noise conditions.

The results reported in this work highlight the limitations of the TDNN-DAE for unseen noise conditions. Different noise types corrupt the signal in different ways and hence the TDNN-DAE is unable to enhance the signal if it contains a noise type that it was not trained for. Unsupervised enhancement techniques like SS and VTS-AM can enhance such signals, since the noise estimation is done on the test utterances. It can be said that training acoustic model with noisy features give better results than training enhancement front-ends in isolation with the same noisy features. However, it possible to achieve performance improvement in case of unseen noise conditions by employing enhancement front-ends also when it is not possible to train acoustic model with noisy data.

4   Conclusions

In this paper, we compared various approaches to achieve robustness in presence of additive noise for ASR task. We compared various enhancement front-end architectures and techniques, namely, DNN based DAE, TDNN based DAE and T-F masking based DNN. We also compared the performance of such front-ends with multiconditioned training of acoustic model. In our experiments we observed that using front-ends gave significant performance improvement in case of seen noise conditions, while it degraded the performance in the case of unseen conditions. We have also used enhanced TDNN-DAE, where the TDNN-DAE is trained with speech signals enhanced by an enhancement method to improve the performance of such front-ends in unseen conditions. Two enhancement methods, namely SS and VTS-AM have been compared for this purpose and it was found that the VTS-AM performed better than the SS. It was also found that while the enhanced TDNN-DAE improved the performance of the ASR significantly in unseen noise conditions, it slightly underperformed the TDNN-DAE for seen noise conditions. Based on a SNR measure, a robust front-end processing approach was implemented that provided better results than the TDNN-DAE in case of unseen noise conditions, while maintaining the performance of the TDNN-DAE in case of seen noise conditions. Although the enhanced TDNN-DAE with SNR measure performed the best among the front-end techniques, it still underperformed compared to the multiconditioned training. However, if multiconditioned acoustic models are not available due to some reason, then the front-end techniques can be relied upon to provide significant performance gain in noisy conditions.

References

1. Berouti, M., Schwartz, R., Makhoul, J.: Enhancement of speech corrupted by acoustic noise. In: Acoustics, Speech, and Signal Processing, IEEE International Conference on ICASSP 1979, vol. 4, pp. 208–211. IEEE (1979)

2. Boll, S.: Suppression of acoustic noise in speech using spectral subtraction. IEEE Trans. Acoust. Speech Signal Process. **27**(2), 113–120 (1979)
3. Brookes, M., et al.: Voicebox: Speech processing toolbox for matlab. Software [March 2011] www.ee.ic.ac.uk/hp/staff/dmb/voicebox/voicebox.html, vol. 47 (1997)
4. Das, B., Panda, A.: Robust front-end processing for speech recognition in noisy conditions. In: 2017 IEEE International Conference on Acoustics, Speech and Signal Processing (ICASSP), pp. 5235–5239. IEEE (2017)
5. Dean, D.B., Sridharan, S., Vogt, R.J., Mason, M.W.: The QUT-NOISE-TIMIT corpus for the evaluation of voice activity detection algorithms. In: Proceedings of Interspeech 2010 (2010)
6. Do, C.T., Stylianou, Y.: Improved automatic speech recognition using subband temporal envelope features and time-delay neural network denoising autoencoder. In: Proceedings of Interspeech 2017, pp. 3832–3836 (2017)
7. Du, J., Wang, Q., Gao, T., Xu, Y., Dai, L.R., Lee, C.H.: Robust speech recognition with speech enhanced deep neural networks. In: Proceedings of Interspeech (2014)
8. Hirsch, H.G., Finster, H.: The simulation of realistic acoustic input scenarios for speech recognition systems. In: Ninth European Conference on Speech Communication and Technology (2005)
9. Janod, K., Morchid, M., Dufour, R., Linares, G., De Mori, R.: Denoised bottleneck features from deep autoencoders for telephone conversation analysis. IEEE/ACM Trans. Audio Speech Lang. Process. **25**(9), 1809–1820 (2017)
10. Joshi, S., Panda, A., DAs, B.: Enhanced denoising auto-encoder for robust speech recognition in unseen noise conditions. In: International Symposium on Chinese Spoken Languages Processing (2018)
11. Li, J., Deng, L., Yu, D., Gong, Y., Acero, A.: High-performance HMM adaptation with joint compensation of additive and convolutive distortions via vector taylor series. In: IEEE Workshop on Automatic Speech Recognition & Understanding, 2007. ASRU, pp. 65–70. IEEE (2007)
12. Maas, A.L., Le, Q.V., O'Neil, T.M., Vinyals, O., Nguyen, P., Ng, A.Y.: Recurrent neural networks for noise reduction in robust ASR. In: Proceedings of Interspeech (2012)
13. Marchi, E., Vesperini, F., Eyben, F., Squartini, S., Schuller, B.: A novel approach for automatic acoustic novelty detection using a denoising autoencoder with bidirectional LSTM neural networks. In: 2015 IEEE International Conference on Acoustics, Speech and Signal Processing (ICASSP), pp. 1996–2000. IEEE (2015)
14. Mitra, V., Franco, H.: Leveraging deep neural network activation entropy to cope with unseen data in speech recognition. arXiv preprint arXiv:1708.09516 (2017)
15. Mitra, V., Franco, H., Bartels, C., van Hout, J., Graciarena, M., Vergyri, D.: Speech recognition in unseen and noisy channel conditions. In: 2017 IEEE International Conference on Acoustics, Speech and Signal Processing (ICASSP), pp. 5215–5219. IEEE (2017)
16. Mitra, V., et al.: Robust features in deep-learning-based speech recognition. In: Watanabe, S., Delcroix, M., Metze, F., Hershey, J.R. (eds.) New Era for Robust Speech Recognition, pp. 187–217. Springer, Cham (2017). https://doi.org/10.1007/978-3-319-64680-0_8
17. Mitra, V., Sivaraman, G., Nam, H., Espy-Wilson, C., Saltzman, E., Tiede, M.: Hybrid convolutional neural networks for articulatory and acoustic information based speech recognition. Speech Commun. **89**, 103–112 (2017)

18. Narayanan, A., Wang, D.: Joint noise adaptive training for robust automatic speech recognition. In: 2014 IEEE International Conference on Acoustics, Speech and Signal Processing (ICASSP), pp. 2504–2508. IEEE (2014)
19. Panayotov, V., Chen, G., Povey, D., Khudanpur, S.: Librispeech: an ASR corpus based on public domain audio books. In: 2015 IEEE International Conference on Acoustics, Speech and Signal Processing (ICASSP), pp. 5206–5210. IEEE (2015)
20. Peddinti, V., Povey, D., Khudanpur, S.: A time delay neural network architecture for efficient modeling of long temporal contexts. In: Proceedings of Interspeech (2015)
21. Povey, D., et al.: The kaldi speech recognition toolkit. In: IEEE 2011 Workshop on Automatic Speech Recognition and Understanding. No. EPFL-CONF-192584, IEEE Signal Processing Society (2011)
22. Povey, D., Kanevsky, D., Kingsbury, B., Ramabhadran, B., Saon, G., Visweswariah, K.: Boosted MMI for model and feature-space discriminative training. In: IEEE International Conference on Acoustics, Speech and Signal Processing, 2008. ICASSP 2008, pp. 4057–4060. IEEE (2008)
23. Qian, Y., Bi, M., Tan, T., Yu, K.: Very deep convolutional neural networks for noise robust speech recognition. IEEE/ACM Trans. Audio Speech Lang. Process. **24**(12), 2263–2276 (2016)
24. Qian, Y., Yin, M., You, Y., Yu, K.: Multi-task joint-learning of deep neural networks for robust speech recognition. In: 2015 IEEE Workshop on Automatic Speech Recognition and Understanding (ASRU), pp. 310–316. IEEE (2015)
25. Seltzer, M.L., Yu, D., Wang, Y.: An investigation of deep neural networks for noise robust speech recognition. In: 2013 IEEE International Conference on Acoustics, Speech and Signal Processing (ICASSP), pp. 7398–7402. IEEE (2013)
26. Spille, C., Kollmeier, B., Meyer, B.T., Spille, C., Kollmeier, B., Meyer, B.T.: Combining binaural and cortical features for robust speech recognition. IEEE/ACM Trans. Audio Speech Lang. Process. (TASLP) **25**(4), 756–767 (2017)
27. Varga, A., Steeneken, H.J.: Assessment for automatic speech recognition: II. NOISEX-92: a database and an experiment to study the effect of additive noise on speech recognition systems. Speech Commun. **12**(3), 247–251 (1993)
28. Waibel, A., Hanazawa, T., Hinton, G., Shikano, K., Lang, K.J.: Phoneme recognition using time-delay neural networks. In: Readings in Speech Recognition, pp. 393–404. Elsevier (1990)
29. Wang, Z.Q., Wang, D.: A joint training framework for robust automatic speech recognition. IEEE/ACM Trans. Audio Speech Lang. Process. **24**(4), 796–806 (2016)
30. Wang, Z., Vincent, E., Serizel, R., Yan, Y.: Rank-1 constrained multichannel wiener filter for speech recognition in noisy environments. Comput. Speech Lang. **49**, 37–51 (2018)

Label-Driven Time-Frequency Masking for Robust Speech Command Recognition

Meet Soni[✉], Imran Sheikh, and Sunil Kumar Kopparapu

TCS Research and Innovation, Mumbai, India
{meet.soni,imran.as,sunilkumar.kopparapu}@tcs.com

Abstract. Speech enhancement driven robust Automatic Speech Recognition (ASR) systems typically require a parallel corpus with noisy and clean speech utterances for training. Moreover, many studies have reported that such front-ends, though improve speech quality, do not translate into improved recognition performance. On the other hand, multi-condition training of ASR systems has little visualization or interpretability capabilities of how these systems achieve robustness. In this paper, we propose a novel neural architecture with unified enhancement and sequence classification block, that is trained in an end-to-end manner only using noisy speech without having any knowledge of clean speech. The enhancement block is a fully convolutional network that is designed to perform Time Frequency (T-F) masking like operation, followed by an LSTM sequence classification block. The T-F masking formulation enables visualization of learned mask and helps us to analyse the T-F points that are important for classification of a speech command. Experiments performed on Google Speech Command dataset show that the proposed network achieves better results than the model without an enhancement front-end.

Keywords: Robust speech recognition · Time-frequency masking · Label driven masking

1 Introduction

The use of Deep Neural Networks (DNNs) has drastically improved the performance of modern Automatic Speech Recognition (ASR) systems. However, performance of such systems in the presence of degradation conditions such as channel distortions, reverberation, and additive noise is still not on par with the ASR on clean speech signals [11]. There are two major paradigms to achieve robustness to various noise conditions, (a) use of model adaptation techniques to achieve robustness against various degradation conditions [10,11,14,16], (b) use of enhancement front-end to map noisy speech features to clean features [3,6,8,9,13,15,18].

Model adaptation techniques majorly use the representation power of DNNs to train the acoustic model with various degradation conditions. This approach

© Springer Nature Switzerland AG 2019
K. Ekštein (Ed.): TSD 2019, LNAI 11697, pp. 341–351, 2019.
https://doi.org/10.1007/978-3-030-27947-9_29

is reported to work well in wide range of degradation conditions [14,16]. One advantage of such approach is that no knowledge about clean speech is required since the model learns directly from noisy or degraded speech. However, these approaches provide little insights regarding how model achieves robustness due to lack of visualization of their inner operations. Another popular approach to achieve robustness is to employ an enhancement front-end trained either separately from the acoustic model, or fine-tuned along with parameters of the acoustic model. Such approaches are especially useful when it is not possible to train the acoustic model with noisy data. The front-ends generally use the De-noising Autoencoder (DAE) based on various DNN architectures such as DNN-DAE [4], Time-Delay Neural Network (TDNN)-DAE [3], Recurrent Neural Network (RNN) DAE [8,9], or Time-Frequency (T-F) masking-based approaches to enhance the noisy signal [13,18]. To train such front-ends, a parallel corpus containing noisy and clean speech pairs is required. Such front-ends are generally trained to minimize the Mean Square Error (MSE) between output of the front-end and clean speech features. However, it is reported that such front-ends, especially when trained in isolation with acoustic model, do not yield improvement in ASR performance in unseen noisy test conditions [4].

In this paper, we propose a novel neural network architecture that can leverage advantages of both these approaches to achieve robustness. We propose a network with an enhancement front-end block that has a T-F masking *like* formulation in its architecture. We expect that the T-F mask required to achieve clean T-F representation (for speech enhancement purpose) is different than the T-F mask required to achieve robustness in speech classification task. The enhancement block is a fully convolutional network that learns feature detectors to locate important T-F regions for maximizing the correct speech classification probability. The output of this enhancement block is given to an LSTM-based sequence classification block to get class probabilities. The entire network is jointly trained in an end-to-end manner using only noisy data with random parameter initialization without providing the network any information about clean speech data.

The proposed architecture provides access to visualization of the enhancement process by inspection of the T-F mask applied by the enhancement block, and activation maps of convolution filters in the first layer of the enhancement block. This visualization gives insights on the T-F regions that are important for classification of a speech command. Experiments on Google Speech Command dataset [19] demonstrate the effectiveness of the proposed model and its visualization capabilities.

The rest of the paper is organized as follows. Section 2 contains details of our proposed model architecture for label-driven T-F masking, Sect. 3 details the experimental setup, results, and visualization of the enhancement process. Section 4 concludes the paper.

2 Label Driven Time-Frequency Masking

Figure 1(a) shows the network architecture of the proposed model that uses an enhancement block to transform the input T-F representation into an enhanced representation. We use two fully convolutional layers in the enhancement block. The first convolution layer transforms the input T-F representation into a multi-channel spectral representations while the second convolution layer maps the multi-channel representation back to the original dimensions of the input T-F representation. The motivation behind using this architecture is to obtain output of the same dimensions as the input T-F representation by using padded convolution. The first convolution layer filters act as feature detectors that identifies T-F regions required to accurately classify the input speech. The second convolution layer filter combines the output of the first layer filters to give the same dimensions as the input T-F representation.

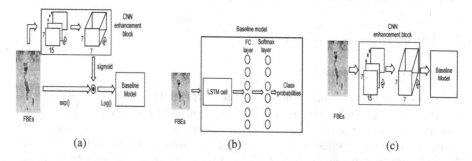

(a)   (b)   (c)

Fig. 1. (a) Proposed architecture with convolutional enhancement block that has T-F masking formulation, (b) the baseline model consist of an LSTM cell, a Fully Connected (FC) layer, and a softmax classification layer. Output of the enhancement block is given as the input to the baseline model, and (c) the same model as (b) without T-F masking formulation for comparison purpose.

We treat the output of the convolutional block as a T-F mask and apply it to the input T-F representation by the following method. We constrain the mask values between 0–1 by applying the sigmoid activation function at the output of the convolutional block. The input to the network is log-magnitude domain T-F representation such as log Mel-Filterbank Energies (FBEs). The input T-F representation is first converted in the magnitude domain by applying the exponential operation and then it is multiplied element-wise with the T-F mask. This operation gives the enhanced T-F magnitude representation [13,18]. This enhanced magnitude representation is converted in log domain by applying logarithm. Mathematically, operations of the enhancement block can be summarized as follows:

$$Y(t,f) = log(exp(X(t,f)) \circ M(t,f)), \tag{1}$$

where $X(t,f)$ is the input T-F representation (i.e. FBEs), $M(t,f)$ is the T-F mask taken at the output of the enhancement block, and $Y(t,f)$ is the enhanced T-F representation.

The output of the enhancement block is given to the baseline classification model. Architecture of the baseline model is shown in Fig. 1(b). The LSTM layer in baseline model takes the enhanced T-F representation $Y(t, f)$ as an input and recurrently encodes the input frames in its hidden states. The final hidden state of the LSTM layer is then propagated to fully connected and softmax classification layer. When used with enhancement block, the model is jointly trained to find the T-F mask that will enhance the input T-F representation for better classification accuracy. Here, the noteworthy observation is that the parameters of classification as well as enhancement block are optimized using the final hidden state of the LSTM block. Hence, the enhancement block tries to enhance the entire T-F sequence, unlike the frame-level enhancement techniques used in previous works. Moreover, it should be noted that this training scheme does not use the clean T-F representation for training the enhancement block. Hence, the T-F mask, and consequently the enhanced T-F mask obtained is solely based on maximizing the output class probability.

3   Experiments and Results

3.1   Database Description

We use Google Speech Command dataset for our experiments [19]. The database consists of 64,727 audio files, each of 1 s duration, and consisting of one spoken command each. The audio files were originally collected by crowdsourcing. Each 1 s utterance was labelled with one of the possible 30 commands, which are divided into 20 main commands and 10 sub-commands. following the original splits provided in the database, 80% utterances were used for training, 10% for validation and 10% utterances were used for testing. Moreover, the dataset provides background noise audio files with white noise, pink noise, and four types of day-to-day noise, namely, running_tap, dude_miaowing, exercise_bike, and doing_the_dishes. Since this dataset was produced for consumer and robotic application purposes, they did not give strict guidelines for quality during crowd-sourcing, other than to record in a closed room. During our initial observations we found that the audio files were already containing little noise. Hence, whenever we add background noise with a particular SNR, the actual SNR will be lower than the added SNR.

To evaluate the robustness of the proposed model we add the provided noises at 15 dB, 10 dB and 5 dB SNR to test utterances. To add the noise in each utterance we randomly select 1 s segment from the noise file and scale its energy to get the desired SNR. We do not add any noise in training data.

3.2   Model Architectures

Baseline Model. We have use a single layer LSTM model as our baseline. As shown in Fig. 1(b) our baseline model consist of an LSTM cell followed by a fully connected layer and a softmax classification layer. Although many approaches have been proposed on the same database using different DNN architectures such as Residual Network (ResNet) [17], TDNN [12], and CNN and Capsule Network (CapsNet) [1], none of the work compare their performance using LSTM based network using uniform experimental setup. Since majority of end-to-end ASR systems use LSTMs to model acoustic information [2,5,7], we selected LSTM as our baseline model. However, the current framework can be easily extended for any kind of classification model.

We have used LSTM cell with 128 units and without any bias parameters. The LSTM layer was followed by a fully connected layers with 128 units. The output layer had 30 units for 30 class classification. All layers except for output layer had Rectified Linear Unit (ReLU) activation function. Output layer had softmax activation for classification. Input to the network were 40 dimensional FBEs of 1 s utterance. FBEs were extracted by taking the frames of 25 ms with 10 ms overlap that gave us total of 99 frames per utterance. Hence, the size of the input sequence was 40×99. The baseline model was trained for minimizing the cross-entropy between class labels and output class probabilities. The model was trained using back-propagation with ADAM optimizer. The learning rate was fixed at 0.001. The model was trained for 10 epochs starting from random parameter initialization, and model that gave the best performance on validation dataset was used for testing.

Model with T-F Masking Enhancement Block. As shown in Fig. 1(a) we use fully convolution layers as enhancement block. The first convolution layer had 60 convolutional filters of size 15×7. The second convolution layer had one convolutional filter of size $7 \times 7 \times 60$. The number of filters and filter dimensions were optimized on validation set. First convolutional layer had ReLU activation function and the second convolutional layer had sigmoid activation for making the output to lie in the range 0–1. The model was trained to jointly optimize the parameters of enhancement and classification block with the similar objective function and training parameters as the baseline model. Results of this model are tabulated under the label "T-F masking enhancement".

Model with Direct Enhancement. We hypothesize that the T-F mask learned by enhancement block will improve the overall performance of the model. However, due to additional parameters in enhancement block, any performance improvement over the baseline model can correspond to the addition of more parameters to the model. To quantify the performance improvement due to increased number of parameters, we trained one additional model as shown in Fig. 1(c). This model had similar blocks, i.e. convolutional enhancement block and classification block. However, instead of treating output of the convolutional block as T-F mask, we used output of the convolutional block directly as the input to the LSTM classification model. Hence, in this case the output of convolutional enhancement block can be directly treated as enhanced representation that will improve the overall classification accuracy. The model parameters and training scheme were same for this model as the model with T-F masking enhancement block. The only difference being the activation function of the second convolution layer. In this case we used linear activation instead of sigmoid activation since the output is not need not be constrained between 0–1. Results of this model are tabulated under the label "Direct enhancement".

3.3 Results

The results of all the models on original validation and test datasets are shown in Table 1. The results suggest that a simple LSTM classifier gives a good performance for speech command classification task. This baseline is stronger than recently attempted CNN and CapNet models [1] trained and evaluated on the same database and train/test condition for classification. We also evaluated our model performance for recognizing 20 main commands to compare our results with [1]. On 20 commands evaluation our LSTM baseline (91.12%) performed significantly better than CNN (77.9%) and CapsNet (87.3%). Moreover, our network had significantly low number of parameters ($\approx$110 K) as compared to models reported in [1] (6M for CNN and 8M for CapsNEt). An improvement over baseline was observed by employing convolutional enhancement block to extract the robust features from input. By using T-F masking enhancement further performance improvement was observed on both validation and test dataset.

Table 1. Classification accuracy (%) of various models on validation and test dataset provided in the database.

Model name	Validation	Test	Test (20 classes)
LSTM baseline	90.93	90.76	91.12
Direct enhancement	91.5	91.47	91.97
T-F masking enhancement	**92.92**	**92.9**	**93.24**

Table 2. Classification accuracy (%) of all the models on noisy test set. All the available noises in the database were added with 15 dB, 10 dB, and 5 dB SNR.

Test noise	LSTM baseline			T-F masking enhancement			Direct enhancement		
	15 dB	10 dB	5 dB	15 dB	10 dB	5 dB	15 dB	10 dB	5 dB
running_tap	75.42	64.74	47.24	82.25	73.46	56.12	81.59	72.60	54.32
dude_miaowing	76.14	65.53	49.26	82.38	73.87	57.41	81.78	73.24	57.82
exercise_bike	76.40	64.30	42.83	83.70	73.91	54.00	81.95	71.60	49.74
doing_dishes	82.53	73.01	56.27	86.26	79.90	67.90	83.96	75.62	59.25
pink_noise	85.44	7.15	68.31	89.20	85.62	77.51	86.83	83.07	73.72
white_noise	72.07	58.26	35.48	79.75	68.01	45.94	79.41	67.90	44.92
Average	78.00	55.50	49.90	**83.92**	**75.80**	**59.81**	82.59	74.01	56.63

Table 2 shows the results of evaluating the trained models on noisy dataset. Performance of LSTM baseline degraded significantly in the presence of noise. By employing CNN enhancement block, the results on noisy database improved significantly. While T-F masking-based enhancement gave the best results on the noisy test dataset. The results indicate that while significant improvement can be achieved using enhancement block in the model, T-F masking based formulation can provide further improvement to achieve more robustness in all type of noise conditions. For certain noise types such as doing_the_dishes, T-F masking gave huge performance improvement over directly using employing enhancement, while in some noise like white_noise, the performance improvement was not significant. For noises added with 5 dB SNR, the T-F masking enhancement gave significantly better performance than direct enhancement model.

3.4   Visualizing the Enhancement Process

The proposed architecture allows us to easily visualize the enhancement process learned by enhancement block. To demonstrate this we present Fig. 2 which

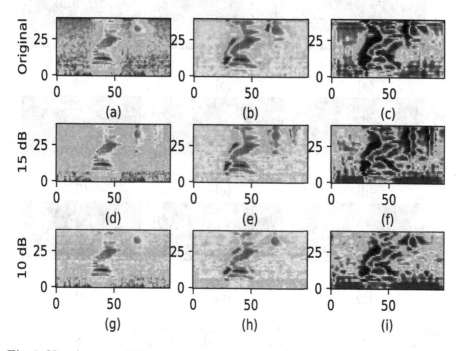

Fig. 2. Visualization of the enhancement process applied by propose model. (a) Input FBEs as T-F representation for original utterance in test set. The spoken command is word "right". (b) Enhanced representation $(Y(t, f))$ taken at the output of the enhancement block. (c) T-F mask $(M(t, f))$ learned by the enhancement block to achieve $Y(t, f)$. Similarly (d)–(f) and (g)–(i) are show the same plots after adding running_tap noise in the original utterance at 15 dB and 10 dB SNR respectively. (Vertical axis corresponds to frequency and horizontal axis is the time axis.)

shows the outputs and T-F masks learned by the enhancement block for an original test utterance as well as noisy versions of it. It can be observed that the original utterance shown in Fig. 2(a) taken from test dataset already has some noise. The enhancement block gives the output shown in Fig. 2(b). This enhanced representation is achieved by applying T-F mask learned by the enhancement block, shown in Fig. 2(c), on the input T-F representation. Figure 2(d)–(f) and (g)–(i) show similar plots for the same utterance with 15 dB and 10 dB additive noise of type running_tap, respectively.

Visual inspection of the enhanced representation and T-F mask suggests that the enhancement block tries to achieve two things: (1) locating the important T-F points in the input T-F representation where acoustic information about spoken word is present. (2) locating the boundary between spoken word and non-speech region. It can also be observed that the enhancement block does not try to remove or suppress noise in the silence regions, which is expected from the traditional enhancement front-end trained with minimizing Mean Square Error

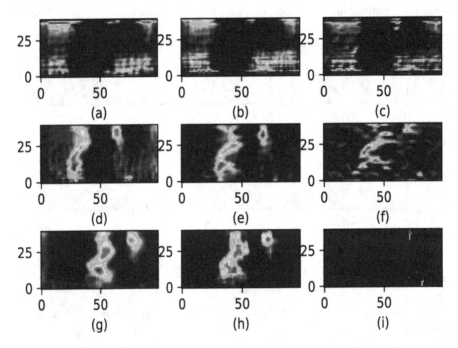

Fig. 3. Visualization of the activation maps of 9 selected filters in the first layer of the enhancement block. (a)–(c) show the output of the filters that find outs the T-F region that contains the acoustic information of the spoken word. (d)–(f) show the filters that locate the boundary between speech and non-speech T-F regions. (g)–(h) show the filters that try to locate the T-F regions where the important acoustic information about spoken command is present. (i) shows the activation of a filter that did not contribute for the classification purpose. (Vertical axis corresponds to frequency and horizontal axis is the time axis.)

(MSE) between enhanced and clean speech features. The T-F masks for original as well as noisy utterances are fairly similar except for some T-F regions with very less SNR. Here, it is noteworthy that the parameters of CNN enhancement blocks are learned only using original utterances, still the enhancement block is able to perform well in the case of utterances with additive noise of lower SNR.

Now, we observe how enhancement block achieves the T-F mask and the subsequently enhanced representation by visualizing the activation maps of convolution filters in the first layer. Figure 3 shows the activation maps of 9 selected filters out of the 60 convolutional filters, for the utterance in Fig. 2(a) as input. Figure 3(a)–(c) suggest that the underlying filters tries to locate the T-F regions where spoken command is present. Figure 3(d)–(f) show that the underlying filters are locating the boundaries between acoustic information of spoken command and non speech T-F regions. While Fig. 3(g)–(h) show the activation of filters that are finding out the important T-F points where acoustic information of a spoken command is present. Figure 3(i) shows the activation of a filter that is not significant for enhancing and classifying this utterance. We found that majority of the activation maps resembled Fig. 3(a)–(c), i.e. trying to locate the T-F regions where spoken command is present. Other filters resembled Fig. 3(d)–(f).

These visualizations suggest that enhancement for robust speech classification is different than traditional enhancement. While traditional enhancement front-ends try to remove or suppress noise, the label driven enhancement approach focuses on finding out important regions in T-F representation that are significant to increase classification probability.

4 Summary and Conclusions

In this paper, we proposed a novel neural network architecture with a fully convolutional enhancement block and LSTM-based classification block for robust speech command recognition. Unlike traditional front-ends that are trained in isolation or jointly with acoustic model using parallel clean and noisy speech corpora, we trained our model directly on noisy data to jointly learn the enhancement and classification block. The enhancement block had T-F masking like formulation for enhancement purpose. This model gave significant performance improvement over LSTM baseline model for both original as well as noisy test dataset. Moreover, the visualization of enhancement process for improving classification accuracy gave significant insights on the working of the proposed network. We observed that instead of removing or suppressing noise present in the noisy T-F representation, the enhancement block locates the important regions in the input T-F representation. In particular, the enhancement block tries to locate the boundary between spoken command and non-speech regions in addition to T-F points that contains acoustic information. This enhancement process is different than traditional enhancement that tries to remove or suppress noise.

For our future work, we plan to extend this study to medium and large vocabulary speech recognition in the end-to-end framework. Since majority of end-to-end frameworks employ LSTM or other recurrent architectures, it would be interesting to observe the performance of the proposed approach on continuous ASR tasks.

References

1. Bae, J., Kim, D.S.: End-to-end speech command recognition with capsule network. In: Proceedings of Interspeech 2018, pp. 776–780 (2018)
2. Bahdanau, D., Chorowski, J., Serdyuk, D., Brakel, P., Bengio, Y.: End-to-end attention-based large vocabulary speech recognition. In: 2016 IEEE International Conference on Acoustics, Speech and Signal Processing (ICASSP), pp. 4945–4949. IEEE (2016)
3. Do, C.T., Stylianou, Y.: Improved automatic speech recognition using subband temporal envelope features and time-delay neural network denoising autoencoder. In: Proceedings of Interspeech 2017, pp. 3832–3836 (2017)
4. Du, J., Wang, Q., Gao, T., Xu, Y., Dai, L.R., Lee, C.H.: Robust speech recognition with speech enhanced deep neural networks. In: Proceedings of Interspeech (2014)
5. Graves, A., Mohamed, A.R., Hinton, G.: Speech recognition with deep recurrent neural networks. In: 2013 IEEE International Conference on Acoustics, Speech and Signal Processing (ICASSP), pp. 6645–6649. IEEE (2013)
6. Janod, K., Morchid, M., Dufour, R., Linares, G., De Mori, R.: Denoised bottleneck features from deep autoencoders for telephone conversation analysis. IEEE/ACM Trans. Audio Speech Lang. Process. **25**(9), 1809–1820 (2017)
7. Kim, S., Hori, T., Watanabe, S.: Joint CTC-attention based end-to-end speech recognition using multi-task learning. In: 2017 IEEE International Conference on Acoustics, Speech and Signal Processing (ICASSP), pp. 4835–4839. IEEE (2017)
8. Maas, A.L., Le, Q.V., O'Neil, T.M., Vinyals, O., Nguyen, P., Ng, A.Y.: Recurrent neural networks for noise reduction in robust ASR. In: Proceedings of Interspeech (2012)
9. Marchi, E., Vesperini, F., Eyben, F., Squartini, S., Schuller, B.: A novel approach for automatic acoustic novelty detection using a denoising autoencoder with bidirectional LSTM neural networks. In: 2015 IEEE International Conference on Acoustics, Speech and Signal Processing (ICASSP), pp. 1996–2000. IEEE (2015)
10. Mitra, V., Franco, H.: Leveraging deep neural network activation entropy to cope with unseen data in speech recognition. arXiv preprint arXiv:1708.09516 (2017)
11. Mitra, V., et al.: Robust features in deep-learning-based speech recognition. In: Watanabe, S., Delcroix, M., Metze, F., Hershey, J. (eds.) New Era for Robust Speech Recognition, pp. 187–217. Springer, Cham (2017). https://doi.org/10.1007/978-3-319-64680-0_8
12. Myer, S., Tomar, V.S.: Efficient keyword spotting using time delay neural networks. arXiv preprint arXiv:1807.04353 (2018)
13. Narayanan, A., Wang, D.: Joint noise adaptive training for robust automatic speech recognition. In: 2014 IEEE International Conference on Acoustics, Speech and Signal Processing (ICASSP), pp. 2504–2508. IEEE (2014)
14. Qian, Y., Bi, M., Tan, T., Yu, K.: Very deep convolutional neural networks for noise robust speech recognition. IEEE/ACM Trans. Audio Speech Lang. Process. **24**(12), 2263–2276 (2016)
15. Qian, Y., Yin, M., You, Y., Yu, K.: Multi-task joint-learning of deep neural networks for robust speech recognition. In: 2015 IEEE Workshop on Automatic Speech Recognition and Understanding (ASRU), pp. 310–316. IEEE (2015)
16. Seltzer, M.L., Yu, D., Wang, Y.: An investigation of deep neural networks for noise robust speech recognition. In: 2013 IEEE International Conference on Acoustics, Speech and Signal Processing (ICASSP), pp. 7398–7402. IEEE (2013)

17. Tang, R., Lin, J.: Deep residual learning for small-footprint keyword spotting. In: 2018 IEEE International Conference on Acoustics, Speech and Signal Processing (ICASSP), pp. 5484–5488. IEEE (2018)
18. Wang, Z.Q., Wang, D.: A joint training framework for robust automatic speech recognition. IEEE/ACM Trans. Audio Speech Lang. Process. **24**(4), 796–806 (2016)
19. Warden, P.: Speech commands: A public dataset for single-word speech recognition. Dataset available from http://download.tensorflow.org/data/speech_commands_v01 (2017)

A Comparison of Hybrid and End-to-End Models for Syllable Recognition

Sebastian P. Bayerl and Korbinian Riedhammer[⊠]

Technische Hochschule Nürnberg Georg Simon Ohm, Nuremberg, Germany
{sebastian.bayerl,korbinian.riedhammer}@th-nuernberg.de

Abstract. This paper presents a comparison of a traditional hybrid speech recognition system (kaldi using WFST and TDNN with lattice-free MMI) and a lexicon-free end-to-end (TensorFlow implementation of multi-layer LSTM with CTC training) models for German syllable recognition on the Verbmobil corpus. The results show that explicitly modeling prior knowledge is still valuable in building recognition systems. With a strong language model (LM) based on syllables, the structured approach significantly outperforms the end-to-end model. The best word error rate (WER) regarding syllables was achieved using kaldi with a 4-gram LM, modeling all syllables observed in the training set. It achieved 10.0% WER w.r.t. the syllables, compared to the end-to-end approach where the best WER was 27.53%. The work presented here has implications for building future recognition systems that operate independent of a large vocabulary, as typically used in a tasks such as recognition of syllabic or agglutinative languages, out-of-vocabulary techniques, keyword search indexing and medical speech processing.

Keywords: Speech recognition · Language model · CTC · End-2-End · Syllables

1 Introduction

Modeling syllables instead of words is a frequent choice for languages of syllabic nature. However, modeling syllables instead of words can also improve tasks related to automatic speech recognition (ASR) such as keyword search or identifying out-of-vocabulary (OOV) words [20,22]. Agglutinative languages, such as Turkish, Finish or Swahili, which form words by putting long successions of word units together can benefit from good syllable recognition as they regularly build new words from basic morphemes [5, p. 293]. Furthermore, speech therapy often relies on assessing different granularities of speech from phrases, words, syllables down to phones. For example, fluency in speech is often measured in terms of (dis-)fluent syllables or their durations [2,11,12,27].

Traditional word-based ASR systems typically depend on prior knowledge in form of pronunciation dictionaries. While these can grow up to millions of words, the resulting systems still regularly face OOV events. Phoneme recognition could

© Springer Nature Switzerland AG 2019
K. Ekštein (Ed.): TSD 2019, LNAI 11697, pp. 352–360, 2019.
https://doi.org/10.1007/978-3-030-27947-9_30

help to avoid those, however error rates are typically around 20–35% and thus not reliable enough [13]. This forms the motivation for syllable recognition. A languages such as German has about 40 phonemes and, due to its feature to form compound words, a near infinite vocabulary. Although it is hard to come up with a definite number, datasets suggest that about 3000 syllables – most of them of rare count – are sufficient to model large vocabularies.[1] The average length of German words are 1.83 syllables [5, p. 87].

End-to-End models have become increasingly popular in speech recognition over the last couple of years. Their success suggests that modeling prior knowledge of natural language has become insignificant. Especially Baidu's *Deep Speech* implementation has taken great part in establishing end-to-end speech recognition as a viable alternative to the traditional hybrid systems that combine hidden Markov models (HMM) and deep neural networks (DNN) [3,10]. These systems work under the assumption, that they are able to learn the acoustic model (AM) and the language model (LM) in a combined effort without the need for specialized prior-infused systems for each task. Results on large datasets indicate that no explicit language model is needed and prior knowledge about the language is in fact not important to successfully create ASR systems [3,6,9,21]. Due to the complexity of the models and the vast amount of data necessary, end-to-end systems require substantial resources to train which makes it relatively expensive to adapt these systems to new requirements, such as a different vocabulary or domain. A huge advantage of the traditionally structured systems is that they can in part be trained very quickly and easily adapted to a new context or new requirements. Another drawback of most end-to-end approaches is that they lack accurate time alignment information, which is needed for applications such as keyword search or paralinguistic speech processing.

Our Contribution. The contribution of this paper is a detailed comparison of a traditional hybrid HMM/DNN system and end-to-end multi-layer long short-term memory (LSTM) network trained using connectionist temporal classification (CTC) for syllable-based ASR using a medium-sized corpus of spontaneous German speech.

2 Data

For all experiments conducted for this paper, the Verbmobil (VM) corpus was used which comprises of recordings of the *VM1* and *VM2* partitions. It contains recordings of spontaneous dialogs of people making appointments and general travel planning over the phone. All systems were trained and evaluated on the published training and evaluation partitions.[2] The dataset used consists of 24435 utterances in 962 dialogs spoken by 629 speakers, the provided lexicon contains 9036 German words. The training set amounts to about 46 hours of audio. All audio data was sampled at 16 kHz and is exclusively in German [26]. We chose

---

[1] The vocabulary of the later used Verbmobil data consists 2825 distinct syllables.

[2] Dataset definitions can be obtained from `bas.uni-muenchen.de`.

the Verbmobil data over the larger Voxforge corpus since written text, and thus its read speech, is much more structured and fluent than spontaneous speech – which is the typical data for the applications described above. Since the LSTMs will jointly learn the language model, we preferred to stick to data which is closer related to the applications in question.

The lexicon with hand-labeled syllable boundary information was provided by the Friedrich Alexander University (FAU). It is a result of merging lexica that were created for the research projects EVAR [14], Verbmobil [26], SmartKom [19] and SmartWeb [25]. Guidelines used in its creation closely match the ones described in [4]. The lexicon itself was incomplete since it contained only words from the VM1 partition of the dataset. The missing 2963 entries in the lexicon were generated by using the phonetisaurus grapheme-to-phoneme (g2p) model trained on the FAU syllable lexicon.[3] For about 40 words, the g2p model was unable to produce a proper syllable representation and those were thus manually generated. The syllable transliteration of the training text were obtained by translating the text using the previously generated German syllable lexicon for the VM corpus.

3   Method

The experiments in this paper were conducted using the Kaldi [17] and SRILM toolkits [24]. The end-to-end systems were trained using the multi-purpose machine learning toolkit TensorFlow [1], using the same Kaldi-generated features. We use two "views" on the data: Six experiments were conducted using all (2825) syllables and six experiments were conducted using a subset of 199 syllables. This was done to reduce the number of targets for the CTC training and to reduce model size of the hybrid system. This split may seem arbitrary at first but was made because 80% of the dataset consisted of the most common 199 syllables. The remainder of the syllables amounted to only 20% of the data. Even though structured models handle many syllables well, it is interesting to study how that number affects their performance and to do a full fair comparision of the two modeling approaches.

The features used for both systems are 40-dimensional Mel Frequency Cepstral Coefficients (MFCC "hi-res") with cepstral mean and variance normalization (CMVN) applied. Although i-vectors result in slightly better performance [15], we did not include those since the point of our experiments is to compare traditional hybrid and end-to-end models.

3.1   Hybrid System

The setup of the kaldi speech recognition system is based on the kaldi Wall Street Journal (WSJ) recipe, which is a hybrid HMM/DNN system. For the training of the AM, the "nnet3 chain" implementation was used, which uses a time-delay

---

[3] G2P tool available online at https://github.com/AdolfVonKleist/Phonetisaurus.

neural network (TDNN) architecture with maximum mutual information (MMI) sequence-level objective function [16,18]. The targets for the DNN training are the context-dependent states obtained by forced alignments of an HMM/GMM baseline system.

For the reduced syllable set, the less common syllables were removed from the lexicon and therefore regarded as unknown (unk). Additionally, silence, laughter, noise, vocalized noise and unintelligible sounds were added to the lexicon. The basis for the experiments was a common word-based speech recognition system trained on the VM dataset yielding a word error rate (WER) of 8.7% with a lexicon containing 9036 words using a 4-gram word based LM with a perplexity of 59.53. Based on this system, the lexicon was replaced by the previously generated syllable lexicon, and the language model was replaced by a syllable-based language model.

Table 1. Syllable language model perplexities

	Reduced set	Full set
0-gram	201	2835
1-gram	88.97	287.59
4-gram	21.49	19.97

3.2 End-to-End System

Long short-term memory (LSTM) units are a special kind of unit in recurrent neural networks (RNN) that are able to learn long-term dependencies through a specific gating mechanism. The connectionist temporal classification (CTC) loss function uses a blank symbol and an enumeration of all possible alignments. This makes it slower but independent of per-frame time alignments and allows training deep neural networks for tasks that require long context [6]. For the end-to-end training, the original word-based transcripts were mapped to syllable transliterations.

The basic network type used in this paper were bidirectional LSTMs. This is especially useful in situations when future events can help to disambiguate current events. They were chosen because they produce good results for ASR [7,8]. The script used for training the models was based on Ford deepDSP's *deepSpeech* implementation[4] which is based on Deep Speech 2 [3]. All end-to-end models were trained using an ADAM optimizer. Learning rate decay was used to adapt the learning rate as training progressed from 0.001 down to 0.00003. The experiments were performed with three different network topologies. For the first two end-to-end experiments, a network with a single hidden layer and 256 nodes, was used. The following two experiments were conducted with three fully

---

[4] Base implementation source code available online under https://github.com/fordDeepDSP/deepSpeech.

connected hidden layers of 196 nodes each. For the final two experiments, we added regularization in form of dropout at training time (50%). Otherwise, the network still consisted of 3 hidden layers with 196 nodes each. Figure 1 shows the final topology. The output of the network was taken as is and no post-processing applied. At the time of writing, no lattice generation or LM-based prefix beam search was performed with the output of the bLSTM networks.

4   Experiments

4.1   Hybrid System

The baseline models to be compared to the end-to-end models that are assumed to learn AM an LM in one training, 0-gram (no prior) and 1-gram (weak prior) LMs were trained. The average length of German words is about 1.83 syllables [5, p. 87], thus a 4-gram syllable LM represents contextual knowledge about the composition of words plus some context. Perplexities for the language models evaluated on the test set can be found in Table 1. The LMs for all experiments always used the complete training set with either a complete or a reduced syllable set.

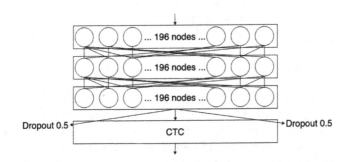

Fig. 1. Topology of the CTC-trained bLSTM network

The results for experiments performed with kaldi can be found on the left part of Table 2. As expected, the experiments with the 0-gram language model show very weak performance since they foremost rely on the AM. This confirms the important role of the LM in hybrid systems. The WER[5] for models with more syllables is consistently better; likewise, higher order LMs consistently perform better. With a WER of 10% the model with the 4-gram LM and the complete lexicon yields the best result overall. There is a huge improvement in WER from the 0-gram to the 1-gram model. Even a very simple LM with no contextual information leads to this huge improvements. With fewer syllables, the WER still improves but also shows problems of LM that rely on learned

---

[5] For the remainder of this article, WER is computed w.r.t. the syllable transcription.

sequences and lose some of their power when facing lots of unknown words. The test dataset consists of about 37,000 syllable instances of which about 6,800 instances were regarded as OOV (about 18%). This helps to put results for the reduced syllable experiments into perspective since decoding performance suffers significantly from a high OOV rate.

4.2   End-2-End System

Table 2 shows the WER results for the CTC-trained bLSTM experiments using three different network topologies. The results indicate that more layers lead to better performance, with a best WER result of 27.53% using the reduced number of syllables, dropout for regularization and three hidden layers. This confirms the assumption that deeper networks perform better and the network does better with fewer training targets. The difference in performance between reduced and full syllable sets almost vanishes for the networks where no dropout was performed. However, the reduction of targets does not appear to be a deciding factor: Relative improvement is only about 7.5% in WER and does not appear reasonable compared to the amount of information lost. On the other hand, adding dropout and more layers leads to a 24% relative improvement in performance for the experiments with the complete target set.

Table 2. WER results for experiments with the hybrid system compared to the end-to-end systems

System	Hybrid			End-to-End		
	0-gram	1-gram	4-gram	1 Layer	3 Layer	3 Layer + dropout
Reduced set	44.6	43.0	32.9	37.22	33.89	**27.53**
Full set	58.7	35.2	**10.0**	39.36	33.96	29.76

5   Discussion

A surprising observation is that the number of training targets (ie. syllables) does not seem to have a strong impact on the WER results as previously assumed for the bLSTM training. With more layers, the difference between decoding results almost vanishes just by adding additional layers. Dropout improves performance up to 18%, showing the importance of regularization and also confirming the assumption that depth is important [3, 8]. The bLSTM results are a bit worse than expected which could be due to the relatively small dataset.

The hybrid ASR system generally performs better with more targets as soon as it has some useful context information through the LM. This shows the huge impact of the LM on the decoding results. As expected, the results for the decoding with more unknown syllables are much worse than with all targets and a

4-gram LM. Also, the flexibility of the hybrid model is to be mentioned. Training times for the bLSTM networks were extensive, especially when compared to the swiftness of LM training and decoding graph generation. The hybrid system can easily be adapted to fit a new lexicon and language model. The results for this medium-sized dataset were significantly better.

Even though syllables and words are units of different size and error rates are not directly comparable without performing post-processing on the syllable recognition results, it is still interesting to see that error rates for syllable recognition are only slightly worse than the results for word recognition on this dataset. For future work, it might be important to evaluate the accuracy of the time alignments which are important to many downstream tasks such as keyword search or paralinguistic analyses.

6   Conclusion and Outlook

The direct training of an end-to-end system for syllable recognition is feasible but not as reliable as the hybrid system using a LM, which may be different with more training data. For this specific task with on a medium-sized corpus, the hybrid approach yields significantly better results. To achieve better performance with the bLSTMs, its output needs to be combined with LM based prefix beam search, or to train the syllable network along with a LM as proposed in [23].

For future experiments, we plan to investigate syllable-to-word transduction in order to build an end-to-end system that has high word accuracy while requiring little memory and CPU usage.

References

1. Abadi, M., et al.: TensorFlow: large-scale machine learning on heterogeneous systems (2015). https://www.tensorflow.org/, software available from tensorflow.org
2. Amir, O., Shapira, Y., Mick, L., Yaruss, J.S.: The speech efficiency score (SES): a time-domain measure of speech fluency. J. Fluency Disord. **58**, 61–69 (2018)
3. Amodei, D., et al.: Deep speech 2: End-to-end speech recognition in English and Mandarin. In: International Conference on Machine Learning, pp. 173–182 (2016)
4. Batliner, A., Möbius, B., Schweitzer, A., Goronzy, S., Rapp, S., RegelBrietzmann, P.: Guidelines for 'text-to-phone' (TTP) conversion, i.e., the sampa inventory plus some other conventions for the smartkom lexicon version 1.0. Technical report, Friedrich-Alexander-Universtität Erlangen Nürnberg (2001)
5. Crystal, D.: Die Cambridge Enzyklopädie der Sprache. Zweitausendeins Frankfurt a.M. (2004)
6. Graves, A., Fernández, S., Gomez, F., Schmidhuber, J.: Connectionist temporal classification: labelling unsegmented sequence data with recurrent neural networks. In: Proceedings of the 23rd International Conference on Machine Learning, pp. 369–376. ACM (2006)
7. Graves, A., Jaitly, N., Mohamed, A.R.: Hybrid speech recognition with deep bidirectional LSTM. In: 2013 IEEE Workshop on Automatic Speech Recognition and Understanding (ASRU), pp. 273–278. IEEE (2013)

8. Graves, A., Mohamed, A.R., Hinton, G.: Speech recognition with deep recurrent neural networks. In: 2013 IEEE International Conference on Acoustics, Speech and Signal Processing (ICASSP), pp. 6645–6649. IEEE (2013)
9. Hannun, A.Y., et al.: Deep speech: scaling up end-to-end speech recognition. CoRR abs/1412.5567 (2014). http://arxiv.org/abs/1412.5567
10. Hannun, A.Y., Maas, A.L., Jurafsky, D., Ng, A.Y.: First-pass large vocabulary continuous speech recognition using bi-directional recurrent DNNs. arXiv preprint arXiv:1408.2873 (2014)
11. Jani, L., Huckvale, M., Howell, P.: Procedures used for assessment of stuttering frequency and stuttering duration. Clin. Linguist. Phonetics **27**(12), 853–861 (2013)
12. Jones, M., Onslow, M., Packman, A., Gebski, V.: Guidelines for statistical analysis of percentage of syllables stuttered data. J. Speech Lang. Hear. Res. JSLHR **49**, 867–878 (09 2006)
13. Lopes, C., Perdigao, F.: Phoneme recognition on the timit database. In: Speech Technologies. InTech (2011)
14. Niemann, H., Brietzmann, A., Mühlfeld, R., Regel, P., Schukat, G.: The speech understanding and dialog system evar. In: De Mori, R., Suen, C.Y. (eds.) New Systems and Architectures for Automatic Speech Recognition and Synthesis, pp. 271–302. Springer, Heidelberg (1985). https://doi.org/10.1007/978-3-642-82447-0_10
15. Peddinti, V., Chen, G., Manohar, V., Ko, T., Povey, D., Khudanpur, S.: JHU aspire system: Robust LVCSR with TDNNS, IVECTOR adaptation and RNN-LMS. In: 2015 IEEE Workshop on Automatic Speech Recognition and Understanding, ASRU 2015, Scottsdale, AZ, USA, 13–17 December, 2015, pp. 539–546 (2015)
16. Peddinti, V., Povey, D., Khudanpur, S.: A time delay neural network architecture for efficient modeling of long temporal contexts. In: Sixteenth Annual Conference of the International Speech Communication Association (2015)
17. Povey, D., et al.: The kaldi speech recognition toolkit. In: IEEE 2011 Workshop (2011)
18. Povey, D., et al.: Purely sequence trained neural networks for ASR based on lattice free MMI (author's manuscript). Technical report, The Johns Hopkins University Baltimore United States (2016)
19. Reithinger, N., et al.: Smartkom: adaptive and flexible multimodal access to multiple applications. In: Proceedings of the 5th International Conference on Multimodal Interfaces, ICMI 2003, pp. 101–108. ACM, New York (2003)
20. Riedhammer, K., Do, V.H., Hieronymus, J.: A study on LVCSR and keyword search for tagalog. In: INTERSPEECH 2013, 14th Annual Conference of the International Speech Communication Association (ISCA), Lyon, France, August 2013
21. Sak, H., et al.: Learning acoustic frame labeling for speech recognition with recurrent neural networks. In: 2015 IEEE International Conference on Acoustics, Speech and Signal Processing (ICASSP), pp. 4280–4284. IEEE (2015)
22. Smit, P., Virpioja, S., Kurimo, M.: Improved subword modeling for WFST-based speech recognition. In: Proceedings of Interspeech 2017. Interspeech: Annual Conference of the International Speech Communication Association, pp. 2551–2555. International Speech Communication Association, August 2017
23. Sriram, A., Jun, H., Satheesh, S., Coates, A.: Cold fusion: training Seq2Seq models together with language models. arXiv preprint arXiv:1708.06426 (2017)
24. Stolcke, A.: SRILM - an extensible language modeling toolkit. In: Proceedings of the 7th International Conference on Spoken Language Processing (ICSLP 2002), pp. 901–904 (2002)

25. Wahlster, W.: SmartWeb: mobile applications of the semantic web. In: Biundo, S., Frühwirth, T., Palm, G. (eds.) KI 2004: Advances in Artificial Intelligence, pp. 50–51. Springer, Heidelberg (2004)

26. Wahlster, W.: Verbmobil: Foundations of Speech-to-Speech Translation. Springer, Heidelberg (2013). https://doi.org/10.1007/978-3-662-04230-4

27. Yaruss, J.: Clinical measurement of stuttering behaviors. Contemp. Issues Commun. Sci. Disord. **24**(24), 33–44 (1997)

LSTM-Based Speech Segmentation
for TTS Synthesis

Zdeněk Hanzlíček$^{(\boxtimes)}$, Jakub Vít, and Daniel Tihelka

New Technologies for the Information Society, Faculty of Applied Sciences,
University of West Bohemia, Pilsen, Czech Republic
{zhanzlic,jvit,dtihelka}@ntis.zcu.cz
http://www.ntis.zcu.cz

Abstract. This paper describes experiments on speech segmentation
for the purposes of text-to-speech synthesis. We used a bidirectional
LSTM neural network for framewise phone classification and another
bidirectional LSTM network for predicting the duration of particular
phones. The proposed segmentation procedure combines both outputs
and finds the optimal speech-phoneme alignment by using the dynamic
programming approach. We introduced two modifications to increase the
robustness of phoneme classification. Experiments were performed on 2
professional voices and 2 amateur voices. A comparison with a reference
HMM-based segmentation with additional manual corrections was performed. Preference listening tests showed that the reference and experimental segmentation are equivalent when used in a unit selection TTS
system.

Keywords: Speech segmentation · Speech synthesis ·
LSTM neural networks

1 Introduction

The aim of speech segmentation is to determine phone boundaries in a speech
recording when its orthographic transcription is given, i.e. phones are time-
aligned with speech. Sometimes, particular words could have more than one
correct pronunciation form. Then, an important task of the segmentation process is the selection of the accurate phonetic transcription which is closest the
actual pronunciation. And last but not least, the segmentation process could
also involve insertion of pauses and other non-speech events.

An accurate speech segmentation is important for many application in the
field of speech processing. A typical application is speech synthesis, especially
unit selection method [12] where the segmentation accuracy directly impacts the
quality of produced speech.

This research was supported by the Technology Agency of the Czech Republic, project
No. TH02010307 and by the Ministry of Education, Youth and Sports of the Czech
Republic project No. LO1506. Access to computing and storage facilities owned by
parties and projects contributing to the National Grid Infrastructure MetaCentrum
provided under the programme CESNET LM2015042, is greatly appreciated.

K. Ekštein (Ed.): TSD 2019, LNAI 11697, pp. 361–372, 2019.
https://doi.org/10.1007/978-3-030-27947-9_31

For a long time, HMM-based speech segmentation [3] with various modifications [2,10,17] was a predominant method [1]. Competitive methods were based e.g. on DTW [14], neural networks [4,21], or combined more methods [15].

Recently, neural networks play an important role in almost all fields of machine learning. One of the most employed type is long short-term memory (LSTM) recurrent neural network [9] which is good for modeling time series data, i.e. it is also suitable for speech processing applications [5]. It was already used for phone classification [7] or speech recognition [6] which are similar tasks to speech segmentation which could be wieved as speech recognition in forced-alignment mode.

The purpose of our research is to use LSTM-RNN for segmentation of speech corpora that were recorded for a unit selection TTS system. The language of the data is Czech and the research described in this paper is partly language dependent, e.g. it is related to the Czech phonetic alphabet. We suppose, it should be adjustable for different languages or generalizable to a language-independent system. However, this is far out of scope of this paper.

A reference segmentation created by a HMM-based segmentation system is available for our experimental data. However, the objective of this work is not a comparison of the HMM-based and LSTM-based segmentation methods, since the reference segmentation is a result of a complex process with several post-processing procedures and contains also a lot of additional manual corrections, whereas the experimental system is a core method with several basic improvements. The purpose of this research is to verify whether a LSTM-based system can produce a segmentation comparable with the reference one.

This paper is organized as follows: Sect. 2 briefly describes the neural network architecture. Section 3 gives an overview of the segmentation process and procedures for increasing the segmentation robustness are proposed in Sect. 4. Experiments and the evaluation are described in Sect. 5. Conclusions and plans for the future work are given in Sect. 6.

2   Network Architecture

For acoustic modeling, the network architecture stack consists of multiple bidirectional LSTM layers followed by linear projection and softmax activation – see Fig. 1. During training, cross entropy loss is minimized. The network tick rate is 200 Hz (5 ms one frame). The network's inputs consists of 13 normalized MFCCs. The audio waveform is downsampled to 16 kHz and preprocessed by preemphasis filter.

For duration modeling, we used another two-layer bidirectional LSTM network with additional linear projection and softmax activation – see Fig. 2. The network inputs a sequence of phones and outputs the distribution of duration for particular phones. The distribution has form of a relative histogram with 10 ms wide bins.

3   Segmentation Process

The network at Fig. 1 outputs a classification score matrix M_A (*alphabet matrix*), in which each row corresponds to one phone and columns correspond to the particular parameter frames. The matrix size is $N_A \times N_F$, where N_A is the number of phones in the alphabet and N_F is the length of the utterance in frames.

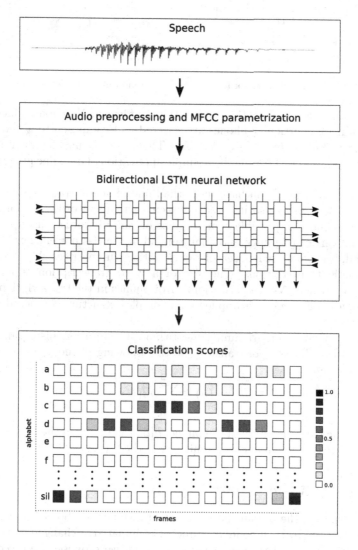

Fig. 1. Neural network for generating classification scores.

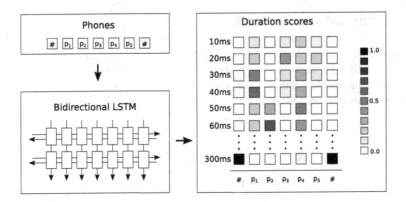

Fig. 2. Neural network for generating phone duration histograms.

According to given phonetic transcription T of length N_P phones, lines of M_A corresponding to particular phones are selected and composed to a new matrix M_T (*transcription matrix*) of size $N_P \times N_F$. Then, the optimal alignment between frames and phones can be found by a simple application of dynamic programming on M_T.

However, each word can have more than one phonetic transcription and an optional pause can be also inserted between particular words. For longer sentences, the number of possible combinations of various word transcriptions and pause insertions can be huge and analyzing all of them is not efficient.

Instead, we composed a set of transcription submatrices M_T for particular phonetic transcriptions. The size of a word transcription submatrix is $N_P(T) \times N_F$, where $N_P(T)$ is the number of phones in the transcription. Then, the dynamic programming is applied on a complex structure composed of these submatrices.

For the dynamic programming algorithm, the duration histograms h are turned to probabilities p_t of transition to the following phone

$$p_t(n) = \sum_{i=1}^{n/2} h[i] \tag{1}$$

where n is the running length of the phone, $h[i]$ is the value in the i-th histogram bin and the reason for upper sum limit $n/2$ is the 2 frames (10 ms) bin width[1].

4   Increasing Robustness

In natural speech, the pronunciation is not always perfect. Some phones can be heavily influenced by their context, reduced, assimilated or changed to a different (but similar) phone[2]. To cope with this problem, we proposed 2 procedures to

---

[1] The shape of the histogram can be interpolated to a one-frame resolution but it has only a marginal effect on the resulting alignment.

[2] The pronunciation could also be variously distorted or the text and speech could not match exactly. However, this problem is out of scope of our research.

increase the segmentation robustness. Both are based on an utilization of phone similarity. This section is partly language-dependent since it is proposed for the Czech phonetic alphabet. However, we believe this approach can be adjusted to most other languages, as well.

4.1   Reduction of Phonetic Alphabet

Some phones are acoustically similar. In speech synthesis, especially unit selection, distinguishing such phones is relevant for naturally sounding resulting speech. Compacting the phonetic alphabet so that all phones are well recognizable and distinguishable can increase the robustness of the segmentation process [8,11]. Haubold [8] performed detection of selected well-recognizable phones to cope with an improper text transcription. Hoffmann [11] increased the robustness by clustering the phones into phonetic groups.

We used a similar approach as Hoffmann [11]. We manually selected a set of basic phones and the remaining phones were replaced with the most similar basic phones. The reduction process can be expressed by the following substitutions (SAMPA notation [23] is used).

- unifying long and short vowels
  a: → a   e: → e   i: → i   o: → o   u: → u
- splitting diphthongs to vowels
  a_u → a + u   o_u → o + u   e_u → e + u
- splitting affricates
  d_z → d + z   d_Z → d + Z   t_s → t + s   t_S → t + S
- unifying selected voiced and unvoiced fricatives
  G → x   Q \→ P \
- unifying syllabic and non-syllabic consonants
  l= → l   m= → m   r= → r
- unifying similar nasals
  F → m   N → n

The default and reduced alphabets are listed in Table 1. The default alphabet contains 48 phones (10 vowels + 3 diphthongs + 35 consonants), the reduced alphabet consists of 29 phones (5 vowels + 24 consonants). The phonetic transcription by using the resulting reduced alphabet remains well-readable, which is a significant practical advantage. Besides, the lower size of alphabet reduces also the computational and memory demands.

We did not perform any throughout research to find an optimal reduced alphabet; the decision was based on subjective phone similarity. The level of reduction could be higher or lower, e.g. some other voiced-unvoiced consonant pairs could be unified. It is possible that results could be different for various voices, e.g. a more reduced alphabet could be suitable for speakers with a less precise pronunciation.

Using a reduced alphabet for segmentation has a significant limitation: since the reduction process is one-way, several originally different word transcription

Table 1. Default and reduced phonetic alphabet.

Default alphabet	Reduced alphabet
a, e, i, o, u a:, e:, i:, o:, u: a_u, e_u, o_u	a, e, i, o, u
p, b, t, d, c, J\, k, g, ? t_s, d_z, t_S, d_Z f, v, s, z, S, Z, j P\, Q\, x, h\, G r, l, l=, r= m, n, N, J, F, m=	p, b, t, d, c, J\, k, g, ? f, v, s, z, S, Z, j P\, x, h\ r, l, m, n, J

may collapse into one reduced transcription and the return into full phonetic alphabet (that is needed for the purposes of speech synthesis) is ambiguous.

Therefore we used the reduced alphabet only for an initial segmentation. Then, an additional segmentation with the full alphabet can be performed on smaller parts, e.g. on speech between pauses, words or just on phones that cannot be unambiguously turned back to the full alphabet. In our experiments, we simply applied the additional segmentation with the full alphabet on speech segments between pauses. Other alternatives may better utilize the previous robust segmentation; we intend to perform more experiments in the future.

4.2 Combining Classification Score of Similar Phones

The difference between some phonetic alternatives may be lost when the reduced alphabet is used. Therefore, the full alphabet must be used for the final selection of actual phonetic alternative.

The similarity of phones can be also utilized to increase the robustness in the scope of the full alphabet. The main idea is that phones that are supposed to be similar should have also similarly high scores. We propose a simple formula to combine the classification score p of similar phones

$$\bar{p}(i,j) = \max\{p(i,j), 0.9 \cdot p(i_1,j), \ldots 0.9 \cdot p(i_k,j)\} \tag{2}$$

where $i_1 \ldots i_k$ are indices corresponding to phones similar to i-th phone, j is frame index. The factors 0.9 are used to preserve a difference between similar phones. Otherwise, all similar phones would have an equal score and we could not effectively select from them.

4.3 Detection of Suspicious Units

During the segmentation process, the most suitable phonetic transcription of each word should be selected. However, only standard alternatives are taken into account during this procedure. In the case of a mispronunciation or a text-speech mismatch, the selected phonetic transcription does not exactly correspond to the spoken word.

For unit selection speech synthesis, such problematic speech segments should be detected and not included in the unit inventory; otherwise, using these improperly segmented phones can result in a significant degradation of produced speech.

We proposed a simple procedure for detection of such improperly segmented units. Since the actual reason for the misalignment cannot be determined, those segments/units are referred to as suspicious. The procedure analyses the classification score of all frames aligned with particular phones. For a perfectly segmented data, the highest score for each frame should correspond to the aligned phone. However, this is not always fulfilled even for audibly correct professional recordings. The highest score corresponds sometimes to a less-or-more similar phone and the aligned phone has a worse score.

We define the following simple condition for a correct segmentation: A phone is correctly segmented when the 1st or 2nd highest score corresponds to this phone or to a similar phone in the majority of its speech frames. The majority of speech frames was experimentally set to 2/3 and similar phones were considered analogously as in Sects. 4.1 and 4.2.

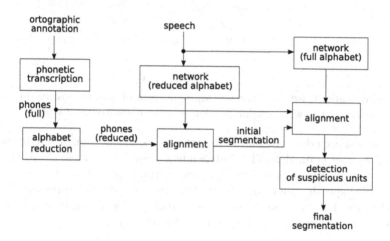

Fig. 3. An overview of the full segmentation process.

5   Experiments and Results

For our experiments, we utilized the following Czech speech data

- 7 large speech corpora recorded by professional voice talents (3 male and 4 female voices) for the purposes of unit selection speech synthesis [19];
- 16 smaller speech corpora recorded by amateur speakers recorded for various experiments with speech synthesis [13].

Speech data was supplemented by a phonetic segmentation created by a HMM-based segmentation procedure with various correction procedures [16,18]. Since the professional voices have been utilized for many years in a TTS system [20] and lots of additional manual corrections have been made over time, the phonetic transcription and segmentation can be considered very accurate. This phonetic segmentation was used as a reference segmentation for the following evaluation.

We selected 2 professional voices (male MP and female FP) and 2 amateur voices (male MA and female FA). For a detailed description of selected voices, see Table 2. The remaining (unselected) speech corpora have a similar size and content.

Table 2. Description of experimental speech data. The total speech duration [hh:mm:ss] is without initial and terminal pauses.

Speaker	Duration	#sentences	#words	#pauses	#phones
MP	14:43:50	12,129	156,607	13,684	624,592
FP	15:22:20	12,050	145,509	3,568	621,397
MA	1:54:17	1,962	18,063	1,039	73,277
FA	1:29:22	1,801	16,445	841	67,019

Since we cannot use the reference segmentation of selected voices during the training process, the whole segmentation process consisted of 2 stages.

1. We used speech data (including the reference segmentation) from unselected speakers and trained speaker-independent neural networks. Then, the segmentation process depicted in Fig. 3 was performed for the selected voices.
2. We added speech data from the selected speakers with the segmentation created in the 1st stage and trained new speaker-independent neural networks. Then, the segmentation process was performed again.

5.1 Objective Evaluation

To evaluate the similarity/difference between the reference and new segmentation, we computed statistics of the deviation between corresponding phone boundaries – see Tables 3 and 4. In both cases, all statistics improved significantly after the second stage, i.e. the final segmentation is closer to the reference one.

The effect of selecting the proper phonetic transcription during the segmentation process is illustrated in Table 5. Again, one can see an appreciable contribution of the 2nd segmentation stage – the final segmentation got closer to the reference one. An interesting issue is a big difference in pauses in the 1st stage segmentation for 3 of 4 speakers.

Table 3. Comparison of the reference and new segmentation after 1st and 2nd stage – absolute segmentation difference [ms].

Speaker	1st stage	2nd stage
MP	6.89 ± 9.99	4.09 ± 5.63
FP	5.33 ± 9.02	3.36 ± 4.88
MA	7.48 ± 10.42	6.41 ± 9.81
FA	6.85 ± 8.50	5.80 ± 8.83

Table 4. Comparison of the reference and new segmentation after 1st and 2nd stage – relative number [%] of units with segmentation difference in various intervals.

Speaker	1st stage				2nd stage			
	≤5 ms	≤10 ms	≤20 ms	≤50 ms	≤5 ms	≤10 ms	≤20 ms	≤50 ms
MP	53.94	81.22	94.90	99.31	73.24	93.82	98.77	99.83
FP	64.51	88.71	96.98	99.38	81.50	96.83	99.16	99.84
MA	50.12	78.05	94.31	99.19	57.32	83.75	95.64	99.29
FA	52.58	80.33	95.09	99.47	60.59	85.76	96.44	99.54

Statistics on suspicious units detected in particular speech corpora are presented in Table 6. The effect of removing suspicious units is illustrated by computing the absolute segmentation difference without those units. Compared to Table 3 with statistics for all units, all values are lower. Despite we did not do any deeper analysis, a proper boundary detection is obviously problematical for suspicious units. As expected, amateur voices contained (relatively) more suspicious units than professional voices. This is mainly caused by the speaking skills, recording conditions and the overall thoroughness of the recording process.

Table 5. Comparison of the reference and new segmentation after 1st and 2nd stage – the relative number [%] of different words, pauses and phones. The number of different phones was calculated as the Levenshtein distance with deletion/insertion and substitution costs equal to 1.

Speaker	1st stage			2nd stage		
	Words	Pauses	Phones	Words	Pauses	Phones
MP	2.79	3.67	0.83	2.20	2.08	0.61
FP	1.86	30,79	0.65	1.83	8.72	0.49
MA	2.32	20,13	1.02	2.82	11.62	0.94
FA	2.80	20.02	1.10	2.52	14.74	0.88

Table 6. Detection of suspicious units and its effect on the segmentation – absolute segmentation difference without suspicious units. The total number of units is given as phones + pauses.

Speaker	All units	Susp. units		Abs segmentation difference [ms]
	#	#	%	
MP	638,276	414	0.06	4.08 ± 5.58
FP	624,965	188	0.03	3.35 ± 8.80
MA	74,316	318	0.94	6.28 ± 8.89
FA	67,860	431	0.88	5.66 ± 7.82

5.2 Listening Test

Although many segmentation methods described in the literature improve the segmentation accuracy (in relation to a reference segmentation), the real impact on the TTS system performance (speech quality) is not always evident [1]. The best way to evaluate a new segmentation method is a perceptual test.

We conducted a simple preference test for a direct comparison of the reference and new segmentation. Ten sentences were synthesized by a unit selection TTS system [20] for each voice, i.e. test contained 40 pairs of utterances. 15 listeners took part in this test. Results are presented in Table 7. Although there are slight preferences for particular voices, there is no definite global preference.

Table 7. Results of the listening test.

Speaker	Ref. segmentation	No preference	New segmentation
MP	28.8	42.4	28.8
FP	34.4	35.6	30.0
MA	26.9	48.1	25.0
FA	22.5	40.0	37.5
All	28.2	41.5	30.3

6 Conclusion

This paper presented an initial research on neural network based speech segmentation. We performed experiments with 4 voices and compare resulting segmentation with a reference segmentation created by a HMM-based segmentation system. However, the objective of this paper was not a comparison of the HMM-based and LSTM-based segmentation methods, since the reference segmentation is a result of a complex process with tuned additional postprocessing and contains also some manual corrections, whereas the experimental system is a core method with several basic improvements. The purpose of this research was rather to verify whether a LSTM-based system can produce a segmentation comparable with the reference system.

The reference and experimental segmentations were also compared by their application in a unit selection TTS system. A preference listening test proved comparable results, i.e no segmentation was significantly preferred.

In our future work, we will focus on issues that need to be dealt with more thoroughly, e.g. the phone similarity and alphabet reduction was proposed only by our subjective decision. However, it should be rather based on a proper data analysis. The way of using the initial segmentation in the following stage was too trivial, most information was untapped. After comparing statistics from the 1st and 2nd stage, one could expect further iterative improvements; this is also worthy of further experiments.

We also intend to work with speech data that was not originally recorded for the purposes of speech synthesis, such as audio books, radio broadcasting, presentations etc. Such data are difficult to process [11,22] since it contains often very long recordings, the text annotation is not always fully correct and the speech quality or recording conditions may be unstable.

References

1. Adell, J., Bonafonte, A., Gómez, J.A., Bleda, M.J.C.: Comparative study of automatic phone segmentation methods for TTS. In: Proceedings of ICASSP, pp. 309–312 (2005)
2. Brognaux, S., Drugman, T.: HMM-based speech segmentation: Improvements of fully automatic approaches. IEEE/ACM Trans. Audio Speech Lang. Process. **24**(1), 5–15 (2016)
3. Brugnara, F., Falavigna, D., Omologo, M.: Automatic segmentation and labeling of speech based on hidden Markov models. Speech Commun. **12**, 357–370 (1993)
4. Finster, H.: Automatic speech segmentation using neural network and phonetic transcription. In: Proceedings of IJCNN (1992)
5. Graves, A.: Supervised Sequence Labelling with Recurrent Neural Networks. Studies in Computational Intelligence, vol. 385. Springer, Heidelberg (2012)
6. Graves, A., Jaitly, N.: Towards end-to-end speech recognition with recurrent neural networks. In: Proceedings of ICML, pp. 1764–1772 (2014)
7. Graves, A., Schmidhuber, J.: Framewise phoneme classification with bidirectional LSTM and other neural network architectures. Neural Netw. **18**, 602–610 (2005)
8. Haubold, A., Kender, J.R.: Alignment of speech to highly imperfect text transcriptions. In: Proceedings of ICME, pp. 224–227 (2007)
9. Hochreiter, S., Schmidhuber, J.: Long short-term memory. Neural Comput. **9**, 1735–1780 (1997)
10. Hoffmann, S., Pfister, B.: Fully automatic segmentation for prosodic speech corpora. In: Proceedings of Interspeech, pp. 1389–1392 (2010)
11. Hoffmann, S., Pfister, B.: Text-to-speech alignment of long recordings using universal phone models. In: Proceedings of Interspeech, pp. 1520–1524 (2013)
12. Hunt, A.J., Black, A.W.: Unit selection in a concatenative speech synthesis system using a large speech database. In: Proceedings of ICASSP, pp. 373–376 (1996)

13. Jůzová, M., Tihelka, D., Matoušek, J., Hanzlíček, Z.: Voice conservation and TTS system for people facing total laryngectomy. In: Proceedings of Interspeech, Stockholm, Sweden, pp. 3425–3426 (2017)
14. Kominek, J., Bennett, C.L., Black, A.W.: Evaluating and correcting phoneme segmentation for unit selection synthesis. In: Proceedings of Eurospeech, pp. 313–316 (2003)
15. Malfrère, F., Deroo, O., Dutoit, T., Risa, C.: Phonetic alignment: speech synthesis-based vs. viterbi-based. Speech Commun. **40**, 503–515 (2003)
16. Matoušek, J., Romportl, J.: Automatic pitch-synchronous phonetic segmentation. In: Proceedings of Interspeech, pp. 1626–1629 (2008)
17. Matoušek, J., Tihelka, D., Psutka, J.: Automatic segmentation for Czech concatenative speech synthesis using statistical approach with boundary-specific correction. In: Proceedings of Eurospeech, pp. 301–304 (2003)
18. Matoušek, J., Tihelka, D., Psutka, J.: Experiments with automatic segmentation for czech speech synthesis. In: Matoušek, V., Mautner, P. (eds.) TSD 2003. LNCS (LNAI), vol. 2807, pp. 287–294. Springer, Heidelberg (2003). https://doi.org/10.1007/978-3-540-39398-6_41
19. Matoušek, J., Tihelka, D., Romportl, J.: Building of a speech corpus optimised for unit selection TTS synthesis. In: Proceedings of LREC (2008)
20. Tihelka, D., Hanzlíček, Z., Jůzová, M., Vít, J., Matoušek, J., Grůber, M.: Current state of text-to-speech system ARTIC: a decade of research on the field of speech technologies. In: Sojka, P., Horák, A., Kopeček, I., Pala, K. (eds.) TSD 2018. LNCS (LNAI), vol. 11107, pp. 369–378. Springer, Cham (2018). https://doi.org/10.1007/978-3-030-00794-2_40
21. Toledano, D.T.: Neural network boundary refining for automatic speech segmentation. In: Proceedings of ICASSP, pp. 3438–3441 (2000)
22. Wang, L., et al.: Improved DNN-based segmentation for multi-genre broadcast audio. In: Proceedings of ICASSP, pp. 5700–5704 (2016)
23. Wells, J.: SAMPA computer readable phonetic alphabet. In: Handbook of Standards and Resources for Spoken Language Systems, pp. 684–732. Mouton de Gruyter, Berlin (1997)

Spoken Language Identification Using Language Bottleneck Features

Malo Grisard[1,2], Petr Motlicek[3], Wissem Allouchi[2], Michael Baeriswyl[2], Alexandros Lazaridis[3], and Qingran Zhan[3(✉)]

[1] Department of Electrical Engineering, EPFL, Lausanne, Switzerland
[2] Artificial Intelligence and Machine Learning Group, Swisscom, Switzerland
[3] Idiap Research Institute, Martigny, Switzerland
qingran.zhan@idiap.ch

Abstract. In this paper, we introduce a novel approach for Language Identification (LID). Two commonly used state-of-the-art methods based on UBM/GMM I-vector technique, combined with a back-end classifier, are first evaluated. The differential factor between these two methods is the deployment of input features to train the UBM/GMM models: conventional MFCCs, or deep Bottleneck Features (BNF) extracted from a neural network. Analogous to successful algorithms developed for speaker recognition tasks, this paper proposes to train the BNF classifier directly on language targets rather than using conventional phone targets (i.e. international phone alphabet). We show that the proposed approach reduces the number of targets by 96% when tested on 4 languages of SpeechDat databases, which leads to 94% reduction in training time (i.e. to train BNF classifier). We achieve in average, relative improvement of approximately 35% in terms of cost average C_{avg}, as well as Language Error Rates (LER), across all test duration conditions.

Keywords: Bottleneck features · Language identification · Language targets · Deep Neural Network

1 Introduction

Language Identification (LID) is the task of automatically recognizing the language that is being spoken. This task can be carried out using different levels of language representations, whether it can be phones, words, or universal speech features. In the early 1990s, phonotactic models had been proposed, exploiting phone-based acoustic likelihood ratios [8] to identify the language. In the recent years, many acoustic approaches have been proposed, or borrowed especially from Speaker Recognition (SR), often based on Universal Background Model (UBM)/Gaussian Mixture Model (GMM) framework [12]. One of the best performing LID, established today as one of a baseline systems, is based on UBM/GMM I-vector approach [1,4,9]. Nonetheless, the growth in available computational power has shifted the focus, in language identification domain as well, towards neural networks based approaches.

In automatic speech recognition, neural networks have become a widely used technique rapidly expanding to other fields of speech processing. Proposed bottleneck features (i.e. BNF vectors) [7] extracted from a narrow layer of neural network have shown to convey information about phonetic content in a non-linearly

K. Ekštein (Ed.): TSD 2019, LNAI 11697, pp. 373–381, 2019.
https://doi.org/10.1007/978-3-030-27947-9_32

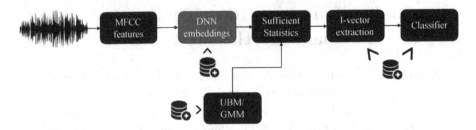

Fig. 1. UBM/GMM$_L$-IV-LR system for language identification. UBM, I-vector extractor and back-end classifier (e.g. logistic regression) are data-driven blocks.

compressed form, which can be directly used as features for GMM modelling. In LID, this approach has shown a remarkable improvement over UBM/GMM I-vector, proposing a linear bottleneck (i.e. phone embedding) layer produced by Deep Neural Networks (DNNs) [3,10,11]. DNNs were trained on phone targets using a small hidden layer representing a phone-embedding (i.e. BNFs). In [11], authors have shown that BNFs when employed as an input to a UBM/GMM i-vector based system, significantly outperform conventional MFCCs on NIST LRE 2007 task [15]. Long Short Term Memory (LSTM) networks were also proposed to take better advantage of the temporal information incorporated in a speech segment [5]. In SR, the aforementioned approach was later adapted by inserting a temporal pooling layer into the network to handle variable-length segments [14]. Inspired by previous work in the LID and SR domains, this paper proposes to extract embedding vectors from a DNN directly trained on language-targets. More specifically we investigate building an embeddings space which can incorporate more information for each language. We hypothesize that extracting BNFs by using phone-embeddings is a sub-optimal approach in language identification. Instead, we presume that the extracted language-embeddings will be more representative for LID task. In practice, when building a DNN to extract bottleneck features, phone targets are replaced by language targets. Additionally, replacing the phone-targets at the output of DNN by language-targets brings a significant reduction in training time.

The remaining of this paper is organized as follows: Sect. 2 presents related work in language identification, together with the baseline LID systems considered in this paper. Section 3 presents the proposed work, while Sect. 4 describes our experimental setup. The results are discussed in Sect. 5 and conclusions are given in Sect. 6.

2   Related Work

The traditional architecture applied in the LID task is shown in Fig. 1. First, statistics from the input speech features are extracted at a frame-level. A DNN is then trained to extract phoneme-embeddings [3,10,11]. The embedding vectors estimated at the frame-level are then projected on an acoustic space to train a UBM/GMM model. An I-vector extractor is then trained to extract the relevant

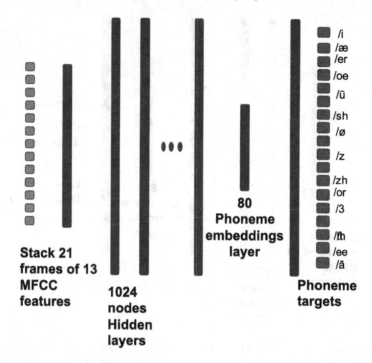

Fig. 2. DNN architecture to extract embedding (BNF) vectors. The neural net is trained on phone targets, thus extracting low dimensional phone embeddings.

information from speech (i.e. projecting a variable-length speech to a fixed low dimensional vector). The low dimensional I-vectors are finally fed to a back-end classifier to detect the language.

2.1 BNF Extraction

Bottleneck features (BNF) trained in the following discriminative framework are used to represent the acoustic space of speech. A DNN model is used, employing seven hidden layers, trained using conventional MFCC features. The DNN is trained to discriminate the phone targets as this is the case in acoustic modelling in Automatic Speech Recognition (ASR) tasks. The weights of the compressed hidden layer of the DNN are considered as phone embedding representations, which are estimated at a frame-level and further applied to train a UBM/GMM model. The architecture of the DNN is shown in Fig. 2.

2.2 UBM/GMM

A UBM is built using the input features to represent the acoustic space of the speech [12]. The UBM is represented by a large number of Gaussian mixtures. It is expected to cover the acoustic space across all languages, if sufficient amount of training data is used.

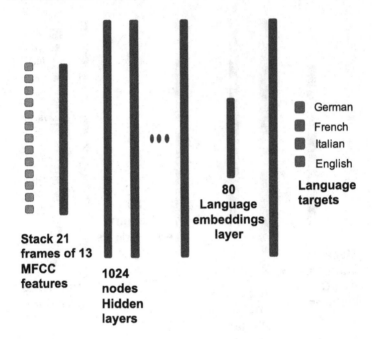

Fig. 3. Proposed DNN architecture used to extract embedding (BNF) vectors. Here, the network is trained on language targets to output a language embedding allowing the network to discriminate among languages directly.

2.3   I-Vector Extractor

The I-vector or total variability space approach is a technique borrowed from the speaker recognition field [1]. It consists of a mapping of a sequence of frames of speech into a low-dimensional vector space, i.e., the total variability space. The motivation for the use of I-vectors in speech is to convey speech information of variable length into a fixed-length feature vector. Unlike joint factor analysis [6], the I-vector approach models all important variability (language, speaker, channel, etc.) in the same fixed dimensional space.

2.4   Language Identification

Most of the related work in LID has focused on extracting features representative of the language fed to a back-end LID classifier to predict the spoken language. Since LID is a closed-set classification task (i.e. with limited number of classes), there is no need to apply Probabilistic Linear Discriminant Analysis (PLDA) [9], often implemented in SR for its inter-class distribution modeling. In [9], Martinez et al. experimented with Support Vector Machines (SVMs) and Logistic Regression (LR) as back-end language classifiers. The results of their experiments led to an optimal performance using LR. LR is deployed in this work as well.

We will consider two different baseline front-ends in this work:

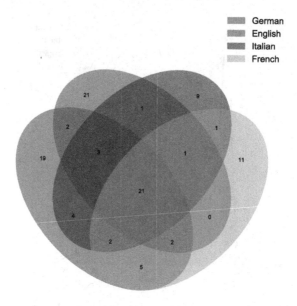

German
English
Italian
French

Fig. 4. Languages' manifolds in the phone space.

Table 1. Language dataset sizes.

Language	Hours	Utterances
German	30.11	108'422
French	25.45	91'612
Italian	17.25	62'127
English	22.64	81'534
Total	93	343'695

- **UBM/GMM-IV-LR** - UBM/GMM I-vector model developed using MFCC features, followed by the logistic regression back-end.
- **UBM/GMM$_P$-IV-LR** - hybrid UBM/GMM I-vector model considering embedding (BNF) vectors extracted using phone-based DNN, followed by the logistic regression back-end.

3 Proposed DNN Embeddings

In this paper, we hypothesize that DNN embeddings can be more relevant for language discrimination if they are trained on language targets rather than trained on phone targets. This paper therefore proposes an architecture to train the LID front-end while reducing the number of target classes (i.e. equal to the number of considered languages). We denote this technique as **UBM/GMM$_L$-IV-LR**, replacing phone targets of the DNN by language targets, as shown in Fig. 3.

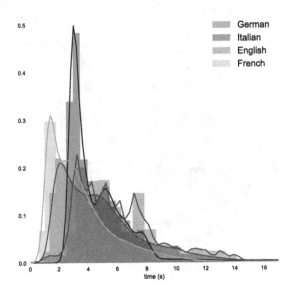

Fig. 5. Utterance duration distribution per language.

Table 2. LID performance for 3 different utterance-length conditions, and the average performance overall data.

Model	C_{avg}				LER in %			
Utterance-length	Avg	$<3\,s$	$[3,\,10]\,$s	$>10\,s$	Avg	$<3\,s$	$[3,\,10]\,$s	$>10\,s$
UBM/GMM-IV-LR	2.40	4.33	1.43	1.29	3.60	8.45	1.84	0.87
UBM/GMM$_P$-IV-LR	1.38	1.72	1.34	1.55	2.09	2.80	1.82	1.46
UBM/GMM$_L$-IV-LR	0.90	1.30	0.72	0.71	1.36	2.47	0.96	0.72

Following the second baseline principle of BNFs, our method proposes a critical reduction in the number of training targets. Keeping training costs in mind, we built our method in such a way that 21 stacked MFCC frames will lead to 1 BNF (i.e. by segmenting speech and zero padding if necessary). Assuming 13 dimensional MFCCs and 80 dimensional embedding layers, the DNN front-end can be seen as a function $Y = F(X)$, where Y is an output matrix of size $(N/21, 80)$ and an input matrix X of the size $(N, 13)$. N is the number of frames of the speech segment. This frame sub-sampling leads to a faster training of the UBM. Not only should the embeddings hold more language information but the neural network training itself is significantly faster.

4   Experiments

During the development, we used two GPU GTX 1080 TI with 12 Intel cores I7 Xseries. The implementation of the models was done using Kaldi[1] toolkit.

---

[1] http://kaldi-asr.org/doc/.

Table 3. Systems' training time comparison.

Model	Total in hours	$\frac{Total}{Total_{Baseline}}$
UBM/GMM-IV-LR	63.75	100%
UBM/GMM$_P$-IV-LR	183.75	288%
UBM/GMM$_L$-IV-LR	70.35	110%

For training and testing, we used respectively 50 K and 10 K utterances from each language which resulted in a training set of 200 K and a testing set of 40 K utterances. Input speech was characterized by 13 dimensional MFCCs with a frame rate of 10 ms, applying 25 ms hamming windows. Voice Activity Detection (VAD) was applied after MFCC feature extraction to remove non-speech frames. Both MFCC and VAD modules were borrowed from Kaldi [13]. **UBM/GMM-IV-LR**, **UBM/GMM$_P$-IV-LR** and **UBM/GMM$_L$-IV-LR** were built with a 1'024 UBM/GMM and 400 dimensional I-vectors. I-vector extractors were trained with 5 iterations using the Kaldi routine from "lre07" example. DNNs were trained with a learning rate of 10^{-4}, patches of size 64 were used. DNNs were trained with cross-entropy loss and the Adam Optimizer.

The "Speechdat" datasets [2] are telephone recordings from both fixed and mobile networks. Each dataset holds the same amount of male and female speakers. The datasets have a vast coverage of speaking styles (e.g., short commands, carefully pronounced speech, spontaneous speech). The audio files are recorded in A-law, 16 bit, 8 kHz format.

The languages used in this work are German, Swiss-French, Italian and British-English. Table 1 presents the amount of data points (utterances) we have used for each language as well as the total hours of speech. In order to build the **UBM-GMM$_P$-IV-LR** baseline, an ASR system was initially developed to obtain a phone alignment, further used to train the phone-DNN front-end. For each language dataset, minor modifications were made to the universal Speech Assessment Method Phonetic Alphabet (SAMPA[2]) dictionary. A diagram shown in Fig. 4 presents the language manifolds in the phone space resulting in 102 classes. The figure reveals that phone classes are not the most language discriminative units to identify the language.

Figure 5 shows the utterance duration distribution of each language set. Class distributions are unbalanced within the 3 speech duration groups, used to evaluate LID systems (i.e. inferior to 3 s, between 3 s and 10 s, superior to 10 s). Keeping the goal to detect the spoken language in real-time, the SpeechDat appears to be an appropriate corpus, as recordings are mostly represented by short utterances.

We apply several performance metrics in this paper. First, Language Error Rate (LER) is computed for each language (i.e. specifically for all 3 speech duration groups, as well as the overall LER). Then we apply the Cost average (C_{avg}), suggested by the NIST evaluation plan [15]. Finally, we also present the training time for each model.

---

[2] https://www.phon.ucl.ac.uk/home/sampa/.

5   Results

Overall, the proposed model **UBM/GMM$_L$-IV-LR** outperforms the **UBM/GMM-IV-LR** and **UBM/GMM$_P$-IV-LR** baselines in terms of LER and C_{avg} and **UBM/GMM$_P$-IV-LR** in terms of the computational load. Table 2 shows the detailed performance of the evaluated models in terms of C_{avg} and LER. As can be seen, significantly better scores are achieved in terms of C_{avg} and LER for all 3 utterance-length conditions.

5.1   Computational Costs

Table 3 shows the computational costs required to train the LID front-ends (i.e. in hours). Obviously, **UBM/GMM-IV-LR** is the most efficient model since no bottleneck features are extracted on top of MFCCs. Nevertheless, **UBM/GMM$_L$-IV-LR** requires only 10% more time while LER is reduced by half. **UBM/GMM$_L$-IV-LR** is lighter than **UBM/GMM$_P$-IV-LR** because the DNN is trained solely on four targets rather than 102 phone targets. The 96% reduction of the number of DNN targets in **UBM/GMM$_L$-IV-LR** led to a reduction in training time by 94%, compared to **UBM/GMM$_P$-IV-LR** baseline.

6   Conclusion

This paper investigates fully adapted embeddings spaces for language identification. We hypothesised that extracting BNFs by using phone-embeddings was a sub-optimal approach. Instead, we presumed the extracted language-embeddings would be more representative for the LID. The results of our experiment validated our hypothesis, as language-DNN front-end significantly increases the LID performance as well as is less computationally expensive. In average, 35% relative reduction in both C_{avg} and LER is achieved across all 3 utterance-length conditions.

Acknowledgement. This work was partially supported by several industrial projects at Idiap and the China Scholarship Council.

References

1. Dehak, N., Kenny, P.J., Dehak, R., Dumouchel, P., Ouellet, P.: Front-end factor analysis for speaker verification. IEEE Trans. Audio Speech Lang. Process. **19**(4), 788–798 (2011)
2. Elenius, K., Lindberg, J.: SpeechDat Speech Databases for Creation of Voice Driven Teleservices. Phonum 4, Phonetics, pp. 61–64 (1997). http://www.speech.kth.se/prod/publications/files/538.pdf
3. Fér, R., Matějka, P., Grézl, F., Plchot, O., Cernocký, J.H.: Multilingual bottleneck features for language recognition. In: Proceedings of the Annual Conference of the International Speech Communication Association, INTERSPEECH 2015, pp. 389–393, January 2015

4. Glembek, O., Burget, L., Matějka, P., Karafiát, M., Kenny, P.: Simplification and optimization of i-vector extraction. In: 2011 IEEE International Conference on Acoustics, Speech and Signal Processing (ICASSP), pp. 4516–4519, May 2011
5. Gonzalez-Dominguez, J., Lopez-Moreno, I., Sak, H., Gonzalez-Rodriguez, J., Moreno, P.J.: Automatic language identification using long short-term memory recurrent neural networks. In: Proceedings of Interspeech, pp. 2155–2159 (2014)
6. Kenny, P.: Joint factor analysis of speaker and session variability: Theory and algorithms. Technical report (2005)
7. Kramer, M.A.: Nonlinear principal component analysis using auto-associative neural networks. AIChEJ **37**(2), 233–243 (1991)
8. Díez, M., Varona, A., Peñagarikano, M., Rodríguez-Fuentes, L.J., Bordel, G.: On the use of phone log-likelihood ratios as features in spoken language recognition. SLT, pp. 274–279 (2012)
9. Martinez, D., Plchot, O., Burget, L., Glembek, O., Matějka, P.: Language recognition in ivectors space. In: Twelfth Annual Conference of the International Speech Communication Association (2011)
10. Matejka, P., Cumani, S., Ondel, L., Mounika, K.V., Silnova, A., Rohdin, J.: BUT-PT System Description for NIST LRE **2017**, 748097 (2017)
11. Matejka, P., et al.: Neural network bottleneck features for language identification. Odyssey, the Speaker and Language Recognition Workshop, pp. 299–304, June 2014
12. Povey, D., Chu, S.M., Varadarajan, B.: Universal background model based speech recognition. In: 2008 IEEE International Conference on Acoustics, Speech and Signal Processing, pp. 4561–4564. IEEE (2008)
13. Povey, D., et al.: The kaldi speech recognition toolkit. In: IEEE 2011 Workshop on Automatic Speech Recognition and Understanding. IEEE Signal Processing Society, December 2011, iEEE Catalog No.: CFP11SRW-USB
14. Snyder, D., Ghahremani, P., Povey, D., Garcia-Romero, D., Carmiel, Y., Khudanpur, S.: Deep neural network-based speaker embeddings for end-to-end speaker verification. In: 2016 IEEE Spoken Language Technology Workshop (SLT), pp. 165–170, December 2016
15. US department of commerce, N.: The 2007 NIST Language Recognition Evaluation Plan (LRE07). NIST Web document, pp. 1–5 (2007). https://catalog.ldc.upenn.edu/docs/LDC2009S04/LRE07EvalPlan-v8b-1.pdf

Dialogue

Question-Answering Dialog System for Large Audiovisual Archives

Adam Chýlek[1]([✉]), Luboš Šmídl[2], and Jan Švec[1]

[1] NTIS - New Technologies for Information Society, Faculty of Applied Sciences,
University of West Bohemia, Pilsen, Czech Republic
{chylek,honzas}@ntis.zcu.cz
[2] Department of Cybernetics, Faculty of Applied Sciences,
University of West Bohemia, Pilsen, Czech Republic
smidl@kky.zcu.cz

Abstract. In this paper, we present our spoken dialog system that serves as a search interface of the MALACH archive. The voice interface and natural language input allow the users to retrieve information contained in large audiovisual archives more comfortably. Especially, finding answers to a more structured question should be easier in comparison with typical search input options. The dialog is build on top of a system that automatically annotates and indexes the archive using automatic speech recognition. These indexes were searchable so far only in a full-text search for any arbitrary text query. Our proposed approach improves this system and leverages named entity recognition to create a knowledge base of semantic information contained in the recognized utterances. We describe the design of the dialog system, as well as the automatic knowledge base generation and the approach to creating queries using a spoken natural language as an input.

Keywords: Knowledge base generation ·
Natural language processing · Question answering · Dialog system

1 Introduction

Nowadays it is easy to collect and store a large amount of audiovisual data. Annotating and searching such archives is a different story. Our research was done on the MALACH archive of Holocaust testimonies[1]. This archive is made of thousands of hours of video footage containing interviews and personal testimonies of Holocaust survivors and witnesses. The archive is maintained by the USC Shoah Foundation[2], its collection was initiated by the Shoah Visual History Foundation founded by Steven Spielberg. It serves as a valuable resource for contemporary historians and future generations.

Focusing on English [13] and Czech [12] part of the archive we have hundreds of hours of video for each language annotated mostly only by manually assigned

---

[1] https://malach.umiacs.umd.edu/.
[2] https://sfi.usc.edu/.

© Springer Nature Switzerland AG 2019
K. Ekštein (Ed.): TSD 2019, LNAI 11697, pp. 385–397, 2019.
https://doi.org/10.1007/978-3-030-27947-9_33

keywords, hence limiting the ability to search the archives only to a sparse subset of handpicked keywords. Although we chose the MALACH archive as our data source, the limited availability of searchable keywords is common also to other archives (e.g. TV or radio broadcast archives) and our approach can be also used in these cases.

Prior to our research, the authors of [14] developed a search engine that allowed searching for any arbitrary text in these archives. Their approach uses automatic speech recognition (ASR) of the audio sources to create a searchable index.

We further improve the indexation by incorporating spoken language understanding (SLU), namely semantic entity detection. We will describe how this creates a knowledge base that stores additional semantic information from the interviews.

We also focus on improving the accessibility of the information stored in the knowledge base. Using the SLU on the archived data alone would still require the user to have specific knowledge about the search query format (e.g. the use of "OR", "NOT" keywords). To mitigate the need for such knowledge, we have developed a dialog system on top of the knowledge base that accepts queries in spoken natural language and presents the results using speech and a graphical interface.

In the following paragraphs, we give the reader an overview of related work, describe how we create our knowledge base, how we map the natural language onto the database queries and how we bind it all into a dialog system. We conclude the paper with future research plans.

2   Related Work

Our research focuses on applying information retrieval, question answering, natural language understanding, database query generation and dialog management on a contemporary problem - searching in large audio-visual archives.

The combination of these parts is usually researched in relation to question answering from the semantic web [3,8] or text comprehension [2] using a statistical approach. The authors of [1] even show promising results learning end-to-end dialog on a common DSTC (Dialog State Tracking Challenge) benchmark [20].

In contrast, we have limited data for the statistical approach. We felt encouraged that systems based on experts' knowledge (e.g. for the dialog management, query templates) are still performing well on the DSTC tasks [6]. Therefore we will stick to the handcrafted knowledge sources and the handcrafted dialog strategy and focus on the ease of extendibility.

The author of [8] explores similarly to us the question answering using a knowledge base from readily available heterogeneous sources. In contrast, we handle the creation of the knowledge base ourselves and from homogenous sources. Constructing a homogenous knowledge base benefits the whole system, as shown in [5].

Regarding the individual parts, our approach to using spoken language understanding for spoken content retrieval comes from an extensive overview in [7] and from the experience our research team has in SLU. The database query generation is inspired by normalized queries from [3] and the dialog management follows loosely dialog acts and flow from [15].

3 Creating the Knowledge Base

The input to our system for the knowledge base generation (Fig. 1) is video footage with an interview that has separate audio channels for the interviewer and the interviewee. In our pipeline, we extract the audio and feed it to an ASR system [17]. This ASR uses an acoustic model trained on the audio from the available footage and language model from the transcribed part of the dataset. We have processed both the English and the Czech parts of the MALACH archive.

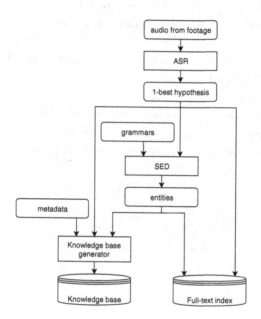

Fig. 1. The schema of the offline knowledge base generation.

The output of the ASR system is a word lattice that is then used as an input to our knowledge base generator. The source footage is processed only upon addition to the system. This means we can use offline processing and do not have to worry about processing times.

We are using a semantic entity detection (SED) approach described in [16] to find the entities in multiple ASR hypotheses using weighted finite state transducers. This approach uses a 1-best hypothesis that our ASR system generates and outputs a list of detected semantic entities.

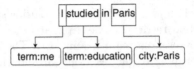

Fig. 2. In an utterance "I studied in Paris" we will detect three entities, represented as strings "terms:me", "terms:education" and "city:Paris". The first two entities belong to the class "terms" that contains important terms and phrases related to the speaker. The last entity belongs to the "city" class.

Table 1. Triples stored for the example from Fig. 2. The subject and the object are written in the form of "value":type tuple. For the sake of clarity of the example, we omitted the metadata and additional properties that we store, e.g. for the Word type we also store the timestamp when the word was uttered and the position in the recognized word sequence.

subject	predicate	object
"I":Word	entityStart	"terms:me":Entity
"I":Word	next	"studied":Word
"studied":Word	entityStart	"terms:education":Entity
"studied":Word	next	"in":Word
"in":Word	next	"Paris":Word
"Paris":Word	entityStart	"city:Paris":Entity
"file8266.1.wav":File	recognition	"I":Word
"id8266":Interview	recording	"file8266.1.wav":File

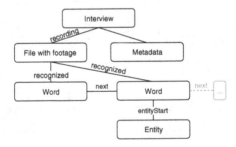

Fig. 3. A simplified schema of the graph of the objects that are stored in the knowledge base. The root of the graph is an object that represents the whole interview, connected to its metadata and files with the interview footage. These files relate to words the ASR recognized in the audio channel. The semantic entities detected in the output of the ASR keep the reference to their original word forms.

The semantic entities are defined in context-free grammars by their word forms (e.g. semantic entity "mother" is described as "mother *OR* mom *OR* ma"). The entities can be arranged in a hierarchy, saying for example that "mother" is a "family member".

We have created grammars for entity classes that we consider to be the most useful to the dialog system in our domain: cities, countries, dates, names, proper nouns, family members, life events (e.g. birth, death, injury), education and other geographical places (e.g. camp names).

We run our algorithms once an audiovisual file is added to the source file storage. Apart from the word index for the previous search engine, we create a new searchable knowledge base from the detected semantic entities.

We process both the English and Czech portion of the corpora the same way. The only language-specific parts are the ASR (trained individually for each language) and the grammars (localized word forms, but the entities and the hierarchy stay the same).

The knowledge base if formed by (subject, predicate, object) triples. Apart from the semantic entities, we also store in the knowledge base the 1-best hypothesis from the ASR, the reference to the audiovisual source file and the metadata that were available for each speaker. For example, from the utterance in Fig. 2 we would store triples that are listed in Table 1. The triples create a graph-like structure for each interview as depicted in Fig. 3.

The design of the database (predicates and types) allows us to find answers to queries that were not possible to find using just a full-text search. We will show that using this structure we can create database queries that answer questions the user may ask. For example, the user can utter a natural language query "Who was born in Paris?" and receive a spoken answer (e.g. "sister") together with video footage where the answer is mentioned.

On the other hand, the index is missing any deeper knowledge inference, e.g. creating instances of family members and representing the facts about them. When we recognize sentences such as "My sister was born in April in Paris, she studied in Bern and later moved to Berlin." we would like to understand the coreference and store that the speaker's sister was born in April in Paris, studied in Bern and moved to Berlin. Right now, we only know that such entities were detected near each other and ignore that they belong to a single instance of the sister entity.

We are not able to extract this knowledge without any deeper syntactic and semantic analysis, but the design of the knowledge base is ready for such additional data.

Preliminary work has been done to assess whether our system will be able to infer and represent some of that knowledge using a tectogrammatical trees generated by TreeX [11]. This semantically oriented structural representation of the recognized utterance should be able capture the relationship between the entities. This expansion of knowledge base shows promises, but it will need to be researched further.

Furthermore, using output of the ASR for the TreeX algorithm is quite challenging, as the algorithm expects sentences with punctuation as its input, but we are only able to provide word sequences from the whole recognized audio segment (ca. 10 min) without any punctuation or sentence boundaries. Nevertheless, we have successfully enriched part of the knowledge base with these trees and created possible templates for the queries, leaving space for future research.

4 Dialog Management

With the information from the footage stored in our knowledge base, we now focus on describing the design of our agent-based dialog system. We describe how the user can use natural language to request information, ask follow-up questions or execute actions on the results. The interaction can be multimodal. We also describe the responses the system presents using a graphical user interface (GUI) and a text-to-speech synthesis (TTS).

We are using our in-house developed modular cloud-based framework Speech-Cloud for speech recognition, spoken language understanding, dialog management and text-to-speech synthesis. This framework also allows us to send messages to and from the graphical user interface. The graphical user interface is created as a web page.

As opposed to the ASR used for the knowledge base generation, this time we are using an online recognition, processing the user's utterance in real time. The ASR's acoustic model was trained on LibriSpeech [10] for the English part and on the archive footage for the Czech part. The language model was created from the transcribed portion of the MALACH archive.

The SLU module uses the same grammars as we use for the knowledge base generation (described in Sect. 3) since we know the user can look only for the things that are contained in these grammars. For the dialog, we need to include only an additional small set of grammars. They contain entities such as question type (who, when, etc.) and dialog actions (go back, repeat, play). To make the input to the dialog system more robust we leverage our ability to augment the recognizer's language model using the words from the grammars that we use for the SLU.

As mentioned in the introduction, we are enhancing an existing search platform that already had a rich graphical interface in form of a dynamic web page. This allows us to create a multimodal dialog - apart from the spoken dialog, we also show the video footage with the results on the screen and allow interaction with them. The structure of the whole system is depicted in Fig. 4. The ASR and TTS interfaces are integrated into that web page and controls to start and to stop the recognition are available to the user. We also allow textual input in natural language.

The framework is event-driven. Each module can dispatch its events and other modules can choose to react to them. The dialog manager reacts to messages from the SLU module and from the GUI. It then updates the dialog state and produces some event (if necessary). These events can be a request to the TTS modules or to the GUI (e.g. play a file, display search results).

The dialog manager itself is designed to be easily extended with event handlers and dialog agents. In the dialog manager, the events from the SpeechCloud framework are passed to the individual event-handling modules (Fig. 4). Some of the events the manager receives and processes are: recognition results with a 1-best hypothesis, results from the SLU module, the level of the input signal, the start or the end of the recognition, the start or the end of the synthesis and finally a change of the playing footage in the GUI.

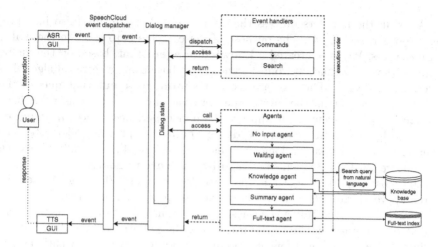

Fig. 4. The schema of the dialog manager reacting to the user's input that we receive as events from the SpeechCloud framework. The event handlers first parse the event's content, alter the dialog state and then the agents react to these changes. Finally, the system reports the responses from the agents to the user using TTS and GUI.

The purpose of the event handling modules is to update the state of the dialog. The dialog manager passes the event to these modules in a predefined order and each module can stop the propagation of the event to the modules that follow. Each module also has access to the state before the event, the current state (changed by the preceding modules) and the history of the states in the dialog.

The structure of the dialog state and the information it contains is maintained mainly by the event handlers and the dialog agents. In our current design, the state will contain most importantly the information what entities the user wants to retrieve and the 1-best hypothesis of the recognized utterance. In the state, there is also the number of "no input" events so far, information whether a search is ongoing, a reference to a currently played source file or dialog action flags that mark whether the user requests help, a repetition of a system's utterance or whether we recognized an affirmative or dismissive utterance.

We have implemented two event-handling modules. The first module handles events that represent dialog commands and GUI actions. The dialog commands are derived from the result of the SLU. The module will parse affirmative and dismissive utterances, requests for help or requests to repeat the system's utterance and change the dialog state accordingly. The events from the GUI contain information what footage is playing and again, this information is stored in the dialog state in case the user references the speaker from that footage.

The other module handles search events. It parses semantic entities that relate to the question-answering portion of the system (e.g. entities from Fig. 2) so that the dialog agents can later use them to perform the database queries.

After all the handlers process the event, we call the agents (also in a pre-defined order, see Fig. 4). The purpose of these agents is to react to the dialog state changes. We have created a **knowledge agent** that, based on the dialog state, retrieves information from the knowledge base using a retrieval algorithm described in Sect. 5. Then we are using a **summary agent** that queries the database for facts about the current speaker that may interest the user. We have also created other agents that improve the user experience: a **no input agent** reacts to the lack of input and a **waiting agent** that provides filler utterance when the search is taking a long time, as suggested in [4]. As a fallback search method, we have also implemented a **full-text search agent**.

The most important agent is the **knowledge agent**. This agent uses the search approach described in Sect. 5 to execute queries on our knowledge base. The search is executed only when the search event handler module parses search-related semantic entities from the user's utterance. Based on the dialog state, the knowledge agent decides what kind of query to use ("when", "what", etc. as in Sect. 5) and which entities should be filled into the template.

The knowledge agent also handles possible references to the current recording based on the dialog state. This allows the user to ask follow-up question regarding the current speaker (if there is any) as seen in Fig. 6. In case that the referenced speaker does not talk about the requested information, we search the whole knowledge base for that information. Then we inform the user that nothing was found for the speaker, but there are other speakers that talk about similar things. This strategy allows us to keep the dialog going and allows the user to explore the knowledge base.

```
MATCH (i:Interview)-->(f:File)-->(e:Entity)
WHERE e.value="city:Paris" RETURN i,f
```

Fig. 5. A Cypher query that retrieves all recordings in our knowledge base that mention the city of Paris.

The **summary agent** is designed to explore the knowledge base for the user in other cases. For example, it gives an overview of the most talked-about topics of the current speaker. This is also possible due to the design of our knowledge base, although we simply count all the classes of the entities that are linked to the speaker and present some of the most occurring ones.

Thanks to our **full-text search agent** we can handle user's requests that do not contain any indexed entities. In this case, we fall back to the full-text search engine, removing certain stop-words from the user's utterance and using the rest as a textual query. The results are then seamlessly presented to the user as if they were contained in our knowledge base, keeping a consistent user experience.

The combination of the event-handlers and the dialog agents results in a dialog manager that allows the user to explore the knowledge base and retrieve information that would be hard to access without it as seen in Fig. 6.

5   Search Queries from Natural Language

As mentioned in the introduction and in the description of the dialog manager, we are not only creating a knowledge base from the detected entities, but we want to query this database using spoken natural language. We are using a Neo4j [19] graph database as a storage for our knowledge base, but the SQL-like Cypher query language [9] that the database uses is far from natural (see Fig. 5).

We must create a mapping from the output of the dialog's ASR system onto the database queries. It would be unfeasible to write direct mapping from utterances (i.e. 1-best output from the ASR) to queries and the dialog would not be natural - the users would have to know specific structure of the phrases from the query templates.

Instead, we have based our mapping on a template selection, similarly to [18]. We had no previous examples of natural language searches in the domain and their mappings onto the Cypher queries. We had to rule out any statistical approach to creating and scoring such templates. But since our knowledge base is by design homogenous, the choice of a template is unambiguous, the templates can be created by experts and there is no need for scoring. The templates and items to be filled are selected solely from the output of the SED in the user's utterance. We base the SED on the same grammars that we use for the indexing (described in Sect. 3).

This approach has several advantages. The structure of the utterance will be more flexible, as we are looking only for entities that allow us to infer the meaning of the utterance and compile the correct query.

For each search, the algorithm requires a semantic representation of the user's input. This information will come from the dialog manager as updates to the dialog state. The state must contain information about what the user wants to retrieve and what restrictions we have received from the user. We will then choose which template to use and what needs to be filled in the template.

We have designed templates for four question types: "when", "who", "where" and "what". These templates contain queries that restrict the type of entities we retrieve as a result:

- "when" retrieves only dates,
- with "who", we are looking only for entities that represent names or family members,
- "where" restricts the results to geographical places (cities, camp names, countries, etc.) and
- "what" returns entities like life events.

If we can't categorize the utterance as one of these four types, we can use a generic template that does not restrict the result type and will return all the entities that were included in the query.

The gist of the templates is that the users are looking for something that connects entities they have uttered. In our implementation of the system, the templates only restrict to a co-occurrence of the entities. This means that the queries are restricted only to such source files that have all the entities near each other, measured by the position in the speaker's utterance.

S: Hello, what can I do for you?
U: \<silence\>
> *The agent that handles a missing input reacts for the system.*

S: You can start the conversation by tapping the microphone.
U: I want to know about deaths in Auschwitz.
> *Utterance is parsed as a search request with entities "death" (terms class) and "Auschwitz" (city class). The knowledge agent executes a database query and presents the results and a question.*

S: I've found 68 records. Do you want me to start playing them?
U: Yes.
> *The command handler finds affirmative keyword and the knowledge agent interprets it as the answer to its question.*

S: \<playback started\>
U: What else is mentioned in this record?
> *The search handler finds the request for a summary and a reference to the current speaker. The summary agent retrieves the summary.*

S: (*person1*) also talks about their father, sister and school.
U: Do they mention Paris?
> *The search handler keeps the reference to the current speaker and a search request for Paris (city class). The knowledge agent fails to find any result for the referenced speaker but searches the rest of the database.*

S: (*person1*) doesn't talk about that. But I have found more than 70 records from others.
S: Do you want me to start playing them?
U: No. Whose sister comes from Paris?
> *The command handler finds dismissive keyword and the search handler finds the request for the question type "whose" with "sister" and "Paris" as the entities the user is looking for. The knowledge agent finds the records and presents the answer.*

S: I've found 10 records. One of the people mentioned is (*person2*)
U: And the other ones?
> *The command handler parses the keyword for the next record and the knowledge agent handles the system's reaction as a continuation of its previous search.*

S: Another person is (*person2*)

Fig. 6. Commented transcript of a dialog. S is the system, U is the user. The commentary is in italics.

We are also able to restrict the search to a certain speaker (e.g. when the user uses the speaker's name). Since the entities are linked to nodes representing each speaker, the queries are then altered to retrieve only these entities.

For example, applying our approach to the sentence "My sister was born in April in Paris, she studied in Bern and later moved to Berlin", we are able to find answers to questions similar to "Where did her sister study?", "Who was born in Paris?" or "When was her sister born?", but we are not able to answer "Tell me about her sister".

Once we select and fill the correct template, we execute the query, retrieve information from the knowledge base and parse the results. Since we are focused on multimodal communication, we are also retrieving links to the video sources that contain the results and the word forms and timestamps of the entities we find. We make them available to the dialog manager that can e.g. present the user the answer together with the video footage in the GUI. This is easy to achieve because the entities in our knowledge base have links to their word forms and the source files.

For queries with the generic template, we retrieve the word forms of all the entities the user was looking for. For example, the query "Find me family members and their education." contains two entities: "family_member":terms, "education":terms. It maps onto a generic query template. The word forms of all the entity pairs will be returned, e.g. ("sister", "grammar school"), ("father", "university").

For queries that have specific result types (when, who, where, what), we retrieve only word forms of these results. To show an example, we can say that "When was his sister born?" contains four entities ("when":keyword, "reference":keyword, "sister":terms, "born":terms). The algorithm will choose the "when" template and fill it with the "terms" entities while restricting the search to the speaker of the current video footage. It will return only word forms of the dates it finds e.g. "April 1968".

6   Conclusion and Future Work

We have presented a modular system that allows the user to retrieve information from large audio-visual archives using spoken natural language queries and explore the knowledge base. We have deployed the system for English and Czech parts of the MALACH archive. A transcript of a dialog with the system that showcases how the information can be retrieved is in Fig. 6.

We can conclude that basing the system on expert-made grammars and query templates is sufficient to create a working system with a reasonable impact on the amount of information that becomes available to the users. The semantic entity detection and augmenting the language model using the grammars results in a dialog that is less prone to errors in speech recognition.

The design of the presented system allows for a quick transfer to a different domain and easy expansion of the knowledge base. The work on using tectogrammatical trees to further enhance the knowledge base, creating a true representation of facts about the objects is still ongoing. Another expansion to our knowledge base that we are planning to incorporate will come from semantic web sources that are related to our domain with focus on keeping our knowledge base homogenous.

Acknowledgement. This work was supported by the European Regional Development Fund under the project Robotics for Industry 4.0 (reg. no. CZ.02.1.01/0.0/0.0/15_003/0000470), by the Technology Agency of the Czech Republic, project No. TE01020197 and by the grant of the University of West Bohemia, project No. SGS-2019-027.

References

1. Bordes, A., Boureau, Y.L., Weston, J.: Learning end-to-end goal-oriented dialog. In: ICLR (2017). http://arxiv.org/abs/1605.07683

2. Choi, E., et al.: QuAC: question answering in context. In: Proceedings of the 2018 Conference on Empirical Methods in Natural Language Processing, pp. 2174–2184. Association for Computational Linguistics, Brussels, Belgium (2018). https://www.aclweb.org/anthology/D18-1241

3. Dubey, M., Dasgupta, S., Sharma, A., Höffner, K., Lehmann, J.: AskNow: a framework for natural language query formalization in SPARQL. In: Sack, H., Blomqvist, E., d'Aquin, M., Ghidini, C., Ponzetto, S.P., Lange, C. (eds.) ESWC 2016. LNCS, vol. 9678, pp. 300–316. Springer, Cham (2016). https://doi.org/10.1007/978-3-319-34129-3_19

4. Gambino, S.L., Zerrieß, S., Schlangen, D.: Testing strategies for bridging time-to-content in spoken dialogue systems. In: Proceedings of the Ninth International Workshop on Spoken Dialogue Systems Technology, pp. 1–7 (2018)

5. Gurevych, I., Porzel, R., Slinko, E., Pfleger, N., Alexandersson, J., Merten, S.: Less is more: using a single knowledge representation in dialogue systems. In: Proceedings of the HLT-NAACL Workshop on Text Meaning, pp. 14–21 (2003)

6. Kadlec, R., Vodolan, M., Libovicky, J., Macek, J., Kleindienst, J.: Knowledge-based dialog state tracking. In: 2014 IEEE Spoken Language Technology Workshop (SLT), No. 1, pp. 348–353. IEEE, December 2014. http://ieeexplore.ieee.org/document/7078599/

7. Lee, L.S., Glass, J., Lee, H.Y., Chan, C.A.: Spoken content retrieval - beyond cascading speech recognition with text retrieval. IEEE/ACM Trans. Audio Speech Lang. Process. **23**, 1389–1420 (2015). http://ieeexplore.ieee.org/document/7114229/

8. Lopez, V.: PowerAqua: open question answering on the semantic web. Ph.D. thesis (2011)

9. Neo4j, Inc: The Neo4j Cypher Manual v3.5 (2019). https://neo4j.com/docs/cypher-manual/3.5/

10. Panayotov, V., Chen, G., Povey, D., Khudanpur, S.: Librispeech: an ASR corpus based on public domain audio books. In: ICASSP, IEEE International Conference on Acoustics, Speech and Signal Processing - Proceedings, vol. 2015, pp. 5206–5210, August 2015

11. Popel, M., Žabokrtský, Z.: TectoMT: modular NLP framework. In: IceTAL, 7th International Conference on Natural Language Processing, Reykjavik, pp. 293–304 (2010). https://ufal.mff.cuni.cz/treex

12. Psutka, J., Radová, V., Ircing, P., Matoušek, J., Müller, L.: USC-SFI MALACH Interviews and Transcripts Czech LDC2014S04 (2014). https://catalog.ldc.upenn.edu/LDC2014S04

13. Ramabhadran, B., et al.: USC-SFI MALACH Interviews and Transcripts English (2012). https://catalog.ldc.upenn.edu/LDC2012S05

14. Stanislav, P., Švec, J., Ircing, P.: An engine for online video search in large archives of the holocaust testimonies. In: Proceedings of the Annual Conference of the International Speech Communication Association, INTERSPEECH, 08–12 September, pp. 2352–2353 (2016)

15. Stede, M., Schlangen, D.: Information-seeking chat: dialogue management by topic structure. In: Proceedings of the 8th Workshop on the Semantics and Pragmatics of Dialogue, pp. 117–124 (2004)

16. Švec, J., Ircing, P., Šmídl, L.: Semantic entity detection from multiple ASR hypotheses within the WFST framework. In: 2013 IEEE Workshop on Automatic Speech Recognition and Understanding, ASRU 2013 - Proceedings, pp. 84–89 (2013)

17. Švec, J., Psutka, J.V., Trmal, J., Šmídl, L., Ircing, P., Sedmidubsky, J.: On the use of grapheme models for searching in large spoken archives. In: ICASSP, IEEE International Conference on Acoustics, Speech and Signal Processing - Proceedings, vol. 2018, pp. 6259–6263, April 2018

18. Unger, C., Bühmann, L.: Template-based question answering over RDF data. In: Proceedings of the 21st International Conference on World Wide Web, pp. 639–648 (2012). http://dl.acm.org/citation.cfm?id=2187923

19. Webber, J.: A programmatic introduction to Neo4j. In: Proceedings of the 3rd Annual Conference on Systems, Programming, and Applications: Software for Humanity, p. 217 (2012)

20. Williams, J.D., Henderson, M., Raux, A., Thomson, B., Black, A., Ramachandran, D.: The dialog state tracking challenge series. AI Mag. **35**(4), 121 (2017)

Crowd-Sourced Collection of Task-Oriented Human-Human Dialogues in a Multi-domain Scenario

Norbert Braunschweiler[1(✉)], Panagiotis Papadakos[2], Margarita Kotti[1], Yannis Marketakis[2], and Yannis Tzitzikas[2]

[1] Toshiba Research Europe Limited, Cambridge Research Laboratory, Cambridge, UK
{norbert.braunschweiler,margarita.kotti}@crl.toshiba.co.uk
[2] Institute of Computer Science, FORTH-ICS, Heraklion, Crete, Greece
{papadako,marketak,tzitzik}@ics.forth.gr

Abstract. There is a lack of high-quality corpora for the purposes of training task-oriented, end-to-end dialogue systems. This paper describes a dialogue collection process which used crowd-sourcing and a Wizard-of-Oz set-up to collect written human-human dialogues for a task-oriented, multi-domain scenario. The context is a tourism agency, where users try to select the more desired hotel, restaurant, museum or shop. To respond to users, wizards were assisted by an exploratory system supporting Preference-enriched Faceted Search. An important aspect was the translation of user intent to a number of actions (hard or soft-constraints) by wizards. The main goal was to collect dialogues as realistic as possible between a user and an operator, suitable for training end-to-end dialogue systems. This work describes the experiences made, the options and the decisions taken to minimize the human effort and budget, along with the tools used and developed, and describes in detail the resulting dialogue collection.

Keywords: Dialogue collection · Crowd-sourcing · Wizard-of-Oz · End-to-end · Exploratory search · Dialogue systems

1 Introduction

One key factor in the development of neural network based dialogue systems is the availability of suitable training material, both in content and volume. More training material is usually associated with better models, but has to be accompanied by sufficient variety and coverage. Despite great progress in this field, especially when it comes to non-task oriented dialogue systems [13,15,18], there is still a lack of high-quality corpora for the purposes of training task-oriented, end-to-end trainable dialogue systems. One challenge in this dialogue collection, is the problem of getting sufficiently realistic dialogues to cover the

© Springer Nature Switzerland AG 2019
K. Ekštein (Ed.): TSD 2019, LNAI 11697, pp. 398–411, 2019.
https://doi.org/10.1007/978-3-030-27947-9_34

wide range of types and styles which are simultaneously influenced or directed by accessing knowledge sources.

The dialogue collection presented here, is designed to provide sufficient training material to train a task-oriented dialogue system in an end-to-end manner. Criteria for the data collection included: (a) realistic dialogues between a user and an operator, (b) the number of dialogues should be a figure in the thousands, (c) multiple-domains, (d) usage of a knowledge base and an expressive interaction paradigm to retrieve and explore information about domains.

To achieve these requirements a dialogue collection was conducted which used a Wizard-of-Oz set-up, in which the role of the dialogue system is played by a human (the "wizard"), and a crowd-sourcing platform to gather a wide range of subjects acting as dialogue system users. A number of trained wizards acted as the dialogue system response generators and used their access to an exploratory search system over a knowledge base, supporting the expressive Preference-Enriched Faceted Search (PFS), to guide their answers.

The contribution of this paper is that (a) it details a dialogue collection process that exploits an expressive interaction model, (b) it explains the selection of certain tools or platforms, and (c) it provides details about the content of the final corpus and the required effort. The rest of this paper is organized as follows: Sect. 2 describes related work, Sect. 3 describes the dialogue collection process, the tools used, and provides some statistics over the collected dialogue corpus. Finally, Sect. 4 discusses the methodology and the results, and Sect. 5 concludes the paper.

2   Related Work

Below, some recently collected datasets are discussed, closely related to the presented dialogue collection here, either in their collection style or content. For a summary of available corpora for building data-driven dialogue systems see [14].

The Maluuba Frames[1] corpus [1], offers roughly 1.3k human-human dialogues in a task-oriented scenario in which users are aiming to book a trip by conversing with an operator who searches a database to find suitable trips. While this collection also uses a Wizard-of-Oz set-up, it includes just 12 participants and it covers only a single domain.

As part of a challenge regarding end-to-end trainable dialogue models [5], Microsoft released a corpus of human-human dialogues collected by crowd-sourcing[2]. The corpus contains 3 domains and about 10k dialogues (movie = 2890, restaurant = 4103 taxi = 3094). The corpus was fully annotated with dialogue intents and slot values, however first challenge results showed modest performances[3].

---

[1] https://datasets.maluuba.com/Frames/.

[2] https://github.com/xiul-msr/e2e_dialog_challenge.

[3] https://xiul-msr.github.io/e2e_dialog_challenge/slides/MS_dialog_challenge_result_outlook_sungjin.pptx.

Another dialogue collection of similar type is [2]. This corpus of written human-human dialogues contains 7 domains and both dialogue belief states/actions are annotated by selected crowd-sourced labelers. Regarding human-to-human based datasets, [2] mentions that these are most suitable for building a natural conversational system, but that many of the corpora released in the past (e.g. [6,11,12]) lack a grounding of the dialogues onto a knowledge base which limits their use for task-oriented systems.

For the dialogue collection described in this paper, the Wizard-of-Oz method [3,4,10] was chosen. In this method a user interacts with a human "wizard" who is acting as the dialogue system response generator. It allows gathering large amounts of text-to-text conversations via crowd-sourcing as shown, for instance, by [2] and previously [19]. While [2] and [19] used an asynchronous set-up in which users and wizards did not have to engage in a coherent dialogue of user-wizard turns, but multiple workers contributed to the same dialogue, the current set-up was synchronous, ensuring more coherent dialogues. Table 1 shows a comparison of the aforementioned four corpora with the one presented in this study (ToshWOZ).

Table 1. Comparison of 4 similar corpora with the one presented in this study.

Corpus	#Dial.	#Turns	Turns/Dial.	#Domains	#Workers	Labeled	Synchron.	Ref.
FRAMES	>1.3k	<10k	14.6	1	12	✓	✓	[1]
MicrosoftE2E	>10k	>70k	7.5	3	?	✓	?	[5]
WOZ2.0	1.2k	<10k	7.5	1	?	-	X	[7]
MULTIWOZ	>10k	>100k	13.7	7	1249	✓	X	[2]
ToshWOZ	>3k	>30k	10.4	4	327 + 9 wiz.	-	✓	-

3 Dialogue Collection Method

To collect dialogues between humans in a goal-oriented setting covering multiple domains, a tourism agency scenario was chosen. Crowd-sourced users were given tasks to find a particular place (e.g. a restaurant or a museum) by written interaction with an operator. The operators were trained agents, who accessed an exploratory system that supported both hard and soft-constraints (i.e. preferences) over a knowledge base, to guide their responses to users. The training of the operators, who where in-house experts, included the usage of the exploratory system while interacting with users and the operation of the dialogue platform, i.e. copying text from users, entering it into the exploratory system, storing it, translating user requests to appropriate hard or soft-constraints in the exploratory system, formulating a response to users, storing it in the knowledge base and submitting it to the web-based dialogue interface.

Using a human-to-human set-up involving many different crowd-sourced workers aims to capture the vast variety of language usage as well as the variability in strategies to achieve a certain information seeking task. To support variety in content during dialogues, 4 domains are covered and for each domain a set of task scenarios was created. The 4 domains are: hotels, museums, restaurants and shops in 4 cities of Japan (Kobe, Kyoto, Osaka, Tokyo). The number of task scenarios are: 11 in hotels, 8 in both museums and restaurants, and 5 in shops.

Each scenario describes the profile and preferences of a customer wishing to find something particular (e.g. a hotel in Kyoto as shown in Fig. 1). Most of the scenarios were created using the information in the knowledge base. However, some scenarios require knowledge not existing in the knowledge base. These scenarios were introduced so that the actions of the wizards operating the knowledge base could be recorded. In addition, workers were encouraged to describe their own preferences.

One of the important aspects here, is the translation of user intents into a number of actions by wizards. These actions can be hard or soft-constraints while wizards are accessing the knowledge base and may be helpful in the training of models mapping user intents to expressive actions. The knowledge base contains structured information linked to these 4 domains. Information is structured into facets, which can be set-valued and can support hierarchically organized values, and labeled or non-labeled intervals as values. The types of their values can be boolean (e.g. free WiFi), numerical (e.g. ratings), geographical for describing actual location, or free text. More information about the way facets are constructed can be found in Sect. 3.3.

The dialogue collection platform had the following 3 main components introduced in detail below: (1) crowd-sourcing platform to access a large user audience, (2) web-based dialogue interface enabling dialogues between workers and wizards and (3) PFS-based exploratory search system over the knowledge base exploited by wizards.

3.1   Crowd-Sourcing Platform

A crowd-sourcing platform can offer a large number of users to which jobs can be disseminated online. Typically, other services are offered as well, such as the selection of user groups with certain features and handling of workers payments. There are many crowd-sourcing platforms available of which some are described in [9,17].

The crowd-sourcing platform MicroWorkers[4] was chosen here instead of the more widely used Amazon Mechanical Turk[5] platform, which was unavailable in Greece, where the data was collected. MicroWorkers appeared to be a viable option since it:

1. Allows a detailed specification of jobs (estimated duration, # jobs per worker, etc.).
2. Allows to reject workers after a quality check.
3. Allows workers to submit a token as evidence that they carried out the task.
4. Comprises of a large community of users (>1.300.000).

---

[4] https://www.microworkers.com.
[5] https://www.mturk.com.

5. Allows selection of specific groups of users, e.g. by regions, worker qualification.
6. Allows tasks on external web-pages.
7. Supports VCODE verification for task validation and payment of workers.
8. Allows to pause, resume and dynamically change the speed of a campaign.

VCODE verification was important to link tasks on external web-pages and workers conducting these tasks, plus quality control and payment of workers. The crowd-sourcing platform provides access to a large user base, but communication between users and wizards needs to be enabled and recorded, which is described next.

3.2   The Web Interface for Collecting Dialogues: Workers and Wizards

The web-interface enabling dialogues between users and wizards resembles a chat platform, in which the communication is synchronous and done by text messages. The free *tawk.to*[6] platform was chosen to connect users and wizards.

Figure 1 shows the web-interface seen by the worker. A small web application was developed, which loads tasks (either particular or random ones) for each of the different domains. The application shows users a description of the task and some general guidelines for the execution of the dialogue. By clicking on the widget at the bottom right of the window, a chat box opened to initiate the discussion with one of the wizards.

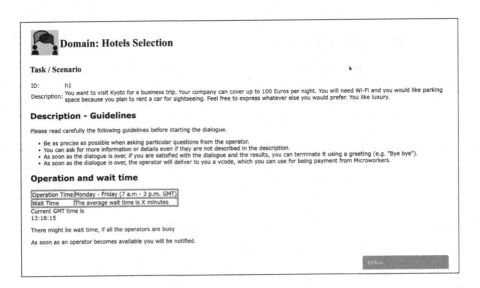

Fig. 1. The chat interface for workers showcasing a task scenario.

---

[6] https://www.tawk.to.

When a worker starts a new dialogue, all the wizards are notified. One (or more) wizards can accept the request and start a dialogue with the user. At that time all the required information for generating a valid VCODE (i.e. the ID of the worker, the ID of the task, etc.), were passed as information tags to the wizards. An indicative screen-shot of the wizard's view is shown in Fig. 2. *tawk.to* can be embedded into a website enabling a live chat functionality.

3.3   Exploring the Knowledge Base: Hippalus

To offer an efficient and easy access to the knowledge base, an exploratory search system called Hippalus[7] [8] was used. Hippalus enabled fast and efficient access to domain specific information, which is an important aspect for task-oriented dialogue systems. Hippalus allows wizards to explore a knowledge base using the Preference-enriched Faceted Search (PFS) [16] interaction paradigm and overview the information space (e.g. hotels) based on their attributes/values and count information. PFS supports actions with hard and soft-constraints enabling users to order facets, values, and objects. Wizards are able to express hard or soft-constraints (i.e. preferences) over attributes that can be multi-valued, intervals with labeled or non-labeled values, or whose values can be hierarchically organized, and Hippalus automatically resolves any conflicts through preference inheritance. Hard-constraints limit the object space to the desired objects, while soft-constraints provide an ordering of the objects/values/attributes. The actual object space is represented in the *Resource Description Framework Schema*

Fig. 2. The chat interface for wizards.

---

[7] http://www.ics.forth.gr/isl/Hippalus.

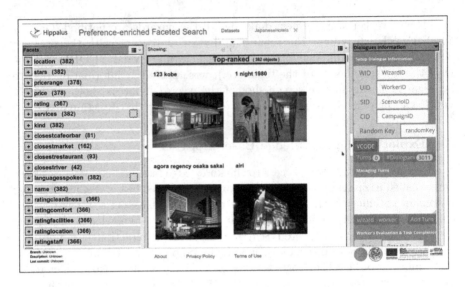

Fig. 3. User interface of `Hippalus`, enhanced to support the recording of dialogues

(RDF/S)[8] and can be realized either by static collections or is the result of SPARQL queries, a query language of the Semantic Web. Apart from the dialogues, the interest was also to collect the corresponding hard or soft-constraints that the wizards performed in `Hippalus`.

The performed preference actions are internally translated to statements in the preference language described in [16] and the respective preference bucket order is computed. Finally, the ranked list of objects according to preference is displayed in the user's browser. For the dialogue collection, `Hippalus` was extended to record all aspects of a dialogue including the turns (i.e. the narratives), the actions performed in `Hippalus` (i.e. preferences, restrictions), the restricted ranked objects, information about dialogues (i.e. wizard and worker ID's, scenarios), and evaluation of the dialogue from the perspective of both wizard and worker.

`Hippalus` was modified to record dialogues, allow wizards to generate a unique token for each dialogue (i.e. UUIDs), generate VCODE tokens which were communicated to workers when dialogues where successfully finished, include tools for inserting turns from workers and wizards, and store all related information and meta-data of each dialogue. Figure 3 shows the enhanced user interface of `Hippalus`. The right panel shows part of the widgets developed for collecting dialogues, the left panel shows some facets in the hotel domain, while the middle panel shows part of the ranked list of available objects. During dialogue collection, `Hippalus` enabled wizards fast and efficient access to domain specific data, an important aspect for task-oriented dialogue systems.

---

[8] http://www.w3.org/TR/rdf-schema.

3.4   The Dialogue Collection Process

The dialogue collection process includes six major steps shown in Fig. 4.

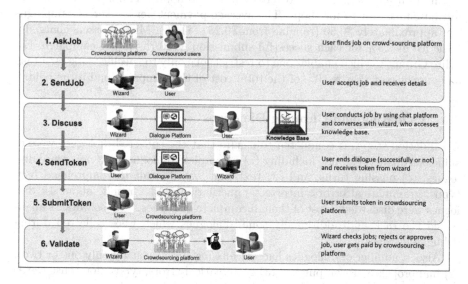

Fig. 4. The processing steps during the crowd-sourced dialogue collection.

To collect dialogues, first the corresponding campaigns had to be created in MicroWorkers. A campaign is a self-contained task submitted to the crowd-sourcing platform. Since MicroWorkers allows creating campaigns for specific groups of workers, a first attempt was made by creating separate campaigns engaging different groups including highly-rated workers from the UK, North-Europe, South-Europe, etc. Unfortunately, these campaigns turned out to be unsuccessful, because they either did not manage to attract workers, or it took a lot of time to get the attention of workers. The same problem remained, despite increasing the amount of money that workers would receive, or reducing the time period in which they would receive the money.

As a result, international campaigns were started without any restrictions, since there where no available highly-rated groups for international workers. Each campaign was referring to a specific scenario in a particular domain. Workers could participate only once in each campaign, ensuring that many different workers would join, to collect different dialogue strategies and as much linguistic variation as possible.

Another issue was the idle time during dialogues when workers did not respond immediately. To ensure a coherent dialogue, it was meant to be carried out in a synchronous manner. However, it turned out to be important to consider potential delays from workers or wizards. In many cases, wizards had to wait for a response from workers. To minimize the occurrence of such idle periods, wizards tried to respond to the initial request from workers, as soon as they initiated the dialogue. Nine persons were trained as wizards, all in-house experts.

In total 49 campaigns were created; 17 for hotels, 11 for restaurants, 11 for museums, and 10 for shops. The average payment per worker in campaigns was approximately $0.50 (ranging from $0.25 – $1.00). MicroWorkers charged a basic fee of 7.5% for each successful submission + $0.75 fee per campaign. For "Hire Groups", which enables one to restrict jobs only to specific workers, a task assignment cost that is 10% of the total cost of the campaign had to be paid.

3.5   Validating and Cleaning Dialogues

A validation step was conducted to ensure that the collected dialogues were of sufficient quality, e.g. not including (a) incomplete dialogues, (b) non-sense dialogues, (c) missing turns, and (d) text that was difficult to comprehend (e.g. typos, grammatical errors, incorrect punctuation). As a result, about 1k dialogues were discarded, most of them incomplete dialogues because workers abandoned the task and additionally some dialogues which were collected during debugging stages.

Also, a number of dialogues had (1) missing turns (usually only one or two), (2) inappropriate user input and (3) grammatical errors, typos, non-sense words and incorrect punctuation. As a result, a final correction and cleaning stage was conducted which included: (1) filling in missing turns, (2) correcting or deleting clearly incorrect user input, and (3) correcting typos in words (e.g. "meseum", "dishses"), incorrect punctuation (e.g. "are there any. hotels"), nonsense words (e.g "wellwith", "facilitiesas"), slang words (e.g. "thnx", "yw") and ungrammatical text. All valid dialogues had to be inspected manually and corrected if needed, which took about 4 h per 100 dialogues.

3.6   Dialogue Data Representation

Dialogues were stored in a relational database using the schema shown in Fig. 5. The tables of the schema are: **Scenarios:** Description of the scenarios with their corresponding domain; **Dialogue:** Meta-data information about the dialogue; **Turns:** Text of the dialogue, either from worker or wizard; **Actions:** Actions conducted by the wizards in `Hippalus` per turn. Each action is described in human-friendly format, the type of the action and the ranked objects after performing it. For subsequent processing, e.g. in a machine learning framework, dialogues can be exported in JSON format.

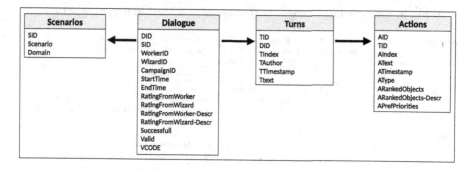

Fig. 5. The schema of the dialogues collection database.

Table 2. Statistics of the collected dialogue corpus.

# dialogues	3010
in domain: hotel	778 (25.8%)
in domain: restaurant	757 (25.1%)
in domain: museum	740 (24.6%)
in domain: shop	735 (24.4%)
Avg. dialogue duration	8 min 52 s
Avg. # of turns/dialogue	10.4
Avg. # User turns/dialogue	5.7
Avg. # Wizard turns/dialogue	4.7

3.7   Statistics of the Collected Dialogue Corpus

Table 2 shows the statistics of the collected corpus. More than 3k dialogues were collected which are roughly evenly distributed across the 4 domains. The average duration for the collection of a dialogue was about 9 min. The average number of turns in a dialogue is more than 10 and there are more than 31k turns in total. The collection was done in a period of 4.5 months. In total, 590 workers participated for all valid and non-valid dialogues. This number is reduced to 327 for the valid dialogues (workers that provided invalid dialogues of very-low quality were black-listed from our campaigns).

Table 3 shows an example of a collected dialogue from the hotel domain with the corresponding scenario listed on top of the table. Wizards were free to decide which action to use (i.e. hard or soft-constraints) in order to provide better feedback to the users. In the given example, the wizard used a hard-constraint for the *freewifi* service, which is available in all hotels and used a preference for the *freeparking* action. By not making a hard-constraint over the *freeparking* service of the one hotel, the wizard can explore a bigger variety of other services offered by the available hotels.

Table 3. Example of a dialogue in the corpus plus selected `Hippalus` actions.

Scenario: *You want to visit Kyoto for a business trip. Your company can cover up to 100 Euros per night. You will need WiFi and you would like parking space because you plan to rent a car for sightseeing. Feel free to express whatever else you would prefer. You like luxury.*

Actor	Text of turn	Hippalus actions
WORKER	*Hello. I am looking for a hotel room in Kyoto for a business trip with a price up to 100 euros. How many options are there?*	`Focus=location: kyoto_prefecture; Add preference action=objects order: term pricerange...{very_cheap, cheap, moderate} best`
WIZARD	Hello, It seems that there are around 47 hotels with the criteria that you mentioned. Would you like to search using some other criteria?	
WORKER	*Well, I would need WiFi and a parking space. Any other available features are also welcome.*	`Focus=services: freewifi; Add preference action=objects order: term services... freeparking best`
WIZARD	All of them offer free WiFi, however only one offers free parking. As regards to other facilities I can find many hotels that have a swimming pool and restaurant inside the hotel. Are you interested in these facilities?	
WORKER	*Well I think I will take the one with the free parking. Can you please give me the address and the telephone number?*	`Focus=services: freeparking`
WIZARD	It is the rihga royal kyoto. The address is shimogyo-ku higashihorikawa-dori shiokoji-sagaru taimatsu-cho 1, japan. Unfortunately I do not have information about the telephone number.	
WORKER	*Ok. Thank you very much. Bye Bye*	
WIZARD	Bye	

4   Discussion

One of the lessons learned during the dialogue collection process was certainly the time consuming aspect of the actual dialogue collection process. The original estimation for the time period needed to collect one dialogue was about 5 min. In reality, it took on average about 9 min, i.e. almost twice the duration originally estimated, mainly due to workers latency to respond and the aim to collect dialogues in a synchronous manner. This also had an impact on the number of dialogues which could be collected in the given time period. However, the chosen set-up ensures a coherent, synchronous dialogue between users and wizards and avoids potential in-coherence which may occur in asynchronous dialogue collection methods such as the one used in [2] and [19].

Conducting a crowd-sourced dialogue collection also depends heavily on the availability and language skills of the workforce. Workers from English-speaking countries do not seem to be readily available, and even when they are, it does not guarantee good quality language skills, since they might not be native speakers of those countries. On the other hand there were some workers from non-native English countries like India, that had excellent language skills, who participated in most of the campaigns, and seem to make a living from crowd-sourcing platforms. Further, the fact that there was a rather large number of "invalid" dialogues and that a cleaning step had to be conducted, shows one of the drawbacks of crowd-sourced data collections: costs to collect relatively large amounts of data can be relatively low, but the quality can also vary significantly.

Analyzing the cost for collecting the dialogues collection showed that 15% of the total budget was spent for development activities, 30% at setting-up, validating and documenting the platforms, datasets and scenarios, 45% for the in-house trained experts that played the role of the wizards, 10% was the cost of the crowd-sourced workers, and finally, 10% was spent for cleaning and validating the collected dialogues. It needs to be mentioned, that a number of workers abandoned the dialogue before completion, and as a result the expensive effort of the experienced wizards was spent for no results. Consequently, reducing the idle time of the wizards (i.e. by early ending non-active dialogues or black-listing low-quality workers) and increasing the percentage of completed, valid and good quality dialogues (i.e. by increasing the percentage of highly rated workers which is a non-trivial task) is important for reducing the total cost of such efforts. Another option is to train workers from the crowd-source platform as wizards which might be a cheaper option. This option was not chosen, because the presented method allowed to better control the efficiency and quality of the wizards results.

Finally, the fact that the current corpus was collected by written communication might introduce a certain bias towards specific ways of interaction and behaviours, as mentioned in [14]. Further, the time needed to post a response is larger for both workers and wizards in written rather than oral communication and the dialogues should be validated and cleaned as discussed previously. The obvious solution is to collect spoken human-human conversations, which is a path to consider for future work.

5   Conclusion

This paper presented the experiences and the lessons learned from the process of collecting expressive and synchronously written human-human dialogues (and their associated meta-data), for a task-oriented multi-domain scenario. The context is a travel agency environment and the dialogues cover four domains (hotels, museums, restaurants, and shops) in Japan. Users were asked to converse with wizards to achieve their tasks (i.e. select the more appropriate resource) via a chat platform, and wizards formulated their responses while accessing a knowledge base via an exploratory system based on Preference-enriched Faceted Search (*PFS*).

More than 4,000 dialogues were collected in 4.5 months. Due to the crowd-source nature of the set-up and the variation in quality of workers input, a significant percentage was invalid or required a clean-up process, leaving at the end a corpus of 3,010 valid dialogues. Each valid dialogue lasted almost 9 min and had on average 10.4 turns. The effort for collecting the above was analyzed, and it turned out, that the cost of the in-house experts that played the role of the wizards was almost 4.5 times more than the cost of the workers for a crowd-sourced campaign.

One distinctive feature of the corpus, is the fact that it recorded the actions taken by wizards, both *hard* and *soft*-constraints, that not only *fill* a slot or restrict the objects, but also *rank* the objects. Consequently the corpus can be exploited for more "refined" training. One future step is to annotate the corpus with dialogue acts, and then use the corpus for training an end-to-end, as well as modular, neural network-based dialogue system, and assessing the value of the corpus.

References

1. Asri, L.E., et al.: Frames: a corpus for adding memory to goal-oriented dialogue systems. In: Proceedings of the 18th Annual SIGdial Meeting on Discourse and Dialogue (2017)
2. Budzianowski, P., et al.: MultiWOZ - A large-scale multi-domain wizard-of-oz dataset for task-oriented dialogue modelling. [Dataset] (2018)
3. Dahlbäck, N., Jönsson, A., Ahrenberg, L.: Wizard of Oz studies: why and how. In: Proceedings of the 1st International Conference on Intelligent User Interfaces, IUI 1993, pp. 193–200. ACM, New York (1993)
4. Kelley, J.F.: An iterative design methodology for user-friendly natural language office information applications. ACM Trans. Inf. Syst. (TOIS) **2**(1), 26–41 (1984)
5. Li, X., Panda, S., Liu, J.J., Gao, J.: Microsoft dialogue challenge: Building end-to-end task-completion dialogue systems (2018)
6. Lowe, R., Pow, N., Serban, I., Pineau, J.: The ubuntu dialogue corpus: a large dataset for research in unstructured multi-turn dialogue systems. In: Proceedings of the 16th Annual SIGdial Meeting on Discourse and Dialogue (2015)
7. Mrkšić, N., Ó Séaghdha, D., Wen, T.H., Thomson, B., Young, S.: The neural belief tracker: Data-driven dialogue state tracking. In: ACL, Vancouver, Canada (2017)
8. Papadakos, P., Tzitzikas, Y.: Hippalus: preference-enriched faceted exploration. In: EDBT/ICDT Workshops, vol. 172 (2014)
9. Peer, E., Brandimarte, L., Samat, S., Acquisti, A.: Beyond the Turk: alternative platforms for crowdsourcing behavioral research. J. Exp. Soc. Psychol. **70**, 153–163 (2017). https://doi.org/10.2139/ssrn.2594183
10. Petrik, S.: Wizard of Oz Experiments on Speech Dialogue Systems. Diploma thesis, Technical University of Graz (2004)
11. Ritter, A., Cherry, C., Dolan, W.B.: Unsupervised modelling of Twitter conversations. In: Human Language Technologies: The 2010 Annual Conference of the North American Chapter of the Association for Computational Linguistics, pp. 172–180 (2010)
12. Schrading, N., Alm, C., Ptucha, R., Homan, C.: An analysis of domestic abuse discourse on reddit. In: Conference on Empirical Methods in Natural Language Processing (EMNLP), pp. 2577–2583 (2015)
13. Serban, I., Sordoni, A., Bengio, Y., Courville, A.C., Pineau, J.: Hierarchical neural network generative models for movie dialogues. ArXiv e-prints (2015)
14. Serban, I.V., Lowe, R., Henderson, P., Charlin, L., Pineau, J.: A survey of available corpora for building data-driven dialogue systems: the journal version. Dialogue Discourse **9**(1), 1–49 (2018)
15. Shang, L., Lu, Z., Li, H.: Neural responding machine for short-text conversation. In: ACL, Beijing, China, pp. 1577–1586 (2015)
16. Tzitzikas, Y., Papadakos, P.: Interactive exploration of multi-dimensional and hierarchical information spaces with real-time preference elicitation. Fundamenta Informaticae **122**(4), 357–399 (2013)

17. Vakharia, D., Lease, M.: Beyond Mechanical Turk: an analysis of paid crowd work platforms. In: Proceedings of the iConference (2015)
18. Vinyals, O., Le, Q.V.: A neural conversational model. In: ICML Deep Learning Workshop, Lille, France (2015)
19. Wen, T.H., et al.: A network-based end-to-end trainable task-oriented dialogue system. In: EACL, Valencia, Spain, pp. 438–449 (2017)

Author Index

Aghaebrahimian, Ahmad 185
Aktaş, Berfin 171
Allouchi, Wissem 373
Arias-Vergara, T. 299
Azarova, Irina 224

Baeriswyl, Michael 373
Bahou, Younès 316
Barth, Volker 274
Bayerl, Sebastian P. 352
Bergler, Christian 274
Bleguith, Lamia Hadrich 316
Böttinger, Konstantin 151
Boughariou, Emna 316
Bouressace, Hassina 127
Bourgonje, Peter 32
Braunschweiler, Norbert 398
Bulín, Martin 287

Cheng, Rachael Xi 274
Chýlek, Adam 385
Csirik, János 127

Debus, Pascal 151
Deksne, Daiga 58
Dobrov, Boris 69

Erjavec, Tomaž 103, 115

Fišer, Darja 103, 115

Gollwitzer, S. 299
Grisard, Malo 373

Hajič, Jan 137
Hanzlíček, Zdeněk 307, 361

Ivanov, Lubomir 45

Jelínek, Tomáš 19
Joshi, Sonal 329
Jouvet, Denis 3
Jůzová, Markéta 91

Kopparapu, Sunil Kumar 341
Kotti, Margarita 398
Kowatsch, Daniel 151

Lazaridis, Alexandros 373
Ljubešić, Nikola 103, 115
Loukachevitch, Natalia 69

Maier, Andreas 274
Malek, Jiri 251
Marketakis, Yannis 398
Matoušek, Jindřich 264, 307
Mirdita, Donika 151
Mírovský, Jiří 197, 236
Motlicek, Petr 373
Müller, Nicolas M. 151
Musil, Tomáš 211

Neilsen, Brandon 45
Nöth, Elmar 82, 274, 299
Novák, Michal 197

Orozco-Arroyave, J. R. 82, 299

Panda, Ashish 329
Papadakos, Panagiotis 398
Pera, Vitor 160
Pérez-Toro, P. A. 82
Přibil, Jiří 264
Přibilová, Anna 264

Riedhammer, Korbinian 352
Rysová, Kateřina 197
Rysová, Magdaléna 197

Scheffler, Tatjana 171
Schmitt, Manuel 274
Schröter, Hendrik 274
Schuster, M. 299
Sheikh, Imran 341
Šmídl, Luboš 287, 385
Soni, Meet H. 329

Soni, Meet   341
Stauder, Andy   185
Stede, Manfred   32, 171
Straka, Milan   137
Straková, Jana   137
Strauss, M.   82
Švec, Jan   287, 385
Synková, Pavlína   236

Tihelka, Daniel   361
Tikhomirov, Mikhail   69
Tzitzikas, Yannis   398

Ustaszewski, Michael   185

Vásquez-Correa, J. C.   82
Vít, Jakub   91, 307, 361

Weber, Michael   274

Zakharov, Victor   224
Zdansky, Jindrich   251
Zhan, Qingran   373
Zikánová, Šárka   236

Printed in the United States
By Bookmasters